Merriam-Webster's

Dictionary

of

ALLUSIONS

Merriam-Webster's
Dictionary
of
ALLUSIONS

Elizabeth Webber
&
Mike Feinsilber

Merriam-Webster, Incorporated
Springfield, Massachusetts

A GENUINE MERRIAM-WEBSTER

The name *Webster* alone is no guarantee of excellence. It is used by a number of publishers and may serve mainly to mislead an unwary buyer.

Merriam-Webster™ is the name you should look for when you consider the purchase of dictionaries and other fine reference books. It carries the reputation of a company that has been publishing since 1831 and is your assurance of quality and authority.

Copyright © 1999 by Elizabeth Webber & Mike Feinsilber

Library of Congress Cataloging-in-Publication Data
Webber, Elizabeth, 1946–
  Merriam-Webster's dictionary of allusions / by
  Elizabeth Webber & Mike Feinsilber.
      p.   cm.
    ISBN 0–87779–628–9
    1. Allusions in literature — Dictionaries. I. Feinsilber, Mike.
  II. Title.   III. Title: Dictionary of allusions.
  PN43.W384   1999
803—dc21   99–33125
                                                    CIP

Made in the United States of America

1234DF:QPV02010099

To

Betty Webber
E.W.

Doris Feinsilber
M.F.

A cknowledgments

This book would not have come about without the encouragement and support of Daniel Rapoport, the midwifery of Paul Dickson, and the knowledge, resources and skill of Merriam-Webster Inc., especially Frederick C. Mish who provided initial guidance on the scope of the book, Mary W. Cornog and E. Ward Gilman for their research and editing help, Jennifer N. Cislo for data input of new material, Kathleen M. Doherty, Daniel J. Hopkins, and Robert D. Copeland for proofreading of the manuscript, and publisher John M. Morse for his guidance and editorial suggestions all along the way. We would also like to thank the gods and goddesses, the beasts both real and mythic, the prophets, poets, kings and clowns—and the ink-stained wretches—who provided the fodder for this work.

Preface

The legendary editor Harold Ross, founder of *The New Yorker*, is said to have once expressed plaintive bewilderment to his magazine's star writer, James Thurber: "Is Moby Dick the man or the whale?" This book is for people like Ross.

Like him, we're not so dumb, we readers, but we don't know everything about everything. We might know what's flotsam and what's jetsam, but not what manner of mammal was Moby Dick. This book will help.

All of us run into (and sometimes use) these sideways references that are intended to add color and vigor to language. But they are lost on us if we have forgotten or never knew what they mean. We could stop reading and hope to find it in a dictionary. More likely, we just make a guess from context and read on in a fog.

This book is a collection of those tricky allusions that appear without accompanying explanations in our daily reading. When your dictionary can't help with *silent spring, the Dreyfus affair, lounge lizard* or the *artful dodger,* turn to these pages. Our collection isn't exhaustive, but it aims to cover much of what an active reader will encounter.

The terms come from literature, sports, mythology, Wall Street, history, headlines, Shakespeare, politics, science, standup comics and the Sunday comics, and venues from the locker room to the board room.

We've tried to convey solid information without being stuffy about it. We show how these terms are used, with examples from magazines, newspapers, books and the odd bit from radio or film. And even if you are familiar with an expression, you are likely to be delighted with the artful, eloquent or humorous uses in our examples.

Oh: the whale was Moby Dick. The man was Captain Ahab. And Ishmael was the narrator, who lived to tell the tale.

Elizabeth Webber
Mike Feinsilber

Pronunciation Symbols

ə . . . . anoint, collide, data

'ə, ˌə cut, conundrum

ᵊ . . . . immediately preceding \l\, \n\, \m\, \ŋ\, as in battle, mitten, eaten, and sometimes open \'ō-pᵊn\, lock and key \-ŋ\; immediately following \l\, \m\, \r\, as often in French table, prisme, titre

a . . . . rap, cat, sand, lamb

ā . . . . way, paid, late, eight

ä . . . . opt, cod, mach

à . . . . French chat, table

ar . . . air, care, laird

aù . . . out, loud, tout, cow

b . . . . bat, able, rib

ch . . . chair, reach, catcher

d . . . . day, red, ladder

e . . . . egg, bed, bet

'ē, ˌē eat, reed, fleet, pea

ē . . . . penny, genie

ei . . . . Dutch eieren, dijk

f . . . . fine, chaff, office

g . . . . gate, rag, eagle

h . . . . hot, ahoy

hw . . . wheat, when

i . . . . ill, hip, bid

ī . . . . . aisle, fry, white, wide

j . . . . jump, fudge, budget

k . . . . kick, baker, scam, ask

ḵ . . . . loch, Bach, German Buch

l . . . . . lap, pal, alley

m . . . make, jam, hammer

n . . . . now, win, banner

ⁿ . . . . shows that a preceding vowel is nasalized, as in French en \äⁿ\

ŋ . . . . ring, singer, gong

ō . . . . oak, boat, toe, go

ò . . . . hawk, bawl, caught, ought

œ . . . French neuf, German Köpfe

œ̄ . . . French deux, German Löhne

òi . . . . oyster, toy, foil

òr . . . core, born, oar

p . . . . pet, tip, upper

r . . . . rut, tar, error, cart

s . . . . sink, bass, lasso

sh . . . shin, lash, pressure

t . . . . top, pat, later

th . . . third, bath, Kathy

t̲h̲ . . . this, other, bathe

ü . . . . ooze, blue, noon

ù . . . . wool, took, should

ᵫ . . . . German Bünde, füllen

ᵫ̄ . . . . German kühl, French vue

v . . . . veer, rove, ever

w . . . . well, awash

y . . . . youth, yet, lawyer

ʸ . . . . shows palatalization of a preceding consonant, as in French campagne \kän-'pänʸ\

z . . . . zoo, haze, razor

zh . . . pleasure, decision

\ \ . . . reversed virgules used to mark the beginning and end of a phonetic respelling

' . . . . . mark preceding a syllable with primary stress: boa \'bō-ə\

ˌ . . . . . mark preceding a syllable with secondary stress: beeline \'bē-ˌlīn\

- . . . . mark indicating syllable divisions

*. . . in theory the [independent counsel's] task is nothing less than to cleanse the **Augean stables** of sin and corruption and restore the national innocence. . . .*

—Gene Lyons

Abelard and Héloïse \\'a-bə-lärd . . . 'a-lə-ˌwēz, 'e-lə-\\ Tragically romantic lovers. Peter Abelard, a great scholar and teacher in France in the Middle Ages, became infatuated with Héloïse, the beautiful, intelligent young niece of Fulbert, canon of Notre Dame. Abelard talked himself into a job as her tutor and seduced her. The two fell deeply in love, and in time Héloïse discovered she was pregnant.

Héloïse was packed off to the country to have the baby, after which she and Abelard were married in secret (although Héloïse thought marriage and philosophy were not compatible). Abelard's in-laws were not happy and arranged for ruffians to attack and castrate him. Héloïse was sent to a convent and eventually became a nun and an abbess, and Abelard became a monk.

Héloïse was one of the most literate women of her day, and her duties as an administrator gave her a successful career as a nun and abbess. Abelard, though brilliant, was a maverick, and his writings were frequently denounced and sometimes burned.

After their separation, he and Héloïse corresponded through letters of love and suffering, which they later collected and published. They are said to have been buried together; they were reburied in the famous cemetery of Pere LaChaise in Paris in 1817. (Jim Morrison of the Doors was there, too, but his body was recently removed because of the damage tourists visiting it had done to other graves. Abelard and Héloïse do not have as many 20th century fans.)

The term in use, by R.Z. Sheppard, *Time,* May 22, 1995, reviewing Gabriel Garcia Marquez' novel *Love and Other Demons:*

> Cayetano is sent as an exorcist, but after one look at the girl's blue eyes and cascading copper hair, all that gets exorcised is his own inhibition. A Latin American Abelard and Héloïse? Not quite.

Another example, also from *Time,* by Nancy Gibbs, April 3, 1995:

> Penn thus becomes the latest school to turn itself inside out over an issue that dates back to Abelard and Héloïse. Through the years so many professors have romanced and often married their students that it seems a quaint, even hypocritical exercise to suddenly try to stop them.

Achilles' heel \ə-'ki-lēz\ A vulnerable point.

In Greek mythology, the hero Achilles was invulnerable to mortal wounds because his mother, Thetis, had dipped him as an infant into the magical waters of the River STYX, which flows around Hades, the underworld. But she held baby Achilles by the heel, and, inevitably, in the war against Troy, Achilles was killed by an arrow which struck him in that one vulnerable spot.

Achilles also gave us his tendon, which joins the calf muscle to the heel bone, and the Achilles reflex, prompted by a sharp tap on the Achilles tendon.

The term in use, by Maj. Gen. William L. Nash, commander of U.S. forces in Bosnia, quoted by Rick Atkinson in the *Washington Post,* April 14, 1996:

> If my Achilles' heel is the low tolerance of the American people for casualties, then I have to recognize that my success or failure in this mission is directly affected by that.

Another example, from Peter H. Lewis in the *New York Times,* March 21, 1989:

> The key to a fax machine's power, and also its Achilles' heel, is that it works over regular telephone lines. Any boor with a fax machine and your phone number can deluge you with unwanted documents.

And from Rick Wartzman, the *Wall Street Journal,* July 24, 1989:

> Some think it's the DC–10's Achilles' heel: a cluster of hydraulic lines that, if cut, can send the plane plummeting.

Acton, Lord Originator of the maxim, "Power tends to corrupt, and absolute power corrupts absolutely." (George Bernard Shaw's view, as reported in *Days with Bernard Shaw* by Stephen Winsten, was: "Power does not corrupt men; fools, however, if they get into a position of power, corrupt power.") A brilliant and quotable Victorian, Acton's full name was John Emerich Edward Dalberg, and he lived in the last two-thirds of the 19th century. As a Roman Catholic, he couldn't attend Cambridge University but later was appointed a professor in modern history there.

A friend of de Tocqueville and other prominent intellectuals of his day and celebrated as one of the most learned men of his age, Acton was an ardent Liberal and a close friend of Gladstone. (*See* GLADSTONIAN.)

In addition to his observation on the corrupting nature of power, this comment on secrecy is attributed to him: "Everything secret degenerates; nothing is safe that does not bear discussion and publicity."

His lordship evoked, by Elizabeth Janeway in her review of Jonathan Yardley's *Our Kind of People* in the *New York Times Book Review,* March 19, 1989:

The WASP group (and I speak from experience since my own kind of people are much like Mr. Yardley's) has combined the comfort of belonging with long dominance of American power and culture. This assumed entitlement naturally infuriates many people. It also complicates its members' lives and visions: reality itself, not mere wishful thinking, has seemed to confirm the rightness of their beliefs and behavior. Here, I suspect, lies the root of that corruption by established power which Lord Acton, a White Anglo-Saxon Catholic, told us humans to fear.

And by columnist Suzanne Fields in the *Washington Times,* April 20, 1997, on the character of Vice President Albert Gore:

Bland ambition quickly becomes blind ambition. To paraphrase Lord Acton: Blind ambition corrupts blindly and absolute blindness corrupts absolutely. It's possible that Al Gore, who begins to see the presidency through a glass darkly, can no longer make distinctions between personal integrity and MACHIAVELLIAN strategies of a politician. [*See* SEE THROUGH A GLASS DARKLY.]

Another example, from Charles Paul Freund in his column "Rhetorical Questions" in the *Washington Post,* April 11, 1989:

Never mind Lord Acton; in Washington, power homogenizes. Look at Newt Gingrich.

Adonis A figure in Greek mythology, so handsome that his name is a metaphor for youthful male beauty.

And like most characters in Greek mythology, his family background was complicated, and his love life was, well, messy. He was the product of the incestuous union of Cinyras, king of Cyprus, and his daughter. He grew up to be beautifully handsome, and Aphrodite, goddess of love, fell in love with him. Beng loved by a goddess was hazardous, however, and Adonis was killed while boarhunting (the boar was reputed to be the jealous war god Ares in disguise). In one version of the story, Zeus arranged for Adonis to spend part of the year with Aphrodite and part with Persephone, queen of the underworld, whose eye he had also caught. This custody arrangement explained the cycle of the seasons.

The term in use, by Brad Hooper in *Booklist,* May 1, 1991, reviewing *Paradise* by Judith McNaught:

When young, Meredith Bancroft was burned in love. A poor little rich girl, the daughter of the owner of a famous department store, she fell for a hometown Adonis who wasn't interested. Then she met Matthew, a mechanic putting himself through school. They had a brief, sour marriage.

And by Ron Fimrite in *Sports Illustrated,* March 18, 1991:

Most players at that time wore at least rudimentary helmets, but not Hobey, who considered headgear too confining. Although there was no contesting the genuineness of his modesty, there, there was a streak of narcissism in being known as "The blond Adonis of the gridiron." His golden hair became his ensign. When joyful spectators cried out, 'Here he comes!' there could be no doubting the object of their excitement. And they could count on Hobey to deliver the goods.

And from the *Springfield (Mass.) Union-News*, August 15, 1990:

Cyndy says if ever there was a relationship addict, she's one. She found herself overwhelmingly attracted to "an Adonis type, really brutally handsome."
"It was major love at first sight," she said. "Failed relationships became a habit."

agitprop \\'a-jət-ˌpräp\\ Political propaganda, and, more specifically, propaganda spread by means of literature, drama, music, or art. A marriage of agitation and propaganda, it's a tactic to arouse the people, and it works through selective and manipulative use of facts and falsehoods.

The term comes from the old Soviet Communist Party. Lenin used it through the *agitatsia propaganda* section of the Central Committee secretariat set up in 1920. Its function was to control the ideological conditioning of the populace.

In English, and generally in Europe and the United States, it is usually a pejorative term used to characterize slanted, prejudicial arguments—often those used by someone on the other side of an issue.

The term in use, by television critic Phil Kloer in the *Atlanta Journal and Constitution,* October 11, 1996:

Either it's blatant agitprop or a courageous take on a subject normally taboo to television. Evaluating *If These Walls Could Talk,* HBO's new all-star drama about abortion, may depend on which side of the picket line or pew you sit.

From Blanche McCrary in the *Village Voice,* October 12, 1993:

Bertha refused to obey any of the rules. She was a true believer, and literature, for her, was about refusing all categories. She could no more write agitprop than she could give up women and start raising rug-rats for some macho stud.

And from Dorothy Rabinowitz in the *Wall Street Journal,* February 14, 1991:

This splendid film is searing in its delineation of Depression-era hardship hitting a farm family. It veers off, to be sure, into a kind of old-fashioned simple agitprop about bosses and migrants now and again. Nevertheless, its social echoes are true and deep.

agonistes \\ˌag-ə-'nis-tēz\\ Being in a struggle, and especially contending with inner conflicts. From a Greek word, meaning combatant or contender.

The root is *agon,* meaning "a gathering place, especially for contests and competitions," and hence the competition itself. *Agonistes* is attached to the name of someone who is a protagonist in a contest or struggle, as in the most famous usage, *Samson Agonistes,* a 1671 poem by John Milton about the blinded Samson and his struggle to renew his faith.

Today, the word is usually a reference to Milton's work. T.S. Eliot used it this way in the title of his poem *Sweeney Agonistes* (1932), as did Gary Wills in the 1970 *Nixon Agonistes.*

The term in use, by John Anderson in *Newsday,* July 28, 1995, reviewing *Double Happiness,* a film about young Chinese in Canada, caught between two cultures:

> Assimilation agonistes: Young, cheeky Chinese-Canadian actress is cast in a drama of family, career, sex and culture, but never gets to play herself.

And by Carlin Romano in the *Philadelphia Inquirer,* reviewing *Democracy on Trial* by Jean Bethke Elshtain, January 15, 1995:

> No, this is not an instant book about Russia in turmoil, Haiti agonistes, or Italy twisted once again into a political pretzel.

And by Jack McCallum in *Sports Illustrated,* April 10, 1995, in a profile of UCLA basketball coach Jim Harrick:

> When he didn't get UCLA to the Final Four, and when he complained publicly that his financial compensation was not in line with that of coaches at other high-profile schools, and when he appeared apoplectic on the sidelines when things went wrong, the coach became an almost tragic figure, Harrick Agonistes, the vise of UCLA pressure tightening year after year as he died a slow death on the bench, one hand on his throat, the other in the air to protest a call.

agora \'a-gə-rə\ A gathering place, especially the marketplace in ancient Greece. In Greek cities, the agora was an open square surrounded by shops and important public buildings. It is this type of open space and bustling commercial activity that the word connotes today.

The term in use, by Robert Plunket in commentary in the *New York Times,* August 17, 1997, on the special status of the Devil in the American South:

> Any Southern politician knows he must always stand up to the devil, unless, of course, the two of them already have a pre-arranged pact, i.e., tobacco. And not just any politician. The other day I was in that agora of Southern life, the 7-Eleven, and when the woman in front of me had her purchases totaled up, they came to $6.66. She became hysterical. The whole store became hysterical. We all had to chip in and give her enough money to

buy another pack of cigarettes—anything to undo that terrible number.

And by Ty Burr in *Entertainment Weekly,* May 9, 1997, on the development of MSN, Microsoft Network:

> Well, MSN is hardly purring yet, but some of the older shows have already grown surprisingly sleek. In direct opposition to AOL's bewildering agora, MSN Onstage offers discrete, shallow-but-fun diversions that coast in on waves of animation, plug-ins, and music. . . .

Ahab \'ā-ˌhab\ A king of ancient Israel, who, with his wife JEZEBEL, is synonymous with wickedness; also Captain Ahab of Herman Melville's *Moby Dick,* identified with fanatical, monomaniacal pursuit of a goal.

As King Ahab's story is told in the Old Testament (I Kings 16:29–22:40), he married Jezebel, a foreigner, who introduced the worship of pagan gods. He soon got into terrible trouble over real estate when he coveted Naboth's vineyard. Naboth didn't want to give the land up, so Ahab, goaded by Jezebel, arranged to have Naboth stoned to death. Ahab took possession of the land but brought down the wrath of God on himself and his wife. The prophet Elijah came to prophesy the fall of the dynasty.

Melville's Captain Ahab is more familiar. As captain of the whaler *Pequod,* Ahab is obsessed with Moby Dick, the mysterious, monstrous white whale that had crippled him years before. The pursuit of vengeance consumes Ahab and eventually all of his crew. Only the narrator Ishmael, who had stood apart from the madness of the rest, survives. Ahab, caught in the rope of the harpoon he has struck into the whale, continues his pursuit even in death.

The term in use, by Murray Kempton in *Newsday,* February 2, 1995:

> For six decades and more the [Fulton] Fish Market has been to racket busters what Moby Dick was to Captain Ahab, a great black whale as endlessly pursued and as incessantly eluding as the great white whale was for the Captain of the Pequod.

Another example, from President Bill Clinton, as quoted in the *Los Angeles Times,* August 26, 1996:

> Through a combination of arrogance, inexperience and political miscalculation, the new president lashed himself—"like Ahab to the whale," in Clinton's words—to the congressional Democratic leadership, which deepened his alienation from the electorate while failing to deliver on his central promises.

And one more from George Will in the *New York Times Book Review,* April 7, 1991:

> Twenty-one years later, thin as a rail and full of purpose, he arrived at the Hub, an adolescent Ahab in baggy flannels pursuing the white whale of perfection.

alarums and excursions \ə-'lar-əmz, -lär- . . . ik-'skər-zhənz\ Stage directions in Elizabethan drama for the noises offstage that simulate the sound
of battle, such as trumpets and the clash of arms, and the movement of
soldiers across the stage. Today the phrase is used to describe clamor,
excitement, or feverishly disordered activity.

Alarum is an old form of "alarm," which was originally a call to arms.
Excursion is also of military origin; it was a sally against an enemy.

The term in use, by Bob Weimer, *Newsday,* March 5, 1989:

> The medium [television] has always been dedicated to the hard
> sell, and that most certainly has not changed. If anything, the
> coming of cable has only introduced a more frenetic quality to
> the pitches, which, like Shakespearean stage directions, are keyed
> to action. Instead of "alarums and excursions," cable television
> has 1-800 numbers. From the herky-jerky glitz of MTV to the
> unrelenting pedagogy of the Discovery Channel, they are the
> punctuation marks of salesmanship.

And Neil Hickey in *TV Guide,* May 17–23, 1986:

> The next day, Willie Nelson walked off the set. Actually, he drove
> off the set in the luxurious bus, trailed by a great, billowing cloud
> of Arizona dust. Yoda had vamoosed, his infinite, saintly patience
> exhausted. Alarums and excursions, as subproducers raced after
> him.

albatross Something that causes persistent deep concern or anxiety or
that is an encumbrance.

Consider the difficulty of getting about with a huge bird tied around
your neck, as was the predicament of the ANCIENT MARINER in Samuel
Taylor Coleridge's 1798 poem, *Rime of the Ancient Mariner. (See quotation under* XANADU). The Ancient Mariner narrates the tale of disasters
that occurred after he willfully shot an albatross. His shipmates punished
him by tying the bird's carcass around his neck. The rest of crew perished;
the mariner finally recognized the beauty of the creatures in the sea and
blessed them. At that moment, the body of the albatross fell from his
neck.

As for the albatross, it is a magnificent and endangered sea bird with a
wing span of six to seven feet and a life span of thirty to forty years. "The
majesty of the wings," writes Simon Barnes in the *Montreal Gazette,* April
14, 1996, "is redeemed by a face of beguiling silliness, a beak like a comic
nose, an expression of mild bewilderment."

The term in use, by Niki Kapsambelis of The Associated Press, August
29, 1996:

> After eight years of learning and relearning the proverb that
> money can't buy happiness, Buddy Post hopes to auction off
> what's left of the $16.2 million jackpot he won in 1988 and free
> himself of the albatross of instant wealth.

In a *Richmond Times-Dispatch* headline, January 23, 1997:

Water main break an albatross for some.

In use again in a *Washington Times* editorial, August 29, 1996:

Despite the fact that Mr. Clinton has adopted a strategy that can perhaps be summed up as 'a program a day keeps Republicans away,' the president will surely be hailed, as former New York Gov. Mario Cuomo hailed him . . . as Captain Bill, the man who lifted the albatross of big government from the neck of the Democratic Party.

Albion *See* PERFIDIOUS ALBION.

Alger, Horatio \hə-'rā-shō-'al-jər\ Resembling the fiction of Horatio Alger in which success is achieved through self-reliance and hard work.

The pattern was repeated so endlessly in Alger's books that a Horatio Alger story became a synonym for a rags-to-riches saga. The term is often applied to someone who has achieved such success, thus blending the author and his creation. Alger's heroes invariably were poor newsboys or bootblacks. Pluck worked for them, but luck figured prominently; a worthy lad would stop a runaway carriage and wind up marrying the rich banker's daughter whose life he had saved.

Alger's first success in the genre he was to make his own—*Ragged Dick: or, Street Life in New York*—was published in 1867. He ultimately wrote some 120 books, most indistinguishable from one another.

The term in use, by Betsy Morris in *Fortune* in a profile of Lou Gerstner, head of IBM, April 14, 1997:

He is drawn to the limelight like a moth to flame, yet he is belligerently private. He has lived a great Horatio Alger story, but doesn't want to tell it.

And by Peter Conn in the *New York Times Book Review,* February 2, 1986:

Royce's rise to prominence seemed to enact a kind of intellectual Horatio Alger tale—from shabby frontier obscurity to international prestige.

Alice in Wonderland A famous character in literature whose name is evoked to describe surreal situations in which people and behavior are comically strange, whimsical, contradictory, and bizarre.

The phrase is from Lewis Carroll's 1865 classic *Alice's Adventures in Wonderland*. Little Alice falls down a well and finds herself in a strange country populated by a collection of human and animal characters who act with insane illogic. Some of the most famous include the White Rabbit, the Queen of Hearts, the Mad Hatter, the March Hare and the CHESHIRE CAT. (*See also* SENTENCE FIRST, VERDICT AFTERWARDS.)

Carroll created further adventures in *Through the Looking-Glass* (1872), in which Alice climbs through a mirror and finds herself in a country where eveything is reversed. Here she meets TWEEDLEDUM AND TWEE-DLEDEE and the Red Queen (*see* RED QUEEN'S RACE).

The term in use, by Ross Clark in the *Times Literary Supplement,* March 29, 1991:

> "Albania may be an Alice in Wonderland charade, but Daniels's next destination, North Korea, confirms what one has long suspected: that as totalitarians, Eastern Europeans are mere amateurs compared to Orientals."

And by Mortimer B. Zuckerman in *U.S. News & World Report,* December 14, 1987:

> "Only in that Alice-in-Wonderland world of spin control can an agreement be promoted as a success when the budget deficit in 1988 will almost certainly be bigger than in 1987."

And from Lewis H. Lapham in *Harper's* magazine, October 1994:

> "Under what Alice in Wonderland rule of illogic did the Americans spend so much money on the care and protection of their health (nearly $1 trillion in 1993) and yet, simultaneously and with no apparent sense of contradiction, so recklessly indulge their passions for alcohol, chocolate, tobacco, and criminal violence?"

alien corn *See* AMID THE ALIEN CORN.

all the world's a stage A line from Shakespeare expressing the thought that all life is theater, and just as actors have parts to play before an audience, so do ordinary men and women.

The phrase is from Shakespeare's *As You Like It,* Act 2, Scene 7, where the exiled duke and his men prepare their meal and discuss their woes. The Duke remarks:

> This wide and universal theatre
> Presents more woeful pageants than the scene
> Wherein we play in.

Jaques, the Duke's attendant and the play's resident cynic, continues the thought:

> All the world's a stage,
> And all the men and women merely players;
> They have their exits and their entrances;
> And one man in his time plays many parts. . . .

Jaques then enumerates the seven stages of a man's life, none of them in very appealing terms, from the "mewling and puking" infant to ignominious, decrepit old age, "Sans teeth, sans eyes, sans taste, sans every thing."

The concept of life as a stage on which players emerge in the limelight (another theatrical reference—to the intense white light produced by heating a piece of lime in an oxyhydrogen flame, once used commonly in theaters) is a journalistic cliché; foreign affairs reporting is awash with references to presidents and prime ministers making debuts on the world stage.

The term in use, by Catherine Fox in the *Atlanta Journal and Constitution,* March 14, 1997:

> If all the world's a stage, then landscape architects are its set designers. They create the outdoor environments in which we live, work and play, encompassing . . . gardens and parks, streets and plazas, college campuses and resorts.

And by Jerry Carroll in the *San Francisco Chronicle,* November 29, 1995, on a well-known San Francisco hotel doorman:

> All the world's a stage—but is that enough? It is a question Tom Sweeney has pondered these 18 years in front of the Sir Francis Drake Hotel on Powell Street. He has decided it is not. He is aware that the media also are necessary if he is to achieve his goal of becoming a truly famous person. His next step in that direction will be a spot on "Late Night With David Letterman."

And by Victoria Irwin in the *Christian Science Monitor,* November 23, 1984:

> Some people think it is daring simply to live in New York City. There are such everyday heroic acts as riding the subway, coping with the anarchistic attitudes of pedestrians and motor traffic, or entering Bloomingdale's during a sale.
>
> But if all the world's a stage, then New York just might hold the record for the wildest opening acts. . . .ranging from a man who scaled the walls of the World Trade Towers, to the dedicated firefighters who risk their lives saving others.

all's right with the world *See* GOD'S IN HIS HEAVEN, ALL'S RIGHT WITH THE WORLD.

alpha and omega The first and last, from beginning to end, the whole nine yards. "Alpha" and "omega" are the first and last letters of the Greek alphabet; thus the reference is to that which is all-inclusive. Originally a reference to the divine—in the Bible (Revelations 22:13), Jesus says: "I am Alpha and Omega, the beginning and the end, the first and the last." The term in use, by John Kean, the *Times Literary Supplement,* June 21, 1991:

> The converse of this point is that representative government as we know it is not the alpha and omega of democratic forms.

And by Lewis H. Lapham in *Harper's,* November 1990:

> To President Bush, the word 'nonpartisan' is the alpha and omega of government by administrative decree: a word for all seasons;

a word that avoids the embarrassment of forthright political argument; a word with which to send the troops to Saudi Arabia, postpone decisions on the budget, diffuse the blame for the savings and loan swindle.

And by Congressman William Clay, D-Mo., quoted in the *St. Louis Post-Dispatch,* April 20, 1997:

> "A balanced budget isn't the alpha and omega," he says—definitely not "if it's going to be balanced on the backs of the poorest people in our society."

alpha male The dominant male in a group of animals.

Whether in a herd of buffalo or in a baboon troop or in a bar, the alpha male is the strongest, the best fighter, the leader of the pack, the guy who always gets the girl (or a whole herd of them, depending on the species). The term has in recent times made the jump from scientific language to general speech, to suggest the strong, powerful, or rich—with a big swagger.

"We're all primates," observed an anthropologist while himself observing the presidential inauguration activities in 1993. "Primates want to be physically close to powerful people and to see the alpha male in person."

The term can arouse strong feelings. In 1996, for instance, an expert on wolves complained to the Minnesota News Council about a *Minneapolis Star Tribune* article which, among other things, referred to him as the "alpha male of wolf research." The council, composed of journalists and private citizens, considers grievances against news organizations. The body found that the article had used "prejudicial language."

The term in use, by Maria L. LaGanga in the *Los Angeles Times,* August 11, 1996, after telling how Republican presidential candidate Bob Dole told his newly selected running mate, Jack Kemp, to make sure he knew which of the two was boss:

> As is clearly evident by the fact that Dole aides went out of their way to relate such a tale, what we have here are two alpha males— two big guys on one small ticket—and a massive struggle for image control by the operatives who would get the pair elected.

And in Maureen Dowd's *New York Times* column, January 23, 1996, on the development of a testosterone patch:

> For just $3 a day your average LOUNGE LIZARD can transform into an alpha male.

And from anthropology professor Lionel Tiger, analyzing the psychology of New York City Mayor Rudolph Giuliani in *Newsday,* March 19, 1995:

> The fact that he cannot abide another alpha male—a police commissioner, for example, who attracts independent attention— suggests he is paying too much attention to his own serotonin

level, and not enough to the realities of civic leadership. It's too bad.

And an example of *alpha* applied to something other than a male, by Amy Finnerty in the *New York Times Magazine,* November 15, 1998:

> A pretty 8-year-old wearing overalls and a deadpan expression vaunted the alpha mom who holds the most-sought-after play-date in her third-grade class: "Backyard. Dog. Full fridge. Mother who plays."

Alphonse and Gaston \\'al-ˌfän(t)s, -ˌfänz . . . 'gas-tən; 'àl-foⁿs . . . gà-'stōⁿ\\ Two people who engage in excessive and sometimes self-defeating deference to each another.

The term originates in two comic strip characters, Frenchmen who did everything with absurd, exaggerated politeness. They were created by Frederick Burr Opper (who also originated "Happy Hooligan") in 1905. According to Coulton Waugh, in *The Comics,* they were national figures, and their elaborate courtesies became catch phrases: "After you, my dear Alphonse!" and "No, after you, my dear Gaston!"

The damage arises when deference turns into destructive delay, as when two baseball fielders defer to each other to the point that the ball falls between them.

The term in use, by Lee Michael Katz in *USA Today,* November 26, 1996:

> A week after the United States vetoed a second term for incumbent Secretary-General Boutros Boutros-Ghali, the selection process has become a diplomatic Alphonse and Gaston routine. So far, no nation has formally submitted a new name for U.N. chief out of fear it will be shot down by his supporters.

Again, from John Rossant and Stan Crock in *Business Week,* June 9, 1997:

> Although American and Iranian officials caution against hopes for any overnight thaw, Khatami's election could pave the way for the first timid move toward a dialogue in a decade. The big question is whether Alphonse or Gaston will take the first step. In the wake of Khatami's election, each side is beckoning the other to make the initial goodwill gesture.

And by Kenny Moore in *Sports Illustrated,* July 22, 1996, on bicycle racer Rebecca Twigg:

> Twigg calls her defining event, in which she had been five times the world champion, "an absolutely pure race" because the cyclists compete in pairs and start on opposite sides of the track. It is therefore free of pack or sprint cycling's damnable drafting and hurry-up-and-wait Alphonse-and-Gaston tactics.

Amazon A woman warrior in Greek mythology. Also a tall, strong, powerful, and aggressive woman, often one with masculine traits. The term
may be evolving into a compliment.

According to Greek mythology, the Amazons were a tribe of warlike
women living in Scythia, an area around the Black Sea. The Greeks per-
petuated the fable that the word means "without breast," claiming that
Amazon girls had their right breasts cut off to facilitate the drawing of a
bow. An Amazon unit fought in the Trojan war on the losing Trojan side;
their leader was killed by Achilles. One of the twelve labors of Hercules
was to steal the girdle (belt) of the Amazon queen Hippolyta. The hero
Theseus fought them and married one.

Recent archeological studies on the steppes of southern Russia indicate
that the legends may have a basis in fact. Dr. Jeannine Davis-Kimball
reported in the January 1997 *Archeology* magazine that she had found
burial mounds in which females were buried with weapons; some skele-
tons showed battle wounds. Tales of these women could well have influenced Greek legends.

Women warriors turn up in various cultures in world history and legend. The Spanish explorer Francisco de Orellana claimed to have encoun-
tered them in South America, and accordingly named the Amazon River
(the world's second largest) for them.

The term in use, by Karen Heller of Knight Ridder newspapers in the
Sacramento Bee, March 22, 1996:

> And the award to the Breast Presenter at the 66th Oscar fete goes
> to . . . Miss Geena Davis! Yes, the Cher Apparent did it again,
> sporting a silver-sequined dress that dipped so far southward that
> even Sherman would have surrendered had he met up with the
> Amazon goddess.

In use again in a *Christian Science Monitor* article, January 5, 1996, by
Elizabeth Levitan Spaid, on Beverly Harvard, chief of the Atlanta Police
Department:

> The Macon, Ga. native wound up in the police force after bet-
> ting her husband $100 that she could become a police officer
> though she was not of Amazon proportions.

amen corner A conspicuous corner in church occupied by fervent wor-
shipers. The most enthusiastic members sit there and lead the "amen"
responses to the minister. By extension it refers to fervent, uncritical followers.

This phrase, an American expression, is the title of a 1955 play by James
Baldwin. It is also the name of a famous section of the Augusta National Golf Club course. The nickname was coined in 1958 in *Sports Illustrated* by Herbert Warren Wind to describe the second half of the 11th
hole, the 12th, and the first half of the 13th, where the most exciting action
had taken place that year. He took the phrase "Shouting at Amen Corner" from an old jazz record.

There is an even earlier amen corner in London near St. Paul's Cathedral. On Corpus Christi Day, the procession of monks began in Paternoster Row, saying the Lord's Prayer (*Pater Noster* is Latin for "Our Father") to the end of the street; they would say "Amen" at the corner of Ave Maria Lane and then continue with the Ave Maria. Most of this area was destroyed by bombing during World War II.

An oft-quoted example, from Patrick Buchanan, columnist, television commentator and presidential candidate, after the Iraqi invasion of Kuwait on August 2, 1991:

> There are only two groups that are beating the drums for war in the Middle East—the Israeli Defense Ministry and its amen corner in the United States.

And by James Kuhnhenn in the *Kansas City Star,* March 14, 1996:

> Forbes gave a lengthy, unscripted defense of his flat-tax proposal Wednesday morning during a planned media event in Washington. He was accompanied by Jack Kemp, the former NFL quarterback and congressman who served as housing secretary under President George Bush. Kemp, a flat-tax advocate, provided a sort of silent amen corner for Forbes, nodding vigorously throughout the speech and later declaring it a "tour de force."

Also in the *Star,* by Kent Pulliam, December 15, 1995:

> Just like the [Kansas City] Chiefs, who have kind of adopted that little piece of real estate as their own little Amen Corner.
>
> "We ought to name it something after the way things have gone for us in that corner," said Hasty, whose 64-yard interception got the whole thing started.

American century The 20th century, in which American influence should work for the good of all. A term introduced by Henry Luce, creator of the Time-Life publishing empire, in *Life* magazine, February 17, 1941:

> . . . to accept wholeheartedly our duty and our opportunity as the most powerful and vital nation in the world, and in consequence to exert upon the world the full impact of our influence, for such purposes as we see fit and by such means as we see fit. . . . [T]he world of the 20th century, if it is to come to life in any nobility of health and vigor, must be to a significant degree an American century.

Luce's statement was a powerful call to a country that had not yet entered World War II and still had strong isolationist impulses.

At the end of the war, when the United States' supremacy in military and economic strength was clear, it did seem that the American century— the PAX AMERICANA—had arrived. From the perspective of the post-Vietnam, post-Cold War present, things look different.

The phrase comes up whenever pundits, with the apparently irresistible tendency to take an event (or a poll) and make it emblematic of an era, examine the American state of mind and ever-fluctuating sense of well-being,

The term in use, in an editorial in the *Economist* reprinted in the *Kansas City Star,* March 18, 1991, in the aftermath of the Gulf War:

> Some are attracted, others frightened, by a caricature of the new world order this might lead to. America thumps any country that gets out of line, shakes down its rich friends to pay for the mugging, gets a meek go-ahead from the cops in the United Nations and tells the Soviet Union to butt out.
>
> Some such hubris is predictable. Already there are mutterings about a unipolar world, a new American century, and how Japan and Germany can be bossed around.

And from Chris Lester in a column in the *Kansas City Star,* January 15, 1993:

> But in the waning years of the American century, inaugurations have become more about business. Big business.
>
> You see, one of the real growth industries in this stagnant economy has become political influence. And inaugural celebrations have become semi-official holidays for those with the money.

And from John B. Judis in the *New Republic,* April 10, 1989, reviewing *The Price of Empire* by J. William Fulbright:

> When Fulbright became a senator during World War II, he was a champion of the American Century. When he left 30 years later, after years as the chairman of the Senate Foreign Relations Committee, he was its foremost critic.

American Dream An expression with about as many meanings as there are Americans to aspire to it, and others to comment on it; generally referring to the ideals of freedom and opportunity on which the United States was founded.

The phrase is often used to express personal pursuit of success—material and otherwise—frequently in a rags-to-riches climb from poverty to recognition, wealth, and honor. It may be a reference to the achievement of comfort and security—a house, a good job, a place in the community. Or the opportunity to achieve great riches. But the expression is also used in talking about the condition of American society, and how well it measures up to its professed ideals of equality and opportunity.

Speechmakers and takers of the public pulse are apt to ask "what happened to the American dream" or "who stole the American dream" or to ponder "whether the dream has become a nightmare" when goals or dreams go awry.

The term in use, by Christopher Swan, the *Christian Science Monitor,* January 8, 1987:

To Cadillac owners and non-owners, the car has always meant something: opulence, even snobbery; magnificent pretension; luxury you couldn't miss.

Cadillac once rolled over all comers as the essential means of transport to the American dream.

And by Les Payne in *Newsday,* February 2, 1996, reflecting on the career of the late William J. Levitt:

The "father of suburbia" brought forth his scheme on Long Island in 1947 in a cradle of 17,447 single-family frame ranch houses. This lily-white development became Levittown, which in time begat the American dream of a one-family home on a little plot of land far away from the teeming city.

Every aspect of the enterprise—even the racial exclusion— was as American as cherry pie.

And in "Comment" in the *New Yorker,* May 2, 1994:

[President Richard] Nixon prided himself on his hard work, stressing his "iron butt" in law school at Duke. But this son of a Whittier storekeeper always felt, and not always wrongly, that those who had it easier were ridiculing him. . . . His struggle was a noir version of the American dream. [*See also* FILM NOIR]

And memorably by Ernest Hemingway in *To Have and Have Not* (1937), describing the despairing descent of those ruined by the Depression and the machinations of a ruthless speculator:

Some made the long drop from the apartment or the office window; some took it quietly in two-car garages with the motor running; some used the native tradition of the Colt or Smith and Wesson; those well-constructed implements that end insomnia, terminate remorse, cure cancer, avoid bankruptcy, and blast an exit from intolerable positions by the pressure of a finger; those admirable American instruments so easily carried, so sure of effect, so well designed to end the American dream when it becomes a nightmare, their only drawback the mess they leave for relatives to clean up.

amid the alien corn Being alone in a foreign land or alien surroundings, a stranger among strangers. Although the phrase sounds like the title of an agricultural horror novel, it's from a famous poem by English Romantic poet John Keats—"Ode to a Nightingale"—which in turn refers to the biblical story of Ruth. After her husband died, Ruth loyally followed her mother-in-law Naomi, speaking to her in some of the loveliest language ever written ("Whither thou goest, I will go," Ruth 1:16). She went to Bethlehem with Naomi and became a gleaner in the fields.

The melancholy poet meditates on the mesmerizingly beautiful song of the nightingale:

Perhaps the self-same song that found a path
Through the sad heart of Ruth, when, sick for home,
She stood in tears amid the alien corn. . . .

The poem has many phrases familiar to us—including "tender is the night," and "for many a time I have been half in love with easeful Death." The term in use, by Matt Nesvisky in the *Jerusalem Post,* July 28, 1995, writing on the life of a Jewish refugee who now lives in the Great Smoky Mountains:

> It's a saga of a refugee, a prisoner, an escapee, a tale of multiple identities, passports and army uniforms, a narrative of international executive life and of tending one's backwoods garden amid very alien corn.

And by sportswriter Bill Conlin in the *Philadelphia Daily News,* November 30, 1990, reporting on the progress of Temple University's basketball team:

> Temple stood in a passive zone amid the alien corn of Iowa, lost to an underwhelming Hawkeyes team in a Big Apple NIT first round game, had its No. 19 ranking stripped away and was dragged back to [coach] Chaney's 5:30 a.m. drawing board.

anal retentive Someone who is orderly, punctual, obsessed with detail, overly conscientious, and excessively frugal. This term from psychological analysis has made its way into general use. While this type might sound like what the world needs more of, it is nevertheless considered a personality disorder.

The problem is thought to arise during the anal stage of psychosexual development, when a primary source of pleasure for the individual is defecation or, in this case, *not* defecating—hence anal *retention.* Yes, the reference is to infants and toilet training.

Anal-retentive personalities are thought by some schools of thought to develop three traits: orderliness (reliability, punctuality, and conscientiousness); parsimony, or avarice; and obstinacy and closely allied traits such as defiance, vindictiveness, and irascibility.

These traits were transformed into comedy by Neil Simon in his play *The Odd Couple* in which a slob and a neat freak become roommates. In fact, Oscar Madison, the slobby sportswriter, is evoked in this use from the New York Times News Service, quoted in the *Sacramento Bee,* May 7, 1995:

> Morgenstern is not an MD, or even a PhD. She's a PO—a professional organizer. With a roll of paper towels, a can of Endust, stacks of multicolored file folders and a focused mind, she transforms offices that seem like homages to Oscar Madison into dream homes for the anal retentive.

And by John MacLachlan Gray, *Maclean's* magazine, February 12, 1996:

One reason for our much-admired social stability is that Canada traditionally provides zones of refuge for disgruntled citizens who have had it up to here with some facet of the country. For example, if you are fed up with a certain, shall we say, anal-retentive quality to the English-Canadian lifestyle, then Montreal is the place for you, an island of European cosmopolitanism two hours from Ottawa.

ancien régime \än s-ya n-rä-'zhēm\ Specifically, the political and social system of France before the Revolution of 1789. Generally, a system or mode no longer in effect.

The term in use, by Tom Teepen in the *Atlanta Journal and Constitution,* March 18, 1997:

You remember the revolution.

It would rescue nature from environmentalists and return it to the care of the industrialists, who are God's chosen stewards. The Education Department was to be destroyed as if it were a suspicious satchel found outside a schoolhouse door. There'd be a televangelist in every classroom, and we'd have federally enforced Victorianism.

The TUMBRELS were lined up and ready to roll to the guillotine liberals, moderates, moral relativists and other corruptions of the ancien régime.

Didn't happen.

Another example, from Fouad Ajami, *U.S. News & World Report,* June 19, 1989, commenting on the death of the Iranian revolutionary leader Ayatollah Khomeini:

Above all, Khomeini was a state builder. The real legacy he leaves is the clerical state he built on the ruins of the ancien régime.

Ancient Mariner An often old and always insistent person or guest determined to relate a long, strange tale. The Ancient Mariner was the narrator and central character of Samuel Taylor Coleridge's poem *The Rime of the Ancient Mariner* (1798). Thin, gray-bearded, and with a glittering eye, the Mariner detains a man on his way to a wedding and forces him to listen to a fantastic tale of woe.

The Ancient Mariner had been a sailor on a ship driven far into the icy seas near the South Pole. When an ALBATROSS, considered a favorable omen, appeared, the ship was able to sail forth through the icebergs to safety—until our man shot the bird with his crossbow. Then things got very bad indeed. The ship was becalmed as if cursed, in Coleridge's famous description:

Day after day, day after day,
We stuck, nor breath nor motion;
As idle as a painted ship
Upon a painted ocean.

His angry shipmates hung the albatross around the Mariner's neck, but even so everyone died except him; his redemption finally began when after a moonlight vision, he saw beauty in the creatures of the sea and blessed them. At this moment the albatross fell from his neck. Once on shore, the Ancient Mariner continued his penance by telling his long tale to others. And nobody got off easily—*The Rime of the Ancient Mariner* went on at length, Parts I through VII. The Wedding Guest finally went on his way "like one that hath been stunned."

The term in use by Tom Shone in the *New Yorker,* March 17, 1997:

> When he is ascending the conversational foothills toward one of his favorite theories—"the Normalizing of the Psychopathic," say, or "the Death of Affect" (he seems to speak in capitals a lot)—his eyes widen a little madly and his laconic drawl rises to an excited declamatory pitch, his white hair shaking loose. The over-all effect is of the Ancient Mariner. . . .

And by historian Stanley J. Kutler in an op-ed piece in the *Los Angeles Times,* August 8, 1989:

> Historian Ronald Steel once wrote that Nixon was the Ancient Mariner, forever tugging at our sleeve, anxious to tell his story. More is to come, as the former President has announced he will publish yet another memoir next spring in which he will discuss his resignation.

angry young man One of a group of English writers in the 1950s, whose works express the bitterness of the lower classes towards the stultifying class snobbery and hypocrisy of the British Establishment. An angry young man is not someone in a temper, but rather one who upsets conventional taste and standards, especially in the arts.

Although the term itself dates to the early 1940s, its use in the 1950s came from the title of a memoir by Leslie Allen Paul, *Angry Young Man.* Another source was John Osborne's play, *Look Back in Anger,* first performed in 1956. According to the back-cover blurb of the play's Penguin Book edition, the hero of Osborne's play, Jimmy Porter,

> plays trumpet badly. He browbeats his flatmate, terrorizes his wife, and is not above sleeping with her best friend—who loathes Jimmy almost as much as he loathes himself. Yet this working-class HAMLET, the original Angry Young Man, is one of the most mesmerizing characters ever to burst onto a stage, a malevolently vital, volcanically articulate internal exile in the dreary, dreaming Siberia of postwar England.

The term in use, by Joe Baltake, the *Sacramento Bee* movie critic, in his April 22, 1994 review of *Backbeat,* a film on the early years of the Beatles:

> Anger is the core of this movie. It's celebrated. It's prized. The one personality here who feels this emotion most acutely is John

Lennon ... presented here as the counterculture, Angry Young Man equivalent to all those characters that Mickey Rooney played in MGM's barn musicals.

And by Karen Campbell in the *Christian Science Monitor,* March 24, 1997:

> Once upon a time, choreographer Bill T. Jones was considered the modern dance world's most visible "angry young man." In works such as "Last Night on Earth," "Last Supper at Uncle Tom's Cabin," and the epic but controversial "Still/Here," his creativity has been fired by hot issues and challenging social concerns.

And by Verne Gay in *Newsday,* November 26, 1995:

> Consider, ladies and gentlemen, the curious and poignant tale of a certain Mr. Rod Serling.
> He was television's first angry young man, a masterful writer who railed against a powerful medium's trivialities and commercialism but who, eventually, succumbed to both.

Anschluss \'än-ˌshlùs\ Annexation, joining, or union. Specifically, the forcible annexation, by Adolf Hitler's Germany, of Austria in 1938. From German, where it has the same meaning. Austria was Hitler's first external conquest, the fulfillment of a vow made in the first paragraph of *Mein Kampf,* to seize his native land "by any means." By extension, *Anschluss* refers to a forced annexation of territory by a stronger nation overpowering a weaker one.

The Austrian government attempted feebly to hold off the Germans; Chancellor Schuschnigg announced a plebiscite on the question of Austrian independence in which only pro-independence ballots would be distributed. Those wishing to support annexation would have to produce their own ballots, an effort that had significant popular support, and that led Hitler to demand a postponement of the election and Schuschnigg's resignation. Unable to control events, the chancellor resigned on March 11, 1938, and was replaced by a Nazi sympathizer. On March 12 the German army invaded. Ruthless revenge was taken on opponents.

A plebiscite conducted by the Nazis after the fact gave a 99.75 percent vote in favor of union.

The term in use, by Christopher Hitchens in a column in the *Los Angeles Times,* August 17, 1997, on Turkey's occupation of a portion of Cyprus:

> As Turkey's paymaster and armorer, Washington has a right and a duty to demand that Ankara's foolish talk of Anschluss be abandoned, and that the Turks and Greeks of Cyprus be given their own fair chance to share in an expanded Europe instead of becoming prisoners of an expansionist Turkey.

And again, by columnist Georgie Anne Geyer of Universal Press Syndicate, December 26, 1995:

Well, first, despite brilliant and courageous coverage of the immediate war—the siege of Sarajevo, for instance—there was virtually no American press in the rest of the "former Yugoslavia" in 1989, '90 and '91, when only a few of us were trying to call the world's attention to the fact that Slobodan Milosevic was well into preparing for a Serbian "Anschluss."

antebellum \‚an-ti-'be-ləm\ Existing before a war. In the United States it always means before the Civil War. An antebellum mansion is one built before 1860. The phrase is Latin.

The term in use, by Florence King, in *Reflections In a Jaundiced Eye* (1989), as quoted by Jonathan Yardley in the *Washington Post*, March 29, 1989:

> I graduated from college qualified to do nothing except crossword puzzles in ink. Though a scholarship student, I received an aristocrat's education, designed for people like the antebellum Ashley Wilkes who have the money and leisure to enjoy it for its own sake.

And by Pete Waldemer in the *Detroit News*, April 11, 1997:

> There in the heart of Georgia's antebellum red clay country, however, it was neither stylish nor de rigueur to have American blacks like Charlie Sifford, Pete Brown or Lee Elder not only traipsing around your expensive, manicured golf links, but (heaven forbid) showering in your locker room or (mercy sakes) eating in your clubhouse dining room.

Antichrist One who denies or opposes Christ; a great antagonist expected to fill the world with wickedness but to be conquered forever by Christ at his SECOND COMING. Mentioned at I John 2:18, 22, 4:3; II John 7; probably at II Thess. 2:1–12, Rev. 13 and 17.

However, the concept of a demonic "man of sin," a devilish figure who will engage God in the final battle at the end of time, is older than Christianity. It is found in ancient Babylonian and Persian traditions and in the prophecies of the Old Testament.

As the Christian church evolved, so did its enemies, and the label of Antichrist was applied to such figures as the Roman emperors Caligula and Nero. In the Middle Ages, the term was used against opponents in religious or political quarrels: during the Reformation, reformers Luther and Calvin charged that the papacy was the Antichrist. The Catholic Church responded in kind.

In more recent times, the term has been applied to contemporary figures such as Kaiser Wilhelm and Hitler. What it comes down to, of course, is that the Antichrist is someone on the other side of a bitter dispute; or, used in a completely hyperbolic humorous sense, is a terrifying person or entity.

The term in use, quoted by Jon Scher in *Sports Illustrated*, April 23, 1997, describing six-foot-seven hockey star Mario Lemieux:

Says the Detroit Red Wings' Tim Cheveldae, still smarting from the three goals Lemieux scored against him in a 9–6 Penguins victory. . . . "They ought to add another six to his uniform. Then he can wear number 666, like the Antichrist. That's what he is. He's the Antichrist."

Another example, from Robert Wright in the *New Republic,* May 24, 1993:

With time this contrast hardened into hacker iconography. Gates was the anti-Christ, a man whose corporate stranglehold on the software industry had left it awash in ugly products. Kapor was a folk hero.

antihero The central character of a work or a notable figure who lacks the traditional attributes of heroes—brains, strength, courage, or other admirable characteristics. Antiheroes may be foolish, cowardly, dishonest, or wicked, but still manage to stir the sympathies of the reader. Famous antiheroes are Yossarian in Joseph Heller's *Catch-22,* the protagonist of Cervantes' *Don Quixote,* and George MacDonald Fraser's Flashman.

The term in use, by Bob Sherwin in the *Seattle Times,* June 4, 1996, on the NBA playoffs and the champions-to-be Chicago Bulls:

Rodman has stolen some of Jordan's thunder, though if you'd ask Jordan he'd say Rodman can have it. Jordan is the hero here while Rodman has emerged as his petulant antihero sidekick.

And by Eugen Weber in a review in the *Washington Post,* March 19, 1989, of *Citizens,* by Simon Schama, a history of the French Revolution:

Speaking from the ruthless precinct of the Committee of Public Safety, Saint-Just, who is one of Mr. Schama's favorite antiheroes, insisted that the Republic stood for the extermination of everything that opposed it.

And by Timothy D. Schellhardt in the *Wall Street Journal,* December 26, 1996:

The show begins with the voice of actor Michael Douglas as Gordon Gekko, the greedy antihero of the movie *Wall Street.*

Apocalypse *See* FOUR HORSEMEN OF THE APOCALYPSE.

Apollonian Having the characteristics of, or pertaining to, the Greek god Apollo. These are such qualities as rationality, intellect, a spirit of justice, creativity. All in all, a cast of mind opposite to DIONYSIAN, which is instinctive, irrational, uninhibited, destructive.

The German philosopher Nietzsche's influential writings on Greek tragedy (*The Birth of Tragedy from the Spirit of Music,* 1872) viewed Apollo and Dionysius as the personification of opposing creative tendencies in man.

Don't confuse this term with the various Apolloniuses who were out and about in the ancient world, writing on science and philosophy. Also be careful if you are introduced to Apollyon at a Hollywood cocktail party; the name is similar but this is a character who was, or is, king of Hell and is described in Revelations as the "angel of the bottomless pit." The term in use, by Lisa Liebmann, *Harper's Bazaar,* August 1, 1996:

> Jasper Johns, whose work will be celebrated in a retrospective that opens October 20 at the Museum of Modern Art, may be the most influential artist of our time, as well as the most elusive. He seems, indeed to be a figure of almost infinite paradox. Johns and his work have again and again been associated with such Apollonian virtues as wryness, remoteness, and intellectualism. And yet his whole career seems to have sprung from the very opposite sort of impulse.

And by Camille Paglia and Neil Postman in *Harper's,* March 1991:

> The history of Western civilization has been a constant struggle between these two impulses, an unending tennis match between cold Apollonian categorization and Dionysian lust and chaos.

And by Robert Hughes in the *Manchester Guardian Weekly,* October 11, 1992:

> People sometimes speak of Matisse's "assurance," his Apollonian, almost inhuman, balance.

apparatchik \ˌä-pə-ˈrä(t)-chik\ A member of the Communist Party organization, whether, functionary, agent, or spy. In contemporary use, the term has broadened to refer to bureaucrats and government officials— functionaries who carry out policy. It's not a friendly word; Western use connotes someone who mindlessly carries out orders from above.

The term in use, quoted by John Hanchette for Gannett News Service, June 28, 1995, on internal disputes within the National Rifle Association:

> One who thinks [NRA official Wayne] LaPierre is Knox's puppet is Osha Dale Davidson, author of "Under Fire," a recent book tracing the NRA's battle against gun control: "Wayne is an apparatchik for the NRA board, and mostly for Neal Knox. He will do whatever they tell him to do. He's a paid lobbyist. That's what his history is. He does what he is told to do."

Another example, from Doug Ireland in the *Nation,* December 5, 1994:

> Whatever the incoming crop of fresh-faced right-wingers lack in experience will be more than made up for by the sophistication of their staffs, drawn from the ranks of the business lobby and the amply funded Republican think tanks, and honeycombed with apparatchik ultras from groups like the Christian Coalition and the Free Congress Foundation.

après moi le déluge \à-pre-mwà-lə-dā-lūēzh\ A French phrase, translated as "after me the deluge," or flood, and meaning (loosely), "after I leave,

all hell is going to break loose." Sometimes this is offered as a simple pre-
diction, and sometimes with the unspoken corollary, "And I don't care
because I'll be dead."

The phrase is usually attributed to Louis XV of France or to Madame
de Pompadour, his mistress. Given how things went for Louis XVI in
the French Revolution, either one couldn't have put the case more suc-
cinctly.

An example, from *Newsday,* November 3, 1996, by John Edgar Wide-
man in a telephone interview:

> He [Clinton] gets into this position of power, and at the first sign
> of real danger to his career, and he adopts this tremendously cyn-
> ical posture of "Apres moi, le deluge."

And as used by "Loose Lips," political columnist of the Washington,
D.C. *City Paper,* captioning a picture of embattled D.C. Inspector General Angela Avant, December 6, 1996:

> Avant le Deluge: The IG will be lucky to make it through the
> holidays.

Aquarius, Age of; Aquarian A new astrological age of freedom, brother-
hood, and community that will also usher in the conquest of outer space;
new astrological era characterized by great changes in society and culture. The Age of Aquarius follows the Age of Pisces, which in the West
corresponds to the Christian era, and may or may not have begun already.
Named for the constellation Aquarius, the water bearer and 11th sign of
the zodiac, the new age will dawn when the sun is in Aquarius at the ver-
nal equinox. An Aquarian espouses the tenets of the new era.

The term was popularized in the 1960s, through the hit musical *Hair*
and other popular and commercial celebrations of the hippie counterculture. These uses of the term suggested a benign view of the changes
anticipated in the new era; harmony, peace, and understanding were to
be the order of the day. The idea retains some life in various New Age
beliefs, an amorphous successor to the '60s originals.

The term today evokes a romantic, naive spirit of optimism—or sneers
at the misjudgments and excesses of the era.

The term in use, by Elinor J. Brecher of Knight-Ridder News Service
in the *Lexington (Ky.) Herald-Leader,* October 10, 1996:

> For eons, a business suit wasn't much to look at: Dark. Boxy.
> Boring. Then, as the Age of Aquarius segued into the Age of
> Arbitrage, businessmen began to discover style. The suit became
> a symbol of success.

And by Secretary of Defense William Cohen, discussing issues of morality in the military in a commencement address at the Air Force Academy, June 2, 1997:

> There are some who now suggest that the military is preaching
> Victorian values in the Age of Aquarius, that our standards are

unrealistic or maybe even undesirable when contrasted with contemporary mores. They would have the military define decency down. I disagree.

And again, from Rick Nichols in the *Philadelphia Inquirer* magazine, July 14, 1996:

> Perhaps it was a matter of time before fresh-squeezed fruit juices and smoothies (with whipped fat-free yogurt or soy milk) would come back in vogue—back from the Aquarian attic.

Ark of the Covenant Something sacred or revered; a revealed truth. The sacred chest representing to the Hebrews the presence of God among them. As described in Exodus:10–12, it was made of wood covered in gold and had four rings to hold the staves used to carry it. The lid of gold was called the mercy seat; two golden cherubim hovered over it. Within the Ark were the two tablets with the Ten Commandments, the basis of the covenant between God and Israel. The ark was regularly carried into battle; for example, it was carried around the walls of Jericho. Kept finally in the Holy of Holies of Solomon's temple in Jerusalem, it disappeared after the fall of Jerusalem in 586 B.C. Its fate is unknown, but Ethiopians believe it rests in the church of St. Mary of Zion at Axum in northern Ethiopia.

The term in use, by British Prime Minister James Callaghan, quoted in *Time,* April 19, 1976, warning the members of his Labour Party that he intended to maintain party unity at all costs:

> I want no cliques. None of you hold the Ark of the Covenant.

Another example, quoted by the *Washington Times,* October 9, 1989, on issues in the Virginia gubernatorial race:

> "They used to call [right to work] the ark of the political covenant" said James Sweeny, a historian at Old Dominion University in Norfolk. "It's a holy of holies. You just don't trifle with the right-to-work law."

And from Murray Kempton, *Newsday,* May 26, 1996:

> Politics is calculation overlaid with the mask of holy faith. To listen to the House debating the minimum wage through two days was to be frozen numb by the winds of theology. . . . As it had been Dick Armey's pleasure to crow the revolution's dawn, it had become his duty now to preach over its descent into the night. Resistance to a higher minimum wage had been the Ark of his Covenant. No fundamentalist divine whose congregants had gagged at the story of Jonah and the Whale could have been more aggrieved at this profanation.

Armageddon \ˌär-mə-ˈgə-dᵊn\ The site of the climactic battle between the forces of good and evil at the end of the world. From the book of

Revelations (16:14–16) in the New Testament, it is used to describe a usually vast, decisive conflict or confrontation.

In fundamentalist Christian belief, "Armageddon theology" prescribes the sequence of events in the coming destruction and re-creation of the world. One step in the sequence is the Rapture, the moment when the select are whisked off the earth by God—out of bed, out of cars, etc.—leaving everyone else to die in the cataclysm. (Apparently out of clothes, too: a T-shirt observed in downtown Washington reads, "In case of rapture, this shirt will be EMPTY!")

Armageddon has become a cliché used to describe nuclear war, as well as other decisive and destructive battles.

The term in use, by Mary Curtius in the *Los Angeles Times,* September 22, 1996, on the effect of closing the San Francisco Central Freeway:

> Then came Aug. 25 and instead of Armageddon, the city experienced something closer to the BERMUDA TRIANGLE of commuting. The freeway closed and 80,000 cars seemed simply to disappear.

And by Matthew McAllester in *Newsday,* reporting on a computer virus scare, August 21, 1996:

> While the highly infectious Hare virus is constructed in a way that could enable it to wipe out every file on a computer's memory, Renert and his colleagues in the antivirus industry counsel caution and safety, not panic. Every day, they note, hackers release thousands of computer viruses that fail to deliver the promised armageddon.

And by *Washington Post* film critic Rita Kempley, reviewing *The War of the Roses,* December 8, 1989:

> *The War of the Roses* is yuppie Armageddon, an explosion of empty values and curdled peevishness that blows a marriage and blasts a decade.

Arnold, Benedict A traitor of the first order.

Benedict Arnold (1741–1801) was a general and military hero in the war for American independence. After serving with distinction in the colonial assaults on Fort Ticonderoga and Quebec and in the Saratoga Campaign, he was passed over for promotion for political reasons. Although he eventually received his promotion, he was highly sensitive to criticism, and General George Washington twice had to talk him out of resigning.

While in command of American troops in Philadelphia in 1778, he incurred heavy debts with his highly social life style. He also married a woman of Loyalist sympathies. His enemies in Congress accused him of improprieties, which eventually led to a court martial. Although most of the charges were dropped, Washington was still obliged to reprimand him. This, combined with his lingering grudge, led him to conspire with General Clinton of the British army. When Arnold learned he would be appointed to the command of the post at West Point, New York (not yet the U.S. Military Academy), he proposed to surrender the fort to the British.

Major John Andre, who was to arrange the details under a flag of truce, was captured and the scheme exposed. Andre was hanged as a spy (he disregarded orders and dressed as a civilian). Arnold fled on a British warship; he later led Loyalist troops on raids in Virginia and Connecticut. In 1781 he left for England, where he received a small pension, and he lived out his life there, disgraced and scorned as a traitor. His wife stuck with him to the end.

The term in use, by Joan Lowy in a Scripps Howard News Service article, May 6, 1996:

> A provision quietly tucked into an immigration reform bill would allow the government to bar wealthy Americans from re-entering the country if they renounce their citizenship to avoid taxes. An estimated two dozen Americans, whom critics have dubbed "Benedict Arnold billionaires," renounce their citizenship each year in favor of countries with more generous tax laws.

And by Brown University professor Darrell M. West in *Newsday,* June 13, 1997:

> The identity of Deep Throat is the greatest remaining mystery of Watergate. Hailed by many as a profile in courage and condemned by others as a modern-day Benedict Arnold, there is little doubt this individual played a crucial role in the greatest presidential scandal of this century

Artful Dodger A streetwise thief, especially a young one; an agile, clever trickster or con artist.

The term comes from a character in Charles Dickens' novel *Oliver Twist.* Artful Dodger was the star of Fagin's gang of child thieves and was the most accomplished pickpocket of them all. His name was Jack Dawkins, but in tribute to his slippery skills he was called the Artful Dodger.

The term in use, by Tony Snow, Gannett News Service, April 1, 1996:

> You hear it everywhere, even in Washington's Democratic salons and saloons: Bill and Hillary Rodham Clinton have a knack for looking guilty. They withhold information, move files, tell silly lies and just do dumb stuff. Although the consensus holds that the Clintons are sweet bunglers rather than artful dodgers, recent events offer tantalizing hints to the contrary.

Another example, from Walter A. Hackett, the *Christian Science Monitor,* March 16, 1989:

> My baggage handler slid up, handed me my stubs. I gave him a $2 tip. "You must be a rich Japanese," he said grinning. He took off like the Artful Dodger.

ashes to ashes, dust to dust A phrase from the graveside rites for the burial of the dead from the *Book of Common Prayer* of the Church of England and the Protestant Episcopal Church in the United States. As earth is cast onto the body in the grave, the recitation is "earth to earth, ashes to ashes, dust to dust; in sure and certain hope of the Resurrection to eternal life. . . . " In a more general sense, the phrase is used to suggest finality, irrevocable loss or decay.

The *Book of Common Prayer* itself has had a lively life, alternately extinguished and restored in its long history. It was first published in 1549 (during the brief reign of little Edward VI, son of Henry VIII); suppressed by Queen Mary; resurrected by Elizabeth I; forced on the stiff-necked Presbyterians of Scotland, who fought the "Bishops' Wars" of 1639-40 over it; suppressed again by Cromwell and the Commonwealth, 1645–60; and made official and compulsory in 1662.

The term in use, by Linda Gorov and Tom Mashberg in the *Boston Globe Magazine,* May 22, 1994, on the debate in post-communist Russia over what to do with the body of Lenin:

> Instigator of world communism, father (and mummy) of the Soviet state, successor to Marx, precursor of Mao, poster man for cryogenics. Forever young at 53. He's also the Kremlin's riddle-inside-the-enigma-within-the-paradox (*See* RIDDLE WRAPPED IN A MYSTERY INSIDE AN ENIGMA) of the 90s: To bury Lenin? . . . Forget ashes to ashes, dust to dust. Forget the Kremlin Wall [where Leonid Brezhnev is interred]. Forget even Madame Toussaud's Wax Museum! With all the hard labor that went into pickling him . . . there are far better uses for Vladimir Illyich. . . .

(The authors go on to suggest that Lenin could be, among other things, a mannequin for car-pool lane cheaters or a spokesperson for the Dukakis 1996 presidential campaign.)

Also from the *Boston Globe,* January 19, 1986:

> Ashes to Ashes and Dust to Dust Department—School Committee member Joe Casper's weekly newsletter, always entertaining, last week concerned a senior custodian in the Boston public schools who "through no fault of his own has been dead for 20 years." Recently a letter was sent to the custodian from the personnel department stating he must notify them if he is coming back or request an extended leave of absence.

And by Lynn Van Dine in the *Detroit News,* October 10, 1996:

> Ashes to ashes, dust to dust, and computer to computer. The virtual funeral is now a reality. A White Plains, N.Y., company has taken all the necessities of paying respects to the deceased and pulled them together in a Web site on the Internet.

Attila the Hun King of the Huns from 434 until his death in 453. His name and that of his people is synonymous with barbarism, cruelty, terror, and destruction. (*See* GOTHIC.)

Attila, also called the "Scourge of God" (in Latin it sounds even worse: "Flagellum Dei"), led his people out of North Central Asia, creating the chaos that pushed along the fall of the Roman Empire. Attila thrust his armies into Greece as far as THERMOPYLAE (where the pass was held) and westward into Gaul (France), where he was finally stopped at the Battle of the Calonian Plains (the exact place is unknown) by the Roman general Aetius who was reinforced by the Visigoths. It was the last great victory of the collapsing Roman Empire and Attila's only defeat. Attila died in his sleep the night after his marriage in 453, and the Hun Empire melted away.

Today, *Attila* is usually a jocular epithet, from the "Attila the Nun" of old parochial school fame to Prime Minister Margaret Thatcher as "Attila the Hen" to the politician "to the right of Attila the Hun." As recently as World War I, Germans were demonized in government propaganda as "Huns" for alleged atrocities against civilians, although the Kaiser himself had set this tone in 1900 with his typical bombast, when he urged troops sent off to China to treat the Chinese as the Huns had.

The term in use, by Christopher Corbett in the *Baltimore Sun,* May 1, 1994:

> In an age in which, if we trust *Time* magazine, most Americans believe in angels and the *Sun* has carried news of people who've had sex with extraterrestrials, there remains a need for the powerful antidote to quackery offered by H.L. Mencken. But the City That Reads doesn't read "the Attila of critics," and so the publication of the first biography of the great iconoclast in a quarter of a century . . . is less of an event than a new John Waters movie. . . .

And from Myrne Roe in an editorial in the the *Wichita Eagle,* December 31, 1992:

> And who can forget the spectacle of the Republican Convention in Houston, with the denizens of the right Pat Robertson, the Quayles, and Pat Buchanan holding forth with ideas that make Attila the Hun seem kinder and gentler. [*See* KINDER, GENTLER.]

Augean stables /ò-'jē-ən/ A condition or place marked by great accumulation of filth or corruption. Where Augean stables are involved, look for a formidable cleanup job, often distasteful.

According to Greek myth, cleaning the stables of King Augeas was one of the twelve heroic labors of Hercules. Just how heroic can be judged from the statistics: the stables housed 3,000 oxen and hadn't been shoveled out in 30 years. Hercules accomplished the task by diverting two rivers and using them to flush out the mess.

A crusading district attorney elected on a pledge to reform an entrenched political machine is said to face a HERCULEAN task in cleaning out the city's Augean stables.

The term in use, by Gene Lyons, reviewing *Firewall: The Iran-Contra Conspiracy and Cover-Up* by Lawrence Walsh in *Newsday,* July 13, 1997:

> Pity the poor independent counsel. In the romantic version of the prevailing myth favored by our nation's political press, his mission is truly a heroic one. Provisionally endowed with the kind of spotless virtue and fierce dedication to Truth, Justice and the American Way that the Washington media normally attribute only to themselves, in theory the I.C.'s task is nothing less than to cleanse the Augean stables of sin and corruption and restore the national innocence. And quickly and dramatically too, lest the audience turn restless and resentful.

And by James Traub, the *New York Times Magazine,* May 9, 1989, referring to a plan to evict suspected drug dealers from public housing:

> It was a new-breeze, clean-the-Augean-stables kind of idea, but civil libertarians have complained that you can't deprive someone of shelter based on an allegation of drug peddling or use.

Augustan Age An illustrious period of Latin literature, from about 45 B.C. to A.D. 18, and also the golden age of any nation's literature.

Augustan refers specifically to the flowering of poetry during the reign of the Roman Emperor Augustus (27 B.C.–A.D. 14). This was the era of Virgil, Horace, and Ovid.

The term is now applied to any period of classical greatness in a nation's literary life. It is frequently applied to the early 18th century in England, specifically the reign of Queen Anne, a period distinguished by Alexander Pope, Jonathan Swift, Joseph Addison, and Richard Steele. It is sometimes extended to take in John Dryden at the beginning and Samuel Johnson at the end.

The term in use, by Marc Schogol in the *Philadelphia Inquirer,* June 30, 1991, reviewing biographies of John F. Kennedy (*Promises Kept,* by Irving Bernstein; *A Question of Character,* by Thomas C. Reeves):

> But in contradiction to those who believe JFK would have developed into a true philosopher-king during a second term in the White House, inaugurating an Augustan Age at home and abroad, Reeves says: "It should be noted that Jack was still incapable of monogamy at the time of his assassination. And it was just as likely that news of the dark side of the president's personal and official activities might have ruined Kennedy's second term. . . . "

And by Justin Kaplan in the *Boston Globe* magazine, May 4, 1980, on the literary history of Boston. On a visit to Boston, Western writer Bret Harte dined with the greats of American literature—Longfellow, Emerson, Dana, Holmes:

After a few days in such company, Harte observed to his host, William Dean Howells, that in this part of the country it was impossible to fire a revolver without bringing down the author of a two-volume work. . . . But it was clear even to Howells, who had come from Ohio as a literary pilgrim and postulant, that Boston culture had entered a post-Augustan age. . . . By the 1870s, New England's great men had become its sacred cows.

auto–da–fé \ˌaú-tō-də-ˈfā, ȯ-tō-də-ˈfā\ The ceremony in the Spanish Inquisition during which judgment was pronounced. Execution followed. The Portuguese term meaning "act of faith" has come to apply both to sentencing and execution. In fact, during the Inquisition, the prisoners—unrepentant or relapsed heretics—were handed over by the church to the government for execution, usually by fire. (*See* TORQUEMADA.) The term connotes unjust, arbitrary, and usually fatal proceedings.

The term in use, by Maureen Dowd in her *New York Times* column, May 21, 1997:

> Lieut. Kelly Flinn will no longer fly B–52 bombers for the Air Force, but her training in hitting the target has not been wasted. . . . She has momentarily saved herself from the auto-da-fe that the Air Force had prepared for her, waging a clever and passionate public relations battle that has sparked an intense national debate on whether the military should be prying into affairs of the heart so avidly, and on whether the generation-old experiment on integrating the sexes has failed.

Another example, James Gleick in *Genius:The Life and Science of Richard Feynman* (1992):

> In less than a decade Oppenheimer himself would lose his security clearance in the classic McCarthy-era auto-da-fé. [*See* MCCARTHYISM.]

avatar \ˈa-və-ˌtär\ The embodiment of a concept, attitude, or view of life.
    It's from a Sanskrit word meaning "descent." In Hindu belief, it refers to the incarnation of a deity on earth.
    The term in use, by Phoebe Hoban in the *New York Times,* July 6, 1997, describing film director John Waters:

> The Baltimore-based director was in town on Tuesday night to sign 25th anniversary video editions of "Pink Flamingos," the scatological film that established Mr. Waters and his leading "lady," Divine, as America's avatars of outrageously bad taste.

And by Henry Louis Gates Jr., in the *New Yorker,* April 8, 1996:

> On the occasions when Ralph Ellison, an avatar of elegance, was invited to college campuses, blacks invariably denounced him for his failure to involve himself in the civil-rights struggle, for his evident disdain of the posturing of Black Power.

axis A real or imaginary straight line about which an object rotates, or a central line along which the parts of a thing or a system are symmetrical. Thus the earth's axis is an imaginary line through the center of the earth marking the North and South Poles. The earth rotates on this axis.

An axis is also a partnership or alliance between nations, groups, power centers, or individuals.

During World War II, Germany, Italy, and Japan called themselves the Axis, with Bulgaria, Hungary, and Rumania as junior partners, all opposing the Allies.

The term in use, by Chuck Taylor of the *Seattle Times,* on media coverage of Jamie Tarses, 33-year-old head of entertainment for ABC, July 23, 1997:

> Some of those covering the semiannual TV-writers meeting here at the Ritz-Carlton Huntington Hotel have been stalking her as though she was Jewel, or maybe a Whitewater figure, or somebody—anybody. But really, she is nobody. Just another media executive. She just happens to be the latest manufactured news of the New York-L.A. media axis.

And by Tom Fiedler in commentary in the *Miami Herald,* December 17, 1995:

> When the history of the 1996 presidential campaign is written, we may look back and find that sometime during the early days of this December the political earth shifted.
>
> For reasons that weren't immediately clear, Bill Clinton went from hapless incumbent to formidable front-runner. . . . Dole, the unmistakable leader of his party's pack and thus president-in-waiting, seemed to step into a deep hole and plummet to near irrelevance.
>
> The changed axis was measured by several polls with similar conclusions.

ayatollah \ˌī-ə-ˈtō-lə, -ˈtä-, -ˈtə-, ˈī-ə-ˌ\ Title of respect for a religious leader among Shiite Muslims. The word is also used to describe a person in a position of authority and an intolerant dictatorial authority.

The word is Persian for "miracle." Ayatollahs serve as spiritual counselors and guides. In the United States and Europe, the word became familiar in 1978–1979 during the revolution in Iran and the taking of American hostages at the U.S. embassy in Teheran. The fierce, dark-browed glare of the Ayatollah Ruholla Khomeini, shown over and over again in the news, combined with the revolutionary regime's hostility to Western—especially U.S.—influence, gave the term a decidedly negative cast.

The term in use, by Senator Alfonse D'Amato (R–N.Y.), quoted by Herbert Gold in the *National Review,* December 9, 1996:

> He [D'Amato] also engaged in a pre-emptive attack on Newt Gingrich and Pat Buchanan, whom he labeled Republican "ayatol-

lahs" for their positions on the environment, immigration, and abortion.

And by William Oscar Johnson in *Sports Illustrated,* April 10, 1995:

They call him the Ayatollah of CBS, and he accepts the label gratefully and with gusto. "Everyone knows," Frank Chirkinian declares in a big bass voice, "that democracy is the least effectual form of government inside a TV control truck. There must be absolutely autocratic rule so there is not confusion as to who is in charge. In short, there must be an ayatollah. And I am he."

*... their amendments were immediately tabled and their bills were consigned to a **Bermuda triangle** of committees.*

—David Shribman

Babbitt; Babbittry A business or professional man who conforms unthinkingly to prevailing middle-class standards. Babbitt was the chief character in the scathing 1922 Sinclair Lewis novel of the same name that looked hard at smug, middle-class, unimaginative, insular, conformist America.

Reread the novel and you'll discover that George Follansbee Babbitt was a little more complicated than that. He was dimly dissatisfied with his life, had a tentative fling with bohemianism, took up a flirtation with an attractive widow, even uttered a few unconventional opinions. Alas, social pressure and fear led him to abandon his small rebellion and settle back into conformity and boosterism. Babbitry means this form of general behavior and outlook.

H.L. Mencken, the acerbic critic, pounced on this character with joy:

> As an old professor of babbittry I welcome him as an almost perfect specimen—a genuine museum piece. Every American city swarms with his brothers. . . . He is no worse than most, and no better; he is the average American of the ruling minority in this hundred and forty-sixth year of the Republic. He is American incarnate, exuberant and exquisite.

The term in use, by Ward Just in the "Camelot" chapter of his 1997 novel *Echo House:*

> Eisenhower's Babbitts had been expelled and discredited, even Nixon gone for good, disappeared somewhere in the California wasteland. Suddenly every Democrat wanted to be in Washington, indisputably the EPICENTER of American life.

And by Terry Teachout in the *New York Times Book Review,* November 26, 1995:

> Powell was born in 1897 in Mount Gilead, Ohio, deep in the heart of the Babbitt Belt. The idyll of her small-town childhood was brought to a harsh end by the death of her mother in 1903.

Babel \\'bā-bəl, 'ba-bəl\\ A confusion or scene of noisy confusion of sounds and voices.

The story of Babel comes from the Bible, Genesis 11:4–9, and explains the variety of languages found on earth. After the Flood, Noah's descendants planned to build a great tower in the land of Babylon that would reach to heaven. Such presumption offended God, and he prevented completion of the project by causing the people to speak in different languages. Unable to understand each other, they couldn't cooperate to complete the tower.

The term in use, by Bill Conlin in the *Philadelphia Daily News,* August 12, 1997:

> You remember what happened when the government deregulated the airline industry and the nation's carriers reorganized themselves into flying cattle cars with a fare structure that seems to have been structured during lunch hour at the Tower of Babel.

Another example, by Margot Hornblower in *Time,* June 21, 1993:

> Their costumes vary: light frocks, skimpy red dresses, glow-in-the-dark Spandex pants. They speak a babel of languages: Czech, Romanian, Bulgarian, Hungarian, German.

babes in the woods Naïve, trusting folks; neophytes. The expression comes from an English play and ballad in the early 17th century, *The Children in the Wood.* The story was about two children whose father left them in the care of his wife's brother. The uncle would inherit a fortune if the children died, so he hired two men to murder them. One of the thugs could not bring himself to do the deed and murdered his partner instead. He then left the children alone in a wood where, helpless, they died.

The term in use, in a *Baltimore Sun* editorial, November 17, 1995:

> Polls show that the American people are (a) for a balanced budget, (b) against tax cuts and (c) for less punitive spending reductions. But the president's attitude toward the coalition is one of dismissive condescension. Nice fellows, to be sure, but such babes in the woods they would give the Republicans the tax-cut issue.

From movie critic Gary Arnold, the *Washington Times,* September 22, 1995:

> Only babes in the wood will mistake *Showgirls* for the eye-opening naked truth about show business in its current state of glittering decadence, as found in meccas of idleness such as Vegas.

And from M.S. Mason, the *Christian Science Monitor,* June 11, 1992, reviewing films "of innocence and experience":

> In *Mr. Smith Goes to Washington,* a young senator, Jefferson Smith, arrives in the nation's capital a babe in the woods—full of patriotism and Jeffersonian ideals untested by adversity.

Babylon A city devoted to materialism and sensual pleasure. From the great city of Mesopotamia, center of one of the most opulent and hedonistic civilizations of the ancient world.

The Bible, Revelation 17–18, speaks of "the whore that sitteth upon many waters." She was decked in purple and scarlet and jewels, and "upon her forehead, was a name written, MYSTERY, BABYLON THE GREAT, THE MOTHER OF HARLOTS AND ABOMINATIONS OF THE EARTH," suggesting disapproval. For Protestants during the Reformation, a movement in opposition to the corruption of the Catholic Church, this reference in Revelations clearly was to Rome and the Papacy. Protestants accordingly called the Roman Catholic Church the "Scarlet Woman" and the "Whore of Babylon."

Now, thanks to the American habit of naming towns after cities of the ancient world, we have a Babylon on Long Island. This phenomenon leads to such wonderful headlines as "Garbage revolt in Babylon." Hammurabi would no doubt understand.

The term in use, by Scott Canon, the *Kansas City Star,* June 23, 1996, describing a hippie-style "Gathering" of the Rainbow Family in the Ozarks:

> They do their best year-round and coast-to-coast to live aside from American consumerism and 9–5 paychecks. They call where you live Babylon.

And from California State Senator Tom Hayden, quoted by Vincent J. Schodolski in the *Chicago Tribune,* June 1, 1994:

> "There is an urgency about the times in which we live," he said in February, when he publicly warned Brown and Garamendi that he would run against them if they didn't focus on the issues he felt were important. "We have become dangerously lost, I think, in the values of Babylon."

And from Ron Rosenbaum in the *New York Times* magazine, August 22, 1993, commenting on the remarkable number of bizarre news stories originating on Long Island:

> What the hell *happened?* What happened to the incredibly boring place I grew up in, where I swear *nothing ever happened?*
> What happened to turn it into this charnel house of sensational spouse slayings; fatally attracted judges. . . . kidnappers with dungeons; horticultural serial killers? A veritable Babylon, and not the colorless stop on the L.I.R.R. right after Amityville, Copiague and Lindenhurst, but a Babylon out of the Book of Revelations, the blood-drenched Mother of Abominations.

Babylonian captivity A lengthy time as a hostage or separated from one's natural home and proper place and under the corrupting control of another. Such a situation is often regarded as self-inflicted and a sellout.

The term refers to the captivity of the Jews in the kingdom of ancient Babylon from 586 B.C. to 538 B.C. The same term was applied to the forced removal of the papacy from Rome to Avignon in what is now southern France; there from 1309 until 1377, the Pope was firmly under the thumb of the French kings.

This action caused a decline in both the power and prestige of the papacy. The rest of Europe regarded these popes as tools of France, and the papal court, while maintaining great splendor, sank into corruption. The papacy returned to Rome but things got even worse when a competing pope was elected. The infighting went on for another 40 years. Even after the division was repaired, the popes of this era were more secular and political than religious in their outlook; and some of them were downright wicked. (*See* BORGIA.)

The term in use, by writer Marshall Frady, quoted in a profile in the *Los Angeles Times*, July 2, 1996, describing his years working in television:

> He now refers to those years as "my electronic Babylonian captivity," in which what he did for a living served up a sense of "ferocious vitality and enormous importance" that was more mirage than reality.

Another example, from theology professor and author Cornelius Plantinga, quoted by Judy Tarjanyi, the *Kansas City Star,* April 4, 1995:

> Plantinga said that when it comes to sin, churches likely have lacked courage in resisting cultural trends away from self-reproach and toward self-esteem. "In this area, the church is in Babylonian captivity to the culture."

And from James H. Billington, the *New Republic,* May 30, 1994, on the role of the Orthodox Church in the Soviet Union:

> The Russian Church defeated early Bolshevik efforts to supplant it by a puppet "renovationist" church, but made its FAUSTIAN BARGAIN with communism in 1927, accepting a narrowly liturgical survival in return for docile support of Soviet policies. A young believer wrote a farewell letter (much discussed in recent months) to his parents explaining why he was going off into the woods rather than accept the Church's new Babylonian captivity. . . .

bacchanal \\'ba-kə-nᵊl, 'bä-; ˌba-kə-'nal, ˌbä-kə-näl\\ Any orgy. The adjective describing such an event is "bacchanalian" \\ˌba-kə-'näl-yən, 'bä-\\.

The term is derived from Bacchus, the Greek and Roman god of wine (and of vegetation and fertility, too). (*See also* DIONYSIAN.) Bacchus was worshiped at Rome in an annual festival called the Bacchanalia, an orgiastic rite, with dancing and singing.

The term in use, by the *Economist,* June 10, 1989, describing the partying at the Indianapolis 500:

> While out-of-town guests of sponsoring companies watch the race from comfortable penthouse boxes lining the track, thousands of Hoosiers, as people from the state of Indiana are known, invade the area inside the oval track. There, nestled in trailer trucks and cordoned off from civilization by metal fences, the natives enjoy what has been called a "blue-collar bacchanal."

And by Tim Sullivan, Gannett News Service, June 25, 1997:

> Plant City was an ideal location for the training of ballplayers. It is warm, but not wild, a Florida oasis from the traumas of tourism and the bacchanal of Spring Break.

Bad Boy *See* PECK'S BAD BOY.

bad day at Black Rock Fateful day that brings complete disaster. The phrase is the title of a memorable 1955 Western directed by John Sturges that has become a deadpan understatement of disaster.

The story is in the classic HIGH NOON form, but set in modern times: a stranger (Spencer Tracy) arrives in an isolated desert town with an evil secret, in this case an old murder. The bad guys (memorably played by Ernest Borgnine, Lee Marvin, and Robert Ryan) are strong; the others are weak and afraid. The stranger has wounds of his own, including a crippled arm. The bad guys close in, and the stranger must stand alone against them. By story's end, quite a few people are dead, but justice has been done.

The term in use, by James Hannah of the Associated Press in the *Cleveland Plain Dealer,* November 21, 1991, reporting on a ban on federal funds for abortion counseling:

> Linda Lombard, president of the group's board of trustees, said several options are being considered, including giving up the federal money in order to continue the counseling.
> "It's a bad day at Black Rock, but the shootout isn't over," she said.

And from John Carman of the Associated Press, in the *San Francisco Chronicle,* May 24, 1994, reporting on CBS-affiliated stations jumping to the Fox network:

> For CBS, it wasn't merely a bad day at Black Rock, as the network's New York headquarters is called. It's an unmitigated disaster.

The allusion is even richer if you know that the CBS headquarters building in Manhattan is dark-gray stone. Located close to NBC at 30 Rockefeller Center, known as "30 Rock," it was natural to christen the CBS building "Black Rock."

Another example, from the *Des Moines Business Record,* September 9, 1996, interviewing an expert in crisis communication for business:

> Twenty years ago, we conducted a whole crisis management training session called "Bad Day at Black Rock." We'd take them to New York under other pretenses, and present them with a crisis. Then we'd spend a couple of days training them.

bad seed An evil person whose wickedness is innate and evident from birth.

The term comes from the 1955 play *The Bad Seed* by Maxwell Anderson (based on a novel by William March), about a little girl who is a calculating murderess.

The term in use, by Myra McPherson, in her examination of the life of serial killer Ted Bundy in *Vanity Fair,* May 1989:

> The major missing link to Bundy, of course, is his unknown father. Who he was might explain Bundy's monstrous nature, a possible genetic "bad seed" misfire.

And by Stephanie Mansfield in *Sports Illustrated,* April 21, 1997, describing the attempted comeback of skater Tonya Harding:

> Her two-minute program—her first public appearance since the 1994 Winter Olympics—was a sort of warmup act for a minor league hockey game . . . and was greeted with equal parts cheers, boos, jeers, catcalls, cowbells and projectiles: a half-full beer cup, a few supermarket bouquets and two black rubber billy clubs.
>
> Appropriately attired en noir, the bad seed of women's figure skating did only one jump, a triple Salchow.

balkanize; balkanization *often capitalized* To break up a region or group into smaller, often mutually hostile units. Originally coined to describe the tragic politics of the Balkan region, *balkanization* now refers to the process of fragmentation of countries, societies, and institutions.

The word first described events on the Balkan Peninsula in the 19th and 20th centuries as the Ottoman Empire broke apart—and then again after the breakup of Yugoslavia in the early 1990s.

Powerful nationalist feelings, religious hostilities, and ethnic antagonisms among the peoples of the regions were suppressed by the influence of powerful neighboring empires—Turkey, Austria-Hungary, and later the Soviet Union. These tensions set the stage for World War I, touched off in the Balkans by the assassination of Archduke Francis Ferdinand of Austria in Sarajevo.

After the fall of Communism, Yugoslavia, the state constructed by the peace settlement after World War I, came apart again in bloodshed and misery.

The term in use, in the *New Republic,* February 3, 1995, on plans to cut public broadcasting with the justification that specialty cable channels—"narrowcasting"—can take its place:

> Narrowcasting also deepens America's political and cultural balkanization. Mightn't the case for subsidizing nationally unifying media actually grow stronger as technological fragmentation prcceeds apace?

And in a *Newsday* editorial, April 4, 1997:

> A dismal reality of the late 20th century is that ethnic and group identity can be even more compelling forces than nationalism

and that artificial attempts to keep diverse people together when they don't wish it are bound to fail, often in showers of blood. Perhaps we should let the Balkans be balkanized again.

And by William J. Cook and David Bowermaster in *U.S. News & World Report,* February 15, 1993:

The near universal acceptance of its software products in a market that has been balkanized by hundreds of small purveyors has pushed Microsoft's stock steadily upward.

bang *See* NOT WITH A BANG BUT A WHIMPER.

Banquo's ghost A troubling reminder of past crimes and misdeeds; someone or some memory that appears to materialize out of thin air, welcome or not.

Banquo and his ghost appear in Shakespeare's *Macbeth,* the ghost at Act 4, Scene 1. A nobleman and general who is a good and loyal man, Banquo is murdered at Macbeth's direction after the witches foretell that Banquo's descendants will rule Scotland; Banquo's son escapes Macbeth's plot to become king.

After Banquo's murder, his bloody ghost appears at a feast, visible only to the horrified Macbeth, who cries: "Thou canst not say I did it; never shake thy gory locks at me." The ghost disappears and reappears, and Macbeth's agitated reactions startle his guests.

The term in use, by David Maraniss in the *Washington Post,* October 7, 1996, describing the audience in the hall for a debate between President Bill Clinton and Republican candidate Bob Dole:

And what might Clinton see if his gaze went beyond the floodlights? The Dole camp hoped he would see Billy R. Dale, their version of Banquo's ghost. While Dale is not exactly a household name, he has symbolic resonance; the former White House travel aide's firing marked the beginning of one of the many Clinton administration mini-scandals.

And by Stephen Birmingham, describing Andy Warhol in the *Washington Post Book World,* October 15, 1989:

All at once I noticed that the Master himself had materialized in our midst. He had not stepped off the elevator, and he had not entered through any door. He had simply appeared, like Banquo's ghost, with his prison pallor, his acne-scarred face, his potato nose, wearing one of his silver fright wigs.

barbaric yawp An aggressive, exuberant shout, a bellow full of confidence and energy, noisy and foolish.

It is a famous expression from American poet Walt Whitman, in *Song of Myself*:

The spotted hawk swoops by and accuses me, he complains of my gab and my loitering.

I too am not a bit tamed, I too am untranslatable,
I sound my barbaric yawp over the roofs of the world.

Tom Wolfe used the expression to sum up American energy and self-confident vulgarity in his 1981 indictment of modern architecture, *From Bauhaus to Our House:*

> In short, this has been America's period of youthful rampage—
> and what architecture has she to show for it? An architecture
> whose tenets prohibit every manifestation of exuberance, power,
> grandeur, or even high spirits and playfulness, as the height of
> bad taste.
>   We brace for a barbaric yawp over the roofs of the world—
> and hear a cough at a concert.

And by *Newsday* columnist Murray Kempton, February 20, 1996, writing about Patrick Buchanan's unsettling effect in the New Hampshire Republican presidential primary:

> He can summon up every barbaric yawp in American political
> history from the Know Nothing Party to Huey P. Long and sea-
> son it with jokes culled from the inspirations of that very morn-
> ing's news wire. No candidate here is so out of date and none
> contrives to sound as up to date. [*See also* KNOW-NOTHINGS.]

And again, by Robert Hughes, art critic of *Time* magazine, describing the work of sculptor Edward Kienholz, May 6, 1996:

> Kienholz didn't believe in refinement. What he believed in was
> a combination of technical know-how, moral anger and all-
> American barbaric yawp.

Barbie and Ken A stereotypically attractive, trendy blond female and her male counterpart, all surface and no substance.
    The Barbie doll is the most commercially successful doll in history. She was introduced to the market in 1959 by the Mattel Corporation and has been a best-seller ever since.
    She has a boyfriend, Ken, and friends, and most important, a gigantic and ever-changing up-to-the-minute wardrobe suited to her up-to-the-minute activities.
    Although millions of little girls love Barbie, she has a figure no mortal female could match.
    The epithet in use, by Beth Tuschak in a profile of NASCAR driver Jeff Gordon and his wife Brooke in *USA Today,* August 2, 1995:

> "I knew the second I met her, no way was I going to let her get
> away; she's the best thing that ever happened to me, and getting
> married was the best thing I've ever done," says Gordon, who
> shrugs off garage-area references to the couple as racing's
> Barbie and Ken.

Another example, from Andrew Ferguson, the *American Spectator,* October 1988:

> The speaker was a fellow named William Paxon, introduced as the candidate for Jack Kemp's seat from Upstate New York. Young Bill stood at the podium with the splendid posture (and haircut) of a Ken doll.

And by Adina Hoffman, in the *Jerusalem Post,* July 22, 1996, reviewing the film *To Die For* in which Nicole Kidman plays a television weather girl who attempts to murder her way to success:

> Kidman plays Suzanne as a homicidal Barbie doll of veritable parade-float proportions.

bare ruined choirs The remnants of earlier glory visible amid the ravages of time. In Sonnet 73, Shakespeare describes old age:

> That time of year thou mayst in me behold
> When yellow leaves, or none, or few, do hang
> Upon those boughs which shake against the cold,
> Bare ruined choirs where late the sweet birds sang.

In Shakespeare's imagery, the bare branches of a tree in winter are likened to the stark remaining arches of a ruined building, and both refer to the destructive effects of age in a human.

A choir is not only the singers, but the place in cathedrals and large churches where the choir sits. In Shakespeare's time, there were many ecclesiastical ruins in England, some still very fresh. When Henry VIII broke with the Catholic Church, he closed all the monasteries and gave church lands to favored members of the nobility. Many of the buildings on these lands were destroyed, leaving the countryside dotted with their broken walls and ruined Gothic arches.

The term in use, by critic John Leonard of *New York* magazine, commenting on the television movie *The Man Upstairs* quoted in the *Miami Herald,* December 13, 1992:

> We all know more than we ought to about [Katharine Hepburn's] medical history, and it's amazing of her to soldier on despite it. . . . But this Constant Nymph as Senior Citizen is hard to take. The wonderful rasp is a quaver. The monkey grin is mummified. What used to be eager and gallant is arch and doddering. What used to be radiant is now just hyper. In the bare, ruined choirs of what she once was, should she really have to put up with a Ryan O'Neal?

And by Houston A. Baker in the *Philadelphia Inquirer,* October 17, 1994, on his memories of his childhood in segregated Louisville during the 1950s:

> On the other hand, I think that critical memory should keep us ever aware of precisely how the human imagination and moral

will can forge a way out of no way, and take the bare, ruined choirs of old, unhappy, far-off things and remake them into the very ark of our salvation.

And by commentator Leon Wynter in National Public Radio's "All Things Considered," in a springtime ode to beleaguered Yankee Stadium, May 29, 1996:

> On sunny Lou Gehrig Plaza . . . we linger at lunch by the courthouse deli where, after 60 years, a few dollars can still put a hot brisket sandwich and a cold Dr. Brown in your hand and the swelling sound of championship baseball in your ear for free. But nobody thinks Bronx brisket, or Bombers, worth the risk of visiting much longer. Up on the concourse we look straight into the upper deck, see the almost bare, ruined choirs and wonder, "Is it us?"

Barmecide feast A disappointing illusion of abundance; a banquet without food.

It's from a story in the *Arabian Nights* in which a wealthy merchant of the Barmecide family of Baghdad asked a poor, starving man to dinner— but served him nothing but empty plates. All the while he discussed the imaginary food and asked the man how he liked it. The poor man played along, pretending to enjoy the nonexistent food. Finally, wine—or rather no wine—was offered, but the poor man said he was already drunk and knocked the Barmecide down. The merchant saw the humor of the situation and then gave the starving man all the food he wanted.

The term in use, by Doug Robarchek in the *Charlotte Observer,* June 8, 1992:

> Oops: Now that it's supposedly ending, the government tells us the recession was worse than they kept telling us it was. . . .
> At the same time, the Bushster says he'll balance the budget by cutting taxes and spending more. This proposal to end America's Barmecide feast (oh, look it up, dammit) comes from the same guy who, when that policy was proposed by Ronald Reagan, called it "voodoo economics."

And from Pat Dailey of the *Chicago Tribune* in the *St. Paul Pioneer Press,* November 28, 1993:

> Holy mackerel! Wordsmiths will have a fine feast—or would it be a Barmecide feast?—with a copy of *Eatioms* by John D. Jacobson.

baroque \bə-'rōk, ba-, -'räk, -'rȯk\ *often capitalized* Of or relating to a florid, extravagant style of European art that dated from about 1550 to 1750. Baroque comes from a French word meaning "irregularly shaped" and was originally applied mostly to pearls. The baroque style is characterized by lots of curving, swirling lines, flocking cupids and cherubim, gilt, and gold. Its most extreme form is called rococo, a decorative style that developed in France in the early 18th century.

Today the word is applied to any creation that is exceedingly ornate, intricate, or elaborate. Saying a politician delivered a baroque speech wouldn't necessarily be a compliment.

The term in use, in a tribute to the late Murray Kempton in the *Deseret News,* May 6, 1997:

> Murray Kempton, a Pulitzer Prize winner who championed underdogs and punctured the powerful in columns of elegant thickly textured and at times baroque prose, has died.

And by Sybil Steinberg in *Publishers Weekly,* March 20, 1995:

> It turns out Chip is a middle-aged pothead living in his mother's seedy beach mansion, whose stoned analysis of televised hostage situations has fueled a baroque kidnapping scheme, into which Harry has stumbled.

And by Dody Tsiantar in *Newsweek,* July 4, 1994:

> You probably saw the headlines: Procter & Gamble lost $102 million trading the pesky things; a Paine Webber bond fund lost $33 million; a Bank America fund, $17.4 million. All three were tripped up by derivatives, those baroque financial instruments that "derive" value from underlying assets.

Bartleby the Scrivener A character in Herman Melville's story "Bartleby the Scrivener" (1853). Bartleby is a suffering clerical drudge and displays "passive resistance"—Melville's phrase.

Bartleby was a clerk employed by the narrator, a lawyer in Wall Street. A scrivener was a professional penman, someone who, in those unthinkable days before word processors, photocopiers, and even typewriters actually copied documents by hand. Scrivener is a tight, tense word that almost makes you feel the writer's cramp, or "scrivener's palsy" that resulted from such work.

Bartleby came to work seemingly mild and cooperative. He was given a desk at a window which faced a brick wall, providing little light and no sense of the world outside. It was not long before Bartleby became rather a brick wall himself and began to reject the menial tasks of copying and proofreading. His famous response was, "I would prefer not to."

He wouldn't work, but he wouldn't leave, and somehow he acquired an ascendancy over the narrator, who couldn't cope with unflagging resistance of such a mild fashion. In desperation he moved his office; Bartleby stayed and drove the succeeding tenant to desperation also. Eventually Bartleby was carted off to prison, where he "preferred not to" eat, and died, leaving his former employer bewildered and feeling vaguely responsible.

The term in use, by John Anderson, *Newsday,* February 12, 1997:

In 1967, Mike Nichols' *The Graduate* seemed to capture the alienated angst of a generation, the character of a time. Ben Braddock—who rocketed Dustin Hoffman to a new kind of stardom—was a Bartleby the Scrivener for the Vietnam generation, the personification of the disillusioned, anti-Establishment ethos that would foment major social change.

And from columnist Anthony Lewis in the *St. Louis Post-Dispatch,* December 13, 1994:

Weakness and vacuity are what we see in the Clinton administration. It moves from day to day, empty of vision, a government without a design. Clinton himself seems more and more like Herman Melville's Bartleby the Scrivener, a dwindling, haunting presence in the White House.

And by Richard Eder, reviewing Calvin Tomkins' biography of artist Marcel Duchamp in *Newsday,* November 24, 1996:

Would the Bartleby of modern art—"I would prefer not to"—have left such a mark had he possessed less wit and allure?

basilisk \\'ba-sə-'lisk, 'ba-zə-\\ A spellbinding, deadly creature. The word comes from the name of a mythical reptile purported to be the king of lizards. It was also called a cockatrice, and it was said to be hatched from the egg of a cock by a reptile. Its best-known qualities are the world's worst case of bad breath and the ability to kill with a glance. The word is frequently used in the phrase *basilisk stare,* the term for a look which is ferociously compelling, frightening, or seductive—or all of the above.

The name was also given to a very large cannon of the Tudor era in England which could fire stone shot weighing 200 pounds. (It was fashionable at the time to name cannon after poisonous snakes.) Certain tropical lizards are now known as basilisks. They can run fast but do not have a drop-dead glare.

The term in use, by Anthony Trollope in *Barchester Towers* (1857) describing the beautiful eyes of one of the most redoubtable sirens of Victorian fiction, La Signora Madeleine Vesey Neroni:

. . . the long, steady, unabashed gaze with which she would look into the face of her admirer fascinated while it frightened him. She was a basilisk from whom an ardent lover of beauty could make no escape.

And by Julian Barnes, in the *New Yorker,* March 5, 1990, describing Margaret Thatcher:

She now sports a large pair of spectacles, which she often holds by the sidepiece while reading an answer, before whipping them off to give the Labour benches a basilisk stare. She has never been a great debater or a great emoter, but she remains a great presence.

And by Karl E. Meyer in the *New York Times Book Review,* April 20, 1986:

> He vanished passively into limbo, his place as party leader usurped by Gustav Husak, who still rules with a mean, basilisk eye.

Bates Motel An isolated and sinister place.

The Bates Motel is the desolate setting of the 1960 Alfred Hitchcock movie *Psycho.* The film, with its famous murder in the shower and artful music, was intended to be a black comedy; Hitchcock wanted to see if he could get away with ground-breaking levels of nastiness. Critics howled at it but soon came around, recognizing its skillful manipulation of the audience. The movie is still able to terrify, even after the oceans of cinematic blood shed since in legions of inferior imitations. The film certainly is potent enough to make millions nervous about showering.

The movie began the trend toward shock and gore and away from suspense; in the hands of less able producers and directors, the genre moved from subtlety to bludgeonry.

The term in use, by Rob Hiaasen in the *Baltimore Sun,* June 1, 1995:

> At Bob Brown's FTS Taxidermy Studio in Forest Hill, the only animal not stuffed is Bob. Think of the lobby of the Bates Motel.

And by Eleanor Ringel, reviewing the movie *Hotel de Love* in the *Atlanta Journal and Constitution,* February 21, 1997:

> *Hotel de Love* is about as much fun as a night at the Bates Motel.

And by Lee Benson, sports columnist of the *Deseret News,* June 12, 1997, commenting on the Bulls-Jazz championship series:

> In hindsight, that's when Jordan and the Bulls should have had a sheet pulled over them—when they were down by double figures in a town that for nearly a week had been the equivalent of the Bates Motel. Practically nothing had gone right from the moment the plane touched down at Salt Lake International.

Bauhaus \\'bau̇-ˌhau̇s\\ A school of design founded in Germany in 1919 in an attempt to bring together technology, craftsmanship, and design aesthetics. The artists struck out in new directions, creating much of what we recognize as modern design in architecture, furniture, and other areas.

Artists and designers associated with the school include Marcel Breuer (as in the chair), Walter Gropius (architecture), Ludwig Mies van der Rohe (architecture and the Barcelona chair), and Wassily Kandinsky and Paul Klee (abstract art).

The school was closed by the Nazis as part of their suppression of modern art, which they regarded as degenerate. But members of the group dispersed to other countries, particularly the United States, where they proved to have lasting influence.

The Bauhaus school (and its spawn, the International Style) became especially strong in the U.S., and indeed is the subject of much controversy. In recent years there has been a reaction against Bauhaus elements—the monotonous boxes, the flat roofs and strip windows flush with the facade, the monolithic and overpowering starkness. Le Corbusier called such a house a "machine for living," and journalist Tom Wolfe spoke for much of the opposition when he said such structures resembled insecticide refineries (*From Bauhaus to Our House*, 1981).

The term in use, by Alessandra Stanley in the *New Republic,* December 12, 1988, "Presidency by Ralph Lauren":

> Snobbery has always sold well. But no one has ever mass-marketed the mystique or so widely popularized the yearning as Bronx-born Ralph Lauren, ne Ralph Lipschitz. . . . The Laurenification of America reaches far beyond clothing. . . . *New York Times* architecture critic Paul Goldberger recently concluded that Ralph Lauren is the "real design symbol" of our age. He calls the clothes designer a "one-man Bauhaus."

And in *Elle,* January 1991:

> For those who are convinced that high tea simply means an opportunity to say "no, thank you" to yet another cucumber sandwich, along comes this sleek teapot with a handle evocative of pure Bauhaus design. Harking back to the recent rage for gleaming high-tech household goods, the comely kettle, made by Kuhn-Rikon, might soon become a classic.

beam me up, Scotty A phrase inspired by the 1960s television series *Star Trek,* usually used to mean "get me out of here," especially from an irrational or bizarre situation.

On *Star Trek,* to "beam up" meant to use the transporter, a device which physically transported people and objects to and from the ship by dematerializing them into twinkling little bits and then rematerializing them moments later at their destination. This was accomplished by a transporter beam. Crew members from the orbiting space ship could be speedily conveyed to the surface of a planet without the muss and fuss of landing the mighty ship.

"Scotty" was Montgomery Scott, the redoubtable chief engineer of the starship *Enterprise.* Actor James Doohan, who created the role on the original series and in movies, says that the line as spoken by Captain Kirk was, "Beam me up, Mr. Scott" and that popular usage changed it to Scotty. It was Doohan who decided that Scott should be a Scotsman, in that nation's tradition of great engineers. *Beam Me Up, Scotty* is also the title of Doohan's autobiography.

The Star Trek series ran on television from 1965 to 1969, a science fiction series on the adventures of the captain and crew of a 23rd-century craft, the starship *Enterprise.* It achieved cult status after going into syndication in the 1970s, with devoted fans ("Trekkies") organizing Star Trek clubs and conventions and collecting memorabilia. This popularity in turn inspired movies and a second television series, more movies, and more TV spinoffs.

A 1970s bumper sticker's variation was: "Beam me up, Scotty. There's no intelligent life on this planet." The expression has been used to describe rapid turnaround or quick communication. For example, Scotty Software was released in 1997 to make Internet connection as fast and easy as possible.

The phrase was in vogue in drug slang during the urban crack epidemic of the 1980s. Sometimes the drug itself would be called *Scotty*. "Beam me up" referred to getting high. For example, a story by Bill Bryan and Joe Holleman in the *St. Louis Post-Dispatch,* May 24, 1995, describes a drug-and-violence-ridden neighborhood:

> Scott and Wade didn't want to give their last names. They appeared to be in their late 30s and sat in lawn chairs outside a car repair shop on Elliott drinking Stag beer at 11 a.m. Tuesday. They offered a simple explanation for the violence.
> "It's dope and gangs and money," said Scott.
> The men were surprised an outsider didn't know why the area was called Beam Street.
> "It's gettin' high on rock crack," explained Scott. "You remember Star Trek? "Beam me up Scotty!"

The term in use by Jonathan Takiff in *Playboy,* May 1994, in describing a new electronic device:

> A home automation standard created to ensure that products from different manufacturers will be on the same wavelength, so to speak, when communicating with one another through power lines, telephone wire, coaxial cable and infared. Beam us home, Scotty, and draw the bath.

And by Jill Rachlin in *Entertainment Weekly,* February 26, 1993:

> Who needs Scotty to beam you up when you can teleport—that is, use your mind to transport yourself from one place to another?

And from Randy Wayne White in *Outside*, April 1993:

> Let's face facts: Theories from the lunatic fringe aside, our forebears did not arrive here on spaceships; Scotty did not beam us down from a foundering Enterprise. We are part and parcel of the biota. Yet the belief that our species is some kind of noxious exotic is being twisted into the national fabric.

beard the lion in his den To confront someone powerful or influential on his or her home ground; to make a bold challenge to someone in a strong position. To beard someone is an old expression, meaning to defy, to be "in one's face" (or beard). Bearding the lion suggests daring to grab Leo by the tuft on his chin.

The phrase is used by Sir Walter Scott in his epic poem "Marmion," about 15th-century Scotland. Marmion is a daring but unscrupulous knight. Lord Douglas, Earl of Angus, snubs him by refusing to shake hands. Marmion is furious with the old man and defies him. Douglas becomes angry in his turn and growls back:

> And dars't thou then
> To beard the lion in his den,
> The Douglas in his hall?
> And hop'st thou hence unscathed to go?

Marmion has to gallop for the gate, dashing out just as the portcullis crashes down.

The term in use, by David M. Kennedy in a review of *The Colonel: The Life and Legend of Robert R. McCormick, 1880–1955,* by Richard Norton Smith in the *New York Times Book Review,* July 13, 1997:

> It was no accident that when [Franklin D.] Roosevelt in October 1937 gave his famous "quarantine" speech, the first of his major public speeches designed to wean his countrymen away from their isolationist illusions, he ventured into Chicagoland to beard the lion in his den (and was forced almost immediately to back off).

And in a headline to a story by Paul Richter in the *Los Angeles Times* August 9, 1995, describing President Clinton's speeches around the country in the home turf of his strongest opponents:

> Clinton Beards Lions in Their Dens in Search of Votes

And by Charles Brock in *USA Today* magazine, January 1, 1996, on the art of Winslow Homer:

> During the 1880s, as Homer's art continued to evolve, his reputation for temperamental reclusiveness emerged. Critics commented that he "affects eccentricities of manner that border on gross rudeness," and that visiting his studio was like "bearding a lion in his den."

beast with two backs, the The sexual act, according to Shakespeare in *Othello,* Act 1, Scene 1—in which IAGO, standing in the nighttime street rouses Desdemona's father with the taunt that she has run off to marry Othello, the Moor: "I am one, sir, that comes to tell you your daughter and the Moor are now making the beast with two backs."

The term in use, by Lawrence Toppman in the *Charlotte Observer,* February 4, 1996, describing a search for cinematic bedroom scenes which are romantic rather than steamy:

> I think sex has its place on film. The terrific *Body Heat* operates on various levels: as an homage to noir [*see* FILM NOIR], as a cracking mystery story, as a story about a man who can think of nothing but making the beast with two backs, as the Bard used to say, and the way he throws his life away for sex.

And by Daniel Webster, music critic of the *Philadelphia Inquirer,* July 1, 1997, reviewing a production of *Faust:*

> In its scene of most-wasted obviousness, the production has Faust and Marguerite making the beast with two backs on the floor, reducing the piece to something like the prom mom's dilemma, rather than some cosmic spiritual battle.

And by John Anderson, reviewing the movie *Murder at 1600* in *Newsday,* April 18, 1997:

> The sex scene sets up the entire impulse behind the movie.
> There they are—and who they are will have to wait—making the beast with two backs in what appears to be the Oval Office.

beat swords into plowshares To make peace; to convert the weapons of war to peaceful uses.

The passage is from the Old Testament:

> They shall beat their swords into ploughshares, and their spears into pruning-hooks: nation shall not lift up sword against nation, neither shall they learn war any more.

This is Isaiah 2:4 in the King James version; it appears in almost the same form in Micah 4:3. These two prophets were contemporaries; Isaiah lived from 742–701 or possibly 687 B.C. Both stood for purity of worship and social justice; and it would seem they freely used each other's material.

The term in use, by Philip Smucker in the *Washington Times,* March 27, 1995:

> The scope and speed of the Aristide government's plans to beat swords into plowshares surprised some North American diplomats. When the international community intervened to toss out Haiti's junta in September, both U.S. and U.N. officials thought they would be engaged in a vast plan to "modernize" the Haitian military.

And again, by the Associated Press, October 18, 1996:

> The same city where Sam Colt introduced firearms more than a century ago has melted down 11,194 guns confiscated or surrendered since 1992 and sculpted the iron into 228 manhole covers in an art project on gun violence. . . . [Artist Bradley] McCallum, of Portland, Maine, considers it a memorial to victims of gun violence as well as an up-to-date version of beating swords into plowshares.

And from Barbara Kingsolver in *Parenting* magazine, March 1995:

> Call it what you will—when ex-spouses beat swords into plowshares and jump up and down at a soccer game together, it makes for happy kids.

And by Allan H. Meltzer in the *Wall Street Journal,* December 18, 1992:

> ... the recovery has labored against sizable defense cutbacks. It has not been possible to beat swords, tanks and airplanes into plowshares or machine tools without making sparks. . . . Reconversion is not a monetary problem. But without reconversion, the recovery would have been faster.

Beau Brummell *See* BRUMMELL, BEAU.

beau geste \bō-'zhest\ A grand or magnanimous gesture, or one that is ingratiating or conciliatory.
Beau Geste was a 1924 novel by Percival C. Wren in which three English brothers (named Geste, actually) heroically join the French Foreign Legion to redeem the family honor. Two of them, including the hero, Michael (nicknamed "Beau," of course), die gallantly in the desert. Hollywood loved the story, and made and remade it; both Ronald Colman and Gary Cooper played the title role.
The term in use, by Cathy Nolan, in *People,* February 20, 1995:

> Delage, a flying instructor, showed his penchant for the beau geste early in life. The son of schoolteachers in a village 50 miles northeast of Paris, he swam the English Channel at age 18—not to make the record books but to be with a girlfriend who had gone to England.

And by Frank Monteleone in *Computerworld,* May 29, 1995:

> Think win. Go for the gusto. Try for major change. Make the beau geste. Re-engineering isn't about seeking modest improvements. It's high risk, high reward.

beer and skittles A situation of agreeable ease. From the expression, "life is not all beer and skittles." It shows up in various forms well back into the 19th century. (*See also* CAKES AND ALE.) Skittles, by the way, here refers not to candy but to a British game of ninepins.
The term in use, by John Hanchette, Gannett News Service, August 15, 1994, on the career of professional baseball player and World War II spy Moe Berg, as recounted in the Nicholas Dawidoff biography of Berg, *The Catcher Was a Spy:*

> Moe Berg was much more—a valued World War II spy for the Office of Strategic Services, the forerunner of the CIA.
> The OSS was a merry band of bright people recruited by founder Wild Bill Donovan for their odd talents and shotgunned into intriguing espionage assignments. It wasn't all beer and skittles for Berg.

And by Jack Patterson, reporting on his ten years of active retirement in *Business Week,* July 21, 1997:

> Have I made my retirement seem all beer and skittles? It's not.

beggar–thy–neighbor *or* **beggar–my–neighbor** A policy or activity that seeks the gain or advantage of one at the expense of others—and ends up hurting everyone, including the originator. "Beggar" here is a verb, meaning to reduce to beggary or to impoverish. (*See also* ZERO–SUM GAME.)

The term in use, in the *New Republic,* December 5, 1994, advocating the abolition of the District of Columbia:

> There is a solution: return the residential areas of the District to Maryland. . . . The areas around the Capitol, White House, monuments and Cabinet agencies could go back to federal control. As citizens of a state, Washingtonians would have taxation with representation. . . . And both jurisdictions could benefit from streamlining redundant services and ending the beggar-thy-neighbor game of luring investment.

And by Frank Petrone in *Newsday,* April 25, 1995:

> A regional approach would help spread out the costs of building these expensive facilities and ensure a constant supply of garbage needed to keep them close to profitability. It would also end the "beggar-thy-neighbor" competition that pits one town against another.

And by historian Paul M. Kennedy in *The Rise and Fall of the Great Powers* (1987):

> If the democracies of the West weathered these storms better, their statesmen were forced to concentrate upon domestic economic management, increasingly tinged with a beggar-thy-neighbor attitude.

bell, book, and candle The elements of the ritual of excommunication, also suggesting any process of condemnation carried out thoroughly and completely.

In the rite of excommunication practiced by the Roman Catholic Church, a bell was rung, a book (the Bible) was closed, and a candle was extinguished to symbolize the darkness to which the excommunicant was consigned. An excommunicated person was thenceforth denied the sacraments of the church and the company of its adherents.

Bell, Book, and Candle is also a 1950 play by John Van Druten about a beautiful modern-day witch who falls in love and loses her supernatural powers.

The term in use, by Geoffrey Mohan in *Newsday,* December 31, 1996, reviewing the year's Long Island news highlights:

> It was less "The Great Impostor" and more "Bell, Book and Candle" in another Long Island courtroom. . . . Nassau County Justice Edward McCarty ruled in June that the two had "engaged in unparalleled character assassination" during their bitter and media-saturated hearing on child custody. To wit: Walter accused Rana of practicing witchcraft. . . .

And by Fleur deVilliers, asserting her view that economic sanctions against nations are not effective in changing their policies, in the *American Spectator,* March 1988:

> Those who wielded bell, book and candle blithely ignored the fact that sanctions without the threat of military intervention have had a dismal record in the conduct of international affairs.

belle epoque \\'bel-ā-'pȯk\\ *often capitalized B&E* A period of high artistic or cultural development, especially such a period in France in the late nineteenth and early twentieth centuries. In French, *belle epoque* means "beautiful era," but specifically it refers to a time nostalgically considered glamorous and elegant. In general today the name evokes the gorgeous sunset of European culture before the horrors of World War I.

However, not for everyone was it so belle. As historian Barbara Tuchman notes in the foreword to *The Proud Tower:*

> The period was not a Golden Age or Belle Epoque except to a thin crust of privileged class. It was not a time exclusively of confidence, innocence, comfort, stability, security and peace. All these qualities were certainly present. . . . Our misconception lies in assuming that doubt and fear, ferment, protest, violence and hate were not equally present. . . .

The term in use, by Irwin Arieff of Reuters, February 15, 1996:

> Chartier, an architectural gem and the first restaurant in Paris created expressly for the working class, this year celebrates a century of good French cooking at modest prices.
>
> Opened in 1896 by Camille Chartier, it draws Parisians and tourists in droves to admire its authentic Belle Epoque decor and boisterous atmosphere that clients lovingly compare to that of a railway station.

And by Paul Chutkow in the *New York Times,* January 3, 1988, in "Belle Epoque Visions in Paris," describing the city's nightlife:

> But the good news for visitors to Paris is that the dance [the cancan] does survive. The Lido, the Moulin Rouge, the Folies Bergere and a handful of smaller halls bravely play on, trying to keep alive a gay Paris still echoing with legendary names . . . a Paris still dancing to the timeless visions of Degas, Renoir and Toulouse-Lautrec.
>
> This may not be the Belle Epoque, but Paris is still good for a night on the town.

bell the cat To do a daring or risky deed. To stick one's neck out. To confront an unpleasant or dangerous foe. The fable illustrates: A mouse suggested to the other mice that they should hang a bell on the cat's neck to warn all mice of approaching danger. "Excellent," quoth a clever young mouse, "but who is to undertake the job?" In other words, who's going to take the risk to save his neighbors?

The expression is an old one. The story appears in *Aesop's Fables* and in *The Vision of Piers Plowman,* written in the 14th century. A hundred years or so later, Archibald Douglas, 5th Earl of Angus, won the nickname "Bell the Cat" when nobles met to determine how to put down upstart favorites of the weakling King James III of Scotland. Lord Gray asked, "Who will bell the cat?" (In other words, who would act?) Responded Douglas, "That will I," and he killed them in the very presence of the king.

The term in use, by John Ed Pierce in the *Lexington (Ky.) Herald-Leader,* March 30, 1997, praising the state's governor for courage in making proposals for education reform:

> Political interference has prevented the existing council from controlling duplication. As a result, we have two dental schools, where we need one at most; three law schools, where one would suffice. . . . It is going to take a tough council, with full official backing, to bell those cats.

And by syndicated political columnist David Broder in the *Washington Post,* August 18, 1993, on the threat to Republicans in Ross Perot's presidential ambitions:

> It also has dawned on Republicans that Perot could be a serious threat for the GOP nomination. Bush put a hammerlock on the 1988 nomination with only 154,000 votes in New Hampshire and South Carolina. In early primaries and caucuses with a half-dozen rivals, Perot's money and grass-roots organization could give him a real shot at finishing first.
>
> Sooner or later, the Republicans will have to try to bell this cat.

bell tolls *See* FOR WHOM THE BELL TOLLS.

bellwether One that takes the lead or initiative; leader; an indicator of trends.

In shepherding, whence the term comes, the bellwether is the leader of the flock and wears a bell around its neck. In politics, they are those precincts which historically have voted for the winner: find out how the bellwethers are voting and you'll know, presumably, whether your candidate is going to win.

In other uses, bellwethers give early evidence of trends, as in this example in the *Wall Street Journal,* December 16, 1987, describing the events of the October 1987 stock market crash:

> But as the bellwether stocks such as IBM were delayed in trading, Mr. Friedman had second thoughts about owning any futures. "All of a sudden, you realized some things were really different here," he says. "There was pandemonium."

And by Constance Sommer, the Associated Press, March 11, 1997:

> In what could be a bellwether for the Academy Awards, the Direc-
> tors Guild of America has saluted a little-known director for the
> critically acclaimed epic *The English Patient.*

below the salt Excluded from upper-class society and restricted to the
company of common folks; the HOI POLLOI, lacking in any outstanding
quality or qualification.

In homes of the medieval upper crust, the salt cellar (container) was
placed in the middle of the long dinner table in the baronial hall. The family and its noble guests would sit at one end (above the salt), and depen-
dents and those of less status would sit at the other, below the salt, with
the lower orders.

The term in use, by humorist Art Buchwald in a July 15, 1995, column
on revelations of access to the White House for political contributors,
recounting a conversation with a rich friend:

> "I have no problem putting the White House on my payroll, and
> if they want to throw in Al Gore as my dinner partner, so be it."
>   Maybe the Democratic National committee is just pulling your
> leg, and after they cash your check, they will seat you below the
> salt—way down at the end of the dining table—next to George
> Stephanopoulos.

And by William H. Gass in his review of *Arabesques* by Anton Sham-
mas in the *New York Times Book Review,* April 17, 1988:

> There are those, of course, for whom the question is never a ques-
> tion, who arrive in the world at a comfortable station and whose
> identity papers are made unnecessary by their wealth, their
> breeding, the games they play, their accents and their clothes;
> there are those, at the other extreme, who are told they are
> untouchable, that they are slaves, Jews, below the salt and
> BEYOND THE PALE.

In another example, E.L. Doctorow comments on Jack London in the
New York Times Book Review, December 11, 1988:

> He was a workaday literary genius/hack who knew instinctive-
> ly that Literature was a generous host, always having room for
> one more at her table. He sits now below the salt, while the cool-
> er, more sophisticated voices of modernist irony take up the con-
> versation.

Belshazzar's feast \bel-'sha-zərz\ A display of opulent excess or wicked
indulgence.

The phrase comes from the Book of Daniel (chapter 5) in the Old Testament of the Bible. King Belshazzar of Babylon held a feast for a thousand of his noblemen, and sent for the gold and silver vessels which had
been looted from the temple at Jerusalem. He and his lords, wives, and

concubines drank wine from the vessels while they praised their own pagan idols. This was not a good way to assure future prosperity, and the HANDWRITING ON THE WALL appeared to foretell his doom.

The tale played a part in the famously dirty presidential campaign of 1884, in circumstances familiar to students of American politics. The *New York World* cartoon by Walt McDougall entitled "The Royal Feast of Belshazzar Blaine and the Money Kings" attacked a lavish dinner that honored the Republican candidate, James G. Blaine, on the eve of the election. The event was attended by the industrial and financial grandees and robber barons of that freewheeling era. The cartoon, which showed the poor shivering outside, resonated with the working-class electorate, which swung strongly to Cleveland. It is probably one of the most influential cartoons ever drawn.

The headline on a wrathful Paul Johnson editorial about an international poverty summit in the *American Spectator,* March 18, 1995, reads: "Mass-murdering Monsters and a Belshazzar's Feast in Copenhagen." Johnson goes on to say,

> Some of the most evil people in the world were there, mouthing lies and humbug in the intervals of stuffing themselves at gargantuan banquets. [*See* GARGANTUA.]

And quoted in the *Boston Globe,* April 18, 1985, in a report of a judge's ruling in a political-legal rumble in the state legislature:

> [Judge] Zobel also said he disregarded "the suggestion that the speaker and plaintiff were the only ones at the legislative Belshazzar's feast," a biblical reference to the last king of Babylon who could not read the handwriting on the wall, which predicted his downfall.

Beltway, the; Beltway bandits A highway skirting an urban area, specifically the beltway around Washington, D.C., as it delimits what is seen as an insular world. In addition to its notoriety for often creating, rather than eliminating, traffic gridlock, the Beltway serves as a geographical, rhetorical, and psychological rampart. "Inside the Beltway" is used pejoratively to suggest an inward-turning, elitist, self-obsessed cabal of insiders who are ignorant of what's going on in the rest of the country. "Outside the Beltway" lies "the real world."

The Beltway is also the locus of the celebrated consultants known as "Beltway bandits." Their offices are located in the glossy buildings which have sprung up in the suburbs around the Beltway. These consultants are often former government experts who have stepped through "the revolving door" between government and private business operations which feed off government activities.

The term in use, by Bob Garfield in *Advertising Age,* July 28, 1997, on former presidential candidate Bob Dole's new career in television commercials:

People who eight months ago thought he was a sourpussed, opportunistic, inside-the-beltway deal-cutter will love him, and people who thought he sold out to the conservative cause will love him.

And by Sarah Booth Conroy in the *Washington Post,* December 11, 1988:

The question came the other day at a Friends of Art and Preservation In the Embassies dinner for George Schultz. The guest who asked it came from Kansas City, the heartland of America, decidedly beyond the Beltway (which ill-informed locals interpret to mean BEYOND THE PALE).

And *Beltway Bandit* in use by Walt Harrington in the *Washington Post* magazine, November 13, 1988:

But Washington's professional work force more and more includes consultants, Beltway Bandits, office managers, stockbrokers, real estate lawyers and others who prosper at the fringes of the government driven prosperity.

And by David Hackworth in *Newsweek,* June 24, 1991:

There is a danger that Beltway Bandits and Pentagon pundits alike will try to substitute technology for man power for the 21st century.

Bermuda Triangle A BLACK HOLE where things inexplicably vanish.

In fact and legend, the Bermuda Triangle is an area of the North Atlantic between Bermuda, Florida, and Puerto Rico, where the disappearance of numerous ships, airplanes, and people is often blamed on mysterious forces. The "lost squadron," six U.S. Navy planes lost on a training mission on December 5, 1945, is but one example. Storms are common in the region, but scientific investigations have produced no other specific phenomena which would make so many things disappear seemingly without a trace.

Even Shakespeare alluded to the region's mystifying reputation. In *The Tempest,* Act 1, Scene 2, a character speaks of "the still-vexed Bermoothes." Shakespeare was influenced by accounts of a hurricane and shipwreck in the recently discovered islands when he was writing.

A scan of the local library catalog reveals a flowering of books on the Bermuda Triangle in the 1970s. Many are categorized as juvenile literature, and many offer hyperventilating theories of space aliens and sea monsters. One author reported that ships were found to have been abandoned so hastily that even pets were left behind—*except for talking parrots!* He speculated that alien kidnappers might have thought that the power of speech indicated a superior species and taken the chatty Pollies along with the humans.

The term in use, by David Shribman in a New York Times News Service article in the *Sacramento Bee,* January 17, 1995:

In North Carolina, where Republican Harold I. Brubaker becomes speaker later this month, the Democrats' control was so strong that the Republicans seldom spoke, their amendments were immediately tabled and their bills were consigned to a Bermuda triangle of committees.

By Marty Munson, *Prevention,* January 1, 1996:

Trigger situations, along with trigger behaviors and trigger foods, form the Bermuda Triangle of dieting—a region where dieters easily lose their way.

And quoted by Gary Rosenblatt, the *Jewish Week,* August 4, 1995:

Avraham Burg is well aware that many political observers thought he committed an act of professional suicide when he left a high position in the Israeli government to become chairman of the Jewish Agency for Israel and World Zionist Organization. Until now, at least, that position has been held by men on their way down from power, as a stepping stone to retirement. Or as Burg put it bluntly during an interview here on Tuesday, "why did I become chairman of the Jewish Bermuda Triangle?"

best and the brightest, the The most intelligent and creative leaders in their professions. The term is sometimes used in an ironic or sarcastic tone, referring to those paragons who are carried by HUBRIS or overconfidence into gross errors of policy. The phrase was given currency in our own time as the title of David Halberstam's best-selling 1973 book on America's slide into the Vietnam war.

Halberstam's title refers to the many men of recognized brilliance brought to government by President John Kennedy, who boasted of the number of Rhodes scholars in his administration. Halberstam explored how decision-making by the brilliant could nevertheless go awry through arrogant self-confidence, misinformation, and unwillingness to examine fundamental policy assumptions.

The origin of the phrase is uncertain. Halberstam says that as far as he can remember he made it up. Mary McCarthy, in a review in the *New York Review of Books,* January 25, 1973, suggested that the author got the title wrong. "Bishop Heber had a better ear; shouldn't it be 'The Brightest and the Best?' " she asked, referring to an Episcopalian hymn written by Reginald Heber (1783–1826), a bishop of the Anglican church.

Halberstam, however, can claim impressive company for his version. Charles Dickens in *Little Dorrit* (1855–1857), referred to the youngest of the Barnacles, a family of unspeakably arrogant and unhelpful bureaucrats in the "Circumlocution Office" as "the best and the brightest of the Barnacles." And Rudyard Kipling, in his poem *The Files* (1903), parodies obituaries of the famous-but-quickly-forgotten:

> Very great our loss and grievous,
> So the best and brightest leave us,
> And it ends the Age of Giants, say the files.

The term in use, by Henry Allen in the *Washington Post,* November 22, 1988:

> And Washington is still full of Kennedy people waiting for the restoration or the resurrection with the ennobling fury of exiles who never feel the need to explain anything to anybody—aging HAMLETS in pinstriped suits, best and bright at law firms and dinner parties and endless booksignings.

Another example, from the *Springfield (Mass.) Morning Union,* December 19, 1986:

> "We have constructed a very ornate edifice for teacher certification," he [Education Commissioner Harold Raynolds Jr.] said. "If it is discouraging the best and the brightest, we have to take off some of the BAROQUE and rococo."

best–laid plans (of mice and men), the A warning that even the most careful plans can be confounded by events.

The phrase comes from Scottish poet Robert Burns—the title of his poem: "To A Mouse, On Turning Her Up in Her Nest With the Plough, November 1775." Poor mouse—"Wee, sleekit, cow'rin, tim'rous beastie"—has had her cozy den wrecked by the plow.

> But, Mousie, thou art no thy lane,
> In proving foresight may be in vain;
> The best-laid schemes o' mice an' men
> Gang aft agley,
> An' lea'e us nought but grief an' pain,
> For promis'd joy!

Burns (1759–1796) was the son of humble cottagers and a laborer himself. He was famous for his poetry in the Scottish vernacular, which vigorously celebrated his love for his country and the life of the peasantry—including drinking with friends and making love in hay-stacks.

Some of his most famous works are "Auld Lang Syne," "Scots Wha Hae," "A Man's a Man for a' That," and "To a Louse":

The term in use, by Mark Heisler, the *Los Angeles Times,* April 28, 1997:

> Of course, the best-laid plans of mice and men are as nothing when a huge, enraged, Superman wannabe like [Shaquille] O'Neal feels like scattering them, as he did Sunday.

And by economist Murray Weidenbaum, writing in the *Christian Science Monitor,* March 10, 1992:

> A final thought: The patron saint of forecasting is Robert Burns, who warned about the best-laid plans of mice and men.

And by Marlys Harris in *Money,* June 1, 1997:

> "The best-laid schemes o' mice an' men gang aft agley," wrote
> Scottish poet Robbie Burns in 1785. He wasn't discussing retire-
> ment, but well he mae ha' ben, since plenty can gang agley. No
> matter how much we strategize in advance, one big mistake can
> turn our post-65 dream into a time of anxiety or even depriva-
> tion. As Burns might say, we can screw op big tyme.

best of all possible worlds, the The credo of the ultimate optimist, that
what is, is the best that can be; and all things happen for the best. It was
the statement of German philosopher and mathematician Baron Gottfried
Wilhelm von Liebnitz (1646–1716), and famously mocked in Voltaire's
Candide (1759). Dr. Pangloss, the tutor to Candide, believes in this completely, regardless of the disasters he suffers, which include the Lisbon
earthquake and being hanged (not quite thoroughly enough, as it turned
out) by the Spanish Inquisition. (*See also* PANGLOSSIAN.)

Usually used as Voltaire did, with a solid dose of irony; also, as another way of stating a hypothetical ideal: under optimum conditions, a particular desirable outcome would occur—but this outcome is very unlikely,
because the conditions stated do not exist.

The term in use, by Craig R. Whitney in the *New York Times Book Review,*
March 19, 1989:

> It seemed like exciting theater in the Brezhnev days when the
> official line was that nothing was wrong in the best of all possi-
> ble worlds.

By Randall W. Forsyth in *Barron's,* March 27, 1989:

> But if this best of all possible worlds is giving way to sluggish
> growth and rising inflation—as the stock market's recent dismal
> action may indicate—the junk market's view of the future is truly
> PANGLOSSIAN.

And by David Whitten in *Wine Spectator,* Octover 31, 1995:

> In the best of all possible worlds, advances in medicine and bio-
> logical science would proceed hand in hand through carefully
> controlled experimental laboratory research and unbiased eval-
> uation of double-blind clinical trials administered by profes-
> sionals whose only interest is the pursuit of truth and discovery
> of new or more effective means to combat human disease and
> promote wellness.

And also from Adam Ulam in *Current History,* October 1992:

> There was to be the best of all possible worlds: democracy
> secured, one-party rule safeguarded, and an (almost) freely elect-
> ed legislature with a firm proregime majority. In any event, it
> did not turn out that way.

Bethlehem *See* SLOUCHING TOWARD BETHLEHEM.

better mousetrap *See* BUILD A BETTER MOUSETRAP.

better to reign in Hell than serve in Heaven The choice of freedom and power in otherwise unpleasant circumstances over life without them in pleasant surroundings. Satan's defiant cry in John Milton's epic poem *Paradise Lost,* 1.362.

As Milton sets the scene in Book I, Satan is a magnificent, PROMETHEAN figure in defeat. He has been cast out of heaven and flung into the lake of liquid fire. His allies lie in stunned confusion, bemoaning the loss of heaven. Satan looks about with his sparkling eyes, rises to his great height, spreads his wings and flies to land. He addresses his rebellious cohorts:

> The mind is its own place, and in itself
> Can make a Heaven of Hell, a Hell of Heaven.
> What matter where, if I be still the same,
> And what should I be, all but less than he
> Whom thunder hath made greater? Here at least
> We shall be free. . . .
> Here we may reign secure; and, in my choice,
> To reign is worth ambition, though in Hell:
> Better to reign in Hell than serve in Heaven.

The term in use, by rocker Warren Zevon, quoted in the *Philadelphia Daily News* by Jonathan Takiff, July 13, 1995:

> Definitely an inspiration for other musicians, Zevon has been backed in the past by devotees ranging from comic Canadian rockers The Odds to Superstars R.E.M., who accompanied him on the "Sentimental Hygiene" and "Hindu Love Gods" albums.
> (Why isn't he out touring arenas with R.E.M. this summer? "It's better to reign in hell," he growls.)

And in an editorial by Bruce Tichinin in the *San Jose Mercury News,* September 9, 1991:

> It seems like only a couple of years ago that Silicon Valley's premiere apologist, Michael Malone, was still spiritually tipsy on the ruling myth that the electronics industry's phenomenal business success has truly enhanced Bay Area quality of life. He justified his proposal to continue indefinitely this area's growth and entrepreneurship-as-usual with the devil-may-care suggestion that "it is better to reign in Hell than to serve in Heaven."

beyond the pale Outside the area or limits within which one is privileged or protected (as from censure). The term comes from the Latin word "palus" which means "stake," thus a palisade, a barrier marking off a territory with defined borders, or an enclosure.

The sense that anything beyond such borders was out of civilization's reach came from the English Pale, a name given to a well-defined area of

Ireland in which there was English settlement and effective control. The settlement had been established by Norman aristocrats from England in the mid-12th century.

The Pale of Settlement was the only area in Russia where Jews were permitted to live, a region created in 1792 by a partition of Poland. During the 19th century, as successive czars alternated between policies of liberalism and repression, Jews were either allowed outside the Pale and into industry and professions or reconsigned to the Pale and subjected to repression that included murderous pogroms.

The term in use, by Susan Caba, Knight Ridder Newspapers in the *Seattle Times,* September 3, 1997, reporting comments on photographs taken of the accident in which Princess Diana was mortally injured:

> "To my mind, there's blood on those photographs," Phil Buncon, editor in chief of the tabloid *Star* magazine, said yesterday, explaining his refusal to buy the pictures. "The person that took those photographs contributed to the accident," he said. "It was beyond the pale."

And from Universal Press Syndicate columnist Maggie Gallagher in the *Kansas City Star,* February 17, 1996:

> The most surprising thing about Patrick Buchanan is not his friends but his enemies: Alone among GOP candidates, the prospect of a Buchanan victory arouses deep ire among the conservative establishment.
>
> Newt Gingrich has said he could be comfortable with any of the GOP candidates—except Patrick Buchanan. The *Weekly Standard* has simply airbrushed the Buchanan candidacy right out of the picture, declaring him beyond the pale of conservatism.

big bang The cosmic explosion that marked the beginning of the universe, according to a theory generally accepted among astronomers. (The big bang was a single event but not an explosion, says astronomer Sten Odenwald in the *Washington Post* "Horizon" section, May 14, 1997.) This theory is based on the observation that distant galaxies are moving away from the Earth—in other words, the universe is expanding. Scientists have worked backward from this observation and concluded there was a point billions (and there are shifting views about how many billions) of years ago at which all the matter in the universe—stars, galaxies, planets—was packed into a single point of nearly infinite energy density. This matter was then dispersed by the event—the big bang.

The term has come to describe a single, cataclysmic event that creates dramatic change. As these examples illustrate, the term has been applied both to economic reforms in former Communist regimes and to major changes in financial markets in London and Tokyo.

The term in use, by David Holley in the *Los Angeles Times,* August 2, 1997, on changes in Japanese investment regulations:

Under the "Big Bang," small-time investors should enjoy a more level playing field and more attractive options. Foreigners will start selling mutual funds in Japan and partnering with banks to compete with brokerages, which may launch price wars.

Another example, from the *Washington Post,* September 3, 1989:

Helmut Norpoth, of the State University of New York-Stony Brook, and Michael R. Kagay, director of news surveys for the *New York Times,* argued that the striking gains of the GOP among young voters "point toward a party realignment in slow motion, not the big bang it may have been at earlier historic moments."

Big Brother An all-powerful government or organization monitoring and directing people's actions.

Big Brother was the Stalin-like dictator of George Orwell's vision of the totalitarian future in his 1949 novel, *Nineteen Eighty-four.* His picture was everywhere, on placards which read "Big Brother is watching you." Television screens were watched—and watched back.

Orwell's novel was his satiric look at the future toward which the extremes of both the Left and Right would lead, given a chance. The story depicts a society perpetually at war, one in which principles of truth and freedom are turned upside down. Manipulative propaganda (*see* -SPEAK; DOUBLESPEAK) taught that:

War is Peace
Freedom is Slavery
Ignorance is Strength.

The term in use, by Amy Harmon, the *Los Angeles Times,* November 22, 1996:

Like God—or Big Brother, take your pick—Bill Gates was everywhere at the giant Comdex computer show here this week, schmoozing at the chili cook-off, listening to his competitors' speeches and delivering his own address over and over again to clusters of attendees gathered around video monitors in the convention center lobby.

And by Kate Lawson in the *Detroit News,* June 12, 1997:

For Daniel Richard and Glenn Cohen, not only is cleanliness next to godliness—it ought to be enforced. Put quite simply, if you're a restaurant or hospital employee, Cohen and Richard want you to wash your hands every time you leave a washroom. To ensure that happens, they've developed an electronic lavatory monitor. Sound like Big Brother?

bigfoot A person of importance able to use his or her position at will to dominate an underling or take over a situation. To act with such domination is to bigfoot. In journalism, for instance, a big-shot reporter who takes over a story from the journeyman who'd been covering it all along when it reaches page-one potential would be said to have bigfooted his way in. Sometimes a bigfoot is simply a VIP, a mover and shaker whose opinion is definitive. (*See* RAINMAKER.)

The original bigfoot or Sasquatch was a large, hairy, manlike—and legendary—creature roaming the mountains, leaving huge, mysterious tracks. The Himalayan version is known as yeti, or the Abominable Snowman. The abominable American bigfoot freely roams the western mountains and allows his picture to be taken for the supermarket tabloids while slyly avoiding all scientific verification.

The term in use, by Tony Snow in a column printed in the *Cincinnati Enquirer,* August 12, 1996:

> For a few shimmering moments, she found herself at the center of the Republican universe. Every party bigfoot materialized at her side, ready to caress her, cajole her, reassure her and, if necessary, grind her into dust—because they considered her the one movable impediment to a compromise on the issue of abortion.

And by Jake Thompson in the *Kansas City Star,* June 4, 1995:

> By this time in the 1980 race, Dole was gearing up to fire the first of his five campaign managers. By spring of 1987, he'd suffered bad publicity over trying to woo GOP bigfoot adviser John Sears as campaign chairman amid objections from his own campaign insiders.

What's the plural of *bigfoot?* Take your pick. Peter Tauber in the *New York Times Magazine,* May 31, 1987, says "Bigfoots"; William Safire, in his syndicated column of February 13, 1991, says "bigfeet."

Big Rock Candy Mountain A place of ease and plenty; the proverbial land of milk and honey.

The phrase occurs in an American folk song popularized by balladeer Burl Ives; and recorded in the 1920s by Mac McClintock, who versified it from hobo stories. "The Big Rock Candy Mountains" sings about hobo heaven, where the handouts grow on bushes, the cigarettes grow on trees, all the boxcars are empty, and there's a lake of stew and of whiskey, too.

The term in use, by Blackie Sherrod in the *Dallas Morning News,* November 9, 1995, on sports teams moving out on their old home towns:

> The Cleveland Browns, with a following that averages 70,000 loyalists per game, have found a big rock candy mountain in Baltimore.

And from Richard Brookhiser in the *National Review,* September 16, 1996, on the choice of Jack Kemp as the Republicans' candidate for vice president:

> Kemp had announced back in February, when Buchanan was riding high, that he could not support a ticket headed by Pat.

Buchanan has endorsed the Dole-Kemp ticket now. But he has been calling Kempery "Big Rock Candy Mountain" conservatism since the late Eighties.

billingsgate Coarsely abusive language. A vocabulary of the sort one would hear at Billingsgate, an old gate in the walls of the city of London and the site of the London fish market.

Therein lies a tale, irrelevant, but irresistible. According to Henry Blyth's *The Rakes,* the sixth Earl of Barrymore was a noted 18th-century rake whose greatest accomplishment was that he produced an entire family of incorrigibles even worse than he was. In a Golden Age of rakes, they stood out.

Their reputations generated colorful nicknames. Who got which when is unclear, but all ended with the suffix "-gate." Richard, oldest and heir to the title, was called "Hellgate" in recognition of his profligacy; he died at 24, having squandered a fortune of 300,000 pounds. Henry, the second son, born with a club foot, was known as "Cripplegate." Augustus, the third son, was "Newgate," after the city's famous prison, which accommodated debtors as well as other prisoners. And Caroline, the foulmouthed daughter, was, inevitably, "Billingsgate." All the names except Hellgate were derived from the names of gates in the walls of the city of London.

Which shows, maybe, that gates got hung on scandalous behavior a long time ago. Today "-gate" is an instrument of American political shorthand, derived from the Watergate, a Washington complex on the Potomac River containing apartments, a hotel, and an office building, where the celebrated burglary of the Democratic National Committee took place in 1972. The suffix *-gate* becomes a convenience; attach it to the appropriate noun and a scandal is implied. Koreagate, Irangate, Troopergate are rather leaden examples.

The term in use, quoted by Jack Betts, in the *Charlotte Observer,* June 26, 1993, reminiscing fondly about a lawsuit brought by an outraged baseball umpire who claimed that injuries in a melee during a game were due to the inflammatory words and actions of the home team's manager. The judge disagreed, and opined:

> Ordinarily, however, an umpire garners only vituperation—not fisticuffs. Fortified by the knowledge of his infallibility in all judgment decisions, he is able to shed billingsgate like water on the proverbial duck's back.

And by Tom Wicker in the *New York Times,* November 8, 1988, commenting on the negative campaigning in the presidential race:

> That went beyond expectable campaign billingsgate into the personal character of Michael Dukakis; it not only vilified him, but in both cases it did so unfairly—with the clear suggestion that Mr. Dukakis deliberately chose to bar the Pledge of Allegiance from Massachusetts schools and visit a murderer on a defenseless family.

bitch goddess Success, especially of the material or worldly variety.
In modern parlance, a bitch is a malicious, spiteful, or domineering woman. William James (1842–1910), American philosopher, physiologist, psychologist, teacher, and brother of author Henry, first used the phrase: "A symptom of the moral flabbiness born of the exclusive worship of the bitch-goddess success."
D.H. Lawrence used the term in *Lady Chatterley's Lover* (1928):

> He realized now that the bitch-goddess of success had two main appetites: one for flattery, adulation, stroking and tickling such as writers and artists gave her; but the other a grimmer appetite for meat and bones.

The term in use, by Verne Gay in *Newsday,* quoting "Twilight Zone" writer Rod Serling, November 26, 1996:

> "Hollywood's a nice place to live," he once wrote, "if you're a grapefruit. . . . My agent, Blanche, warns me not to overdo my subservience to the Bitch Goddess Success, but I honestly don't think Hollywood will spoil me."
> Of course, the Bitch Goddess won.

Another example, where the success being sought is a little less material but no less worldly, from Will Manley in *Booklist,* March 1, 1993:

> Yes, Mr. Bush's work is just beginning. The rest of his life will be spent trying to appease that Bitch Goddess History. It's an impossible task. History is so fickle. . . . Just consider JFK—in 30 short years, he's gone full circle, from martyr to angel to devil and now back to martyr.

bite the bullet To meet or confront a difficult or painful situation directly and courageously. It comes from the practice of having a patient bite on a bullet during surgery when there was no anesthetic.
Quoted by Scott Thurston, Cox News Service, the *Kansas City Star,* March 30, 1997:

> "It's very tough on the business traveler right now," said Ann Lombardi of Global Travel. "If you can keep an unrestricted ticket in the high seven hundreds, they'll wince but bite the bullet."

And quoted by Christina Nifong, the *Christian Science Monitor,* June 5, 1996, on preservation of lobster fisheries in Maine:

> Others, however, are not so sure the change can remove the inherent conflicts between scientists and lobstermen. "Lobster-management measures have been taken over the years, but nobody wants to bite the bullet," says Maine's D. Krous.

And basketball great Rick Barry, quoted in the *Detroit News,* February 8, 1997, on the "knucklehead syndrome" in today's NBA:

Barry said players who show up coaches and act like idiots—whether it's Robert Horry throwing a towel at his coach or Dennis Rodman kicking a cameraman—should be kicked off teams.

"Get rid of these guys," Barry said. "Bite the bullet. Teams should admit they made a mistake and they screwed up."

Black Friday A day of calamity; especially a day of financial disaster associated with a precipitous drop in the stock market; often attached to any day of the week, and other forms of catastrophe.

The original American Black Friday was the financial panic of September 24, 1869, caused when ROBBER BARONS Jay Gould and James Fisk tried to corner the market on gold. They planned to control the supply and bid up the price. They almost succeeded, but the price crashed on September 24, when the U.S. Treasury put $4 million in gold into the market to break their scheme. Fisk and Gould escaped ruin, and left only the innocent to suffer.

Financial history in the U.S. has been darkened on many occasions since, but the most memorable was undoubtedly Black Tuesday: October 29, 1929, the Crash at the beginning of the Great Depression. This is *the* crash, the one that earned its uppercase letter. The volume of trading was so high that the stock ticker ran more than four hours late. At the end of the day, billions had been lost. The market continued to drop after that day and reached its lowest point on November 13, but it is Black Tuesday that is remembered.

Another notable drop took place on October 28, 1987—Black Monday—when the market plunged 22 percent.

Giving days the appellation "black" was not an invention of the financial markets. In England, Good Friday was also known as "Black Friday." And the tag was given to days on which disasters or great storms occurred.

Another use arises from an unrelated association. The Friday after Thanksgiving in the United States is called Black Friday because it is the biggest shopping day of the year, and merchants hope to be profitable—"in the black"—as a result.

The term in use, by Charles A. Jaffe, the *Boston Globe,* October 1, 1995:

> Welcome to October, which is to the stock market what Cajun food is to a menu: Every day is blackened. Okay, so not every October is that bad, but the month that brings us Halloween—and that brought the market Black Monday, Black Friday and a few dark days in between—clearly frightens a lot of investors.

Another example, from Geoff Drake in *Bicycling,* February 1, 1995, on his cycling injury:

> This means that after more than a decade of hard riding, I suddenly find myself doing little more than commuting to work. I have done only a few local group rides, haven't completed a single (or double) century, and haven't pinned on a race number since Black Friday (April 22, the date of my crash).

And in a *Washington Times* editorial, August 21, 1995:

> Aug. 11 might come to be known as Black Friday for national defense. That was the day President Clinton announced that he was disregarding objections from the Joint Chiefs of Staff and other defense experts and forswearing all future nuclear testing.

black hole A hypothetical invisible region in space with a small diameter and intense gravitational field that is held to be caused by the collapse of a massive star, or something that, like a black hole, consumes a resource continually.

The term may also have been influenced by the Black Hole of Calcutta, referring to a cramped, dungeon-like room. This reference comes from an episode in 1756, in which the Nawab of Bengal confined 146 British prisoners in a cell 18 feet by 14 feet 10 inches. All but 22 of the prisoners suffocated.

The term in use, by Nancy Ann Jeffrey in the *Wall Street Journal,* June 2, 1995:

> Many young people believe a high-paying career entitles them to indulgences, such as expensive restaurants, designer clothes, pricey hobbies, high-tech toys and lavish gifts. But these splurges often become black holes that suck up vast amounts of cash.

And by Stephen W. Gibson in the *Deseret News,* June 29, 1997:

> It seems that originally these answering machines were invented so people could get back to you—and not miss a single call. Now it seems that just the opposite effect is in place. . . . I know several people [who] never, never answer their home phone anymore. With their particular kind of machine, they can hear who is leaving a message. If it is a person they want to talk to, they pick up the phone, otherwise the message goes into some black hole.

Black Rock *See* BAD DAY AT BLACK ROCK.

Bladerunner A futuristic urban hell from the name of the 1982 movie *Blade Runner,* set in Los Angeles in the year 2019. In the film, a blade runner is someone whose job it is to hunt and destroy murderous androids.

The film is futuristic FILM NOIR—dark, garishly lit, dreary with rain, befogged by smoke and steam. The streets teem with a multitude of punk-style nationalities, speaking a mishmash of languages. The premise, design, and production of the film created such a striking vision that they have been carried into the language, overshadowing plot and characters. (Director Ridley Scott also prematurely grayed the hair of movie audiences with *Alien*—the tension heightened by the dark, clanking interior of the space freighter *Nostromo,* redolent of a Joseph Conrad tramp steamer, and full of spots for a malevolent space creature to lurk.)

The term in use, by Daniel B. Wood, the *Christian Science Monitor,* April 24, 1997:

Five years after the costliest riots in US history, Los Angeles has become neither the prototype of American urban revitalization that many had hoped nor the "Bladerunner" dystopia others had feared.

And by Debra J. Saunders, giving her views on a congressional move to allow resumption of offshore oil drilling, the *San Francisco Chronicle,* June 23, 1995:

This precipitous vote, supported by House Appropriations Committee chairman Bob Livingston, R–oil-rich Louisiana, only contributes to the party's image of corporate lackey. Why not just call the GOP The Bladerunner Party?

By Tom Maurstad, the *Dallas Morning News,* reprinted in the *Kansas City Star,* January 9, 1996, on pop culture trends:

As we hurtle into our high-tech Bladerunner future, the trend that has swept across music and fashion is 1960s REDUX. Hey, the future is just the past viewed through the irony of the present.

Bligh, Captain William William Bligh (1754–1817) is known as the dictatorial captain of H.M.S. *Bounty,* scene of the most famous naval mutiny in history. His name has become a byword for petty, tyrannical, cruel discipline.

In 1787, Bligh and the *Bounty* were on an expedition to the Pacific to obtain specimens of the breadfruit tree. Although the causes of the mutiny remain unknown, Bligh's extreme, unbending discipline is popularly supposed to have precipitated it. The mutineers, led by Fletcher Christian, set the captain adrift in a small boat with eighteen crewmen loyal to him.

In a tremendous feat of seamanship, Bligh navigated the open boat to safety across nearly four thousand miles of open sea. He was later cleared by a court-martial of responsibility for the loss of the ship.

Bligh continued his career, and was involved in two more mutinies. On May 19, 1797, a mutiny arose throughout the British fleet, and Bligh, like other officers, was put ashore by rebellious crews. This one could hardly be blamed on him, however. The third mutiny took place on terra firma (Australia, actually), where Bligh was serving as governor of New South Wales. After another court-martial, Bligh was promoted to rear admiral. But he never went to sea again.

The story of the *Bounty* gained fame through the 1932 novel *Mutiny on the Bounty* by Charles Nordhoff and James Norman Hall, and its various movie versions, the most memorable of which (1935) offered a scenery-chewing portrayal of Bligh by Charles Laughton.

The captain evoked, by Steve Dale in the *Chicago Tribune,* February 17, 1989, on learning to sail:

Your best friend may seem to speak perfect English until he or she begins shouting instructions during a sailboat ride on Lake

Michigan. You're eager to help until your friend turns into Captain Bligh, yelling at you in another language. "Sheet the jib!" the captain screams. "Come about!"

Another example, by Eliot Asinof in the *New York Times Magazine,* March 26, 1989, writing on baseball manager Dallas Green:

> Green ran the Phillies the way Captain Bligh ran the *Bounty.* No more card playing in the clubhouse; no more ballplayers' children on the field before the game; everyone runs in practice, including the future Hall of Fame pitcher Steve Carlton, who had other ideas about conditioning.

Blimp, Colonel A pompous person with out-of-date or ultra-conservative views; a reactionary. Colonel Blimp was a cartoon character created by British cartoonist David Low after World War I. His name came from the nickname for the observation balloons used during the war. Colonel Blimp was a caricature of the archetypical elderly British Tory, a paunchy, harrumphing John Bull opposed to all change, and rather dim mentally.

The term in use, by William Chapin in *Mother Earth News,* August 18, 1995:

> The commanding officer of Morris Field was a Colonel Gates. He would have been better named Colonel Blimp. Colonel and Mrs. Gates had a rose garden. Almost every morning he would saunter into the weather station and demand to know if we would have a thunderstorm that afternoon. My thunderstorm forecast determined whether or not the colonel felt compelled to water his roses.

A play on the term in the *Economist*, January 28, 1989, as the title of an item on Japanese production of miniaturized airships: "Corporal Blimp."

Another example, from Robert Brustein in the *New Republic,* March 6, 1989, reviewing a London production of Strindberg's play *The Father:*

> John Osborne's adaptation occasionally suffered from Colonel Blimp Anglicisms ("You'll jolly well provide for the child, take it from me") but it's the strongest, most lyrical version of the play I know.

bliss was it in that dawn to be alive The complete happiness of being present at a revolutionary moment. In our sadder but wiser times, the phrase is often used ironically, to imply that even the best revolutions can be full of unpleasant surprises.

The quotation is from William Wordsworth's autobiographical poem, "The Prelude." As a young man Wordsworth spent considerable time in France during the French Revolution. He was much moved by the hope that the people were throwing off tyranny—hope dashed by the REIGN OF TERROR and then the imperialist warfare of Napoleon. But he clearly expressed the joy and excitement of revolution's heady days:

Bliss was it in that dawn to be alive,
But to be young was very Heaven!

The term in use, by R.W. Johnson in the *National Review,* October 18, 1993:

Whatever one may have read about "bliss was it in that dawn to be alive," I can report unhesitatingly that it is no fun at all to live through a revolution like this.

Another example, from Melvin Seiden in the *Humanist,* September 1, 1994:

They—I had no idea who—had chosen me to be a student in a so-called G.I. university in . . . Florence. Though still a private first class . . . I was living like a civilian, indeed like a privileged gentleman and scholar—not scholar enough in 1945, however, to be able to recite: "Bliss was it in that dawn to be alive."

And from an editorial in the *Baltimore Sun,* July 4, 1994:

As *Newsweek* so smugly put it, Thomas Jefferson said all men are created equal, yet he kept slaves: "Anybody got a problem with that?"
    Bliss is it in this dawn to be alive, but to be hip is very heaven. How happily we condescend to the authors of our independence.

blitzkrieg War conducted with great speed and force; specifically a violent surprise offensive by closely coordinated air and ground forces. In German, it means "lightning war." *Blitzkrieg* is the name the Germans gave to their fast-moving attacks on Poland, the Low Countries, and France at the beginning of World War II. After their bitter experience of trench warfare in World War I, the German planners devised a program of sudden attacks by air and ground to surprise and overwhelm their enemies.

The word entered the English language almost immediately. "Blitz" was the name the British themselves applied to the savage Nazi air attacks on London and other British cities during the war. To be "blitzed" is to be struck by a swift, violent attack.

Words of war are often applied to sport, and the blitz quickly became part of the lexicon of American football, referring to a swift charge by defensive players through the opposing line to break up plays.

The term in use, in the *Rocky Mountain News,* November 17, 1996:

Someday—perhaps tomorrow, perhaps in several centuries—death will plunge like a blitzkrieg from the slopes of a Washington volcano.
    Thousands could die, drowned or crushed by . . . a muddy flood of melted glacial water and smashed trees surging through farmland and small towns.

And by James Kuhnhenn in the *Kansas City Star,* March 14, 1996, on presidential primary developments:

> Forbes, a late entry into the presidential campaign last year, struck in blitzkrieg fashion in January. By using his own money, he was able to avoid federal limits on spending and saturated the airwaves in Iowa and New Hampshire with ads critical of Dole.

And by Melissa Healey in the *Los Angeles Times,* January 1, 1995:

> In what Gingrich hopes will be a 100-day legislative blitzkrieg, the GOP plans not only to cut taxes, revamp welfare and reduce regulation, but to overhaul government itself.

blood in the water The traces of blood from an injury which draw sharks in for the kill. Sharks have a powerful sense of smell; it is said they can detect blood in the water from over a mile away and will rush in to finish off the creature whose blood it is. Sometimes this rush to the kill brings on a FEEDING FRENZY.

The expression colorfully describes how in human society, especially public life, a wound or sign of weakness will draw predators (political opponents, perhaps, or the press).

The term in use, by William Endicott in the *Sacramento Bee,* January 27, 1996:

> Political reporters can sometimes be like motorists braking for a better look at a freeway pileup. They gravitate toward conflict like sharks toward blood in the water.

Another example, from Jeffrey Ressner, *Time,* May 13, 1996, on the loss of star clients at a major Hollywood agency:

> Rivals, long resentful of the agency's No. 1 status, are smelling blood in the water.

And from Peter Johnson, *USA Today,* March 14, 1997:

> Add a major defection like Gumbel's to CBS after 25 years at NBC and you've got blood in the water.

blood, sweat, and tears Great effort through great suffering; results achieved at great cost.

The phrase is a slight variation of a quote from Winston Churchill. In a speech to the House of Commons after becoming prime minister, with the British army in France in full retreat before the onrushing BLITZKRIEG of Nazi Germany, he said: "I have nothing to offer but blood, toil, tears and sweat." Similar words had been used by Lord Byron and John Donne, who also knew a thing or two about stirring language.

Churchill shortened the phrase in a collection of his speeches published in 1941: *Blood, Sweat and Tears.*

The term in use, by Jim Van Vliet in the *Sacramento Bee,* December 2, 1995:

After all the hours in the film room and all the hours of blood, sweat and tears that began back in August, Jesuit High School coach Dan Carmazzi could only stand helplessly as he watched the 1995 season slip slowly down the drainpipe.

And quoted by Ted Sickinger, the *Kansas City Star,* March 1, 1997:

"There's no question that my intention was originally to clean this bank up and sell it," he said. "But it has just reached a point where we've got the blood, sweat and tears in the thing. Why not take advantage of the future value?"

And from the *Christian Science Monitor,* May 31, 1994, on difficulties in economic transition from communism in Central Europe:

"After 40 years of communism, people didn't know much about a market. They anticipated an overnight transformation," says Jaroslaw Mulewicz, a Warsaw-based economic consultant. "No one told them that it takes blood, sweat and tears."

bloody shirt *See* WAVE THE BLOODY SHIRT.

Bloomsbury A London neighborhood near the British Museum and the University of London, traditionally an area where writers and intellectuals reside.

References today to "Bloomsbury intellectuals" are often barbed; the term is used to suggest an offbeat Bohemian or radical tinge. The neighborhood has a reputation akin to New York's Greenwich Village or Paris's Left Bank.

Bloomsbury is associated with some famous people who banded together to further their ideas and goals.

One famous group, the Bloomsbury group, in 1904 started meeting in each other's homes. Included were economist John Maynard Keynes and writers E.M. Forster, Virginia Woolf, Lytton Strachey, and Vita Sackville-West.

The term in use, by Rachel M. Brownstein in her review of *Writing for Their Lives: The Modernist Women 1910–1940* in the *New York Times Book Review,* March 12, 1989:

As [authors] Gillian Hanscombe and Virginia L. Smyers see it, not only the wordlings of the Left Bank and Greenwich Village, but Amy Lowell cultivating her garden outside Boston and Marianne Moore in Brooklyn were members of what the authors call "another Bloomsbury," who lived and wrote "anti-conventionally."

bluestocking \'blü-ˌstäk-iŋ\ Any of a group of ladies who in mid-18th-century England held "conversations" to which they invited men of letters and members of the aristocracy with literary interests. The word has come to be applied derisively to a woman having or pretending to have literary or learned interests. The Bluestockings attempted to replace social evenings spent playing cards with something more intellectual. The term probably originated when Mrs. Elizabeth Vesey invited the learned Benjamin Stillingfleet to one of her parties; he declined because he lacked appropriate dress, whereupon she told him to come "in his blue stockings"—the ordinary worsted stockings he was wearing at the time. He did so, and Bluestocking (or Bas Bleu) society became a nickname for the group.

The group was never a society in any formal sense. Mrs. Vesey and Mrs. Elizabeth Montagu became leaders of the literary ladies. Others included Madame d'Arblay (better known as Fanny Burney), Mrs. Frances Boscawen, Mrs. Hester Chapone, and Miss Hannah More, whose poem "The Bas Blue, or Conversation" (1786) supplies inside information about them. Guests included Samuel Johnson, James Boswell, David Garrick, George Lyttleton, and Horace Walpole (who called the women "petticoteries").

The term in use, Kathryn Harrison in *Vogue,* September 1995:

> . . . by the time I was in high school, I recognized the worth of my hair color. It would serve as a correction to anyone's assumption that I was what my grandmother derisively called a bluestocking. If blonds were dumb, and if they had more fun, then perhaps no one would hold my SAT scores against me; perhaps they would overlook that I translated Cicero for pleasure and had never stepped into the local video arcade.

And by Giselle Benatar in *Entertainment Weekly,* November 20, 1992:

> Branagh, who calls this his "most personal film to date," produces, directs, and stars as a self-loathing English writer who writes Hollywood sitcoms for his actress wife, Rita Rudner. . . . Thompson plays a bluestocking publisher looking for someone to love. . . .

And by Myra Stout in the *New York Times Magazine,* May 26, 1991:

> Byatt may be a quintessential English bluestocking, but she differs in that she chooses to "look out" omnivorously. Besides being a bona fide bookworm (she "loves footnotes" and reads even when cooking), she is also passionate about observing people and nature.

B movie A cheaply produced motion picture, often the second movie on a double bill. The B movie was usually an inferior, low-budget effort with lesser-known actors, although many stars got their start in these productions and moved on to bigger things.

The term is often used to describe the actors or production qualities of these films. The most familiar use in recent times, of course, was applied to Ronald Reagan by those who did not admire his work on or off the screen.

The term in use, by Joe Baltake, movie critic of the *Sacramento Bee,* January 19, 1996:

> *From Dusk Till Dawn* is based on the very first script Tarantino ever wrote. It was written in 1981 and is clearly the product of someone who had pigged out on too much B-movie junk.

Another example, in *Sports Illustrated,* October 14, 1996:

> There stood Billy Sims last Saturday afternoon, the autumn sunlight glinting brilliantly off his 1978 Heisman ring as he displayed it for fans behind the Sooners bench in Norman. Not more than 50 yards away was Brian Bosworth. The Boz, an intimidator only on B movie sets these days, hoisted children on his shoulders and gave them pregame walking tours of the sidelines.

Body Snatchers *See* INVASION OF THE BODY SNATCHERS.

boilerplate A standardized text; formulaic or hackneyed language. The standard language that appears in contracts, wills, or other legal forms is a good example.

Use of the term goes back to precomputer days, when "boilerplate" referred to syndicated material (such as features, columns, and editorials) that was widely distributed to newspapers, especially weeklies. It came in plate form ready for the presses, so that the type didn't have to be set, and offered a way to fill out the paper with innocuous stuff.

The term in use, by Kenneth Turan, film critic of the *Los Angeles Times* reviewing *Different for Girls,* September 12, 1997:

> A plot does have to kick in eventually, and as written by Tony Marchant and directed by Richard Spence, what there is is not particularly inspired. It involves an unfortunate arrest, a sadistic policeman, the tabloid press . . . and considerable amounts of sentimental boilerplate that isn't up to the subtlety and sensitivity of the film's best moments.

And by Sidney Blumenthal in the *Washington Monthly,* October 1987, in a review of the writings of columnist George Will:

> Much of this slight book is filled with commonplaces that can be gleaned from the daily newspaper. . . . Most annoying of all, Will puts forth this boilerplate as if it were derived from a close reading of Aristotle.

Boop, Betty A wide-eyed, gold-digging cutie pie with a bouncy 1920s flapper manner out to achieve her own ends. Betty Boop was an American cartoon character created by Max Fleischer in 1915; her name came from the "boop-oop-a-doop" singer Helen Kane.

She was an early hit as an animated cartoon character in the 1920s, and attracted the concern of motion picture censors—when Betty danced the hula, the flowers blushed. She remained a popular character through the 1930s.

Fleischer and his brother (who also created Popeye) were the "anti-Disney" cartoonists. Their waggish humor was considerably more adult, with a hip, New York style. Myron Waldman, who worked as an artist for Fleischer Brothers, recalled that one Fleischer cartoon had a scene in which a dancing hippo kicked her garter into the audience. It was censored in Philadelphia. Waldman noted that, "You weren't allowed to show cow udders at Disney."

The term in use, by Merle Rubin, the *Christian Science Monitor,* June 19, 1996, reviewing *An Echo of Heaven* by Kenzaburo Oe:

> Marie, we learn, was a slim, attractive woman with a free-and-easy manner, a sometimes unsettling outspokenness, an independent attitude, and a warm, wide Betty Boop-like smile accentuated by bright red lipstick.

Another example from *People,* April 6, 1992:

> But in the wider world, Tammy Faye receives little sympathy. She is, after all, the Betty Boop of spiritual sanctimony, who, two months after PTL was declared morally and financially bankrupt, tottered onto Ted Koppel's *Nightline* in high heels and a jungle-print jumpsuit.

And by Richard Corliss in *Time,* on the poignant career of black actress Dorothy Dandridge, September 1, 1997:

> Growing up onscreen, Dorothy was pretty as a Keane picture, vivacious as Betty Boop, and slim—slim as a black actress's chance of movie stardom in the whites-only golden age.

Borden, Lizzie An accused, but acquitted, ax murderess.

On August 4, 1892, Lizzie Borden was charged with murdering her father and stepmother with an ax in their home in Fall River, Massachusetts. There had been great tension in the family among the two daughters and their stepmother and parsimonious father. After the murders Lizzie was discovered burning a dress in the stove.

Following a sensational trial, Lizzie was acquitted but not exonerated; there was wide belief in her guilt. She was ostracized by the folks of Fall River, where she lived until her death in 1927. She did live more comfortably, however—she used her inheritance to purchase a finer house. And, of course, she inspired the famous (anonymous) lines:

> Lizzie Borden took an ax
> And gave her mother forty whacks;
> When she saw what she had done,
> She gave her father forty-one.

The murder was never solved, and Lizzie's guilt or innocence continues to be debated and dramatized in our own time. The story has been the subject of plays, ballets, and even an opera. As with other famous murders, the case is analyzed according to the perspectives of those who study it—

in the 1970s, Lizzie was a feminist heroine; more recently, it was suggested that she and her sister were the objects of parental abuse or incest.

The term in use, by then-Congressman Pat Roberts (R–Kan.) characterizing Indiana Senator Richard Lugar's questioning of agricultural subsidies, the *Kansas City Star,* January 2, 1995:

> Roberts, who is more closely allied with incoming Senate Majority Leader Bob Dole than Lugar, called him "Lizzie Borden Lugar" for demanding that all agriculture commodity programs be put on the table.

And by Michael Farber, *Sports Illustrated,* April 15, 1996:

> There is no neutral ground—you love him or you hate him. Ron Hextall of the Philadelphia Flyers is either the most competitive goalie in hockey, a man whose ability to pass the puck has helped to redefine his position, or a magna cum laude graduate of the Lizzie Borden School of Stickhandling.

Borgia An infamous family of Renaissance Italy renowned for remorseless cruelty in the name of power. They achieved success in the 1400s and 1500s, producing two popes and numerous other church and political leaders, but today their name is a byword for utter ruthlessness: In a time notable for intrigue, betrayal, and murder, they stood out as they changed sides and assassinated their enemies or former allies without compunction.

The most famous Borgias were a sister and brother, Cesare and Lucrezia. They were the illegitimate children of the notoriously wicked Rodrigo Borgia, Pope Alexander VI. Cesare was a cardinal at 17 but resigned after the murder of his older brother, in which he probably had a hand. In 1502 he lured his rivals for power to the castle of Sinigaglia and had them strangled. He was intelligent and vicious, a successful blend of daring and duplicity that was the model for Machiavelli's *The Prince.*

Lucrezia, his sister, was married off for political advantage—three times. The first marriage was annulled by the pope, her father, after the husband changed political sides and charged his wife and father-in-law with incest. The second husband became inconvenient and was strangled by one of brother Cesare's servants while recovering from a previous assassination attempt. Number 3 survived, probably because Lucrezia's career as a serial widow ended in 1503 with the death of her father. Once free of the immediate influence of her family, she turned to religion, became a patroness of the arts, and died calmly at the age of 39. It is thought now that she has been unjustly tainted by family plots in which she was a pawn rather than a player.

The term in use, by columnist Cynthia Tucker, appearing in the *Kansas City Star,* October 12, 1996:

> Women had not gotten over the 1992 Republican National convention—with Pat Buchanan playing pit bull and Marilyn Quayle

doing her Lucretia Borgia imitation—when they were introduced to a Republican House of Representatives with Newt Gingrich at the helm.

Another example, from Phil Elderkin in the *Christian Science Monitor*, January 20, 1981, describing professional football player Ted Hendricks:

> Meeting Hendricks, a 6 foot 7 inch linebacker who weighs 225 pounds and sometimes wears an old German war helmet to practice, rates right alongside having a date with Lucrezia Borgia.

Another example, from Mitchell Owens, the *New York Times*, April 13, 1997:

> Though a footnote today, for nearly 50 years [Daisy] Fellowes, the daughter of a French duke and granddaughter of the sewing-machine magnate Isaac Merritt Singer, was the trans-Atlantic fête-set's No. 1 bad girl.
> Contemporary sources tend to put a Borgia-like spin on the formidably witty Fellowes, painting her as a Molotov cocktail in a Mainbocher suit.

Borscht Belt \\'bȯrsh(t)-\\ The theaters and nightclubs associated with the Jewish summer resorts in the Catskill Mountains near New York City. Borscht (or borsch) is a beet soup (a Yiddish or Russian dish) frequently found on the menus of such establishments, reflecting the taste and origin of many of the patrons.

The Borscht Belt served as the training ground for many comedians, including the likes of Milton Berle and Henny Youngman, so the region came to be associated with rapid-fire one-liners usually with a New York flavor.

Other "belts" turn up here and there as a shorthand way of summing up a region's cultural, ethnic, ideological, or economic attributes. H.L. Mencken is credited with coining the most commonly used of them, the "Bible Belt," in the 1920s to refer to areas where fundamentalist Protestantism flourishes. Later came the "Sun Belt" and the "Rust Belt."

The term in use, by Eric Metaxas in the *Washington Post Book World*, May 4, 1997, describing his experience adapting stories for children's audiobooks—including one recorded by Robin Williams:

> But even before we'd cast Williams I'd thought of this story as an opportunity for me to write something very over-the-top Borscht-belt jokey. . . . Still, I'd have to keep the wackiness somewhat in check. After all, some parents and teachers might actually use the audiobook version to teach kids grammar, no? Enter Robin Williams, fresh from Ork.

And from Michael Lichtenstein in the *New York Times Book Review*, October 14, 1990:

Unfortunately, Mr. Lupica's Borscht-Belt one-liners mar "Limited Partner," and his incessant name-dropping detracts from what would otherwise have been a pretty fair whodunit.

Boswell A person who records in detail the life of a usually famous contemporary. James Boswell (1740–1795) was a Scot who gained fame as a diarist and as the biographer of Dr. Samuel Johnson, the English lexicographer, critic, poet, and conversationalist, whose every witticism he faithfully recorded.

The term in use, by Victor Gold, reviewing Monica Crowley's book *Nixon Off the Record: His Candid Commentary on People and Politics* in the *Washington Times,* August 18, 1996:

> No, whatever Miss Crowley's shortcomings as a witness to history—youth and impressionability being the most obvious—I believe the words and thoughts she ascribes to her mentor are, whether Nixonophiles like it or not, appallingly authentic . . . . Nor does it take much imagination to picture Richard Nixon trying to "relate" to his Generation-X Boswell by adopting the barnyard language he once criticized Harry S. Truman for using.

And by Joanne Lipman in the *Wall Street Journal,* November 5, 1987:

> Just who, or what, is this fabled creature, the bimbo? . . . So . . . we decided to turn to some experts on the subject—and who is more expert, we reasoned, than the bimbo's Boswell, the gossip columnist?

bottom feeder A marine animal that feeds on whatever sinks to the bottom of the sea; someone who feeds on misfortune or exploits the damaged or unsavory; a scavenger.

A fishy term: Bottom-feeding fish are those which literally eat what is on the bottom of the body of water they inhabit, whether microscopic creatures, plants, or dead things. Often they are specially equipped for their work—catfish, for example, have barbels or "whiskers" and paddlefish have a spatula-like nose to facilitate digging. For their eating habits, they are called trash fish, and considered "dirty."

By transference, the term has come to be applied to people who dig in dirt and profit from repugnant things. In real estate, it pertains to buyers who grab distressed properties at better-than-bargain prices. It is also applied to losers, or to those who must survive any way they can, often by preying on others even weaker.

The term in use, quoted by Carol Ostrom in the *Seattle Times,* October 4, 1996, writing about the introduction of a course on abortion at the University of Washington medical school:

> Medical students nationwide were mobilized when they received a pamphlet about abortion providers titled "Bottom Feeders" from an anti-abortion group in 1993, said Patricia Anderson, executive director of Medical Students for Choice.

Another example, from Gaile Robinson, the *Los Angeles Times,* May 4, 1995:

> Wanna-be models, lacking the looks, the will and the sense to understand their precarious position, are junk food for modeling's predators and bottom feeders.

And from Lyall Bush, the *Seattle Times,* December 20, 1996:

> Lots of low, nervous, dying-animal chortling. An unerring antenna for bottom-feeder puns about body parts and bodily functions. Unchecked hunger for more TV, sugar, heavy-metal guitar, fire and fantasies straight from Larry Flynt publications. Yes, it's Beavis and Butthead's spiritual odyssey across America! And it's not all that bad.

bowdlerize \'bōd-lə-ˌrīz, 'baud-\ To expurgate (for example, a book) by omitting or modifying parts considered vulgar.

The term comes from the name of Dr. Thomas Bowdler (1754–1825), a retired doctor and self-appointed literary critic who applied his literary scalpel to the works of Shakespeare and Edward Gibbon's *The History of the Decline and Fall of the Roman Empire,* excising expressions "which cannot with propriety be read aloud in a family" and "whatever is unfit to be read by a gentleman in a company of ladies." He maintained that Shakespeare would have approved.

The Family Shakespeare, published in 1818, became a bestseller in which "God" as an expletive was replaced by "heavens"; famous speeches were severely cut; such major characters as Macbeth, Hamlet, and Falstaff were seriously altered, and some bawdy characters disappeared completely. Sometimes Bowdler had to admit defeat, as he did with *Othello:* The play was "unfortunately little suited to family reading."

Eleven years after his death, his name made its appearance as a verb.

The term in use, by Patt Morrison in the *Los Angeles Times,* June 21, 1996:

> A few neighbors of Caffe Michelangelo wanted the city to order the restaurant to bowdlerize its new 4-foot-high sign, which features Michelangelo's nude statue of David rendered in full and faithful detail.

And by Dennis Cauchon in *USA Today,* May 11, 1994, reporting that 100 offensive words have been removed from the official Scrabble dictionary:

> "They're bowdlerizing the damn thing!" says Charlie Southwell, a top-ranked Scrabble player. "Everyone knows and uses these words."

Bracknell, Lady Fictional character; the mother of Gwendolen Fairfax in Oscar Wilde's *The Importance of Being Earnest.* She is a snob and a tyrant, the epitome of Victorian respectability, and one of the funniest characters in literature.

Jack Worthing, who has asked Gwendolen to marry him, observes, "Never met such a GORGON . . . I don't know what a Gorgon is like, but I am quite sure that Lady Bracknell is one. In any case, she is a monster, without being a myth, which is rather unfair. . . . "

The term in use, by Jan Stuart in *Newsday,* May 6, 1995, reviewing Patti LuPone's performance in *Pal Joey:*

> Her super-diva rendition epitomized a reading of society gal Vera Simpson with enough crusty ennui to suggest a Lady Bracknell separated at birth from Leona Helmsley.

And from Robert Seiple in the *Economist,* May 1, 1993:

> One bomb in the City of London may be regarded as a misfortune, as Lady Bracknell might have put it; two looks like carelessness.

Brahmin \'brä-mən, 'brä-, bra-\ A person of high social standing and cultivated intellect and taste. It comes from Hinduism, where a Brahmin (or Brahman) is a member of the highest, or priestly, caste.

In the 19th century, the term was applied to Boston's close-knit intellectual, social, and political aristocracy by Oliver Wendell Holmes Sr., prolific author (and father of famed Supreme Court Justice Oliver Wendell Holmes). In the bare-knuckle politics of Boston, the term often was used by ethnic politicians taking shots at the blue-blooded elite. Today the link to Boston is diluted; what we are talking about is the Eastern Establishment.

The term in use, in the *New Republic,* November 2, 1987:

> In the October *Atlantic,* investment-banking Brahmin Peter G. Peterson writes the standard CASSANDRA scenario.

And by Eleanor Holmes Norton in the *New York Times Book Review,* November 27, 1988:

> And from another world there was Harris Wofford, the Alabama Brahmin who was the closest thing to a movement "mole" in the Kennedy White House.

brave new world A future world, situation, or development, or recent development or recently changed situation. Used ironically, as Aldous Huxley (1894–1963) did in his satirical 1932 novel by that title, the term evokes a world that is sterile, regimented, without soul. Thus the phrase is often applied pejoratively to unnerving modern social and scientific developments.

The novel *Brave New World* is set in the future, in the year 632 AF (for "After Ford," that is, Henry Ford, the inventor of the assembly line and thus of the modern mass-production, mass-consumption society).

Huxley stood values on their heads to make his point. In the novel, the traditional family is abolished, monogamy and parenthood viewed with horror. Human beings are hatched in laboratories, predestined and programmed for specific classes of society and work. They are anesthetized by promiscuous sex and drugs.

A "savage" who has educated himself reading Shakespeare is found on an Indian reservation. He is brought to "civilization" as an experiment. Thrilled at first, he quotes Miranda in Shakespeare's *Tempest* Act 5, Scene 1. Like him, Miranda has been raised in isolation, and upon meeting the stranger her father has brought, she cries, "O brave new world/That has such people in't."

The term in use, by Jim Bencivenga in the *Christian Science Monitor,* October 31, 1996, reviewing *Idoru* by William Gibson:

> Gibson is known as the father of cyberpunk literature and the originator of the term "cyberspace" (in the summer of 1981). His work poses essentially metaphysical questions for the brave new world spawned by telecommunications/microchip technology.

And by James A. Fussell in the *Kansas City Star,* April 5, 1993:

> Let me say for the record that any flea market with the chutzpah to have a gigantic scowling flea in a red-and-white super hero suit for a mascot deserves my attention for at least a day.
>
> I refer, of course, to Super Flea, Skip Sleyster's brave new world of garage-sale-run-amok commerce on a grand indoor scale.

And by Robert Darnton in the *New York Review of Books,* January 19, 1989, on the bicentennial of the French Revolution:

> Two hundred years of experimentation with brave new worlds have made us skeptical about social engineering.

bread and circuses A palliative offered especially to avert potential discontent. Public spectacles or entertainments distract the public from important issues and may alleviate discontent in the short run, but neither provides fundamental solutions.

The term comes from the work of the Roman satirist Juvenal (ca. A.D. 60–140), who wrote: *Duas tantum res anxius optat/Panem et circenses* (Satires X, 79). ([The people] long eagerly for two things/Bread and circuses.)

The term in use, by Thomas Boswell in a commentary on the Super Bowl in the *Washington Post,* January 22, 1989:

> Nothing stops, or even deflects, the NFL—which did not cancel a single game the week President John F. Kennedy was shot—from fulfilling its self-appointed role as national purveyor of bread and circuses.

And by Dick Williams in commentary in the *Atlanta Journal and Constitution,* September 9, 1997:

Infrastructure just isn't sexy. Reporters, including this one, would rather report the story of a protest . . . than delve into whether the pipes beneath us are sound and safe.

Infrastructure becomes news when it fails or when it isn't available. . . . Bread and circuses are more fun.

break a leg A good-luck wish for a successful performance, a traditional expression from show business. Its origin is obscure, but theories abound. A likely possibility is the superstitious feeling that wishing aloud for something bad will produce the opposite, and will in fact prevent the bad thing from happening.

The term in use, by Samuel Fromartz, Reuter/Variety Entertainment Summary, June 16, 1996:

Andrea McArdle has been performing on Broadway since her days as the original kid star of "Annie" and should know that "break a leg" is not a literal show business term. McArdle has had to drop out of Broadway's "State Fair" after breaking an ankle during a June 5 performance.

And from Jay Gallagher, Gannett News Service, August 15, 1996:

You know you're at a Republican convention when: The New York lieutenant governor tells the governor to "break a leg" before he gives a speech and everyone's afraid she's carrying a club.

Brigadoon A place that is idyllic, unaffected by time, or remote from reality.

The word is taken from the fictional Scottish village of the eponymous 1947 Lerner and Loewe stage musical. Brigadoon is a magical place protected from the outside world by a magic spell from which the village awakens for one day every hundred years. Of course in the story love bridges the gap, and lonely 20th–century boy meets beautiful 18th–century girl, with happiness all around.

Brigadoon evoked, by Stewart Brand, *Time*, March 1, 1995:

Newcomers to the Internet are often startled to discover themselves not so much in some soulless colony of technocrats as in a kind of cultural Brigadoon—a flowering remnant of the '60s, when hippie communalism and libertarian politics formed the roots of the modern cyberrevolution.

By Nancy Shute, the *New Republic*, May 2, 1994, on Russia:

You may no longer need a special propiska stamped in your passport to come here, but Moscow is still nine time zones away. Add to that the fact that parts of the twentieth century have passed Kamchatka by and we're talking Brigadoon with kimchi and borscht.

And from Roger Simon in a commentary in the *Baltimore Sun,* June 4, 1995:

> So did Bob Dole, who is so very concerned about decency and honor in movies, also resign from the NRA?
> He did not. Bob Dole has accepted tens of thousands of dollars from the NRA and hopes for tens of thousands more as he runs for president.
> Did I forget to mention that he is running for president? And that his concern for "traditional values" has surfaced Brigadoon-like just in time for his campaign?

brimstone *See* FIRE AND BRIMSTONE.

Brobdingnagian \ˌbräb-diŋ-ˈna-gē-ən, -dig-ˈna-\ Marked by tremendous size.

It comes from Jonathan Swift's satire, *Gulliver's Travels* (1726) in which Brobdingnag was a country of giants who were twelve times larger than ordinary men.

The term in use, by Steve Rushin in *Sports Illustrated,* May 24, 1993:

> Malone entered the first game with two out in the bottom of the ninth, runners at second and third, and the Brobdingnagian Boog Powell stepping into the box.

By Robert Hendrickson in *Smithsonian,* July 1990:

> He crammed a generous chunk of the mix in his mouth and blew a bubble. The bubble rose, rose higher. It was a big beautiful bubble, a Brobdingnagian bubble, a supercalifragilisticexpialidocious bubble. Diemer had never before seen anything like it. And then it popped.

And by Elizabeth Levitan Spaid in the *Christian Science Monitor,* August 30, 1995, on planning for the Atlanta Olympics:

> But other competitions—from soccer to track and field—will take place on fields and in stadiums where the heat and humidity could be intense. And the concrete sidewalks and streets of Atlanta will likely magnify the temperatures, turning the city into a Brobdingnagian sauna. . . .

brother's keeper, my Taken from Genesis, it is part of the evasive response by the guilty Cain, who has killed his brother Abel, to the question posed by God: "Where is Abel thy brother? And he said, I know not: am I my brother's keeper?" Cain is cursed, always to be a fugitive and wanderer in the earth. (*See also* CAIN, MARK OF.)

The phrase is now most commonly used as a statement: yes, you are your brother's keeper; you should feel responsibility for the well-being of your fellow man.

The term in use, by Carol Stevens in the *Detroit News,* April 27, 1997:

Thousands of politicians, corporate executives and national activists are gathering today in the City of Brotherly Love to convince Americans that—when it comes to helping the nation's troubled youth—they are their brother's keeper.

And in a *Christian Science Monitor* editorial, February 8, 1995, on the plight of refugees throughout the world:

Politicians who can generously bail out banks at home and underwrite loans to countries abroad cannot skirt the question when it is applied to the world's homeless: Am I my brother's keeper?

And by Edward Hoagland in *Harper's,* June 1989:

Most of us realized early on that we are not our "brother's keeper." Yet perhaps we also came to recognize that "there but for the grace of God go I." If the jitters we experience on a particularly awful afternoon were extended and became prolonged until we couldn't shake them off, after a few drastic months we might end up sleeping on the sidewalk too.

Brummell, Beau A dandy, a fop: a fashion-conscious man who gives exaggerated attention to his appearance.

Beau Brummell was a real person, an Englishman named George Poryan Brummell (1778–1840) who was an intimate friend of the Prince Regent, later George IV.

"Beau" is French and means "beautiful," "handsome." Still sometimes used as a term for a lady's male admirer, in the early years of the 19th century it was prefixed to the names of men who devoted themselves to fashion.

In a period of flamboyance in men's dress, Beau Brummell's creed was one of elegant restraint; he believed that a man's attire should not attract attention, at least not overtly. He ushered in the era of tightly fitted jackets and trousers and elaborately tied neck cloths—the recognizable style of the *New Yorker* magazine's Eustace Tilley.

Brummell squandered his inheritance on gambling and high living, and then quarreled with the Prince of Wales in 1812. The story is told that Brummell sauntered by the prince and a companion in the park, saying, "Good morning, Westmoreland, who's your fat friend?" He left the country soon afterward and died in poverty in France.

The term in use, by playwright Nicky Silver, quoted in *Newsday* by Patrick Pacheco, February 28, 1995:

Skipping his senior year, 16-year-old Silver moved to New York to study theater. . . . He also quickly lost 100 pounds, and became, as he puts it, "a Beau Brummell."

And by columnist Richard Cohen in the *Washington Post* magazine, August 31, 1997:

Nor do I recall our current president, and Hillary's current husband, being criticized in print for ditching that clunky Timex sports watch and adopting a whole new clothing style—a modified Italian look recommended, I am authoritatively told, by the political consultant and regular Beau Brummell Robert Squier.

Brute *See* ET TU, BRUTE?.

brutish *See* NASTY, BRUTISH, AND SHORT.

Buchanan, Daisy and Tom Fictional characters; the wealthy, careless couple who help to bring about the tragic end of Jay Gatsby in F. Scott Fitzgerald's novel *The Great Gatsby*. The careless rich.

Beautiful, shallow Daisy is loved by the nouveau riche Jay GATSBY, who has accumulated wealth in order to win her back from her loutish husband Tom. The dream ends in death when Myrtle, Tom's working-class mistress, is accidentally killed by Daisy while driving Gatsby's car. Gatsby remains silent to protect her, but Myrtle's husband traces the car and shoots Gatsby. The narrator, Nick Carraway, is left to bury Gatsby, as Daisy and Tom escape all responsibility for their actions, and go on with their frivolous life.

In Fitzgerald's words, they "smashed up things and then retreated back into their money ... and let other people clean up the mess they had made."

The term in use, by Karl E. Meyer, in a review of books on U.S. policy in Afghanistan, in the *New York Times Book Review,* August 11, 1996:

These books illustrate what deserves to be called the Buchanan strain in American foreign policy. Not Pat Buchanan, but Tom and Daisy.

And by columnist Richard Reeves, appearing in the *Baltimore Sun,* May 26, 1994, on Jacqueline Kennedy:

She was married to an impatient rich boy of surpassing charm whose vocation was mass seduction and whose avocation was serial seduction. Jack Kennedy, boy and man, was "beautiful" and "careless"—in the way F. Scott Fitzgerald used those two words to describe Daisy Buchanan in *The Great Gatsby*.

Buck Rogers *See* ROGERS, BUCK.

build a better mousetrap A shortened version of the saying, "Build a better mousetrap, and the world will beat a path to your door." In other words, come up with a better idea or product, manage to do something better than anyone else, and the world will seek you out; you'll be a success no matter where you are.

The phrase is attributed to Ralph Waldo Emerson (1803–1882) American philosopher, lecturer, and essayist. The quotation is from one of Emerson's lectures, as quoted by Sarah S.B. Yule and Mary S. Keene in *Borrowings,* 1889:

> If a man can write a better book, preach a better sermon, or make a better mousetrap than his neighbor, though he builds his house in the woods the world will make a beaten path to his door.

However, George Seldes in his *Great Thoughts* says that Emerson did not deliver (or write) a lecture using "a better mousetrap." He did write,

> If a man has good corn, or wood, or boards, or pigs to sell, or can make a better chain or knives, crucibles or church organs, than anybody else, you will find a broad, hard-beaten road to his house, though it be in the woods.

The "mousetrap" quote was claimed by Elbert Hubbard, an American writer and publisher.

The term in use, quoted in the *New York Times,* June 1, 1997, in a story on the development of the B-61, a nuclear bomb designed to destroy underground facilities:

> But Ashton Carter, who was assistant secretary of defense for international security for three years until last September, said the bomb was merely intended to perform the same mission as the older weapon, but more safely. The B-61 is not new, Carter said, just "a better mousetrap."

And again, in a *San Francisco Chronicle* editorial, February 6, 1995, on the recently passed presidential line-item veto as a tool to eliminate pork-barrel spending:

> What has been less obvious is that a line-item veto is a two-edged sword. . . . One need only imagine how Richard Nixon, for instance, might have wielded a line-item veto threat against those urging his impeachment. Fortunately, a better mousetrap—or pork trap—exists, promoted by Budget Committee Chairman Pete Domenici and others in the Senate.

And quoted by Diane Stafford, in the *Kansas City Star,* June 8, 1997, on careers in manufacturing:

> "There are a lot of opportunities in the niche marketplace," said Logan Wilson, vice president-legal at Fike Corporation. . . . "Products that are labor- or raw material-intensive may be tough to grow a business with in the U.S., but when you're talking about a product with a high degree of intellectual content or novelty or the proverbial better mousetrap, there's great opportunity."

bullet *See* BITE THE BULLET.

bully pulpit A prominent public position that provides an opportunity for expounding one's views; also, such an opportunity.

The term comes from the irrepressible Theodore Roosevelt, first to call the presidency a bully pulpit. For T.R., "bully" meant just grand, splendid. He understood the modern presidency's power of persuasion and the way it gives the incumbent the opportunity to exhort, instruct, or inspire. Other presidents of this century—Wilson, FDR, Kennedy, and Reagan—followed suit.

The term in use, by Richard S. Dunham in *Business Week,* May 5, 1997:

> What do you do if you're a Big Government activist but don't have the money—or the political clout with Congress—to attack such problems as pollution, joblessness, and illiteracy. If you're Bill Clinton, you use your presidential clout to lean on business to foot the bill for patching the social safety net. "We have to use the bully pulpit to generate enthusiasm for things government can no longer do," says White House Chief of Staff Erskine B. Bowles.

And by Ishmael Reed in his 1988 book *Writin' is Fightin':*

> Councilman Leo Bazile says that if he were the mayor he would use the office as a bully pulpit, and he would see to it that the city manager, who, because of the Oakland charter, runs the government, deals with the crisis effectively.

bunkum *or* **buncombe** Nonsense; insincere or foolish talk. The word comes from a remark made in 1845 by the congressman from Buncombe county, North Carolina, who defended an irrelevant speech by claiming he was speaking to Buncombe.

The word caught on quickly, and has endured; it's often shortened to *bunk.* Similarly, to deflate a nonsensical idea is to *debunk* it.

H.L. Mencken in 1924 famously described political conventions as "a carnival of buncombe."

Henry Ford did *not* say, "History is bunk." He did say, referring to the armistice following the First World War:

> I don't know much about history, and I wouldn't give a nickel for all the history in the world. History is more or less bunk. It is tradition. We want to live in the present, and the only history that is worth a tinker's damn is the history we make today.

Another example, from Joe Barton and Jon D. Fox in *USA Today,* January 4, 1995:

> Here are five key cautions for GOP honchos giddy with the ideological champagne they're drinking in Washington this week:
> Forget the buncombe about upcoming generational realignment. Maybe Jefferson, Jackson and Lincoln launched generation-long political supremacies, but you won't.

And by Adam Pruzan in the *Washington Times,* October 2, 1995, stating his objections to the charge that Republican tax cuts would help the rich: "It comes as no surprise that Democrats have flocked to peddle this buncombe."

bunker mentality A state of mind, especially among members of a group, that is characterized by chauvinistic defensiveness and self-righteous intolerance of criticism. A bunker is a military dugout, a fortified chamber designed to withstand attack. The most famous bunker of all, of course, was Hitler's heavily fortified shelter in Berlin, where he committed suicide on April 30, 1945, as Soviet forces took the city.

In politics, a bunker mentality is an embattled frame of mind, often accompanied by an aggrieved sense of being unfairly under attack. The term is most often applied to American presidents who suffer political reverses and assume a surly defensive posture—all critics are enemies; if you're not for us you're against us, etc., etc.

The term in use, by conservative commentator Bill Kristol in the *Washington Post,* July 22, 1997, discussing dissension in right-wing ranks:

> "There is a type of thinking on the right that if you don't agree with everything, you're a traitor to the movement," says Kristol, a former GOP operative whose magazine is financed by another conservative, Rupert Murdoch. "There's a certain kind of bunker mentality up there [on the Hill]. . . . "

And quoted by Martha T. Moore in *USA Today,* June 19, 1998:

> Mayor Rudy Giuliani wants a new emergency command center for the city, but all he's getting is howls of laughter. . . .
> "He already has the bunker mentality; now he has the bunker," says leftist lawyer and radio talk show host Ron Kuby, whose listeners quickly dubbed the facility The Nut Shell. "What next, nukes?"

Burkean Of or pertaining to Edmund Burke (1729–1797), and his moderate political views. A British parliamentarian, statesman, and friend of the American colonies, Burke was a moderate who felt revulsion for the excesses he saw in the French Revolution and spoke in defense of traditional institutions and political restraint. Prudence, he said, is "in all things a Virtue, in Politicks the first of Virtues."

Burke was born in Dublin, the son of an attorney and the product of a mixed Catholic-Protestant marriage. He was elected to Parliament in 1766, where he opposed the government's uncompromising policy toward the American colonies, calling instead for cooperation and reconciliation. He wanted to give the colonies a parliament of their own under the British crown—essentially the dominion status later granted to Canada and Australia.

Burke wrote papers on the appalling poverty of his native Ireland and advocated Irish legislative independence, cautioning that, "If laws are their enemies, they will be enemies to law."

Contrary to what Barry Goldwater would say almost two centuries later about moderation (that in defense of liberty, it is no virtue), Burke found it a commendable quality, "not only amiable but powerful . . . a disposing, arranging, conciliating, cementing Virtue."

Here's some typical Burkean advice: "Dare to be fearful when all about you are full of presumption and confidence."

The term in use, by Bruce Nussbaum, reviewing Michael Lind's *Why the Right Is Wrong for America* in *Business Week,* September 2, 1996:

> The reason to read Lind is that he is an apostate, one of the millions of young, well-educated, and well-off people who joined the GOP in the 1980s to build a new mainstream conservatism only to see the party taken over by extremists in the 1990s. Their inclusionist dreams were replaced by exclusionist hatreds. Their Burkean ideals were displaced by YAHOO racism, contempt for the poor, and immigrant-bashing.

And again, by Adam Gopnik in the *New Yorker,* December 12, 1994:

> Any Burkean conservative knows why a right-wing political triumph cannot stop . . . social change; electoral politics has a very limited effect on the real world—the life of parliaments doesn't have much to do with the life of the mind or the heart. . . . Conservatives in America, however, continue to hold the extremely unconservative belief that electing congressmen can change a culture.

butterfly effect The enormous impact that a very small change or disturbance can have in the course of events. The term was coined by meteorologist Edward Lorenz, who developed the concept of chaos theory. Lorenz observed that certain systems—such as the weather—defy analysis by conventional scientific methods. Chaotic systems, he said, showed an "exquisitely sensitive dependence on initial conditions and minute but unpredictable variables." In a lecture in 1970, Lorenz posed his famous question as to whether the delicate motion of a butterfly's wings in the Amazon could cause a tornado over Texas.

James Gleick popularized the butterfly effect concept in his 1987 book *Chaos: Making a New Science,* but noted that the idea *had* been around before, quoting the old rhyme:

> For want of a nail, the shoe was lost;
> For want of a shoe, the horse was lost;
> For want of a horse, the rider was lost;
> For want of a rider, the battle was lost;
> For want of a battle, the kingdom was lost!

Another version, complete with butterfly, comes from Ray Bradbury's short story, "A Sound of Thunder," in the collection *The Golden Apples of the Sun* (1953). A hunter goes on a time-travel safari to shoot the ultimate big game, tyrannosaurus rex. All care is taken to avoid changing the future; hunters do not touch the ground, and only animals already destined to die at that time are selected for hunting. But things go awry. T-rex charges, the hunter panics and steps off the platform onto the jungle floor. When he returns to his own time, he senses a change. Something in the air . . . then the spelling in a sign. Then the outcome of the recent election is changed, now won by a Fascist. The hunter looks at his boot in horror—in the caked mud of the ancient jungle is a single dead butterfly. "It fell to the floor, an exquisite thing, a small thing that could upset balances and knock down a line of small dominoes and then big dominoes and then gigantic dominoes, all down the years across Time."

The term in use, by Stephanie Hawthorne in *The Independent,* June 14, 1997, on the financial implications of the drowning death of British media tycoon Robert Maxwell, which exposed the theft of his employees' pension funds:

> Sally Bridgeland, of the actuarial firm Bacon & Woodrow, compares pensions to the butterfly effect: 'A single flutter escalates to cause a catastrophic weather system somewhere else in the world. Here, a splash in the ocean [Maxwell's death] has led to a flood of legislation in the pensions system.'

Byronic Like or pertaining to the English Romantic poet George Gordon, Lord Byron (1788–1824). Byron made a name for romantic sensuousness and self-indulgence and was described as "mad, bad and dangerous to know" (by one of his paramours, Lady Caroline Lamb, no slouch in that category herself).

Byronic heroes are usually handsome, melancholy, brooding, a bit cynical, theatrical, defiant of social convention, and apparently haunted by some mysterious sorrow, which of course makes them devilishly attractive. As the poet himself puts it in *Lara:*

> There was in him a vital scorn of all:
> As if the worst had fall'n which could befall,
> He stood a stranger in this breathing world,
> An erring spirit from another hurl'd.

Depending on whom you read, Byron was notable for his physical beauty, which was only enhanced by his club foot or decidedly unhandsome, short, and chubby, with a limp. Much of his life was spent abroad, where he wrote, hobnobbed with the poet Shelley, had numerous affairs, and championed the causes of Italian and Greek nationalism. Byron died in Greece, where he had gone to aid the struggle for independence.

His most famous works include *Childe Harold, The Corsair, The Prisoner of Chillon, The Destruction of Sennacherib,* and *Don Juan.*

The term in use, by Tom Wolfe in his 1987 novel, *The Bonfire of the Vanities,* in which hungover reporter Peter Fallow contemplates his reflection:

> Head on, he looked a young and handsome thirty-six rather than fortyish and gone to seed. Head on, his widow's peak and the longish wavy blond hair that flowed back from it still looked . . . well, Byronic . . . rather than a bit lonely at the dome of his skull.

And by Michael Sauter in *Entertainment Weekly,* October 3, 1996:

> Marlon Brando was unlike any other leading man Hollywood had ever seen. He was more intense, more animalistic—and more iconoclastic. "What are you rebelling against?" someone asks him in *The Wild One* (1954). Brando's answer: "What have you got?" Pauline Kael once described him as "a Bryonic Dead End Kid. . . ."

And from columnist George Will in the *Washington Post,* September 28, 1989, on rocker Mick Jagger:

> Jagger, a Byronic figure for generations unschooled in poetry, excited young people 25 years ago as someone mad, bad and dangerous to know.

And by Darryl Pinckney in his 1992 novel, *High Cotton:*

> Sometimes my parents came home and, instead of finding me mowing the lawn, saw me loafing in front of the house with a secondhand Edwardian treasure, lolling in a shopping mall in a hippie-boutique version of Byronic drag: frilly prom shirt, shoes and belts with big buckles, and a knock-off of an Inverness cape.

Byzantine \'bi-z°n-,tēn, 'bī-, -,tīn; bə-'zan-,, bī-'\ *often not capitalized* Of, relating to, or characterized by a devious and usually surreptitious manner of operation; intricately involved or labyrinthine.

The term, as it describes human activity, is derived from the style of bureaucracy and internal politics of the Byzantine Empire, rife with coups, plots, murders, and intrigue.

The Byzantine Empire was the eastern segment of the Roman Empire, its capital Constantinople (now Istanbul), founded in A.D. 330 by the Roman Emperor Constantine on the site of the ancient city of Byzantium. Constantine hoped to strengthen the entire Roman Empire by creating an eastern capital. In A.D. 395, the Empire was divided into East and West and never reunited.

Despite roiling intrigue, daggers in the harem, and a nexus of sex and politics in the imperial court that even novelists couldn't dream up, the Byzantine Empire lasted long after the collapse of Rome in A.D. 476. Christian in belief and Greek in culture, during the European Dark Ages, it was a beacon of civilization, culture, and wealth, and a bulwark against barbarian invasion. Constantinople finally fell to the Turks in 1453.

The term in use, by Andrew C. Miller in the *Kansas City Star,* May 30, 1993:

> In one respect, the House Rules Committee is like the National Football League's byzantine playoff system. Everybody pretends to understand how it works, but few do.

And by Jill Leovy in the *Los Angeles Times,* October 3, 1995:

What the business lacked in subtlety, Silgan made up for with Byzantine debt schemes and a head-spinning corporate structure.

Again, by J. Hampton Sides in Washington, D.C.'s, *City Paper,* April 29, 1988:

Founded in 1974 with a $500,000 grant from the Rockefeller Brothers' Fund, the Worldwatch Institute has always been an anomaly in the Byzantine world of the Washington think tanks.

Perhaps American commercial television never was a shining city on a hill. But increasingly it seems a valley of slums.

—Tom Shales

cachet \ka-'shā\ An indication of approval or a feature carrying great prestige.

It's a French word, originally the seal on letters or documents which made them both official and secret. Lettres de cachet were orders of the king of France, and they did not usually confer prestige. Rather they were used to order punishment or imprisonment without trial. (The ANCIEN RÉGIME was not troubled by concepts like habeas corpus and due process.) The letters were often issued blank; local officials had the authority to fill in the names.

Today the meaning is much cheerier: a mark or quality of celebrity and prestige.

The term in use, by Stephen Labaton, the *New York Times,* April 20, 1997:

> The list of former friends may seem long for a politician who built his career on hundreds of personal relationships. . . . And for many, of course, the mutual loyalties are still in place.
>
> Still, being a Friend of Bill had considerably more cachet during Mr. Clinton's first administration.

And from Lorraine Woellert, the *Washington Times,* January 12, 1997:

> A fine silk scarf adorned with Italian designs draws big dollars at Fifth Avenue department stores, but stitch a "Made in China" label into the hem and it suddenly has all the cachet of a Kmart blue-light special.

By F.E. Satir, Gannett News Service, December 18, 1996:

> While the White House Christmas card is the most sought-after in Washington, it's not the only valued one. In fact, collecting holiday cards from senators, congressmen, ranking administration officials and the nation's other political high and mighty carries a certain amount of cachet.

Caesar's wife A person above reproach and free from any semblance of wrongdoing. Julius Caesar divorced his wife Pompeia because of an episode in which a man had been admitted illicitly and without Pompeia's knowledge to Caesar's house during a women-only religious rite. The man was tried for sacrilege, and even though neither Caesar nor his wife knew anything of the crime, he divorced his wife. When asked why, he responded that Caesar's wife should not be subject even to suspicion of wrongdoing.

The term in use, by J.B. Dixon in the *Detroit News,* June 7, 1993:

> Politically for women, the Caesar's Wife syndrome can be deadly. To accept a standard of political perfection for female candidates in the clear absence of such a standard for male candidates ... is to bid for political powerlessness.

And from *People,* September 22, 1986, quoting defense attorney Oscar Goodman:

> "I have certain defined enemies out there," he says, "and if I were ever anything less than Caesar's wife, beyond reproach, I think I would be nailed quicker than wallboard. I like to think my life-style is working hard at the office and going home to my family."

Cain, mark of A stigma; the distinguishing mark or brand of a criminal or outcast.

In Genesis 1:1–16 in the Bible, Cain, first child of Adam and Eve, murdered his younger brother, Abel, and became an exile and a fugitive.

As the Bible tells the story, when the Lord asks the guilty Cain about his brother, Cain responds, " 'I know not; Am I my BROTHER'S KEEPER?' And He said, 'what hast thou done? The voice of thy brother's blood crieth unto me from the ground.' " The Lord put a mark upon Cain so that he would be identified as the killer of his brother but would also be protected in his wanderings. As the term is used today, the idea of a protective mark has been lost; only the negative sense of a mark of shame or criminality remains.

The term in use, by Washington lawyer Leonard Garment, quoted in the *New York Times,* August 23, 1988, on the political hazards in seeking psychiatric care:

> Even the fact of having consulted a psychiatrist on an intermittent basis or after some kind of tragedy becomes a label. It is among a number of things that Washington punishes people for that make no sense. Almost anything these days can become a mark of Cain.

And by Pamela D. Schultz in commentary in *Newsday,* March 31, 1995, on what she saw as the dubious value of laws requiring notification of communities of the presence of convicted child molesters:

> A released molester is merely moved from one prison to another. Branded with a modern mark of Cain, he has no place to go, no one to turn to. It becomes impossible for him to relinquish his past and start over.

cake *See* LET THEM EAT CAKE.

cakes and ale The good things in life; material pleasures. The most famous reference is in Shakespeare's *Twelfth Night,* Act 2, Scene 3. The roistering rogue Sir Toby Belch inquires of the priggish Malvolio, "Dost thou think, because thou art virtuous, there shall be no more cakes and ale?"

"Cake" in those times was more like fancy bread, not necessarily the sugary concoction we think of today; Sir Toby would have loved corn chips.

Cakes and Ale is also the title of W. Somerset Maugham's 1930 novel satirizing English literary life.

The term in use, by George Brockway in the *New Leader,* June 3, 1996:

> For my part, I do not think that there shall be no more cakes and ale, and I doubt that either the Chairman [of the Federal Reserve] or the Speaker thinks so.

And by William Safire in his syndicated column, January 24, 1992:

> It's a dilemma. If the CIA advice is to provide only technical and emergency aid, that would suit the Bush-Baker inclination to bad-mouth foreign aid while piously deploring isolationism; but if the CIA virtuously damns the politics and endorses the pro-Yeltsin opinion of its Slav-Eu experts, there may be no more clandestine cakes and ale.

Caligari, Dr. Director of an insane asylum in the 1919 film *The Cabinet of Dr. Caligari*—a famous German horror film and a pioneer of the genre. The film's strangely angled abstract sets create a dreamlike and disorienting atmosphere, which must have been a great shock to moviegoers of the time, who were much less accustomed to abstract art and the idea of movie dream sequences than we are today.

The film tells the story of a carnival performer who controls a sleepwalker who commits murders. But then the sinister Caligari appears as the director of an insane asylum; and in a final twist, the whole story is revealed to be the dream of a patient in the asylum.

The term in use, by Herbert Muschamp in the *New York Times,* October 11, 1996:

> You can get lost in lower Manhattan. The streets are not named after numbers. They disregard the Manhattan grid. They bend, twist and turn back on themselves, creating looming, demented perspectives on a scale Dr. Caligari never dreamed of.

Another example, from the *London Observer,* May 5, 1996, in a review of the autobiography of the actress Billie Whitelaw:

> Her first husband was the menacing actor Peter Vaughan, whose best friend, the late Donald Pleasence, lived with them for a time; it must have been like sharing a house with Doctor Caligari and the Boston Strangler.

Camelot The site of King Arthur's palace and court, and thus a time, place, or atmosphere of idyllic happiness. The Camelot of legend is a beautiful medieval castle with pennants flying, the king surrounded by the gallant knights of the Round Table. Bravery, gallantry, beauty and tragic love are part of the legend, probably based on the unknown general whose victories at the end of the 5th century A.D. checked the Saxon invasion of Britain for about fifty years.

For Americans today Camelot is inextricably linked to the presidency of John F. Kennedy. The Lerner and Loewe musical *Camelot* was a Broadway hit at the time the president was assassinated and less than a month later his widow Jacqueline spoke of the couple's fondness for the music and how they played it when alone together in the evenings. The closing song's reference to the "one brief shining moment that was known as Camelot" became identified with the glamor and tragedy of the Kennedy years.

This wasn't the first time Camelot found itself hitched to high politics. The legend struck a powerful emotional chord in England, where a street fight over it is reported between locals and visiting French clergy in Cornwall in 1146. England's kings often buttressed claims to the throne with "proof" of their descent from King Arthur. Early in the reign of Richard II, Arthur's tomb was supposedly found, and the site became an instant, lucrative tourist attraction.

The term in use, in *Maclean's* magazine, July 12, 1993:

> During the campaign, Clinton promised all sorts of things. . . .
> He was going to be strong and decisive and true to the ideals of
> public service symbolized by his hero, John F. Kennedy. Camelot
> was only around the corner.

Another example, from Reuters, April 26, 1996, on reasons for the wild bidding for the possessions of the late Jacqueline Kennedy Onassis:

> Were they just victims of mass hysteria as one British critic said?
> Everyone seems to have a different answer—but trying to recapture the spirit of the bold Kennedy Camelot seems to play a major part.

And, looking back to another kind of Camelot, this from *Basketball Digest,* May 7, 1993:

> The Official Boston Celtics 1992–93 Greenbook . . . flashes back
> to "Camelot," Larry Bird's first eight seasons in the league, when
> he led the Celtics to three NBA titles and treated fans across
> America to a battle royale with Magic Johnson and the Lakers.

canary in a mine shaft/coal mine First warning of danger. In earlier times miners took canaries down into coal mines to detect poisonous gases. Because the birds were more sensitive to these gases than people, they served as a warning device; if the birds died, the miners were in jeopardy and had better get out.

The term in use, by Eve Brooks, president of the National Association of Child Advocates, quoted in a November 20, 1996, statement on recently passed welfare legislation:

> The gap between rhetoric and reality make[s] it clear that shifting power to the states is a risky experiment—especially for children who will bear the consequences. Welfare reform treats kids like canaries in a mine shaft.

And again, by Thomas Matthews, writing about Beaujolais nouveau in *Wine Spectator,* December 31, 1992:

> The frenzy signals the importance wine merchants give to this frivolous wine. It's the wine-world equivalent to the canary in a coal mine, an indicator of the health of the market. So far, it seems, so good.

Canute A person who makes preposterous statements, especially pronouncements of his own importance and power. Derived from a king of Denmark and England who, legend has it, commanded the tide not to turn—a deed misinterpreted as an example of arrogant pride.

Not so, according to the original 12th–century story. Canute, rather, demonstrated to his subjects the limits of a king's power by ordering the tide to hold back. He knew it waited for no man. Modern versions frequently stand the original lesson on its head.

Canute the Great, as they called him, died in 1035. He became the king of England in 1016, of Denmark in 1018, and of Norway in 1028. He ruled wisely and maintained peace, a significant achievement in those turbulent times.

The term in use, by Michael Kinsley in *Time,* September 4, 1995, on proposals to reform Medicare:

> Of the proposals that actually are under discussion, some are variations on what might be called "the King Canute solution": just order the tide of Medicare spending to stop.

And by Christopher Andreae in the *Christian Science Monitor,* January 29, 1996:

> Resisting technology is like King Canute commanding the waves. Technology, in its ever-advancing waves, is here.

Capraesque Characteristic of, or similar in spirit to, the work of the American movie director Frank Capra (1897–1991) whose works were warmhearted comedies, parables celebrating the values and essential goodness of the common man. His films were utterly American in their settings and characters.

Though often referred to as "Capra-corn," these Capra films of the 1930s and 1940s were not just sentimental: they were masterful blends of comedy and darkness in which ordinary folks survived despair and crisis by standing up for their ideals and helping out their fellow man. Capra classics include *It Happened One Night* (1934), *Mr. Deeds Goes to Town* (1936),

You Can't Take It With You (1938) and, probably the best-known, *Mr. Smith Goes to Washington* (1939) and *It's a Wonderful Life* (1946).

The term in use, by Yvonne Zipp, in the *Christian Science Monitor,* reviewing new television series, September 19, 1996:

> Three dramas set out to prove that one person can make a difference. These could build a following if viewers can swallow a somewhat hokey premise. The best of these, Early Edition (CBS), is a good-natured, Capraesque piece that poses the question: What would happen if tomorrow's newspaper were delivered today?

And from Jack Garner, Gannett News Services, November 13, 1995:

> Whether you know Capra's works or not, you'll be able to savor many "Capraesque moments" in *The American President*. It's the best Frank Capra movie, well, since Frank Capra.

captains and the kings depart, the A warning against national arrogance. "Recessional" was written by Rudyard Kipling in 1897 as part of the celebration of Queen Victoria's 60 years on the throne. A recessional is the hymn sung at the end of a church service. Kipling's message, at that great moment in the history of the British Empire, was a warning against hubris and overconfidence: "The tumult and the shouting dies/ The Captains and the Kings depart," says the poet, as he reminds readers that "all our pomp of yesterday/ Is one with Nineveh and Tyre," once-mighty empires of the ancient world.

The term in use, by James Walsh, reporting in *Time International,* June 9, 1997, on the end of British rule in Hong Kong:

> The captains and the kings depart, but recessionals can at least have some style. Certainly the frills will be full-blown when Christopher Francis Patten and his family board the H.M.S. Britannia on June 30 as clocks in Hong Kong tick toward midnight.

And by columnist George Will, in the *Washington Post,* September 2, 1996:

> Well, the tumult and the shouting dies, the captains and the kings depart, and perhaps the banality of contemporary politics should be a national boast. The deflation of politics is not a bad coda to this century.

Capulets *See* MONTAGUES AND CAPULETS.

carpe diem \\'kär-pe-'dē-ˌem, -'dī-, -əm\\ A Latin phrase meaning "seize the day." It is taken from the work of the Roman poet Horace (65–8 B.C.), who in his *Odes* offered the thought, "carpe diem, quam minimum credula postero"—or, "enjoy today, trusting little in tomorrow." In other words, enjoy today because tomorrow is uncertain. It's a variation of "eat, drink and be merry, for tomorrow you may die."

The term in use, by Chris McCosky, The *Detroit News,* March 31, 1998, on professional basketball player Grant Hill:

> Hill is blossoming into quite a wordsmith. He shared his recently adopted credo for getting through the ups and downs of the NBA season: "The past is history. The future is a mystery. This moment is a gift; that's why it is called the present. Focus on the present."
> Carpe diem never sounded so good.

And another reference from professional basketball, from Mr. Know-It-All (sports columnist Doug Robinson) in the *Deseret News,* September 15, 1997:

> Caller: What do you think about the Jazz re-signing all of their players from last season?
> Mr. Know-It-All: Sure, the Jazz are together again, but they're older than Congress. The Jazz had two choices: a) win now, pay later; b) try to trade somebody (Jeff Hornacek?) to begin mixing in more youth for the future. The Jazz chose the carpe diem plan. They're going to pay through the nose in a couple of years. My advice: Enjoy it while it lasts, Jazz fans.

carpetbagger A Northerner in the South after the American Civil War, usually seeking private gain under reconstruction government. Also, an outsider or new resident, especially one who meddles in politics. The name derives from the "carpetbag" traveling bags, actually made of carpet, that were common in the 19th century. The governments instituted in the defeated Southern states, with newly enfranchised blacks and Northern Republican officeholders, were called "carpetbagger governments."

Today the term, applied frequently in the context of a political campaign, labels a candidate an outsider, an opportunist who has come into a state or district merely to win an election.

The term in use, in the *Los Angeles Times,* October 20, 1996, describing a hotly contested race for the U.S. House of Representatives:

> He [incumbent Robert Dornan] scoffs at Sanchez as inexperienced, naive and uninformed about the issues. He calls her "a carpetbagger from Palos Verdes" and has attacked her for associating with a convicted felon.

And by L.J. Davis in the *New Republic,* April 4, 1994:

> In Little Rock the whole Whitewater affair is treated as something of a hoot—the Yankee carpetbagger press, with the reality of Arkansas staring it in the face—has gone and missed the real story again.

Cartesian \kär-'tē-zhən\ Of or relating to Rene Descartes or his philosophy. Descartes, a 17th–century French logician, formulated the famous

"Je pense donc je suis," "I think, therefore I am." It is most frequently quoted in its Latin form, "Cogito ergo sum."

Descartes' philosophy can be summed up in two words: systematic doubt. He, along with Francis Bacon, used modern techniques of analysis to study the world about them.

Their new methods challenged the Aristotelian method of the Middle Ages, which stated a general proposition then sought to discover what further knowledge could be deduced from that accepted idea. Descartes and Bacon reversed the process, believing that the truth ought not to be stated at the outset but should emerge from a process of investigation and experimentation. This was the beginning of the scientific method.

To aid the search for truth, Descartes called for systematic doubt, which was to sweep away past ideas and allow philosophers to consider things afresh.

The term in use, by Norman Sherman in "Pity the Poor Vice President," an op-ed piece in the *Washington Post,* January 20, 1988:

> Vice presidents frequently are sent to funerals of heads of state to represent our country. Their visits with living heads of states are only marginally more productive. Yet, vice presidents all brag about what those visits mean. I can deal with a head of state, therefore, I myself can be a head of state. It is a kind of Cartesian proof of both existence and importance, but it is nonsense.

And in a *Los Angeles Times* piece, June 30, 1996, in which prominent people are asked to select the movies they believe sum up the American character, Mexican novelist and essayist Carlos Fuentes offered the following:

> *Singin' in the Rain*—The supremely optimistic U.S. film. Almost Cartesian: I sing and dance, therefore I am. (Fuentes also suggested *Citizen Kane* and *Taxi Driver*.)

Casey at the Bat A hero, usually the heavy hitter, who through arrogance and overconfidence falls flat on his face at the most critical possible moment, to the huge disappointment of his fans.

This was the title of Ernest Lawrence Thayer's beloved 1888 poem, published first in the *San Francisco Examiner,* and recited with relish ever since.

Mighty Casey, the star of the Mudville team, steps to the plate before his adoring fans. With two men on base, in the next-to-last inning, Mudville is two runs down. He lets two pitches go by—two strikes. The tension is unbearable. He swings mightily at the last pitch and misses, and the results are told in the famous last lines of the poem:

> Oh somewhere in this favored land the sun is shining bright,
> The band is playing somewhere, and somewhere hearts are
>   light;

Cassandra 102

And somewhere men are laughing, and somewhere children
   shout,
But there is no joy in Mudville; Mighty Casey has struck out.

Shakespeare it ain't, but it sure is fun. Thayer could never understand why it was so popular, and refused to take royalties from it. "All I ask," he said, "is never to be reminded of it again."

The term in use, by Peter Hakim in a column in the *Christian Science Monitor,* September 22, 1993:

> There is joy in Mudville. Casey's at the bat. President Clinton has finally taken the field for the North American Free Trade Agreement, promising to put his full weight behind efforts to gain congressional approval of the pact.

And by Kenneth Turan, film critic of the *Los Angeles Times,* November 3, 1995:

> *Total Eclipse* is the art-house equivalent of "Casey at the Bat." Considerable ability has gone into a potential home run scenario, but the result is a big whiff all the way around.

Cassandra \kə-'san-drə, -'sän-\ Someone endowed with the gift of prophecy but fated never to be believed. Also one that predicts misfortune or disaster.

Therein lies a myth, Greek of course. Cassandra, daughter of Priam, king of Troy, spurned the romantic advances of the god Apollo. He cursed her for this in a particularly cruel way: he gave her the power of prophecy, but assured that her forecasts, while invariably accurate, were inevitably ignored. Today the word is applied to those who foretell disaster.

The term in use, by John Simons in *U.S. News & World Report,* February 17, 1997, anticipating computer chaos for the year 2000 (the shorthand version: Y2K):

> [Consultant Peter] Jager, who has become the Cassandra of corporate computing, worries that only a quarter of all U.S. firms have earmarked budgets for tackling their Y2K problem.

And by Charles Mann in the *Atlantic,* February 1993:

> How many people is too many? Over time, the debate has spread between two poles. On one side, according to Garrett Hardin, an ecologist at the University of California at Santa Barbara, are the Cassandras, who believe that continued population growth at the current rate will inevitably lead to catastrophe.

casting couch The locus of sexual favors given by aspiring actresses or actors and demanded or accepted by directors, especially in the Hollywood film industry, with the hope on the givers' part that advancement will result.

The term in use, by William B. Falk in *Newsday,* December 15, 1996, describing the career of Evita Peron:

> The more jaundiced biographers theorize, but offer no real proof, that her ascent was speeded by the effective use of the casting couch.

Another example, from the *Detroit News,* June 3, 1996:

> Former Playboy playmate of the year Jenny McCarthy had a tough time landing a speaking job in front of a camera. "I can't even begin to tell you how many casting couches I was attacked on," McCarthy says in *TV Guide.*

casus belli \\'kä-səs-'be-,lē, 'kä-səs-'be-,lī\\ An event or action that justifies or is held to justify a war or conflict. It's a Latin phrase meaning "occasion of war."

The term in use, by Michael J. Ybarra in the *Los Angeles Times,* September 3, 1996, describing the controversy over a plan by the new San Francisco Public Library to discard numbers of old books and to discontinue its card catalog:

> In the meantime, the original casus belli slumbers peacefully on the second floor of the old beaux-arts library, which is slated to become the Asian Art Museum. Librarians call the [card] catalog a disaster.

And in the *Economist,* June 21, 1997:

> The air was pierced with ear-splitting roars, banshee wails and thunderous explosions. And that was just Boeing and Airbus insulting each other. With all its noisy fighters, sleek missiles and other boyish toys, the biennial Paris Air Show usually lets more testosterone into the atmosphere than is conducive to civilized commercial competition. But this year the international aerospace industry has another casus belli. Politics, which has long governed the defence part of its business, has now determinedly entered the civil side as well.

cat *See* BELL THE CAT.

catbird seat, in the A position of great prominence or advantage.

The slang expression is strongly associated with the late Red Barber, the longtime radio sportscaster, who also gave us "tearing up the pea patch."

Barber once said that he acquired the term in a poker game in which his opponent kept meeting every raise he offered and raising back. At show time, Barber revealed he had only a pair of eights with nothing in the hole. His opponent had an ace showing and an ace in the hole. "Thanks for all those raises," he told Barber. "From the start I was sitting in the catbird seat."

Years later, Barber wrote in *Saturday Review:* "Inasmuch as I had paid for the expression, I began to use it." Humorist James Thurber gave it further currency in a short story, "The Catbird Seat," published in 1942.

The term in use, by Carl Hartman of the Associated Press, April 24, 1997:

> Four of the five surviving U.S. poets laureate met Thursday to read their work on what may be the birthday of William Shakespeare. The four were celebrating the 60th year of what is called American poetry's "catbird seat"—the job of consultant in poetry that half a century later gained the title of poet laureate.

The expression quoted, by Jeff D. Opdyke in the *Wall Street Journal,* May 22, 1996:

> Also, the company's association with software giant Microsoft "put Micrografx in the catbird seat," says David Hayship, director of equity research at Sunpoint Securities in Longview.

Also from the *Journal,* by James M. Perry, December 11, 1995, writing on Iowans' views of Washington politics:

> The Democrats—Messrs. Knott, Riedman and Hunsaker and Ms. Niles—support Mr. Clinton, tepidly. "At least," says Mr. Hunsaker, "he's not Ted Kennedy." Notes Mr. Knott: "He's in the catbird seat and doesn't even know it. We're with him. All he has to do is move ahead with moderate change."

And from an editorial in the *Baltimore Sun,* November 17, 1995:

> Not only would Ms. [U.S. Senator Barbara] Milkulski carry the authority of her office, she's in the legislative catbird seat.

catch–22 *often capitalized* A problematic situation for which the only solution is denied by a circumstance inherent in the problem or by a rule; an illogical, unreasonable, or senseless situation.

The expression originated as the title of Joseph Heller's 1961 novel about World War II. Yossarian, the book's hero, is a captain in the Army Air Corps desperately trying to avoid the increasing odds that he will be killed. He seeks to get out of flight duty by claiming to be insane. An army doctor tells him he is following the correct approach, that the army will ground someone who is crazy. But he adds that there's a catch in the regulations. "Catch–22," he tells Yossarian (thus suggesting there are at least 21 other such illogical catches). "Anyone who wants to get out of combat duty isn't really crazy." Consequently Yossarian is doomed to continue trying. If he becomes truly crazy he will be eligible for grounding, but he won't be sane enough to apply for it.

The term in use, by Myra McPherson in the *Washington Post,* September 2, 1988, writing about the revival of alligator hunting in Florida and the determination of state game officials that hunters be qualified:

There's an admitted Catch–22 in trying to find out just who is a gator expert. Since it has been illegal to hunt alligators for a quarter of a century, it is hard to find anyone who admits to having done it.

And from Chris Weller, a college women's basketball coach, quoted in the *New York Times,* March 31, 1989, on playing opportunities for women in the 1960s:

The girls had "honor teams," she recalled, with just a trace of scorn. "You could play six games a year. I asked why and they had no arguments. It was a Catch–22. You had no interest so you couldn't have a gym so you had no interest."

And by Dick Lilly in the *Seattle Times,* April 25, 1997:

Seattle School board members wonder if they are trapped in a Catch–22 as they try to decide the level of school funding the voters might approve next year. . . . The bottom line: The board gets heat for not doing what reluctant voters won't give it the money to do.

Caulfield, Holden Fictional character and teenaged protagonist and narrator of J.D. Salinger's 1951 novel *The Catcher in the Rye.* Holden has become an icon of youthful angst and alienation for having called attention to the hypocrisy and ambiguity of the adult world. He is asked to leave his prep school (the fourth such failure for him) and goes to New York City; the novel is his account of his weekend of wandering, trying and failing to establish contact with others.

Holden is isolated from his contemporaries and repelled by the adult world: he sees phoniness and hypocrisy everywhere. But he is unable to look inward to examine himself. The only person he trusts is his little sister Phoebe. He cherishes a romantic idea in which he is "the catcher in the rye" who saves little children from falling off a cliff as they play in a field of rye. Ultimately he returns home, has an emotional breakdown, and is institutionalized.

Holden evoked, by Maureen Dowd of the *New York Times,* in a column in the *Arizona Republic,* August 7, 1995:

When others moved on to Mick Jagger, I was still lipsynching with Hayley Mills. When others wallowed in the angst of Holden Caulfield, I was luxuriating in *The Parent Trap.*

Another example, from Mark Anderson, the *Kansas City Star,* December 7, 1996:

Was it Holden Caulfield who said the problem in life was all the crap. He was speaking, of course, of something of more substance than junk mail and telephone solicitation.

And by Eugene Marino, Gannett News Service, November 10, 1994, writing on the television series *My So-Called Life:*

> Told mostly from the point-of-view of a sort of female version of Holden Caulfield, it vividly evokes the surreal world of high-school students—the morning-till-night angst, the unfocused rebelliousness, the sexual stirrings, the crumbling of childhood friendships and the building of daringly new ones.

center cannot hold, the A cry of prophecy and despair at a world of chaos and terror, spinning out of control—the structure of civilization as we know it breaking apart under the forces of extreme dissension and distrust.

The phrase is from "The Second Coming," by Irish poet William Butler Yeats (1856–1923), a poem that perfectly expresses contemporary angst:

> Things fall apart, the center cannot hold;
> Mere anarchy is loosed upon the world,
> The blood-dimmed tide is loosed, and everywhere
> The ceremony of innocence is drowned;
> The best lack all conviction, while the worst
> Are full of passionate intensity.

Critics associated the poem with various contemporary calamities—the Easter Rising of 1916, the Russian Revolution, the rise of fascism, and political decay. The poem has become such a favorite in political speechifying that there have been calls to give Yeats a rest, but it seems unlikely. (*See also* SLOUCHING TOWARD BETHLEHEM.)

The term in use, by Bill Harley, in commentary on National Public Radio's *All Things Considered,* September 6, 1994, describing a ruthless game of veggie baseball, played with buckets of overripe tomatoes and overgrown zucchini at the height of the garden harvest:

> It's not pretty. Everyone runs for cover. There is a hoarding of tomatoes. Players circle each other, searching for advantage. . . . Innocent bystanders are dragged into the fray. . . . Blatant contempt for fans. The spectators rush the field. Someone puts a tomato down the back of another player's pants and paddles a rear end with a zucchini bat. Screams of protest, but there's no rules. The center cannot hold. The game goes on and on, but it's only a matter of time until the bucket is emptied. Everyone lies on the ground, licking their wounds, horrified at what has happened. Someone asks, "What's for dinner?"

By Leonard Silk in the *New York Times,* October 18, 1987:

> Wall Street, plunging into a downturn that many analysts and investors feared was the end of the big bull market of the last five years, behaved last week as though the center would not hold.

And from Kevin Phillips in the *New York Times Magazine,* April 12, 1992:

> Frustration politics, even in its more extreme forms, represents a sort of PRIMAL SCREAM by the electorate that major party politics must heed if the center is to hold.

central casting A stereotype, a standard, expected image; someone whose looks so perfectly match the popularly imagined idea that a film director would cast them for the part. In other words, your appearance is so much like the popularly imagined one, you would be cast as a fictional version of yourself. Got that?

The expression comes from Hollywood history. There was once a Central Casting Corporation. It was set up in 1926 as a pool for supplying extras, and those on its lists were classified according to type, as in "hick" or "dumb blonde."

The term in use, by Dusty Saunders, broadcasting critic of the *Rocky Mountain News,* March 31, 1997, reviewing a Discovery Channel series on the Central Intelligence Agency:

> Among the most outspoken [of the former CIA agents] is Duane (Dewey) Clarridge, who retired in 1987 after 30 years with the agency. Clarridge, with his white hair, blue blazer, yellow breast-pocket handkerchief and always-present cigar, looks to be out of central casting for a Hollywood spy movie.

And by Mimi Sheraton in *Time,* paying tribute to James Beard, February 4, 1985:

> With his tall and portly frame, his gleaming bald head and jovial, Buddha-like countenance, James Beard was central casting's dream of a food writer come true.

Cerberus, sop to \\'sər-b(ə)rəs\\ A conciliatory or persuasive bribe, gift, or gesture.

In Greek mythology, Cerberus was the three-headed watchdog at the gates of hell. Vergil's *Aeneid* tells how this ferocious dog was put to sleep (just a nap) by a drugged honey and poppyseed cake tossed to him by a sibyl (a prophetess) who was leading the hero Aeneas through the underworld. Aeneas and she could then pass safely. The Greeks buried honey cakes with their dead to quiet Cerberus.

Incidentally, one of the twelve labors of Hercules was the capture of Cerberus. (For another Herculean task, see AUGEAN STABLES; see also HERCULEAN.)

The term in use, by William Safire, in his essay "Telemarketing Dukakis" in the *New York Times,* August 29, 1988, and speaking, of course, of the 1988 Democratic candidate for president:

> His far-left supporters know this moderate pose is only a sop to Cerberus, and smile at the campaign-time conversion.

And by Michael Saunders in the *Boston Globe,* June 30, 1997, on the Supreme Court's decision to overturn the Communications Decency Act, which attempted to regulate objectionable material on the Internet:

> The digerati had pounced on the CDA, as the act is known, before it landed on President Clinton's desk last year. Cynics in some forums on the Well and other on-line services initially branded the bill as Clinton's sop to Cerberus, a choice bone thrown to conservatives that would also appease pro-family forces among moderates and liberals.

Chance *See* TINKER TO EVERS TO CHANCE.

Charge of the Light Brigade A heroic but doomed effort. An incident in the Battle of Balaclava (1854) in the Crimea in which a brigade of British cavalry, following ambiguous orders, charged a heavily defended position knowing they had little chance of survival. The catastrophe was immortalized in the 1855 poem by Alfred, Lord Tennyson.

The actual event took place during the Crimean War (*see* THIN RED LINE) and was presided over by two military figures who became famous for lending their names to articles of clothing rather than for their abilities as soldiers.

The Light Brigade was commanded by George Brudenell, the Seventh Earl of Cardigan, who obtained command through family influence, and then set out to make his regiment one of the most fashionable in the British army. He came up with the design for the knitted woolen Cardigan jacket. Lord Raglan had overall command, and was blamed by many for the ill-fated charge. But his most lasting fame is the design of an overcoat without shoulder seams that bears his name.

Through a mix-up the regiment was sent directly into Russian guns. Cardigan questioned the order, but when it was repeated he led the charge (and survived, unlike forty percent of his men). As Tennyson wrote:

> Not tho' the soldier knew
> Someone had blundered:
> Their's not to make reply
> Their's not to reason why,
> Their's but to do and die. . . .

The term in use, by C.W. Nevius, the *San Francisco Chronicle,* October 26, 1997:

> Tomorrow [San Francisco 49ers quarterback] Steve Young will attempt to beat the stacked deck. If he pulls it off again he will add another volume to his sporting lore. But what will we say if he doesn't?
>
> Remember "The Charge of the Light Brigade"? Wonderful, inspirational story of roaring into the face of nearly impossible odds. Of course, they were completely wiped out, but you have to admire their grit.

Another example, from Robert Marquand, the *Christian Science Monitor,* October 3, 1986, reporting the volunteer cleanup campaign at the University of Massachusetts Library:

> Spirits were high by all accounts, starting on Thursday night with the "Charge of the Light Brigade," a surge by the football team 28 floors up to distribute light bulbs throughout the building.

Charybdis *See* SCYLLA AND CHARYBDIS.

chautauqua *often capitalized* An institution that flourished in the late 19th and early 20th centuries, providing popular education combined with entertainment through lectures, concerts, and plays either outdoors or in a tent. A place gave its name to the movement. Chautauqua is a resort town in western New York State where in 1874, the Chautauqua Institution was established as camp-meeting training for Methodist Sunday-school teachers. The program grew to include adult education and correspondence courses, and attracted many outstanding speakers.

Similar groups, called chautauquas, blossomed around the country. At the turn of the century there were more than 400 of them, and many speakers and performers traveled the Chautauqua circuit. The movement declined after the mid-1920s, perhaps a casualty of radio. Nevertheless, the Chautauqua movement remains a monument to the American desire for self-improvement and education—as well as entertainment. The institutions at Chautauqua, New York, continue to provide a variety of educational programs, and many related programs around the country are enjoying renewed popularity.

The term in use, by Hal Espen, the *New Yorker,* August 21–28, 1995:

> Grateful Dead tours became an American institution, a traveling Chautauqua of electric musicianship and communal, cross-generational joy.

And by David Sterritt, the *Christian Science Monitor,* November 1, 1982:

> So where have the Karamazovs been all these years? Traveling from town to town, participating in Chautauqua-type carnivals in the Northwest, and refining their routine before a wide range of audiences.

Checkers speech A speech in which a politician portrays him- or herself as unjustly victimized and plays on emotion to gain sympathy. Such manipulative speeches often are fraught with self-pitying personal detail embarrassing to the listener and render the speaker as much a figure of ridicule as of sympathy.

The original Checkers speech was a nationwide television address given by Richard Nixon in 1952 when he was Dwight D. Eisenhower's vice presidential running mate. In the speech, Nixon dealt with charges that he was the beneficiary of a secret political fund. As news coverage of the issue mushroomed, Eisenhower first stood aloof, then reportedly said that

Nixon would have to prove himself "clean as a hound's tooth" in order to avoid being dumped from the ticket.

Nixon's decision to respond to the situation on television was innovative. In a 30-minute speech he described the fund and went into lugubrious detail about his modest personal finances. Mrs. Nixon did not have a mink coat, he said, but a "respectable Republican cloth coat."

And his family had also been given a dog:

> It was a little cocker spaniel dog . . . black and white, spotted, and our little girl Tricia, the six-year-old, named it Checkers. And you know, the kids, like all kids, loved the dog, and I just want to say this, right now, that regardless of what they say about it, we are going to keep it.

Response to the speech was overwhelmingly warm; Nixon stayed on the ticket.

The term in use, by the *Washington Post,* July 9, 1987, commenting on the testimony of Oliver North during congressional hearings on the Iran-contra affair:

> A new classic in the annals of melodramatic political rhetoric, Lt. Col. North's appearance before the Iran-contra committees yesterday ranks right up there with Richard Nixon's "Checkers speech."

And by Ira Robbins in *Newsday,* May 31, 1995, on Michael Jackson's latest recording:

> "Childhood," which Jackson wrote and recorded as the theme for the forthcoming movie *Free Willy 2,* is the most blatantly personal public appeal for tolerance and consideration in recorded memory, a virtual Checkers speech from the world of self-analysis.

Cheeveresque; Cheever country The life, manners, and morals of middle-class suburban America as described by writer John Cheever (1912–1982) through fantasy and ironic comedy. Cheever wrote in clear, elegant, carefully crafted prose, and his subtle, ironic short stories and novels feature the landscape of affluent suburbia, particularly the WASP communities of suburban Connecticut.

The term in use by Joseph Berger in the *New York Times,* January 13, 1997, describing a raid by building inspectors on a Hasidic school in Monsey, New York:

> Most students were forced out by a court order, but the November raid by inspectors added one more strain to already tense relations between the Hasidic and Orthodox Jewish community and its more Cheeveresque suburban neighbors in Rockland County.

And by Blaine Harden in the *Washington Post,* August 4, 1997 (dateline: Greenwich, Connecticut):

> There is a spot of trouble here in Cheever country, the suburban promised land where moneyed executives ride the train to Manhattan and return each evening to sprawling homes and cool breezes off Long Island Sound.

And again, by Drew Jubera, television critic of the *Atlanta Journal and Constitution,* reviewing the latest edition of the British detective series "Prime Suspect," February 9, 1996:

> This "Prime Suspect" instead knocks heads with the insular hanky-panky of suburban London's country club set. This is Cheever country with an accent and a murder weapon.

Chernobyl \chər-'nō-bəl, cher-\ The scene of the worst nuclear reactor disaster in history, on April 26, 1986.

A nuclear power plant exploded in the town of Chernobyl, in what was then the Soviet Union (now Ukraine), 60 miles north of Kiev. The explosion caused a fire and the release of massive amounts of radiation that drifted across northern Europe, affecting the inhabitants and food grown in the entire region. The area around the plant was evacuated permanently, and the damaged reactor entombed in millions of tons of cement. The long-term scope of the disaster continues to unfold.

There's an ironic biblical twist to the name, as noted by the *Christian Science Monitor,* April 20, 1989:

> Chernobyl means "wormwood," the biblical name given to the great star in Revelation 8:10–11 that fell from heaven "burning as if it were a lamp" when the third angel sounded his trumpet. According to Revelation, the star poisoned one-third of the Earth's waters "and many men died of the waters, because they were made bitter."

The term in use, quoted in the *Christian Science Monitor,* November 15, 1995, in an article describing the growth of theme parks world-wide:

> When Disneyland Paris opened in April 1992, French intellectuals moaned that it would be a "cultural Chernobyl."

Another example, from Robert Houston's review of *The Cloning of Joanna May* by Fay Weldon, in the *New York Times Book Review,* March 25, 1990:

> They band together to readjust their lives and their men, share what children they have and begin at last to have a good time, while Carl goes down in his own private, ego-triggered Chernobyl.

And quoted by Thomas Brandt in the *New York Times,* September 21, 1997, describing an illness spreading in trout in the western United States:

The whirling disease threat to American trout has been raised to a possible "biological Chernobyl," leading Alberta, a huge province of Canada, to shut its border to live trout from the United States . . . to protect its own trout streams.

Cheshire cat A broadly grinning cat in Lewis Carroll's *Alice's Adventures in Wonderland* (1865). The Cheshire cat could appear and disappear, and its pronouncements were enigmatic, or at least ambiguous. The cat sometimes leaves only its grin behind.

The origins of the phrase go back further than that, but no one is certain of the source, although theories abound. One is that cheeses from the English county of Cheshire were molded in the shape of a cat or were stamped with a grinning cat. Others say that an inept sign painter in Cheshire made all of his lions look like cats, or that a county forest warden named Caterling presented himself at the hangings of poachers, grinning "like a Cheshire caterling" which was then shortened to "cat."

The term in use, by Frances Fitzgerald in *Rolling Stone* February 25, 1988, reviewing the Reagan presidency:

Yet he has never chided any one of his appointees for betraying the public trust. His smiling face has hovered over them all like that of a Cheshire cat.

Another example, from David Maraniss in the *Washington Post,* October 7, 1996, reporting the scene at a presidential candidates' debate:

The Dole camp planted their smile specialist, Sen. John McCain, (R–Ariz.) in a prime seat inside the hall with the sole mission of beaming so broadly that [Dole] might notice the crescent flash of whiteness in the audience. McCain performed the same Cheshire cat role during a crucial debate in the South Carolina primary. . . .

And quoted by Anastasia Toufexis in the *Detroit News,* February 4, 1997, in a piece on single women wary of marriage:

One unmarried woman said she saw too many "Cheshire cat" women. When they're in relationships they tend to disappear around the edges until all that's left is their smile.

chestnut An old joke or story or piece of music repeated to the point of staleness. It's a 19th-century slang expression, probably American. One theory is that it was popularized by an American actor who quoted a punch line from a long-forgotten play about either a chestnut tree or a cork tree: "I have heard you tell the joke twenty-seven times, and I am sure it was a chestnut."

The term in use, by Joe Chidley, *Maclean's* magazine, July 22, 1996, on sexual behavior at the Olympics:

Denying oneself, the theory goes, sharpens focus or builds up tension to be released in competition. And for some athletes, the old chestnut of no-sex-the-night-before still applies. "Sex makes you happy," American miler Marty Liquori once said, "and happy people don't run a 3:47 mile."

And by Rance Crain in *Advertising Age,* April 21, 1997:

Ralph conjured up that old chestnut from Philadelphia department store owner John Wanamaker, who said more than 90 years ago he knew half his advertising was wasted, he just didn't know which half.

chiaroscuro \kē-ˌär-ə-ˈskyu̇r-(ˌ)ō, kē-ˌar-, -ˈsku̇r-\ Pictorial representation in terms of light and shade without regard to color. An Italian word meaning "light-dark," it produces the effect of depth and distance in a painting or drawing. The technique was developed by Renaissance artists in the great change from earlier flat, one-dimensional painting. The term is also used to suggest an atmosphere, style, or mood created through the interplay or contrast of dissimilar qualities such as mood or character.

The term in use, by Richard Eder in *Newsday,* October 15, 1995, reviewing *Eveless Eden* by Marianne Wiggins:

"Mixed" is my reaction to her turbulent new novel. . . . It is not an average "mixed," a gray balance of black and white. It is more of a blinding chiaroscuro: blinding both when it dazzles and when the light goes out and it merely churns.

And by *Washington Post* film critic Stephen Hunter, August 10, 1997, on the genre of conspiracy films, specifically Orson Welles' masterpiece *The Third Man:*

It was not the first but it was surely one of the most sophisticated films to evoke the universe of the conspiracy visually. For to watch it is to feel oneself absorbed into the vortex of plot and counterplot, to be drawn through LABYRINTHS both literal and metaphorical, to enter a world of dappling chiaroscuro where light and shadow marbleize into each other almost effortlessly. . . .

chicken in every pot, a A political promise of prosperity for all.

The phrase has a long history. It originated with Henry IV of France, who survived cruel religious and civil wars to become king in 1589. He is considered one of the ablest kings in French history. He protected the rights of French Protestants, and sought to improve the welfare of the people. He said, "I wish that there would not be a peasant so poor in all my realm who would not have a chicken in his pot every Sunday," and was nicknamed "King of the chicken in the pot."

Henry was politically astute, and knew when to make a change (*see* PARIS IS WELL WORTH A MASS).

In the United States, the promise is associated with Herbert Hoover, who never said it. However, during his campaign for president in 1928, he *did* say, "The slogan of progress is changing from the 'full dinner pail' to the full garage." Of course, the stock market crash the following year and the Great Depression soon assured that huge numbers of Americans had no car, no full dinner pail, no job, no Sunday chicken. This was a point that the Democrats did not hesitate to make, and variations of the theme were tied to Hoover for decades thereafter: "Two chickens in every pot, two cars in every garage."

The term in use, by Michael Fumento, the *Washington Times,* September 11, 1995:

> Moreover, you would also have students paying off their college loans even as their own children were going off to college. Instead of a chicken in every pot, Mr. Clinton's promise is two generations of student loans in every family.

And by Ross Atkin, the *Christian Science Monitor,* July 28, 1980:

> In a twist to the old "a chicken in every pot" theme, the US Olympic Committee (USOC) has come up with a gold medal for every pocket. . . . The medals, to be presented on the steps of the Capitol July 30, are just one reward for the athletes denied the opportunity to compete in the Moscow Olympics.

Children's Crusade An unsuccessful attempt to take control of the Holy Land back from the Muslims waged in 1212 by thousands of French and German children. Their weapons were love and purity, but they perished in disaster.

The crusades—wave after wave of Christian pilgrims and armies seeking to oust the Muslims from the Holy Land—lasted for almost 200 years, from 1096 to 1274.

The Children's Crusade was one of the saddest episodes of the era. It was set in motion by a French shepherd boy named Stephen who was inspired by a vision of Jesus. Stephen attracted a following of an estimated thirty thousand children. A second group of at least twenty thousand (some estimates are as high as forty thousand) headed for the Holy Land under the leadership of a 10-year-old German boy.

The French children proceeded to Marseilles, expecting the Mediterranean to part as the Red Sea waters had for Moses. Instead, the children fell into the hands of slave traders who shipped them to the North African slave markets. The German children crossed the Alps, where they split into smaller groups headed to various ports to find ships. Some were refused transport; others were sold into slavery; a few were met by the pope, who took pity and released them from their vows so they could return home. Their story may have been the inspiration for the tale of the PIED PIPER of Hamelin.

The religious fervor generated by the children helped inspire the Fifth Crusade in 1218, a military disaster conducted by adults.

Children's Crusade has come to mean any enterprise led by the inexperienced and idealistic young. Most notably, the name was applied to the grassroots political campaign undertaken by antiwar college students in support of presidential candidate Eugene McCarthy in 1968. McCarthy came close to upending President Lyndon B. Johnson in the New Hampshire primary; shortly after, LBJ decided not to seek reelection.

The term in use, by Casey Combs of the Associated Press, August 18, 1997:

> Children from a pacifist Christian commune who used computers and faxes to draw supporters stepped off Monday on a march to fight the death penalty. Despite being sheltered from television and most movies, the youngsters from the Bruderhof communities waged a high-tech campaign of faxes, e-mail and even a Web site to promote their three-day, 30-mile march to the state prison near Waynesburg [Pa.]. The "Children's Crusade to Death Row" began Monday morning with an estimated 500 participants.

And by Steve Jacobson in *Newsday,* June 30, 1996, on the hazards of intense physical training on child athletes:

> It's not the fault of gymnastics, which has a lot of good values at gyms with sanity around the country. It's the way championships are determined and the attitude of the coaches and the parents who send their girls to these coaches on a Children's Crusade for the gold.

chimera \\'kī-mir-ə, kə-\\ An imaginary monster compounded of incongruous parts; an illusion or fabrication of the mind. Something that is fantastically visionary, improbable, or the product of an unchecked imagination is called chimerical.

In Greek mythology, the chimera was a monster: the front third was a lion, the midsection a goat, the rear end a serpent. Luckily it was slain by the legendary hero Bellerophon, riding the winged horse Pegasus. (Incidentally, the *Bellerophon* was a 74-gun British man-of-war, which participated in the Battle of Trafalgar. And it was the captain of the *Bellerophon* to whom Napoleon made his final surrender after defeat at Waterloo.)

Bellerophon would be shocked to learn that research into animal cloning has now created sheep/goat and sheep/cow combinations, as reported in the *New York Times,* June 3, 1997—and they are called chimeras.

The term in use, in a *Christian Science Monitor* editorial, January 16, 1992, in opposition to using lotteries as an easy way to help finance public schools:

> It is also about lacking the fortitude to make some significant sacrifices. . . .
>
> The promise of a few thousands or millions from gambling is a chimera. Those who see it as more than the shadow of a true commitment are misled and misleading.

And by Gary Chapman, in an opinion piece in the *Los Angeles Times,* July 8, 1996, on what he saw as the fallacies of "Star Wars" anti-missile technology:

> Nevertheless, Bob Dole continues to deliver stump speeches calling for ballistic missile defense. This is yet another bone thrown to the far right in his party, who have been weirdly obsessed with this chimera since the 1960s.

Chinese wall A strong barrier; a serious obstacle to understanding. From the Great Wall of China, probably the world's greatest public works project, a massive, 1,500-mile rampart built along the border of ancient China to keep out barbarian invaders.

The term is used in the financial world, to describe the insulation required between the mergers and acquisitions departments of brokerage and finance houses and their stock trading activities. A "Chinese wall" separating the two divisions is intended to keep stockbrokers from picking up inside information about takeover attempts, information they could use to purchase stock before it rises in price as a reaction to the acquisition or merger.

The term in use, from the *New York Times,* November 16, 1984:

> The union had insisted on retaining the so-called "Chinese wall" clause, which prohibits the sale in the metropolitan area of milk processed elsewhere.

And quoted in the *Christian Science Monitor,* February 27, 1997, in a story on political fundraising improprieties, and barriers which may not be so impassable:

> "The line between national party committees and the White House has always been an invisible Chinese wall," says Henry Graff, a presidential historian at Columbia University in New York. "It is a curious notion that you can separate the actions of the president as president from the actions of the president as politician."

Cincinnatus Roman citizen-soldier, a model of simplicity, ability, and republican virtue.

The original Cincinnatus was a legendary Roman (ca. 519–430 B.C.), a farmer summoned from his plow to become Dictator in order to save the Roman Republic from invaders. He served for sixteen days. Having saved his country, he returned to farm, without reward and expecting none. This agrarian virtue is often evoked to contrast with today's professional legislators.

George Washington is often called "the American Cincinnatus" and served as the first president-general of the Society of the Cincinnati, founded in 1783 by a group of officers serving in the Continental Army. Its motto is, translated from Latin, "He left all to preserve the republic." The society still exists today, with headquarters in Washington, D.C.

The term in use, by historian Robert Dallek, in a commentary on the presidential ambitions of H. Ross Perot, in the *Los Angeles Times,* July 21, 1996:

> Perot . . . would have us believe that his selfless determination to benefit the nation is the only consideration making him run. No doubt Perot believes his own rhetoric; but anyone who thinks this hugely egotistical Texan is our modern-day Cincinnatus would do well to consider the man's long history of self-serving actions.

And by and about Harry Truman, quoted in the *Christian Science Monitor,* in John Budris' review of David McCullough's *Truman,* June 12, 1992:

> Leaving the White House with only a $100-a-month Army pension, he went home to the farm—like his hero the mythic Roman warrior Cincinnatus who put down his sword and took up his plowshare. Decades earlier in one of the many courting letters to young Bess Wallace, farmer Truman wrote, "Who knows, maybe I'll be like Cincinnatus."

And again, from Jon Talton, Gannett News Service, April 29, 1994:

> Whatever history's judgment of Nixon—and it will not come from newspaper columns or TV soundbites—the 37th president was no Cincinnatus. . . .
> Richard Nixon . . . was part of a generation of ambitious, mid-century professional politicians who killed off the aspiration that government service would be limited, that leaders would come from private life and return to it.

cinema verité \\'si-nə-mə-ˌver-i-tā; si-nā-'mä-ve-rē-'tā\\ The art or technique of filming a motion picture so as to convey candid realism. The French phrase means "cinema-truth."

The film directors in this movement attempted to provide a film experience that closely resembled life rather than a make-believe image. Filmmakers would frequently record sound separately, taping actual conversations or interviews, and then put the audio and visual elements together in the editing process. In television, this style was pioneered in such shows as "Hill Street Blues" with its grubby sets and action in background and foreground.

The term now is sometimes turned back upon itself, describing real events that are viewed as drama—life imitating art.

The term in use, by Stephen Frantzich and John Sullivan in *The C-SPAN Revolution* (1996):

> During election campaigns, C-SPAN offers its viewers political events in their entirety, cinema verité coverage of candidates on the campaign trail, analysis of political advertising, and call-in programs.

And by Linda Shrieves of the *Orlando Sentinel,* November 30, 1994:

> Tune in sometime to MTV's "Real World," a cinema verité experiment in which a handful of twentysomethings are thrown together in an apartment so that their every move can be recorded on videotape.

city on a hill Utopia. A community based on and living by ideals, and a shining example for all the world. (*See also* UTOPIA.)

It's from the Sermon on the Mount, Matthew 5:3–7:27, in the New Testament:

> Ye are the light of the world. A city that is set on an hill cannot be hid. Neither do men light a candle, and put it under a bushel, but on a candlestick; and it giveth light unto all that are in the house. Let your light so shine before men that they may see your good works, and glorify your Father, which is in heaven.

John Winthrop, rallying his band of Puritans crossing the Atlantic to found the Massachusetts Bay colony, turned to the phrase, conscious of founding a godly society that would be watched by the world: "We must consider that we shall be a City Upon a Hill, the eyes of all people are upon us."

The term in use, by art critic Robert Hughes in *Time,* May 6, 1996, reflecting on the work of artist Ed Kienholz:

> Actually, he was at least as American as his critics —a compulsive Puritan who realized that the City on a Hill had been built in a mudslide area.

And by television critic Tom Shales, in the *Washington Post,* December 7, 1988, bemoaning sleazy new television programs:

> Perhaps American commercial television never was a shining city on a hill. But increasingly it seems a valley of slums.

cloud–cuckoo–land A realm of fantasy or whimsy or foolish behavior. The expression is from *The Birds,* a comedy by the Greek comic playwright Aristophanes (445–ca. 388 B.C.). Cloud–cuckoo–land was a city in the clouds that the birds were persuaded to create by two fugitives from Athenian taxes and litigation.

The term in use, by British military historian John Keegan, writing about D–Day and the challenge posed by German defense measures in *Esquire,* June 1, 1994:

> Rommel may have called the wall a "cloud–cuckoo–land" of the Fuhrer's imagination, but to the infantrymen who had to land underneath its concrete pillboxes and artillery bunkers, any single sector of it had a menacing reality.

And by Arthur Frommer, in his column "Dollar-Wise Travel," in *Newsday,* April 30, 1989:

In short, to wander the airport car rental counters of America, looking for informed comment on third-party liability insurance, is to enter a cloud-cuckoo-land of ignorance and doubt, ranging from minimal knowledge to innocent deception ("the car is insured").

cloud like a man's hand, a An indicator, or portent now small and distant, of great turmoil to come.

It comes from the Old Testament, I Kings 18:44–45:

And it came to pass at the seventh time, that he said, Behold, there ariseth a little cloud out of the sea, like a man's hand . . . and it came to pass a great rain.

The term in use, by Dave Rossie for Gannett News Service, February 28, 1996, on a bookstore's tea party alternative to the Super Bowl:

While the bookstore event—let us resist the urge to call it the Tea Bowl—may be a cloud no larger than a man's hand, it could be a portent. And if it is, the lords of professional football, television and the advertisers who buy television time will have only themselves to blame.

And by Wesley Pruden in the *Washington Times,* February 2, 1997, on the shadow of scandal over the inauguration of President Clinton:

[Special prosecutor] Kenneth Starr did not ride in one of the limousines . . . but he did not have to. His presence is felt all over town, as the cloud, now considerably larger than a man's hand, remains settled stubbornly in its earthly orbit over the White House.

clouds of glory *See* TRAILING CLOUDS OF GLORY.

cloven hoof The sign of a devilish character, from the traditional representation of Satan.

Thus a mention of the cloven hoof conjures up the Devil; however the Devil might disguise himself, he cannot hide his cloven hoof.

The term in use, by Deirdre Donahue in *USA Today,* May 15, 1996, reviewing John Grisham's novel *The Runaway Jury:*

But at this point, many Americans believe that cigarette makers have their clothes specially tailored to hide their cloven hoofs and pointed tails.

And from Gene Lyons, in *Newsday,* October 20, 1996:

Besides registering Clinton's lack of cloven hoofs and horns, [Clinton biographer Martin] Walker also recognizes his wide-ranging curiosity, intellectual self-confidence, tactical brilliance and sheer dogged determination.

coal mine *See* CANARY IN A MINE SHAFT/COAL MINE.

coals of fire *See* HEAP COALS OF FIRE.

coals to Newcastle Something that is redundant; something taken or offered where it is already plentiful.

The expression refers to the city of Newcastle-upon-Tyne in Great Britain, in a region noted for its abundance of coal and hence in no need of importing any more. The phrase is an old one, showing up as early as the 17th century.

The term in use, by Brian Burnes in the *Kansas City Star,* September 5, 1996:

> Yet there are many fine doughnut proprietors in eastern Jackson County, not the least of which is LaMar's. . . . Perhaps bringing doughnuts anywhere close to LaMar's is a sticky, greasy version of coals to Newcastle. But the chiefs at the Krispy Kreme insist they have several selling points.

And from syndicated columnist George Will, in the *Washington Post,* July 11, 1996:

> The idea of a nonbinding initiative to measure public opinion is subject to the coals-to-Newcastle criticism. Does anyone think that there is insufficient measurement of public opinion?

coat of many colors A colorful garment. While now applied to anyone's colorful outfit, this reference comes out of the Old Testament story of Joseph (Genesis: 37-50). Joseph, the 11th of the 12 sons of Jacob and his father's favorite, was given a beautiful "coat of many colors," undoubtedly an expensive gift. His older brothers resented this favoritism and sold the boy into slavery, showing the garment to Jacob as proof that Joseph was dead.

Joseph was taken to Egypt and sold to Potiphar, a high government official. Joseph rose to a position of trust in the household until the advances and rape allegations of POTIPHAR'S WIFE caused him to be imprisoned.

However, he achieved freedom, as well as power and success, through his ability to interpret the pharaoh's dreams. The pharaoh had dreamed of seven lean cattle who swallowed up seven fat cattle and seven lean ears of corn which consumed seven ripe ones. Joseph's interpretation was that this meant seven years of prosperity to be followed by seven years of famine. This analysis prompted Pharaoh to appoint Joseph to administer the stockpiling of food to prepare for the predicted years of shortages. Joseph's interpretation was correct, and when the famine came, Egypt was well prepared. Joseph's brothers came to Egypt from Canaan to ask for help, having no idea that this great man in the kingdom was their lost brother. After more complications, Joseph was generous to them, and brought them to live in Egypt.

The term in use, by Andres Viglucci in the *Miami Herald,* November 1, 1997:

> Terry is resplendent in his coat of many colors: a garage-sale waiter's jacket, painted by his students in the style of the modern masters. It has a Tahitian beauty by Gauguin over the heart, a Cubist head by Picasso on the flank.

And by Chris Satullo in a tribute to his mother in the *Philadelphia Daily News,* February 26, 1998:

> She loved the Berkshire mountains of Massachusetts, particularly how her special mountain looked from her breakfast room, dappled in morning light, clad in autumn's coat of many colors.

And by Bob Swift in the *Charlotte Observer,* November 23, 1986, reviewing his life history with neckties:

> Eventually I saw a beautiful necktie in a store window and bought it. It resembled Joseph's coat of many colors, being extremely wide with a pattern of large concentric interlocking circles in various garish hues.

cold *See* COME IN FROM THE COLD.

Colonel Blimp *See* BLIMP, COLONEL.

colossus of the north The United States in its relations, especially economic, with the countries of Central and South America, perhaps in a bullying or intrusive way.

The term *Colossus,* meaning "a statue of gigantic size and proportions," was originally applied by the Greek historian Herodotus to the huge statues of ancient Egypt. But the most famous reference is to the Colossus of Rhodes, a statue of the god Helios (Apollo) and one of the Seven Wonders of the ancient world. The statue which was more than 100 feet high, stood at the entrance to the harbor of Rhodes and was completed about 280 B.C. Legends arose centuries later that the figure stood astride the harbor entrance so that ships sailed between its legs, and that the harbor was destroyed when it fell.

Shakespeare evoked this very image in *Julius Caesar* Act 1, Scene 2, when Cassius says of Caesar:

> Why, man, he doth bestride the narrow world
> Like a Colossus, and we petty men
> Walk under his huge legs, and peep about
> To find ourselves dishonourable graves.
> Men at some time are masters of their fates:
> The fault, dear Brutus, is not in our stars,
> But in ourselves, that we are underlings.

Colossus now describes anything vast, large, or awesome, or someone of immense talent, power, or influence.

Although in the early 19th century "colossus of the north" may have referred to Russia, these days the United States can claim the overwhelming majority of references.

The term in use, by David Clark Scott in the *Christian Science Monitor,* July 1, 1992:

> No other issue inflames political passions more in Mexico than an affront to sovereignty. With a long history of being invaded, bullied, and fooled by the imposing colossus of the north, Mexico jealously guards its territorial integrity.

And by Thomas Powers in the *New York Times Book Review,* February 18, 1990:

> What followed was the largest American military operation in nearly 20 years, cost the lives of 23 United States soldiers and several hundred Panamanians and set the stage for another generation of Latin American resentment toward the colossus of the north.

comédie humaine \kò-mā-dē-ēē-men\ Human comedy; the whole variety of human life. A French phrase with the same meaning. The 19th-century novelist Honore de Balzac (1799–1850) gave this phrase as title to his works, which provide a sweeping and realistic view of France from many perspectives. Thus comédie humaine means the entire spectrum of human behavior.

Balzac's characters and plots are romantic, extreme, passionate, and melodramatic. Like Dickens, he draws memorable pictures of human failings and virtues.

The term in use, by Max I. Dimont in the introduction to *Jew, God and History* (1979):

> This book attempts to portray the broad sweep of Jewish history, the grandeur and humor of the Jewish *comédie humaine,* and to present Jewish history through the eyes of a twentieth-century Western man rather than a sixteenth–century ghetto Talmudist.

And by David L. Ulin, on the works of Beat author Jack Kerouac in *Newsday,* March 19, 1995:

> Kerouac, in fact, viewed *On the Road* and his other novels as installments in a multi-volume "Comédie Humaine" he called the "Legend of Duluoz"—"one vast book . . . seen through the eyes of poor Ti Jean (me), otherwise known as Jack Duluoz, the world of raging action and folly and also of gentle sweetness seen through the keyhole of his eye."

come in from the cold In espionage, to leave a lonely, exposed, or dangerous undercover position for one of safety or comfort.

The expression is particularly tied to the spying game of the Cold War, where agents engaged in dangerous secret work could be brought back by their own side. The expression was popularized by the 1963 novel by John le Carré, *The Spy Who Came in from the Cold,* about a weary British agent operating behind the Iron Curtain who wishes to return to the West.

The term in use, by Michael Hiestand, in *USA Today,* July 24, 1996:

> The Rose Bowl has come in from the cold. In an agreement announced Tuesday, the winners of the Big Ten and Pacific 10 conferences will no longer be locked into an automatic trip to Pasadena, Calif., when that means forgoing a national title bowl matchup.

And from David W. Marston in the *Baltimore Sun,* July 9, 1995, reviewing *Explaining the Unexplainable: The Rodent's Guide to Lawyers,* by The Rodent, an anonymous author:

> Speaking of skulking, Rodent, why don't you just come in from the cold? . . . And after all, hiding behind a NOM DE GUERRE is fine if you're Che Guevara or The Jackal, but if you're just another paper-pushing lawyer killing yourself in an impossible quest for partnership that will be ultimately unfulfilling even if you somehow get it, why worry about being fired?
>   Unless, maybe, you're really a Big Cheese.

And by Bruce Stanley in the *Christian Science Monitor,* July 18, 1995:

> After years of isolation, Communist-run Vietnam is coming in from the cold, and fast.

come up and see me sometime A famous movie invitation to sexual dalliance. It was delivered by the inimitable Mae West in *She Done Him Wrong* (1933) to Cary Grant, playing a virtuous Salvation Army officer, who accepted. A furor ensued, and Mae (as the scandalous saloon singer) triumphed over the local prudes. The film was based on her stage hit *Diamond Lil,* a spoof of the Gay 90s.

The West persona was utterly unique in American VAUDEVILLE and films. She wrote her own material, controlled her productions and picked her leading men. Her double entendre-laden material was a major cause for movie codes adopted in the 1940s. Her films showcased her as both an irresistible femme fatale and a self-parody.

Invariably she played a saloon chanteuse or con artist with a heart of gold who mocked and baffled the prating moralists. Her langorous demeanor, amused vulgarity and hilarious one-liners were as famous as her hourglass figure, which inspired the nickname for World War II's inflatable life jackets.

The phrase in use, by Richard Lacayo in *Time,* July 1, 1991, writing on the prospects for Supreme Court actions to overturn the legacy of the Warren court:

> A court that approves challenges to settled law tends to invite more of them. To anyone unhappy with the legacies of the old

Supreme Court, the new Supreme Court appears to be sending this message: come up and see me sometime.

computer virus A computer program usually hidden within another seemingly innocuous program that produces copies of itself and inserts them where they usually perform a malicious action (such as destroying data). A term coined by American researcher Fred Cohen in 1984. They are often triggered by specific dates, and affected computer screens show only repetitive flashing messages or patterns. Computer viruses are aptly likened to viruses infecting living organisms because they can spread through casual contact, such as infected disks and downloaded transmissions.

That's about all the knowledge we have on the technical point. But for language, the good news is that the term has come to describe subversive, destructive, and mischievous agents in other settings.

The term in use, by Richard Eder in *Newsday,* November 11, 1996, reviewing a biography of artist Marcel Duchamp:

> Marcel Duchamp was a computer virus in the modernist program; a graceful saboteur of the cult of artist as hero/creator/ prophet that ran from the romantic movement up through Renoir and Manet, Van Gogh and Gauguin, Matisse and Picasso and the abstract expressionists.

Another example, from Bill Tammeus, the *Kansas City Star,* March 15, 1996:

> But it's been nice to see that a place like the Pelican Cove Motel can stand up to the vast army of Motel 6's, Super 8's and other even-numbered motel chains now multiplying faster than a computer virus on STEROIDS.

And in an example in which the allusion refers to its biological root to further explain a concept, an Associated Press story reported in the *St. Louis Post-Dispatch,* April 15, 1997:

> Genes blamed when breast cancer runs in families may do their damage by infecting the genetic coding system with a biological version of a computer virus, according to a study by the University of Tampere in Finland.

Comstockery Strict censorship of materials considered obscene; censorious opposition to alleged immorality.

George Bernard Shaw is given credit for making a noun out of the name of Anthony Comstock (1844–1915), an American crusader against smut, birth control, and gambling in the late 19th and early 20th centuries. Shaw was quoted by the *New York Times,* September 26, 1905, as saying, "Comstockery is the world's standing joke at the expense of the United States." (Comstock had objected to Shaw's play, *Mrs. Warren's Profession,* dealing with organized prostitution, when it was produced in New York that year.)

Comstock was an organizer of the New York Society for the Suppression of Vice, and was personally credited with the destruction of 160 tons of dirty pictures and literature. He was a leader in pressuring Congress to enact laws against sending pornography through the mail—the "Comstock laws."

The term in use, by Jeffrey Rosen discussing court challenges to the Communications Decency Act, federal legislation to regulate pornography on the Internet, in the *New Republic,* March 31, 1997:

> The best argument for upholding this electronic Comstockery can be summed up in a single word: zoning. Solicitor General Walter Dellinger, in his brief, and Lawrence Lessig of the University of Chicago, in a series of powerful articles, urge us to view the CDA as an Internet zoning ordinance that channels indecent material away from children while guaranteeing full access to adults.

And from Dave Michaels in the *Dallas Morning News,* August 17, 1997:

> In spite of the best efforts of Disney's in-house comstockery unit, the Insane Clown Posse has found a home—at Island Records.
>
> Disney-owned Hollywood Records gave the Detroit group's naughty *The Great Milenko* the post-facto heave-ho two months ago and pulled the album from stores. Island then did its own computations and decided the payoff from the hype over the pseudo-rappers was well worth the fuddy-duddy fulminations *The Great Milenko* is sure to attract.

conspicuous consumption Lavish or wasteful spending intended to enhance social prestige.

The concept was introduced in 1899 by Thorstein Veblen in his book *Theory of the Leisure Class.* To test whether an expenditure fell within this classification, Veblen said one must merely ask "whether, aside from acquired tastes and from the canons of usage and conventional decency, its result is a net gain in comfort or in the fullness of life." By that standard, most of the consumer spending in the wealthy nations of the world would be conspicuous indeed.

Veblen maintained that spending for status and show exists in all classes of society, but his term is usually applied to extremely flamboyant spending. At the time Veblen wrote, the wealthy constructed huge, ornate mansions, entertained lavishly, and competed in expensive excesses of all kinds. Reformers of the day loved to cite the Bradley Martin costume ball staged in the Waldorf Hotel at a cost of $368,000. It took place in February 1897 in the depths of an economic depression and was attended by guests wearing costumes costing as much as $10,000. That's the sort of showy expenditure evoked by Veblen's phrase.

The term in use, by Jim Motavalli in *E* magazine, March 13, 1996:

And because television has so successfully spread the religion of conspicuous consumption, the world consumed as many goods and services in the 46 years since 1950 as had all previous generations together.

And from Playthell Benjamin, the *Village Voice,* November 8, 1988, describing the lifestyle of drug dealers:

And they are prepared to commit bloody murder to attain the status symbols dictated by the amoral materialist ethos spawned by a uniquely American culture of narcissism. It is an ethos that prizes style over substance and thrives on conspicuous consumption.

Cook's tour A quick tour in which attractions are viewed very briefly or cursorily; a quick cursory scanning.

The expression comes from the travel agency founded by Thomas Cook (1808–92), an English missionary. Cook began his career as a travel agent when he organized a train excursion to a temperance meeting in 1841.

A package tour business caught on; in 1855 Cook conducted tours to the Paris exhibition and later organized tours all over Europe and later the world. The success of his company in handling complex travel arrangements led the British government in 1884 to hire Cook to convey an 18,000-man army to the Sudan to relieve General Charles George Gordon, who was besieged at Khartoum. The trip was accomplished, although the mission was not—Gordon and his army were slaughtered by the rebel armies of the Mahdi two days before the arrival of the relief column, a detail it would be unfair to lay at the door of the travel agent.

Today, Thomas Cook Group operates in more than 100 countries.

The term in use, by Robin Knox in *Colorado Outdoors,* January/February 1993:

Also the daily take of waterdogs (gilled form of tiger salamanders) was reduced from 120 to 20 to help protect their populations.

Well, there you have it. A cook's tour of major changes. The Division of Wildlife will be scrutinizing the changes during the next three years, realizing that we are close to the maximum of regulations that anglers may tolerate.

By William J. Gatens, in a review for *American Record Guide,* September 19, 1996:

The one really important genre not represented here is the English madrigal. Apart from that omission, this is a Cook's tour of Elizabethan music.

And by John Vincent, the *Times Literary Supplement,* September 21–27, 1990:

His book, though, is not all denunciation. The question posed in his subtitle, "Who runs Britain?", is an excuse for a Cook's tour of those elite institutions which, while influential, manifestly do not run Britain: the dukes, the gentry, the bishops, the Brigade of Guards, Oxbridge, Royalty, the judiciary, the BBC. . . .

cordon sanitaire \kȯr-dōⁿ-sà-nē-'ter\ A protective barrier (as of buffer states) against a potentially aggressive nation or a dangerous influence (such as an ideology). The phrase is French, and originally meant an area quarantined to prevent the spread of disease. The term is still used to describe a zone that serves as a barrier to keep an unwelcome someone or something hemmed in or fenced out.

The term was applied to the ring of small states, from Finland to Romania, created by the Paris peace conference in 1919 along the borders of Russia to contain Bolshevism.

The term in use, in "The Perils of Public Art" by Herbert Muschamp, in the *New Republic,* August 8, 1988:

> With its blank, fortress-like walls, its green *cordon sanitaire* of clipped golf course grass, the museum building embodies the idea of art as something isolated, set apart from its surroundings and from the history that produced it.

And in the *Economist,* March 16, 1996, on attempts to control Internet use in Asia:

> China has already gone a step further than Singapore, requiring all Internet users as well as providers to register. It too is looking at how to put a cordon sanitaire around the Internet. Like Myanmar and Vietnam it is particularly concerned about the campaigning activities in cyberspace of exiled dissidents.

And from Reuters, April 11, 1997, reporting on the British elections:

> Prime Minister John Major poked fun at Tony Blair Friday, taunting [him] with avoiding the press like the plague—or New Black Death.
> Major, in good spirits at his daily election news conference, accused Blair's media handlers of throwing a "cordon sanitaire" around the Labor [Party] leader to spare him unwanted grillings.

corpus delicti \'kȯr-pəs-di-'lik-ˌtī, -(ˌ)tē\ A lugubrious Latin phrase referring to evidence establishing that a crime has been committed; in Latin, it literally means "the body of the crime." This evidence may in fact be the body of a victim done in by foul means, as suggested by the similarity to the word "corpse"—but not always. The corpus delicti may also refer to evidence of embezzlement, or any other crime, with or without bloodshed.

The term in use, by Norman Podhoretz, in *Commentary,* March 1, 1996, musing on the state of the neoconservative movement of which he is a leading intellectual:

> In proposing to deliver a eulogy in honor of neoconservatism, I am obviously implying that it is dead. But is it? There are those who think that neoconservatism is still very much with us. . . . Others might say that instead of trying to bury neoconservatism alive, I have come to orate over an empty coffin; maybe neoconservatism is not dead but only temporarily missing, which would leave us with a kind of corpus delicti problem.

And by Elizabeth Kirsch, reviewing an exhibit of self-destructing art by Marcie Miller Gross in the *Kansas City Star,* October 4, 1996:

> These photos become like evidence, or scenes from a crime, demonstrating an earlier, healthier life of the now shredded, peeled and decaying artworks lying dormant on [the art gallery's] cement floor. Gross produces an aesthetic corpus delicti, for these works gently, but unmistakenly, allude to the "ASHES TO ASHES, DUST TO DUST" part of life we humans try so assiduously to avoid thinking about.

Cory, Richard The fictional subject and title of a poem by Edwin Arlington Robinson, an American poet who lived from 1869 to 1935. He lived in poverty much of his life and was forced to cut short his stay at Harvard. Theodore Roosevelt admired his work and secured a job for him in the Custom House in New York (which had also employed Herman Melville). His poetry tends to have a dark, ironic tone.

"Richard Cory" is one of Robinson's best-known works. Elegant, impeccably mannered Richard Cory was "imperially slim" and "glittered when he walked." He seemed to have everything—but one calm summer night he "went home and put a bullet through his head." Robinson's lyric phrases show up often to describe elegant, suave characters who nevertheless have a darker side.

The term in use, in a *Detroit News* editorial, November 20, 1996, commenting on the death of Alger Hiss, who was convicted of perjury in a celebrated espionage case of the McCarthy era. Hiss spent the rest of his life denying his guilt:

> He [Hiss] had clerked for Justice Oliver Wendell Holmes, Jr., and was a trusted aide in the State Department. He was handsome, sartorially elegant and, like E.A. Robinson's "Richard Cory," he was "imperially slim."

And by Jan Breslauer, the *Los Angeles Times,* January 26, 1997, describing playwright Tina Howe:

> She is imperially slim, like E.A. Robinson's Richard Cory, fashionably arrayed in flowing garments of black jersey and dark brown crushed velvet. . . .

And by James R. Kincaid in the *New York Times Book Review* November 10, 1996, reviewing Jackson L. Benson's *Wallace Stegner: His Life and Work:*

> But Mr. Benson does not stop with the preface or with the inner man: he finds Stegner's exterior just as admirable: possessed of "a beautiful voice," Stegner was "a strikingly handsome man— one is tempted to add that he 'glittered when he walked.' " That's a temptation one should resist, as the allusion to "Richard Cory" suggests not only a suicidal darkness beneath the glitter but a superficiality in those who mistake the glitter for the man.

cottage industry An industry whose labor force consists of families or individuals working at home with their own equipment; or, increasingly, a small and often informally organized industry.

Cottages were once rural dwellings for farmers or laborers, and cottage industries were activities such as weaving and making soap and candles. With the arrival of factories in the Industrial Revolution, weavers in particular suffered from the displacement of their livelihood to such large-scale industries. Some, like the LUDDITES, violently resisted the shift and smashed the machines which had taken their work.

The term in use by Joanne Kaufman, the *Wall Street Journal,* November 19, 1996, on Sarah Ferguson, former wife of the Duke of York:

> Fergie's fall from grace has sold millions of newspapers and spawned a veritable cottage industry of books about the most famous redhead since Lucille Ball.

Another example, from Linda Feldmann in the *Christian Science Monitor,* April 17, 1996:

> In a nation obsessed with predictions, the presidential prediction business has become a sort of cottage industry in recent years.

And by Kenneth J. Garcia, in the *San Francisco Chronicle,* February 5, 1997, writing about the murder trial of celebrity O.J. Simpson:

> And it has spawned a cottage industry for lawyers, authors, jury members and former associates of the victims and the plaintiffs— a group more than happy to cash in on instant fame regardless of the sorry circumstances.

Coxey's Army A motley, disorganized group with a single purpose. The original army was a group of unemployed men who marched on Washington in the spring of 1894 to demand the creation of jobs through public works programs after the Panic of 1893 had caused enormous unemployment and hardship.

Jacob Coxey was the well-to-do owner of a sandstone quarry and a horse breeder from Massillon, Ohio. He was also a populist and believed that a $500 million federal employment program of road building could alleviate the problem. When his plan was rejected by Congress, he vowed: "We will send a petition to Washington with boots on."

His army was one of a number of such groups of the ragtag unemployed to march on Washington in those difficult times.

Coxey's group marched peacefully from Massillon to Washington, picking up sympathizers along the way. They numbered several hundred when on May Day they arrived and marched to the Capitol. There they were assaulted by police. Coxey was arrested for walking on the grass and carrying a banner; he was not permitted to complete his speech.

Coxey lived until 1951. He had the satisfaction of completing his speech on the steps of the Capitol on May 1, 1944, and of seeing his concept of public works employment accepted as a routine way to relieve cyclical unemployment.

The term in use, by R. Reagan in *Video Librarian,* September 11, 1996, reviewing video guides for collectors:

> Like Coxey's army, hordes of collectors march on libraries expecting to be served. While identification guides and price books are essential, videotapes offer patrons the advantage of seeing their adored collectibles in full color and three dimensions.

And by Stan Isaacs in *Newsday,* September 4, 1988, on comments by tennis great/commentator Tony Trabert on TV coverage of tennis matches:

> Trabert has some suggestions for CBS in its coverage of tennis. He says he doesn't like the network's Coxey's army approach. . . .
> "Sometimes we have three people in the booth and two people in the studio downstairs commenting on the same match."

Crane, Ichabod A tall, skinny man with a beaky nose; nervous, inept, and a figure of some ridicule, like the fictional character created by Washington Irving in the short story "The Legend of Sleepy Hollow," published in *The Sketch Book* (1819–20).

Ichabod Crane was the scarecrow-like Yankee who came to Sleepy Hollow, near Tarrytown, to be the schoolmaster. In this prosperous 18th-century community of canny Dutchmen, Ichabod paid court to a local belle and incurred the enmity of her chief admirer, Abraham Van Brunt, known as Brom Bones.

Many tales and legends of ghosts and hauntings were told locally, but the greatest was the legend of the Headless Horseman. One night, on his way home from a party, the nervous Ichabod saw a strange horseman who kept pace with him and who seemed to be carrying his head. As the schoolmaster desperately whipped his horse along, the apparition threw the head at Ichabod, knocking him to the ground.

The following morning the schoolmaster's horse was found grazing nearby; there was a broken pumpkin lying in the road—but Ichabod Crane was never seen again. Brom Bones got the girl, and laughed heartily whenever the story was told.

The term in use, by Jan Stuart in *Newsday,* July 3, 1997, in a tribute to actor James Stewart:

> The Jimmy many of us will choose to remember is the clown giant, the gangly 6-foot-plus bumbler locked in a constant, Ichabod Crane-ish struggle with his own body.

And again, by columnist Tony Snow in the *Detroit News,* March 11, 1996, describing presidential candidate Bob Dole:

> The lugubrious parliamentarian remains a mystery to most of us. He has a certain charm, a scorpion wit, a heroic biography and a long history of public service. He combines Don Rickles' warmth with Ichabod Crane's vivacity. Yet he has a poignant side.

And by Kenneth Turan, reviewing the presidential campaign documentary *The War Room,* in the *Los Angeles Times,* November 6, 1994:

> With his impish grin and the personality of a sardonic Ichabod Crane, James Carville, Bill Clinton's preeminent campaign strategist, is a natural actor.

critical mass A size, number, or amount large enough to produce a particular result. The term comes from physics, where it refers to the point at which an atomic pile is capable of producing a sustained nuclear chain reaction.

The term in use, by humorist Dave Barry in the *Washington Post Magazine,* September 14, 1997, on family vacations:

> On our trip we encountered numerous families that, after many hours together in the minivan, had reached Critical Hostility Mass.

Another example, from an October 10, 1989 *New York Times* story quoting a report on hiring minority faculty members at Yale University:

> The lack of a "critical mass" of minorities on the faculty deprives undergraduates of role models, reinforces perceptions of minorities as marginal or tokens and reduces the opportunity for colleagueship, the report said.

crocodile tears False or affected tears; hypocritical sorrow.

The expression stems from an ancient myth that the crocodile sobs like a being in grievous distress to lure its prey, and then sheds tears as it devours its victim. A reference appears in Shakespeare, in *Henry VI, Part II.*

The term in use, by columnist Kevin Phillips, appearing in *USA Today,* April 3, 1995:

> Term limits have just been defeated in the House because top Republicans—despite gallons of crocodile tears—don't want to

go back to Spokane or Syracuse any more than the Democrats did.

And in an editorial in the *Economist,* April 8, 1995, on the ruin of Iraq:

> The country is in a terrible way—and what money there is often ill-spent. On palaces for Saddam, for a start: while shedding crocodile tears for children dying of malnutrition, the dictator has repaired and added to the PLEASURE DOMES created for himself.

Croesus \\'krē-səs\\ Someone who possesses enormous wealth. The expression most often heard is that a person is "rich as Croesus."

In about 550 B.C., Croesus was the king of Lydia, a kingdom of ancient times located in a region that is now western Turkey. The Lydians have the distinction of having invented money. They had been using coins for about a century when Croesus came along and introduced gold and silver coins in 550. He was, as the saying goes, filthy rich, and his name is a byword for that condition.

His court attracted many artists and wise men, including perhaps Aesop (of *Fables* fame). SOLON was supposed to have visited as well. Historians say this is not chronologically possible, but it makes a good story, and serves up a lesson that the rich are not always smart. Solon supposedly told Croesus, his host and the king who thought he had everything: "Account no man happy before his death." This was not what Croesus liked to hear and he threw the lawmaker out of his court.

Croesus was planning a war, and inquired of the oracle of Delphi (*see* DELPHIC) about the prospects for success. The oracle responded that "When Croesus crosses over the river Halys, he will overthrow the strength of an empire." Croesus assumed this meant victory, but he was defeated and his own empire overthrown by the Persians. Sentenced to death, Croesus recalled with regret the advice given by Solon. As the story goes, King Cyrus of Persia heard the tale and commuted the death sentence, and made Croesus one of his closest advisers.

The term in use, by Michelle Green and Linda Kramer in *People,* November 14, 1988:

> Jack Kent Cooke was a twice-married Croesus in his waning years; Suzanne Martin was a comely blond of 29. They met by a swimming pool at Miami's Palm Bay Club, and within days he was plying her with flowers and billets-doux.

And by John Greenwald in *Time,* December 23, 1985:

> The consolidation craze has created opportunities for sudden Croesus-style riches. For aiding Pantry Pride in its fight for Revlon, financial advisers and lawyers stand to gain more than $100 million.

And by Daisy Maryles in *Publishers Weekly,* November 28, 1994:

Croesus wannabes are flocking to the stores for a best-seller wannabe. One of the titles just below our nonfiction hardcover list is Robert G. Hagstrom Jr.'s *The Warren Buffett Way: Investment Strategies of the World's Greatest Investor,* published Nov. 18 by Wiley.

cross of gold The figurative crucifixion of one economic class for the enrichment and protection of another.

This arresting image comes from a speech by William Jennings Bryan, one of the great stem-winders of American history, nicknamed the Boy Orator of the Platte. At a raucous Democratic Convention in Chicago in 1896, Bryan gave the speech that catapulted him into the nomination for the presidency at the age of 36. Bryan urged free coinage of silver to expand the money supply and assist struggling farmers and debtors. Republicans backed the gold standard. Bryan also spoke against the rule of a privileged elite. His oratory, biblical in tone, electrified the convention: "You shall not press down upon the brow of labor this crown of thorns, you shall not crucify mankind upon a cross of gold."

William McKinley, the Republican nominee, conducted a "front porch" campaign, delivering speeches literally from his front porch in Canton, Ohio, while his campaign raised unheard-of sums of money—estimates range as high as $15 million, compared to the $300,000 spent by Bryan. Eastern newspapers described Bryan as a radical and the Democrats as JACOBINS and madmen. McKinley won, soundly; Bryan did not carry a single state outside the West and South.

Ironically the increase in the money supply that Bryan advocated came about anyway through gold discoveries in South Africa and improved refining techniques. The economy boomed with this influx of capital.

The term in use, by financier Felix Rohatyn, quoted in a *Newsday* editorial, September 1, 1996:

> The more you have an economy that has to deal with brutal competition on a global scale, the more you need intelligent, active government to deal with the social dislocations that business isn't set up to deal with. Beginning with education, public works, pensions, etc. And ultimately, if you don't we are going to have social dislocations all over the western world—because of this cross of gold that's being created by us for global capitalism.

And by Alan Ryan in the *New Republic,* April 18, 1994, reviewing Robert Skidelsky's biography of John Maynard Keynes, who had gained fame with his prophetic 1919 work *The Economic Consequences of the Peace:*

> Once Winston Churchill decided in 1925 to crucify the British economy on a cross of gold, Keynes let fly with the second of his devastating pamphlets, *The Economic Consequences of Mr. Churchill....*

cross the rubicon *See* RUBICON.

cult of personality Great devotion to a single person and his ideas and movement. A term made famous by Soviet leader Nikita Khrushchev in his 1956 "secret speech" denouncing the policies of the deceased dictator Josef Stalin. Khrushchev accused Stalin of having created a "cult of personality" by making himself the nearly godlike central figure of government, feared and venerated, and superseding collective leadership in a betrayal of the Russian revolution and Communist Party principles. The speech signaled the beginning of "destalinization" of the Soviet Union.

The term has since taken on a more casual meaning, describing someone who is building power by making himself or herself the focus of attention and adulation rather than subordinating his or her personal image to that of the institution.

The term in use, by Burling Lowrey in the *Washington Post,* March 17, 1989, defining the word "charisma":

> We apparently needed a word to convey the chemistry that a public speaker exudes, and this seems to fit the bill. In America it has taken on an added significance because of the emphasis in the political realm placed on "attractive" candidates and those who "come across well on television."
> It's the Cult of Personality reborn.

And by Laurie Winer, theater critic of the *Los Angeles Times,* October 28, 1995:

> Broadway musical stars often inspire a cult of personality, where the singer, the song and the role all meld to create an intensity that is ether to an adoring audience.

curate's egg Something which is part good, part bad; a mixed bag. The expression comes from a 19th-century cartoon in the British humor magazine *Punch*: A nervous young curate (in Britain, a junior-grade clergyman who is usually an assistant to a more senior member of the clergy) is served a bad egg while a guest at his bishop's breakfast table. Asked whether the egg is to his liking, he stammers: "Parts of it are excellent!"

The term in use, by the *Economist,* April 5-11, 1986:

> Band-Aid's band of volunteers feel that even the best of agencies resemble the curate's egg, a view that professionals in the aid business find hard to take from a beginner.

And by R.W. Johnson in the *Times Literary Supplement,* July 31, 1987:

> Melinda Camber Porter's book is more of a curate's egg—a collection of thirty-three interviews, some of which are genuinely interesting.

By book reviewer Nicholas P. Brooks in *Speculum,* January 1993:

> This is a bold, fascinating, and intensely irritating curate's egg of a book.

And from Myles na Gopaleen (Irish author Flann O'Brien), sounding a different tone in *The Best of Myles* (1968):

> Do you feel hot and angry when some unspeakable hack writes: 'This book is like the curate's egg—good in parts'? Does that hideous cliché make you close your fist in murderous resolve?

cutting-room floor The place where rejected pieces of a project go. It's an expression from the motion picture industry, referring to the room in which films are edited. During this process, "rushes" or the raw film is trimmed, rearranged, and sometimes dramatically cut. Whole scenes may go; sometimes an actor's part will be shrunk or eliminated. Laments are heard about what has ended up on the cutting-room floor—or what should have gone there, but didn't.

A famous example is the editing of the film *The Big Chill* (1983). Kevin Costner, then an unknown young actor, saw his hoped-for breakthrough role shrink to a few moments' appearance as a corpse during the opening credits.

The term in use, quoted by David Judson, Gannett News Service, March 14, 1996, reporting congressional deliberation on farm legislation:

> "Our hope is that the land preservation provisions don't wind up on the cutting-room floor," said Farr, who drafted the original language now adopted only by the Senate. "We'll see."

And by Charles Levendosky, appearing in the *Rocky Mountain News,* March 1, 1998, on proposed legislation to restrict harassment of celebrities by press photographers:

> This nation needs thoughtful legislation regarding social ills, not grandstanding for the glitterati. Leave these bills on the cutting-room floor.

And by Ellen Joan Pollock in the *Wall Street Journal,* February 22, 1995:

> Indeed, as independent counsel Kenneth Starr moves ahead with his investigation and refines his legal case, what is most noteworthy is how many of the biggest Whitewater headlines appear to be heading toward the cutting-room floor.

Cyclops \'sī-ˌkläps\ Any of a race of giants in Greek mythology with a single eye in the middle of the forehead.

Some of them worked at the forge for Hephaestos, the god of fire, forging the thunderbolts that enabled Zeus to defeat the Titans. The most famous Cyclops is Polyphemus, who appeared in the *Odyssey*. He brutally devoured several of Odysseus' men when they entered his cave; Odysseus escaped by blinding him.

One-eyed? The term inevitably invites use when writing about television, as in a *Newsday* editorial, October 6, 1996, by Kenneth Omiel:

When the candidates step onto the stage tonight to face off in the first of this year's presidential debates, they'll take a deep breath, stare into the camera's cyclops eye, and hope to hell they avoid a gigantic blunder.

In use again, by Jay Mariotti, the *Chicago Sun-Times,* November 19, 1996:

If we must hide the kids at Halloween, cover all photographers with hardhats and risk ruffling the tender ego of Frank Thomas, so be it. As a desperate franchise heading for a crash, the White Sox have no choice but to sign the volatile cyclops known as Albert Belle, hoping he does more damage to baseballs than the human beings around him.

Cyrano A gallant, extravagantly chivalrous and romantic swashbuckler, one of the great characters in literature. Cursed with an enormous nose, Cyrano used his own eloquence to woo the woman he loved on behalf of another.

Cyrano de Bergerac was a real person, a 17th-century French novelist and satirist. He wrote fantastic adventures about visits to the sun and moon, and fought many duels over insults to his very large nose. Cyrano was recreated in heroic scale in modern times by Edmond Rostand in his verse drama *Cyrano de Bergerac* (1897).

In the play, Cyrano is the boldest of the bold and utterly true to his honor. He deeply loves the beauteous Roxanne, but does not speak his love to her when she tells him of her fascination with the handsome young Christian. Instead, to serve the happiness of his loved one, Cyrano uses his eloquence in composing speeches and letters on behalf of the dim, tongue-tied Christian. Christian dies in war; Roxanne mourns for years, and realizes too late that the eloquent voice and noble spirit she loves belong to Cyrano, who dies in her arms.

As we see here, references to Cyrano often simply play upon the theme of the monstrous, disfiguring feature; others refer to his romantic eloquence on behalf of another, and still others to his panache, the fearless poet and warrior. All are Cyrano.

The term in use, by syndicated columnist Chuck Stone in the *Philadelphia Daily News,* December 30, 1994:

In retirement, [former President] Carter reflects a quality that eluded him during his presidency: class. It is hard to define. As diaphanous as gauze and as regal as a monarch, class is Cyrano de Bergerac's quality that goes "caparisoned in gems unseen."

Another example, from Russ DeVault in the *Atlanta Journal and Constitution,* October 11, 1996:

But the new Venture—along with its domestic siblings, Pontiac Trans Port and Oldsmobile Silhouette, and exports, Opel and Vauxhall Sintras—has a sensibly short front end instead of those

Cyrano de Bergerac-like noses that characterized previous GM offerings.

And in a *Christian Science Monitor* editorial, September 18, 1987:

In this media age, even TV anchors, employed at high salary for their authoritative demeanor, utter lines researched and crafted by others. An industry of Cyranos exists to woo corporate Roxannes.

*. . . the Net/Web can also entangle browsers in misinformation, and even **disinformation.***
—Christian Science Monitor

Dada \\'dä-(,)dä\ A movement in art and literature based on deliberate irrationality and negation of traditional artistic values. Dadaism developed in the years after World War I, with the goals of making fun of existing art, breaking the rules, and seeking to shock the sensibilities of the middle class, the critics, and the pundits. It was a protest against the wastefulness and madness of the war.

And shock the Dadaists did. Exhibitions of Dada art were scenes of total confusion and nonsense, incorporating junk and common household items. Dada music was a deliberate cacophony. And the critics and the public reacted with gratifying apoplexy.

The movement ultimately self-destructed. When the only rule is "there are no rules," and when incoherence is a virtue, a legacy is unlikely. Dadaism's leaders quarreled or drifted off into other pursuits—surrealism was founded by Dadaists and produced artists such as Salvador Dali (*see* DALIESQUE). American artist Man Ray was a participant in both movements.

The movement was given its name by the poet Tzara and the artist Arp, who stuck a knife at random into a French dictionary and fortuitously struck upon "dada," French for "hobbyhorse."

The term today generally is applied to deliberate nonsense.

The term in use, by Sandra Chereb of the Associated Press, August 27, 1997, describing the annual "Burning Man" festival in Nevada:

> More than 15,000 people are expected to attend the esoteric mix of pagan fire ritual and sci-fi Dada circus where some paint their bodies, bang drums, dance naked and wear costumes that would draw stares at a Mardi Gras parade.

Again, from Lee Gomes of the *San Jose Mercury News,* December 21, 1991, on whimsical screen saver designs:

> Some are practical—you can float the company logo or a message to a colleague. Some are meant to be eye-catching. . . . And some are downright Dadaesque, like the winged flying toasters that have become Berkeley System's unofficial mascots.

And by Michael Hirschorn in *Spy,* February 1989, "Mr. Stupid Goes to Washington," on Spy's list of the ten dumbest members of Congress:

[Congressman Joseph] Kennedy unscripted is hopped-up gibberish, an almost dadaist assortment of sentence fragments, expletives and exaggerated bonhomie. . . .

Daliesque \ˌdä-lē-'esk\ In the style of surrealist Spanish artist Salvador Dali (1904–1989), and thus characterized by fantastic or incongruous imagery through unnatural and unusual combination and settings.

Dali was a painter and etcher, and experimented with many styles (including "bulletism"—in which a 16th–century blunderbuss is loaded with graphite and fired at an etching plate). He was influenced by Freud and his ideas about the role of dreams and the subconscious mind. His images were realistic but presented in dreamlike and irrationally bizarre settings. His most famous work is probably "The Persistence of Memory" (1931), a painting depicting drooping, melting clocks sagging over a barren landscape.

In an era of experimental silliness—this is the period of DADA, after all—Dali stood out. He had a great gift for self-promotion and a flair for creative stunts. With his flamboyant pointed mustache, his physical appearance contributed to his image.

The term in use, by Dan Rodricks in the *Baltimore Sun,* October 4, 1995:

> Hey, listen, I'm a collector of late-40s neckwear, owner of nearly 200 splashy numbers with palm trees and Daliesque motifs.

And by Mark Binelli, for the *Atlanta Journal and Constitution,* September 10, 1995, describing the Dolly Parton theme park Dollywood in Pigeon Forge, Tennessee:

> Or you can just bask in the loopy surrealism of all that is Dolly. Listen to her very own radio station—yes, WDLY. Spend her very own legal tender—yes, Dolly Dollars. . . . After a day in the park, the terms Dolly-esque and Dali-esque might start to become oddly interchangeable.

And by Denise Flaim in *Newsday,* October 6, 1996, describing her tour of the West:

> We started in the Dalmatian-spotted hills of New Mexico, snaked west to Arizona's much-hyped Grand Canyon, darted into Utah to hike the Dali-esque rock formations of Moab and window-shopped the Victorian storefronts of Durango, Colo.

Damascus *See* ROAD TO DAMASCUS.

Damocles *See* SWORD OF DAMOCLES.

Damon and Pythias \'dā-mən . . . 'pi-thē-əs\ A celebrated pair of friends in Greek legend who came to stand for the willingness to sacrifice oneself for the sake of a friend.

In the Greek legend of the 4th century B.C., Pythias was condemned to death by Dionysius, the ruler of their city (*see* SWORD OF DAMOCLES), but Damon pledged his life for that of his friend. So impressed was Diony-sus with the strength of their friendship that he pardoned them both.

The term in use, by Ross K. Baker, commenting on institutional dif-ferences between the House and Senate, in the *Philadelphia Inquirer,* Jan-uary 28, 1995:

> And even if Dole and Gingrich were as close as Damon and Pythias—which they surely are not—the built-in constitutional tensions will make themselves felt.

danegeld \\'dän-ˌgeld\\ *often capitalized* An annual tax believed imposed originally to buy off Danish invaders in England or to maintain forces to oppose them but continued as a land tax. The tax was levied at the end of the 10th century by King Ethelred (famed as Ethelred the Unready). The idea probably was to use the funds to buy off the Danes, who were attacking England and establishing settlements; the term has been used ever since to describe political blackmail or an appeasement policy. And it didn't work: Ethelred bolted for Normandy in 1013, and the English acknowledged the Danish king, Sven, as king. His son CANUTE became king in 1017, altogether an improvement. Canute continued to collect the tax and apply it to defense. Later kings continued to collect it for use as they saw fit.

As Rudyard Kipling wrote in his poem "Dane-Geld":

> It is always a temptation to an armed and agile nation
> To call upon a neighbour and to say;—
> "We invaded you last night—we are quite prepared to fight,
> Unless you pay us cash to go away."

The term in use, by Richard Segall in the *Economist,* June 4, 1994, deploring policies allowing North Korea to become a nuclear power:

> The Danegeld option is even more desperate. This holds that a large enough collection of inducements . . . might persuade Kim Il Sung to give up his bomb-making plans.

Dangerfield, Rodney Pop-eyed BORSCHT BELT comedian whose SHTICK is the lament "I don't get no respect." It has turned his name into a code word for someone who is—justly or unjustly—not respected.

The term in use, by *Washington Post* columnist Colbert I. King, blast-ing Washington, D.C.'s mayor and council for taking a vacation in the middle of budget deliberations, July 19, 1997:

> Barry and the council's disappearing act gives legitimacy to the low regard Congress has for them. Explaining his reason for abandoning the city . . . Barry offered the lame excuse, "I don't have any influence on this debate at all." Rodney Dangerfield couldn't have said it any better!

And from Jim Murray, in the *Los Angeles Times,* June 20, 1996, on much-traveled baseball player Rex Allen Hudler:

He'd be the Rodney Dangerfield of major league baseball—
except that, compared to him, Rodney Dangerfield would be the
Rose Parade marshal.

And again, a quote in *Money,* April 1, 1997, about Chase Manhattan:

> "It's my favorite stock because it's trading at a 20% discount to
> the average bank stock," says analyst George Salem at Gerard
> Klauer & Mattison in New York City. "Chase is the Rodney Dan-
> gerfield of bank stocks," he adds. "It don't get no respect."

Dantesque \\'dän-'tesk, 'dan-\\ Characteristic of or resembling the work of
the great poet Dante Aligheri (1265–1321)—in particular his masterpiece
The Divine Comedy, in which the poet is conducted through the intrica-
cies of Hell, Purgatory, and Paradise. Dante's picture of Hell *(The Inferno)* is the most famous section. Over the door is written the legend:
"Abandon All Hope Ye Who Enter Here." Hell has several levels, to which
sinners are assigned according to their transgressions. Those in the lowest circles are the worst—frauds, thieves, hypocrites, and traitors.
  The term in use, by Jay Carr in the *Boston Globe,* June 5, 1992, on Federico Fellini's film *La Dolce Vita:*

> On the surface it's autobiographical, as Fellini sends his favorite
> surrogate, Marcello Mastroianni, tumbling through a sybaritic
> Rome in Dantesque fashion.

And by James R. Bean, reviewing Sherwin B. Nuland's book *The Wisdom of the Body* in the *Lexington (Ky.) Herald-Leader,* May 4, 1997:

> This book is written like a Dantesque journey through the human
> body's intricate anatomy (structures) and physiology (function-
> ing), a literary and scientific Fantastic Voyage to the human's
> inner recesses and thoroughfares.

dark night of the soul A state of hopelessness and despair. The phrase
comes from the writings of St. John of the Cross (1542-1591). He was an
originator of Christian mysticism, a process of becoming closer to God
in which visions and voices come into play. Part of that process was a
period in which the individual finds himself utterly alone—without God
or hope or even the ability to pray. "Dark Night of the Soul" was the title
of one his poems describing this state. Eventually, the soul achieves spiritual union with God.
  The term in use, by Anthony Burgess in the *New York Times Book Review,*
August 27, 1989, describing the life of Gerard Manley Hopkins:

> There was no compromise in his religion either. His family was
> heartbroken when he left Anglicanism and turned Roman
> Catholic. His fellow Jesuits didn't understand him. He knew the
> dark night of the soul.

And by Jim Holt in *Harper's,* November 1994, discussing theories of cosmology:

> Whether the existence of the world is a mysterium tremendum et fascinans or a mere tautology, it continues to exercise the imagination of philosophers and theologians, not to mention stoned undergraduates and insomniac yuppies having a Dark Night of the Soul.

And by Craig Offman, writing about the Clintons in *George,* October 1997:

> And when a dark night of the soul befell the first couple after the GOP's 1994 congressional victory, Williamson gave chin-up advice at Camp David.

dark satanic mills English poet William Blake's phrase evoking the ugly, dispiriting working conditions in the mills of the Industrial Revolution—crowded, poorly lit, cruel, dirty, dangerous places. The phrase, from an 1804 poem, has become shorthand for the hellish harshness of industrialization in any era.

The term in use, by James Atlas in *Travel & Leisure,* April 1, 1996:

> I got in my rental car and tuned the radio to 98.7, WFMT, "Chicago's fine arts station." . . . I loved the distinction between the highest achievements known to man—Joan Sutherland in *The Magic Flute,* followed by the Stuttgart Symphony . . . and the dark satanic mills of Chicagoland spreading out from the highway on both sides: factories, bungalows, drive-in restaurants with their garish signs ablaze in the smoky light.

And by Sandra Gilbert in the *New York Times Book Review,* May 4, 1986:

> "Life in the Iron Mills" [is] Rebecca Harding Davis's superb narrative of working-class life in the dark satanic mills flung up by America's Industrial Revolution.

D'Artagnan \där-'tan-yən\ A protagonist of *The Three Musketeers* by Alexandre Dumas *père,* and a thoroughly gallant, swashbuckling character.

The bold novel tells the exploits of four heroic friends in the service of king Louis XIV—and especially his queen—of France in the mid–17th century.

D'Artagnan is based on a real hero of the time, Charles de Baatz de Castlemore (1623–1673), but Dumas's account of the young hero must be regarded as primarily fiction.

The term in use, by Chris Kaltenbach in the *Baltimore Sun,* October 22, 1995:

> Lewis Shaw knows swords. Like the one he's twirling in his hand right now, a rather plain number with a black wire-wrap grip. It

looks sturdy but unspectacular—until Mr. Shaw slashes the air with it a few times, looking for all the world like a 20th-century D'Artagnan, complete with wire-rimmed glasses and curly blond hair.

Darth Vader An arch-villain or ANTICHRIST; someone of dark and sinister appearance, the personification of evil.

This memorable character, a renegade knight who serves the forces of darkness, was created by George Lucas in his *Star Wars* trilogy of films in the late 1970s and early 1980s. Darth Vader, like Satan, is a fallen angel in science fiction mode. He is deliciously sinister, with his great stature, black armor and cape, and rich, velvet voice with a mysterious mechanical wheeze.

The term in use, by Sarah Lyall in the *New York Times,* May 4, 1997, describing the cast of characters in a documentary about the Royal Opera House of London's Covent Garden:

> And backstage, Keith Cooper, the company's new, Darth Vader-like public-affairs director, fumes that the box-office manager, Andrew Follen, "has neither the seniority nor the intelligence" for the job—and promptly dismisses him, as the camera watches from a decorous distance.

And by Ralph Nader, quoted in the *Progressive,* October 1, 1995:

> "These Republican governors are the Darth Vaders of the contemporary political scene—they are slick, they are cruel, and they are bought," says consumer advocate Ralph Nader.

And by Peter Grier, the *Christian Science Monitor,* March 20, 1996:

> They're the Darth Vaders of downsizing, corporate hit men in black hats, merchants of greed who slash jobs by the thousands while pocketing millions in take-home pay.

David and Goliath An underdog opposing and defeating a giant.

The Biblical story of David in I Samuel 17 places the story during the wars between the PHILISTINES and Israel. Goliath of Gath was a gigantic warrior of the Philistine army—ten feet tall. When no one else would answer Goliath's challenge to single combat, the youth David stepped forward, without armor and with a slingshot as his only weapon. He hit the giant in the forehead with a stone from his sling, and killed him. David went on to become king of Israel.

The story has been a comfort to underdogs ever since.

The term in use, by columnist Molly Ivins, in the *Houston Chronicle,* April 15, 1996, commenting on upsets in the Texas primary:

> In the Ron Paul-Greg Laughlin brawl for the GOP slot in the 14th Congressional District race, I claim a real victory for the people. Paul may be a formerly Libertarian weirdo (take no

offense, Libertarians, that is not a redundancy), but Laughlin was surely the Establishment Goliath.

And by Norman Hildes-Heim, in the *New York Times,* July 7, 1997:

> British crews won 12 of the 16 cup finals at this year's Henley Royal Regatta in Henley-on-Thames, England yesterday, and the most memorable was Britain's 12-inch upset of the University of Washington in a David-and-Goliath Ladies Challenge Plate race.

day of infamy Moment of supreme disgrace or evil. A reference to December 7, 1941, and the Japanese surprise attack on Pearl Harbor.

The phrase comes from President Franklin D. Roosevelt's speech to Congress asking for a declaration of war after the attack: "Yesterday, December 7, 1941—a date which will live in infamy—the United States of America was suddenly and deliberately attacked by naval and air forces of the Empire of Japan."

The attack, at 7:55 a.m., with a second wave of bombers an hour later, caught America with its guard down. Most U.S. planes on the Hawaiian island of Oahu were destroyed; eight battleships, three destroyers, and three cruisers were put out of action; two more battleships were damaged; 2,323 U.S. servicemen were killed. With only one vote in opposition, Congress gave Roosevelt what he sought.

The term in use, by Mike DiGiovanna in the *Los Angeles Times,* September 15, 1996:

> But despite suffering one of the worst collapses in baseball history late last season, Angel first baseman J.T. Snow finds himself pining for those days of infamy.

And by Georgia State Representative Billy McKinney, an African-American in Congress, quoted on July 17, 1996, after a Supreme Court ruling that Georgia had unconstitutionally used race as a factor in drawing a Congressional district:

> I think it's a day of infamy for us, for black people in the South. . . . I'm saying that four racist white people and one Uncle Tom [on the Supreme Court] made this decision.

dead man's hand Really rotten luck; a sign of unforeseen and unintended disaster.

The phrase refers to the poker hand held by Wild Bill Hickok at the moment he was shot in the back by Jack McCall in Deadwood, South Dakota, on August 2, 1876. There is some controversy about the cards Hickok was holding, but they are thought to have been black aces and black eights, two pairs, and the combination became known as the "dead man's hand." Another version has it as two jacks and two eights.

The term in use, by Mickey Spillane (yes, really) in *Men's Health* (yes, really), January 1, 1996:

Sometimes, the big-ticket items you buy can reach up and grab you around the throat like a dope-crazed fiend in a blind alley. Choosing a house can be like that. . . . Nothing's worse than getting dealt a dead man's hand when you're not even sitting at the table. Take me, 1989. Hurricane Hugo. . . . I go back to where my house was. Hugo got it and tossed it into a Mixmaster.

And by Ron Borges of the *Boston Globe,* glooming about the New England Patriots football team, December 10, 1984:

From their inception, it seems, the Patriots have held the Dead Man's Hand, and never was that truer than yesterday when they played like cadavers and ended up resembling one after losing to the Philadelphia Eagles. . . .

death by a thousand cuts A slow death by the torture of many small wounds, none lethal in itself, but fatal in their cumulative effect.

This torture was a form of execution in ancient China, reserved for the most heinous crimes. The more literal translation from the Chinese is "one thousand knives and ten thousand pieces," the scariest possible description, designed to deter criminals.

The term quoted in the *Baltimore Sun,* August 2, 1994:

But Mr. Alexander said he was troubled that the controversy was a "newspaper-driven phenomenon" in which Ms. Stansel and Chavis' opponents were using the sexual-harassment charge to subject the 46-year-old director to the "death of a thousand cuts."

And by David Barton, the *Sacramento Bee,* January 9, 1996:

A broken car window, a spray-painted garbage can, a defaced wall—all part of the vandals' bill of goods—may not be seen as serious crimes, but their overwhelming effect is "death by a thousand cuts," each tiny indignity piling on each small, inconveniencing mess until the resentment and sense of violation are almost overwhelming.

deep six A place of disposal or abandonment—used especially in the phrase "give it the deep six," meaning get rid of it completely: it's hot, it's dangerous, or it's incriminating. In naval slang, the phrase means to toss something overboard. One theory says it is inspired by U.S. Navy regulations requiring that burial sites at sea be at least 100 fathoms, or 600 feet, down.

As a verb it attained fame and a political tinge in the Watergate era. Former White House counsel John Dean III told the Senate Watergate Committee on June 25, 1973, that his former colleague John Ehrlichman had advised him to "deep six" a briefcase found in the White House safe of Watergate burglar E. Howard Hunt Jr. Testified Dean:

I asked him what he meant by "deep six." He leaned back in his chair and said: "You cross the [Potomac] river at night, don't you? Well, when you cross over the river on your way home, just toss the briefcase into the river."

The term in use, by Sherry Bebitch Jeffe in a *Los Angeles Times* editorial, September 29, 1996:

[Gov. Pete] Wilson's action could help establish his bona fides for 2000—if he could brag about making California the "first state in the nation" to deep six the highly unpopular welfare system.

And from a movie listing in *TV Guide,* December 30, 1995:

"Better off Dead." (1985) Uneven comedy about a lovesick teenager (John Cusack) who is mortified when his friend deep-sixes him for someone more popular.

Defarge, Madame \di-'färzh\ A character in Charles Dickens' 1859 novel of the French Revolution, *A Tale of Two Cities.* A symbol of vengefulness and revolutionary excess. She sits outside her Paris wine shop endlessly knitting a scarf that is, in effect, a list of those to be killed; she incorporates in the scarf's pattern the names of hated aristocrats who are soon guillotined. Her revolutionary zealotry was so intense that her name became a synonym for the type.

Mme. Defarge is an implacable and merciless fanatic for the Revolution. "Tell Wind and Fire where to stop," says she, "but don't tell me."

She is a fictional example of the famous "tricoteuses," or knitters—Parisian women who attended revolutionary meetings and urged the crowds on to greater bloodshed, knitting all the while.

The term in use, by Nat Hentoff, in the *Village Voice,* March 13, 1990:

In the Madame Defarge stage of the Red Scare (guillotine first, proof of guilt afterwards), the press in the 1950s did a great deal to start the flames reaching toward the heretics at the stake.

And by columnist Christopher Matthews in the *Detroit Free Press,* January 12, 1995, on Democrats in the House of Representatives rallying after losing their majority in the 1994 elections:

David Bonior, Madame Defarge's bearded Michigan cousin, was the first to fight. Learning four days before Christmas that speaker-to-be Newt Gingrich was about to grab a $4.5-million book advance, the Democratic whip pounced.

defenestration \(ˌ)dē-ˌfe-nə-'strā-shən\ The act of throwing a person or a thing out a window. Today the word has come to be applied to any sudden and involuntary ejection from high office or prominent position.

A famous example, known as the Defenestration of Prague, occurred in Bohemia in 1618 and was one of the aggravating elements leading to the Thirty Years' War. Bohemia was under the rule of the Hapsburgs, and discontent was widespread. In a fracas with a group of local citizens, two representatives of the government were thrown out of a window of Prague Castle. They fell 50 feet to the moat but weren't seriously hurt and managed to escape with their lives.

Defenestrations are "something of a Prague specialty," says David Binder, a *New York Times* reporter, old Czechoslovakia hand, and our source on this subject. Binder says there was an earlier case in 1419, in which a mob of Hussites (followers of church reformer Jan Hus, who was burned at the stake in 1415) stormed the Prague City Hall after someone from inside threw a stone at a peaceful demonstration. Once inside, the Hussites grabbed members of the city council and tossed them out the window. The mob outside killed them.

In the modern era, Jan Masaryk, the foreign minister of post-World War II democratic Czechoslovakia, died in Prague on March 10, 1948, in a fall from his office window shortly after the Communist coup in his country. His death was explained as a suicide, but the circumstances remain mysterious to this day.

The term in use, by columnist Nat Hentoff in the *Washington Post,* September 10, 1997, on his son's college newspaper experience with "language correctness":

> He was being pressured by his staff to mandate that the term "freshperson" be used henceforth to identify all incoming students. "Freshman" would be tossed into the dustbin of sexist history. "Freshwoman" would also somehow be discriminatory.
>
> Tom, even at the risk of defenestration, would not be moved, insisting that language should not be politicized.

And from Jane Bryant Quinn in *Newsweek,* June 15, 1992:

> The number of early retirees is huge.... Growing numbers of younger men are also on the beach, thanks to the mass defenestration of middle management.

déjà vu \ˌdā-zhä-ˈvü\ The illusion of remembering scenes and events when experienced for the first time. Among medical professionals this condition is also referred to as *paramnesia. Déjà vu* can also refer to a feeling that one has seen or heard something before or to something overly or unpleasantly familiar. It's French for "already seen."

Yogi Berra, beloved for his MALAPROPISMS, is said to have exclaimed, "It's déjà vu all over again!"

The phrase is commonly used when history repeats itself, as in this example from a New England Patriots football player after his team's defeat by the Buffalo Bills, quoted by the *Boston Globe,* October 24, 1988:

> "Déjà vu," sighed offensive tackle Bruce Armstrong. After watching the Bills' Scott Norwood beat New England for the second time this season with a last-minute field goal.

The term in use, closer to its dictionary definition, by singer Judy Collins, quoted by Robert Greenman, *Words That Make A Difference* (1983):

"Send in the Clowns" was two years old when I first heard it, Miss Collins recalls, and Sinatra had already recorded it. But as soon as I heard it, I knew it belonged to me. I have that feeling of déjà vu sometimes about a song. It's almost as though I knew it from another life.

Delphic *often not capitalized* Ambiguous, obscure; sometimes double-edged in meaning.

In ancient Greece, the oracle at Delphi made pronouncements that were so obscure or vague that more than one interpretation was possible. So "delphic" has come to describe statements that are ambiguous or enigmatic, real head-scratchers.

The term in use, by Tom Mathews in *Newsweek,* April 29, 1991:

Encouraged, Galbraith then tried to score a meeting at the National Security Council, too. With delphic evasiveness, a top Mideast hand told him, "Our policy is not to overthrow the regime, it's to get rid of Saddam Hussein." And when the hapless Kurds arrived at the State Department, Schifter was "regrettably" busy.

Another example, from the *Economist,* March 4, 1989:

For umpteen years everyone has known that Israel possesses nuclear weapons. For umpteen years Israel has denied it, intoning instead its Delphic promise to be neither the first country, nor the second, to introduce nuclear weapons to the Middle East.

desert air *See* WASTE ITS SWEETNESS ON THE DESERT AIR.

deus ex machina \'dā-əs-ˌeks-'mä-ki-nə, -'ma-, -ˌnä; -mə-'shē-nə\ A person or thing (as in fiction or drama) that appears or is introduced suddenly and unexpectedly and provides a contrived solution to an apparently insoluble difficulty.

Literally the phrase means "a god from a machine," and it refers to a god of classical Greek drama who was lowered onto the stage by means of a crane, the machine, to sort out the insoluble dramatic problem.

The term in use, by columnist Richard Cohen, reflecting on Watergate in the *Washington Post,* May 3, 1992:

It was an extraordinary event, a scandal caused by a truly corrupt and mendacious president. Whoever Deep Throat is, he cannot be the deus ex machina of the Nixon era, the person who speaks for the forces that toppled a president, when those "forces" were the crimes and lies of Richard Nixon himself.

And from Molly Haskell, writing in the *New York Times Magazine,* September 24, 1989, about her husband's driving:

These are perfectly normal, everyday, garden-variety accidents, the responsibility for which is legally and quite plainly his, but which he must dramatize by invoking a *deus ex machina* to exonerate the dummy in the machine.

diaspora \dī-'as-p(ə-)rə, dē-\ The breaking up and scattering of people, whether by conquest, migration, or forced removal.

That is its general meaning. Capitalized, the word refers to the dispersal of the Jews from Palestine following the BABYLONIAN CAPTIVITY and the unsuccessful Jewish revolts against Roman rule, or to the Jews living in countries other than Israel.

The term in use, by Jay Mathews in the *Washington Post Book World,* April 14, 1996, reviewing *East to America: Korean American Life Stories* by Elaine H. Kim and Eui-Young Yu:

> The Korean diaspora, sadly made newsworthy by the 1992 Los Angeles riots, emerges here as no Up-With-America fairy tale, despite the misplaced inclination of Americans like me to make it so.

And by E.J. Dionne Jr. in the *Washington Post Magazine,* October 12, 1997, pondering Wisconsin cheesehead culture:

> A band named Johnny Belmont and the Fabulous Cheeseheads . . . proudly advertises itself as "one of the only bands in Door County without an accordion." Johnny and his friends hail from Chicago, and are thus part of the Cheesehead diaspora.

Dickensian Characteristic of or similar to the writing of novelist Charles Dickens (1812–1870)—with humor and pathos in the portrayal of odd, often extravagant and picturesque character types usually from the lower strata of 19th–century English society.

Dickens, one of the great English novelists of the Victorian age, wrote books noted for their implicit social commentary. Through his eyes we see the misery of the London slums, the harsh life of workers in the mills, the evils of child labor, the nonsensical and maddening toils of the law. His novels are filled with a multitude of characters remarkable in appearance or speech or personality—some notable for their kindness and virtue, others even more for shocking cruelty, often cloaked in pious statements of morality. The names of his villains are wonderfully suggestive: HEEP, Squeers, Merdstone, Bounderby.

The term in use, by Luaine Lee in the *Detroit News,* December 20, 1996, in a profile of actor Daniel Day Lewis:

> At first acting was a way of escaping what he considered a Dickensian existence. "I discovered it when I wasn't happy at all," he says. "I was at boarding school, and it seemed to me like a very grim place to be."

By Glenn Lovell in the *San Jose Mercury News,* reviewing the film *Murder in the First,* January 20, 1995:

There has been a lot of talk lately about the Dickensian conditions of our maximum-security prisons, about how these penal
institutions do more to create criminals than rehabilitate them.

And by Joe Klein in *Newsweek,* December 6, 1993:

As for the rest of the country—well, have you come across anyone who wasn't rooting for the flight attendants? Such nice
cheery rebels! By contrast, management appeared Dickensian.
Robert Crandall, a perfect road-company Uriah HEEP, had lost
his airline a lot of money by cutting fares unduly and was trying
to make some of it back by squeezing the workers.

die is cast, the Chance has determined the outcome; the choice of action
is irrevocable. There's no turning back now.

The phrase comes from gambling with dice (one of a pair of dice is a
die). Once the dice are thrown, the cast can't be taken back or changed,
and the thrower must live with the results.

The statement (in Latin, "Jacta alea est") is attributed to Julius Caesar
in 49 B.C. as he crossed the Rubicon with his army, an act regarded by
the Roman Senate as an act of war. The act eventually made Caesar emper-
or. As Plutarch put it in his *Lives:*

Using the proverb frequently in their mouths who enter upon
dangerous and bold attempts, "The die is cast," he took the river.

Shakespeare used the phrase also in *Richard III,* (1592) in Act 4, Scene
4: "I have set my life upon the cast/And I will stand the hazard of the die."

The term in use, by Mary McCarthy, in the *New York Review of Books,*
January 25, 1973, in a review of David Halberstam's book on the Vietnam
war, *The Best and the Brightest:*

His [Halberstam's] determination to view Vietnam as an American tragedy means that the outcome is ineluctable, foreordained
(cf. the "would's" and "were to be's"), and that all those Rubi-
cons should be invisible to the participants; nobody ever says,
"Well, the die is cast."

Another example, by Jean Marbella, in the *Los Angeles Times,* November 12, 1989, writing on gender differences in human beings:

The genetic die is cast at conception, but it takes a couple of
months before the net result becomes apparent.

Dien Bien Phu \͵dyen-͵byen-ˈfü\ The fortified site of a disastrous military
defeat, the result of willful, arrogant miscalculation.

Dien Bien Phu was a French military outpost in northern Indochina
before the French colony became independent North Vietnam. In 1954
the garrison was besieged for 55 days by the Vietminh, the communist
guerrilla army led by Vo Nguyen Giap. The French troops surrendered
in May 1954.

French military strategists had devised what they thought was a trap to bring the elusive Vietminh into the open for a European-style battle in which superior French technology would destroy a primitive guerrilla force. The French established their position in a valley and left the high ground to the Vietminh in the serene conviction that the guerillas had no artillery, and if they did, they would not know how to use it. Both assumptions were false, and the French suffered the consequences.

The term in use, by Charles Paul Freund in the *New Republic,* January 25, 1988:

> However long the siege of Khost lasts, Afghan rebels have won an important battle, a psychological Dien Bien Phu.

different drummer *See* MARCH TO THE BEAT OF A DIFFERENT DRUMMER.

dine out on To use as a subject of conversation, as if at a dinner table. Making conversation with a late-night television host on an airplane, for example, could give one something to dine out on for years to come.

The term in use, by Christopher Corbett, reviewing a biography of H.L. Mencken in Mencken's own *Baltimore Sun,* May 1, 1994:

> *The Sun* and *Evening Sun,* having dined out on Mencken's legacy for most of this century, turned on him, denouncing the most influential journalist of the 20th century as a wicked sinner.

And by G. Gordon Liddy in the *New York Times Book Review,* August 22, 1993:

> It may seem a bit early, but why not revisit the cold war? After all, successful authors have been dining out on World War II for half a century and, if memory serves, they didn't wait long to start.

Diogenes \dī-'ä-jə-₁nēz\ Greek philosopher (ca. 412–320 B.C.) and founder of the Cynics, a school of philosophers advocating asceticism, self-sufficiency, and moral zeal. In legend he went about with a lantern in broad daylight, searching for an honest man. A modern-day Diogenes searches for honesty and truth.

As a Cynic, Diogenes believed that true happiness was to be found through virtue, self-control, and independence. Only later did cynicism take on the sense of contemptuous distrust of human nature and motives.

True to his belief that the virtuous life was the simple life, Diogenes, it is said, lived in a tub. He was also capable of nervy put-downs: Alexander the Great, a great admirer, asked if he could do anything for the philosopher. "Yes," said Diogenes, shaded by the conqueror, "move out of my sunshine."

The term in use, by William F. Buckley, in the *National Review,* February 3, 1992:

> I hereby summon a joint session of the Democratic and Republican National Committees, and I give them this mandate.

Deputize someone, an anti-Diogenes, to go out in search of the man so dishonest as to pronounce current capital-gains tax policy as defensible.

And from George Will in his syndicated column of May 9, 1986:

Epstein, editor of the *American Scholar,* says the virtucrat is "a modern Diogenes who, in search of one good man, knocked off after turning his lantern on himself." Epstein says that "anti-war" and "pro-life" are labels of virtucratic self-advertising, announcing that the holder of the particular political view is large-hearted and great-souled. . . .

Dionysian \ˌdī-ə-'ni-zhən, -'ni-shən, -'nī-sē-ən\ Being of a frenzied or orgiastic character. An adjective taken from the name of Dionysus, the Greek god of wine and fertile crops (or Bacchus, the name of his Roman counterpart) (*see* BACCHANAL). According to mythology, Dionysus invented wine and encouraged cultivation of grapes. He was worshiped at festivals celebrating the return of spring. Greek drama, tragic and comic, is thought to have originated in the ceremonies performed in the god's honor.

The frenzied worship of the followers of Dionysus could take frightening turns: in Euripides' play *The Bacchae* (408–406 B.C.), the king of Thebes is killed, torn to pieces by his own mother and aunts during the rites. In Rome, the festivals (Bacchanalia) were notable for their drunkenness and generally uninhibited behavior. So today Dionysian or bacchic orgies are wild, licentious, drunken parties.

The term in use, by Lance Morrow in *Time* magazine, January 11, 1988, looking back on the year 1968:

In the great collision of generations, the young created their own world, a "counterculture," as historian Theodore Roszak first called it, and endowed it with the significances and pseudo-profundities of a New World. No one had ever had sex before, no one had ever had the Dionysian music, the sacramental drugs, the world struggling back to its protomagical state.

Another example, also characterizing this period, from culture critic Camille Paglia, in *Mother Jones,* January 11, 1996:

The Dionysian '60s went too far against the Apollonian '50s and so we've swung back again. Our ideals were too simplistic for political realities and we got out of touch, which made Republicans become the voice of the people.

Dirty Harry A tough guy who tends to overreact in stressful situations, never hesitating to break the rules.

Dirty Harry is a murderous, free-lancing fictional cop, the eponymous hero of a 1971 action movie directed by the masterful Don Siegel starring iconic, laconic Clint Eastwood. The film struck a chord, or perhaps a national revenge fantasy, and spawned a series of successful sequels. In one of those sequels, *Sudden Impact,* Dirty Harry's terse threat to a slimy punk, delivered from behind his .44 magnum—"Go ahead, make my day"—made the crossover to politics in a Ronald Reagan speech to a group of business leaders in which he dared the Democratic Congress to send him a bill increasing taxes.

Spoke the President:

> Let them be forewarned. No matter how well-intentioned they might be and what their reasons might be, I have my veto pen drawn and ready for any tax increase that Congress might even think of sending up, and I have only one thing to say to the tax increasers: "Go ahead, make my day."

The term in use, by Francis X. Clines in the *New York Times,* December 20, 1996, describing Clinton aide Harold M. Ickes:

> Raspy-edged in strategem and speech, he played a blue-eyed Dirty Harry kind of character in the White House inner sanctum.

Another example, from Richard Cohen, the *Washington Post Magazine,* April 27, 1997:

> He [Mark Fuhrman] participated in his own stereotyping: He told Laura Hart McKinney, with whom he was developing a screenplay, that he was a foul-mouthed racist, a nitro-violent and Dirty Harryish brute who beat on perps and hated black people.

discontent *See* WINTER OF OUR DISCONTENT.

disinformation False information deliberately, often covertly, spread (as by planted rumors) to influence public opinion or obscure the truth. The term became popular in the Cold War. The word also occurs in Russian, *dezinformatsiya,* part of the title of a special branch of the Soviet secret service. It describes misinformation spread for political motives or to characterize what the opposition on an issue is saying.

During the Cold War, the United States frequently accused the Soviet Union of planting disinformation in the press of Third World countries to spur anti-American sentiment. For example, the Soviets circulated stories that accused the Pentagon of creating the AIDS virus. But the United States also used the technique, and in some cases such plants by American agents abroad have been picked up by American reporters. Such stories reported back to the United States as fact were referred to as "blowback."

The term in use, in a *Christian Science Monitor* editorial, August 15, 1997, about the hazards of information on the Internet:

> CASSANDRAS have long warned that the Net and its key, the Web, are well named. For all its wonderful near-instantaneous access

to useful information, skeptics say, the Net/Web can also entangle browsers in misinformation, and even disinformation.

Another example, in a case in which the American government planted stories abroad that U.S. military action was imminent against Libyan leader Gadhafi. As described by Bob Woodward in the *Washington Post,* October 5, 1986:

> A former CIA officer said that the agency normally undertakes small, low-level disinformation campaigns in a few countries or a single country. But in the current anti-Gadhafi plan, the former officer said, "the fire of disinformation was supposed to sweep across the Middle East and Europe . . . and no one was supposed to notice? They were kidding themselves."

dismal science Economics. The expression was coined by Thomas Carlyle (1795–1881). Economics is the study of the distribution of resources in response to demand, and it often seems to be the study of shortages in the face of demand. In Carlyle's era, English economists David Ricardo and Thomas Malthus both held particularly pessimistic views on the ability of food production to keep pace with population growth. (*See* MALTHUSIAN.) This gloomy outlook undoubtedly inspired Carlyle's coinage.

Carlyle was born in Scotland and wrote a number of histories, essays and commentaries, the best-known being *The French Revolution.* (*See* WHIFF OF GRAPESHOT.) He distrusted democracy and was skeptical of the reform movements of his day. He was an advocate of the "great man" theory of history: "The history of the world is but the biography of great men." Carlyle is also famous for his biting style and striking figures of speech.

The term in use, in the *Economist,* March 14-20, 1987:

> It is that, in 1981, a new president [Ronald Reagan] decreed that Americans should keep about 5% more of their incomes than they had been doing. Being a kindly man, he forgot two rules of the dismal science: increase pay after productivity has increased, not before; and never cut taxes merely on the hope rather than the reality of expenditure cuts.

And by Michael Lewis in the *New Republic,* October 14, 1996:

> It is as if [vice presidential candidate Jack] Kemp chose his economic theory not by its plausibility but by his ability to sell it in a language he speaks. ("Did you ever see anybody so enthusiastic about capitalism?" he shouts to the crowds.) In Kemp's hands economics ceases to be the dismal science, concerned with allocating scarce means to alternative ends and becomes . . . football!

And by Daniel Kadlec in *Time,* June 2, 1997:

> As bash fodder, economists are right there with lawyers, politicians and stockbrokers. Economists predicted nine of the last

five recessions, remember? Studies show they have less than a 50% success rate predicting whether interest rates will go up or down. That's dismal science, all right.

Disraeli, Benjamin \diz-'rā-lē\ A British statesman and novelist who championed expansion of the Empire. He lived from 1804 to 1881 and twice served as prime minister (1868, 1874–80). His nickname was Dizzy.

He was of Italian-Jewish descent, but his father's quarrel with a synagogue led to Benjamin's baptism as a Christian—making his political career possible, since Jews were excluded from Parliament until 1858. (This brings to mind a Disraeli riposte to a slur by Daniel O'Connell in 1835: "Yes, I am a Jew, and when the ancestors of the right honorable gentleman were brutal savages in an unknown island, mine were priests in the temple of Solomon.")

As the author of flamboyant novels, Disraeli cut quite a figure in London society with his extravagant dress and affected manners. His first four attempts to win a seat in Parliament failed, but he was finally elected as a Tory. His unconventional style and appearance were not popular with colleagues at first, but eventually he rose to positions of leadership; he became prime minister for the first time in 1868.

His rivalry with William Gladstone (*see* GLADSTONIAN), leader of the Liberal Party, defined the issues of the Victorian age. As James Morris put it in *Heaven's Command: An Imperial Progress* (1973):

> They might have been cast by some divine theatrical agency for their parts in the drama, so exactly suited were they to their roles. . . . They represented two complementary impulses in the British political genius: the idealistic impulse, which wished to make Britain the paragon of principle, [and] the urge for glory, which fed upon the exotic, the flamboyant, even the slightly shady.

Disraeli opted for the glory of imperial expansion. The English, he stated in 1872, had a choice: to be the subjects of an insular and comfortable England or of an empire that commanded the respect of the world. He charmed Queen Victoria and had her assume the title Empress of India, a title she relished.

Political columnist Mark Shields evokes Disraeli's shrewdness (and ability to turn a phrase) in his column in the *Washington Post,* June 27, 1988:

> These candidate chronicles recall Benjamin Disraeli's formulation concerning the two requisites for political leadership: That a man . . . know himself and that he also know his times. Four years ago, the Democratic presidential contest between Gary Hart and Walter Mondale, according to analyst Alan Baron, pitted one candidate who completely understood the times but didn't know how old he was against another who knew himself thoroughly but thought 1984 was 1936. This year, the question is, do Michael Dukakis and George Bush pass the Disraeli test?

And by Michael Lind in the *New Republic,* August 21, 1995:

> In 1871, Benjamin Disraeli told the House of Commons that inequality in Britain was grossly exaggerated. "The working classes are not paupers. . . . Their aggregate income is certainly greater than any other class."
>
> This year's Benjamin "Dizzy" Disraeli Award for Effrontery in Economics goes to Michael Novak. The neoconservative scholar recently argued in the *Wall Street Journal* that inequality of wealth in the United States is exaggerated by liberals who don't take into account "the publicly owned wealth that belongs to all Americans. . . . "

Doctors' Plot An elaborate but trumped-up attempt to accuse someone of nefarious conspiracy. The original involved the arrest in 1952 of nine prominent Soviet doctors on charges that they intended to murder high Soviet and Communist officials. It was a frame-up.

In January 1953, *Izvestia* reported that nine doctors had been arrested and charged with the poisoning deaths of two officials and the attempted murder of others. The doctors, at least six of whom were Jewish, were accused of working for American and British intelligence.

These arrests presaged another of Stalin's bloody purges, but he died on March 5, before the doctors could be tried. In April *Pravda* reported that the charges had been investigated and found to be false and that the doctors' confessions had been obtained through torture. The doctors were cleared and released, except for two who had died under interrogation.

In his secret speech before the 20th Party Congress three years later, Nikita Khrushchev accused Stalin of personally ordering the investigation of the doctors on spurious grounds.

The term in use, by Charles Paul Freund in the *New Republic,* June 6, 1988:

> [Reagan administration Attorney General Edwin] Meese's firing of Terry Eastland, lest Eastland quit first, has a sad Doctors' Plot air about it. Even the *Washington Times* thinks the Justice Department is going down the drain.

dog in the manger A person who selfishly withholds from others something useless to himself.

The expression comes from a fable about a dog who settled himself in a manger and would not let the ox eat the hay, even though the dog couldn't and wouldn't eat it himself.

The term in use, by commentator Thomas Sowell in the *Detroit News,* November 5, 1995, on complaints that the Internet is dominated by the English language:

> What does it mean to be "at a disadvantage"? No one is worse off than before the internet was developed and many are better

off. Is dog-in-manger resentment to be raised to the level of a guiding principle?

And by F. Scott Fitzgerald in a letter dated March 4, 1938:

> "Gatsby" was made into a movie with Warner Baxter in 1927. Clark Gable wants to do it, but Paramount is playing dog-in-the-manger about the rights.

Dogpatch A backwoods, backward place, completely naïve and utterly unsophisticated.

The original was the isolated community of hillbillies created by cartoonist Al Capp in his satirical comic strip "Li'l Abner." The residents lolled about with their pigs, distilled their potent liquor, and smoked their corncob pipes while coping with social climbers and frauds from the outside world. Capp's hero, Li'l Abner, had stupendous muscles but was childlike and innocent. Male characters were usually simple-minded and oblivious to women, while the women were statuesque, scantily clad, libidinous, and a lot smarter.

"Li'l Abner" ran from 1934 to 1977; Capp's targets ranged from his fellow cartoonists (he ruthlessly mocked "Dick Tracy" with the antics of Fearless Fosdick, a comic strip within a comic strip) to attacks on anti-Vietnam War activists. He created many characters and ideas that entered our language and culture, from the Shmoo to SADIE HAWKINS DAY. Other memorable creations were Joe Bftsplk, who went about with a permanent rain cloud over his head, and Lower Slobbovia.

The term in use, by *Arkansas Times* reporter Ernie Dumas on National Public Radio's *Weekend Edition,* March 24, 1996:

> [There] is the suggestion that Arkansas is somehow different from other states, that it's kind of an ethical dogpatch where government is run for the benefit of a very few people and they all scratch each others' back.

And by Lisa Riley Roche, in the *Deseret News,* August 4, 1996:

> Atlanta, the self-proclaimed capital of the New South, saw itself mocked in the media for turning the world's premier sporting event into a shabby street fair, a place where "Dogpatch meets the world."

More Atlanta bashing, by Steve Kelley, the *Seattle Times,* July 22, 1996:

> What do you get if you cross the infield of a NASCAR race with a flea market and a county fair? You get the host city of the Centennial Olympics. This is Dogpatch on STEROIDS. Atlanta should be drug tested.

dogs of war A figure of speech for the horrors of war, the phrase comes from Shakespeare's *Julius Caesar,* Act 3, Scene 1. Mark Antony is left alone with the body of Caesar. While he had controlled himself in the presence of Brutus and the other murderers, he now gives way to grief and rage for revenge: "O, pardon me, thou bleeding piece of earth, That I am meek and gentle with these butchers!" Then he prophesies bloody war for Rome:

> Cry 'Havoc!' and let slip the dogs of war,
> That this foul deed shall smell above the earth
> With carrion men, groaning for burial.

The term in use, by Marvin Hier and Abraham Cooper in *USA Today,* February 24, 1997, on revelations about uneven Swiss neutrality during World War II:

> Neutrality also meant cashing in on the dogs of war. The Swiss made it clear that only those few refugees who could pay their own way were welcome.

And again, by Madeleine Albright, then U.S. Ambassador to the United Nations, in a speech on the U.N., NATO, and crisis management, April 29, 1996:

> [F]or every mission there should be a plan not only of how to get in but of how to get out. . . . But an exit strategy alone is no strategy at all. There must also be a political strategy that will heal the wounds of war while the dogs of war are leashed.

The expression is applied also to mercenary soldiers, drawn from the popular Frederick Forsyth novel *The Dogs of War* (1974) and the movie based on it.

The term in use in Forsyth's sense, by Richard Meares, of Reuters, on "private sector war" in Africa, January 10, 1997:

> Mercenaries, private armies and security firms are today's armed helpers. You can find many of them in the Yellow Pages. Most are a far cry from the charismatic "dogs of war" such as "Mad" Mike Hoare who blustered into Africa to fight civil wars that followed independence in the 1960s.

dog that didn't bark, the A nonaction or nonevent which is significant precisely because it *didn't* happen.

The phrase comes from the most famous fictional detective in the world, Sir Arthur Conan Doyle's Sherlock HOLMES. In the story "Silver Blaze," a valuable racehorse is stolen from a well-guarded stable, which also had a watchdog. Holmes and Dr. Watson have this exchange:

> Watson: "Is there any point to which you wish to draw my attention?"
> Holmes: "To the curious incident of the dog in the night-time."
> Watson: "The dog did nothing in the night-time."
> Holmes: "That was the curious incident."

In other words, the dog, which should have barked, did not; the thief, therefore, was probably someone the dog knew.

The term in use, by Jonathan Alter in *Newsweek,* July 21, 1997, describing the efforts of major media companies to suppress unfavorable stories in the publications they own:

> So the story is quietly killed, or watered down to mush, or somehow never gets assigned in the first place. No fingerprints. But once in awhile, the dog barks. The suppressors are caught red-handed.

And by Ramesh Ponnuru in the *National Review,* in a guide to 1996 election issues, October 14, 1996:

> Affirmative action has been the dog that didn't bark in this campaign.

Don Juan \\'dän-(h)wän, *chiefly British & in poetry* dän-'jü-ən\\ A womanizer, a seducer, a libertine; a man who is irresistible to women (or thinks he is) and pursues them constantly.

The name is taken from the tale of Don Juan Tenorio, first appearing in a 1630 play by Tirso de Molina, *The Libertine of Seville and the Stone Guest,* and since then Don Juan has been the subject of numerous poems, operas and plays. According to legend, Don Juan was the son of an aristocratic family who killed the commandant of Ulloa after seducing his daughter. Don Juan tauntingly invites the statue of the murdered man to a feast; the statue comes to life, and drags him off to Hell.

The tale has inspired many great works, including Mozart's *Don Giovanni,* Lord Byron's *Don Juan* and George Bernard Shaw's *Man and Superman.*

The term in use, by Sam Walker in the *Christian Science Monitor,* August 28, 1995, on controversy over state and local tax benefits used to lure industry:

> Tax breaks are like roses to Don Juan—cities and states rely heavily on them to court new manufacturers.

And by Patricia McLaughlin in commentary in the *Kansas City Star,* August 8, 1993:

> [J]ust by promising transformation, the ad raises a seductive possibility, starts you thinking how nice it would be to be so cool. . . .
> It's one reason shopping for clothes is so exhausting. It's like going out with Don Juan: you have to be fighting off these enticing but totally empty promises every minute.

do not go gentle into that good night Don't give up or acquiesce, especially to death, without a struggle. The title and first line of a poem by Welshman Dylan Thomas (1914–53). Thomas attained fame for the beauty of his poetry and for the exuberance and pathos in his prose, as well as for his stormy domestic life and alcoholism. From the 1952 poem:

Do not go gentle into that good night,
Old age should burn and rave at close of day;
Rage, rage against the dying of the light.

The term in use, by Hugh A. Mulligan of the Associated Press, September 22, 1996, on the dilution of the tradition of the Irish wake:

The Irish do not go gentle into that good night. They revel against the dark.

And from Anne Scott, the *Des Moines Business Record,* June 24, 1996:

Moreover, the market for cosmetic surgery is expanding thanks to aging Baby Boomers. Nobody expected that the Boomers would go gentle into that good night, and they aren't.

And by Stephen Hunter, in the *Baltimore Sun,* April 2, 1995, writing about the 1969 film *The Wild Bunch:*

They go down with guns in their hands, under the impression that that's what's expected of them and that they had no choice; and, to put it mildly, they do not go gently into that good night.

Dooley, Mr. A fictional Irishman, a homely philosopher. Invented by American journalist and humorist Finley Peter Dunne (1867–1936) in the *Chicago Tribune,* Mr. Dooley presided over a small saloon on Chicago's West Side and offered biting commentary on the events and personalities of the day, from the Spanish-American War to World War I to the shams and hypocrisies of contemporary society.

As Gene Shalit notes in his 1988 humor anthology, *Laughing Matters,* "Dunne never could have jabbed the rich and powerful men and the mores of his time in his own voice—the *Tribune* would not have published it. But to have it from Mr. Dooley—who could take seriously anything said by an Irish bartender on Chicago's Archer Road? Everybody, that's who."

Samples of Mr. Dooley's drollness, in the Irish brogue Dunne gave him:

A man can be right an' prisident, but he can't be both at th' same time.
Histhry always vidicates th' Dimmycrats, but nivir in their lifetime. They see th' thruth first, but th' trouble is that nawthin' is iver officially thrue till a Raypublican sees it.

Dooley evoked, by Robert Kuttner in the *New Republic,* March 6, 1989, reviewing Brooks Jackson's book, *Honest Graft: Big Money and the American Political Process:*

This is a good tale, wise to the folkways of American politics, chock full of delightful anecdotes, and, in the spirit of Plunkitt of TAMMANY HALL and Finley Peter Dunne's Mr. Dooley, not without a storyteller's appreciation of a good rogue.

And by Godfrey Sperling, in commentary in the *Christian Science Monitor,* April 20, 1993:

> "Politics ain't beanbags," as Peter Finley Dunne's Mr. Dooley once commented. And what we're hearing from Clinton and Perot sounds like they both have put on their brass knuckles.

doppelgänger \\'dä-pəl-, gäīē-ər, -geīē-, ₁dä-pəl-'\\ A ghostly counterpart of a living person; a double or alter ego. A doppelgänger often represents the evil or unpleasant aspect of a person's nature. From the German words "doppel," meaning "double," and "gänger," meaning "walker."

The term in use, by Richard Brookhiser, in *Time,* December 11, 1989:

> A specter is haunting conservatives—the specter of the end of Communism. Our nightmare, our adversary, our dark doppelgänger for the past 40 years seems to be fading away.

Another example, from Kurt Anderson, profiling James Fallows in the *New Yorker* magazine, March 31, 1997:

> Nicholas Lemann is both Fallows's professional doppelgänger (Harvard *Crimson* president, *Washington Monthly* writer, *Atlantic* correspondent, author of important nonfiction books) and an old friend.

double helix A helix or spiral consisting of two strands in the surface of a cylinder that coil around its axis; especially the structural arrangement of DNA.

In scientific circles, the term describes the molecular shape of DNA, the building block of genes. The double helix structure was discovered by Francis Crick and James Watson in 1953, for which they received the Nobel Prize.

Helix comes from Greek via Latin and means "spiral." The shape of the double helix is usually described as similar to a spiral staircase.

The term in nonscientific use, by Robert Heilbruner in the *New York Times Book Review,* May 11, 1986:

> Here we begin to distinguish the public and private themes that become the double helix of Keynes's personality—the public Keynes, building on the traditions of his family and of Eton . . . and the private Keynes, emerging in passionate homosexual involvements. . . .

And by Luaine Lee, in a profile of actor Daniel Day-Lewis in the *Detroit News,* December 20, 1996:

> The 39-year-old Day-Lewis . . . is the son of England's former poet laureate C. Day-Lewis and actress Jane Balcon.
> The double helix of both sides is evident in the thin, dark, intense man.

doublespeak Language used to deceive usually through concealment or misrepresentation of truth; also gobbledygook. The word is a hybrid of *newspeak* and *doublethink,* two words from George Orwell's novel *Nineteen Eighty-four* (1949). Newspeak was the language created by the dictatorship, drained of historic meaning; doublethink was the ability to hold two conflicting ideas at the same time, a useful habit of thinking cultivated by BIG BROTHER, the Stalinesque dictator in Orwell's totalitarian vision.

The term *doublespeak* won national attention at the annual meeting of the National Council of Teachers of English in 1971, according to Walker Gibson, Professor Emeritus of the University of Massachusetts at Amherst, who was in attendance. There it was defined as "dishonest and inhumane uses of language" and was an outgrowth of concern expressed by delegates about a lack of candor by the U.S. government in communicating with Americans about the Vietnam War. Clearly this was a problem crying out for a descriptive name; *doublespeak* has since come into wide use. Sometimes it is attributed mistakenly to Orwell himself. (*See* -SPEAK.)

The term in use, by *Kiplinger's Personal Finance* magazine, quoted in the *Deseret News,* March 30, 1997, on the Social Security trust fund:

> The problem is that when accounting for bonds held by everyone else, the government calls it debt. The money owed the trust fund is called an asset because the government owes the money to itself. This political doublespeak doesn't affect the value of the trust fund, but it does disguise the true size of annual budget deficits.

And by Hugh Carter Donahue in *Commonweal,* July 14, 1995:

> The "privatization" of "public" broadcasting now being proposed in Congress is a concept worthy of ORWELLIAN doublespeak.

double whammy *See* WHAMMY.

down the rabbit hole Into a bizarre, surreal or strange situation, episode or series of events. The phrase is the heading of Chapter One of *Alice's Adventures in Wonderland,* the 1865 classic of Lewis Carroll. Alice's adventures begin when she follows the White Rabbit down a large rabbit hole, "never once considering how in the world she was to get out again."

She follows the hole like a tunnel for some way, and then suddenly falls down what seems like a very deep well, The descent is slow enough for her to see pictures, bookshelves and cupboards along the sides. After a long, slow drift downward she suddenly lands at the bottom and her peculiar adventures begin in earnest.

The term in use, by William Plummer in *People,* July 29, 1991:

> For 10 years, virtually since that night at Little Joe's when he fell down the rabbit hole of cocaine addiction, Steve Howe has been trying to regain the ground he held with the Dodgers in the early '80s, when he was one of the top relievers in the game.

And by James Ridgeway in the *Village Voice,* October 15, 1991:

> Like any investigative reporter disappearing down the rabbit hole of Iran-contra or the OCTOBER SURPRISE, Danny Casolaro had entered a world of shadowy grudges and wispy suspicions that are often difficult to follow, much less prove.

Also, from the *New York Times Book Review,* May 8, 1988, in a review of *What They Owed to the Scandal Sheets* by Justin Kaplan:

> He probes a strain of pre-Civil War popular literature and culture that he calls "subversive," as distinguished from the genteel, conventional and conformist. He shows the subversive to have been a nurturing subsoil for the major writers and, farther down the rabbit hole, an underworld of eroticism, bizarre fantasy and radical impulse that disturbed and darkened their imaginations.

And in the headline of Ken Ringle's description of the scene in the Senate impeachment trial of President Clinton, in the *Washington Post,* January 21, 1999:

> Down the Rabbit Hole and Into the Senate Trial

doyen; doyenne \'dȯi-ən, -(y)en; dwä-yən\ The senior member or leader of a body or group, such as a diplomatic corps. In this regard, the word has been used to refer to someone who is specifically or tacitly allowed to speak for the body or group. Also, a person uniquely skilled by long experience in some field of endeavor. A French word; the English equivalent is "dean," which also refers to officials in educational or ecclesiastical institutions. Doyen is the masculine form, doyenne the feminine.

The masculine form in use, by Aram Bakshian Jr., in the *American Spectator,* May 1989, reviewing *The Lyre of Orpheus* by Robertson Davies:

> If you are among the growing number of readers who resort to fiction as a mental muscle relaxant, Robertson Davies is not your kind of novelist. The doyen of Canadian authors refuses to succumb to the trite or trendy.

The feminine form in use, by Dominick Dunne in *Vanity Fair,* June 1996:

> Linda Deutsch, the doyenne of crime reporters, said to me one day about the Simpson case, "It was a story of damage. Everyone connected with the case was damaged by it."

draconian \drā-'kō-nē-ən, drə-\ *often capitalized* Of, relating to, or characteristic of Draco or the severe code of laws held to have been framed by him; cruel or severe.

Draco was a lawgiver of Athens in the 7th century B.C. appointed to stop the practice of individual revenge for wrongs suffered and to replace it with a more uniform, objective system of public justice and punishment. His code, noted for its use of the death penalty for many offenses, was said to have been written in blood, not ink. Most of Draco's code was abolished by another Athenian lawgiver, Solon.

The term in use, by William Branigin in the *Washington Post,* June 22, 1997, on the brutal rule of the Khmer Rouge in Cambodia in the 1970s:

> Having waited so long to seize power, Pol Pot and his colleagues began at once to implement their bizarre and Draconian social reforms. Within a day after taking the capital, the party ordered most of its 2 million citizens—including many hospital patients—into the countryside to plant rice, create new villages and perform other menial labor according to a brutal schedule.

And in a *New York Times* editorial on air pollution control, August 15, 1988:

> Air in the New York region, breathed by 17 million people, sometimes contains 50 percent more ozone than permitted. The law provides for sanctions, but they are so Draconian that in practice Congress won't let them be applied.

dragon's teeth *See* SOW DRAGON'S TEETH.

Dreyfus; Dreyfus affair \'drī-fəs, 'drā-\ Alfred Dreyfus (1859–1935) was the protagonist of the wrenching political scandal that dominated French politics and caught the world's attention at the turn of the 20th century. The Dreyfus case stands as an example of gross and cruel injustice, vicious bigotry, and complicit government malfeasance.

Dreyfus, an officer in the French army, was accused in 1894 of passing military secrets to the Germans. Although Dreyfus adamantly maintained his innocence and the evidence against him was thin, he was convicted of treason, stripped of his rank and honors in a humiliating public ceremony, and imprisoned on Devil's Island. His persecutors had found him easy to suspect and convict because he was a Jew; the French army, like French society, was rife with anti-Semitism.

Gradually evidence developed which clearly indicated that another officer, Major Ferdinand Walsin Esterhazy, had forged the evidence in question. The army could no longer suppress the case against Esterhazy and court-martialed him, but he was acquitted in minutes. At this point, the Paris newspaper *L'Aurore* published Émile Zola's famous open letter "J'ACCUSE", in which the noted writer charged the government and military with covering up the truth.

The case divided France along its deepest FAULT LINES. Royalist, militarist, nationalist, and Roman Catholic elements of French society lined up in support of the army; republican, socialist, and anticlerical forces supported Dreyfus.

New evidence came to light and Esterhazy fled. Dreyfus was tried again (1899), but the military court found him guilty again. Public outcry increased, and Dreyfus was pardoned, but public opinion in France and around the world demanded more. Dreyfus was ultimately exonerated by the Supreme Court of Appeals in 1906 after years of personal suffering for him and political agony for France. His rank was restored, and he was awarded the Legion of Honor. German documents finally published in 1930 established that Esterhazy was indeed guilty.

The term in use, by Robert C. Maynard in the *Washington Post Book World,* reviewing Taylor Branch's *Parting of the Waters,* November 20, 1988, discussing the FBI's allegations of Soviet influence against Stanley Levison, a friend of Dr. Martin Luther King:

> To this day, the evidence on which Hoover based his allegations of Soviet influence on King associate Stanley Levison has never been released by the FBI, and Levison remains an American Dreyfus.

Another example, from Mark Silk, in the *New York Times Magazine,* April 19, 1987, on a dispute within the history department of Princeton University:

> As the German historian James Joll has pointed out, the case became "a kind of historical Dreyfus affair . . . in which the original issues have often been obscured by the personal virulence and moral indignation with which Abraham has been attacked and the bitter and polemical tone of his replies."

droit du seigneur \drwä-dūē-se-n^{y}œr\ A supposed legal or customary right of a feudal lord to have sexual relations with a vassal's bride on her wedding night. From French, meaning "the lord's right." The term is used satirically to describe someone asserting rights or authority in a grandiose or overbearing fashion. In medieval Europe, the custom appears to have existed on a theoretical basis, if at all, and chiefly to raise revenue: the lord of the manor willingly accepted payments instead of insisting on his right.

The term in use, by Michael Kelly in the "TRB" column in the *New Republic,* June 6, 1997, on the sexual harassment case against President Clinton brought by Paula Corbin Jones:

> His [Clinton's] is the class that came of age possessed by a conviction that it was equipped to remake the world. . . . When a member of this class does something a little eyebrow-raising—makes $100,000 on a sweetheart commodities deal, say, or exercises his droit du seigneur with a working girl—the better sort of people avert their eyes.

And by Mary Battiata in an interview with British actor John Hurt in the *Washington Post,* May 23, 1988, on his home in Kenya:

> It's not unheard of for newcomers to this somewhat baronial way of life to feel a twinge of uneasiness at how far their First World dollars go in a country where high unemployment and crushing rural poverty still dovetail with a kind of post-colonial droit du seigneur. Hurt is no exception.

DuBois, Blanche \'blanch-dü-'bwä\ The central character in Tennessee William's 1947 Pulitzer Prize-winning play *A Streetcar Named Desire,* which charts her mental and moral disintegration and her ultimate ruin. Sex and violence underlie the pervasive atmosphere of romantic gentility; her neurotic, genteel pretensions are no match for the harsh realities symbolized by her brutish brother-in-law, Stanley Kowalski.

Blanche comes to live in New Orleans with her sister Stella and Stella's husband, Stanley. Stanley is affronted by Blanche's airs; Blanche believes that Stella has lowered herself by marrying the crude Stanley. Stanley dashes Blanche's hopes of marriage to his friend Mitch with cruel lies about her past; when she confronts him, he rapes her. Stella does not believe her sister, and Blanche collapses mentally—not that she had far to fall. At the end of the play, she is taken off to an asylum, telling the doctor that she has "always depended on the KINDNESS OF STRANGERS."

The play was successfully translated to film in 1951, with the roles of Blanche and Stanley indelibly played by Vivien Leigh and Marlon Brando. The impact of Leigh's performance becomes more eerie as audiences watch the actress who had played ur-Southern belle Scarlett O'Hara twelve years before translate herself into Blanche.

The term in use, in the *Memphis (Tenn.) Commercial Appeal,* June 23, 1996:

> Pink elephants reside in closets everywhere. They're those frothy bridesmaid's gowns we never wear again because they don't look right for anything except tea with Blanche DuBois.

And in the *San Jose Mercury News,* November 23, 1995:

> West Marine had a Blanche DuBois rally Wednesday—like the character in "A Streetcar Named Desire," its stock benefited from the kindness of strangers. The "stranger," in this case, was PaineWebber Group analyst Aram Rubinson, who began coverage of the Watsonville retailer of recreational boating supplies with a "buy" rating.

Dunkirk A retreat to avoid total defeat, or a crisis situation that requires a desperate last effort to forestall certain failure.

Dunkirk was the scene of the greatest military evacuation in history. During World War II, from May 26 to June 4, 1940, the main body of the British army and the remaining French, Polish and Belgian troops, in full retreat before advancing German forces, abandoned the European mainland. About 340,000 men were rescued from the beach by a ragtag armada of Royal Navy ships, ferries, fishing boats, and yachts while under attack by vast formations of German bombers.

The term in use, by David Stockman, the first budget director of the Reagan administration, warning of the hazards of tax cutting without budget cutting. In his 1986 book *The Triumph of Politics: How the Reagan Revolution Failed,* Stockman describes the circumstances:

This foreboding sense of being overtaken by events and economic conditions motivated the alarmist tone of my GOP economic Dunkirk memo. The split between tax cutters and budget balancers was already gaining new intensity within the recently victorious conservative governing coalition. A Dunkirk-scale economic setback might be the final outcome by November 1982.

And from *U.S. News & World Report,* January 26, 1987:

Israeli officials for whom spats with Washington are viewed as the diplomatic equivalent of Dunkirk, welcomed the conciliatory message.

dust bowl A landscape desolated by extreme drought. It is the name given to the Great Plains region of the United States, and to an era of severe drought in the 1930s.

Fragile grasslands, extending from the Dakotas to Texas, had been plowed for grain production during World War I. A slump in agricultural prices followed the war, followed by the Great Depression. When drought struck in the 1930s, the soil had no grass cover, leading to dust storms so heavy they were known as "black blizzards." These storms blotted out the sun and carried away tons of soil.

Thousands of farmers lost their land and homes, as memorably described by John Steinbeck in *The Grapes of Wrath* (1939). Measures to restore the soil were undertaken by the New Deal, including the planting of shelter belts of trees, taking fragile land out of production, and promoting use of soil-conserving farming practices.

The term in use, by Howard Schneider in the *Washington Post,* September 14, 1997, describing environmental destruction caused in Canada by an exploding population of snow geese:

Land that once bloomed with gentle blue gentian and white Grass of Parnassus flowers now has a dust-bowl quality, covered with mats of a purple weed and the skeletal twigs of dead willow bushes.

And by Mac Margolis in the *Christian Science Monitor,* August 26, 1983, on drought in Brazil:

Five years of relentless drought have turned an area five times the size of Italy into a dust bowl.

And by *Christian Science Monitor* film critic David Sterritt, January 3, 1985, reviewing *The River:*

It's just a coincidence that three movies in one year have chosen the subject of farm families struggling to save their land—this isn't really a 'dust bowl trilogy,' as Hollywood-watchers have dubbed it. But even a strong topic wears thin when treated too often in too short a time.

dybbuk \'di-bək\ A wandering soul believed in Jewish folklore to enter and control a living body until exorcised by a religious rite. It's a Hebrew word meaning "evil spirit," or "a clinging thing."

In premodern times, any unfortunate who went insane, became hysterical, or suffered epileptic or other seizures was thought by Jewish folklore to have been invaded by a dybbuk, just as Christians feared witchcraft or possession by the devil. Dybbuks can be cast out by holy men in specific rituals not unlike the procedures used by the Roman Catholic Church to exorcise demons.

The Dybbuk by S. Ansky is a classic play of Yiddish literature; the more recent *The Tenth Man* (1959), by Paddy Chayefsky, is also about a dybbuk.

The term in use, in a contemporary political context in a *Philadelphia Daily News* editorial on the field of gubernatorial candidates, October 21, 1994:

> Despite their party affiliations, Republican Tom Ridge and Democrat Mark Singel often appear to be centrist twins whose better selves have been taken over by an evil dybbuk who's done polls.

And by New York Times News Service columnist Anna Quindlen, appearing in the *Detroit Free Press,* January 30, 1992:

> Enter any neonatal intensive care unit . . . and at first glance all the machines and monitors obscure the person they are there to serve, a baby as small and translucent as a sheet of bond paper. That is what some parents believe has happened; the technology, like a kind of modern dybbuk, has taken control.

*Not only did the best team win Super Bowl XXXI, but the right team won. The Lombardi trophy is going home. It's like **Excalibur** is returning to the rock.*
—Tony Kornheiser

East Lynne A melodramatic and moralizing tale of the fall of virtue. To say "Tonight we play *East Lynne*" is to suggest that one is about to be treated to a tear-jerking display of bathos and purple prose. It comes from *East Lynne,* a hugely popular English novel by Mrs. Henry Wood published in 1861, which became a hugely popular play. The story was a sentimental, multiple-hanky weeper in which the heroine abandons her husband for another man but returns in disguise to care for her children.

Clifford A. Ridley, theater critic of the *Philadelphia Inquirer,* said it "may be the most disparaged play in the history of the American theater" as well as one of the most popular. In the *Inquirer* of July 25, 1991, Ridley offers some examples of mocking references:

> A Chicago movie critic writes of a character's "chuckling fiendishly—an effect that hasn't been heard with this much relish since the last road company of *East Lynne* closed down." A Long Island opera critic describes a singer's "bulging eyes, . . . posturing, and other histrionics right out of a turn-of-the-century production of *East Lynne.*"

And from Thomas M. Disch in the *Nation,* April 23, 1988, in a review of a made-for-TV movie on homelessness:

> They sink to ever more fearful and life-threatening depths of the welfare system, until the mother is faced with a final soul-crushing choice: to save her daughter's life she must seem to abandon her. The last scenes rival *East Lynne* for their capability of putting a lump in the throat, but a drama about homelessness that did not invite pathos would be an act of cowardice.

eat the seed corn To use up the amount of this year's harvest that should be saved to provide seed for next year's crop; shortsightedly squander the means of future growth or prosperity. If you eat your seed corn, you destroy your ability to plant a future crop, which would yield in time much more food and wealth than the seed corn itself.

The term in use, in a *Detroit Free Press* editorial, September 5, 1995:

> We're prepared to believe that some research money can be prudently pruned. . . . But a number of categories come under the heading of investment—seed corn for the future, if you will—and scientific research is one of them.

In use again, by Democratic Senator Tom Daschle, quoted by the Associated Press, March 31, 1995:

> To cut off aid to children, to cut off aid to educational opportunities for children is, as we say in South Dakota, eating the seed corn.

And quoted in *Maclean's* magazine, October 21, 1996:

> GM [General Motors] was in such dire straits that it delayed new car programs to preserve cash, what one writer called "eating your own seed corn."

Eden Paradise; an unspoiled, idyllic, peaceful place. In Genesis, the Garden of Eden was the first home of Adam and Eve, whence they were expelled when they had sinned. When they were evicted, however, Eden was not destroyed, and much interest, research, and legend have been devoted to finding it in a few millennia of human escapism.

"Earthly paradise" was an idea much in vogue in the Middle Ages. One candidate for the spot was a sort of SHANGRI-LA of peace, beauty, and immortality that was the domain of Prester John, a legendary monarch of fabulous wealth. The spot was thought to be in Asia; Marco Polo mentions him, as do other travelers. When he was not found in Asia, myth shifted him to Africa. His land is always in the next undiscovered place, and, for all we know, he's out there still.

The term in use, by Chris Kelley in the *Dallas Morning News,* December 6, 1995:

> By his calculations, Detroit and 23 other American cities have reached the point of no return, says Mr. Rusk, the former mayor of Albuquerque, N.M.
>
> Dallas is Eden compared with these cities. But Dallas is showing increasing signs of Detroit's distress. . . .

And by Stephen Hunter, film critic of the *Baltimore Sun,* reviewing the film *Casino,* November 22, 1995:

> *Casino* is really "Paradise Lost" Vegas-style, a study of monumental and character-driven folly. Its majestic chronicle tracks two men who inherited the Garden of Eden and managed in a very short time to destroy everything for no more cogent reason than their own bitter and unmalleable pride, which goeth before the fall every darn time.

And by Jonathan Rowe in the *Christian Science Monitor,* March 21, 1990:

> Most fans probably date baseball's Lost Eden to 1966. That was the year a contentious labor lawyer named Marvin Miller took over the Major League Players Association and led it down the path of militancy and confrontation.

Edsel Unsuccessful model made by the Ford Motor Company starting in 1957. It turned out to be a huge marketing blunder; an expensive investment in a product which no one wanted and everyone ridiculed.

The Edsel was launched onto the market with much fanfare in September 1957. Its unusual name was a tribute to Edsel Ford, son of the company's founder.

The car was full of gadgets like a push-button transmission, but its most memorable feature was the shrieking "O" grille. It was also introduced in a price range in which there was the most competition at the same time that the country was in a recession and the American consumer's attention was beginning to focus on small European cars like the Volkswagen Beetle. In short, Ford had designed a car for a market that was not there.

The term in use, by Glen Slattery in the *Atlanta Journal and Constitution,* June 24, 1996:

> You get weird about the Punch List. On the one hand, you want to cite each and every imperfection in your home and force the builder to make good. Then again, if you find too many problems, there's this feeling that you're trapped inside a giant Edsel.

And by Peter N. Spotts, the *Christian Science Monitor,* December 7, 1994, on the performance of the Hubble Space Telescope:

> The latest findings cap "a spectacular year" for the repaired Hubble, Ms. Kinney says. Astronomers once were concerned that the instrument might become the orbiting Edsel of observatories.

Edwardian Of, relating to, or characteristic of Edward VII (reigned 1901–1910) of England or his age; especially clothing marked by the hourglass silhouette for women, long narrow fitted suits and high collars for men.

The period followed the Victorian era and was characterized by a relaxation of the conservatism that marked the reign of Edward's mother, Victoria. Edward embodied the spirit of the era: he was charming and fond of good food, good company—especially that of beautiful women—yachting and horse racing. He supported philanthropic causes, traveled widely to promote peace, and was popular with his people. Edward's reign was a period of opulence and elegance, at least for the wealthy few, and is viewed nostalgically as a time of tranquility before the horrors of World War I.

But changes were afoot. Writers like George Bernard Shaw and H.G. Wells were challenging old ideas and values; expansion of the vote was bringing the Labour Party increasing representation in the House of Commons; and militant women were demonstrating for the right to vote. Abroad, the rising power of Germany, Japan, and the United States was leading to great changes in the international order.

The term in use, by Norman Mailer in *Esquire,* August 1, 1994, speaking of himself in the third person, describing a photo shoot with Madonna:

Mailer, like many an upstart before him, maintained a secret gentleman in a closet—the nice part of himself, so to speak. This Edwardian was puffed with outrage by the imposition on Madonna. It was not that her breast had been exposed—Mailer, along with much of America, had seen her bare breasts looking splendid more than a hundred times in film, video, magazines and books. It was just that this was not the time for Madonna to be seen.

Another example, from the *New York Times,* January 18, 1982, in Phil Gailey's profile of Washington insider Craig Spence:

Mr. Spence, who is something of a mystery man who dresses in Edwardian dandy style.

Electra complex A term from Freudian psychoanalysis, describing the unconscious tendency of a daughter to attach herself to her father, or a father-figure, and to be hostile toward her mother. The comparable effect for boys is known as the Oedipus complex. (*See* OEDIPAL.) Both expressions are drawn from Greek myth.

Electra was the daughter of Agamemnon, king of Mycenae, and his wife Clytemnestra. The story is told in drama by each of the three great Greek playwrights, Aeschylus, Sophocles and Euripedes, and in many other famous retellings, including Eugene O'Neill's play *Mourning Becomes Electra* (1931).

The royal family of Mycenae, the house of Atreus, was a dysfunctional family of the first order, and a lot of incest, murder, revenge, and suicide already had bubbled under the bridge before Electra came along. But the immediate issue arose because Agamemnon had sacrificed Electra's sister Ephigenia before departing for ten years to fight the Trojan war. Clytemnestra never forgave him, took a lover and murdered Agamemnon when he returned. Electra had sent her brother Orestes into hiding, and after he grew up he returned to kill Clytemnestra and her lover with Electra's help.

The term in use, by Brad Darrach in *People,* October 23, 1989, describing cinema grande dame, Bette Davis:

In her middle teens, huge-eyed and ethereal, Bette glowed like a nymph in a pre-Raphaelite painting. But she loathed her looks and behind every boy she glimpsed the specter of her disapproving father. She had an Electra complex, a terrified fascination with strong males that became more acute as she grew older and kept her wavering in their presence between fight and flight.

And by *National Review* columnist Florence King, reprinted in the *Minneapolis Star Tribune,* February 1, 1996, siding with her father's views of Prince Charles in his disputes with Princess Diana:

I always sided with my father. The psychobabblers no doubt will say I'm "threatened" by Princess Diana, that she has unearthed my "unresolved conflicts" and "buried anxieties." Maybe so, but a recent book claims that eccentrics have no unresolved conflicts or buried anxieties. . . . In any case, I am an unabashed Anglophile; if Paris is worth a mass, London is worth an Electra complex. [*See also* PARIS IS WELL WORTH A MASS.]

Also from Susan Isaacs, reviewing *Lovely Me,* Barbara Seaman's biography of Jaqueline Susann in the *New York Times Book Review,* March 29, 1987:

> Nor is Ms. Seaman's use of pop psychology any more satisfying, like the explication of Susann's Electra complex. She claimed to have walked in on one of her father's many adulterous liaisons.

elevator music Instrumental arrangement of popular songs often piped in (as to an elevator or retail store). Bland, soothing music—and nowadays something so boring that it is insultingly devoid of interest; so soothing, in other words, as to be irritating.

Elevator music was actually developed in the 1930s to calm nervous elevator passengers and is now artfully programmed for commercial establishments to produce specific results (usually involving spending money). The term elevator music is often applied to "easy listening" music, the butt of jokes about bourgeois lack of taste.

The term in use, by Mark Lorando, in the *New Orleans Times-Picayune,* February 15, 1992:

> The 1992 Winter Olympics TV sportscasting hosts, Tim McCarver and Paula Zahn, have turned the events into the athletic equivalent of elevator music.

And by syndicated columnist George Will, October 11, 1996, after the campaign debate between Democratic Vice President Al Gore and his Republican rival, Jack Kemp:

> In the "debate" (Americanspeak for a meandering, triangular conversation with Jim Lehrer) with droning Al Gore, who is the elevator music of American politics, Kemp sometimes rose from incoherence, only to espouse the indefensible.

elysian fields \i-'li-zhən\ *often capitalized E* The landscape of paradise; an abode of delight, an idyllic place. In ancient Greek and Roman mythology, Elysium (Greek, meaning "happy, delightful") was the place where heroes and those blessed by the gods went after death. According to Homer, Elysium lay "at the world's end," where life was always comfortable, where temperate breezes wafted through the gardens and groves, and the cares of ordinary earthly existence never intruded.

The Elysian Fields are also famous earth addresses. The most renowned is found at Avenue des Champs-Elysees in Paris. Originally laid out as gardens in the 1660s, the Champs-Elysees is one of the most famous streets in the world. Elysian Fields is also a famous neighborhood in New Orleans;

it is the slum setting of Tennessee Williams' play *A Streetcar Named Desire*. Blanche DUBOIS arrives, nervous and uncertain. Asked if she is lost, she repeats the directions she was given to find her sister's house: "To take a streetcar named Desire, and then transfer to one called Cemeteries and get off at Elysian Fields."

The term in use, by Lewis H. Lapham in *Harper's*, September 1994:

> Over the course of the summer I had occasion to reread Marshall McLuhan's *Understanding Media*, and although the argument of the book made a good deal more sense to me in 1994 than it did in 1964, it wasn't until I saw the white Ford Bronco proceeding majestically north on the San Diego Freeway under a royal umbrella of helicopters that I knew why. McLuhan had announced mankind's happy return to the Elysian fields of primitive consciousness, and here was his word being made flesh in the southern California twilight. Well before the procession moved through the Santa Monica Interchange, the news of O.J. Simpson's whereabouts had reached Tokyo and Rome (i.e., the villagers in the distinct precincts of McLuhan's GLOBAL VILLAGE), and the reverent crowd gathering under the eucalyptus trees on Sunset Boulevard had come to pay homage to what passes in late-twentieth-century America for the presence of divinity.

And by Sy Montgomery in *International Wildlife*, March-April 1989:

> Yearly rainfall at Brookfield Park ranges from less than 3 inches to as many as 21. Within a single season, the wombat's habitat can careen from billiard-table-bare soil and rock to waving elysian fields of grass.

And by John D. Thomas in the *Village Voice*, November 5, 1991:

> What better time to note that a diverse collection of baseball greats decomposes throughout the New York region, some in appropriately grand surroundings, some in surroundings less than grand, and some just sort of there, rotting in obscurity. Join us, if you will, as we embark on a brief sojourn from the playing fields to the Elysian fields. It's time we visited New York's most legendary players as they while away the eons on baseball's permanent DL.

éminence grise \ā-mē-nä^{n}s-grēz\ A confidential agent, especially one exercising unsuspected or unofficial power.

A French expression, it means "gray eminence." The term originated with Père Joseph, secretary and confidential agent of Cardinal Richelieu, the powerful minister of King Louis XIII. Père Joseph wore a gray habit, which earned him the nickname "Éminence Grise" in contrast to Richelieu, who was know as "Éminence Rouge," from his red habit.

In American politics, the expression has been applied to backstage political operators such as Mark Hanna, an Ohio businessman who devoted himself exclusively to putting William McKinley into the White House. Once he succeeded, he held great influence over the president.

The term in use, by John A. Byrne in *Business Week,* April 28, 1997, profiling lawyer Ira Millstein:

> When most lawyers his age are happiest swinging a golf club, Millstein is at the top of his professional game. An éminence grise of corporate governance, he now spends well over half his time on board [of directors] issues.

By Michael Weisskopf in *Time,* August 4, 1997:

> If Washington's shadowy power brokers operate best in secret, Joe Gaylord is losing his mystique. It was bad enough when Gaylord, éminence grise to Newt Gingrich, was blamed for isolating the House Speaker, antagonizing enough Republican brethren to threaten Newt's leadership post earlier this month.

And by Jill Abramson in the *Wall Street Journal,* November 9, 1992:

> Felix Rohatyn, the Lazard Freres chieftain and eminence grise of municipal finance, is considered to have a serious shot at being named to a top economic post.

emperor's new clothes, the A set of new clothes, actually nonexistent and therefore invisible, which everyone pretends to see for fear of being thought a fool. Something meaningless or nonsensical or wrong that is automatically and uncritically agreed with. From the fairy tale by Hans Christian Anderson. In the tale, the emperor is given a set of clothes and told they are visible only to people who are not fools. Word gets around; no one wants to admit he cannot see the clothes and thus admit to be a fool. Both emperor and subjects praise the wonderful new duds for their elegance and beauty. Finally an innocent child pipes up with the truth—that the emperor has no clothes on—and pretense collapses in hilarity.

The term in use, by Marvin Kitman in *Newsday,* May 4, 1997, on the fad for 3–D television programs:

> This month's 3–D rage is the latest example of the emperor's new clothes TV is wearing while the bored audience erodes away. In my humble opinion, it is a sham, the last refuge of programming scoundrels. [*See* LAST REFUGE OF SCOUNDRELS.]

And again, by Dave Gagon in the *Deseret News,* April 27, 1997, commenting on the Whitney Museum's Biennial exhibit:

> Van Gogh was crazy, but he left behind works of art that cry out to be experienced. They give, and will continue to give, lasting pleasure to the soul of the viewer. Nothing at the Biennial does this. Everything is trendy; everything is perishable. And I can't

help feeling that as I stood there listening to people discuss the exhibit I was experiencing the Emperor's New Clothes.

empty suit Someone of no substance, despite an impressive facade, who takes on and promotes whatever ideas prevail at any given moment; an anonymous functionary. *Suit* was 1960s slang for an F.B.I. agent; thus it became a term for a man for whom a business suit was a uniform as well as a sign of class distinction in the work place. It's not a friendly term—picture the blue-collar types in their coveralls making jokes about the anonymous middle-manager in his—or her—business suit. In yet another context, *suits* (homicide detectives) and *uniforms* (street cops in uniform) are staples of television's version of police work.

The term in use, by Larry Wheeler of Gannett News Service, August 7, 1996:

> First elected to the Senate in 1988, [Florida Sen. Connie] Mack was dismissed by some as an "empty suit" who was incredibly lucky to beat his Democratic opponent by virtue of absentee ballots.

And by columnist Fred Barnes, quoted by the *Washington Times,* September 22, 1995:

> Fred Barnes says . . . that Sen. Bob Kerrey, Nebraska Democrat, will be a highly visible antagonist of the White House as long as Bill Clinton is there.
> "The truth is Kerrey took the measure of Clinton, perhaps when they were governors (1982–86), perhaps later, and decided he's an empty suit."

endgame The stage of a chess game after major reduction of forces; also the final stages of an action.

The term in use, reported by David Espo of the Associated Press, December 14, 1995:

> After months of tumult, House Speaker Newt Gingrich said the extended budget battle was nearing its endgame.

By Stefan Halper in the *Washington Times,* December 9, 1994, on the NATO role in Bosnia:

> In the case of NATO, the Bosnia endgame may be a blessing in disguise. Both the charter and the mission [of NATO] need review in a changed world. . . .

And by John Barth in *Harper's,* July 1990:

> The century now ending with fashionable treatises on the end of history and the end of nature opened with whispers . . . of the end of art. In such an endgame ambience, it understandably may come to seem not only that "less is more" . . . but that least is most.

enemy of the people, an A person officially declared a danger to the common good in a socialist or totalitarian state and prosecuted as such; someone who tells unpalatable truths the resentful majority does not want to hear, believing that truth is more important than popular approval.

Here is a case in which history imitates art. *An Enemy of the People* is an 1882 play by Henrik Ibsen. It tells the story of Dr. Stockman, who is voted "an enemy of the people" by his fellow townsmen because he insists on proclaiming that the baths of the town's spa, a major source of municipal income, are dangerous to public health.

The phrase appears again in George Orwell's 1949 novel, *Nineteen Eighty-four,* in a description of a propaganda session—the "Two Minute Hate" directed at Emmanuel Goldstein, "the Enemy of the People" who had once been a leader of the party but who had become a counterrevolutionary traitor.

Orwell had the modern totalitarian states of Nazi Germany and Soviet Russia as models, soon followed by the People's Republic of China. Under these regimes, to be an enemy of the people was not a metaphorical position; it was lethal. Dictatorships still find it useful, as related in Barbara Bradley's account of a visit to Burma in the *Christian Science Monitor,* December 29, 1994:

> As we drove through the funereal streets, emptied by a 10 p.m. curfew, the huge red-and-white billboards proclaimed—in both Burmese and English—varying versions of "The Enemy of the Army Is the Enemy of the People."

And from Rick Atkinson, the *Washington Post,* May 9, 1996, reporting on Germany's prosecution of American Gary Lauck, the "Farm-Belt Fuehrer," for distribution of racial hate materials:

> "We've intercepted more stuff from him than anyone else," Hartmut Wulf, the chief prosecutor in Hamburg, said in an interview. "I don't want to elevate Lauck to the status of enemy of the people or someone who represents a great danger. But we're well advised not to underestimate the right-wing radicals, nor overestimate them."

England expects . . . The start of Lord Nelson's signal to the British fleet from his flagship *Victory* as they sailed to fight the Spanish and French fleets at the battle of Trafalgar, October 21, 1805: "England expects that every man will do his duty." Nelson's original message began "England confides. . . . " The signal officer requested the change in order to save seven flag hoists, since "confides" was not in the signal book.

The Royal Navy won a great victory that day, one that established its supremacy for the next century. Nelson was fatally wounded.

The term in use, by Jim Murray in the *Los Angeles Times,* January 24, 1997, looking forward to Super Bowl XXXI:

He [Patriots coach Bill Parcells] subscribes to the Lombardi the-
orem that the name of the game is block-and-tackle. Like England, he expects every man to do his duty.

enigma *See* RIDDLE WRAPPED IN A MYSTERY INSIDE AN ENIGMA.

Enlightenment, the A philosophic movement of the 18th century in
Europe and America marked by a rejection of traditional social, religious,
and political ideas and an emphasis on rationalism; also called the Age of
Reason.

The noun *enlightenment* means an act or means of being freed from
ignorance and misinformation. The leading thinkers and politicians of the
Enlightenment believed that the goals of the enlightened, rational individual were knowledge, freedom, and happiness.

Their outlook was in part a reaction to the religious wars and persecutions of the 17th century, and they turned their minds from spiritual
matters to practical ones. Religious tolerance grew, and the absolute power
of the clergy waned. While leading philosophers did not deny the existence of God, they often saw the Creator as a great watchmaker who set
the universe in motion rather than the personal, all-knowing deity of the
medieval church.

Some of the Enlightenment's major figures were radical. Voltaire
assaulted the traditional Christian concept of the world and wrote his *Universal History* from a purely secular point of view. He viewed Christianity as a social phenomenon and observed, "If God did not exist, it would
be necessary to invent him."

The leaders of the American Revolution and of the infant United States
were products of this age: Thomas Jefferson, John Adams, and Thomas
Paine eloquently stated their belief in reason and their commitment to
freedom of thought.

The term in use, by Mark Lilla, in the *Washington Times,* March 2, 1997,
in a review of Frederick C. Beiser's book *The Sovereignty of Reason: The
Defense of Rationality in the Early English Enlightenment:*

> For two centuries now, the modern Enlightenment has served as
> a convenient scapegoat for social and psychological ills facing
> the human race. The charges leveled against it are many and usu-
> ally contradictory.

And by Robert Orsi in his review of *People of God: The Struggle for
World Catholicism* by Penny Lernoux, published in the *Voice Literary Supplement,* June 1989:

> With *People of God,* Lernoux joins the circle of post-modern polit-
> ical tragedians who, decrying the desiccation of liberalism, look
> to religion as the hope of a new political culture. Lernoux believes
> that Enlightenment traditions are dead. In the "developed" coun-
> tries, she argues, the liberal mainstays of "tolerance and free-

dom" have emptied out into materialism, consumerism, and conformity.

envelope *See* PUSHING THE ENVELOPE.

epicenter The part of the earth's surface directly above the focus of an earthquake; the center of some activity, interest, or condition.

The term in use, by Guy Trebay, in the *Village Voice,* September 15, 1987:

> After 18 years on Broadway, Speakeasy Antiques is closing shop. . . .
> "Can you believe we're supposed to be leaving in five days?" asks Bob Brand, surveying a sales floor that makes FIBBER MCGEE'S CLOSET seem spare. . . . Proprietors of New York's kitsch epicenter, the Brands are natural collectors who met and fell in love over a $3 oak bucket in Vermont.

And by Leigh Montville in *Sports Illustrated,* November 4, 1996:

> I am with Madonna's personal trainer! . . . I am at the epicenter of a trend that grows bigger by the day: people hiring people to help them exercise, sweat, diet, rebuild themselves into whatever they want to be.

epiphany \i-'pi-fə-nē\ A usually sudden manifestation or perception of the essential nature or meaning of things; an illuminating discovery.

As a religious term, *epiphany* refers to a Christian festival commemorating the manifestation of Christ to the Gentiles at the coming of the Magi. Epiphany is celebrated on January 6.

Use of the term in a literary context is particularly associated with James Joyce. It is the moment in which "the soul of the commonest object . . . seems to us radiant" and may be manifested through any chance word or gesture.

The term in use, in commentary by Michael Eric Dyson in the *Washington Post,* October 13, 1996:

> One year after the epiphany of the Million Man March—a dramatic testament to the magnitude of black male hunger for racial rescue and moral requirement—the bright light it spread through our nation continues to illumine the efforts of black communities.

And in the *New York Times,* August 19, 1987, by Michiko Kakutani, reviewing *Herself in Love* by Marianne Wiggins:

> The heroine experiences a bizarre epiphany while strolling on the shore: she comes to see a dying, beached whale as a symbol of her own mismanaged life, and she begs, with nearly religious fervor, that it (and presumably she) might be granted a second chance.

And by Mona Behan in *Parenting,* September 1995:

These small epiphanies are what I've come to think of as Eureka Moments, those times when all doubt melts away and a parent becomes certain she has discovered the perfect preschool for her child.

Eton *See* PLAYING FIELDS OF ETON.

Et tu, Brute? \et-'tü-'brü-te\ Words of Julius Caesar when he recognized his friend Marcus Junius Brutus among his assassins. A reproach for an act of treachery or betrayal by a friend or ally. It's Latin and means "And you too, Brutus?" The phrase is best known from Shakespeare's *Julius Caesar*, but is quoted by the Roman historian Suetonius in *The Lives of the Caesars.*

The term in use, by Congressman David Hobson, (R–Ohio), quoted in the *Washington Post's* recounting of an attempt by disaffected Republicans to oust House Speaker Newt Gingrich, July 28, 1997:

> It was Hobson who sounded the alarm bells. He located [former Congressman Robert] Walker and told him Paxon was involved with the dissidents.
> "That can't be," Walker exclaimed.
> "Et tu, Brute," Hobson replied.

The phrase often shows up as "Et tu, __?" with the name of the betrayer in the blank, as in this example from columnist Richard Cohen in the *Detroit Free Press,* October 5, 1993:

> Et tu, Bill?
> You could almost hear that question being asked by the National Rifle Association, as yet another prominent politician, this time Massachusetts Gov. William Weld, a Republican, called for a measure of gun control.

Another example, from Kathy O'Malley and Hank Gratteau, in the *Chicago Tribune,* November 12, 1989:

> Et tu, Bruce? Anti-establishment comedy writer Bruce Vilanch, known for the edgy one-liners he writes for people like Bette Midler and Cher, is collaborating with (you may want to sit down) The Osmonds!

Evers *See* TINKER TO EVERS TO CHANCE.

everyman *often capitalized* The typical or ordinary person. John Q. Public, the man in the street, not rich or brilliant or exceptional—just one of us.

The term comes from one of the MORALITY PLAYS of the 15th century, allegorical dramas that served as popular entertainment and provided religious and ethical instruction to the unlettered public. Everyman, the central character, is, of course, the ordinary person. Other allegorical characters represent virtues, vices, and good and bad influences.

In the play, Everyman receives a summons from Death and calls on his friends—Beauty, Fellowship, Kindred and Worldly Goods, among others—to accompany him. Only Good Deeds agrees to attend Everyman to the grave. Not too subtle, but neither was the audience.

The term in use, by Verlyn Klinkenborg in the *New York Times Magazine,* August 3, 1997:

> One of the unmentionable pleasures of modern life is the increasing video coverage of natural disasters. . . . Someday, thanks to the proliferation of home-video cameras, we'll get the taped testimony of some Everyman who will forever stand for being in the wrong place at the wrong time.

And by Phillip Lopate in the *New York Times Book Review,* January 21, 1996:

> Mr. Gould's "I," as he chooses to represent himself, is first of all, a mensch: the public-school Jewish kid from Queens, a "dinosaur nut" . . . , who became a lover of tolerance and reason, a "humanist at heart," a "meat-and-potatoes man." Layered over this earthly Everyman is a proud, prickly researcher not above tooting his horn. . . .

everything you always wanted to know . . . A catch phrase, meaning a work, study, or description which thoroughly illuminates a topic, and often provides much more information than the ordinary person would perfer to know.

The phrase was popularized by the title of a 1969 best-seller by Dr. David Reuben, *Everything You Always Wanted to Know About Sex (But Were Afraid to Ask).* It was on the *New York Times* best-seller list for many weeks. A 1972 movie of the same title was directed by and starred Woody Allen. The film featured a series of comic sketches, including Gene Wilder as a doctor enamored of a sheep and Woody Allen as a sperm in a tour of the male body.

The term in use, by Karlyn Bowman in *Roll Call,* March 12, 1998:

> Everything You Always Wanted to Know About Sex (and the Pollsters Weren't Afraid to Ask). We've come a long way from the days when pollsters rarely asked about sex or did so in delicate ways.

And by John Ray in the *Times Literary Supplement,* December 4, 1992:

> *The Giant Book of the Mummy* is clearly designed as a Christmas present for a precocious toddler, and its purpose is to tell him or her everything he or she always wanted to know about mummification and funerary charms. This is perhaps the reason why it approximates to a small child in size, and this gives the book the added advantage that if the infant continues precocious it can be used as a blunt instrument.

And by Thomas E. Young in *Movie Theater,* May 1997:

> May the force hyperlink you to the official THX site from Lucas-film. You will find everything you always wanted to know about commercial film sound technology and THX here, including everything from technical white papers to lists of THX-certified theaters around the world.

Evil Empire The Soviet Union, or any archenemy, real or imagined. Cold Warrior Ronald Reagan gave the name to the Soviet Union—and it stuck. It has come to be applied to any large, powerful entity looked upon with a mixture of hostility, suspicion, fear, and disdain.

Reagan used the term in a speech to the National Association of Evangelicals in Orlando, Florida, in March 1983:

> I urge you to beware the temptation of pride, the temptation of blithely declaring yourself above it all and label both sides equally at fault, to ignore the facts of history and the aggressive impulses of an evil empire, to simply call the arms race a giant misunderstanding and thereby remove yourself from the struggle between right and wrong and good and evil.

Given Reagan's years in the movie industry and his delight in the medium, the name was undoubtedly influenced by the enormously popular *Star Wars* trilogy of the late '70s and early '80s, created by George Lucas, in which the valiant heroes and their lovable robots fought and ultimately defeated a totalitarian enemy known simply as "The Empire."

The term in use, quoted by Charles Bosworth Jr. in the *St. Louis Post-Dispatch,* March 9, 1996:

> Calling Thomas Venezia's multimillion-dollar gambling operation an "evil empire" that corrupted elected officials, lawyers and judges, District Judge William D. Stiehl . . . gave Venezia an extended sentence of 15 years in prison. . . .

And by Amy Harmon, in the *Los Angeles Times,* November 22, 1996:

> Vilifying Microsoft as the Evil Empire is a cliché in the computer industry.

Excalibur The sword of King Arthur. A weapon of might and mystery which confers kingship on its possessor. Mythical heroes tend to have swords with famous names, and they are usually endowed with magical powers that give the owner of the sword victory, bravery, power, etc. In one version of the legend of Arthur, Excalibur is embedded in a stone from which only the king of England can draw it out. Arthur succeeds, and is proclaimed king.

Informal research leads to a big question: Why is "Excalibur" such a popular name for seedy nightclubs? The term seems to turn up mostly in newspaper reports of police calls.

The term in use, by Tony Kornheiser in the *Washington Post,* January

27, 1997, describing the Green Bay Packer victory in the 1997 Superbowl:

> Not only did the best team win Super Bowl XXXI, but the right
> team won. The Lombardi trophy is going home. It's like Excal-
> ibur is returning to the rock.

By F. King in the *Economist,* March 28, 1992, reviewing William
Broad's book *Teller's War:*

> Dr. Teller put the new president and the nascent super-weapon,
> which went by the code-name Excalibur, in touch with each
> other. His enthusiasm for the X–ray laser helped to bring about
> the Strategic Defense Initiative.
>   The fact is that Excalibur has, to date, stayed resolutely in its
> stone, and efforts to remove it have all but ceased.

And by John Updike in his collection of essays *Hugging the Shore* (1984):

> The totem-image of the poet that Whitman prophesied and
> appeared to embody still lies at the core of American poetry, for
> any who attempt to unriddle it—a kind of Excalibur that none
> but the pure of heart can seize and wield.

ex cathedra By virtue of or in the exercise of one's office or position. In
Latin, it means "from the chair," and was originally applied to the decisions of popes issued from their seats, or thrones. It does not necessarily
mean (as the phrase seems to suggest) that one is shouting out the cathedral door.
     In Roman Catholic doctrine, when the Pope speaks ex cathedra, he is
addressing matters of Church doctrine on faith or morals, and speaks with
infallibility. In general usage, the phrase is applied to statements uttered
by authority and may be used ironically to describe dogmatic, self-
certain statements.
     The term in use, by columnist George Will in the *Washington Post,* Jan-
uary 23, 1992, on the proposed auction sale of a three-hole outhouse seat
bearing paintwork said to have been done by artists Willem de Kooning
and Jackson Pollock:

> A connoisseur of de Kooning says, "As soon as I saw it I knew
> it was of his hand." But even the cognoscenti can't be sure about
> the contribution of Pollock, he of the famous canvases of dribs
> and drabs.
>   The *New York Times,* speaking ex cathedra, announces, "The
> seat is executed in a style of the two masters."

And by South African writer J.M. Coetzee, in the *New Republic,* January 8 & 15, 1990, reviewing *Save the Beloved Country* by his countryman
Alan Paton:

excursions

Paton was turned, not wholly unwillingly, into a sage and oracle.... The effects can be seen not only in the increasingly ex cathedra tone of his pronouncements, and in his tendency to think, speak, and write in brief, easy-to-chew paragraphs, but in his failure to break new ground and to develop as a writer.

excursions *See* ALARUMS AND EXCURSIONS.

*He married during his first term, and the press turned his honeymoon into the kind of **feeding frenzy** we see today.*

—Peter Andrews

Fabian tactics The style of warfare of the Roman general Quintus Fabius Maximus Cunctator, known for his defeat of Hannibal by the avoidance of decisive contests; cautious, dilatory strategy. "Cunctator" means "delayer" in Latin, and that is what Fabius did during the Second Punic War (Rome vs. Carthage, 218–201 B.C.). Things were not going well for Rome; they were facing an invading force commanded by Hannibal, one of the great military commanders in history, who had brought a force (including elephants) over the Alps.

Fabius was elected dictator and decided to fight in a new way that is sometimes called "masterly inaction." He avoided pitched battles and dodged around in the hills where Hannibal's cavalry couldn't be used effectively, and he harassed supply lines. Rome used the time he bought to recover and rebuild, and ultimately prevailed.

The Fabian Society, a group formed in London in the 1880s to advance the cause of socialism, used these same tactics of patience and selected opportunity to gain political victory over stronger forces. Early members of the society included famous intellectuals George Bernard Shaw and Beatrice and Sydney Webb.

Washington Post publisher Katherine Graham's memoir, *Personal History* (1997), notes this description of the headmistress at Madeira School:

> Miss Madeira had some advanced ideas and attempted to broaden our horizons. . . . She used her BULLY PULPIT to try to mold us into some species of "Shavian Fabian". . . .

The term in use, in its tactical sense, by Ramesh Ponnoru, the *National Review,* September 2, 1996:

> The Clintons have pursued this objective with essentially Fabian tactics.

And from Takashi Oka, the *Christian Science Monitor,* June 21, 1988, on U.S.–Japan trade negotiations:

> So Takeshita adopted Fabian tactics, offering just enough concessions to the Americans to keep the talks barely alive, while gradually wearing down resistance among farmers and legislators representing them.

Fabulous Invalid, the The theater, especially the New York theater world, whose health and future seem forever to be on the verge of financial and artistic collapse. For all its death notices, New York's legitimate theater manages to revive and survive year after year.

The term in use by Jay Carr in the *Boston Globe,* November 18, 1988, reviewing *The Land Before Time,* an animated feature movie:

> Animation, the movies' Fabulous Invalid, gets a real boost from *The Land Before Time.*

And by Craig Wilson, in *USA Today,* October 2, 1997, on the *New Yorker* cartoonist Bob Mankoff:

> As for the future of cartooning, Mankoff says it's fine, maybe even better than fine with all the technology available to cartoonists now. "Cartooning," he says, "like Broadway, is the fabulous invalid."

Another example, from the headline of a February 11, 1990 *New York Times* story on an effort to abolish the House of Lords of Britain's Parliament:

> "That Fabulous Invalid, the British House of Lords"

face that launched a thousand ships, the An extremely beautiful woman for whom, presumably, men would be willing to fight and die. The reference is to Helen of Troy, said to have been the most beautiful woman in the world. She was married to Menelaus, the king of Sparta, but was abducted by (or eloped with) Paris, Prince of Troy, thus precipitating the Trojan War, according to legend and the *Iliad.* Other Greek heroes and city-states joined forces with Menelaus and Sparta to make war against Troy.

Archeology has shown that there was a war against Troy in the 12th century B.C., in reality probably over the lucrative trade routes dominated by Troy. Was there a Helen, whose name is now synonymous with matchless beauty? Probably not.

The phrase comes to us from Elizabethan dramatist and poet Christopher Marlowe, in *The Tragical History of Dr. Faustus* (first performed 1588, published 1601). Having sold his soul for magical powers, Faust is able to summon up the beauteous Helen. Looking on her, he says: "Was this the face that launched a thousand ships/And burnt the topless towers of Ilium?"

The term in use, by Shelden Sevinor in *USA Today Magazine,* September 1, 1994:

> Eleanor Roosevelt, Golda Meir, Indira Ghandi, and Margaret Mead became attractive with age. None of these women were graced with "a face that would launch a thousand ships," but their charm, talent, and intelligence transformed them in the eyes of their beholders.

From Elise Armacost, in commentary in the *Baltimore Sun,* July 9, 1995, on the heroines of Disney feature cartoons:

> Belle, Ariel, Jas, Poca—no wonder little girls love them. They all have faces to launch a thousand ships and bods over which wars could be fought.

And, in one of a countless number of possible variations, by Michael Alexander in *People,* December 7, 1987:

> Is this really the face that launched a thousand rumors? Yes, but apparently through no fault of her own, alas. In 1984, when she bopped with the Boss in Springsteen's *Dancing in the Dark* video, drooling dweebs kept coming up to her and saying "You're Bruce's new girlfriend, right? Or his sister, right? Or his daughter, right?" Wrong on all counts.

fall on one's sword Sacrifice oneself. Voluntarily take full responsibility—and voluntarily pay the price—for a disastrous turn of events. For example, to acknowledge a grave error by resigning from office.

From the Roman custom of committing suicide by falling on one's sword when one failed in a big way. Frequently the fallers were generals or high officials who felt honor-bound to take their lives if they were responsible for a defeat in battle or a failed conspiracy.

Distinguished examples from history include Brutus, who is best known for his part in the stabbing assassination of Julius Caesar. (*See* ET TU, BRUTE?) He was subsequently defeated by Octavian and Mark Antony at the battle of Philippi in 42 A.D. Recognizing that all was lost, Brutus threw himself on a friend's blade.

During the reign of Augustus, the Roman general Varus led three legions into a trap while attempting to quell a revolt in the German provinces of the Empire. The Roman army was massacred and Varus paid the price: he fell on his sword.

Nowadays, when someone falls on his sword, he usually lives to tell the tale, as illustrated below.

The term in use, by Ben Brantley in the *New York Times,* June 1, 1997, on the Broadway season:

> In the heady spate of Broadway openings crammed into the month of April—to qualify for nominations for the 51st annual Tony Awards . . . the recurrent image was one of regal talents falling on their own swords. Harold Prince, John Kander and Fred Ebb, Stockard Channing, Wendy Wasserstein: some of the most critically and commercially reliable artists in the American theater issued forth in productions that could seem truly tragic for the wrong reasons.

And by a city official, quoted by Tinah Saunders in the *Atlanta Journal and Constitution,* March 20, 1997, on the furor caused by cutting down two trees on a city street:

"I thought everybody was in agreement about this, but I guess I'm left holding the bag," Jones said. "I'll fall on my sword if that will solve things."

Falstaff; Falstaffian A fat, convivial, roguish character in Shakespeare's *Merry Wives of Windsor* and *Henry IV*, or having the traits of him. His death is reported in *Henry V*. Engaging, witty, he's a rogue who takes robust pleasure in drinking, wenching, and other such "sins." He is shamelessly self-indulgent and a monumental liar, but his zest for life makes him irresistible.

The term in use, by R.Z. Sheppard in *Time*, April 24, 1989:

> But Welles was not made for that more contemporary medium, TV. His Falstaffian girth, so impressive on stage and screen, seemed grotesque when stuffed into the small tube. The voice that shivered the old Philco during the Depression sounded hokey when it was used to seduce would-be sophisticates of the '70s.

And by CBS News anchor Dan Rather, paying tribute to Charles Kuralt in the *New York Times*, July 13, 1997:

> Charles, who died on July 4 at the age of 62, was not the Falstaff of CBS News, however, as some might think. Yes, he loved playing the bon vivant, and his "On the Road" crew sometimes seemed as much a band of rogues as Pistol, Bardolph and Hal.

Another example, by Peter J. Boyer on National Public Radio's *Morning Edition*, February 28, 1989, describes the *Today* show's ebullient weatherman Willard Scott as "the Falstaff of morning television."

far, far better thing, a An act that transcends one's normal standard of behavior especially in moral quality, often with a sense of self-sacrifice. From the closing lines of Charles Dickens' novel of the French Revolution, *A Tale of Two Cities*. As Sidney Carton ascends the guillotine to be executed in the place of Charles Darnay, these are the words he speaks:

> It is a far, far better thing that I do, than I have ever done; it is a far, far better rest that I go to, than I have ever known.

Carton is a cynical, self-destructive alcoholic who loves Lucie Manette. Lucie loves the upright and good Darnay, who is condemned to die during the REIGN OF TERROR. Carton visits Darnay in prison, exchanges places, and sees to it that the unconscious Darnay is smuggled to safety. By this act of unselfish love, Carton transforms his dark and aimless life.

The term in use, by Bill Berkrot, Reuters, November 20, 1995, on German tennis star Steffi Graf:

> But the year was so full of tennis triumph—including an emotional U.S. Open final victory over Monica Seles she now considers a far, far better thing than she has ever done—that Graf insists she will remember it as "the best year of my career."

And by columnist Florence King in the *National Review,* April 8, 1996, mocking presidential candidate Bob Dole's habit of speaking of himself in the third person:

> Considering how rapidly language horrors spread in this country, the Third-Person Diminutive is likely to catch on, but before it gets carved in marble we should test it on a sampling of notables and listen carefully:
> "Nat Hale only regrets that he has but one life to give for his country."
> "Johnny Paul Jones has not yet begun to fight."
> "It's a far, far better thing Sid Carton does than he has ever done."

far from the madding crowd A peaceful locale, away from the frenzied hurly-burly of normal existence. This phrase is from the poem "Elegy Written in a Country Church Yard," by Thomas Gray, published in 1751. It's a favorite cliché of travel writers, used to describe "get-away-from-it-all" vacations. But keep in mind that the rural life of Gray's time was very different—most of the denizens of small, quiet villages were truly isolated from the outside world. Their talent, ambition, or beauty were known only to a few:

> Far from the madding crowd's ignoble strife,
> Their sober wishes never learned to stray;
> Along the cool sequestered vale of life
> They kept the noiseless tenor of their way.

Thomas Hardy chose the phrase as the title of his 1874 novel of life in rural Dorset.
The term in use, by Robert A. Erlandson, in the *Baltimore Sun,* June 7, 1995:

> Two years ago, determined to secure the future of their 15-acre paradise, far from the madding crowd, Ms. Woodward, 46, a lawyer, and her husband, Robert W. Devlin, 51, a real estate agent, made a unique proposal to county officials—that their farm be designated a historic district.

And by Patrick Marshall in his computer advice column in the *Seattle Times,* March 2, 1997:

> I checked again with several service providers and, unfortunately, didn't find any that have immediate plans to provide toll-free access to your community. . . . For those who choose to live far from the madding crowd, that means toll calls.

fascism; fascist An anti-democratic, authoritarian, nationalistic and sometimes racist movement in politics and government that glorifies the state over the individual; or a movement or philosophy that shares some or all of these traits. Characteristics may include a dictatorial charismatic leader, celebration of military conquest, and mystical glorification of national history, race, and destiny. Government typically controls business, and there is little or no tolerance for opposition of any kind.

The term is often loosely applied to right-wing views, or to tactics and characteristics such as ruthlessness, cruelty, and racial and religious hatred considered typical of a fascist movement.

Fascism was the name taken by an Italian extreme nationalist party formed in 1919 to oppose communism. The Fascists took their name and emblem from the "fasces," a symbol of authority in ancient Rome—a bundle of wooden rods containing an axe. The Fascists controlled Italy from 1922 to 1943 under the leadership of Benito Mussolini.

The ascendancy of Fascism in Italy foreshadowed the rise of Nazism and Adolf Hitler in Germany a few years later.

Given the horrific history of Fascism, "fascist" is a highly charged epithet, but perhaps our distance from the reality of Hitler and Mussolini and the irresistible urge to overstate a grievance have led to the devaluation of this important word, as these examples may illustrate.

The term in use, by Gloria Steinem on the subject of *Hustler* publisher Larry Flynt, quoted by Jim Sullivan of the *Boston Globe,* in the *Detroit News,* January 18, 1997:

> In a subsequent telephone interview, Steinem says she doesn't think she's raising Flynt's profile by contributing to the public debate. "His profile is already there," she says. "It's whether people perceive him as First Amendment hero or sexual fascist."

And by Deb Price, the *Detroit News,* April 11, 1997:

> Chris has fallen victim to what author Michelangelo Signorile terms "body fascism," pressure to conform to a very narrow notion of attractiveness.

And an interesting twist from the Associated Press, April 12, 1997, quoting a mob in Tehran:

> Chanting "Death to fascist Germany," thousands of Iranians marched to the German Embassy on Friday, and Iran's president vowed that a Berlin court ruling that Tehran was behind the murder of dissidents "will not remain unanswered."

Faulknerian \fȯk-'nir-ē-ən, -'ner-\ Resembling the characters, themes, settings, or style of William Faulkner, American novelist and short story writer (1897–1962) who won the Nobel Prize for Literature in 1949 and two Pulitzer prizes.

His characters are prisoners of their pasts, their society, their personalities. As Malcolm Cowley noted in his introduction to *The Portable Faulkner* in 1946: "They also carry, whether heroes or villains, a curious sense of submission to their fate. . . . They are haunted, obsessed, driven forward by some inner necessity. . . . "

Faulkner was born in Mississippi and lived there most of his life. His

writing explored the Southern past, the burden of slavery and the catastrophe of the Civil War, conflict between the old ways and modern life,
and relations between the races.

The setting for his stories is the imaginary Yoknapatawpha County of
Mississippi, where he created a rich, detailed variety of characters: decaying aristocrats and cunning, avaricious and unscrupulous white trash (*see*
SNOPES). His novels and stories are characterized by tragic themes and
bizarre and melodramatic violence.

His style produced a dense narrative, the result of rapid shifts in point
of view, repeated counterpoint of themes and motifs, echoing memories—
the sense of an underlying emotional chaos.

The term in use, by Jack Kroll in *Newsweek,* October 15, 1989:

> The resonant expressionist setting is perfect for the Faulknerian
> texture of the play that takes in the lynch-hungry rednecks, their
> virago wives, the murderous sheriff who's driven his wife to reli-
> gious hysteria.

And by Fred Hobson, reviewing *The Politics of Rage: George Wallace,
the Origins of the New Conservatism, and the Transformation of American
Politics,* by Dan Carter, in the *Los Angeles Times,* January 28, 1996:

> Nearly a Faulknerian character in the single-minded devotion to
> his "design," Wallace determined early to become governor and
> set out to do whatever was necessary to accomplish that.

fault line A split or rift; geologically, a fracture in the crust of a planet or
a moon with displacement of one side of the fracture relative to the other.
Many of these lines occur where TECTONIC PLATES have bumped together in their vast geological minuets around the globe.

The term also describes deep divisions in society or among nations.
Fault lines are sources of earthquakes—in both geological and extended
senses.

The San Andreas fault in California is the best known geological fault
line in the United States, but there are some other fascinating ones, such
as the Dead Sea Transform, where the Arabian Plate and the African Plate
lie uneasily side by side. This fault line illustrates both senses of the term:
it is not only geological but cultural as well. Historically it has separated
the Hebraic and Arabic traditions. The Golan Heights result from a slip
along this complex of faults. The fault is still active, advises our staff pale-
ontologist with dry understatement.

Another fault is the wonderfully named Indus/Tsangpo Suture, the line
where India collided with Asia, leaving chunks of seabed protruding at
the headwaters of the Indus River in the Himalayas.

The term in use, by David Hoffman, the *Washington Post,* May 13, 1996:

> Stalin still symbolizes a fault line in Russian politics—dividing
> those who want reform, often described as "de-Stalinization,"
> from those who resist it.

Another example, from the *New Republic,* December 30, 1996:

> In a widely quoted article three years ago in *Foreign Affairs,* the prominent Harvard political scientist [Samuel P. Huntington] argued that the fault lines between civilizations rather than borders between states represent the battle lines of the future.

Faustian bargain \\'faù-stē-ən, 'fȯ-\\ A bargain made or done for present gain without regard for future cost or consequences; a pact with the Devil—selling one's soul in order to gain power, knowledge, wealth, beauty, eternal youth, or another desired goal.

It is an age-old theme: one may gain short-term delights, but the Devil always comes to collect in the end.

The term comes from a body of literature about a quasi-legendary 16th century German magician who became the subject of numerous literary and musical works. In 1587 *The History of Dr. Faustus, the Notorious Magician and Master of the Black Arts* appeared and became popular; Christopher Marlowe used him as the central character in his *Tragical History of Dr. Faustus* in the late 16th century. In the 19th century, Goethe developed the theme of the struggle between the best and worst elements of man's nature, and Wagner, Berlioz, Gounod, and others wrote operas on the subject, the best known of which is Gounod's *Faust.*

The term in use, by Joan Ryan in the *San Francisco Chronicle,* November 2, 1995:

> To grasp the depth of the Faustian bargain that players make with the NFL, spend an afternoon in the trainer's room of any pro team. The career-threatening injury to fullback William Floyd's knee last Sunday has pointed up with frightening clarity what every player knows: He has sold more than his skills to the NFL. He has sold his body.

And in a *Seattle Times* editorial of August 25, 1997, against the American Medical Association's endorsement of products of the Sunbeam Corporation for a substantial fee. The AMA had contended the deal would make funds available for education and research:

> AMA leaders announced last week that they've reconsidered the product-endorsement arrangement. But Sunbeam has signaled it won't let the medical lobby off the hook so fast.
>   Faustian bargains are hard to undo. That is something foolish AMA lobbyists should have considered before they signed Sunbeam's dotted line.

Fawkes, Guy \\'fȯks\\ English conspirator (1570–1606) in the famed Gunpowder Plot of 1604–05.

A small group of Roman Catholics planned to murder King James I of England and members of Parliament by exploding a large cache of gunpowder in the cellars under the House of Lords on November 5, when the king would appear at the opening of Parliament. Fawkes was in the cellar, ready to strike the match, when he was arrested. (Historians suggest that the king's intelligence network had discovered the plot much earlier, but let it go to the last minute in order to achieve the maximum political advantage.)

Fawkes was tortured to obtain the names of his coconspirators and was executed in front of the Houses of Parliament before a large crowd. Parliament established a day of thanksgiving for its deliverance. The British now celebrate Guy Fawkes night on November 5 with fireworks and bonfires in which "guys," or effigies of Guy Fawkes, are burned.

Guy Fawkes evoked, by Pat Truly in commentary in the *Lexington (Ky.) Herald-Leader,* August 12, 1996, on opposition to legislation to place taggants, or tracers, in explosives to assist law enforcement authorities:

> We can track cliques of suspicious foreigners and figure out who blew up the World Trade Center. But we play heck trying to trace a simple black powder pipe bomb constructed by some angry native-born n'er-do-well with a grudge against humanity. Any would-be Guy Fawkes who wants his moment in the limelight stands a good chance to get away with it.

And by Dave Wood in the the *Philadelphia Daily News,* June 6, 1990, reviewing Roy Blount Jr.'s novel *First Hubby,* a tale told by the husband of the first woman president:

> *First Hubby* gets off to a fast start as its narrator, Guy Fox, a Southern writer who inherited at least some of Guy Fawkes' proclivities, records in his journal how he met the beauteous Clementine in the troubled '60s and how Clementine got to be president of the United States a quarter-century later.

feeding frenzy An intense, usually wild, agitated, disorderly bout of eating; also the excited pursuit of something by a group. Predators under the effects of a feeding frenzy may become so violent and uncontrolled that they blindly tear and rend anything within reach, including each other.

Applied to human activity, the expression characterizes a hyper-enthusiastic fad, mob mentality, or hysteria in which some purpose is pursued en masse with a frantic energy. The term often describes news coverage overkill, where vastly disproportionate resources are summoned to pounce on an incident or personality which has suddenly captured public interest. The level of excitement and coverage, and the damage done to the subjects of such an onslaught, are often not at all related to the importance of the issue.

The term in use, by Peter Andrews, writing about Grover Cleveland in *American Heritage,* October 6, 1994:

> Once in office, however, he found an insistent press particularly vexing. He married during his first term, and the press turned his honeymoon into the kind of feeding frenzy we see today.

And by Martin McNeal in the *Sacramento Bee,* May 22, 1996:

When the team sported the tie-dyed shirts on the medal stand, it sparked a clothing feeding frenzy of sorts that prompted a 1996 re-run. The shirts became the most sought-after items on the streets of Barcelona. . . .

Another example, quoted by Esther Schrader, Knight-Ridder/Tribune News Service, in the *San Jose Mercury News,* August 20, 1996, on investment prospects in Mexico:

"We're not going to see a feeding frenzy," said analyst Marla Marron, a Latin America expert at Salomon Brothers investment firm in New York.

feet of clay A flaw of character that is usually not readily apparent.

The term comes from Daniel 2:33, in the Old Testament. Nebuchadnezzar, king of Babylon, dreamed of an image which had a head of gold, breast and arms of silver, belly and thighs of brass, legs of iron, and feet of iron and clay. According to Daniel's interpretation, the feet were the image's weakness, and the dream foretold the fall of Nebuchadnezzar's empire.

The term in use, by Tom Baxter in his "On Politics" column in the *Atlanta Journal and Constitution,* June 6, 1997, on the revelation that a Republican candidate for governor previously touted for his integrity had been involved in a 10-year adulterous affair:

The prospect of a GOP struggle between a thrice-married, twice-defeated businessman and a party-switching straight arrow with feet of clay is enough to set Democrats to hugging themselves. . . .

Another example, from the *Washington Post,* December 8, 1989, quoting reaction to racist and anti-Semitic statements in the just-published diaries of H.L. Mencken:

"This hero has not only feet of clay, but feet of mud," said Laurence M. Katz, president of the Baltimore Jewish Council. "Any respect I ever had for him is shattered."

Felliniesque Fantastic, dreamily erotic, surreal, characteristic of or resembling the work of Italian film director Federico Fellini, with obscure, intensely personal fantasies and numbers of physically grotesque extras to enhance the bizarre context of his stories.

Some of his most famous films are: *La Strada* (1954); *La Dolce Vita* (1959); *8½* (1963); *Satyricon* (1969); and *Amarcord* (1973). In its portrayal of a decadent social scene in late 1950s Italy, *La Dolce Vita* foreshadowed the frenzied media pursuit of the famous and infamous. In fact, the word *paparazzi* was born in this film; Paparazzo was the name of a street photographer.

The term in use, by Don Kardong in *Runner's World,* January 1, 1994, describing the American Airlines Miami Mile, which features, among other things, a human-canine event:

In the park behind the grandstands, the circus atmosphere extends to live music, assorted food and more entertainment for those who aren't entertained enough by the sight of their mayor trying to dribble a basketball for a mile. . . . And then it's your turn. This has had the ambience of a track meet to this point, albeit a Felliniesque one.

And by John Mintz and Sandra Saperstein in the *Washington Post,* December 8, 1987, describing the scene in Washington during the visit of Soviet leader Mikhail Gorbachev:

It was a Felliniesque scene: a woman clad in a garbage bag over her full-length fur coat pacing Lafayette Park from rally to rally, a man calling himself "Mr. Wake-Up America" hiring a plane with banner to take his message to the skies, and an outraged Afghan in a curbside argument with a top D.C. police official yelling, "You will be Soviet slaves."

fellow traveler One that sympathizes with and often furthers the ideals and program of an organized group (such as the Communist Party) without belonging to the group or taking part in its activities. Not, as it might seem, someone who sits next to you on the plane. Historically, the term was an attack, labeling someone a Communist sympathizer. The expression is now used more generally, but still with a negative tone, to imply that someone is close to a suspect cause.

Leon Trotsky coined the reference in criticizing Russian authors he believed were not sufficiently dedicated to the revolution: "They are not the artists of the proletarian revolution, but only its artistic fellow travelers."

The term in use, by William Safire in a *New York Times* column, February 16, 1997:

A decade from now, will America's smug supporters of China's dominance be reviled as naive fellow travelers who neglected America's strategic interests while betraying our principles?

And in an editorial in the *Columbus (Ga.) Ledger-Enquirer,* July 25, 1997, on attempts by Republican insurgents to unseat House Speaker Newt Gingrich:

. . . members of the GOP Class of '94 and their fellow travelers could do themselves and the country a lot of good by behaving like adults. There is a time and place for everything. The thing to do when you have the power to govern is to govern, not squabble publicly over political philosophy.

And by Dotty Griffith in the *Dallas Morning News,* January 18, 1995, on comedienne Beth Donahue:

Fibber McGee's closet

196

If Ms. [Susan] Powter is the drill sergeant of the lean and fit, Ms. Donahue is the fellow traveler to those suffering from dieting failure and fatigue.

Fibber McGee's closet A closet into which anything and everything has been jammed without order and out of which everything tumbles when the door is opened.

One of the most durable comedies of radio's Golden Age, *Fibber McGee and Molly* was on the air 1935–56, starring the real-life husband and wife team of Jim and Marian Jordan. The show's famous running gag centered around Fibber's overstuffed closet, the contents of which crashed down on anyone opening it, to appropriate sound effects. The Broadcast Pioneers Library of the University of Maryland calls the show's humor "vaudevillian." (*See* VAUDEVILLE.) The show gave America a catch-phrase (from Molly's mouth): "'Tain't funny, McGee."

The McGees' address at 79 Wistful Vista also was famous for their windbag neighbor, Throckmorton P. Gildersleeve, who was so popular a character that he had his own spinoff series, *The Great Gildersleeve.*

The term in use, by Dan Keating in the *Miami Herald,* January 17, 1996, describing the Internet:

The world's biggest computer network makes Fibber McGee's closet look like the work of a neurotic neatnik. Disorganization, chaos, and maelstrom don't begin to describe it.

And by Patty Fisher of the *San Jose Mercury News,* May 29, 1995, in an editorial in support of a school bond proposal:

My daughter's Palo Alto school is an example. From the outside it looks OK. But inside it's Fibber McGee's closet.

fifteen minutes of fame A statement of the expectation that everyone will be famous for something in this media-driven era, but not for long.

A phrase originating with the ineffable Andy Warhol (1927?–1987)—artist, filmmaker, professional trendsetter, and self-professed weirdo. In a prophetic comment on our era of instant, fleeting, and insubstantial celebrity, he observed: "In the future everyone will be famous for fifteen minutes."

Warhol was one of the creators of pop art, based on commercial art. He and his fellow pop artists painted photograph-like images of soup cans, comic strips and other icons of commerce, in which all personal elements of the artist's view were deliberately omitted. He also produced garishly colored multiple images of Marilyn Monroe and other celebrities.

With his talent, silver wig, and idiosyncratic manner, he was well beyond a caricature of himself; rather he was a poseur whose poses were struck throughout his life and work. He knew it, we knew it, and he knew that we knew it, and he knew that we would still buy it. One final quotation: "I always thought I'd like my tombstone to be blank. No epitaph, and no name. Well, actually I'd like it to say (figment.)"

The term in use, by Molly Ivins, in the *Progressive,* November 11, 1995:

> Speaking of Texas, we're awfully proud of Judge Sam Kiser of
> Amarillo, who achieved his fifteen minutes of fame by telling a
> bilingual mother that speaking Spanish in the home constitutes
> child abuse and she could lose custody over it.

Another example, indeed the one that Warhol himself could not improve
on, from the *Los Angeles Times,* April 4, 1995, on Kato Kaelin of the O.J.
Simpson case:

> "While I think that he's getting his fifteen minutes of fame right
> now, he may be able to parlay that into a short-term career,"
> [casting director Marc] Hirschfeld continues.

And by Michael Kimmelman in the *New York Times,* March 28, 1997:

> Andres Serrano's 15 minutes are up. An artist whose reputation
> grew, above all, from the enemies he made in public office, he
> was defended by people who evidently believed that to endorse
> him was somehow brave or correct, never mind that his pho-
> tographs . . . were trite and mean.

fifth column A group of secret sympathizers or supporters of an enemy
that engage in espionage or sabotage within defense lines or national borders.

The term comes from the Spanish Civil War (1936–39). In an interview,
rebel General Emilio Mola described the four columns of troops advancing on Republican-held Madrid in October 1936. When asked which column would take the city, he said, "The fifth," referring to sympathizers
within the city who would rise up when the time was right.

The Fifth Column was the title of Ernest Hemingway's only play (1938).
The phrase was applied to Nazi sympathizers in Western Europe, and is
now used in the broader sense of hidden traitors within an organization.

The term in use, by David Awbrey in the *Wichita Eagle,* February 24,
1991:

> The question is whether Democratic legislators will join the gov-
> ernor's merry band and funnel millions of tax dollars into the
> pockets of some of the state's most affluent citizens. If they do,
> it will mean that Democrats in Kansas have become traitors in
> the class war, a fifth column for the affluent.

And from Dick Cooper in a guest column in the *Philadelphia Inquirer,*
September 25, 1994, describing his battle with a squirrel gnawing on his
porch:

> As with the creeping Red Menace of the 1950s and social decay
> in general, it took a while before we realized the true danger we
> were in. It was just a little scratch, a tiny gnaw.
> But this fifth-column rodent kept coming back when we

weren't around. By the end of the week, it was clear that this was not just a casual bite.

And in a *Washington Post* story, April 18, 1988, on the troubles of Continental Airlines:

> [Continental president Frank] Lorenzo complained about the difficulty of "trying to run an airline when you have two fifth columns within your airline," whom he identified as the pilots and the mechanics.

film noir \\'film-'nwär\\ A genre of crime film featuring cynical, malevolent characters in a sleazy setting and an ominous atmosphere conveyed by shadowy photography and foreboding music; also a film of this type. Film noir developed out of the American crime/mystery/thriller movies of the 1940s. Frequently filmed in black and white in seedy urban settings, these films make use of flashbacks and voice-over narrations, usually by the cynical, world-weary hero. The phrase is now used to suggest the atmosphere, style, or characters typical of these films.

The term, literally "black film" in French, was coined by French film devotee Nino Frank in 1946. Classics of the genre include *The Maltese Falcon* (1941), *This Gun for Hire* (1942), *Laura* (1944) and *Out of the Past* (1947).

The endings in these movies are not always happy and the hero does not always unambiguously overcome. Leading men such as Humphrey Bogart, Dana Andrews, Robert Mitchum and Alan Ladd made their mark in these movies, portraying tough, laconic characters in rumpled trenchcoats with cigarettes dangling from their lips. They roamed the night streets, which always gleamed with fresh rain in the harsh light of street lamps. These flawed heroes struggled to unravel, but frequently became entangled in, the schemes of bad men and wicked women.

Sometimes "noirish" is used alone to describe the look, mood, or style. The term in use, by Natalie Angier in the *New York Times,* July 15, 1997:

> For most pregnant women, the routine prenatal ultrasound scan is an event of unalloyed pleasure, sweeter by far than a blood test, amniocentesis, or the monthly weigh-in at the obstetrician's office.
>
> Assuming you can make sense of the grainy film-noir images on the sonogram screen, it is thrilling to see the fetus thrash about like a real baby and stick its thumb in its mouth. . . .

And by Vic Sussman in a description of the horrors of the Motor Vehicle Division of the District of Columbia government in the *Washington Post Magazine,* September 18, 1988:

> Sometimes people begin with a little story. My car was stolen, or booted, or my permit went through the washing machine, or my dog ate the title. The clerk, leaning on the counter like a film noir bartender, listens, then ships them out to other rooms: 1063, 1065. . . .

final solution *often capitalized* The Nazi program for extermination of all Jews in Europe through a systematic program of mass murder in concentration camps.

According to Robert Leckie in *Delivered from Evil: The Saga of World War II* (1987), the term was coined by Reinhard Heydrich, the Nazi leader assigned by Hitler the "housecleaning" detail of deciding the fate of three million Jews in the portion of Poland that Germany shared with the Russians. "Heydrich began with the Jews by deporting them to German labor camps, but in his first report to Hitler he used the now notorious and chilling phrase, 'the final solution' of the Jewish problem," Leckie writes.

With its ghastly associations, the term is definitive in characterizing as utterly reprehensible schemes to eliminate (literally or figuratively) those of opposing views or values.

The term in use, by Matthew Bigg for Reuters, April 25, 1997:

> A U.N. aerial search confirmed Friday that some 85,000 Rwandan Hutu refugees fled into the Zairian jungle and aid agencies accused Tutsi-dominated rebels of seeking a "final solution" by condemning them to die.

And a hyperbolic and vitriolic use, by conservative activist James Carrett in the alternative Dartmouth College student newspaper, the *Dartmouth Review,* October 19, 1988, likening Dartmouth president James Freedman to Hitler:

> Der Freedman would need such a weapon to carry out his most precious dream—the "Final Solution" of the Conservative Problem at Dartmouth.

fin de siècle \ˌfan-də-sē-ˈe-kəl; faⁿ-də-syeklᵊ\ Of, relating to, or characteristic of the close of the 19th century, especially its literary and artistic climate of sophistication, world-weariness, and fashionable despair. In French, it means "the end of the century." While the phrase once referred to progressive ideas and customs, it now connotes decadence, fatigue, the end of an era, and sometimes angst.

The term in use, by Ira Berkow in the *New York Times,* May 18, 1997:

> The first organized women's basketball game was held at Smith College in 1892. Signs were posted outside the gymnasium: MEN ARE NOT PERMITTED TO WATCH. And the hoopsters wore long dresses.
> It's a long, long way from the fin de siècle.

And by Laura Berman in the *Detroit News,* January 9, 1997, protesting the vogue for cigar smoking:

> What began as a kind of retro macho celebration in private clubs and at special "cigar parties" has become an oppressively noxious

trend. Now a cult of the few is smoking out the rest of us.
Is this—swank as stank—the most imaginative form of fin de
siècle decadence Americans can come up with?

finest hour, their A moment of surpassing greatness and courage; a
rising to the occasion in a terrible test of character and endurance.
The phrase comes from Winston Churchill, addressing the embattled
British people on June 18, 1940. Days before the British army had barely escaped disaster in the evacuation of DUNKIRK. Nazi Germany was
triumphant on the Continent, and Britain stood alone. Speaking in the
House of Commons, Churchill told his people the Battle of Britain was
about to begin:

> Hitler knows he will have to break us in these islands or lose the
> war. Let us therefore brace ourselves to our duties, and so bear
> ourselves that if the British Empire and its Commonwealth last
> for a thousand years, men will still say, "This was their finest
> hour."

The term in use, by veteran broadcast reporter Daniel Schorr recalling
the role of the press in the Watergate scandal, reported by Gannett News
Service, August 7, 1994:

> To Schorr, this was life at its best. "I thought it was journalism's
> finest hour. Also, the FBI's finest hour, the finest hour of the
> Senate."

Another example, from the *Manchester Guardian Weekly,* February 2,
1992:

> During the Suez crisis—the *Observer's* finest hour—when Astor
> led the fight against Eden, the paper lost both Jewish readers and,
> more importantly, advertisers, who started seeing the paper as
> too left-wing.

Finlandization A foreign policy of neutrality under the influence of the
Soviet Union; the conversion to such a policy.
This Cold War term describes the negative view of some in the West of
Finland's situation. Finland is a democratic country sharing a long bor-
der with the former Soviet Union; the Soviets exerted considerable control within Finland. The term was coined by German politician Franz-Josef
Strauss to reflect the fear that Soviet influence was growing in Western
European countries and influencing their foreign policy even while their
democratic and capitalistic systems remained intact.
Finland's view was different: as a tiny country in the shadow of a nuclear
superpower, the Finns sought to preserve their democracy—and had no
choice but to take into account the needs, demands and moods of their
giant neighbor. As David J. Lynch of *USA Today* described it, March 19,
1997, "Finland was the international equivalent of the frightened home-
owner living next door to a gangster."

The term in use, applied to U.S.–Canadian relations by Allan Fotheringham in *Maclean's* magazine, December 7, 1992:

> Since we have just seen our last Grey Cup, it moving to San Anto-
> nio or Sacramento next year, it is time to contemplate. Our semi-
> American Prime Minister is now being emulated by our
> semi-American Canadian Football League, which feels com-
> pelled to commit self-immolation by moving south of the bor-
> der. . . .
> This fits in perfectly with the Finlandization of Canada, a minor
> blip on the world horizon whose Gross Domestic Product next
> year will be roughly equivalent to Madonna's income.

And by Takashi Inoguchi in the *International Herald Tribune,* May 19,
1997:

> Conciliation does not have to mean Finlandization. But if Asians
> get any softer toward China, Beijing could begin objecting to any
> alliance it takes to be anti-Chinese in inspiration or intent.

fire and brimstone The torments suffered by sinners in hell. From the
New Testament Book of Revelation. Brimstone is sulfur—so picture something like a volcanic lake of stinking, smoking molten lava.

To preach a "fire-and-brimstone" sermon is to threaten the congregation or others with damnation in hell for their sins, or to send such a message in a passionate, fiery style.

The term in use, quoted by Doyle McManus in the *Los Angeles Times,*
February 22, 1996:

> Clinton aides said that they do not believe Buchanan is likely to
> win the Republican nomination. But they are licking their chops
> over the prospect that the fiery columnist will continue picking
> up delegates during the remaining primaries and play a major
> role at the GOP convention. . . .
> "If you liked Houston, you'll love San Diego," crowed one,
> referring to Buchanan's fire-and-brimstone speech at the 1992
> convention which turned many voters away from the party.

And by Sarah Durkin and James Plummer in the *Detroit News,* December 1, 1996:

> Now that the holiday season has officially arrived, expect the
> Center for Science in the Public Interest to celebrate life's boun-
> ty by doling out generous portions of fire-and-brimstone-
> evoking guilt in those who dare to eat traditional holiday treats.
> To remain in the public eye, the center must resort to scare tac-
> tics and threats of coronary disease to bring in the season.

fire wall A wall constructed to prevent the spread of fire. The term is also
used to describe a barrier designed to stop the spread of a problem or to
insulate one part of a business operation from another to avoid questions

of conflict of interest. In the computer age, it refers to programs which prevent intruders from gaining unauthorized access to computers or data. The term in use, in *Communications Week,* October 14, 1996:

> Network security is more critical than ever, and a bigger business than it used to be. Fire walls—the new darling of the network security arsenal—have catapulted onto the front line of network defense as corporations clamor for Internet and intranet access.

And quoted in the *Houston Chronicle,* July 31, 1996, on the Federal Reserve's proposed changes in bank regulations:

> "The Fed addressed exactly the fire walls that have been hamstringing banks in securities underwriting," said Larry LaRocco, managing director of the ABA Securities Association, a unit of the American Bankers Association that represents 20 of the largest U.S. banks.

And Rolando Bonachea, acting director of Radio Marti, quoted in the *Los Angeles Times,* August 20, 1996, on the decision to move the station (similar to Radio Free Europe, aimed at Cuba) from Washington to Miami:

> And he defends the move to Miami as logical and economical. Radio Marti staff members, he said, work behind "a fire wall of protection that ensures that our journalists can operate free from outside influences or internal pressures."

fire when ready, Gridley A phrase giving authorization to begin. The words were first uttered by Commodore George Dewey, commanding the American fleet at the Battle of Manila Bay in the Philippine Islands on May 1, 1898. (Gridley was the captain of Dewey's flagship.) Actually, the quote is, "You may fire when you are ready, Gridley."

The outcome of this battle of the Spanish–American War was a foregone conclusion: the Americans won a great victory over a vastly inferior force without losing a single man. Dewey's statement has since become a catch phrase in situations where victory is assured with minimal effort.

An example, from Michael Dolan, writing in Washington, D.C.'s *City Paper,* May 5, 1989:

> Nobody goes into journalism to *work;* if all a newshawk has to do to avoid having to open all those envelopes is pay out some money, then fire when ready, Gridley.

By Alan Lupo in the *Boston Globe,* August 6, 1989:

> The Republican State Committee says it has prepared radio advertisements, mailing and even a slogan—"The less sense they make, the more sense we make." It ain't "Damn the torpedoes, full speed ahead," or even "Fire when ready, Gridley," but it could prove catchy.

And, with a slight variation, by Sandy Grady in the *Pittsburgh Press,* January 9, 1991:

> They'll bloviate for hours on the meaning of a U.S.–Iraq blood-fest—whether its oil, aggression, jobs, or Bush's latest reason, to ease the U.S. recession. In the end, they'll write Bush his ticket: Fire when ready, Chief.

flat–earther Person who believes the Earth is flat. In the opinion of some, militant benighted ignoramuses; nincompoops; those considered to be doggedly ignorant, who deny obvious facts which contradict their beliefs. Or, more kindly, those who hold beliefs well outside the mainstream.

This is an epithet with a history. In fact, it is itself based on a historical misperception: the belief that everyone in Europe thought the Earth was flat until Columbus made his voyage. This canard was popularized by Washington Irving's *History of the Life and Voyages of Christopher Columbus* (1828). Historians have demonstrated that there were very few scholars in ancient and medieval times who believed the Earth was flat.

"Flat-earth man" began showing up in the mid-19th century as a label for someone utterly wrongheaded. Supporters of Darwin's theory of evolution compared the views of their religious opponents to the alleged medieval belief that the Earth was flat; they saw religion as the enemy of science and thus of truth.

Rudyard Kipling had fun with the conceit in his 1917 story "The Village That Voted the Earth Was Flat": London newspapermen get a speeding ticket in the village of Huckley. They avenge themselves by publishing a trumped-up story that the villagers had voted the Earth was flat. Never mind that the reporters made up the whole thing—the newspaper increased circulation and the town is derided throughout the country.

One final note: there *is* a Flat Earth Society—in Southern California, of course.

The term in use, by Frank Hayes, in *Computerworld,* January 20, 1997:

> We've all heard about the studies that show . . . since the dawn of desktop computers, how corporate productivity has barely inched up at all. . . . This amazing, blind faith has made IT departments the Flat Earth Society of the corporate world. We've seen the pictures from space; we just can't believe it's true.

And by C. Fraser Smith in the *Baltimore Sun,* April 23, 1995:

> A coalition of organizations and private citizens succeeded in pulling the Assembly another step away from its flat-Earth approach to a problem that leaves 17,000 or so Americans dead and many more seriously injured each year.

Fleet Street The London press. Named after the street in London which is the center of the London newspaper district. Today it is a synonym for English journalism, although the newspapers themselves have moved elsewhere.

The term in use, by Marvin Kitman in *Newsday,* February 5, 1996, on press magnate Rupert Murdoch:

> Wherever he has been, Australia, the United Kingdom, establishing a news presence is the first thing he does. In England, to gain a news presence, he destroyed the craft unions. Who needs Fleet Street when you can bounce things off satellites and print anywhere? He destroyed Fleet Street.

And by Michael Neill and Michelle Green in *People,* July 15, 1996, profiling Mark Phillips, ex-husband of Britain's Princess Anne:

> In 1973—before Charles and Di, before Andrew and Fergie—Princess Anne and her Royal Dragoons officer had their royal wedding. Fleet Street raved about the dashing commoner who had landed the willful Anne. . . . As with so many Windsor marriages, though, the magic evaporated.

flotsam and jetsam Wreckage of a ship or its cargo that is floating, has sunk, or has washed ashore. In general, miscellaneous debris or wreckage, unimportant odds and ends, lost or drifting people and things.

The terms are from admiralty law, which pertains to ships, their cargoes, and the sea. In law, flotsam and jetsam have specific meanings.

Flotsam (derived from the same root as "float") refers to floating goods from a ship that has been wrecked or sunk; jetsam (a variant of "jettison," from the Latin word meaning "to throw") refers to goods deliberately thrown overboard in an attempt to stabilize and save a ship in distress.

The term in use, in an editorial in the *New Republic,* January 30, 1995, on the government of Boris Yeltsin in Russia:

> But his loyal "power ministries" of defense, interior and intelligence are the ones most staffed by the flotsam and jetsam of "Weimar Russia": generals, spies, industrial commissars and incompetents inclined toward fantasies about a reborn Russian superpower, blind mistrust of the West, intrigue and DISINFORMATION.

And by Marvin Kitman in *Newsday,* July 1, 1996, reviewing *The Rosie O'Donnell Show:*

> Her frame of reference is totally TV. This can be annoying. But I understand: She is a child of TV. Her unconscious is filled with the flotsam and jetsam of TV viewing. She can't help it. Whatever anyone says, it reminds her of TV.

Foggy Bottom The U.S. Department of State, so called from the neighborhood in Washington, D.C., where the State Department is located.

Lower reaches of the area were marshy and flat, generating the mists that gave the place its name. While historians and geologists insist the area was not completely a swamp before, enemies of the Department of State bureaucracy would undoubtedly contend that it is now: the name is irresistibly suggestive of obscure language, muddled thinking, and bureaucratic lassitude.

The term in use, in a *Washington Times* editorial, February 23, 1997:

> Foreign policy-minded Republicans complain that the leadership has shown precious little interest over the past four years in doing anything but criticize and oppose whatever proposal has come out of the White House or Foggy Bottom.

And by Charles Lane in the *New Republic,* July, 29, 1996:

> Christopher's stewardship at Foggy Bottom was not supposed to culminate on such an ambiguous note.

food chain An arrangement within an ecological community according to the order of predation in which each organism uses the next, usually lower, member as a food source. What, or who, is eaten, in what order, and by whom.

It's a term from biology, referring to the sequence of organisms through which energy and materials are passed, as those organisms eat and are eaten in their turn. At the bottom of the food chain are plants, then plant eaters—herbivores; higher up are the carnivores and omnivores. And some carnivores eat other carnivores or omnivores.

The chain can also be pictured as a pyramid, since the total mass of the organisms decreases as you move up the chain: there is much greater mass of green plants in the environment than there is of the animals that feed on the plants. And there is a greater mass of herbivores than of the carnivores that prey on them. At the top of the food chain are the fiercest chompers of all—lions and tigers and bears and their ilk.

The term has come to describe the human PECKING ORDER (to use an animal behavior term). The biggest predators are the guys at the top of an organization who consume the most resources, or the tough guys with the biggest teeth, metaphorically speaking.

The term in use, by Mark Bechtel in *Sports Illustrated,* June 25, 1997, on the commercial success of basketball player Dennis Rodman:

> "There is a place in the marketing food chain for Rodman." In fact, Rodman is one of its biggest carnivores, having earned an estimated $9 million in endorsements in 1996.

Another example, by Jerry Heaster in the *Kansas City Star,* April 25, 1997, on government reform in Kansas City:

> Meanwhile, the loftiest layers of City Hall's bureaucracy came to be perceived as growing fat at the expense of those further down the food chain.

And by Draper Hill in the *Detroit News,* January 12, 1997, describing the effects of a state term limits law:

Lansing veterans worry about the loss of "institutional memory," an increase in the power of staff, lobbyists and bureaucrats, and an unseemly scramble for jobs all along the political food chain.

force majeure \‚fōr-smä-ꞌzhər, ‚fȯr-, -smə-\ Superior or irresistible force; an event or effect that cannot be reasonably anticipated or controlled. A French phrase, meaning "superior force." In insurance law, it's an act of God or an unavoidable event or accident.

The term in use, by Philippa Fletcher, Reuters, April 25, 1997, concerning the Russian government's request for help in destroying its stockpiles of chemical weapons in accordance with an international treaty:

> The Duma [the Russian parliament] appealed to the signatories of the convention not to exclude Russia from its deliberations because of its failure to ratify, which it blamed on "force majeure" circumstances.

Another example, from the *Long Beach Press-Telegram,* August 2, 1993, on Reggie Jackson's induction into the Baseball Hall of Fame:

> As a player, Reggie was force majeure, an overpowering presence who lifted his teams out of the ordinary.

fort *See* HOLD THE FORT.

forty acres and a mule Settlement promised to freed slaves at the end of the Civil War but never given. An unfulfilled promise of future wealth; pie in the sky.

Land was one of the forms of assistance—often never given—to freed slaves after the American Civil War to enable them to become independent. General William Tecumseh Sherman issued a field order in January 1865 directing that every family should have a plot of not more than 40 acres of tillable ground, on land confiscated from rebel landlords. Then during Reconstruction, a bill providing that freedmen should have parcels of unoccupied land in the defeated South, up to 40 acres, was vetoed by President Andrew Johnson.

The term in use, by Patricia Hills in the *Los Angeles Times,* April 27, 1997, reviewing art critic Robert Hughes' television series *American Visions:*

> Such empathetic pictures of blacks disappeared from the art scene by 1870, at the very time when the optimism among abolitionists collapsed. Forty acres and a mule didn't happen; the plantation owners were not about to let their land be confiscated for the sake of the economic independence of the freed slaves.

And again, by Ira Berlin in the *Washington Post,* June 29, 1997, on the proposal that the government issue an official apology to African-Americans for slavery:

Some on the left dismiss an apology as simply not enough; what happened, they ask, to 40 acres and a mule?

for whom the bell tolls Poetic statement of the interdependence of all humans, and of their importance to each other. From the ritual tolling of the church bell at a funeral. The phrase, from John Donne's religious work *Devotions,* is one of the most frequently quoted passages in the English language:

> No man is an island entire of itself; every man is a piece of the Continent, a part of the main; if a clod be washed away by the Sea, Europe is the less, as well as if a promontory were, as well as if a manor of thy friends or of thine own were; any man's death diminishes me, because I am involved in Mankind; and therefore never send to know for whom the bell tolls; it tolls for thee.

Donne (1572–1631), an English poet of the Metaphysical school and dean of St. Paul's Cathedral, wrote satirical and love poetry in his youth ("Go and catch a falling star"). In 1614 he converted from Catholicism to the Anglican church, and became an eloquent and influential preacher.

"For whom the bell tolls" was adopted by Ernest Hemingway as the title of his 1940 novel set in the Spanish Civil War. *Death Be Not Proud,* a book by John Gunther about the death of his child, takes its title from another Donne passage:

> Death be not proud, though some have called thee
> Mighty and dreadful, for thou art not so. . . .

Powerful stuff. It puts Donne in the front rank of those who provide meat for allusion.

The term in use, by Ralph Ellison in the *New York Times,* March 12, 1989, in a collection of statements by writers on behalf of Salman Rushdie, a writer forced into hiding as a result of a death sentence by Muslim religious leaders who objected to Rushdie's book, *The Satanic Verses:*

> This story of a man alone against worldwide intolerance, and a book alone against the craziness of the media, can become the story of many others. The bell tolls for all of us.

In a lighter vein, the phrase is often used in any story associated with bells, as in this example from Tom Greenwood in the *Detroit News,* July 9, 1996:

> Any child in America can tell you the answer to the question:
> "Ask not for whom the bell tolls."
> It tolls for ice cream.

Four Horsemen of the Apocalypse War, famine, pestilence, and death personified as the four major plagues of humankind. They are allegorical figures in the New Testament Book of Revelation 6:2–8, in which St. John envisions the apocalypse, the end of the world. War rides a white horse, Pestilence a red horse, Famine a black horse, and Death a pale horse.

The Spanish novelist Vicente Blasco Ibanez used the phrase as the title of his 1916 book on World War I. But the most famous application was the handiwork of sportswriter Grantland Rice (1880–1954), in which he describes a football victory by Notre Dame over Army in the *New York Tribune,* October 18, 1924:

> Outlined against a blue-gray October sky, the Four Horsemen rode again. In dramatic lore they were known as Famine, Pestilence, Destruction and Death. These are only aliases. Their real names are Stuhldreher, Miller, Crowley and Layden.

The cast of characters is a little off, but Rice probably had forgotten to take his New Testament with him to the game.

Contemporary use of the term is generally in the same humorous vein; it is applied to any four characters united in an enterprise. A remarkable exception to this pattern comes from a speech given by Senator Margaret Chase Smith on the floor of the Senate in 1950. This was her famous "declaration of conscience" against the tactics of Senator Joseph McCarthy (*see* MCCARTHYISM) then at the flood-tide of his power. Senator Smith said:

> I don't want to see the Republican Party ride to political victory on the four horsemen of calumny—fear, ignorance, bigotry, and smear.

Another example, by Hendrik Hertzberg in the *New Republic,* February 27, 1989, on *From: The President* (1989), a collection of memos from the Nixon White House:

> *From: The President* contains pungent memos by H.R. "Bob" Haldeman, John Ehrlichman, Pat Buchanan, and Chuck Colson—the Four Horsemen of the Nixonian apocalypse—but the best are from the master himself, alone and hunched over his dictaphone far into the night.

fourth estate *often capitalized* The public press. The expression was attributed to Edmund Burke by Thomas Carlyle in 1841; here is what Carlyle said Burke said:

> Burke said there were three Estates in Parliament, but in the Reporters' Gallery . . . there sat a fourth Estate more important far than them all.

There is an earlier report of its use in Parliament by Lord Brougham in 1823 or 1824. *Fourth estate* was also used to refer to the army or the mob. In 1752, Henry Fielding wrote:

> None of our political writers . . . take notice of any more than three estates, namely Kings, Lords, and Commons . . . passing

by in silence that very large and powerful body which form the fourth estate in the community—the Mob.

Today, the term consistently refers only to the press. While it recognizes the power of the press, it is often employed with ironic solemnity.

Estate refers to the historical division of the body politic in many European countries, for which there were variations from country to country. In England the divisions of representation in Parliament went like this: first, the Lords Spiritual—the clergy; second, the Lords Temporal—knights and barons; third—the commons. In France, the divisions were first, the clergy; second, the nobility; third, the townsmen.

All of these estates are long out of style *except* the nonhistorical *fourth estate.*

Rudyard Kipling, an ink-stained wretch himself, summed it up:

> Remember the battle and stand aside
> While thrones and powers confess
> That King over all the children of pride
> Is the Press—the Press—the Press!

The term in use, by Edwin Chen and Maria L. LaGanga in the *Los Angeles Times,* November 6, 1996:

> The very next day at a Houston rally, the statesman with a history of good media relations lashes out on camera about a Fourth Estate that he claims simply does not care and, in fact, goes out of its way to pamper the president.

And quoted by Alex Taylor III in *Fortune,* December 9, 1996:

> This is the sort of deflating analysis that drives Chrysler nuts. "We are so radically different that it pains me to see the fourth estate lump us together with our success-challenged competition from across town," [Chrysler's] President Robert Lutz recently told a group of journalists.

Frack *See* FRICK AND FRACK.

fragging Throwing a fragmentation grenade at one's own military officers, often while they are sleeping.

The term originated in the Vietnam War. Fragmentation grenades were the favored instrument for these maimings or killings; the grenade was tossed under the bed or into the tent of the target while he was asleep.

Fraggings were often aimed at getting rid of individuals who were considered threats to the unit through incompetent or overzealous leadership. Estimates of deaths from fragging vary widely, from about 1,000 to less than 100 actually confirmed by the Pentagon.

The term is more widely applied to a sudden, sneaky, and devastating attack.

The term in use, by Albert Eisele in the *Hill,* June 4, 1997:

Shortly after then-Sen. Eugene McCarthy (D–Minn.) became the unlikely catalyst for the anti-Vietnam War movement by fragging President Johnson in the 1968 New Hampshire primary, his ragtag campaign distributed copies of a Beatles record album to a handful of reporters who had covered McCarthy's lonely underdog odyssey. The album's title was altered to read "Gene McCarthy's Magical Mystery Tour". . . .

And in the *Washington Post,* February 2, 1988, quoting an Iowa politician on the power of the *Des Moines Register* in the Iowa precinct caucuses:

"The *Register* is capable of fragging you," says Iowa's Democratic speaker of the House, Donald Avenson, who is working in Missouri Rep. Dick Gephardt's campaign. "They can open the door, throw in the grenade, and boom, you're finished."

Frankenstein One who creates, and is ultimately destroyed by, a technological marvel or scientific advance. In common use, the creation is often conflated with creator, so that the word also can refer to a monstrous creation or a work that ruins its originator.

Victor Frankenstein is the central figure of the GOTHIC novel *Frankenstein* (1818), by Mary Wollstonecraft Shelley (1797–1851). He constructs a being of parts of dead bodies and succeeds in bringing it to life. But Frankenstein's monster is rejected by humans, including its creator, and becomes vengeful. Ultimately it kills Frankenstein's wife and brother, and Frankenstein himself dies in attempting to destroy it.

The story has been told numerous times in wildly and widely varying cinematic versions, so that the tale is well known even though few read the novel. Shelley's powerful themes—the dangers of unbridled and reckless technology, and the responsibility of scientists for their work—reverberate with the public more than ever as our dependence on, and vulnerability to, new and complex technologies grows.

The term in use, in *Time,* April 4, 1988, reporting the death of Patrick Steptoe, a British obstetrician who (with Robert Edwards) developed in vitro fertilization:

To those who feared his achievements would lead to the baby-breeding farms envisioned in Aldous Huxley's *Brave New World,* Steptoe replied, "I am not a wizard or a Frankenstein. All I want to do is help women whose child-producing mechanism is slightly faulty."

And by Stephen Brush, in the *New York Times,* May 29, 1988:

Madonna's success has been a relatively endless 15-minute event. She's been called the ultimate Frankenstein product of MTV: Calculatedly tasteless (when it suits her), relentlessly energetic—coming at you in bright, noisy, media blips.

Also, from Jonathan Alter in the *San Francisco Examiner,* October 13, 1987:

> Alexander Haig, a Republican candidate for president, had been spotted parking his car in a zone reserved for the handicapped.
> Haig the heartless? Wheelchairgate?
> With the revelations last week about the Rev. Pat Robertson's personal life, the hulking "character issue" was turning into the Frankenstein monster of U.S. presidential politics.

free fall The condition of unrestrained motion in a gravitational field; the part of a parachute jump before the parachute opens; a rapid and continuing drop or decline.

The term in use, by James L. Hickman, *Inc.,* August 1, 1995:

> Long before the collapse of the Soviet Empire threw Russia into both economic free fall and a free-market free-for-all, even a casual visitor could see signs of a fledgling, if amateur, entrepreneurial class.

And quoted by *Maclean's* magazine, January 2, 1995:

> Federal Fisheries Minister Brian Tobin said that dwindling stocks continue to head toward oblivion and that he had no choice but to respond with even stricter conservation guidelines. "Our conscience could allow us to do no less," added Tobin. "The fishery is in free fall."

And by Sidney Blumenthal in the *New York Times Book Review,* June 22, 1997, reviewing *The Year the Dream Died: Revisiting 1968 in America* by Jules Witcover:

> This was the opening for [Vice President Hubert] Humphrey to demonstrate his independence, which was what the voters wanted of him. From June to August, he went into free fall, down to 29 percent in the polls.

Freudian slip A slip of the tongue that is motivated by and reveals some unconscious aspect of the mind. Freud believed that there were no simple accidents, and that such events reveal unconscious wishes or conflicts. In popular use the term is applied to statements or behavior not only of people but of even larger entities—towns, companies, nations. And it is applied broadly to include any unintended, embarrassing action or accident.

The term in use, by Mark Simon in the *San Francisco Chronicle,* February 14, 1997:

> NOT SO FREUDIAN SLIP: The masthead of the February 10 edition of the Stanford Daily listed the day as "Moanday," and we all know what they meant by that.

And from Brook Adams in the *Deseret News,* September 21, 1996:

I did a search on "hair dye," "hair coloring" and "gray hair" on the World Wide Web. Many hits I got back, unfortunately, had to do with dogs—Scottish deerhounds and Tibetan mastiffs, bearded collies and dachshunds.

Does the Internet make Freudian slips?

And from Garry Wills, in the *Washington Post,* April 27, 1997:

If any culture is to be understood, historians must read it by judging what it chose to honor. The ancient Greeks did not praise warriors alone. They honored philosophers. Medieval statues were of saints. The Renaissance brought classical gods back down to earth. Though we Americans do not think of ourselves as a militaristic people, the outdoor statues in Washington are overwhelmingly of generals. Is that an unwitting self-revelation, a kind of "Freudian slip" in stone?

Frick and Frack A closely linked or inseparable pair; two of a kind.

Frick and Frack were a comedy skating duo whose long career began in the 1930s. Werner Groebli (Frick) and Hans Mauch (Frack) were born in Switzerland but traveled the world, performing remarkable and hilarious stunts on the ice.

The term in use, in *Newsday,* August 27, 1996:

Bosom buddies, partners in crime, Frick and Frack. There were many names for what we were: pals.

Another example, from Lenore Skenazy, the *New York Daily News,* in the *Portland Oregonian,* April 16, 1996:

No, let's go over to eggs and butter, the Frick and Frack of cholesterol.

friendly fire The weapons fire of one's own side. The term gained currency during the Vietnam War when casualties were reluctantly admitted to have been killed by such friendly fire. To civilians, the thought that any fire that killed could be called friendly was a painful oxymoron. Perhaps the obfuscatory quality of the word blunted the pain, as in the response of a Gulf War general to a question about casualties from friendly fire: "fratricide prevention is not a zero-defect operation."

The term now refers to lethal blows of any kind delivered by one's own side.

The term in use, by David Espo of the Associated Press, reporting on a campaign for the U.S. Senate in Minnesota, July 29, 1996:

Republicans are in the midst of a fresh televised attack on Minnesota Democrat Paul Wellstone, but may be wounding themselves with friendly fire in the process.

And by Richard Lacayo in *Time,* March 4, 1996:

From the start, Buchanan has been expecting his primary-season opponents to gang up on him. But the scale and intensity of the not-so-friendly fire have been more than he counted on.

And from an editorial in the *St. Louis Post-Dispatch,* February 13, 1997:

This is an example of the other type of school violence, the kind that results from unintentional friendly fire rather than peer conflict.

And from the Associated Press, March 21, 1997:

A blip on a radar tape purported by friendly fire theorists to prove that a missile brought down TWA Flight 800 was actually a passing Navy reconnaissance plane, the FBI's lead investigator said Thursday.

frisson \frē-'sō^n\ A brief moment of emotional excitement: a shudder or thrill. In French, a shudder, but in English, a shiver of delight, fear, or excitement, perhaps a slightly naughty thrill like the one that causes prickles up your neck during a scary movie your parents told you not to watch.

The term in use, by Ian Wilmut, a scientist who produced Dolly, the first cloned sheep, quoted in the *Washington Post,* March 5, 1997:

There's a *frisson* of excitement that this will happen with humans. But let's put it into context. What will this actually let us do that we couldn't do before.

Another example from Barbara Walder's column "Women Shouldn't Box" in *Newsday,* February 9, 1997:

So while fragile literary ladies may get a frisson from the fight game, to take this at best marginal sport for men and try to make it seem mainstream for women is ridiculous.

And from Henry Louis Gates Jr. in the *New Yorker,* April 8, 1996:

And a great many blacks—who, suborned by "solidarity," had trained themselves to suppress any heretical thoughts—found Murray's book oddly thrilling: it had the transgressive frisson of SAMIZDAT under Stalinism.

full–court press An aggressive pressuring defense employed in basketball over the entire court area; an all-out effort, especially in politics and government. The term refers to a basketball tactic designed to keep the offense from moving the ball downcourt or to take the ball away. Offensive players are covered throughout the court—as opposed to just the defense's half—in hopes of forcing a turnover.

In politics and other fields, the phrase seems to have lost its defensive connotation; it is simply a no-holds-barred, all-out effort.

The term in use, by Jonathan S. Landay in the *Christian Science*

Monitor, November 22, 1995, on efforts to achieve a peace accord in the
Balkans:

> Negotiators for Bosnia's Muslims, Serbs, and Croats reached the
> agreement Nov. 21 after US mediators mounted a last-ditch full-
> court press to break a deadlock that had appeared to doom the
> three-week-long talks at Wright-Patterson Air Force Base in Day-
> ton, Ohio.

And by Jack Mathews in *Newsday,* May 3, 1995, reviewing the movie
Panther, about the Black Panther Party of the 1960s:

> *Panther* . . . covers about the first 18 months of the party's exis-
> tence, from its formation after one-too-many police assaults on
> peaceful black protesters to the full-court press put on it by J.
> Edgar Hoover's FBI.

Fu Manchu \ˌfü-(ˌ)man-ˈchü\ Chinese villain in stories by "Sax Rohmer"
(A.S. Ward). Later, a criminal mastermind; and, today, a campy reference
to a cultural relic. Dr. Fu Manchu was a lurid fictional character in a long
series of popular mystery novels beginning in 1912. Fu Manchu's brilliant
and elaborate plans aimed at establishing an empire of crime were continually being foiled by the redoubtable Englishman Dennis Nayland
Smith.

The stories are a bundle of roaring cultural affronts, displaying all the
stereotypes and bigotries of the author's time. Also typical of the era are
the popular movies made from the novels, in which the doctor was played
by non-Asian actors—Harry Agar Lyons and Boris Karloff were British,
Henry Brandon was American, and Warner Oland was Swedish. Oland
went on to a long career playing Charlie Chan. Myrna Loy did a turn as
Oriental vamp in *The Mask of Fu Manchu* in 1932. The evil doctor also
gave his name to a style of long, drooping mustache, a continuing blight
on the male physiognomy.

At the end of Rohmer's career in the late 1950s, Fu Manchu—always
adaptable—had evolved into a strong anti-communist. In a final plot twist,
Sax Rohmer died during the Asian flu epidemic of 1959 of complications
from the bug. Really.

The term in use, by Richard Corliss in *Time International,* September
23, 1996, on a retrospective of Vietnamese films:

> The U.S. officers in *The Wild Field,* set during the American con-
> flict, are played by Vietnamese actors, looking feral and deca-
> dent as they stroke their beards and plot the deaths of sensitive
> villagers. They are an Asian Marxist updating of an old Asian
> cliché: G.I. Joe as Fu Manchu.

And by Richard Alleva in *Commonweal,* January 26, 1996, reviewing
Oliver Stone's movie *Nixon:*

The nature of the filmmaker is here, undistilled: the paranoia, the pretentiousness, the simple-minded views of recent American history and institutions, the spasmodic flashes of real talent, the shrewdness in selecting and directing actors, and—above all—the unbounded confidence of the man as he tries to explain all the historical convulsions of the last three decades by evoking the Fu Manchu nefariousness of a few organizations. . . .

Furies Merciless, relentless avengers. The term is often applied to cruelly vengeful females, as well as to the mental and emotional tortures of the guilt-ridden—as in "pursued by the Furies"—when it is really the conscience doing the pursuing. In Greek and Roman mythology they were three goddesses, Tisiphone (the Avenger of Blood); Alecto (the Implacable); and Megaera (the Jealous One). They continued to pursue transgressors even beyond death.

They were so feared that the Greeks did not refer to them by their real names, but rather as "the kindly ones."

The term in use, by Tom Mathews in *Newsweek,* June 22, 1994:

Watergate was tragedy with scattered moments of low comic relief. Its causes tracked back to the furies of Vietnam and the obsessions of a man whose paranoia sorted badly with his patriotism.

And by Molly Haskell in the *San Francisco Examiner,* August 21, 1994:

Their vision of women as sexual Furies bent on destruction may play well to a world confused by the emergence of women as professionals, but reality still favors men, and what Mamet and Crichton really seem to be angry about is the refusal of women to play traditional roles as stay-at-home wives or submissive helpmeets.

And by Amy Tan in *The Kitchen God's Wife* (1991):

For all those years I had imagined how it would be to have my mother know: She would be upset that this had happened to me. She would be angry that I had not told her sooner. She would try to find reasons why this illness had struck me. She would be vigilant in her pursuit of a cure.

I had imagined all this, and I was wrong. It was worse. She was the Furies unbound.

future shock The physical and psychological distress suffered by one who is unable to cope with the speed of social and technological changes.

The term was coined by Alvin Toffler and used as the title of his 1970 book, which offered strategies for coping with the phenomenon. Toffler said he came up with the term in 1965 "to describe the shattering stress and disorientation that we induce in individuals by subjecting them to too much change in too short a time." He based the idea on "culture shock," the sense of disorientation one feels when plunged into a radically different culture in which familiar reference points and norms of behavior are completely lacking.

The term in use, by Henry Allen in the *Washington Post,* February 27, 1989, exploring future shock withdrawal:

> What future? What shock?
>
> These are dog days in America. Nothing seems to be happening. This is not to say that nothing is, in fact, happening—one assumes the rough beast of the future is always slouching around (*see* SLOUCHING TOWARD BETHLEHEM) out there somewhere. But nothing seems to be happening. After lifetimes of shock and/or delight at upheaval and invention, we are putting our ears to the ground and hearing little more than our own heartbeats.

And by Mark Binelli, reviewing film soundtracks in the *Atlanta Journal and Constitution,* June 10, 1995:

> Talk about future shock. The new Keanu Reeves cyberthriller, *Johnny Mnemonic,* offers a nightmarish vision of things to come, all right, but it has nothing to do with murderous bands of data pirates or Reeve's increasingly robotic acting.
>
> No, the scariest notion, judging by this soundtrack at least, is that future doings will be played out to the strains of obvious industro-metal.

 *... we have to experience it in the social context. We have to capture the **gestalt**, get the big picture. We've got to go out and drink too much and boogie.*
—P.J. O'Rourke

Galahad \\'ga-lə-ˌhad\\ The knight of the Round Table who successfully seeks the HOLY GRAIL; also, one who is pure, noble, and unselfish. A perfect knight errant, the man of valor and honor, uncompromisingly devoted to the highest ideals.

In the legends of King Arthur, Sir Galahad was the purest of heart, the noblest of nature. Because of those qualities, he alone succeeded in the quest for the Holy Grail.

The term in use, by Marianne Catalano in *Newsday,* April 9, 1996, on the travails of attending a wedding as a single woman when the dancing begins:

> Couples eagerly leave the dinner tables to strut their stuff while I sit conspicuously waiting for the father of the bride or some other kindly Sir Galahad to rescue me.

And by Alan Bunce, in the *Christian Science Monitor,* July 5, 1996:

> I was ushered into the literary world of animals partly through the works of Albert Payson Terhune. His books about the collies on his rolling estate in New Jersey and beyond—like *Lad: A Dog* and *Bruce* sang of their heroism, and intelligence.... But early on I began to suspect that the line between reality and fantasy was a trifle blurred in Terhune's works. A kind of pre-Disney anthropomorphizing imbued his nonhuman characters with Galahad-like natures, complex motives, and long-term agendas.

game face A tough, intimidatingly aggressive expression or attitude assumed in competitive situations. The idea is to cow the opposition, and to conceal one's own doubt, pain, or anxiety.

The term in use, in the *Portland Oregonian,* May 16, 1996:

> The 6-foot-1-inch, 180-pound senior at Hillsboro High School swears he doesn't try to look angry.
> "I guess I'm just kind of serious about it," Brunswick said. "It's just a game face."

In use again, by Harry Levins of the *St. Louis Post-Dispatch,* January 25, 1996, writing about American troops:

Yet, in Bosnia, the word seems to be that soldiers must wear their game faces—along with their helmets and rifles—until next December. Small wonder they're griping.

Gang of Four A term of opprobrium first applied by Chinese Communist authorities to four leaders held responsible in 1976 for the excesses of the Cultural Revolution and accused of trying to seize power following the deaths of Mao Tse-tung and Chou En-lai. The best known of the group was Mao's widow, Chiang Ching.

Today the term can be pejorative but is often jocular and applied to any group of four people engaged in a joint enterprise or strongly advocating a point of view. (We also frequently see references to Gangs of Three, Five, etc.)

The term in use, by Alan Cooperman and Tim Zimmermann in *U.S. News & World Report,* July 1, 1996:

> They were called Russia's Gang of Four, the Party of War, the Kremlin Shadows, a Collective RASPUTIN, the Powers behind Yeltsin's Throne. Now, the key members of Boris Yeltsin's hard-line inner circle are just history—unlike the Russian president, who is poised not only to win re-election but also to redeem his reputation as a democratic reformer.

And from Carl Weiser, Gannett News Service, October 29, 1996:

> The U.S. Chamber of Commerce has endorsed Wittig, and this month targeted Hinchey as one of its "Gang of Ten: the most vulnerable anti-business members of Congress."

And by Susan F. Rasky, in the *New York Times,* July 27, 1989:

> First there was the Gang of 17, a bipartisan group of House members, Senators and officials of the Ronald Reagan Administration who brokered a deal on taxes and spending that got the 1982 budget through Congress.
>
> Now there is the Gang of Six, half a dozen Democrats on the House Ways and Means Committee who have created a political crisis for their party leaders by joining the panel's 13 Republicans to support a capital gains tax cut favored by President Bush.

Gantry, Elmer The title and central character of a 1927 novel by Sinclair Lewis. Elmer Gantry starts out as a greedy, shallow, philandering Baptist minister, turns to evangelism, and eventually becomes the leader of a large Methodist congregation. En route, he meets up with other religious hypocrites, becomes romantically involved, and is often exposed as a fraud. The name has since come to describe corrupt, manipulative evangelical preachers. Gantry is handsome and charming and becomes a successful evangelist. But he is also unscrupulous and plagiarizes sermons, deludes his naive followers, and steals their donations.

The term in use, as quoted by the *New York Times Magazine,* April 23, 1989, in a profile of Boston University president John Silber:

> Silber is quick to deride "Elmer Gantry" fundamentalism, but what he calls "religious literacy" is so basic to his understanding of education that, as an ethics professor, he would quiz his students on central points in the Bible and church history *before* they studied Christianity—"to illustrate their ignorance."

And by John Omicinski, Gannett News Service, July 20, 1996:

> As he moves into the heat of yet another of a lifelong string of political campaigns, President Clinton is warming into his Billy SUNDAY/Elmer Gantry preacher mode.
> Lately, when exiting church services in Washington, he's taken to lifting The Good Book high over his head, showing it off in a Gantry-like wave so photographers assembled for the ritual president-leaves-the-church-with-or-without-smiling-wife photo won't miss it.

Gargantua \gär-'gan(t)-sh(ə-)wə\ A giant, notable for his voracious appetite and fantastic adventures; in general anyone or anything of prodigious size or gluttony. "Gargantuan" is its adjective form.

His name is taken from "garganta," the Spanish word for "gullet." He originated in medieval tales and is a character in the 16th-century satire *Gargantua and Pantegruel* by Francois Rabelais.

There's a reference in Shakespeare, in Act 3 of *As You Like It:* "You must borrow me Gargantua's mouth first before I can utter so long a word; 'tis a word too great for any mouth of this age's size."

The term in use, by Karen Uhlenhuth in the *Kansas City Star,* April 5, 1998, describing Pennsylvania Avenue in Washington, D.C.:

> "The Pennsylvania Avenue that unfurls to the southeast from the White House and runs smack dab into the Capitol is monumental, gargantuan, self-important. This, let us not forget, is the route for the quadriennial inaugural parade."

Another example, from John M. Barry's *Rising Tide: The Great Mississippi Flood of 1927 and How It Changed America* (1997), a description of the levee break at Greenville, Mississippi:

> "One last train tried to escape. But outside the city the crevasse water was roaring over the railroad embankment, washing it away in its entirety, leaving the rails turned upright like a picket fence. A mile beyond the city limits the train derailed. It would remain there, a twisted Gargantua lying helpless, for months."

And in a *Christian Science Monitor* editorial, May 12, 1995:

"Ideally, the budget-deficit Gargantua would be attacked with a spirit of national unity and determination akin to the effort to put a man on the moon or to win the war against fascism 50 years ago."

By Louis Bayard, reviewing *The Last King of Scotland* by Giles Foden in the *Washington Post Book World,* January 24, 1999:

Gargantua, buffoon, mass murderer, polygamist, PLO champion—Idi Amin Dada was many well-documented things during his 1970s reign of terror over Uganda.

Gaston *See* ALPHONSE AND GASTON.

Gatsby; Gatsbyesque The central character, or in his style, of *The Great Gatsby,* a 1925 novel by F. Scott Fitzgerald, about a self-made man who flaunts his wealth while remaining silent about his past. The novel offered a devastating picture of wealthy society in the 1920s, a society of greed, tinsel extravagance, and what H.L. Mencken called "glittering swinishness." Critics have judged the work to be one of the most finely constructed novels in American literature.

The mysterious Jay Gatsby moves into a luxurious mansion on Long Island and entertains lavishly at parties. He was once simply Jay Gatz of a poor family in the Midwest, but with ill-gotten millions he has created a new past for himself. He spends lavishly to win the love of Daisy Buchanan and to impress rich friends, but they bring about his downfall. (*See* BUCHANAN, DAISY AND TOM.)

The term in use, by Ann Butler in the *Pittsburgh Press,* July 16, 1990:

At 42, New Yorker Jim Erwin has the Gatsbyesque dash of a man to the manor born. Who knows what his background is? This man looks the part. Tanned and trim with amused blue eyes and longish hair, he makes a white polo shirt and white Bermuda shorts look simply smashing.

And from *Mike, Before Mickey,* by Frank Rose, a profile of Hollywood bigwig Michael Ovitz, excerpted in the *Los Angeles Times,* September 3, 1995:

He showed a Gatsbyesque desire to reinvent himself.

gaucherie \ˌgō-sh(ə-)-rē\ A tactless or awkward act. French for "left" or "left-handed"—and clumsy.

The term in use, by Steve Jacobson in *Newsday,* April 19, 1996, on the Stanley Cup hockey playoffs:

With 5.5 seconds on the clock, Ranger fans stood in the aisles and before they turned to climb out of the pit of despair, many of them flung their blue and red souvenir caps onto the ice. This was not the HAT TRICK they expected. . . .

"If I was a fan, I'd be upset, too," Colin Campbell, the coach of the sudden underdog, said. Then he counted off a list of gaucheries his team committed, which were something like committing suicide on center ice.

And by Matt Wolf of the Associated Press, January 2, 1994, reviewing the television production of Armistead Maupin's novel *Tales of the City* portraying San Francisco in 1976:

> Devotees of Maupin's fictional 28 Barbary Lane, will find their beloved characters on screen—grace, innocence, and occasional gaucherie intact in the script by Richard Kramer, a writer for "Thirtysomething."

gauntlet, run the \\'gȯnt-lət, 'gänt-\ To undergo a severe trial or ordeal; to be made to run between a double file of people facing each other who strike at the runner with clubs or other weapons. It was originally a Swedish term that came into English as "gantelope," used as a military punishment in the Thirty Years War (1618–1648). "Gantelope" eventually became replaced with "gauntlet" by a process known as folk etymology, whereby an unfamiliar word is replaced with a more familiar similar-sounding word, in this case the older "gauntlet"—drawn from French meaning "glove." "Running the gauntlet" means, more broadly, passing through harassment, or receiving criticism or punishment from all directions.

The term in use, by Reuters, in the *Baltimore Sun,* August 22, 1995:

> Critics have accused China of denying visas to those it sees as troublesome applicants or forcing them to run a bureaucratic gauntlet.

Another example, quoted by Timothy J. Mullaney, also in the *Sun,* November 10, 1995:

> "Our employees and visitors feel they're running a gauntlet to go to lunch, a ballgame or the theater," she said. "The reality is that we have homeless and panhandlers on what seems like every corner downtown."

And from Jim Bovard, in the *Washington Times,* April 5, 1994:

> This April 15, hard-working Americans will once again be forced to run a gauntlet of IRS regulations, penalties and bureaucratic incompetence.

gauntlet, throw down/pick up the To issue or accept an open challenge. It comes from the conventions of medieval combat. A gauntlet was a glove, part of one's armor. To challenge someone to combat, a knight would throw his glove at another knight's feet. The second knight would take it up if he intended to accept the challenge, in which case a jousting match might ensue.

The term in use, in an editorial in the *Baltimore Sun,* July 13, 1995:

Well, Newport [Rhode Island] may just be willing to pick up the gauntlet. Newport bills itself as the sailing capital of the world, but the city's director of tourism, Evan Smith, acknowledges that Annapolis, alone of all other U.S. cities, has a right to argue about that.

And from Gene Mueller, in the *Washington Times*, January 31, 1994:

Hunters, particularly, had better study the outfits that will throw down the gauntlet. Anglers also would be wise to find out who the groups are that even frown these days on sport fishing, calling it a "cruel" activity.

genius loci \\'jēn-yəs-'lō-ˌsī, -ˌkē; 'jē-nē-əs-\ The pervading spirit of a place, or the tutelary deity of a place. A Latin phrase with the same meaning.

The ancient Romans believed that protective spirits were assigned to watch over specific places and what went on there. (Only later did "genius" come to mean extraordinary intellectual ability or creativity.)

The term in use, by Henry Allen in the *Washington Post*, June 24, 1987:

. . . true Washingtonians love the heat. Heat is a kind of local god, a guardian angel, a genius loci. We love our heat the way San Francisco loves its fog or New York loves its neurosis. . . . Paris is the City of Light, Washington is the City of Heat.

And by Timothy Ryback in the *New Yorker*, December 30, 1991:

Later in the day, Herbert Fartacek, the Vice-Mayor of Salzburg, who has issued the permit for Thuswaldner's proposed tribute to the town's genius loci, strolled over to Mozart Square to see how the project was faring.

gentle *See* DO NOT GO GENTLE INTO THAT GOOD NIGHT.

gestalt \gə-'stält, -'shtält, -'stólt, -'shtólt\ A structure or pattern of physical, biological, or psychological phenomena that are integrated to form a unit with properties that transcend the sum of its parts. It comes from a German word meaning "shape" or "form."

Gestalt has given its name to a field of psychotherapy that rejects the Freudian approach to analysis of the patient's past and concentrates instead on the senses and on complete experience of the present.

The term in use, by P.J. O'Rourke, *Holidays in Hell* (1988), as a reporter for *Rolling Stone* describing Poland:

I said, "Zofia, there's only one way to cover this story. We have to get inside it, we have to experience it in the social context. We have to capture the gestalt, get the big picture. We've got to go out and drink too much and boogie."

"Your magazine pays you for this?" she said.

And by Jeff Morgan in *Wine Spectator*, March 31, 1996:

In addition to pragmatic methodology intuition is no small factor in decision making here. "You need to see the grapes and the gestalt of the harvest to make decisions, too," Dyer says.

Gilded Age, the The title of a novel of social and political criticism published in 1873 and, from it, the name of an era of gross materialism and blatant political corruption.

The novel, jointly written by Mark Twain and essayist-editor Charles Dudley Warner, describes speculators and their greedy schemes in post-Civil War America. The book captures the excesses of its day (the 1870s), and its title came to sum up the vulgar extravagance of the era.

The phrase is particularly apt—"gilded" suggesting excess, as in "GILDING THE LILY" as well as the idea of superficial splendor; a gilded age, after all, is not a truly "golden" one, merely a showy imitation.

The term in use, by Laurence I. Barrett in *Time,* January 23, 1989, discussing the political legacy of Ronald Reagan:

> Looser ethical standards and the adoration of capitalism led to a wave of scandals in and out of government that rivaled the excesses of the Gilded Age.

And from E.J. Dionne Jr. in *Commonweal,* February 23, 1996:

> There is a final difficulty with the new conservatism that goes largely undiscussed: Its program has been tried before and found wanting. That is the importance of realizing that the new laissez faire is simply Gilded Age conservatism dressed up in the finery of a high-tech age.

gilded youth Wealthy, privileged youth—those touched with gold; often, meaning young wastrels, or those who do not wear their privileges with grace or restraint. Sometimes used in the positive sense of a "golden" youth who is virtuous, handsome and talented; or a privileged childhood. However "gilded" more often suggests a showy veneer of wealth, not solid character.

Often referred to using the French phrase, "jeunesse doree," a term first applied to a group of wealthy young men who ranged the streets of Paris following the downfall of ROBESPIERRE and the end of the REIGN OF TERROR. These well-dressed young men were counter-revolutionary hooligans. They wielded lead-weighted clubs and carried out violence against the SANSCULOTTES who so recently had been the bloody mobs of revolution. (*See also* THERMIDOR.)

The term in use, quoted by Sylvia Adcock in *Newsday,* April 12, 1998, on the first international automobile race held in the United States. (The Vanderbilt Cup Race was held on Long Island in 1904.):

> "In order that the speed-madness monomaniacs may drive their man-maiming engines at an excessive and illegal pace, the residents and taxpayers of the island are bidden to keep off the road," the New York *World* fumed. "It is an extraordinary condition of

affairs when a coterie of idlers, rich men's sons and gilded youth can take possession of public highways."

And by Richard Stengel in *People,* November 11, 1985, on the occasion of the visit of the Prince and Princess of Wales to the United States:

> Diana herself, over the course of four years of marriage, has undergone a transformation. She began as a reticent, slightly plump kindergarten teacher from Sloane Square, the trendy headquarters of London's gilded youth.

By Murray Kempton in *Newsday,* September 9, 1992:

> When Truman's campaign train stopped at Concord, N.H., Exeter's entire contingent of jeunesse doree was there to meet him with the boos and scurrilities their headmaster, a Saltonstall, had unleashed them for hurling.

gild the lily Also, to "paint the lily." To add unnecessary ornamentation to something already beautiful, and thus to detract from, cheapen, or spoil its beauty; to excessively embellish an object, making it gaudy, vulgar, or overdone. (Gilding is a thin layer or edging of gold.)

The expression comes from Shakespeare's play *King John,* Act 4, Scene 2, when Lord Salisbury admonishes the king for staging a second coronation for himself:

> Therefore, to be possess'd with double pomp,
> To guard a title that was rich before,
> To gild refined gold, to paint the lily,
> To throw perfume on the violet,
> To smooth the ice, or add another hue
> Unto the rainbow, or with taper-light
> To seek the beauteous eye of heaven to garnish,
> Is wasteful, and ridiculous excess.

The term in use, Congressman Jim Kolbe of Arizona, quoted by Gannett News Service, July 25, 1996, proposing to cut $20 million out of funds budgeted for a government project in his state:

> "The Central Arizona Project provides the water that has become our life-blood," Kolbe said on the House floor. "That doesn't mean, however, that we have to gild the lily.
>
> "We don't have to add things to the project that have nothing to do with delivering water to central Arizona," the Arizona Republican said.

And by Andrew Ferguson in the *National Review,* September 11, 1995, mocking the effusive response to the death of Jerry Garcia of the Grateful Dead:

> "What bound the generations of Deadheads together?" wondered the editorialist, his thumb raw and red from ferocious sucking.

A fondness for sandals, yes, and a lack of cabfare, of course. But this intellectual insecurity, too: a desire to gild the lily, to pretend that our slightest diversions involve the greatest intensities of feeling.

Gladstonian Of, related to, or characteristic of the politics and policies of William Gladstone; also, of or characteristic of a politician of extreme probity and talent. The word comes from the name of William Ewart Gladstone (1809–1898), four times prime minister of Great Britain. Known as the "Grand Old Man" or "G.O.M.," he was one of the most capable men of his age and one of its leading orators. As leader of the Liberal Party, he is remembered for his decades-long rivalry with Benjamin DISRAELI, leader of the Tories.

Gladstone originally intended to follow the Church of England as a vocation, but instead moved into politics, where he strove throughout his life to serve the principles of his religious faith, especially those of unfailing integrity and courage. Courage was needed for the causes he espoused—reform in Ireland, extension of the vote, and opposition to Britain's imperial expansion in the late 19th century.

One of the supreme moments of his career came late in his political life, during the so-called "Midlothian campaign." Gladstone had retired from politics in 1874, but in 1879 he made a comeback. In a series of great speeches to his Midlothian constituency in Scotland, he addressed not only the electors but the nation at large—something new in political campaigns. Gladstone's sincerity and argumentative skill carried the Liberals into power, and returned him to the post of prime minister.

Unlike Disraeli, Gladstone was never able to charm Queen Victoria, and as the years passed her aversion grew. In 1892 she described him as "an old, wild, and incomprehensible man of 82½." (She was a glum and reclusive 73.)

The Grand Old Man evoked by the *Economist,* April 8, 1989, in a discussion of the U.S. budget deficit:

> If the federal budget were in balance, not counting social security, the federal government would be in overall surplus and this would be a form of national savings. The government would reduce its outstanding debt, freeing capital for private investment. But there are two crucial provisos—besides the political impossibility of such Gladstonian rectitude.

And by Scott Syfert in the *Charlotte Observer,* May 15, 1997:

> Many of the themes of the Republican revolution have been borrowed, either explicitly or implicitly, from Victorian values. The calls for greater self-reliance, religious devotion and "renewing civil society" owe less to our Founding Fathers than to 19th-century Gladstonian liberalism.

glass *See* SEE THROUGH A GLASS DARKLY.

glass jaw Vulnerability (as of a boxer) to knockout punches. A person's or institution's critical point of weakness. It's an ACHILLES HEEL.

The term comes from boxing: a fighter who could not withstand a blow to the chin was said to have a glass jaw.

The term in use, quoted in a Cal Thomas column in *Human Events,* August 25, 1995, discussing the decision of Senator Bill Bradley not to run for another term:

> [A Republican consultant] recalled Bradley's near loss in 1990 to the then-unknown Christie Whitman and told *Human Events:* "Bradley is out because he has a glass jaw."

Another example, by Deron Snyder in *Baseball Weekly,* March 30, 1994, reviewing prospects for the San Diego Padres:

> But pitching could eventually be their glass jaw.

And by political consultant Dick Morris in his book *Behind the Oval Office* (1997), on 1996 Republican presidential candidate Steve Forbes:

> Forbes might have come closer had he kept his wits about him. Instead he proved fragile—the political glass jaw—vulnerable to a knockout punch.

Glick, Sammy The main character of Budd Schulberg's 1941 novel, *What Makes Sammy Run?:* tough, hard-driving, unprincipled, the crass son of a Jewish immigrant, who clawed his way from his humble New York origins to Hollywood success in the movie business.

The term in use, by Karen DeYoung in the *Washington Post,* April 23, 1987, on British author-politician Jeffrey Archer:

> Well-dressed, clean-shaven and tanned, Archer, 47, appeared during several days on the witness stand to be precisely what he is—a clever, tightly controlled, relentless achiever with a bit of the Sammy Glick about him.

And from David Margolick, commenting on Robert Burt's *Two Jewish Justices: Outcasts in the Promised Land,* in the *New York Times,* December 22, 1989:

> Brandeis, according to Mr. Burt, remained in, and even relished the role of outsider, or, to use the political philosopher Hannah Arendt's term, "pariah." . . . Frankfurter, on the other hand, was the "parvenu," in Miss Arendt's terms, a judicial Sammy Glick, so desperate for acceptance that he became, Mr. Burt wrote, "an overeager apologist for the existing order."

global village The world viewed as a community in which distance and isolation have been dramatically reduced by electronic media. The concept was offered by communications theoretician Marshall McLuhan in 1960. (*See also* MEDIUM IS THE MESSAGE.)

McLuhan's idea was that reading the printed page, a very private and isolated form of communication, ended the earlier communal forms of oral communication. He believed that radio and television would restore the old sense of community and link all mankind in a "global village." And now there's the Internet—are we there yet?

The term in use, in *Essence,* September 5, 1995:

> Need more information? The global village is friendly. Post a shout-out to a news group or a bulletin board or in AOL's ebony chat rooms, and your mailbox will overflow with advice, ideas and opinions.

And by Guy Trebay in the *Village Voice,* February 22, 1994:

> Too jet-lagged to go walking in the shuttered city, I'm channel-hopping across the face of the global village. On 5 is an Indonesian import, half of whose characters are gods. On 30 there's a winter polo match being played on snow and beamed from San Carlos de Bariloche, Argentina.

gnomes of Zurich Swiss international financiers and bankers, who exercise great economic power in anonymity. The expression originated with George Brown, a member of the British House of Commons, during a currency crisis in 1964. It's not a compliment, since gnomes are ageless and often deformed dwarves of folklore who live in the earth and usually guard treasure. (There also are garden gnomes, who inhabit gardens—along with plastic flamingoes and those plywood cutouts of ladies with watering cans.)

Gnomes in finance had more power over currency in the days of Brown's annoyance because currency values were fixed, pegged to the dollar and the price of gold. In 1971 the United States allowed the dollar to float on the currency market and so was born the wonderful world of day-to-day value changes. Today the gnomes of Zurich still inhabit their ultra-discreet banking houses, although their reputation for probity is somewhat tarnished. The term is applied broadly, often playfully, to describe anyone, from a bureaucrat to a dark conspirator, who wields power in secret.

The term in use, by David Walter, *New Statesman,* December 6, 1996:

> Still, plenty of sober-suited gnomes of Zurich seem content to ride on the trams.

And in an editorial in the *Long Beach Press-Telegram,* July 24, 1997:

> It took a little nudging from a former Federal Reserve chairman and a lot of nudging from Jewish groups, but the gnomes of Zurich continue to discover bits and pieces of the billions in gold that was plundered by Nazis during World War II.

goal posts *See* MOVING THE GOAL POSTS.

God's in his heaven, all's right with the world A line from Robert Browning's *Pippa Passes* (1841), a long dramatic poem. The line is from a song sung by Pippa, a poor young girl who works in a silk mill. The line is quoted in many senses—to speak of the absolute rightness of a moment; or to suggest a smug, insufferable certainty; or, with irony, to suggest that things are very far from what they ought to be.

Browning was no cornball optimist, and excelled at revealing characters through his dramatic monologues; his poem is more complicated than you might think. The story is about Pippa's chance appearance at critical moments in the lives of the characters. When she passes, singing her songs, she changes the lives of those who overhear her.

> The lark's on the wing;
> The snail's on the thorn:
> God's in his heaven—
> All's right with the world!

This is her first song, overheard by two guilty lovers who have just murdered the inconvenient husband. They promptly quarrel in the face of such sweetness and light.

The term in use, by Lucy Soto, the *Atlanta Journal and Constitution,* September 8, 1995, recounting a football battle between Arizona and Georgia Tech:

> Six minutes were left to play, Georgia Tech had a 19–7 lead, God was in His heaven and all seemed right with George O'Leary's world. Then all hell broke loose.

Another example, from Jim Murray, the *Los Angeles Times,* February 1, 1996, on Magic Johnson's return to basketball:

> A guy with a smile as broad as the Atlantic and a heart as big as Texas had the ball in his hands and a song in his heart and, as the poet said it, God was in his Heaven and all was right with the world.

And from columnist George Will, mocking the Senate inquiry into the failure of the University of Wyoming's football team to receive a postseason bowl bid, in the *Washington Post,* May 29, 1997:

> In year three of the Republican ascendancy, being virtuous is a snap, and almost everything—everything but the Bowl Alliance—is right with the world.

Godzilla A rampaging monster of great size and destructive aggressiveness, hard to stop and even harder to kill, or a person with such traits.

Godzilla was the creation of the Japanese Toho movie studios, a monster who seemed to combine King Kong and Tyrannosaurus rex. The 1954 original was conceived with the dangers of the nuclear era very much in mind, and specifically the atomic bombs dropped on Hiroshima and Nagasaki.

Godzilla is awakened from his prehistoric nap in the ocean depths by hydrogen bomb testing. After he has wrought terrible destruction, an experimental super-weapon, the "oxygen destroyer," reduces the monster to a skeleton. The scientist who created the weapon commits suicide to prevent the dread technology from becoming a further threat to the world.

The movie was a great hit in Japan and also in the United States in 1956, with Raymond Burr spliced in as a newsman breathlessly reporting on the monster's progress. The bad dubbing, and particularly the clumsiness of the monster, obviously a man clad in a tyrannosaur suit, added a camp appeal and made the movie fun for kids and hilarious for adults. But there was a message: no mindless, terrifying *Alien* here, no creature from outer space; Godzilla was the product of the destructive and dangerous actions of man—nuclear testing. Evils in subsequent movies, such as the Smog Monster, were due to pollution.

Sequel followed sequel, and Godzilla evolved from threat to protector, battling other foes such as Mothra, Rodan, and Monster Zero to protect Japan and the earth.

The monster evoked, by *Time* magazine art critic Robert Hughes, May 6, 1996, on a retrospective show of the works of American artist Edward Kleinholz:

> Moving through the show is like being alternately slugged and hectored by a redneck Godzilla with strong libertarian-anarchist convictions.

And by Chris McCosky, in the *Detroit News,* November 13, 1995, on Detroit Pistons coach Doug Collins:

> As a player, he would dive across broken glass to get a loose ball and take it to the hole against Godzilla—whatever it took, regardless of personal cost.

go gentle *See* DO NOT GO GENTLE INTO THAT GOOD NIGHT.

Goldberg, Rube Reuben Lucius Goldberg (1883–1970), an American cartoonist best known for his complicated, ramshackle contraptions that performed simple tasks in intricately, ludicrously complex ways. His name has become an adjective meaning "accomplishing by complex means what seemingly could be done simply."

Goldberg's cartoons—he published nearly 50,000 of them in 72 years, during which time he smoked 118,700 cigars at a cost of $47,480—satirized the technology of modern times. Biographer Peter C. Marzio (who calculated the cigar consumption) in *Rube Goldberg: His Life and Work* (1973), sums up Goldberg's comic contribution: "For Americans, complex machinery has been ever present and ever growing, but few Americans until the arrival of Rube Goldberg saw it as a subject for comedy."

Here's Rube's explanation from a typical cartoon, showing a process in which the whiskers of a bearded man, seated in a chair atop a balloon, brush off the suit of a man standing before him. It starts with a lit candle under a jug:

Heat from flame (A) expands home brew in bottle (B) and cork (C) flies out with attached safety razor blade (D), which cuts string (E)—weight (F) drops on strength-testing machine (G) ringing bell (H)—boxing dog (I) thinks round is starting and jumps off chair (J) falling on head of spike (K)—point (L) punctures balloon (M), dropping chair (N), which bobs up and down on spring (O), causing whiskers (P) to brush off clothes with neatness and care. (The cartoon is captioned, "Try our new patent clothes brush.")

The term in use, by Charles Krauthammer in the *Washington Post,* January 6, 1989, commenting on congressional devices to dodge difficult decisions:

Take three elementary functions of the government: 1) balancing the budget, 2) closing obsolete military installations and 3) regulating congressional salaries. Hopelessly afraid of acting on any of these, Congress has constructed an elaborate set of Rube Goldberg devices, to do what has to be done while taking no responsibility for having done it.

And by David B. Ottaway and Warren Brown in a *Washington Post* story on the history of automobile airbags, June 1, 1997. Automobile magnate Henry Ford II had authorized development work on air bags, but was furious when the device did not inflate during a demonstration:

When Ford read about it in the next day's newspapers, [automobile safety advocate Joan] Claybrook added, "he went berserk and then killed the program. He said he didn't want any Rube Goldberg device in his car."

golden calf *See* WORSHIP THE GOLDEN CALF.

golden oldie One that was a favorite in the past. Often warm and nostalgic feelings are evoked when it is viewed or heard or experienced again. This is a term particularly familiar to radio listeners, encountering Baby-Boom-boosted "golden oldies" stations playing music of the '50s to the '80s. This is a trend which undoubtedly will continue until aging Boomers experience total hearing loss (probably soon), or Daddy takes the T-bird away.

A golden oldie is a moveable feast; each generation must have its own comfort foods, and new golden oldies arise with each succeeding wave.

The term in use, by President Bill Clinton in a debate with Republican Bob Dole, October 6, 1996:

And you know, this "liberal" charge, that's what their party always drags out when they get in a tight race.

It's sort of their "golden oldie," you know. It's a record they think they can play that everybody loves to hear.

And by veteran newsman Daniel Schorr, commenting on the release of additional Watergate tapes on National Public Radio's *All Things Considered,* May 19, 1993:

> A cancer growing on the presidency, twisting slowly, slowly in the wind. What did the president know and when did he know it? Headlines from the golden oldies of 1973, a rush of nostalgia. [*See* TWIST SLOWLY IN THE WIND.]

Golgotha \\'gäl-gə-thə, gäl-'gä-thə\\ The Place of the Skull; the place of Christ's crucifixion. An experience or a place of intense mental suffering. It is the Aramaic form of the Hebrew word for skull. The Greek and Latin word is "calvaria," thus "Calvary." Both words, as proper nouns, are most familiar to us from the New Testament as the place where Jesus was crucified. It is not known if the site took its name from its function as a place of execution, or possibly from the skull-like contour of the ground, and its exact location is not known.

Both words also are used to designate graveyards or places of execution, and to describe places or times of great mental suffering or public excoriation.

The term in use, in the *New Yorker,* February 3, 1997, in a caption to a reproduction of a painting by Elizabeth Peyton:

> "Hotel," her recent portrait of John Lennon, captures the singer at a Chicago hotel, in August 1966, during his personal Golgotha, as the press clamored for an apology for his declaration that the Beatles had become "more popular than Jesus."

Another example, from *Shrouds of Glory: From Atlanta to Nashville: The Last Great Campaign of the Civil War,* (1995) by Winston Groom, a description of the casualties after the battle of Franklin:

> A big autumn moon rose up and loomed over the Winsted Hills, bathing the Golgothan scene with an eerie silver glow.

Goliath *See* DAVID AND GOLIATH.

Golightly, Holly The chief character in *Breakfast at Tiffany's;* an amoral, rootless young woman of great style and charm. Adrift in the big city, she finds peace and safety in the hushed, conservative opulence of Tiffany's jewelry store, and eventual happiness in a traditional female role.

She was created by Truman Capote in his 1958 story and made immortal by Audrey Hepburn in the 1961 film.

The term in use, by Ilene Rosenzweig in *Forward,* November 4, 1994, in a profile of Elizabeth Wurtzel, author of *Prozac Nation: Young and Depressed in America:*

> Dressed for a party following our interview, she is sporting a fringed black suede jacket and diamond-chip nose ring, her pony tail swinging. She has the air of a downtown Holly Golightly. I had expected her to look more, well, depressed.

And again, by Laurie Winer, reviewing Lisa Loomer's play *The Waiting Room* in the *Los Angeles Times,* August 12, 1994:

> Wanda is perhaps the most disturbing character of all. In a stunning performance by Jacalyn O'Shaughnessy, this is a Holly Golightly who's had her cheeks done, as well as her nose, her jaw and her breasts (three times), and yet who has some basic grasp of feminist thinking.

Gomorrah *See* SODOM AND GOMORRAH.

go native To assume the way of life of the indigenous inhabitants of a place, often in the sense of an alien in a foreign land who adopts the practices of the place he visits. In politics or business: an outsider who takes up the ideas and habits of an institution or system different from his place of origin. This sense is used negatively of a turncoat who abandons original principles and takes up those of his new surroundings for his own advantage. It is also spy jargon for an agent who goes over to the other side.

The term in use, in the *Economist,* November 26, 1994:

> The Republican-controlled Congress could easily go native and guard the institution's power.

And by Walter Shapiro in *Esquire,* November 1, 1994:

> During the [1992] campaign, Clinton treated the Congressional leadership like his brother Roger—keeping them off center stage as much as humanly possible. But once he hit Washington, perhaps out of insecurity, certainly egged on by fresh-from-Capitol-Hill advisers, Clinton went native.

And by columnist Maggie Gallagher in the *Washington Times,* August 4, 1996:

> Conservatives, on the other hand, have a consistently different experience: of supporting pols who talk a good limited-government game, but once elected, "go native," i.e., help expand the power and prerogatives of the governing class.

gonzo \'gän-(ˌ)zō\ Idiosyncratically subjective but committed to a cause; bizarre. Also, characteristic of a style of journalism that mixes fact and fiction, allegedly produced by a writer in a crazed state, sometimes induced by the excessive consumption of drink and/or drugs. The term is now used to describe an intense, off-the-wall, or surreal experience, mood, or style.

The preeminent practitioner of gonzo journalism is the quasi-legendary Hunter S. Thompson, the political reporter for *Rolling Stone* magazine in the 1970s, who gained fame for producing his copy while under the influence of Wild Turkey bourbon and a variety of drugs. Thompson's works include *Fear and Loathing in Las Vegas* (1971) and *Fear and Loathing on*

the Campaign Trail 1972 (1973). His writing is characterized by outra-
geously false allegations about public figures and grotesque and exaggerated descriptions of events. His legend has been embellished by the
character of Duke in the comic strip "Doonesbury."

The term in use, by Tim Carvell in *Fortune,* January 13, 1997:

> Since the sweeps months are so important for these local sta-
> tions, it is hardly surprising that they tend to go a little gonzo to
> draw viewers to the set.

And by Paul Greenburg, editorial page editor of the *Arkansas Gazette,*
in commentary in the *Kansas City Star,* March 29, 1996:

> What's with the *Wall Street Journal's* editorial page? It's more than
> knowledgeable about a wide range of economic, political and
> social topics from foreign affairs to the economy—it can be sharp,
> urbane and sensitive. But get it on the subject of Whitewater,
> and . . . Gonzo City! It's Paranoids-of-the-World Unite! time.

And by R.Z. Sheppard, *Time,* October 17, 1988, in a review of P.J.
O'Rourke's *Holidays in Hell:*

> The papa of gonzo is, of course, Hunter S. Thompson, who at 49
> seems to have lost his bite. . . . For true spite and malice one must
> now turn to P.J. O'Rourke, 40, a baby boomer who seems to have
> teethed on brass knuckles and suckled on bile.

good cop, bad cop A method designed to wear down an opponent by alternating a kind, compassionate approach with a harsh, unrelenting attitude.
The expression comes from police interrogation techniques, in which one
police officer assumes a hostile manner while a second officer disarms
the subject with sympathy.

The term in use, by Walter Shapiro in *Esquire,* March 1, 1994:

> At times, the Clintons play off each other at meetings, Hillary
> pressing a line of questioning in search of more candid answers
> than a president usually receives. Good cop, bad cop.

And by political columnists Jack Germond and Jules Witcover in the
Baltimore Sun, June 7, 1994, on the teamwork between President Clinton
and Vice President Gore:

> In one sense, it was nothing more than the old good cop/bad cop
> routine, with Gore playing the heavy. But the sense of outspo-
> ken independence that Gore conveyed, with Clinton's approval,
> was a clear measure of how far the vice presidency has come in
> the hands of these two political partners.

good night *See* DO NOT GO GENTLE INTO THAT GOOD NIGHT.

Good Samaritan One who selflessly assists another, especially a stranger
in trouble.

It is taken from the parable of Jesus in the New Testament, Luke 10:25–37. "Love thy neighbor as thyself," said Jesus. A question then came (from a lawyer), "And who is my neighbor?" In response, Jesus told this story: A man traveling on the road from Jerusalem to Jericho fell among thieves. He was robbed, stripped of his clothes, wounded, and left to die. As he lay by the side of the road, passersby (including a priest) ignored his plight and crossed to the other side of the road.

The man is finally saved by a Samaritan who binds up his wounds, takes him to an inn, and cares for him. The story is particularly pointed because the traveler was Jewish and Samaritans and Jews were generally hostile to each other.

In American law, there are "Good Samaritan laws," statutes aimed at protecting from lawsuits medical personnel who give emergency medical treatment without consent, or those who use force on another in a reasonable belief that it is necessary to prevent a suicide.

The term in use, by Michael Sauter in *Entertainment Weekly,* April 28, 1995:

> Driving their getaway car straight off a bridge, they find themselves stranded among Good Samaritan yokels who, idiotically, don't realize that these boys are the bank robbers.

And by Michael Small in *People,* March 16, 1987:

> It often seems that there is nothing a Samaritan can do but pass by. Confronted everyday, on television and in the mailbox, by pleas for help to relieve nearly every conceivable form of social and private suffering—from homelessness and hunger to child abuse, drug addiction, mental retardation—the most conscientious citizen often feels impotent.

goody two-shoes A person who is affectedly good or proper; a person who is uncommonly good. Maybe just a mite too good and a bit too optimistic and a tad too nice?

In an 18th-century nursery tale, believed to have been written by Oliver Goldsmith, the (Irish-born) English novelist, poet, and playwright, Goody Two-shoes is very poor and has but one shoe. When she is given a pair she is so happy that she tells everyone that she has "two shoes"— hence, her name. She later becomes wealthy, in the way of worthy nursery-tale children.

Thus a goody two-shoes is someone like her: properly behaved, happy, cheerfully optimistic, nice. As you might guess, the term has acquired a negative aura: someone too nice to be completely sincere.

The term in use, by Washington Redskin Brian Mitchell, to express his dismay after a defeat, quoted in the *Washington Post,* December 10, 1996:

> We've got to have more guys with attitude. We've got too many guys worried about being goody two-shoes.

In use again, by Marli Murphy in the *Kansas City Star,* January 21, 1996, in an article about good neighbors in which citizen Susan Talbert described an acquaintance who delivers dinner to someone who's had a baby, makes grocery runs for folks, and organizes neighborhood happenings:

> "I don't mean to make her sound like a goody two-shoes, because this girl knows how to have fun," Talbert added. "Can she ever throw a football party."

Gordian knot \\'gȯr-dē-ən\\ An intricate problem, especially one insoluble on its own terms. A knotty problem. "Cutting the Gordian knot" means taking decisive, swift action to resolve a complicated problem once and for all.

In Greek legend, Gordius was a peasant who became king of Phrygia, now central Turkey, an ancient country with interesting procedures for selecting leaders. Gordius won his throne by fulfilling a prophecy that whoever drove up to the temple of Zeus in a wagon would become king. Gordius, in gratitude, dedicated his wagon to Zeus. The wagon was secured to the temple by an intricate knot, and it was said that whoever could undo it would rule all Asia. Many tried to untie the knot without success until Alexander the Great arrived on the scene and cut the knot with a single stroke of his sword. Thus, a quick, thorough resolution to an apparently insoluble problem.

The term in use, by Karl Hess Jr. in *Reason,* June 1, 1995, commenting on land-use issues in the American West:

> This is why the West is at war with itself. . . . But all the federal might in the world cannot and will not unravel the Gordian knot of how best to allocate the West's resources—the rivers, range-lands, and mountain peaks that are the sources of its livelihood, happiness, and identity.

And in *Newsweek,* July 6, 1992:

> Could a foreign military operation really slice through the political Gordian knot and get help to Sarajevo's people? It wouldn't be that simple.

Gorgon Any of three snake-haired sisters in Greek mythology whose appearance turns the beholder to stone. Also, an ugly or repulsive woman—someone scary and mean.

In Greek mythology, the Gorgons were three hideous and terrifying sisters with snakes for hair and terrible teeth and claws. The best-known of the trio was MEDUSA. A glance from, or at, one of them could turn a person to stone.

The term in use, by Meryl Streep, quoted by Clifford Rothman in *USA Today,* February 4, 1997:

> He [Dustin Hoffman] always talks in pugilistic terms about working with me. Like he's girding for battle with the Gorgon or something.

In use again, in Adina Hoffman's review of the movie *To Die For* in the *Jerusalem Post,* July 22, 1996:

> Meanwhile, the people around her are all kind, decent souls, a little pathetic perhaps, though basically nothing more than innocent victims of this dressed-for-success Gorgon.

gothic Of or relating to a style of fiction characterized by the use of desolate or remote settings and macabre or violent incidents. Frequently applied in a jocular way to lurid, peculiar, uncouth, or barbarous people or goings-on; also, capitalized, pertaining to an architectural style of the Middle Ages in Europe.

The term Gothic applies to the architecture of Western Europe in the 12th-16th centuries, characterized by the pointed arch, soaring high ceilings, and flying buttresses, as seen in such great cathedrals as Chartres and Notre Dame de Paris.

Gothic novels are often set amid medieval trappings; gloomy castles and wild landscapes are almost mandatory. Indeed, Horace Walpole's *The Castle of Otranto* (1764), the first of the genre in English, was subtitled *A Gothic Story,* reflecting its themes of dark passions and wanton cruelty. Mary Shelley's *Frankenstein [q.v.]* (1818) is another famous example. Gothic elements are also found in the works of the Brontë sisters, and continue to appear in fiction today. The term also is frequently applied to the modern genre of romance novel known as "bodice rippers."

Tania Modleski, in *Loving with a Vengeance,* a study of soap operas and paperback gothic novels, writes:

> Gothics can be identified by their cover illustrations: each portrays a young girl wearing a long, flowing gown and standing in front of a large, menacing-looking castle or mansion. The atmosphere is dark and stormy, and the ethereal young girl appears to be frightened. In the typical Gothic plot, the heroine comes to a mysterious house, perhaps as a bride, perhaps in another capacity, and either starts to mistrust her husband or else finds herself in love with a mysterious man who appears to be some kind of criminal.

But why are the novels or the architecture called gothic or Gothic, anyway? The Goths were a barbarian tribe that invaded Europe in the declining days of the Roman Empire, sacking and pillaging as they came. So "Gothic" as an adjective came to mean "primitive," "uncouth," and "barbarian." The adjective was attached to medieval architecture in general during the Renaissance of the 14th through the 16th centuries; the bright stars of the new era applied the term retroactively and pejoratively to let the world know that the old styles were very backward. You can bet that the master builder of Chartres did NOT call the cathedral Gothic.

At any rate, the adjective has spread well beyond novels and architecture, as the examples illustrate:

From Tom Shales in the *Washington Post,* April 3, 1989:

. . . plans to colorize *Kane* fell through when lawyers for the Welles estate managed to block it. "The tests looked great," Turner insists. But doesn't he concede that *Citizen Kane* has a dark, stark gothic look that makes it an extremely poor candidate for what Welles on his deathbed allegedly called "Ted Turner's crayons"?

And by Robert Marquand in the *Christian Science Monitor,* July 31, 1997, on increasing news coverage of bizarre and violent events:

Whether due to public fascination with the gothic details of crime, or to a sales strategy by media marketers, the era of defining deviancy on Page 1 seems to be more pervasive.

Götterdämmerung \ˌgə(r)-tər-ˈde-mə-ˌrün, -da-\ A collapse (of a society or a régime) marked by catastrophic violence and disorder. Literally in German, "twilight of the gods." The day of doom, the end of life as we know it, total destruction.

In Norse mythology, the destruction of the world is to be preceded by a battle between the good and evil gods, and the good gods are all to die heroically. Afterward, a new world is to be born.

The term in use, from Jeanine Basinger, writing in the *New York Times,* July 3, 1989:

The new police movies reflect the fear the average citizen feels, and the helplessness. The screens show an operatic panorama of explosion, death, destruction and blood, a Götterdämmerung removal of crime.

And a play on the term: When the *New Republic* ran a contest to find an appropriate name for the Iran-contra scandal in December 1986, someone nominated "Gipperdammerung" as in "the twilight of the Gipper" (a Reagan nickname), suggesting that the scandal was so cataclysmic as to mark the end of Reagan, the fall of a political idol. (*See* WIN ONE FOR THE GIPPER.)

And by Jonathan Alter, writing about a more recent political scandal in *Newsweek,* December 28, 1998:

The consequences of this era of bad feeling will be felt for years by the president, the Congress and the press. All have been demythologized in unhealthy ways. . . .

Meanwhile, in the real America, people are scratching their heads. . . . No matter what fate befalls Bill Clinton—no matter how loud our gauche *Götterdämmerung*—this will always be seen as a transitional era between the fall of the Berlin wall and whatever overarching global drama comes next.

Gradgrind \ˈgrad-ˌgrind\ Someone interested only in cold, hard facts. Thomas Gradgrind is a character in *Hard Times,* a novel by Charles Dickens. The novel, published in 1845, is Dickens' most ferocious exposition of the hardships caused by the Industrial Revolution. Gradgrind is a businessman, and while he does not intend to be cruel, the education he imposes on his children leave them starved for affection and without a moral compass. Both his son and his daughter go astray; through their experience and the kindness and loving nature of Sissy Jupe, a poor child taken into the house as a servant, Gradgrind begins to understand his error.

The term in use, by Wendy Lesser in *The State of the Language* (1990):

> On the negative side, there is something ludicrous, if not downright offensive, about having a group that serves meals to the homeless (or carries out some other obviously philanthropic service) fill out quarterly reports describing the cost-benefit ratio of the operation. This is Hard Times Gradgrindism at its worst.

And by Paul Baumann in *Commonweal,* June 2, 1995, on the removal of advertising posters from New York's subway cars:

> I will miss all this eccentric exhortation. But I will especially miss the efforts of the New York State Health Department to dissuade the young from, as it is so delicately put, "doin' it." In a touching display of Gradgrind-like faith in the magical powers of "facts, facts, facts," the Health Department recently put up an eye-catching poster. "Everybody's not doin' it," the poster announces in big bold red letters."

And also from Elizabeth Hardwick in the *New Yorker,* May 8, 1995:

> A great many bricks of Gradgrind fact, whether laudatory or dismissive, are bound to destroy the fluid nature of human lives, yet facts are the stuff of biography.

Grand Guignol \ˌgräⁿ-gēn-ˈyȯl, -ˈyōl\ Dramatic entertainment featuring the gruesome or horrible. In today's use, an expression meaning generally gruesome, macabre, and bloody. It comes from the gory plays that were performed in Paris in a theater called the Grand Guignol, a name that apparently springs from an 18th-century puppet theater in France similar to Punch and Judy in England and frequently violent. The main character was named Guignol.

The term in use, by Robert Bianco, in a Mother's Day salute to Hollywood's scariest moms, in the *Philadelphia Daily News,* May 13, 1995:

> *Die! Die! My Darling!* (1965): One of the more ghoulish sub-genres of American film is the *Baby Jane*-inspired rash of star-struck Grand Guignols, in which aged divas found a temporary career boost playing torturers, victims, or a combination of both.

Another example, in a *Christian Science Monitor* editorial, June 6, 1995:

> Restrictive laws or court decisions will never be the ultimate answer to ending the widespread fascination, especially among

the young, with today's form of Grand Guignol—shock theater. But that doesn't mean nothing can be done.

And by David Falkner in the *New York Times,* August 4, 1989, on baseball's Baltimore Orioles:

> Only eight of the players currently on the roster were here for the Grand Guignol losing streak last year.

grasp *See* MAN'S REACH SHOULD EXCEED HIS GRASP, A.

grassy knoll The conspiracy theory about the assassination of President John F. Kennedy. No longer a cliché for describing a landscape, these two words are forever associated with the feverish suspicion surrounding the assassination in Dallas, Texas, November 22, 1963.

The grassy knoll is believed by many (the Warren Commission findings notwithstanding) to be the place from which assassins (in addition to or instead of) Lee Harvey Oswald fired shots at President Kennedy.

In fact, as conspiracy theories grow ever more popular to explain ever more events and mysteries, "grassy knoll" has become a shorthand term for all conspiracies or for the state of mind attracted to such theories. It is also, inevitably, the name of a musical group which plays numbers with such conspiracy-dripping titles as "Black Helicopters" (all-purpose government evildoing) and "Roswell Crash" (space aliens).

The term in use, by Matt Roush in *USA Today,* November 15, 1996, reviewing an upcoming episode of the television series *The X-Files:*

> Deftly playing a revisionist-history game . . . this episode revives key players from the show's and the nation's past, from the grassy knoll to the Super Bowl.

And again, by Alan Wartofsky in the *Washington Post,* October 27, 1996, in a commentary on Michael Collins, ambiguous hero of Irish independence:

> Collins's assassination that summer in an ambush in West Cork became a symbol of the pointlessness of the fratricidal conflict. It also gave rise to persistent grassy knoll theories that biographer [Tim Pat] Coogan refers to as "the great Irish whodunit industry."

Gray, Dorian One who leads a life of sin and depravity but maintains an outward appearance of innocence and naïveté.

The name comes from the central character of a GOTHIC novel by Oscar Wilde, *The Picture of Dorian Gray* (1891). In the story, a portrait is painted of the young Dorian Gray, an elegantly handsome man who leads a thoroughly degenerate life.

Gray expresses a wish that he always remain as attractive and young as he is in the portrait. As he sinks deeper into his life of vice, the ravages of corruption show on the portrait, but his own living face remains unblemished. In the end, the tormented Gray kills the artist and stabs the painting, but it is Gray who is found at the foot of his portrait with the knife in his heart, his face grotesquely aged. And the picture is once again that of a young and handsome man.

The term in use, by columnist Russell Baker in the *New York Times,* March 13, 1989, commenting on the behavior of major league baseball players:

> Such things do not evoke visions of the boys of spring. They describe the lives of the rich, the arrogant and the corrupt. Dorian Gray stalks the diamond.

Another example, from Cathy Campbell, the *Village Voice,* November 7, 1989, on the updating of Quaker Oats' advertising ICON, Aunt Jemima:

> The mammylike image of Aunt Jemima—an immaculate deception (*see* IMMACULATE CONCEPTION)—has functioned as the inverse to Dorian Gray's portrait: never aging, never directly reflecting the sins of the master or the socio-economic gains (however limited) of black Everywoman [*see* EVERYMAN].

And actor Ed Begley Jr., quoted in the *Los Angeles Times,* April 14, 1996:

> I've been recycling since 1970. Most of us have stuff we'd like to throw away, but where is "away"? The landfill? Landfills serve us the way the portrait served Dorian Gray: They allow us to cavort in an orgy of consumerism until the final day of reckoning, which is today or tomorrow, depending on where you live!

gray flannel suit *See* MAN IN THE GRAY FLANNEL SUIT.

Great American Novel, the The mythical magnum opus—often capitalized because it's Important— that will somehow define completely the American experience and character. The term is often used in an ironic or joking tone—that someone is naïve or foolish or vain enough to think he or she knows what the Great American Novel is, and that he or she could actually sit down and write it.

This concept seems to be an American thing; we never hear about the Great English Novel, or its Russian or French counterpart.

Novelist Philip Roth finessed the problem by simply titling his 1973 novel *The Great American Novel.*

The term in use, by Darryl Rehrer, *Popular Mechanics,* August 1, 1996:

> The sounds of the marvelous old manual typewriter echo through the dimly lit room. Pounding the keys with heavy hands is a writer who is hardly in the process of creating the Great American Novel, but there is no doubt that he's using a Great American Machine, which is putting some real muscle into his prose. If he were using a modern word processor, would it feel the same?

And from architect Thierry Despont, quoted by Karrie Jacobs in the *Los Angeles Times,* August 25, 1996:

> Despont speaks earnestly about "capturing elements of the perfect house, the dream house one is always after like a writer is always after the great American novel."

And by *Celestine Prophecy* author James Redfield, quoted by Marci McDonald in *Maclean's* magazine, June 10, 1996:

> Once again, reviewers have lamented Redfield's simplistic summaries and impoverished style. But, in a protest perhaps unique among fiction writers, he insists they are no accident. "I keep explaining it's not a great American novel," he says.

Great Game, the Power politics, intrigue, high-stakes espionage, and cloak-and-dagger skirmishing between and among the great powers.

The phrase was coined by a British officer, Captain Arthur Conolly, to describe the dark, secret combat of the 19th century between the empires of Britain and Russia over control of Central Asia. The Russians were constantly probing toward India, the British pushing back. Conolly was a daring participant in those struggles and suffered the penalty: in 1842 he was imprisoned, tortured, and beheaded in the great square of Bukhara.

The phrase was popularized by Rudyard Kipling in his novel *Kim* about an Irish orphan who is raised as an Indian and who achieves renown as an agent in the Great Game.

The term in use, by Phil Kloer, in the *Atlanta Journal and Constitution,* March 31, 1997:

> It was all part of "The Great Game," as the retired agents refer to the spy vs. spy days of the Cold War.

And from television news anchor Dan Rather, in the *Economist,* March 19, 1994, reviewing Dilip Hiro's book *Between Marx and Muhammad: The Changing Face of Central Asia:*

> The new "Great Game" resulting from the collapse of the Soviet Union is one reason that the region is so interesting.

And by Patrick Tyler, the *New York Times,* March 23, 1997:

> In the spy-versus-spy atmosphere of the cold war, countless millions of readers everywhere followed the modern world's Great Game, both the reality of it and the fiction of it.

Great Leap Forward Capitalized, it was an enormous, painful, and ultimately catastrophic campaign in China from 1958 to the early 1960s aimed at promoting rapid economic development. Today, without capitals, the term is used to describe any great and dramatic change, especially (but not only) in economic policy, often arbitrarily instituted.

In China, wildly unreachable goals were set for increasing industrial output, often based on impractical means. One example: an effort to increase iron and steel production through the use of small backyard smelters. Simultaneously, China's rulers sought to combine cooperative farms into large agricultural communes—another disaster. A horrifying famine resulted in which an estimated 30 million people died.

Failure of the Great Leap Forward led to conflict among China's Communist Party leadership, and eventually to Mao Tse-tung's launching of the Cultural Revolution to restore purity. In 1966 Mao created the Red Guards, youthful fanatics whose rampages led to beatings, public humiliation, imprisonment, or death for those believed to be opposing the dictates of Chairman Mao. Chaos reigned until 1970, when the authorities began to move the country toward normalcy.

The term in use, by Don Sherman in *Popular Science,* April 1, 1996, on the latest model of the Ford Taurus:

> [We] gathered test cars and scheduled a date at the track to answer what may be the most important question on the minds of family-sedan buyers all over America: Is the new Taurus another great leap forward?

A play on the term, in *Newsweek,* June 19, 1989, reporting on political turmoil in China, and the suppression of student advocates of democracy in Tiananmen Square:

> The great leap backward sent reverberations through financial centers around the globe.

And by Thomas J. Bray in the *Detroit News,* December 31, 1995:

> But when historians look back on the mid-1990s, and 1995 in particular, I suspect they will see the most important story as the great leap forward in telecommunications—in particular, the emergence of the Internet.

Great White Fleet A show of strength, especially naval. From American naval history: At the direction of President Theodore Roosevelt, a force of 16 battleships and four destroyers of the U.S. Navy's Atlantic fleet—all reinforced with steel plates, all painted a dramatic white—took a 14-month global cruise starting in 1907. The journey was a public relations triumph, alerting the world to America's arrival as a major power. The show of strength, recalled the *National Journal* of April 21, 1984, also intimidated Japan (at least for a while) into honoring the status quo in the Pacific. The phrase is still evoked in contemporary flexings of American naval muscle.

The term in use, in an editorial in the *New York Times,* July 28, 1983:

> There is a cold-blooded case for sending a great white fleet to the Caribbean. It is a comparatively low-cost way of sending a message to the Managua Marxists and their friends in Havana and Moscow.

And more whimsically, by David W. Dunlap in the *New York Times,*
December 2, 1981:

> The New York Transit Authority's "great white fleet," the first
> of the Flushing-line subway trains to be painted only white, suf-
> fered a minor graffiti attack Monday.

Great White Hope A long-awaited champion and savior, the unproven
hero of a cause, who is invested—and burdened—with the unrealized
hopes and expectations of adherents.

The term came into being after Jack Johnson, a black man, won the
world heavyweight boxing championship in 1908. White supremacists
couldn't abide the notion and launched a search for a "great white hope"
to take the crown from him. Their first candidate was Jim Jeffries, a former champ lured out of retirement. Johnson knocked him out and dis-
posed of other hopefuls as well (including Victor McLaglen, who later did
better as an actor).

Johnson further infuriated his enemies with his flamboyant way of life
outside the ring, including his marriages to white women. Prosecutors
went after him; he was convicted of violating the Mann Act (for trans-
porting a woman, who later became his wife, across a state line for sexual purposes), spent several years in exile in Europe, and eventually served
a year in Leavenworth Prison. In 1915 another great white hope, Jess
Willard, finally dethroned Johnson, although Johnson was later to claim
that he threw the fight. Today we often see the phrase minus the racial
connotation or the ugliness of its origins.

The term in use, by Camille Paglia in the *New Republic,* March 4, 1996,
in a pop-psychology sketch of Hillary Rodham Clinton:

> Ice queen, drag queen: the Great White Feminist Hope is a far
> more conflicted and self-destructive creature than either her
> admirers or revilers understand.

However, racial connotations are often in evidence, as in this use by
Carrie Rickey in the *New York Times Book Review,* December 11, 1988:

> Drafted by the Boston Celtics in 1978, Mr. Bird was touted as
> the great white hope of the N.B.A., in which 70 percent of the
> players then were black.

And a play on the phrase from Robert Parker in *Parker's Wine Buyer's
Guide* (1989):

> Oregon has proven to be the only place outside of Burgundy
> where high-quality Pinot Noir grapes can be grown with consis-
> tent success. Chardonnay, Riesling, and Sauvignon Blanc have
> done well in Oregon, but the great white hope here is the Pinot
> Gris. . . .

Greek chorus A company of singers and dancers in Athenian drama par-
ticipating in or commenting on the action. The chorus's contributions

were often highly emotional. Also, those who function in a similar role—commenting, explaining, criticizing, carping, bemoaning—outside the theater.

Through the ages, playwrights have continued to use the device. In *Henry V*, Shakespeare reduced the chorus to one person to speak the prologue and epilogue and to explain and comment on events.

The term in use, by Michael Kinsley in *Time*, March 17, 1997:

> C. Boyden Gray, White House counsel in the Bush Administration, has become a sort of Greek chorus of the Clinton fundraising scandal. He pops up in the newspapers after each new revelation to intone self-righteously, We never did that in our day. This generally turns out to mean, We never did exactly that.

And by Linda Feldmann, the *Christian Science Monitor*, July 18, 1996:

> As if the latest polling numbers aren't bad enough, Bob Dole faces a Greek chorus of GOP brethren with little nice to say about their likely nominee's run for the White House.

And in *Business Week*, by Howard Gleckman, May 13, 1996:

> . . . Representative Edward J. Markey (D-Mass.) calls for a windfall profits tax on oil companies. And a sort of Greek chorus of congressional committees vows hearings to get to the bottom of the price hike.

Grendel \\'gren-dᵊl\\ A monstrous man-eating descendant of Cain (*see* CAIN, MARK OF) slain by Beowulf in the Old English poem *Beowulf*. A fearsome, evil, destructive ogre.

The heroic tale *Beowulf* is the earliest surviving composition of any length in the English language, probably composed in the 8th century.

Grendel would frequently rush into the castle of King Hrothgar and kill and devour many of his warriors as they slept, and for twelve years held the kingdom in terror. Beowulf arrived to help, and fought the monster with his bare hands. He defeated Grendel by tearing the monster's arm off; Grendel fled to his marshy lair.

All rejoiced. But the joy was premature, because Grendel's even more unpleasant mother emerged from her home at the bottom of a dark lake to avenge her son. Beowulf pursued her to the bottom of the lake and killed her after a desperate fight; he then beheaded the fugitive Grendel and returned to his companions.

The term in use, by Frederick D. Robinson in an editorial in the *Atlanta Journal and Constitution*, November 13, 1996:

> Written off with no chance of winning, his [Evander Holyfield's] defeat of Mike Tyson was as remarkable as Beowulf's slaying of the fearsome dragon Grendel.

And by Vincent Czyz in *Sports Illustrated*, November 13, 1995:

There is something primal about wrestling, whether it involves the naked Beowulf grappling with the bestial Grendel in a misty swamp or former New York Giant linebacker Lawrence Taylor straining against pro wrestling bad boy Bam Bam Bigelow for pay-per-view millions.

Gresham's Law \'gre-shəmz-\ An observation in economics: when two coins are equal in monetary value but unequal in intrinsic value, the one intrinsically worth less will stay in circulation, the other will be hoarded; a process by which inferior products or practices drive out superior ones. Or, bad money drives out good.

This principle was named for Sir Thomas Gresham (ca. 1519–1579), English financier, merchant, and adviser to Queen Elizabeth I. Gresham was credited with authorship of the "law" by economist H.D. MacLeod in 1857, who did not know that the same observation had been made earlier by others, including Copernicus.

The term in use, by Julie Chao in the *Wall Street Journal,* June 7, 1995:

> But to some Usenet veterans, that trend is akin to a kind of electronic Gresham's Law, in which the bad drives out the good.

And by Matthew Miller, in commentary on political promises on the economy in the *Los Angeles Times,* February 4, 1996:

> It's not that we're short of numeric goals worth fighting for. But there's a perverse "Gresham's Law" at work in political rhetoric, where silly but nice-sounding promises drive out room for goals that would mean something—such as reducing the number of Americans with no health insurance; or raising wages stagnant in real terms for two decades.

And from *Village Voice* film critic J. Hoberman, December 12, 1989:

> There is a Gresham's law of images: the facile ones drive the tougher ones out of circulation.

Gridley *See* FIRE WHEN READY, GRIDLEY.

griot \'grē-ˌō\ Musician-entertainer of Western Africa whose performances include tribal histories and genealogies. Griots, poets and musicians, through oral recitations preserve local traditions, memories, tales, history, and genealogy.

The term in use, by Ken Ringle in the *Washington Post,* January 7, 1997:

> As a Gulf Coast sunset gilds the waterscape behind him, W.E.B. Griffin, the grizzled griot of the warrior breed, sets down his glass of cabernet and begins explaining how the Nazis smuggled their World War II loot into Argentina.

Another example, from Green Bay Packer veteran Sean Jones on the eve of the NFC championship game, as quoted in the *New York Times,* January 12, 1996:

That's what the old guys are for. We're like the griots who passed down oral history. We sit here at the locker rapping, explaining to the young guys what this thing is all about.

And by Rick Perlstein in *Nation,* December 18, 1995:

Michael soon discovered he had a gift for listening empathetically to the stories lonely old farmers would tell him; so, incongruously, this child of the upper middle class soon found himself a griot of upper-Midwestern agrarian history.

And, finally, by Stevie Wonder, quoted by David Ritz in *Rolling Stone,* July 13, 1995:

"I love rap," Wonder says. "I learn from rap. I'm not saying I like the way some rappers address women, but I believe that rappers are the griots, the African storytellers in the village. They're verbal historians telling tales that are clear and real and need to be heard."

Griselda *See* PATIENT GRISELDA.

grok \\'gräk\\ To understand intuitively, empathetically; to establish rapport with. Often used in the computer world to mean to scan or encompass all available information and to form an opinion. The verb (in the Martian tongue) was coined by Robert A. Heinlein in his science fiction classic, *Stranger in a Strange Land* (1961): "Smith had been aware of the doctors but had grokked that their intentions were benign." The novel is about a young man who is raised by Martians and returns to earth.
   The term in use, by Ty Burr in *Entertainment Weekly,* February 4, 1994:

But test audiences, unable to grok the concept of Nick Nolte singing and dancing, reportedly gave a thumbs-down to the musical numbers.

And in *Computer Life,* October 1994:

Are you a disgruntled baby boomer? One who just doesn't grok today's twentysomethings? Or are you a Generation X-er who's had it with how much mindshare Baby Boomers still get? Either way, you're not alone. . . .

And in *Newsweek,* September 4, 1995:

When you're a trend-savvy neologizer like Douglas Coupland, you get to do cool things like grok new words. In his new book, *Microserfs,* Coupland employs "intercapping"—capitalizing a letter in the middle of a word like WordPerfect, NetManage or Compu-Serve to make it look more high-tech.

Grub Street The world or category of needy literary hacks.
   The term comes from Grub Street in London, where, in the 18th century, writers of trash congregated. Samuel Johnson defined Grub Street

as: "Much inhabited by writers of small histories, dictionaries, and temporary poems; whence any mean production is called grubstreet."

The term in use, by Gaylord Dodd, reviewing Dan Wakefield's memoir *New York in the Fifties* in the *Wichita Eagle,* July 12, 1992:

> It seems hard to believe, but New York in the '50s was both safe and affordable. . . . Cheap meals could be had in bistros, lunch counters, and at innumerable sidewalk cafes that catered to students, artists and writers, and to those members of the Grub Street fraternity lucky enough to have an assignment.

And by Anthony Burgess in the *New York Times Book Review,* April 21, 1991:

> There was for him, as later for me, a grim pleasure in being a Grub Street man: one touched the grubby paw of Samuel Johnson. He introduced me to subliterary modes of earning the odd pound.

Grundy, Mrs. Imaginary English character who typifies the censorship by conventional opinion at work in everyday life. A tyrant of propriety. The name is from a 1798 play by Thomas Morton, *Speed the Plough.* Mrs. Grundy is the neighbor, never seen onstage, whose opinion Mrs. Ashfield fears. She therefore constantly asks, "What will Mrs. Grundy say?"

The term in use, by Patt Morrison in the *Los Angeles Times,* August 6, 1995, applying new rock music ratings to Broadway musicals:

> "I Get a Kick Out of You" from *Anything Goes.* Substance abuse, high tolerances for cocaine, and later, champagne. He (Cole Porter) provided a whole COTTAGE INDUSTRY to the Mrs. Grundys; "Love for Sale" was banned from radio for years.

And by Judith Dunford, commenting in *Newsday* on the popularity of Robert James Waller's *The Bridges of Madison County* (1992), January 29, 1995:

> Middle-aged people loved the idea that Waller's principals were no longer young (although in excellent shape), that their little lines just made them more beautiful. Even Mrs. Grundies had their day. Just like in the (old) movies, the adulterous lovers choose (gasp!) duty over personal happiness. . . .

Gucci Gulch \'gü-chē-\ Congressional lobbyists and the turf on which they operate. Used especially of the well paid, elegantly dressed, and expensively shod (hence the reference to Gucci shoes) practitioners who linger in the corridors when important legislation is being crafted.

The term is a wonderful play on the titles of innumerable Western movies of the *Shootout at Tombstone Gulch* ilk. The term was coined during House Ways and Means Committee deliberations on a massive revision of federal tax law in 1986, an enterprise that brought forth swarms of lobbyists, waiting in their tasseled shoes outside the committee room.

A lawmaker making his way through this crowd was said to be running the Gucci Gauntlet (*see* GAUNTLET, RUN THE), and the battles fought during this version of the Gulch Wars was definitively described by *Wall Street Journal* reporter Jeffrey Birnbaum in *Showdown at Gucci Gulch* (1988). The term in use, in a *Wall Street Journal* editorial, September 30, 1994:

> Better that the telecom industry develops as amazing Silicon Valley did in the 1980s, driven by new technology and the demands of the marketplace, not by the dictates of Gucci Gulch.

And by Jerry Heaster in the *Kansas City Star,* May 10, 1995:

> Not all of those people clogging congressional offices and hallways are high-paid lobbyists from Gucci Gulch. Many are obviously from the provinces. . . .

gulag \\'gü-ˌläg\\ The penal system of the former U.S.S.R. consisting of a network of labor camps; a labor camp. Often the term describes primitive, isolated, oppressive, or otherwise grimly horrible and prisonlike conditions.

The term gained notoriety in the English-speaking world with the publication of Alexander Solzhenitsyn's 1973 novel, *The Gulag Archipelago.* "Gulag" is a Russian acronym for the chief administration of labor camps in the Soviet Union. "Archipelago" means a group of islands, or a sea with many islands. Thus the image of the archipelago is of a chain of camps—like islands in the vast ocean of the Russian landscape.

The term in use, by Richard Hoffer in *Sports Illustrated,* October 12, 1992:

> "He's businesslike," says Esiason, "which is what it takes to win." Of course, it's not like Shula's running a gulag, either. Before he scheduled the minicamps, he consulted with Esiason about any possible conflicts with his summer vacation plans.

Another example, from Donna Foote in *Newsweek,* July 4, 1994:

> "J" is a prisoner in the largest juvenile-justice system in the world—the California Youth Authority, a teen gulag with 9,000 inmates in 11 training schools, including the Nelles School, and four conservation camps.

And quoted by Lew Powell in the *Charlotte Observer,* December 31, 1995:

> "He took a college that had been run like a plantation and turned it into a gulag." Political science professor Andy Koch, citing embattled president Anthony DiGiorgio as one of his reasons for leaving Winthrop University.

guru \\'gu̇r-(ˌ)ü\\ A personal religious teacher and spiritual guide in Hinduism; a teacher and guide in matters of fundamental concern; a leader or expert. A Hindi word for a spiritual adviser or teacher. Now used of anyone from the head of a religious cult to the possessor of expertise—

or at least opinions—on virtually anything. In fact, the word is used so freely of charlatans and schemers that it can be a sneer rather than a compliment.

The term in use, by Lenore Skenazy, the *New York Daily News,* in the *Portland Oregonian,* April 16, 1996:

> I'm scared of food. I'm scared of what's in it, what's on it, where it came from and how it got to be that color. (Especially orange.) Health gurus, newspaper articles and those ever-watchful consumer groups have led to the only possible conclusion: You eat, you die.

From John A. Byrne, *Business Week,* August 26, 1996:

> Suddenly, the idea of rising above the tumult of day-to-day business to ponder the future of markets and competitors is looking attractive again. Reengineering consultants with stopwatches are out. Strategy gurus with visions of new prospects are in.

Business writing seems infested with gurus. Another example from Simon Forge, in *Futurist,* June 1, 1996:

> The whole guru-SPEAK phenomenon seems to be a characteristic of the mid-life crisis facing management science today, with the invasion of the initiative snatchers, the management gurus.

Guy Fawkes *See* FAWKES, GUY.

*I thought I knew all about political **hardball**. . . .
In 1972, I learned about a new kind of dirty politics . . .*

—Tip O'Neill

Hail Mary A play in football in which the quarterback throws the ball far down the field in the hope that some one of his teammates will catch it. A desperation move. Named after the best-known prayer of Roman Catholicism, the term has migrated from sports to politics.

This description from Robert Falkoff in the December 30, 1994, *Houston Post* captures the essence of the play as well as any we've read, this time in basketball:

> Christmas came late for the Rockets and Vernon Maxwell delivered the biggest and best gift of all. Houston's designated miracle man did it again Thursday night, delivering an improbable, twisting, 3-point Hail Mary with 1.9 seconds remaining to give the Rockets a 126–124 victory over Golden State before 16,611 stunned fans at The Summit.

Again, by political analyst Charles Cook, commenting on the presidential campaign, quoted in the *Kansas City Star,* August 4, 1996:

> Given the size of Dole's poll deficit, I think it's Hail Mary time.

And by Mark Lander in the *New York Times,* June 30, 1997, on AT&T Corporation's attempted merger with SBC Communications:

> "This was a Hail Mary pass," Daniel Reingold, a Merrill Lynch analyst, said. "AT&T was attempting to declare peace on one front so it could defend all its other fronts."

hair shirt A shirt made of rough animal hair worn next to the skin as a penance; something that irritates like a hair shirt. It is similar to the idea of sackcloth and ashes, sackcloth being coarse and irritating; ashes sprinkled on the head are an extra. The Biblical sackcloth was a dark cloth of goat or camel hair.

Real hair shirts are not much in vogue now, but metaphorically they show up everywhere. As for modern penitential wear, go no further (bunions permitting) than stiletto high heels.

The term in use, by Anita Lienert, the *Detroit News,* March 19, 1997:

> Up until now, Volvo cars have been the hair shirts of the auto industry, the kind of serious vehicles you drove when you were feeling burdened by the "responsibilities" of family and career.

By Tom Teepen in the *Atlanta Journal and Constitution,* April 6, 1997:

> Run for your life. That "thump, thump, thump" you hear behind you is a holier-than-y'all moralism chasing us down with lumberjack boots.
>
> The latest galloping moralist is, implausibly, Bill Clinton, rejiggered during the last election as Dr. Stern, scourge of wayward citizens and national hair-shirt-in-chief.

And from Jeremiah O'Leary, the *Washington Times,* January 4, 1991, commenting on the then-new-on-the-scene Rush Limbaugh:

> Just when I thought it was safe to go back in the water, I have discovered a new hair shirt of the air waves in the voice and persona of Rush Limbaugh, King of the Daytime Radio Talk Shows.

halcyon days \'hal-sē-ən\ Calm, peaceful days, a happy golden period; prosperous, affluent times.

Halcyon is the Greek name for the bird we know as the kingfisher. The ancient Greeks believed the bird nested at sea at the winter solstice and calmed the waves while it incubated its eggs. This halcyon period lasted fourteen days.

There is an explanation in Greek mythology, of course. Halcyon was the daughter of Aeolus, god of the winds. She was married to a mortal who died at sea, and threw herself into the ocean to be near him. The gods changed them both into kingfishers—it's unclear whether this was an act of compassion or anger!

The term in use, by David Holahan, *USA Today,* March 11, 1997:

> Hearken with me to yesteryear and those straightforward times when NFL football referees made calls, stood by them and the games played on.
>
> In those halcyon days, the men in stripes didn't congregate like doo-wop groups on street corners to mull over calls.

And again, by James J. Fisher of the *Boston Globe,* in the *Kansas City Star,* October 8, 1995, writing about automobile nameplates that have disappeared:

> In the years since, another postwar car, the Tucker, has gotten most of the ink, despite a total production run of 50-plus cars. The Kaisers and the Frazers, though, were the cars that Americans really embraced in those Halcyon days of the late 1940s.

half-life The time required for half of something to undergo a process of disintegration or elimination. Most often the term appears in physics and refers to the decay of radioactive substances. The term also describes, sometimes playfully, the period of usefulness, growth, or prosperity before decay or decline sets in.

The term in use, in "Walter Scott's Personality Parade" in *Parade,* July 28, 1996:

The half-life of most pop groups is extremely short, but Garbage may be here to stay.

And by Vincent Canby in the *New York Times Book Review,* January 6, 1991:

In Ms. Hepburn, Mr. Ryson found an extraordinary woman who also possesses a face structured by bones with a half-life of forever. The years pass but not the beauty. A face for Mount Rushmore, he calls it.

Hamlet A legendary Danish prince and hero of Shakespeare's play *Hamlet,* or someone who behaves like the Shakespearean character—soul-searching, melancholy, and tortured by indecision.

Hamlet's father, the king of Denmark, has been murdered by his own brother Claudius, who has taken the throne and married the king's widow, Gertrude. The ghost of his father appears to Hamlet, tells him of the crime, and demands revenge. The prince struggles to decide whether or not to believe the spirit (it was thought in those times that ghosts were agents of the devil sent to deceive and damn the unwary). At the conclusion of this story of passion and revenge, very few of the characters are left standing.

The play also contains some of the most famous characters in Shakespeare (*see* POLONIUS) and some of the most familiar passages in the English language.

The term in use, by A.N. Wilson, author of *The Rise and Fall of the House of Windsor,* in commentary on the death of Diana, Princess of Wales, in the *New York Times,* September 3, 1997:

Prince Charles is not the monster portrayed in popular newspapers. He is a Prince Hamlet, agonized, self-doubting, self-critical.

And by Jacob Heilbrunn in the *New Republic,* August 23, 1993:

In 1984, for example, he engaged Weinberger in a protracted and bitter public dispute over the use of force, declaring that the United States could not become the "Hamlet of nations," fretting over when to exert its power.

During his long political career as Democratic governor of New York, Mario Cuomo was frequently characterized as a Hamlet for his public indecision about whether to run for the presidency. He was referred to as the Hamlet of the Hudson or the Hamlet of Albany. In fact, he has become an allusion himself, as in this example from John F. Stacks, *Time,* July 10, 1995, on the possible presidential candidacy of General Colin Powell:

This reluctance, in the jujitsu of American politics, is a huge plus for the time being. A dithering Powell would become the Hamlet of the 1996 race, a kind of Mario Cuomo with medals.

handwriting on the wall, the An omen of one's unpleasant fate. A portent of disaster.

It is from the book of Daniel (4:9) in the Old Testament. Belshazzar, king of Babylon was holding a great feast in his palace for his noble guests, when they saw a vision of a man's hand writing these Aramaic words on the wall: "mene, mene, tekel, upharsin." Daniel, a Jewish prophet who was a captive in Babylon (*see* BABYLONIAN CAPTIVITY), was summoned to translate. He said that the words foretold the fall of the king: "God hath numbered thy kingdom, and brought it to an end; thou art weighed in the balance and found wanting (another allusion originating in this tale); thy kingdom is divided and given to the Medes and Persians."

(*See* BELSHAZZAR'S FEAST for details of how this story became part of American presidential politics during the Cleveland-Blaine campaign of 1884.)

The term in use, by Ivan Ludington, on the sale of his family business, quoted by George Hunter in the *Detroit News,* May 15, 1997:

> But it was either sell or see the company go under completely. Over the last year and a half, things were really getting tough. I could see the handwriting on the wall.

And by Linda Feldmann in the *Christian Science Monitor,* September 11, 1996:

> But administration officials also point out that the rise in teen marijuana use began during the Bush administration. According to [Dr. Lloyd] Johnson, the handwriting was on the wall in 1991, when surveys showed that declining numbers of teenagers viewed drugs as dangerous.

hardball Baseball. Also, forceful uncompromising methods employed to gain an end. Rough, tough tactics, often in politics.

The term became popular in the Watergate era. It originates, no doubt, from the differences between the games of baseball and softball. Baseball is played with a harder, faster ball and thus is often called hardball to distinguish it from the slower, more widely played version of the sport. Hardball is a tougher game and is played mostly by professionals and semi-professionals. Its political counterpart is practiced on the local as much as on the national level.

The term in use, by Robert Shogan in the *Los Angeles Times,* August 19, 1997:

> When Richard G. Lugar won the mayoralty of Indianapolis in 1967, newspaper cartoonists depicted him in his old Boy Scout uniform, complete with short pants, confronting a menacing gang of political bosses.
>
> But despite the perception that he was too genteel for hardball politics, Lugar tamed the bosses during his two terms in City

Hall and went on to become one of the U.S. Senate's most influential policymakers.

And in *Man of the House* (1987), by Tip O'Neill with William Novak, in which the former speaker of the House complains of the tactics employed by the Nixon White House:

> I thought I knew all about political hardball. Hardball was ballot-stuffing in Illinois during the 1960 presidential election. Hardball was when you pressured somebody to make a donation on the basis of your friendship. Hardball was when organizations feuded and tried to destroy each other. Hardball was repeat voters being run in and out of the polls in Boston. In 1972, I learned about a new kind of dirty politics in the Republican camp.

Sometimes the term is applied outside the field of politics, as in this use quoted by Neil Hickey and Bill Burns in *TV Guide,* December 14, 1991:

> "They are the ultimate hardball corporation," says one Hollywood studio executive of G.E. "They would sell the body parts of NBC piecemeal in Grand Central Station if that would improve G.E.'s bottom line."

Hardy, Andy The fictional all-American boy in the all-American family. The name, like OZZIE AND HARRIET, evokes that idealized image of safe, happy life in a safe and happy community.

Andy Hardy and his family were the basis for a highly popular MGM movie series starting in 1936 and continuing through and past World War II. The series featured fine performances, especially by Mickey Rooney as Andy and Lewis Stone as kindly Judge Hardy, who was firm but fair.

The setting was Carvel, a fictional town of 25,000. As *Magill's Survey of Cinema* describes it, Carvel was "an apparently exclusively white community which has never had to face school busing, teenage alcoholism, drug addiction, war protests on campus, premarital sex, or women's liberation." And Hollywood being Hollywood, the girl next door was Lana Turner. Judy Garland also came to visit so Andy could say, "Hey, let's put on a show!"

The last film in the series was made in 1958, when the grown-up Andy returns home, but it was not successful; no one really wanted Andy to grow up.

The term in use, by Denise Topolnicki, *Money,* January 1, 1996, rating the best public school districts in the U.S.:

> Is everything absolutely perfect in our top 100 districts? Of course not. . . . But a handful of places are straight out of Andy Hardy. At Hesston High in Kansas, for instance, computers are not anchored to the tables, and most kids don't even have locks on their lockers.

And from John Blake, in the *Atlanta Journal and Constitution,* July 15, 1996, on FILM NOIR:

> Lee Server, a pop culture critic who wrote the book's introduction, said noir films were a corrective to the Hollywood of "candy-colored optimism and Andy Hardy values."

And from Owen Gleiberman, *Entertainment Weekly,* May 19, 1995, reviewing the film *The Englishman Who Went Up a Hill But Came Down a Mountain:*

> Displaying the can-do enthusiasm of an Andy Hardy musical, they trudge up and down the hill, hoisting buckets of earth from their own gardens.

harm's way *See* IN HARM'S WAY.

harpy A foul, malign creature in Greek mythology that is part woman (head) and part bird (body). Also, a predatory person, leech; or a shrewish woman. Greek legend has it that harpies snatched food from the blind king Phineus until they were frightened away by the Argonauts, the heroes who sailed with Jason to recover the Golden Fleece.

The term in use, by the *Sunday Telegraph* of London, September 17, 1989:

> The French have allowed Mrs. Thatcher to develop into a creature of myth—La Dame Fer, a combination of Harpy and Red Queen constantly blocking the moves of the rest of the Euro chess pieces and ready to savage her opponents. [*See also* RED QUEEN'S RACE.]

And by Nanci Hellmich in *USA Today,* July 29, 1994, in a profile of nutrition advocate Jayne Hurley of the Center for Science in the Public Interest, a group which has objected to some of America's most cherished foods:

> At 5 feet 6 and 120 pounds, Hurley, 37, looks like a fashion model, not a nutrition heavyweight. Or—as some columnists have described—a "skinny harpy" or one of CSPI's "killjoys. . . . "

And from the *Economist,* October 7, 1989:

> Ms. Peggy Pascoe of the University of Utah challenges the myth that frontier women were either the non-beings their absence from the history books would imply, or the harpies and angels that western films have painted them.

Harriet *See* OZZIE AND HARRIET.

Haskell, Eddie Character in the popular TV series *Leave It to Beaver* notable for smarmily obsequious behavior.

The term in use, by Tim Sullivan, Gannett News Service, February 21, 1997, on volatile baseball player Albert Belle:

Albert Belle's best behavior is boring, like a volcano during a dormant period or Eddie Haskell in the presence of June Cleaver. It is less dangerous, to be sure, but dreadfully dull.

And by Ronald Brownstein in the *Los Angeles Times,* August 12, 1996:

Through a powerful presentation of Clinton's biography, they transformed the public perception of him from a sharpie who glided through Georgetown, Oxford and Yale (think of Eddie Haskell with good board scores) into a small-town boy who was at once a product and the champion of "the forgotten middle class."

Hastings, Battle of A battle between the armies of King Harold of England and Duke William of Normandy. The Norman victory changed the course of world history.

The battle took place in 1066 near the English seaport of Hastings on the English Channel. It was the culmination of a dispute over the succession to the crown of England after King Edward the Confessor died childless.

On one side: Harold, Earl of Wessex, the most powerful nobleman in the kingdom, who had apparently been designated heir by Edward on his deathbed, and confirmed King by the parliament of Saxon nobles. On the other: William, Duke of Normandy (a region in northern France on the English Channel), who claimed that Edward had promised *him* the throne. There was also the matter of an oath of loyalty Harold had made to William two years before. (Keep in mind that historians are *still* arguing about these events.) Halley's comet made an appearance, giving everyone a fright, and was interpreted as a portent in favor of William because of the business of the broken oath (complete polling data not available).

The outcome: While Harold watched England's south coast in anticipation of William's invasion, Harold's rebellious brother Tostig and the king of Norway landed a horde of Vikings 200 miles to the north. Harold rushed his army north in four days and defeated these ferocious invaders, but William took advantage of the opportunity and landed his army in the south.

Harold's weary army marched south again, and the battle was joined. After a long fight Harold's offensive line was finally broken by wave upon wave of Norman arrows. Legend says Harold fell, dead or wounded, with an arrow in his eye, and his army collapsed.

Through William's control of Normandy, England became a power on the continent; the struggles of later English kings to maintain, expand, or regain territories in France set up centuries of war and diplomatic rivalry between the two countries.

The battle brought a new, Norman, ruling class to England and with it a more centralized and organized feudal government. From this time on England had a strong monarchy that promoted order (not always successfully), the growth of towns, merchant classes, and other familiar institutions.

The outcome of the Battle of Hastings also produced a new language, English, which possesses the largest vocabulary in the world, thanks to the confluence of French (based on Latin) and Anglo-Saxon (a Germanic language).

The term in use, by Nat Hentoff in the *Village Voice,* March 21, 1989:

> For years after the previously unimaginable horrors of Hiroshima, the print and broadcast press carried stories about American children afraid they would be incinerated before they grew up. I have seen no such stories for a long time. To today's kids, Hiroshima and Nagasaki are as remote as the Battle of Hastings, and most of them never think of that historic turning point either.

And by Ed McNamara in *Newsday,* May 5, 1996, on horse trainer D. Wayne Lukas:

> Lukas sends out his horses in waves, the way William the Conqueror ordered his Norman knights up the hill against the Saxons at the Battle of Hastings in 1066.

Hatfields and McCoys Families in the Appalachian Mountains of Kentucky and West Virginia engaged in a long and bitter feud. Now synonymous with two bitterly opposing groups, those engaged in a seemingly irreconcilable feud. The Hatfields and the McCoys were the real thing, and in the last twenty years of the 19th century their battles attracted national attention. (*See also* MONTAGUES AND CAPULETS.)

These two families were neighbors, of course: the Hatfields lived in Kentucky, on one side of the Tug Fork, and the McCoys lived in West Virginia, on the other side.

The origins of the feud seem to be obscure, but the story does have its Romeo and Juliet: there evidently was a romance between Rose Anna McCoy and Johnson Hatfield in 1880 which the McCoys broke up.

The quarrel got out of hand in 1882 when Ellison Hatfield was shot. This event set off a spiral of revenge. Things began to quiet down after 1888, although there continued to be occasional outbreaks of violence.

The term in use, quoted by John Martellaro in the *Kansas City Star,* March 25, 1996, on the advertising war between Advil and Tylenol:

> So which company's ads are misleading?
>
> "It seems like they both are. It's always fun to watch," said Michael Leff, editor of "Consumer Reports on Health," a monthly newsletter published by Consumers Union. "It reminds me of the Hatfields and McCoys what these two are doing."

Another example, from Chuck Green, in the *Denver Post,* August 23, 1992:

When I was watching TV this week, I wasn't sure whether I was tuned into a rerun of Family Feud or the Republican National Convention.

Or was it an updated, made-for-TV version of the Hatfields and the McCoys?

hat trick The retiring of three batsmen with three consecutive balls by a bowler in cricket. Also, the scoring of three goals in one game (such as hockey or soccer) by a single player; or a succession of three victories, successes, or related accomplishments. Three repeated successes.

The term actually originated in British cricket; a player accomplishing this feat is entitled to a new hat at the expense of the club, rather like earning a letter in sports in the United States. Broadcasting's baseball announcers also borrow the term to refer to a player who gets three hits in three times at bat.

The term in use, by Lois Romano in the *Washington Post,* February 24, 1988, describing the troubles of Evan Mecham, governor of Arizona:

> He is desperately hanging on to his political life and will need nothing short of a political hat trick to survive. He faces a Senate impeachment trial next week, a criminal prosecution next month and a May recall election.

And by Mark Simon in the *San Francisco Chronicle,* August 22, 1997:

> Stanford law school officials are quite tickled about what Rosenfield called a judicial "hat trick." In addition to Rehnquist, the chief justice of the California Supreme Court, Ron George, is also a Stanford law graduate. So is Proctor Hug, Jr., chief judge of the U.S. Court of Appeals in San Francisco, the largest of the federal appellate courts.

heap coals of fire To react with kindness and generosity to insult or injury, thus undermining the enmity behind the act and mortifying the perpetrator with the awareness of his or her wrong.

The expression comes from the Old Testament, Proverbs 25: 21–22:

> If thine enemy be hungry, give him bread to eat; and if he be thirsty, give him water to drink; for thou shalt heap coals of fire upon his head, and the Lord shall reward thee.

St. Paul's Epistle to the Romans 12: 20 offers the same counsel:

> . . . for in so doing thou shalt heap coals of fire upon his head. Be not overcome of evil, but overcome evil with good.

The term in use, by Jerry Useem in *Inc.,* December 1, 1996, describing an Amish businessman's method of dealing with a bad debt:

> So when a customer stiffed Sam Stoltzfus for $12,000, Sam chose the obvious alternative to hiring a lawyer or a collection agency. He baked him a loaf of bread.

"He gave it as a symbol of love," Michael explains matter-of-factly, as if that were standard procedure for collecting outstanding accounts receivable. . . .

The Amish call that debt-collection method "heaping coals of fire on his head" (rough translation: The MOTHER OF ALL guilt trips).

And from Doug Crichton of the Associated Press, January 23, 1996, quoting a psychology professor on increasing incidents of violence between drivers on the highway:

"[T]urn the whole thing around," Tedford adds. "Make it a challenge not to react. Do good unto those who hate you and you'll heap coals of fire on their heads. That is, smile at someone who is giving you the finger."

heart of darkness The deepest part of the jungle in Joseph Conrad's *Heart of Darkness* (1902). Also the dark, depraved, primitive side of human nature.

The term comes from the darkest jungle into which the narrator of Conrad's story goes in his search for Kurtz, the mysterious and powerful white trader who lives deep in the jungle in what was then the Belgian Congo. The term also refers to the utter depravity the narrator finds when he reaches Kurtz.

Marlow, the narrator, recounts his search and also describes the cruelties of the colonial regime and of Kurtz's own particular regime. Kurtz, we learn, had been celebrated for his enlightenment and humanity, but has now descended to violence and brutality. (*See* HORROR, THE HORROR.) The story was adapted by Francis Ford Coppola for his 1979 film *Apocalypse Now,* with the scene changed to the Vietnam War.

The term in use, by William McGurn in the *American Spectator,* March 1989, on travel in the Third World:

Yet there exist lands where an L.L. Bean knapsack only singles one out as a likely mark, places where credit ratings are unknown and life (human, at least) is cheap. Here in the heart of darkness, with no Arthur Frommer to clear the way, the adventurer stands alone.

And by Ellen Willis, reviewing *Without a Doubt,* Marcia Clark's account (with Teresa Carpenter) of the prosecution of the O.J. Simpson murder case, in the *New York Times Book Review,* June 15, 1997:

And throughout her book that passion hints at a story that never quite emerges—an epic of disastrous confrontation with America's heart of darkness, centered on the metaphorical resonance of the Simpson trial.

hearts and minds Conviction felt in every way, emotional and intellectual, thoroughly and completely. The phrase came into currency in the

Vietnam era to describe how and to what extent the people of Vietnam had to be wooed away from communism. As President Lyndon Johnson put it in 1965:

> . . . so we must be ready to fight in Vietnam, but the ultimate victory will depend on the hearts and minds of the people who actually live out there.

Earl Warren (1891–1974), then chief justice of the United States, incorporated the phrase in the 1954 ruling on *Brown v. Board of Education* outlawing segregated schools.

William Safire, in his *Political Dictionary,* attributes the origin of the phrase to Theodore Roosevelt, who explained his popularity to his young aide, Douglas MacArthur, as his ability "to put into words what is in their hearts and minds but not in their mouths." James S. Olson's *Dictionary of the Vietnam War* attributes the phrase, albeit reversed, to John Adams' description of the American Revolution: "The Revolution was effected before the war commenced. The Revolution was in the minds and hearts of the people. . . . (Letter to Hezekiah Niles, 1818)"

The term in use, by George Lardner Jr. in the *Washington Post,* April 12, 1989, writing about the dramatic confrontation between Iran-contra scandal defendant Oliver North and prosecutor John Keker:

> Throughout the day, the two men, both Marine Corps veterans of the Vietnam War, battled head-on for the jurors' hearts and minds.

And by Alan Wolfe in *Commonweal,* May 23, 1997:

> No rulers, even the most authoritarian, we generally believe, can exercise power in a vacuum; modern totalitarian regimes, in both their Fascist and Communist forms, relied on propaganda as well as terror, as if winning the hearts and minds of their subjects were as important as coercing their obedience.

heaven *See* GOD'S IN HIS HEAVEN, ALL'S RIGHT WITH THE WORLD.

Heep, Uriah Fictional character in Charles Dickens' autobiographical novel *David Copperfield* (1849–1850); obsequious villain, the standard for an unctuous hypocrite. Heep is a smarmy, toadying villain, the clerk in the law office of Mr. Wickfield. While he constantly proclaims how "umble" he is, he plots to gain a financial hold over Wickfield and marry his daughter Agnes. Heep's machinations are foiled by the wonderful Mr. MICAWBER, and Agnes and David marry (and live happily ever after).

The character is so vividly realized that "Uriah Heep" has become virtually a brand name for a fawning sycophant.

The term in use, by Joanna Underwood, the *Economist,* November 13, 1993:

> So the White House has gone on the offensive. In particular, and many months too late, it has dared say Boo to its Texan bugbear,

Ross Perot. The vice-president, Al Gore, was the one who volunteered to fight Mr. Perot before that Uriah Heep of referees, Larry King.

And from Molly Ivins, the *Progressive,* May 1, 1996:

> And consider Bob Dole, Uriah Heep as undertaker. We now get to watch some of the finest minds of our time, not to mention some of the most expensive, try to convince us that Bob Dole is warm and fuzzy.

hegira \hi-'jī-rə, 'he-jə-rə\ A journey, especially when undertaken to escape from a dangerous or undesirable situation; exodus. An Arabic word meaning departure or flight to a more congenial place. In Islamic theology, the Hegira (with a capital H), refers to the flight of Muhammad the Prophet from Mecca to Medina with his followers on July 2, 622 A.D. to escape persecution, the event that marks the opening of the Muslim era. In a general sense, the word is applied to long and arduous journeys undertaken to escape to safety.

The term in use, by Jonathan Yardley in the *Washington Post,* January 13, 1997, remembering a visit to Mississippi in 1972:

> The names on the signs at interstate exchanges included some of the most infamous stations along the civil rights hegira: Meridian, Philadelphia, Neshoba, Jackson itself. Black Mississippians working for civil rights had been killed in some of these places not long before, as had whites trying to help them.

And by Mark Muro in the *Boston Globe,* December 15, 1988, reviewing John Feinstein's book *One Year in College Basketball:*

> But even so, this 464-page hegira plods on with little of the elegance and still less of the junkie's religiosity that might make it transcend numbing logistics.

Heimlich maneuver The manual application of sudden upward pressure on the upper abdomen of a choking victim to force a foreign object from the windpipe. Also, action administered to remove a dangerous obstruction—like a foot in the mouth—or to deal with the mental choke, the name for a self-defeating panic sometimes experienced by athletes in crucial events.

The Heimlich manuever in its original form is named for its originator, Dr. Henry Heimlich, who perfected the technique in the mid-1970s.

The term in use, in the *Seattle Times,* June 1, 1996, on the Seattle Supersonics basketball team's prospects in the NBA playoffs:

> If they lose tomorrow, after a 3–1 lead, this will be the tsunami of collapses. The Sonics would complete the Heimlich Trifecta. . . .

And by *Boston Globe* syndicated columnist Ellen Goodman, March 27, 1992:

There is a touch of pleasure in watching the Bush people gag on their very own gag rule. The rule that was designed to cut off free speech about abortion is now making it harder for the Republicans to clear their throats. Somebody out there better perform a political Heimlich maneuver on the party.

And by Doug Robinson in the *Deseret News,* March 21, 1997:

Stanford and Utah were falling all over themselves, throwing passes out of bounds, falling, dribbling off their feet, blowing easy layups. If the KEYSTONE KOPS had played ball, this is what it would look like. For a while there you wondered if they were going to stop the game and perform a group Heimlich.

Heisenberg principle The complete title: Heisenberg uncertainty principle. A principle in quantum mechanics: it is impossible to discern simultaneously and with high accuracy both the position and the momentum of a particle (such as an electron). Determining either one alters the other. Or, the very act of observing changes what is being observed. It is a scientific term, the understanding of which is beyond the capacity of many laypeople, including your authors. Nonetheless, it has entered the world of allusions and is employed to describe situations in which the act of observing something—particularly human behavior—changes that which is being observed.

In quantum mechanics the only way to observe an atomic particle is to measure it. The process of measuring the particle disturbs it, therefore producing a minimum uncertainty in the measured state of the particle or its whereabouts. It is this uncertainty that was formulated in 1927 by the German mathematical physicist Werner Heisenberg (1901–1976). Outside of quantum mechanics, however, observing something does not necessarily alter it, although this truth is unlikely to crimp the style of nonscientific writers and commentators.

The Hawthorne Effect is probably a better reference to illustrate the impact of observation on people. From the late 1920s through the 1930s, the effects of workplace improvements on productivity were studied at the Hawthorne Works of the Western Electric Company in Cicero, Illinois. The researchers noted that the research—the worker's perception that they were being observed and specially treated—had greater impact than the workplace improvements and led to a temporary increase in productivity. On the other hand, televising congressional proceedings. . . .

The term in use, by Michiko Kakutani in the *New York Times,* September 16, 1997, reviewing Don DeLillo's novel *Underworld:*

All of Mr. DeLillo's trademark themes are here, from real and imagined conspiracies to the media's Heisenberg effect to the threat of terrorism and random violence.

And by Lance Morrow in *Time,* July 10, 1995:

The summer of 1995 may be remembered as the moment when Heisenberg Tourism achieved a sort of global CRITICAL MASS. A few weeks ago, a monk at St. Katherine's Monastery on Mount Sinai looked gloomily at the tourist and stated the new Heisenberg Principle: "They come, and everything changes."

Héloïse *See* ABELARD AND HELOISE.

hemlock A poisonous preparation made from the hemlock plant and drunk as a way of committing suicide.

That's how death came to the Greek philosopher Socrates. In 399 B.C., he was tried and sentenced to death on charges of corrupting the morals of youth and committing religious heresies. Resisting all efforts to save his life, he willingly drank the cup of hemlock poison given him. His life and death were recorded by his most famous student, Plato.

The term is typically used in the phrase "drink hemlock," and the phrase more widely describes an act that is deliberately destructive of one's own interests.

The term in use, by Barbara Tuchman in *The Proud Tower,* setting the scene for the historic vote in 1910 in which the British House of Lords gave up its power of veto over the House of Commons:

> On August 10, the day for drinking the hemlock, the temperature reached a record of a hundred degrees and tension at Westminster was even higher, for, unlike previous political crises, the outcome was in suspense.

Another example, from Mary McGrory, in the *Washington Post,* September 14, 1989, on partisan battles in the U.S. House of Representatives:

> While they were groaning through this silly exercise, the Democrats were sipping hemlock on the capital gains tax, an issue on which their position has been dramatically different from that of the Republicans.

And television producer Dick Wolf, quoted by Alan Bash in *USA Today,* September 6, 1994:

> Dick Wolf has a dream to tape all his shows on location in New York City, even though he knows "any studio would practically drink hemlock before they came in here."

Herculean \ˌhər-kyə-ˈlē-ən, ˌhər-ˈkyü-lē-\ Of, relating to, or characteristic of Hercules; or (often not capitalized) of extraordinary power, extent, intensity, or difficulty. From the name of the mythic Greek strongman Hercules. The meaning comes from the tales of his adventures and his twelve labors, which were very difficult indeed. Hercules is the Latin form of his name, Heracles the Greek form, but thanks to those domineering Romans, their version is more familiar.

Hercules was the son of Zeus and a mortal lady, Alcmena, who caught his eye while her husband was away. She gave birth to twins—Hercules, the son of Zeus, and Iphicles, the son of her husband. Hercules showed his heroic stuff even as an infant when he strangled in his crib two snakes that Zeus's jealous wife Hera had sent to kill him.

Among the most famous of the labors of Hercules: He killed the Hydra, a many-headed monster; when one head was cut off, another grew in its place. (*See* HYDRA-HEADED). He cleansed the AUGEAN STABLES and captured the girdle of Hippolyta, the queen of the AMAZONS. He went down into the underworld and captured Cerberus, the three-headed guard dog. (*See* CERBERUS, SOP TO). And as his last labor he stole the golden apples of the Hesperides. (The Hesperides were three sisters who guarded the apples along with the standard-issue dragon.) The apples had been a wedding present to Hera, who just kept on being angry at Zeus and out to punish Hercules.

The term in use, quoted by Dexter Filkins, in the *Los Angeles Times,* May 16, 1997, on allegations of voter fraud:

> The only way to assure the accuracy of the records, Florman said, would be to manually check the files of tens of thousands of people with names identical to those on the Orange County voter roll. Florman said that could take several months.
>
> "It would be a truly Herculean task," Florman said. "And even then, we might not get 100% reliable results."

And by Kristine F. Anderson, in the *Christian Science Monitor,* June 20, 1996, on the task of feeding 10,000 athletes at the Atlanta Olympics:

> To meet the Herculean demands for food production, more than 1,100 workers will staff the kitchen and dining tent.

Herodotus \hi-'rä-də-təs\ Greek historian, who lived about 480–425 B.C., called "the father of history."

He was the first to research the past and to treat events as history rather than myth. He is famous for his highly readable chronicles of the wars between the Persian Empire and the Greek city-states. George Seldes in *Great Thoughts* notes that the first historian was also the first MUCKRAK-ER, exposing bribery of the oracle at Delphi (*see* DELPHIC) by military men seeking favorable predictions for the outcome of battles.

Employed as an allusion, he appears in the *Village Voice,* "Jockbeat," February 21, 1989, in a quotation of A.J. Liebling to the effect that writer Pierce Egan was "the Herodotus of pugilism."

And from Marvin Kitman in *Newsday,* June 22, 1995:

> In February, Bill Moyers started doing commentaries on "The NBC Nightly News." Three times a week, "Bill Moyers' Perspective" tried to make some sense out of the totally insane world. Moyers was Herodotus compared to what was usually heard on commercial TV.

high noon The time of day when the sun is at its height, of course; and the most advanced, flourishing, or creative stage or period; but thanks to the 1952 movie starring Gary Cooper, it is also the moment of the decisive showdown.

High Noon tells the story of Will Kane, a marshal who stays to fight the vengeful bad guys, due to arrive in town at high noon. As the clock ticks away the time, the townsfolk desert Kane, and his Quaker bride (Grace Kelly) pleads with him to run away. Ultimately he must face the gang alone.

The screenplay was written by Carl Foreman, one of the Hollywood Ten blacklisted during the McCarthy era. The movie is thought by some to convey a message about being deserted in a crisis by one's friends and left to stand alone. John Wayne, by the way, hated the film.

The term in use, from an editorial in the *San Francisco Chronicle,* November 14, 1995:

> Those are the real stakes in the showdown in Washington, as the high-noon hijinks run the risk of eroding confidence of financial markets in the ability of government to function and to pay its bills on time.

Another example, from the *New Hampshire Business Review,* October 27, 1995, reporting pharmacists' protests against insurance companies:

> About half the state's 50 independent pharmacists draped their windows in black flags to dramatize "high noon for your local pharmacy."

Hindenburg Total catastrophe. Hindenburg, the man, was the president of the weak German republic that preceded Hitler. His name was given to a German dirigible that crashed horribly, with great loss of life. The crash has made Hindenburg a byword for disaster or total failure.

Field Marshal Paul von Hindenburg was chief of staff of the German armies during World War I and was elected president of Germany in 1925. The aged Hindenburg made attempts to resist Adolf Hitler's takeover, even defeating him when reelected in 1932, but he was forced to appoint Hitler chancellor, and Hitler assumed the presidency after Hindenburg's death in 1934.

The dirigible *Hindenburg* crossed the Atlantic but exploded on May 6, 1937, as it approached its mooring mast in Lakehurst, N.J. Thirty-six people perished in a fiery catastrophe—an event that was broadcast memorably on the radio. The mode of travel was set back irretrievably.

The term in use, quoted by the *Boston Globe,* August 22, 1987, describing the reaction of former staff members to rumors that Gary Hart, damaged by personal scandal, might resume his campaign for the 1988 Democratic presidential nomination:

> Former policy chief David Dreyer said of reentry, "It's absurd. If this is a trial balloon, it's the Hindenburg of trial balloons."

And by Paul Rogers in the *San Jose Mercury News,* July 22, 1994, describing the process of installing a giant window at the Monterey Bay Aquarium:

> Tense onlookers dreaded a repeat of the fish tank industry's Hindenburg disaster—the 1990 Big Easy window smashup. That year, a cable snapped while hoisting an eight-ton acrylic window at the Aquarium of the Americas in New Orleans, sending the $135,000 panel exploding to the floor.

hit the wall To reach the point in a marathon at which the runner feels utter mental and physical exhaustion, usually around the 20-mile mark. This unpleasant state of affairs is probably brought about when the body uses up its fuel, muscle glycogen.

Runner Bill Rodgers describes it this way in *Marathoning:*

> When you hit the wall, you suddenly catapult into a whole new world. When I talk about the wall, I mean the psychological impact you encounter when you start to fall apart. Sometimes it hits you very suddenly. Usually you can feel it building up. There is a tightening in your legs and a dizziness. You are mentally fatigued and your perspectives and your goals change very drastically.

The term in use, by columnist and marathoner Colman McCarthy in the *Washington Post,* November 7, 1988:

> The marathon has become an athletic rite of passage, the personality's run-in with mediocrity. It is the metaphor of choice in the presidential race now stumbling in hit-the-wall and hit-the-fan exhaustion to Election Day's 26.2 mile finish line.

And by Howard Anderson in *Computerworld,* June 19, 1995:

> It is axiomatic that every technology company will hit "The Wall." Has Microsoft hit its wall or is it immune? . . . Today Microsoft is essentially bulletproof. This is not because the CHILDREN'S CRUSADE up in Redmond didn't make mistakes, but because its competitors, time and again, made more.

Hobbesian \\'häb-zē-ən\\ Of or relating to the English philosopher Thomas Hobbes (1588–1679) or to Hobbism, his philosophy.

Hobbes wrote treatises on the nature of man and government, and in his best-known work *Leviathan* (1651) he supported a strong, secular monarchy. (*See* LEVIATHAN.) Hobbes advocated a controlling governmental authority because he believed that without it society would collapse into anarchy; and the life of man, in his famous phrase, would be "solitary, poor, nasty, brutish and short." It is that grimness about human nature and human life that is "Hobbesian." (*See also* NASTY, BRUTISH, AND SHORT.)

Hobbes's view is not surprising, since he lived through the 17th-century religious and political wars between King Charles I and Parliament. Charles was beheaded in 1649, and the Commonwealth was proclaimed with Cromwell as Lord Protector. Charles II was restored to the throne in 1660, pledging tolerance, but prosecutions continued. In 1666, Hobbes himself was in trouble for the secularist views he expressed in *Leviathan*. The House of Commons established a committee to consider a bill "touching such books as tend to atheism, blasphemy, and profaneness, or against the essence and attributes of God" and mentioning Hobbes in particular. They considered reviving a 15th-century law on the burning of heretics to deal with him, but the bill was defeated.

The term in use, by Patrick Glynn in *Commentary,* August 1, 1994:

> Everywhere throughout the world of ethnic and communal struggle . . . one finds the pervasive figure of the "warlord" and his followers, young armed men, usually not terribly sophisticated or at all disciplined, men who have become, in the Hobbesian conditions of civil war, a law unto themselves.

And by Roger P. Winter, in the *Christian Science Monitor,* June 14, 1995:

> Now the enemy is more amorphous. Some have described it as "anarchy" or "chaos"—a Hobbesian environment in which the brutes with the biggest guns rise to the top.

Hobson's choice An apparently free choice when there is no real alternative; often also used to refer to a situation presenting a choice among unpleasant alternatives.

The expression comes from Thomas Hobson, a livery stable operator in England, who required that every customer take the horse nearest the door; no horse could be taken out of turn.

The term in use, by columnist Jonathan Yardley in the *Washington Post,* January 18, 1997, meditating on a visit to Mississippi:

> Twenty-five years ago when I pulled off for lunch, the choice might have been a barbecue pit or a Moon Pie and a Dr. Pepper. Now the choice is McDonald's or Wendy's, a Hobson's choice if ever there was one.

And again, by Norman Ornstein in *USA Today,* February 18, 1996, giving his view of proposal for a flat tax:

> The flat tax would create a Hobson's choice for those—including many conservatives—who believe that some limited government role in the social policy arena is either appropriate, inevitable or both.

hoi polloi \ˌhȯi-pə-ˈlȯi\ The general populace; masses. In Greek, literally, the many, but in common use a sneering term for the common people, the rabble.

Purists point out that since the word means literally, "the many," to use it with the English article *the* is redundant. However, whatever the literal meaning of *hoi polloi* in Greek, *hoi* does not mean *the* in English. In fact, Greek has no definite article, and many earlier writers who were well-versed in Greek, such as John Dryden and Lord Byron, used the article *the* with *hoi polloi* even when writing the word in Greek letters. Moreover, *hoi polloi* alone in English can look and sound awkward, and the use of *the* is idiomatic.

The term in use, by Robert Strauss in the *Philadelphia Inquirer,* July 15, 1994:

> Haddonfield has long thought of itself as the most sophisticated of burgs: South Jersey's Main Line and all that.
> But despite its wonderful cache of Victorian and Colonial architecture, this is much more a town of the hoi polloi than the hoity-toity would like to admit.

And by Lance Morrow in *Time,* September 15, 1997, on the nature of celebrity:

> Fame has style, glamour, money, attention; ignites the sudden light of recognition in strangers' eyes, commands the comic deference of headwaiters as they sweep you past the serfs and hoi polloi to the best table.

hoist with one's own petard \pǝ-'tär(d)\ Destroyed by the weapon one planned to employ against someone else; caught in one's own trap.

Petard is French for a minelike explosive device used in medieval times. It was packed with gunpowder and attached to doors and gates to blow them up—just the thing for breaking into an enemy's castle to end those tiresome sieges as warfare was getting acquainted with guns and gunpowder. The problem was that these contrivances tended to blow up the unlucky person assigned to touch them off. As Shakespeare put it in *Hamlet* Act 3, Scene 4:

> For 'tis sport, to have the engineer
> hoist with his own petar. . . .

By the way, *hoist* in this phrase is the past tense and past participle of the verb *hoise,* which means "to hoist."

The term in contemporary use, by James K. Glassman in the *New Republic,* April 11, 1988:

> A year ago, at a *New Republic* editorial meeting, I predicted that Ronald Reagan would run for a third term and win (I still think that if the ridiculous 22nd Amendment, passed by vengeful Republicans now hoist with their own petard, were repealed Reagan could win this time around).

Other prepositions are often used in the place of *with,* as in this used by Stephen Jay Gould in *Natural History,* September 1990:

> Now I am finally hoist by my own petard (blown up by my own noxious charge, according to the etymologies).

And by Virginia Wilson in *Newsweek,* October 8, 1990:

> The flight of American capital abroad is yet another consequence of our total disregard for the buildup of debt. We are hoist on our own platitudes. . . .

hold the fort To maintain a firm position under fire; or to take care of usual affairs.

The phrase was immortalized by General William Tecumseh Sherman during the Civil War. After the fall of Atlanta, the Confederate army commanded by John Bell Hood struck at the railroad lines connecting Sherman's army to Chattanooga. One of these attacks was on a Union outpost at Allatoona commanded by General John M. Corse. Word reached Sherman at Kennesaw Mountain, and he signaled Corse from the mountaintop: "Hold the fort. I am coming." Corse held his position until reinforcements arrived.

The need to protect railroads and territory already fought over convinced Sherman to cut loose from his lines of supply, ignore Hood, and march to the sea, slashing through the heart of the Confederacy. "I can make the march," he said, "and make Georgia howl!"

The term in use, by basketball player Danny Manning, quoted in the *Baltimore Sun,* November 28, 1994:

> The Phoenix Suns didn't have Charles Barkley again. Instead, Danny Manning took center stage . . . again.
>
> "Every night we have somebody else step up," says Manning, who scored 10 of his 18 points in the fourth quarter of the Suns' 115–110 victory over New Jersey last night. . . . "I think we can hold the fort until they come back."

And by sportswriter Jim Murray in the *Los Angeles Times,* March 28, 1996:

> The job of any 18th hole is to hold the fort, guard the integrity of the game, sort out the ribbon clerks, restore order and golf monarchy, put the peasants in their place.

Holmes, Sherlock A fictional character created in 1887 by Sir Arthur Conan Doyle who became the prototype for the modern mastermind detective. The brilliant English detective's adventures were recounted in a series of stories beginning with *A Study in Scarlet.* Doyle not only created the eccentric, arrogant protagonist, but Holmes's loyal friend and biographer, Dr. John H. Watson, and his archenemy, the equally brilliant and supremely evil Dr. Moriarty.

Holmes's greatest qualities were his powers of observation and deduction and his knowledge of arcane science, but he was prone to boredom and was a cocaine addict. The character was hugely popular, and has remained so ever since, in Doyle's books and in films and plays in countries and languages around the world.

To be a Sherlock Holmes is to display the superior observational and analytical powers of the Doyle character. A Sherlock Holmes may also describe the solution to a knotty problem as "elementary," his most characteristic utterance.

The term in use, by Carol Rosenberg in the *Miami Herald,* July 24, 1997, on the publication of lists of Holocaust victims' accounts in Swiss banks, secret since World War II:

> In Argentina and Brazil, Jewish leaders met the publication of names with wary hope, as they embarked on the daunting task of trying to track down the owners.
>
> "It's a job worthy of Sherlock Holmes," said Manuel Tenenbaum, director of the Latin American Congress in Buenos Aires. "These are names from before 1945. Many of these people have moved or are dead. You have to look for the heirs."

And by K.C. Cole in the *Los Angeles Times,* July 15, 1997:

> Science, as the late Carl Sagan pointed out, is a strange business, requiring its practitioners to be two contrary things at the same time: complete skeptics, believing nothing that isn't proven beyond doubt, and wild dreamers, willing to risk everything on a hunch and a prayer. It is equal parts guesswork and high precision, looking for hidden patterns and inventing clever gadgets, rational Sherlock Holmes-style sleuthing and a game of Kick the Can.

Holy Grail The cup or platter used according to medieval legend by Christ at the Last Supper and thereafter the object of knightly quests. Also, the object of an extended or difficult quest.

A grail is usually thought of as a cup or chalice. The one that tradition says Jesus used at the Last Supper vanished and became the subject of numerous legends and romances in the Middle Ages. Versions differ, but the basic tale goes like this: Joseph of Arimathea (who offered his own tomb for Jesus's burial) took the cup, called the Holy Grail, to what is now England, where he founded Glastonbury Abbey and worked to convert Britons to Christianity. The Grail disappeared, and the search for it became part of the legend of King Arthur and his Knights of the Round Table (*see* GALAHAD).

The term in use, by Bud Collins in the *Washington Post,* September 14, 1997, recounting the long rivalry in men's tennis between Australia and the United States in competition for the Davis Cup:

> Washingtonian Donald Dell ascended to the U.S. captaincy promising "a crusade" to regain the grail.

And by political consultant Dick Morris in his book *Behind the Oval Office* (1997), his account of the 1996 Clinton presidential campaign:

> While Clinton and I were focused on getting a budget deal—our fruitless quest for the Holy Grail—nothing seemed to move Dole

from his determination to run against the deficit rather than cure it, even though the numbers between the two sides on the budget were very, very close.

And by Steve Scott in *Washington Monthly,* December 1996, describing a fight in California over campaign reform:

California seemed the perfect place to pursue the Holy Grail of campaign reform—a direct challenge to the U.S. Supreme Court's *Buckley v. Valeo* decision, which effectively banned any form of mandatory limits on campaign spending.

Homeric Of, relating to, or characteristic of the Greek poet Homer, his age, or his writing. Also, of epic proportions. Larger-than-life; mythic.

From the name of Homer, the ancient Greek bard commonly accepted as author of the *Iliad* and the *Odyssey,* epic poems relating the stories of gods and heroes in the Trojan War and in the adventures of Odysseus.

Little is known of the real Homer—not even whether he actually lived, or if so, when. According to legend, he was blind. The poems are among the Western world's greatest literary works.

The term in use, by Russell Baker in the *New York Times,* March 13, 1989:

There has been a gaudier baseball show than usual this spring, with players carrying on like nasty rich kids. . . . From the Yankees, stories about Homeric boozing.

And by Bob Finnigan in the *Seattle Times,* August 18, 1996:

Griffey's was the third of a [H]omeric trio which gave the Mariners a team-record 183 home runs this season and helped Seattle pound New York 10–3 yesterday at Yankee Stadium.

Homer sometimes nods *or* **even Homer nods** Even the best sometimes turn in a subpar performance. The phrase is a translation of a line from *Ars Poetica* by the Roman poet Horace: "Quandoque bonus dormitat Homerus."

Homer was an epic poet, the giant of ancient Greek literature, creator of the *Iliad* and the *Odyssey*. As Horace put it: "I think it shame when the worthy Homer nods; but in so long a work it is allowable if drowsiness comes on."

The term in use, by Michael S. Malone, in commentary on the future of Silicon Valley in the *San Jose Mercury News,* December 29, 1996:

Moreover, Microsoft, as a hierarchical organization at the mercy of a single business genius, is vulnerable to the weaknesses of that solitary figure. As the saying goes, even Homer nods. So will Bill Gates.

And by syndicated columnist James J. Kilpatrick Jr., putting the needle to the *New York Times* in the *Charlotte Observer,* June 5, 1993:

Ask anyone who keeps up with the media: Which is the greatest newspaper in the nation? The answer more often than not, is the *New York Times*. . . .

But it was said of Homer, the greatest epic poet of them all, that even Homer nodded. A surprising lot of snoozers occupy desks at the greatest paper in the land. The *Times* has problems with elementary grammar. . . .

And by Philip Klass in the *New York Times Book Review,* March 18, 1990, reviewing *Essays in Disguise* by Wilfrid Sheed:

But if Homer can nod, Mr. Sheed, unfortunately, can shrug.

Horatio Alger *See* ALGER, HORATIO.

Horatius at the bridge One who heroically holds a defensive position against overwhelming odds.

Horatius Cocles was a legendary hero of the ancient Roman republic, supposed to have saved Rome when the city was attacked by the Etruscans led by Lars Porsena, in the 6th century B.C. The predominant version tells that Horatius and two companions held off the entire Etruscan army while the Romans chopped away at the wooden bridge behind them to cut off the enemy's access to the city. Horatius then swam the Tiber to safety, having sent his companions back earlier. Thomas Babington Macauley popularized this version in *The Lays of Ancient Rome,* which immortalized these and other exploits for the Victorian era.

Even if you didn't read Macauley's poem in your youth, you have probably heard this refrain somewhere, spoken as Horatius prepares to swim to safety:

Oh, Tiber! father Tiber!
To whom the Romans pray,
A Roman's life, a Roman's arms
Take thou in charge this day!

The term in use, by Florence King in the *National Review,* July 1, 1996:

We talk incessantly of "heroes" and seem to have a plentiful supply, but they're a far cry from Horatius at the Bridge. Ours is the age of the passive hero. Get yourself taken hostage, shot out of the sky, buried in an avalanche, trapped on a runaway roller coaster, or wander off and fall in a hole, and you are sure to end up on the morning shows as the latest hero. . . .

And by Kenneth T. Walsh in *U.S. News & World Report,* November 27, 1995:

President Clinton, playing Horatius at the bridge against the Republican hordes, is finally winning some favorable reviews.

Horatius is sometimes confused with another fictional character, Hamlet's Shakespearean pal Horatio. (As in, "Alas, poor Yorick. I knew him, Horatio.") But Horatio belongs in Denmark with his melancholy friend, and not on the bridge.

One final point. Many historians now agree that the story of Horatius was something cooked up by the Romans to rationalize, if not cover up, their own aggression against the Etruscans. Alas, poor Lars Porsena; but it's the winners who write the history.

horror, the horror The dying whisper of Kurtz, the renegade white man of Joseph Conrad's novel *The Heart of Darkness*: "The horror! The horror!" The words represent his despair at his encounter with the depths of human depravity—his own and others'—the heart of darkness. (*See also* HEART OF DARKNESS.) In current use, Kurtz's cry of "intense and hopeless despair" is used ironically to express a usually humorous annoyance at some passing irritant rather than to reflect the dark vision of human evil in Conrad's novel.

Kurtz is the central figure of the story, which is set in the Belgian Congo in the late 19th century. Marlow, the narrator, journeys up the Congo River to the remote trading station where Kurtz holds sway. Kurtz has a reputation as a man of great humanity, culture, and learning, dedicated to improving the lot of the natives under his jurisdiction.

When Marlow arrives at the trading station, he finds Kurtz in failing health. Moreover, Kurtz has embraced savagery, and he rules the natives with a cruel hand in bloody sovereignty. Marlow's party carries Kurtz onto the boat to take him back downriver, but he dies—filled with despair at the blackness of evil at the heart of humanity. (A year later Marlow carries a packet of letters to Kurtz's fiancee in Belgium, who remembers him as he once was and begs to know his last words. Marlow, kindly, lies and tells her that Kurtz's last word was her name.)

The term in use, by Garry Trudeau in *Time* magazine, June 16, 1997:

> Spinning, feinting, jabbing, the lawyers for Paula Jones and Bill Clinton spent the week negotiating in public—leaving the rest of us to wonder what backstage progress was being made to spare us the horror, the horror, of a trial now that the Supreme Court won't stop it.

And by Alan Bash in *USA Today,* April 24, 1995:

> Inspired by the enduring appeal of "Star Trek" and "The X-Files," TV's "clone-it" mentality is going into overdrive for next season. Expect any number of quirky new aliens, bizarre new worlds. The horror, the horror.

hors de combat \ˌȯr-də-kōⁿ-ˈbä\ Out of combat; disabled. A French phrase with the same meaning.

The term in use, in the gossip column of the *Chatham Courier,* Chatham, New York, September 15, 1988:

> A prominent Kinderhook ladies' man will be hors de combat for the next two weeks. He checked in Monday at a Boston hospital for the works—hernia, vasectomy, hair transplant. . . .

Another example, from Martin Pave in the *Boston Globe,* January 21, 1989:

> Losers of three straight and with three of last year's starters rendered hors de combat, the Celtics needed somebody to step forward in crunch time—which lately had resembled crumble time in Chicago, Detroit and Philadelphia.

horseback *See* MAN ON HORSEBACK.

hotdog To perform in a conspicuous or often ostentatious manner, especially involving fancy stunts and maneuvers. This is not the wienie but the verb meaning "to show off," particularly in athletics. It can also be a noun—*hot dog*—meaning "a person who shows off" as in "She's such a hot dog."

Hotdogging was first a form of skiing that involved extravagant in-air maneuvers. The term has also been translated into other sports and activities to describe all attention-getting hijinks, such as prancing about the end zone after scoring a touchdown.

The term in use, by super baseball fan Mike Volpe (he dubbed himself a "free agent fan" and offered his loyalty to the team that showed him it deserved his fandom), quoted by Dave McKenna in *City Paper,* a Washington, D.C. free weekly, April 11, 1997:

> "I was shocked by what the Giants did, just crushed. [They'd sent longtime San Francisco player Matt Williams to the Cleveland Indians.] I mean Matt Williams was a great player, but more than that he was a guy who didn't complain, a guy who hit a lot of home runs but didn't hotdog."

In use as a noun by Joe Gilmartin in the *Phoenix Gazette,* January 25, 1995:

> Once upon a time, there was only one Deion Sanders, and nobody much liked him, except maybe the fans.
> He was too spicy a hot dog for most tastes. A showboating, strutting, boasting taunter/dancer who seemed to epitomize much of what some see as wrong with sports today.

hot stove league Baseball's off season—all talk, no action in this league. The baseball season is over, snow is on the ground, there is nothing to do but sit around a hot stove, real or imagined, and talk about seasons ancient, just past, or soon to come.

The origin of the expression is uncertain; it was applied to baseball around the turn of the century. *The New Dickson Baseball Dictionary* (1999) by Paul Dickson also reports references to horse racing's off-season.

The term in use, by Paul Hirshon in the *Boston Globe,* September 12, 1989:

> The party is expected to attract the political junkies and lots of talk from the hot stove league of presidential politics.

And by Patrick Quinn, reviewing Robert Palmer's *Rock 'n' Roll: An Unruly History* in the *Wichita Eagle,* November 12, 1995:

> Readers will be torn between tucking it safely away on the shelf or leaving it out on the coffee table, but there isn't any doubt that it belongs in the house. Let's be honest. "Who's Left Out?" is a game that can and should be played with every book ever written on this subject, it's the musical equivalent of baseball's Hot Stove League.

Houdini \hü-ˈdē-nē\ American magician; the ultimate escape artist.

Harry Houdini (born Ehrich Weiss in 1874) is probably the most famous magician of all time. He was born in Budapest, Hungary, but his parents emigrated to Wisconsin where he began a circus career in 1882. His conjuring act debuted in 1890 and his specialty was escapes—from handcuffs, ropes, safes, crates lowered into water. Houdini's death in 1926 remains puzzling: a backstage visitor punched him hard in the stomach before Houdini was ready to receive a stomach punch as part of his act. He died of the resulting peritonitis.

Now his name is applied to someone who shows a special knack for getting out of dicey situations.

The term in use, quoting historian Arthur M. Schlesinger Jr. on President Clinton, in the *New York Times Magazine,* December 15, 1996:

> Where Schlesinger really grabs my attention is when he predicts that there will be "storms ahead" for Clinton and then adds that the president has shown a resource for dealing with such adversity: "His Houdini-like agility in getting out of tight spots."

And by Michelle Emery, the Associated Press, February 12, 1997, reporting proceedings against a canine perp in Portsmouth, New Hampshire:

> Prince, whom Kristiansen nicknamed "Houdini" for his ability to escape from cages and leashes, was labeled a vicious dog under a city ordinance because he killed a rooster in May.

How many divisions has the Pope? The paraphrase of a question posed by Soviet dictator Joseph Stalin that mockingly dismissed the moral and spiritual strength of Christianity. The question is used to pose the dilemma of physical versus moral power, and seemingly to dismiss the latter.

The source of the story is Winston Churchill's history of World War II, *The Gathering Storm* (1948). Churchill says that French premier Pierre Laval went to Moscow in 1935 to see Stalin. They had lengthy discussions about troop strength, and Laval asked Stalin if he could do something to encourage religion in the U.S.S.R. It would help in relations with the Pope, explained Laval. "Oho!" said Stalin. "The Pope! How many divisions has *he* got?"

The term in use, by Jim Mann in the *Los Angeles Times,* November 16, 1994, on a Pacific region free-trade pact:

> If one country wants to preserve its trade barriers, none of the other Pacific nations can do anything about it. A defiant leader can merely come up with his own adaptation of the old line "How many divisions does the Pope have?"

Another example, in which Arthur Waldron gleefully sends up the Colin Powell presidential boomlet, touting him for pope in the *Economist,* September 30, 1995:

> He does not bow the knee to Larry King or David Frost; indeed his ring still gleams with the kisses they have planted there. "How many divisions has the pope?" sneered Stalin. Under Pope Colin, better not ask.

hubris \\'hyü-brəs\\ Exaggerated pride or self-confidence. This is the pride that goes before a fall, an excessive, overweening, I-can-make-the-Red-Sea-part, arrogant pride.

In Greek tragedy, hubris is a prideful refusal to accept the authority of the gods. When the central character begins to believe that his achievements result from his own powers and virtue rather than from the favor of the gods, he is guaranteed to be laid low.

The term in use, by Gene Smith in *American Heritage,* September 1993:

> The first time he talked to a Belmont exercise boy about Ruffian, Whitely said something very strange, for it is an ageless tradition of racing that an owner or trainer should never speak too highly of a horse. Such a display of hubris can bring down the wrath of the gods who control the draw for post positions, determine whether your jockey makes his move too early or too late, and rule who wins by a nose and who doesn't.

Another example, from Melvin Maddocks' review of David Halberstam's *The Best and the Brightest,* in *Time,* November 27, 1972:

> Like all proper tragedies, *The Best and the Brightest* begins with hubris: the certainty of a young and ebullient President Kennedy and his New Frontiersmen that they constituted an elite, "a new breed of thinker-doers" who could handle the world, to say nothing of what President Johnson was to refer to as "a raggedy-ass little fourth-rate country."

And by Alan Tonelson in the *Atlantic,* June 1993:

> To think that Washington could have strengthened the Iraqi dictator just enough to contain Iran but not enough to fuel his own imperialism reflected considerable hubris.

Humbert Humbert The pedophile protagonist of Vladimir Nabokov's novel *Lolita* (1955). A middle-aged lecher obsessed with preteen-aged girls. Humbert Humbert is the pseudonym of the narrator of Vladimir Nabokov's *Lolita*. Both Humbert and LOLITA have passed into the language as eponyms.

Humbert Humbert is a shocking character in a shocking novel; he schemes to exploit a child sexually, something that remains difficult for even jaded readers to cope with. At the same time his obsession and his sometimes pathetic bumbling add comic tones to the story. He bullies Lolita, yet his romantic passion gives her great power over him while she is able to remain remote.

The term in use, by Alice Steinbach, in the *Baltimore Sun,* March 2, 1994:

> ... March is the time of year when the fashion industry trots out its vision of what the well-dressed woman can look forward to wearing.
>
> Suffice it to say that Humbert Humbert would go gaga over this year's look.

And by Tony Snow in the *Washington Times,* May 2, 1994, on jogging trail etiquette:

> There is nothing rarer on a jogging trail than actual eye contact. People gaze carefully at every ripple of the anatomical landscape but the eyes. Nevertheless, men should not gawk at sun-bronzed women in halter tops or other scanty garb. Such behavior is tacky and lecherous, not to mention dangerous in the presence of fathers, husbands, boyfriends and Janet Reno.
>
> It is politically and socially unacceptable for males to act like Humbert Humbert—unless they're president.

Humpty Dumpty A nursery-rhyme character, who sat on a wall and had a great fall. By extension, someone who sits in an insecure position; or some one or some thing which, once broken, is difficult to reassemble, even when great resources are brought to bear—all the king's horses and all the king's men. Also, in hyphenated form, it is an adjective meaning short and broad, like the physique of the egg-man character in the nursery rhyme.

The nursery rhyme's origins are obscure, but the character shows up in various European languages. Humpty also makes an appearance in Lewis Carroll's *Through the Looking-Glass* (1872) and encounters Alice:

> "When I use a word," Humpty Dumpty said, in rather a scornful tone, "it means just what I choose it to mean—neither more nor less."
>
> "The question is," said Alice, "whether you can make words mean so many things."
>
> "The question is," said Humpty Dumpty, "which is to be master—that's all."

The nursery rhyme is referenced in the title of Robert Penn Warren's novel *All the King's Men* (1946) set in the American South of the 1920s and 1930s, in which a central figure is a Huey Long-like politician, Willie Stark. Stark rises to power, becomes corrupt and falls to his doom.

The term in use, by Tim Folger in *Discover*, October 1993:

> Black holes have a confounding humpty-dumpty property that makes it impossible, even theoretically, to put them—or anything that falls into them—back together again once they evaporate.

And by Richard Corliss in *Time*, July 6, 1987:

> On the subject of unpleasant expression, Reagan has said no such thing. Indeed, he has exerted all his political suasion to put the Humpty-Dumpty of traditional morality back together again. His administration has aligned itself with Fundamentalist vigilantes, and it created a commission that studied and in 1986 condemned pornography.

And echoing Lewis Carroll's Humpty is Marshall H. Tanick in the *Minneapolis Star Tribune*, October 26, 1997:

> The consternation of those who defend the telephone calls, coffee klatches, and other fundraising activities engaged in by President Clinton and Vice President Al Gore at the White House and executive offices is reminiscent of the words of Humpty Dumpty, speaking to Alice in Wonderland: "When I use a word, it means just what I choose it to mean—nothing more nor less," he roundly said to an awed Alice.

hundred flowers *See* LET A HUNDRED FLOWERS BLOOM.

Hyde *See* JEKYLL AND HYDE.

hydra-headed Having many heads. The Hydra was a monstrous serpent in Greek myth. The creature was killed by Hercules—it was one of his twelve HERCULEAN labors. When he chopped off a head, two more grew back. Hercules succeeded by having his charioteer apply fire to each wound to prevent the regrowth.

The expression is applied figuratively to situations in which problems repeat themselves, or appear at many points.

The term in use, by Elizabeth Drew in the *New Yorker*, June 15, 1992:

> There are some technical problems with the Clinton campaign: it still seems headless—or, perhaps more accurately, hydra-headed.

And from Marilyn Chase in the *Wall Street Journal*, September 17, 1986:

> The tests looked at AZT's use by patients with recently diagnosed AIDS, and AIDS-related pneumocystis carinii pneumonia. So

even optimistic results might not be applicable to patients with other forms of the hydra-headed disease.

And by Eleanor Perenyi in *Green Thoughts* (1981):

The Egyptian onion is a curiosity. From a single bulb it sends up half a dozen stout, hollow stalks each of which sprouts a bulb cluster rather like shallots. When the weight of these brings them to the ground, they root in their turn and in no time you have a hydra-headed monster ready to take over the whole garden.

And by Paul Vitello in *Newsday*, January 24, 1999 on the scene at the impeachment trial of President Clinton:

Shoulder-to-shoulder under bright TV lights that gave it all a cinematic glamor shuffled reporters, politicians, staff, camera operators. Each was in search of, or locked onto, some detail about Social Security or defense spending or the impeachment that would be quickly fed to some arm of the hydra-headed media to which they were all connected by phone or cable wire.
    The sound of it was like a hurricane.

I

I can hear myself think, and I'm thinking: Did that TV screen grow overnight? . . . It's looming over the living room like some seductive incubus.
—Diane Werts

Iago \ē-'ä-(ˌ)gō\ The villain of Shakespeare's tragedy *Othello.* One of the most purely malevolent characters in literature; a clever and scheming provocateur.

Iago, an aide to the Moorish general Othello, is bitterly disappointed when Othello chooses Cassio as his lieutenant instead of himself. Iago plots vengeance. Although pretending loyalty and honesty, Iago cunningly manipulates Othello and fosters his suspicions that his wife, Desdemona, is being unfaithful to him with Cassio. Mad with jealousy, Othello kills his wife, and then kills himself when he realizes she is innocent.

The term in use, by Bernard Holland in the *New York Times,* May 18, 1997, reviewing a PBS documentary on the Royal Opera:

> Keith Cooper, the new director of public affairs (and still on the job) plays Iago with relish. The act of firing faithful employees he describes as a solemn, painful duty, but the glint of pleasure in those steely eyes is unmistakable.

And from David Denby, writing in *Premiere,* October 1989, on Alfred Hitchcock's 1943 film, *Shadow of a Doubt:*

> Uncle Charlie [Joseph Cotten], however, has not only a cruel temperament but a cruel point of view. Genial and sociable, he is nevertheless tormented by the awfulness of existence. "Do you know the world is a foul sty? Do you know if you ripped the fronts off houses you'd find swine? The world's a hell," he rants in the extraordinary, Iagolike aria that he delivers to his niece in a cheap bar.

Icarus \'i-kə-rəs\ Someone who flies high, disregards warnings, and pays the price for HUBRIS and pride.

It's a Greek myth. Icarus was the son of Daedalus, an artisan who built the LABYRINTH for King Minos of Crete. The king then kept Daedalus and his son imprisoned lest they reveal the key to the maze. But Daedalus devised a clever escape plan: he constructed wings of wax and feathers so that he and his son could fly away from Crete. He warned his son not to fly too high—to fly too close to the sun would melt the wax of the wings. But Icarus ignored his father's warning, and fell to his death when his wings came apart.

The term in use, by Frank Luksa in the *Dallas Morning News,* April 9, 1995, on the career of golfer Curtis Strange:

> Prematurely gray even then, Strange now tells of being prematurely successful in his mid-30s. Like Icarus, he flew too close to the sun, and rare altitude led to a career FREE FALL.

And by William Safire in the *New York Times Magazine,* March 22, 1987:

> The attempted suicide of former national security adviser Robert C. McFarlane changed the perception of that character from a tinhorn Kissinger to a bureaucratic Icarus whose judgment melted when he flew too high.

icon \'ī-ˌkän\ A conventional religious image. Also, an object of uncritical devotion; an idol. An emblem or symbol. Someone who has achieved such fame and or authority in his field of endeavor that he is accorded wholehearted adoration; or someone who has become a symbol of a movement or idea or issue.

In Greek, the term means "image." In the Eastern Orthodox Church, it refers specifically to a sacred representation of Jesus, a saint, or an angel. These icons may be mosaics, paintings, or low-relief sculptures and may range from simple to richly ornate. Typically they are accorded the burning of candles and incense.

The opposite of reverence for icons is iconoclasm (Greek for "image-breaking"), which is the opposition to the religious use of images, for fear that the practice will lead to idol worship. In contemporary use, an iconoclast is one who tears down popular figures, cherished beliefs, or traditional institutions.

In the computer era, an icon is the small image representing an option on the computer screen.

The term in use, by Marc Fisher in the *Washington Post,* October 23, 1997:

> The Rolling Stones—gray, pale, bowed by the weight of three decades as pop icons—mount the mammoth stage.

Another example, from Andrea Barnet in the *New York Times Book Review,* June 2, 1996:

> . . . she [Gertrude Stein] became a cult figure, an icon whose radical credo and hermetic writing style were the very symbol of modernist experimentation.

And by Kevin Sherrington, writing about the Nike Corporation in the *Dallas Morning News,* August 6, 1995:

> He [Nike president Phil Knight] started at the feet of athletes like Too Tall [Jones] and Phil Chenier, whose busts can be found among those of Michael Jordan and Bo Jackson and Charles

Barkley, the cast generally credited with turning a shoe company into a cultural icon.

id One of the three divisions of the psyche in the psychoanalytic theory of Sigmund Freud that is completely unconscious and present at birth. It is the source of psychic energy derived from instinctual needs and drives, such as the sex drive, hunger, and aggression. In Freudian theory, the other two aspects of human personality are the ego (the conscious mind) and the superego (the externally imposed standards and regulations that humans live by).

The term in use, by Jim Hoagland in the *Washington Post,* September 20, 1988, discussing former Carter advisor Zbigniew Brzezinski's joining the presidential campaign of George Bush:

> You will recall Brzezinski as the id of the Carter administration's divided foreign policy brain, constantly battling the superegos in Cyrus Vance's State Department. Those battles created the shambles that helped bring Ronald Reagan and George Bush to the White House nearly eight years ago.

And by Jay Carr in the *Boston Globe,* paying tribute to the work of Orson Welles, October 14, 1985:

> Welles' grand yet bleak Falstaff serves as his epitaph, making a "Lear" redundant. Falstaff is 300 pounds of id, bloated with excess, not of worldliness but of innocent unawareness of consequences.

idiot savant \'ē-ˌdyō-sä-'vän, 'id-ē-ət-sə-'vänt, -'vant\ A mentally defective person who exhibits exceptional skill or brilliance in some limited field. Such people usually demonstrate their extraordinary ability in music, mathematics, feats of memory, or extrasensory perception. By extension, the word has come to refer to a person who is highly knowledgeable about one subject but knows little about anything else.

The term is French, meaning "learned idiot."

Idiots savants (or idiot savants) should not be confused with prodigies, who frequently show signs of genius at an early age. Mozart, who was composing at age 5, was a prodigy.

The term in use, by Stanley Kauffmann in the *New Republic,* May 9, 1988, reviewing a movie:

> Mess though it is as a total experience, *The Moderns* is worth discussing for two reasons. First, [director Alan] Rudolph has become (if it's possible to become one) an idiot savant of cinematics.

And by Stephen Manes in the *New York Times,* November 12, 1995:

> The computer world often seems to be run by arrogant idiot savants who understand everything about their products except how they behave when human beings try to use them.

ignorant armies Forces blindly fighting with each other with no under-standing of whom they are fighting or why. Often used to describe bitter political disputes where all is conflict, contention and confusion.

The expression is taken from Matthew Arnold's poem "Dover Beach" (1867). Arnold mourns the loss of the faith of earlier centuries, and is skeptical of the benefits of "progress"—19th-century industrialization, science and worldliness. He says to his love that they should be true to one another because the new world which seems to offer so much

> Hath really neither joy, nor love, nor light,
> Nor certitude, nor peace, nor help for pain;
> And we are here as on a darkling plain
> Swept with confused alarms of struggle and flight,
> Where ignorant armies clash by night.

Norman Mailer alluded to Arnold in his 1968 work *The Armies of the Night: History as a Novel, the Novel as History,* an account of a massive anti-Vietnam War march on the Pentagon in October 1967.

The term in use, by Jonathan Alter in *Newsweek,* January 4, 1999:

> The history of the 1990s, so peaceful and prosperous for most Americans, will be of "ignorant armies sounding confused alarms" over nothing much at all.

And by James Deakin, in a tribute to Jacqueline Kennedy Onassis, May 22, 1994:

> There is a lesson here for Bill and Hillary Clinton, but it's not necessarily a lesson of despair. It is that presidents and first ladies who try to do something—actually try to improve things—bring wrath down upon themselves, from the ignorant armies that clash by night. The same venom was visited on Franklin and Eleanor Roosevelt—and on Abraham Lincoln.

And by Charles Colson, quoted by Charles C. Haynes, Gannett News Service, November 3, 1997:

> A number of years ago, following the killing of a doctor who worked in an abortion clinic, Christian evangelical leader Charles Colson warned that the crime "was not only senseless, it was sym-bolic—its message was that a democracy poisoned by hatred and division can be as dangerous as the streets of Sarajevo . . . our public square threatens to become Matthew Arnold's darkling plain, where ignorant armies clash by night."

Immaculate Conception The conception of the Virgin Mary in which, as decreed in Roman Catholic dogma, her soul was preserved from original sin by divine grace. Contrary to popular misconception among non-Catholics, this does not refer to the Virgin Birth—the birth of Jesus—but to the (pre-birth) conception of the Virgin Mary.

There had been widespread belief in the immaculate conception of Mary for centuries, although it was argued about by scholars throughout the Middle Ages. Thomas Aquinas didn't accept it; Duns Scotus did (and doctrinal disputes being bitter then as always, adherents of Duns Scotus were called *dunsers,* which then became *dunces*).

The Pope finally settled the issue (so to speak) in 1854 with the PAPAL BULL entitled *Ineffabilis Deus* (essentially, "God who is incapable of being expressed in words"), which agreed with the dunsers.

In contemporary use, the term refers with sarcasm to something which comes into being in an unconventional manner or with no apparent rational explanation—something that miraculously appears.

The term in use, by Reagan administration budget director Richard Darman in the *Washington Post,* October 26, 1987, discussing the need for an agreement to reduce the budget deficit:

> Now what's needed is to arrange the political equivalent of an immaculate conception: a compromise that materializes without any politician having to take the blame.

And by Senate Majority Leader Trent Lott, quoted by the Associated Press, April 7, 1997 on lack of progress on budget negotiations between the Congress and the president:

> Despite talk of bipartisanship, "somebody's got to stand up and say 'let's do it,' " Lott said. "That someone should be the president. . . . It's not going to happen by immaculate conception."

And the head of an insurance firm offering policies against alien abduction, and other unusual policies, quoted by Edith Lederer of the Associated Press, October 24, 1997:

> "We insure virgins against immaculate conception; prostitutes against loss of earnings from headache and backache; conversion to a werewolf or vampire; death or serious injury through paranormal activity; and unfaithful husbands against Bobbitting," he said. This was a reference to John Bobbitt, whose wife severed his penis in 1993.

incubus \\'iŋ-kyə-bəs, 'in-\ An evil spirit that lies on persons in their sleep; especially one that has sexual intercourse with women while they are sleeping. Also, a nightmare, or feeling that oppresses like a nightmare. The term's sexual connotation comes from medieval times; the existence of the incubus was recognized in church and civil law. Testimony of medieval victims of the demon is not unlike contemporary accounts of alien abduction.

The female counterpart is the succubus, from the Latin word *succumbere,* to lie under.

Trouble can result from not knowing things like this. The Reebok Corporation, to its enormous embarrassment, in 1997 was forced to withdraw a women's athletic shoe which they had named *Incubus.*

The term in use, by Jim Murray in the *Los Angeles Times,* November 30, 1995:

> Death by boxing glove is all too common. It hovers over the sport like an incubus.

Another example, from Diane Werts, *Newsday,* April 23, 1995, on her experiment with living without television for a week:

> Boy, is it quiet. I can hear myself think, and I'm thinking: Did that TV screen grow overnight? Why does it seem so suddenly enormous? It's looming over the living room like some seductive incubus.

in flagrante delicto \ˌin-fləˈgrän-tē-di-ˈlik-(ˌ)tō, -ˌgran-\ In the very act of committing a misdeed; red-handed. Also, in the midst of sexual activity. In Latin, it means while the crime is blazing. It's frequently applied to noncriminal but embarrassing situations.

The term in use, by Christopher Buckley in his review of *From: The President, Richard Nixon's Secret Files,* edited by Bruce Oudes, in the *New York Times,* February 26, 1989:

> *From: The President* is pretty much everything you would expect it to be: fascinating, appalling, boring every now and then, but mostly fascinating, showing human beings caught in the act of being themselves, or rather, laboring with considerable lack of success not to be themselves; history in *in flagrante delicto.*

And by Mary Alice Daniels, guest columnist in the *Kansas City Star,* July 10, 1996:

> The White House statement reveals a sophisticated grasp of a principle of damage control that is indispensable to anyone taking a side trip from the path of righteousness. When caught in flagrante delicto, a wily transgressor always apologizes fulsomely when taking responsibility for a documentable lesser offense.

The term often appears without the *in,* as in this use by Thomas Bass in *Smithsonian,* December 1988:

> Meanwhile, catfish and other predators lurk in the nearby rocks, hoping to pick off distracted cichlids caught flagrante delicto.

in harm's way In a dangerous place or situation. Particularly applied to members of the armed services in war or in threat of war.

The phrase comes from America's Revolutionary War naval hero, John Paul Jones. In a letter dated November 16, 1778, he wrote, "I wish to have no connection with any ship that does not sail *fast;* for I intend to go *in harm's way.*" He was in France at the time, seeking a ship; the French offered him several, prizes taken from the British. He finally took the ship he named *Bonhomme Richard.*

The phrase in use, quoted by Beth Shuster and James Rainey in the *Los Angeles Times,* March 1, 1997:

> Time and again in a morning of extreme violence, policemen and policewomen stepped from behind cover with their light sidearms to face the suspected bank robbers, who launched a blazing gun battle that ranged across several blocks of a North Hollywood neighborhood.
>
> "The thin blue line is made out of the men and women who are out there who put themselves in harm's way every day," Police Chief Willie L. Williams said later in the day. . . .

And by Gary Fields and Cathy Chestnut in *USA Today,* March 24, 1994:

> For most of the last four years, troops from Fort Bragg, N.C., have been in harm's way around the world. Wednesday, harm's way was at home.
>
> At least 16 Army troops from the 82nd Airborne, the 18th Aviation Brigade and other Fort Bragg units preparing for jumping exercises at Pope Air Force Base were killed and 82 injured when they were showered with fragments and burning metal from an air crash.

Invasion of the Body Snatchers A situation in which normal behavior is strangely lacking or altered. From a sci-fi movie classic (1956): a small town is taken over by alien replicas of the residents which emerge from giant pods. The copies are perfect but passionless, zombielike.

As the story unfolds, we learn that the only way to avoid being metamorphosed into a pod is to stay awake. Soon the only real people left are the town doctor and his girlfriend. But then she dozes off. . . .

Based on the novel *The Body Snatchers* by Jack Finney, the movie has suffered two inferior remakes. Do not be fooled by soulless replicas. The original is a gem of Cold War paranoia, combined with the terror of loss of self. Hard enough to root out Communists, but if your friends and neighbors and the corner grocer turn into aliens, how can you tell—and who can you trust? From another viewpoint, the film is seen as a statement against the deadening power of conformity. As director Don Siegel observed, "People are pods. Many of my associates are certainly pods. They have no feelings. They exist, breathe, sleep."

Two final notes: body snatcher is another term for grave robber. In the 18th and 19th centuries, "resurrection men" robbed graves for corpses to sell to medical schools and anatomists. Occasionally they didn't wait for the burial and resorted to murder. Also, during the Vietnam War, the term was bestowed on medics who came to pick up the wounded or the dead.

The term in use, by Rahm Emanuel, an aide to President Bill Clinton, quoted by Walter Shapiro, *USA Today,* August 14, 1996:

> "Did you see what [vice presidential candidate Jack] Kemp said last night about affirmative action?" Emanuel asked

eagerly. . . . "This Kemp flip-flop is like the Invasion of the Body Snatchers."

Another example, from Patric Hedlund, in the *Los Angeles Times,* March 11, 1997:

> If you remember the dead-eyed aliens taking over in *Invasion of the Body Snatchers,* you may have a glimpse into how it feels to be among the 2,000 people every day who contact credit bureaus to report that someone has stolen their identity.

And by Michael McCabe in the *San Francisco Chronicle,* June 17, 1995:

> "Chez Louis . . . is a victim of the times," Borel said, "changing zoning plans, changing neighborhoods and the implacable onslaught of chain restaurants taking over El Camino like a scene from the movie *Invasion of the Body Snatchers.*"

invisible hand The doctrine of enlightened self-interest of Adam Smith, the *laissez faire* economist.

Smith, writing in 1776, argued that individuals seeking to further their self-interest would be led "as if guided by an invisible hand" to achieve the best for all—the altruism of the marketplace.

Smith opposed government interference with free competition and foreign trade, arguing that a policy of "laissez faire" (French, meaning basically "to let things alone") would promote individual freedom, encourage the best use of economic resources, and enhance economic growth. Critics of the invisible hand proposition say it might work under conditions of perfect competition, but those conditions do not exist in the real world.

The term in use, by commentator Tom Scheibley on National Public Radio's *Morning Edition,* June 7, 1996, on the impact of deregulation on the airline industry:

> Most people don't need a theorist to tell them that flying 27-year-old planes that have been cast off by other companies, sometimes with inadequate maintenance records, is not a great idea. Farming out aircraft maintenance to subcontractors can only add to the problem. It's important to acknowledge that these troubling developments, too, are the work of the invisible hand.

And reporter Jerry Knight in the *Washington Post,* December 6, 1988:

> Car salesmen are just investment bankers with white shoes, the way I figure it. Undercoating, underwriting, it's all the same. The invisible hand of the free market gets into your pocket one way or another. . . .
> So I offered this guy the same kind of deal that Kohlberg Kravis Roberts & Co. made to RJR Nabisco—you know, where they bought $25 billion worth of company with $15 million of their own money. I said I'd give him $15 down on a $25,000 car.

iron triangle A source of entrenched power and opposition; the formal or informal collaboration of forces to define and determine policy and practice; friendly/incestuous/sometimes corrupt mesh of communication and support among lobbyists, government agencies, and the members of Congress who oversee the activities of the agencies. It's one of those expressions dear to Washington.

A classic example is the linkage of defense contractors, officials of the Department of Defense and members of Congress who sit on committees with jurisdiction over the department or its appropriations. Also part of the formation are other members of Congress who have important contractors or a significant military installation in their districts. Many times Defense Department employees, and sometimes former senators or representatives, go to work for the contractors. They provide each other with information useful in winning or keeping a contract. Or they might provide inside information on budget cuts under consideration so that opposition can be mounted even before decisions have been made. The upshot is that changes in policy, especially spending cuts, become very difficult to make.

Iron triangles work the same way throughout the government, from agriculture to banking regulation to health care to transportation.

The term in use, by Sonni Efron in the *Los Angeles Times,* November 20, 1996, reporting on political scandals in Japan:

> In terms of taxpayer yen squandered, this scandal is by no means the largest to have rocked Japan in recent years. But . . . it follows a parliamentary election campaign in which every political party promised to curb the powers of the overreaching Japanese bureaucracy and thus weaken the corrupt ties that bind bureaucrats, politicians and industry in an "iron triangle."

And in commentary by Jon Talton, Gannett News Service, December 25, 1994:

> Establishment Washington—including many Republicans—has grown rich on the tax money of the American people. The "iron triangle" of congressional staff, regulatory agencies and lobbyists kept the scam going for decades.

*It was an alter-ego thing, like **Jekyll and Hyde**. My bad
part overwhelmed me.*

—John McEnroe

J'accuse \zhà-kū̄ez\ A dramatic and impassioned accusation of wrongdoing and cover-up. The French phrase, meaning "I accuse," comes from
a celebrated open letter by writer Émile Zola expressing outrage and
protest at government actions and denouncing the French army general
staff in the infamous DREYFUS affair. "J'accuse" is one of the most famous
and successful polemics ever written.

Publication of the letter on the morning of January 13, 1898 electrified
Paris. The newspaper *Aurore,* in a special edition, printed it in bold letters under the headline "J'accuse," a title taken from the litany of charges
in the conclusion of the letter, each beginning "I accuse. . . . " Its publication marked a turning point in the epic struggle that had gripped France.

Zola accused the government and army of convicting Dreyfus on the
basis of a secret document which Dreyfus had no opportunity to rebut;
of conducting an elaborate, criminal cover-up; and of misleading the press
and people to conceal these actions. He denounced the "odious anti-Semitism from which the great liberal France of the rights of man will die if
it is not cured."

Zola was himself then successfully prosecuted in the courts and forced
to flee the country. He was vilified as a foreigner who took up the cause
of Dreyfus for mercenary reasons, when in fact it nearly ruined him finan-
cially. But his role was pivotal in turning the tide toward eventual justice
for Dreyfus and in forcing the public and government to confront the
truth.

The term in use, by Matt Roush in *USA Today,* reviewing a report by
Peter Jennings of ABC News on the failures of United Nations peace-
keeping efforts in Bosnia, April 24, 1995:

> This is Jennings' J'accuse, strongly and convincingly argued. It
> should leave you shamed, shaken, angered and hoping there will
> be no need for another rebuke from the newsman a year from
> now.

And by Alexander Wolf, giving a humorous glossary of terms for basketball referees in *Sports Illustrated,* November 15, 1996:

> The Bird Dog. The j'accuse, finger-pointing gesture a ref makes
> when booking a player for a foul.

And by Jay McCormick in *USA Today,* January 9, 1997:

Stumbling across a computer Web site put out by Georgia Tech University's campus in Metz, in the eastern region of Lorraine, the Association for the Defense of the French Language and the Association for the Future of the French Language cried "J'accuse!"

The charge is that the Web site is mostly in English. That might violate a 1994 French law against advertising or selling products in a foreign language unless accompanied by a French translation.

Jacobean \ˌja-kə-'bē-ən\ Of, relating to, or characteristic of the reign of James I of England (1603–1625). The adjective is applied particularly to the literature and architecture of the time. The word is drawn from *Jacobus,* the Latin form of the name James.

The Jacobean era was a period of great achievement, producing some of the finest writing in the English language: Shakespeare's great tragedies, the poetry of John Donne and Ben Jonson, the essays of Francis Bacon, and the King James Version of the Bible.

The period was cautious and somber, however, in contrast to the booming optimism of the Elizabethan years. This new tone reflected the growing tensions in English society over religion and values. Guy FAWKES and the other members of the Gunpowder Plot tried to blow up Parliament and the king; growing quarrels over the king's authority and the divergence of values between the pleasure-loving court and its Puritan critics in Parliament would ultimately lead to the Civil War and the execution of King Charles I in 1649. "Jacobean melancholy" shows up in the tragic themes of contemporary plays which provide some of the most memorable portraits of evil in the history of drama. Today plots or dark scenes of bloody murder and vengeance are frequently characterized as Jacobean.

The term in use, by Eleanor Ringel and Steve Murray, in the *Atlanta Journal and Constitution,* August 22, 1997:

> If absolute power corrupts absolutely, the same could be said for a spare "Y" chromosome, preppy blond hair and a blandly handsome face.
>
> Those are the weapons Chad (Aaron Eckhart, in a career-making performance) uses in *In the Company of Men* as he plays a game that's as clean and mean as a Jacobean revenge tragedy: He and his mousier colleague . . . embark on a seduce-and-abandon scenario with . . . a hearing-impaired secretary, simply for the pleasure of breaking a heart in retaliation for the times women have spurned them in the past.

And by David Delman, reviewing Walter Mosely's mystery *Black Betty,* in the *Miami Herald,* June 26, 1994:

> As a prose stylist, Mosely defies pigeon-holing. Dealing with children, he can be restrained, tenderly eloquent. Turn a page, and

you may find him ranting like a Jacobean, spilling blood as if violence were as necessary to him as air.

Jacobin \\'ja-kə-bən\\ A member of an extremist or radical political group, originally a member of a group advocating egalitarian democracy and engaging in terrorist activities during the French Revolution. The Jacobins started out in 1789 as relatively moderate democrats, but soon became the radical leadership of the French Revolution and ushered in the REIGN OF TERROR. Their name is now synonymous with extreme radicalism and revolutionary zeal.

The Jacobin group, formally the Society of Friends of the Constitution, was one of many political clubs active during the Revolution. They met in a former Dominican convent; the nickname Jacobin comes from the Parisian name for the Dominicans (the Dominicans had first become established in the Rue St. Jacques; the Latin for Jacques is Jacobus— hence Jacobin). The club's members included some of the most influential leaders of the National Assembly: Mirabeau, Danton, Marat, and ROBESPIERRE among them.

Initially the Jacobins sought merely to limit the powers of the king, but they grew increasingly extreme. The Reign of Terror, 1793–1794, a wartime dictatorship to preserve the republic against counterrevolutionaries, sent thousands to the guillotine. Ultimately, popular discontent led to the overthrow of the government installed by Robespierre and others.

The term in use, quoted by Peter Canby in the *New York Times Book Review,* May 18, 1997, reviewing *Che Guevara: A Revolutionary Life* by Jon Lee Anderson:

> Mr. Galeano wound up labeling Che the Jacobin of the Cuban revolution, and Che did, in fact, have a frightening cruel streak.

And again, by political pollster Guy Molyneux in commentary in the *Los Angeles Times,* April 28, 1996, on support for an increase in the minimum wage:

> In a sure sign of a changing political climate, 23 Republicans from the House—the Jacobin nerve center—came out for a hike 10 cents more generous than that proposed by President Bill Clinton.

Javert \\zhä-'ver\\ A relentless, merciless prosecutor; one who never gives up in his or her pursuit of someone who has committed a crime. Javert is a character in Victor Hugo's novel *Les Miserables* (1862). Hugo was one of the greatest novelists of the Romantic era, and his work reflected his belief that art should lead and guide and that artists should have a role in politics. His work is marked by compassion for the downtrodden, and the epic *Les Miserables* is a stunning statement of his view.

The novel's hero Jean Valjean is pursued by the policeman Javert. Born in prison to a convict, he is monomaniacally committed to the law, even when it is unjust or cruel. Valjean is a peasant who has stolen a loaf of bread to feed his sister's family. He emerges from years in prison and the galleys a hardened, embittered criminal. His rehabilitation begins when he is treated kindly by a bishop; he becomes successful in business and the mayor of his town. But when his identity is revealed, the implacable Javert resumes his pursuit.

Javert knows no charity or mercy, and accepts neither atonement nor redemption; the law is the law. The pursuit continues for years, including the famous scenes of Valjean's flight through the sewers of Paris during the Paris insurrection of 1848. Javert corners his quarry at last, but Valjean escapes again, having saved the policeman from rebels bent on killing him as a spy. This act of mercy shatters Javert's raison d'etre, and he commits suicide.

The novel has achieved modern popularity through various cinematic versions, and, most notably, as a theatrical musical by Claude-Michel Schoenberg and Alain Boublil first performed in 1980. The musical achieved huge commercial success when produced by Britain's Royal Shakespeare Company in 1985. Since that time the work has been performed worldwide.

The term in use, one of many, many characterizations of Independent Counsel Kenneth W. Starr, in a *Washington Times* editorial, November 20, 1998:

> Even if Mr. Starr were the Javert that the Democrats would have us believe, it wouldn't change the fact that Mr. Clinton repeatedly lied under oath and encouraged others to do the same.

Another, by Ruth Marcus of the *Washington Post,* January 30, 1998:

> Is Starr, as the White House and its allies contend, an overzealous and politically motivated prosecutor hounding the Clintons like Victor Hugo's Inspector Javert pursued Jean Valjean, relentlessly "scratching for dirt" as first lady Hillary Rodham Clinton put it last week.

Jekyll and Hyde One having a two-sided personality, one side of which is good and the other evil; the good and evil sides of an individual, and, by extension, of a group, an organization, or a class. The names are drawn from the most famous literary rendering of such a dual personality, Robert Louis Stevenson's 1886 novel, *The Strange Case of Dr. Jekyll and Mr. Hyde.*

The virtuous Dr. Jekyll is fascinated by the idea of good and evil and develops a drug which transforms him into the terrifying Mr. Hyde, a distillation of the evil latent in his nature. Jekyll also has an antidote which allows him to restore himself, but the evil side gradually takes over and the antidote proves useless. Hyde commits a terrible murder; Jekyll is unable to obtain one of the ingredients necessary for the antidote and commits suicide.

The expression in use, by retired tennis terror John McEnroe, quoted by Franz Lidz, *Sports Illustrated,* September 9, 1996:

He needed a publicist. He needed an exorcist. "I'd think, You're going out to play, and you're not gonna yell at the umpire," he says. "And within two games I'd be pissed and yelling at the umpire. It was an alter-ego thing, like Jekyll and Hyde. My bad part overwhelmed me."

And a quote in the *Christian Science Monitor* cited by Mark Clayton, August 23, 1995:

"It's almost like a Jekyll-and-Hyde economy," says Jayson Myers, chief economist for the Canadian Manufacturers' Association.

By Walter Nicholls in the *Washington Post,* May 28, 1997, describing the growth cycle of sockeye and king salmon:

Weird changes occur in the fish in just a matter of days upon entering the river itself—a dramatic Jekyll/Hyde metamorphosis. . . . The salmon become bigger and more aggressive. . . . They grow an ugly hooked nose and a hump on their back. Their teeth lengthen half an inch. It's not a pretty sight.

jeremiad \ˌjer-ə-ˈmī-əd, -ad\ A prolonged lamentation or complaint. Also, a cautionary or angry harangue. It is drawn from the Old Testament prophet Jeremiah, who foretold doom and gloom in lengthy lamentations and harangues, and was right.

He told his countrymen to abandon futile political resistance to Babylon and attend instead to reform and matters of religion. Such advice was unpopular, and he was put in prison. Israel was conquered by Babylon anyway, and Jeremiah was released from prison after Jerusalem fell, in 586 B.C. Later he was forcibly taken to Egypt, where he died. Despite his contentious career, toward the end of his life, Jeremiah expressed hope for the future of his people and their own land.

The term in use, by Leigh Montgomery in a review of Robert Bork's *Slouching Towards Gomorrah: Modern Liberalism,* in the *Christian Science Monitor,* December 12, 1996:

America possesses a "hedonistic," "enfeebled" culture, he says. Modern liberalism, from the 1960s, is the root of the problem. His jeremiad covers varied subjects such as crime, radical feminism, rap music and the Supreme Court.

Another example, from Steven Pinker in the *New Republic,* January 31, 1994:

It is ironic that the jeremiads wailing about how sloppy language leads to sloppy thought are themselves hairballs of loosely associated factoids and tangled non sequiturs.

Jesuitical Of or relating to the Society of Jesus, a Catholic order of priests founded by Ignatious Loyola in 1534. While originally referring to matters pertaining to the order, the word also has a negative sense, meaning devious, cunning, prevaricating. It may also be used to suggest intense, hairsplitting analysis.

The Society of Jesus was established as a counter to the Protestant Reformation and was particularly active in missionary and educational endeavors. The society was well organized, highly disciplined, and secretive and became a considerable political force. This led to conflicts with civil authorities, and the Jesuits were expelled from England and various European countries. They were suppressed by the Pope in 1773, but revived in 1814.

In recent times Jesuits have continued their strong identification with education and have often been involved with progressive social causes.

The term in use, by Anne McElvoy in the *Independent,* August 19, 1998:

> Bill Clinton, with his easy courtliness and his Jesuitical meanderings on the nature of what is and is not sex, would have been a perfect 19th-century president, while Hillary has updated the serviceable historical model of tough political comrade-in-arms.

And conservative Republican Tom Pauken questioning the conservative credentials of Colin Powell, quoted in the *Washington Times,* October 30, 1995:

> They can use all the Jesuitical logic to try to rationalize how Powell is really one of us, but that's nonsense.

And by Allison Pearson in the *Daily Telegraph,* February 16, 1998:

> I have stood in my local park and seen mothers who are afraid to chastise their own young, even when they are being a danger to themselves and others, because they are under the impression that it will do untold psychological damage. "Because I say so" is no longer an acceptable clincher; instead, arguments of Jesuitical nicety must be deployed to persuade little Matthew to stop pouring sand into Alice's ear.

jetsam *See* FLOTSAM AND JETSAM.

Jezebel \ˈje-zə-ˌbel\ The Phoenician wife of AHAB who, according to I and II Kings in the Old Testament, pressed the cult of Baal on the Israelite kingdom but was finally killed in accordance with Elijah's prophecy. Also, usually uncapitalized, an impudent, shameless, or morally unrestrained woman.

The original was the infamous wife of King Ahab of Israel (circa 874–853 B.C.). She was a bad influence on him, and her name is now synonymous with her reputation.

The prophet Elijah foretold the end of the house of Ahab—correctly. But because Ahab had repented, the Lord postponed punishment until the reign of Ahab's son. There was a coup, but Jezebel was defiant. She painted her eyes, and attired her head, and spoke defiantly (and seductively?) out the window at the conqueror. He ordered her thrown down, and she was eaten by dogs—just as the prophet Elijah had foretold.

The term in use, by Erin Arvedlund in *Fortune,* March 3, 1997, in a story on a gangland-style murder of an American businessman in Moscow:

> Leggy Russian Jezebels strolled in and out of the hotel's retail stores, looking bored and fetching in Chanel suits and impossibly high heels.

And by Naomi Barry, in an article about Dolley Madison in *Gourmet,* December 1989:

> . . . but Dolley rouged her cheeks like a jolly jezebel. She also took snuff from a carved mother-of-pearl snuffbox in public, daintily dusting the last grains from each nostril with a fine lace handkerchief.

jihad \ji-'häd, *chiefly British* -'had\ A holy war waged on behalf of Islam as a religious duty. Also, a crusade for a principle or a belief. It's the Arabic word for a crusade or holy war against infidels (unbelievers).

The term in use, by Eric Alterman in *Rolling Stone,* March 23, 1995:

> The Get Rid of the Agency Entirely camp is led by a New York Democrat, Sen. Daniel Patrick Moynihan, who has conducted a one-man jihad against the agency ever since he discovered how badly it misread the Cold War and exaggerated the strength of the U.S.S.R.

And by Sarah Durkin and James Plummer in the *Detroit News,* December 1, 1996:

> As the season of good cheer and good eating arrives, the Center for Science in the Public Interest, the self-proclaimed "food police" is sure to strike again. . . .
>
> The center's most recent anti-fat jihad targets dinner house grills such as Chili's, Bennigan's, Applebee's, and the Hard Rock Cafe.

Jim Crow Ethnic discrimination, especially against blacks by legal enforcement or traditional sanctions. The body of laws enacted in the South after the end of Reconstruction in 1877 to enforce segregation of the races in virtually every aspect of public activity—in schools, restaurants, theaters, transport, parks, cemeteries, drinking fountains. The purpose was to insure that blacks and whites would not meet as equals. These laws were sanctioned by the Supreme Court in its decision *Plessy v. Ferguson* in 1896, with its "separate but equal" finding. De jure segregation was not ended until the 1960s, after long and difficult campaigns in the courts, in Congress and state legislatures, and in public facilities.

The term is derived from a song made popular by Thomas Dartmouth Rice. Rice was a white man, an itinerant actor who caught on with a blackface song-and-dance act, "Jump Jim Crow," first performed in 1828. This act was the germination of the popular minstrel shows, in which white actors performed in black makeup. Rice toured with great success in the United States and Britain, and the song was so popular that it was translated into French.

"Jim Crow" became a derogatory term for blacks and then served as the nickname for the segregation laws. As an epithet for both overt and subtle forms of discrimination and segregation, it is alive and well. It is also a transitive verb; that is, someone can be Jim Crowed.

The term in use, in a column by DeWayne Wickham, *USA Today,* June 3, 1996:

> No amount of sucking up is likely to change [South Carolina Senator] Thurmond. Having once been a disciple of Jim Crow, Thurmond is now a follower of his baby-boom offspring. Jim Crow was an in-your-face bigot, but Jim Crow, Jr., practices a more subtle form of racism.

By U.S. Navy Captain Rosemary Mariner, in a guest editorial in the *Washington Post,* May 11, 1997, on the role of women in the armed forces:

> As with racial separation, the idea of keeping people "with their own kind" has nothing to do with combat readiness or stopping harassment. The purpose of Jim or Jane Crow policies is to keep an institutionally inferior group in its place.

In use as a verb, by World War II day-care center operator Mary Willett, quoted by Doris Kearns Goodwin in her 1994 book, *No Ordinary Time:*

> We had Indian children, Mexican children, and black children. I remember one big black woman whose son, Freddy, was in the program. She was so happy to know that, for the first time in Freddy's life, he was not being Jim Crowed.

jingoism Extreme chauvinism or nationalism marked especially by a belligerent foreign policy. Cocky, pugnacious, shrill, xenophobic, chest-thumping patriotism.

The term originated in British politics. In 1876, Disraeli threatened the Russians with war if they continued interfering in Turkey. The London music halls rang with the refrain:

> We don't want to fight,
> But by Jingo, if we do,
> We've got the ships,
> We've got the men,
> We've got the money, too.

The song and theme made their appearance in the United States in the late 19th century as the country experienced its own surge of imperial exuberance. James G. Blaine, secretary of state (1889–1892) under President Harrison, earned the nickname "Jingo Jim." The jingle made an appearance in this period during a fishing dispute with Britain and Canada in this Americanized version:

> We don't want to fight,
> But by Jingo, if we do,
> We'll scoop in all the fishing grounds
> And the whole Dominion too.

The term in use, by Norman Chad in "Sportswaves" in the *Washington Post,* September 20, 1988, discussing television coverage of the Olympics:

> NBC largely has steered away from the jingoism, brought us admirable camera work and presented a balanced picture of the proceedings.

And by Robert W. Duffy of the *St. Louis Post-Dispatch,* June 18, 1995:

> "Made in America," the special exhibition that opened Friday at the St. Louis Art Museum, is not an exercise in artistic jingoism. Rather it is a great big good-natured pat on our national back, a celebration of "our" culture, mounted with 160 or so American works of art. . . .

Job \\'jōb\\ The hero of the Old Testament book of Job who endures afflictions with fortitude and faith. His story is the exploration of why, if suffering is punishment for sin, do the good suffer?

At the outset, Job is a wealthy man when God permits Satan to test Job's faith. Job's wealth disappears, his children die, he is afflicted with boils, but his faith never wavers, and eventually he is rewarded. Now his name is used to allude to someone who suffers a succession of woes. As an adjective, describing cumulative misfortune, the word is *Jobian.*

The term in use, by Letitia Baldridge, in *Town & Country,* September 1, 1994, on the art of aging gracefully:

> Keep a sense of humor about everything, including the fact that you may have lost a couple of inches in height, you feel like the Sufferings of Job when you wake up in the morning . . . and you seem to be having a "bad hair day" every day.

Another example, by Dave Herring in the *Christian Science Monitor,* October 28, 1994, quoting Rabbi Victor Reichert on his friend, poet Robert Frost:

> Frost was a "Jobian man with Jobian experiences," Reichert says. Yet Frost did not whine—he sought to transform his hardship into art of beauty and depth.

And by political columnist Tony Snow in the *Detroit News,* March 11, 1996:

> Think of Dole as a latter-day Job. . . . He strode off to war looking like a young Charles Atlas, but returned a skeleton—

shrunken, deprived of the full use of his right arm. . . . Experts said he'd die. He didn't. They said he'd never walk. He did. They said he'd never win the Republican nomination: You get the idea.

Jonah \\'jō-nə\\ An Israelite prophet who according to the book of Jonah in the Old Testament resisted a divine call to preach repentance to the people of Nineveh, was swallowed and vomited by a great fish, and eventually carried out his mission. The book of Jonah recounts his adventures, which were considerable. His name is now forever associated with whales, but a jonah is also someone who is believed to bring bad luck. The word is even used as a verb—to jonah someone is to jinx them.

Jonah was commanded by God to go to Nineveh to foretell its destruction, but he didn't want to go and instead boarded a ship. A violent storm ensued. The sailors decided that Jonah was to blame, and threw him overboard. He was then swallowed by a whale and lived three days and nights in its belly, praying like mad. The whale then spewed Jonah up safely on dry land.

The term in use, by John Gould in the *Christian Science Monitor,* September 13, 1996, recounting a Maine tale of a 1920s car salesman attempting to make a sale:

> But the Fordson tractor was a white elephant, a Jonah! It wasn't something to drive a distance, so Phil would fetch prospects to the Bickfords' garage and demonstrate it in the street. Not the best way. Phil got the big ha-ha every day, and the Fordson was still in the inventory.

Another example, from David Brauer in *Finance,* June 1, 1994:

> Like Jonah and the whale, banking executives Bob Weiss and Dave Peterka knew enough about the insides of big banks to want to get out. Trouble is, they kept getting swallowed up.

Judas goat \\'jü-dəs\\ Goat that leads other goats to slaughter. Also, one who entices into danger and betrays others. The name of course is an allusion to Judas Iscariot, who betrayed Jesus for thirty pieces of silver.

The term in use, from former conservative Congressman Robert K. Dornan (R–Calif.) on the 1996 presidential race, quoted in the *Washington Times,* April 24, 1995:

> "But I am not going to do for Dole what I did for Bush, and be a Judas goat, taking conservatives— particularly military ones and pro-lifers who trust me—and . . . march them into Dole's camp," he said.

And by Florida Governor Lawton Chiles, quoted in the *Tallahassee Democrat,* May 7, 1995:

> Gov. Lawton Chiles planned a visit to Washington this week to
> warn of "Judas goat" governors leading the sheep in their ranks
> to fiscal slaughter.

juggernaut A massive, inexorable force, campaign, movement, or object
that crushes whatever is in its path.

The word comes from Hindi; its origin lies in Jagganath, a Hindu god,
the Lord of the World. The city of Puri in eastern India is the site of an
annual festival in his honor at which the image of the god is carried on a
gigantic wheeled vehicle 45 feet high drawn through the streets by pilgrims. It was said (mostly inaccurately) that fanatical followers would
throw themselves under the wheels; this image has contributed to the
meaning of the word in English.

The term in use, in the *Deseret News,* June 10, 1997:

> For many in the investors group, buying into the Chicago Bulls
> in 1985 was a way to fulfill a fantasy.
>
> At the time of the purchase, the National Basketball Associa-
> tion was hardly a business juggernaut.

And by Ted Anthony of the Associated Press, May 18, 1997, reviewing
Andrew F. Smith's book *Pure Ketchup,* a history of the condiment:

> "The more I got into ketchup, the more I fell in love with the
> story," [Smith] says. "It's got foreign intrigue, mean adulterators,
> captains of industry. All the elements of a great story are there."
>
> He goes on to deal with the Heinz juggernaut and, of course,
> the 1980s ketchup debacle, when the condiment was declared a
> vegetable by the Reagan administration to save money on the
> federal school lunch program.

*. . . these political conventions . . . are our version of a **Kabuki** dance.*

—Tom Brokaw

Kabuki \kə-'bü-kē, 'kä-bù-(ˌ)kē\ Traditional Japanese drama with singing and dancing performed in a highly stylized manner. By extension, an activity or drama in real life carried out in a predictable, ritualized fashion. Kabuki also refers to the white face makeup used by the actors.

Kabuki originated in Japan during the 17th century. It is characterized by elaborate, colorful costumes and makeup. The plays are traditional and deal with historical themes. All parts are played by men, which has been the rule since the mid-17th century. The actors mime their parts while narrators speak the lines.

The term in use, quoted by Eric Pianin and Clay Chandler in the *Washington Post,* on congressional budget negotiations, August 5, 1997:

> The talks were all posture and little progress— "budget kabu-ki," as Kasich and Domenici came to call it.

And quoted by the Associated Press, August 14, 1996, on news coverage of party conventions:

> "As we've been saying for some time, these political conventions, Democrat and Republican, are our version of a Kabuki dance," NBC anchorman Tom Brokaw said in a telephone interview early today.

And by the Kitchen Guy in the *Detroit News,* July 28, 1997:

> The Kitchen Guy has to confess that he grew up drinking tea and not coffee. Consequently, drinking a cup or two of espresso gets him so wired he can actually hear conversations on airliners passing overhead.
>
> Even so, when the KG tires of visiting Royal Oak's approximately 843 coffee shops—all staffed by the same shaved-head, multi-earringed, "wo/men in black" sporting the wan New York Kabuki look—he prefers to whip up his own espresso, cappucino or caffe latte at home.

Kafkaesque \ˌkäf-kə-'esk, ˌkaf-\ Of, relating to, or suggestive of Franz Kafka or his writing; especially, having a frighteningly surreal, complex, bizarre, or illogical quality.

From the name of author Franz Kafka (1893–1924), whose work was characterized by nightmarish settings in which individuals were crushed by nonsensical, blind authority. Kafka's work foreshadowed the horrors of the modern police state and expressed vividly the 20th-century emotions of alienation, powerlessness, and fear. In *The Trial* (1925), an innocent man is deprived of the means of defending himself, condemned, and stabbed to death by polite executioners; in *Metamorphosis* (1915), a young man wakes up to find that he has turned into a gigantic cockroach.

The term in use, by Susan Blaustein in *Harper's,* May 1994:

> All of the evidence gathered against Bower was circumstantial; potentially exculpatory evidence mysteriously disappeared before the trial. Although within days of his conviction witnesses began coming forward with new evidence supporting Bower's innocence, his lawyer, off on a Mexican vacation, failed to meet the thirty-day deadline. Bower's harrowing trial experience, followed by a decade spent studying the cases of his neighbors on the row, has persuaded him that inside Texas's sometimes Kafkaesque criminal-justice system, one's innocence can have astonishingly little bearing on one's fate.

And by Richard Conniff in *Time,* October 3, 1988, reviewing a study of public bathrooms in Washington, D.C., by architecture professor Alexander Kira:

> The tour adjourns to the Martin Luther King Memorial Library downtown, a large, gloomy building in the soul-crushing modernist style. Here the search for a rest room takes on a literary character, mainly Kafkaesque: a visitor finds the men's room down a darkened corridor on the third floor, just past the security cameras, but it's locked and a sign on the door says AFTER 5:30 USE MEN'S ROOM ON A-LEVEL.
>
> A librarian supplies directions: take that elevator there, cross the lobby, take another elevator to the A-level, and bingo, you're there. But the second elevator has a sign on it: OUT OF SERVICE. PLEASE USE ELEVATOR AT OTHER END OF BUILDING. The stairs are handier, but they lack directional signs and so lead the uninitiated to an underground garage. Back up one flight, through a vast, empty room, into another room containing only a security desk (unattended), just in time to see the ostensibly broken elevator arrive. . . .

Kansas *See* WE'RE NOT IN KANSAS ANYMORE.

karma \\'kär-mə *also* 'kər-\\ The force generated by a person's actions, held in Hinduism and Buddhism to perpetuate transmigration and in its ethical consequences to determine the nature of the person's next existence. Wrongful actions may go unpunished in one life, but the moral debt remains and payment is exacted in the future.

The Sanskrit word came into vogue in the United States in the 1960s as part of the period's fascination with Eastern religions. Today the term is used loosely to mean fate or destiny, or to explain events or circumstances, or to refer to the aura felt to emanate from persons, places, or things—good (or bad) vibrations.

The term in use, by Mark McDonald, in the *Philadelphia Daily News,* October 22, 1997:

> Police commissioner Richard Neal's tango with bad karma continued apace yesterday when he failed to show up for a City Council meeting on crime in the neighborhoods.

And from David Margolick in the *New York Times,* December 1, 1989:

> After seven years of litigation, there is still some dispute over whether toxic solvents dumped at a tannery in Woburn, Mass., found their way into the municipal water supply and caused six deaths from leukemia. But there is no denying that bad karma from the case has seeped even further than the chemicals. . . .

Ken *See* BARBIE AND KEN.

Kevorkian \kə-'vȯr-kē-ən\ Doctor known for assisting the terminally ill to commit suicide. Also, a force of suicide or an agent of death.

Dr. Jack Kevorkian, a retired pathologist in Michigan, became notorious in the 1990s for his willingness to assist ill or disabled persons to commit suicide.

After he began publicizing his activities in 1990, his actions and the resulting deaths created endless controversy and resulted in several unsuccessful prosecutions for murder and a conviction in 1999. His aggressive advocacy of his point of view and his refusal to stop made his name a jocular byword for a sinister purveyor of doom. Undoubtedly this association was enhanced by the doctor's unusual surname, which rolls richly off the tongue and requires no other modifiers. Would it have happened if he were named Smith? Unlikely.

Presidential candidate and right-wing opinionmeister Patrick Buchanan was one of the first to use the reference, quoted in the *Christian Science Monitor,* February 22, 1993:

> Clinton's program is the son of [former budget director] Dick Darman, the Dr. Kevorkian of the Bush administration.

And on a more lighthearted note, by Ray Magliozzi, of *Car Talk,* in the Magliozzi brothers' car advice column, appearing in this case in the *Deseret News,* July 18, 1997:

> And for the record, we don't condone shooting a car between the headlights. That's undignified. When the time comes, we simply recommend making an appointment at Kevorkian Motors.

And in the *Seattle Times,* July 13, 1997:

> The joke circulating in Silicon Valley in the aftermath of the ouster of Apple Computer's chief executive was not a pretty one.

Who's on the short list to be chief executive of Apple?
Dr. Kevorkian.

Keystone Kops A group of cinematic policemen known for defeating themselves through chaotic physical antics. People—often those in authority—who display such clownish incompetence.

The term comes from high-velocity comedies of the early days of moving pictures. These films were the creation of Mack Sennett and his Keystone Studio, founded in 1912.

Sennett is known for broad, fast-moving pratfall humor—in one of his "Keystone Comedies" the first cinematic custard pie was thrown. Many future stars worked for Sennett, including Fatty Arbuckle and Charlie Chaplin. Sennett described his enterprise as being "as well-organized as a national chain of lemonade stands operated by small, dishonest boys."

The Keystone Kops roared about in open automobiles, clinging to the running boards while dodging dizzily through haystacks and weaving wildly in front of speeding trains. They waved truncheons and fell over each other under the direction of their goggle-eyed leader, and they still generate huge laughs.

The term in use, by Sarah Lyall in the *New York Times,* May 4, 1997, reviewing the documentary, *The Royal Opera House:*

> Some critics said the programs proved what they had suspected all along: that the people who run the Royal Opera and the Royal Ballet were the stage equivalent of the Keystone Kops, doomed to missteps and pratfalls of the highest order.

And from Richard Teitelbaum, *Fortune,* August 19, 1996:

> The Boston SHOCK TROOPS of aggressive investing are starting to look a lot like the Keystone Kops. Fidelity's growth funds— for decades the industry's premier franchise—have been slipping.

And by Laurence I. Barrett, reviewing Pete Earley's book *Confessions of a Spy: The Real Story of Aldrich Ames,* in *Newsday,* March 16, 1997:

> Earley is neither a CIA-basher nor a gee-whiz fan in the Tom Clancy manner. By simply laying out the weird facts, he confirms negative stereotypes about the agency's culture. The slow, serpentine investigation was not so much a game of cat and mouse as it was Keystone Kops versus klutz.

kill/shoot the messenger To punish the bearer of bad news, even though the person has done no more than deliver the information. While the messenger is not the cause of the bad tidings, he or she is the one within reach. The phrase has been offered by the news media as an explanation for public hostility to them; the media merely report bad news, but the public blames them for it.

The concept comes from Sophocles, the Greek tragic poet who wrote in *Antigone* (ca. 442 B.C.), "None love the messenger who brings bad tidings."

The term in use, in an editorial in the *Atlanta Journal and Constitution,* July 17, 1996:

> The CDC [Centers for Disease Control and Prevention] has funded some of the most comprehensive research on firearm injuries, including studies on the numbers of child firearm deaths each year and the risks of keeping a gun at home. . . .
>
> But the House Republicans, fearing the facts, want to kill the messenger. Last year, they tried to kill funding for all injury research just to stop the study of firearm injuries. . . .

And quoted by Carl Cannon and Nelson Schwartz in the *Baltimore Sun,* January 7, 1995:

> But hiring and firing new [White House] press secretaries, according to presidential historian Stephen Ambrose, signals more than just a problem in getting out the message.
>
> "There is a kill-the-messenger quality to it," Mr. Ambrose said. "The president wants better press, and the frustrations he feels are easiest to take out on the press secretary."

Kilroy A character whose name turns up everywhere but is otherwise unknown.

During World War II, the graffito "Kilroy was here," was found wherever American troops went. One popular explanation for the phenomenon has it that a shipyard inspector named Kilroy in Quincy, Massachusetts, chalked the words on all the materials he inspected, and that the entire U.S. military picked up the habit.

The term in use, by Michael Lind, the *New Republic,* March 11, 1996:

> There's only one thing wrong with this happy scenario: Kemp has been wrong about almost everything in his career. Over the past quarter-century, he has been present at the creation of practically every awful idea the right has foisted on America. He is the Kilroy of conservative public policy quackery.

And by Holly Crenshaw in the *Atlanta Journal and Constitution,* June 5, 1997:

> It's the local equivalent of "Kilroy Was Here"—an outgrowth of that strong human impulse to leave a distinguishing mark behind. Or maybe it's nothing more than a bit of inspired copycat goofiness.
>
> There must be some explanation for such weird phenomena around town as the place in Little Five Points where for years, people have tied pairs of shoes together by the laces and heaved them over the power lines. Left to dangle there, the discarded footwear loom overhead like the ghosts of punk-rockers past.

kinder, gentler Nicer. A term used by George Bush in accepting the Republican presidential nomination at the GOP national convention in New Orleans on August 18, 1988. Speechwriter Peggy Noonan, on loan from President Ronald Reagan, coined the term. Its apparent purpose was to distance Bush from his MENTOR, whose popularity had softened and whose image, as unsympathetic to the plight of the poor, had hardened.

"Where is it written," Bush asked, "that we must act as if we do not care, as if we're not moved? Well, I am moved. I want a kinder, gentler, nation."

The phrase caught on, and was soon widely used, sometimes ironically, sometimes sarcastically, sometimes with a wink. By the following spring, Bill Kole, an Associated Press reporter, noted new road signs in Detroit admonished motorists to be "kinder, gentler, safer drivers." A strip joint in Windsor, Ontario called itself a "kinder, gentler adult entertainment center." A billboard in South Carolina advertised a "kinder, gentler plumbing company."

And it had staying power. It was applied in 1989 to a hair style, in 1991 to the recreational drug Ecstasy, in 1992 to the British popular singer Donovan, in 1994 to the newspaper movie *The Paper,* in 1996 to the landscape of mid-Wales, in 1997 to a computer operating system, and in 1998 to the entourage of communist APPARATCHIKS who accompanied Jiang Zemin on the Chinese president's eight-day tour of the United States.

The term in use, by Janet Malcolm in the *New York Times Magazine,* November 6, 1994:

> Revisionists have traditionally wanted a kinder, gentler Freud, and they have wanted a softer, more inclusive, less elegant theory—that is, they haven't wanted a theory.

And by Robert MacKenzie in *TV Guide,* June 23–29, 1990, in a review:

> This ABC series (Thursday at 8 p.m. [ET]) has a slight case of the cutes—its central characters are a priest and a nun who call each other Frank and Steve—but if you're looking for a kinder, gentler crime show, this is it.

kindness of strangers, the An allusion to the parting words of the mentally broken Blanche DUBOIS as she is taken away to an institution. When the doctor and the matron arrive, she flees to her bedroom; Stanley Kowalsky taunts her and the hospital matron pins her arms. The doctor intervenes and directs the matron to release Blanche. He speaks gently to her, and she leaves, supported on his arm. She tells the doctor: "I have always depended on the kindness of strangers."

The term in use, quoted in the *St. Louis Post-Dispatch,* November 1, 1998:

> San Francisco independent filmmaker Marc Huestis says it does seem that credits are getting longer and longer, and his films are no exception. "Everybody needs to be thanked, if they've do-

nated food, money or time," he says. "We live by the good graces and kindness of strangers."

And by Darienne L. Dennis in *Fortune,* August 17, 1987:

As befits a city long on charm, New Orleans has always been able to rely on the kindness of strangers. Just as the port began to decline in the late 1970s, along came the second oil boom to prop up the economy. But not for long.

Know-Nothings Members of a 19th-century secret American political organization hostile to the political influence of recent immigrants and Roman Catholics. Today, the term is applied more broadly to include those who take a reactionary political position based on bigotry, ignorance, and emotion.

Dislike of immigrants was rooted in fears of cultural dilution, economic competition, and the immigrants' growing political power, but the chief element was anti-Catholicism. Agitation started in the 1830s with the publication of anti-Catholic newspapers and books, the stonings of Catholic institutions, and the burning of the Ursuline Convent School in Charlestown, Massachusetts, in 1834.

Secret groups sprang up to resist the perceived menace. The Sons of America, the Druids, and others united to form the Order of the Star Spangled Banner. Because members were sworn to secrecy and refused to answer questions about their activities, they were called Know-Nothings.

In 1854 and 1855, the movement captured several state legislatures, elected several governors, and claimed the allegiance of at least 75 congressmen. In 1856, as the American Party, it won a quarter of the popular vote for the presidency under the candidacy of former President Millard Fillmore. The movement faded as the nation became embroiled in the slavery issue, and the idea of America as a place of religious refuge reasserted itself.

Today charges of know-nothingism surface periodically when xenophobia and anti-intellectualism arise.

The term in use, by Lance Morrow in *Time,* October 24, 1988, on the presidential campaign:

Bush used to be a moderate Republican. Now, inheriting the Reagan legacy, he is constrained to run as a right-winger. He trumpets right-wing "values"—and panders unapologetically to the Know-Nothing instincts in the crowd, but one listens to him always with a smudge of doubt: Does he really believe that?

And by Steve Chapman in the *St. Louis Post-Dispatch,* January 26, 1995:

And if you forget that, the new chairman of the House Agriculture Committee is Pat Roberts—of yes, Kansas—who notes that all those dollars add up to a petty 0.6 percent of federal outlays. Roberts also fumes that you critics of farm spending are "agriculture know-nothings" who "complain about agriculture with your mouths full."

Kristallnacht \kri-stäl-'nä̲k̲t\ The night of November 9, 1938, when the windows of thousands of Jewish shops and homes were shattered across Germany and Austria. In German, the "Night of Broken Glass."

The attack on Jewish homes, businesses, and synagogues was carried out by the Nazis. Their pretext was revenge for a fatal attack two days earlier by a 17-year-old Polish Jew, Herschel Grynszpan, on Ernst vom Rath, a third secretary in the German embassy in Paris.

Researchers estimate that over three hundred Jews died that night, at least 1,100 synagogues were vandalized or destroyed, and approximately 30,000 people were arrested and later taken to concentration camps.

The event was a prelude to the Holocaust and is looked at with horror today, not only because of violence toward people guilty of nothing except being themselves, but also because of the failure of the rest of the population—or the world—to protest. While there are many individual stories of aid to victims, there are many more of bystanders who watched passively or joined in the violence.

The term was used by then-Senator Albert Gore Jr., in a guest editorial on the environmental crisis in the *New York Times,* March 19, 1989, entitled "An Ecological Kristallnacht." Gore went on to evoke not only Kristallnacht but MUNICH and the Holocaust to dramatize the urgency of the problem.

The term in use, by Norman Mailer in *Esquire,* August 1, 1994, on a controversial appearance by Madonna on the David Letterman show:

> She was on his program . . . and the results produced a two-day Kristallnacht in the media. Madonna, once again, was being called sick, sordid, depraved, unbalanced, out of control, offensive, outrageous and stupid. So wrote all the boozers, cokeheads, and solid suburbanites who do the TV columns. . . .

Kulturkampf \kùl-'tùr-ˌkäm(p)f\ Conflict between civil and religious authorities, especially over control of education and religious appointments. The word is German, meaning "struggle for civilization."

This was the term for the conflict in the 1870s between Chancellor Otto von Bismarck and the Roman Catholic hierarchy in Germany.

An encyclical issued by Pope Pius IX in 1864 touched off the clash. The Pope set forth what he didn't like about the 19th century (just about everything) and asserted church control over culture, science and education; denounced freedom of conscience and of worship and religious tolerance; and maintained that the church was free of all state control. In 1870, to top things off, the Pope also asserted the doctrine of papal infallibility.

In Germany, these edicts set off a struggle between the newly formed empire and the church. Bismarck would admit no exceptions to the sovereignty of the German state and took measures to make his point clear, saying, "Have no fear—to Canossa we shall not go, either in body or spirit." (In January 1077, Henry IV, emperor of the Holy Roman Empire, stood barefoot as a penitent at Canossa, a castle in northern Italy, for three days awaiting the absolution of Pope Gregory VII in another church-state dispute. "Going to Canossa" has come to mean humiliation, or eating humble pie, definitely not in the diet of Otto von Bismarck.)

The crisis lasted until Pius died in 1878 and was replaced by a more diplomatic, more liberal pontiff, Leo XIII.

The term in use, by Susan Sontag in her book, *AIDS And Its Metaphors* (1989):

> Although these specialists in ugly feelings insist that AIDS is a punishment for deviant sex, what moves them is not just, or even principally, homophobia. Even more important is the utility of AIDS in pursuing one of the main activities of the so-called neo-conservatives, the Kulturkampf against all that is called for short (and inaccurately) the 1960s.

Another example, from Hendrik Hertzberg, writing on President Bush's inaugural address in the *New Republic,* February 13, 1989:

> One of the subtexts of Bush's speech was an effort to declare peace in the Kulturkampf of the past 20 years—a laying down of arms made weirdly explicit the next night, when Ron Wood of the Rolling Stones ceremonially presented his guitar to Lee Atwater, chairman of the Republican National Committee, after Atwater had played and sung with the likes of Percy Sledge and Joe Cocker at an inaugural rhythm-and-blues bash.

And in an editorial in the *Boston Globe,* September 18, 1993, on a speech by presidential candidate and political commentator Patrick Buchanan:

> Though Buchanan may not know, or may not want to remember, that the term originated in Bismarck's "kulturkampf" against the German Catholic Church, he left no doubt about his passion for combat. . . . As for the enemy, Buchanan defined it as "multiculturalism," a force that has perpetrated "an across-the-board assault on our Anglo-American heritage."

*Movies are the **lingua franca** of the twentieth century.*
—Gore Vidal

labyrinth A place made up of intricate passageways and blind alleys; a maze.

In ancient history and legend the Labyrinth was built under the great palace of King Minos on the Mediterranean island of Crete. The king may have been mythological, but the palace is real; excavations have shown it to be the seat of a magnificent civilization, called the Minoan.

Legend says that at the center of the vast Labyrinth was the Minotaur, a ferocious man with the head of a bull. The Greek hero Theseus slew the creature, finding his way into and back out of the Labyrinth with a ball of thread given to him by the princess Ariadne.

The term in use, in the *New Orleans Times-Picayune,* September 9, 1996:

> With its future clouded by the upcoming gambling referendum and its financial footing equally precarious, Harrah's Jazz Co. will struggle mightily in the next few weeks to push its restructured plan for a New Orleans land casino through a labyrinth of city and state agencies.

In use again by Matt Campbell and Christine Vendel in the *Kansas City Star,* March 8, 1996:

> The caucuses didn't actually elect delegates so much as they elected people who will elect delegates to the Democratic National Convention. It's a labyrinth, but the caucuses served as a preference poll that will determine Missouri's 93-member delegation to Chicago in August.

Lancelot A knight of King Arthur's Round Table and lover of Queen Guinevere. A flawed hero. (*See* GALAHAD *for perfection.*) Lancelot du Lac, or Lancelot of the Lake, stood first among the knights of the Round Table. He was the greatest fighter of them all, gallant and brave, a model of chivalry according to Arthurian romance; but he fell in love with Queen Guinevere, and she with him. The story is told in many ways, but the result of the affair was the breakup of the Round Table, war, the end of the magic of CAMELOT, and the death of Arthur.

The term in use, by Daniel Sneider, the *Christian Science Monitor,* February 8, 1993:

Deep in the bowels of the Moskva department store, a four-story concrete box on this capital's Leninsky Prospekt, a glittery private grocery store has opened up. The refrigerated glass cases are filled with items that in another era were sought by Muscovites with the zeal of Sir Lancelot searching for the HOLY GRAIL.

And from Phil McCombs, in the *Washington Post,* April 25, 1997, discussing his enthusiasm for the movie *Shane:*

Undoubtedly you'll first think of Alan Ladd, who played the mysterious drifter Shane in the classic '53 Western, which is a quintessentially American take on Arthurian legend. But it isn't the fast-shooting Lancelot-ish good guy Ladd, with his cute little frilly cowpoke vest and white hat, who interests me.

La Pasionaria Pseudonym of Delores Ibarruri (1895–1989), Spanish communist and political radical. The term today means "a passionate female revolutionary." It is a Spanish term, meaning "the Passionflower." Dolores Ibarruri was a Spanish seamstress and cook who became a political radical and a leader in the Spanish Communist Party. She was a national figure in the Spanish Civil War and was famed for her fiery speeches. A sample of her rhetoric: "It is better to die on your feet than to live on your knees."

The term in use, in the *New York Times Magazine,* May 26, 1996, describing Svetlana Gorycheva, a rising figure in the resurgent Communist Party in Russia:

Gorycheva is one of the only prominent women in the Communist Party—"La Pasionaria of the anti-democratic resistance." She has no trouble combining a newfound Orthodox faith with hardline Communism.

Another example, from Michael Neill and Michael Haederle in *People,* October 11, 1993, in the title of a profile of author Barbara Kingsolver:

La Pasionaria: Barbara Kingsolver writes about a West where women are women and none of the heroes are cowboys.

Lares and Penates \\'lar-(ˌ)ēz, 'ler- . . . pə-'nā-tēz, -'nä\\ Roman gods of the household. The phrase is now used to refer to cherished personal belongings or household effects, or to the comforts of cozily staying at home.

The *Lar* (the singular form) *familiaris* was the permanent protective spirit of the founder of the house; there were other Lares of roads and of seafarers as well. Penates were guardians of the inner rooms of the house, particularly the storerooms for food. Special places were reserved for these deities in the home, and they were given offerings of wine, incense, cakes, and honey on special family occasions. They were linked with Vesta, the goddess of the hearth, who protected homes and families.

The term in use, by Celestine Sibley, in the *Atlanta Journal and Constitution,* October 22, 1995:

> A friend of my daughter's who learned that she had cancer, the quick, incurable kind, told everybody that she had no intention of dying until she could get home and clean out her attic. As I recall, she made it. Clearing out boxes and baskets of old papers is a brutal business for surviving relatives, I know, and I have launched my children on a campaign to get their own lares and penates out of the house while I'm still around to take a hand.

And by Frederick Brown, in a review of *Jean Renoir: Letters,* in the *New Republic,* August 14, 1995. Renoir, a famous French filmmaker, was the son of August Renoir, the even more famous Impressionist painter:

> The elaborately framed images of nudes, children, flowers and landscapes that hung side by side in the Renoir household defined the boundaries of Jean's world, separating kin from alien, like TOTEMS or lares and penates. They pervaded the boy's consciousness of himself to such an extent that the sale of canvases— especially those that pictured his family—filled him with grim forebodings.

last hurrah A final, often valedictory effort, production, or appearance. The term is taken from Edwin O'Connor's 1956 novel, *The Last Hurrah,* about a politician and lovable rogue who, on his 72nd birthday, announces his intention to run for mayor one last time.

The main character, Frank Skeffington, is thought to have been based on Boston's four-time mayor, James Michael Curley. Curley was more rogue than lovable, however, and made his way in politics with brass-knuckle tactics, graft, and corruption, which earned him two terms in prison.

The term in use, by Jackie King in the *Des Moines Business Record,* May 15, 1995:

> Promoters of the Court Avenue River Party [CARP] say that unless they find more financial support within the business community, this year's festival could be their last hurrah.

Another example, from Leonard Weiner in *U.S. News & World Report,* December 13, 1993:

> There's still a few expense-account last hurrahs. Business meals through New Year's Eve are 80 percent deductible; after that, 50 percent.

And from Amy Fine Collins in *Vanity Fair,* July 1996:

> The Black and White Ball, in fact, did sound the death knell of an elite culture founded on privacy, exlusivity, and breeding and heralded the emergence of another, more raucous one, devoted

to publicity, celebrity, and big money. It was the last hurrah of the glamorous go-go phase of the 60s, the optimistic era of Camelot, space launches, "the Great Society," horizonless prosperity, and a certain sophisticated, irretrievable naivete.

last refuge of scoundrels A pronouncement of the acerbic Samuel Johnson (1709–1784): "Patriotism is the last refuge of a scoundrel." Johnson's biographer, BOSWELL, explained:

> ... he did not mean a real and generous love of our country, but that pretended patriotism which on so many, is a cloak for self interest.

The practice of loudly professing patriotism to gain political advantage or to conceal wrongdoing is alive and well today; the phrase is also transplanted onto other themes as illustrated below.

The phrase in use, by Scott Simon on National Public Radio's *Weekend Edition,* September 16, 1995, commenting on the phone-in poll planned by the Miss America Pageant on their swimsuit competition:

> Maybe patriotism is the last refuge of the scoundrel, but sometimes public opinion polling can be close. Any Miss America telephone poll would seem to be, please pardon the expression, "a stacked deck."

And by ABC newsman Ted Koppel on *Nightline,* October 3, 1997, introducing a program on the Promise Keepers, a men's religious movement:

> It has long been held that patriotism is the last refuge of scoundrels. I'm inclined to believe that patriotism actually comes in a poor second behind religion. . . . If a man claims to be operating in God's behalf, only the two of them know the truth of the matter. . . .

lay an egg To fail utterly, especially in front of an audience. The phrase is used particularly in the theater, where it means "to flop, to bomb, to leave the audience totally cold." There are a couple of theories about its origin: in World War I, to "lay an egg" meant to drop a bomb, hence, to bomb. Interestingly enough, a bomb in British usage is a big success, while in American usage it is a major failure. Another theory of the origin of the American usage has it arising from sports as a shortened form of "goose egg"—meaning a zero, a failure to score; it is still used in sports.

A famous use of the expression came in a *Variety* headline after the 1929 stock market crash: "Wall Street Lays an Egg."

Another example, quoted by Mike O'Hara, in the *Detroit News,* November 17, 1996:

> "The deciding factor in our season will be how we do in our next two games," tight end Wesley Walls says. "We've shown we can win at home but we haven't shown a thing on the road. If we go

out and lay an egg these next two weeks, we'll spoil everything
we've done up to this point."

Lazarus \'laz-rəs, 'la-zə-\ A New Testament figure who was raised from
the dead by Jesus, recounted in John II. Lazarus fell ill, and his sisters,
Mary and Martha sent for Jesus, but Lazarus died before Jesus arrived.
Reproached by Martha, Jesus responded: "I am the resurrection and the
life; he who believes in me, though he die, yet shall he live, and whoever
lives and believes in me shall never die."

Jesus ordered the stone rolled away from the tomb and commanded
Lazarus to come out. And Lazarus emerged, still wrapped in his burial
shroud. His name now implies a remarkable recovery or a return from
disaster, either professional or personal.

The term in use, from *The Proud Tower* (1966), by Barbara Tuchman,
in a description of the return of Captain Alfred Dreyfus from imprisonment on Devil's Island to be retried on charges of spying. (*See* DREYFUS;
DREYFUS AFFAIR, J'ACCUSE.) As the judge summoned the accused, all
eyes turned to the door:

> Every gaze fastened on it with a kind of shrinking awe as if fear-
> ful to look upon a ghost. . . . For five years he had been present
> in all their minds, not as a man but as an idea; now he was going
> to walk through the door and they would look on Lazarus.

And by columnist Tony Snow, in the *Detroit News,* July 10, 1997, commenting on hearings investigating campaign finance abuses:

> The lip-smacking irony of the whole affair is that Republicans
> may succeed in creating an unlikely and (to them) unwanted
> Lazarus. Think about it: Who benefits most if people get tired
> of campaign-finance corruption, disgusted with windbag law-
> makers, suspicious of foreign intriguers and hungry for plain
> talk? . . . Ross Perot.

lean and hungry look An appearance of readiness to fight or act, an attitude of grasping ambition. The phrase is from Shakespeare's *Julius Caesar,* Act 1, Scene 2. Caesar observes to Antony:

> Let me have men about me that are fat;
> Sleek-headed men, and such as sleep o'nights.
> Yond Cassius has a lean and hungry look;
> He thinks too much. Such men are dangerous.

Caesar was right, of course. Gaius Cassius Longinus had opposed Caesar in the war against Pompey, but had nevertheless been pardoned by
the victorious Caesar and given office. Despite this, it was Cassius who
initiated the plot to kill Caesar and who drew Brutus into it.

That lean and hungry look, therefore, is really a state of mind, as illustrated by the term in use by Jaime Diaz in *Sports Illustrated,* April 17,
1995, describing the golfer Billy Casper:

At 63 he has a fleshy face anchored by some all-world jowls, but his narrow, crystalline eyes still have a lean and hungry look.

And by Walter Shapiro, *Esquire,* July 1, 1994, on presidential hopeful Senator Phil Gramm:

The best you can say about Gramm's presidential chances is that he has the lean and hungry look of a contender.

Lear Legendary king of Britain and one of the greatest characters in literature. From Shakespeare's *King Lear,* his name has become a byword for the tragic follies and passions of age.

Lear when old decides to divide his kingdom among his three daughters. But first he demands that they declare their love for him. The first two, Goneril and Regan, insincerely profess their love in the most flattering and excessive manner. Cordelia, the third daughter and her father's favorite, disappoints him by stating her love more simply.

Honest Cordelia is penalized by having her portion divided between the flatterers. Lear realizes his error when Goneril and Regan begin to treat him with contempt; he descends into madness in a scene set in a storm on a desolate, "blasted" heath. The story is unremittingly tragic; Cordelia comes to her father's rescue but dies; Goneril poisons Regan and kills herself; Lear himself dies, brokenhearted.

The term in use, by Christopher Buckley, reviewing *Nixon Off the Record: His Candid Commentary on People and Politics,* by Monica Crowley, in the *New York Times Book Review,* August 25, 1996:

But alas, the Rodney DANGERFIELD of Saddle River got no enduring respect from the Clintons. That realization came when they did not attend the funeral of Mrs. Nixon. It's a harrowing and poignant moment, Lear on the blasted heath. . . .

And by John B. Judis, also in the *New York Times Book Review,* in a review of Lawrence E. Walsh's *Firewall: The Iran-Contra Conspiracy and Cover-up,* June 29, 1997:

By then, Walsh had become a Lear figure, roaming the moors of Washington, railing privately against Bush, the senate minority leader Bob Dole and his other detractors.

lebensraum \\'lä-bənz-,raùm, -bən(t)s-\\ Space required for life, growth, or activity. Also, territory believed, especially by Nazis, to be necessary for national self-sufficiency. In German, it means "living space."

The word summed up Hitler's justification of Germany's aggressive policy of territorial expansion, the rationale being that Germany was crowded and, as the national home of the master race, was entitled to take what it needed.

The term, with a more neutral feel, in use in a *Boston Globe* editorial, December 1, 1985, lauding a company's decision to scale back a building project:

The company evidently decided that neighborliness and civic roots outweighed the need for corporate lebensraum. It has chosen a uniquely Boston solution, respecting the scale and character of the Back Bay.

And by Alan Vonderhaar, reviewing the Nissan Altima for Gannett News Service, September 2, 1997:

It feels like a compact, but still not excessively confining. . . . It's called a five-passenger machine, but you'd need a gun to get three adults into the rear. Two would manage all right if the folks up front were willing to sacrifice a bit of lebensraum.

Legion, my name is "There are many like me." Often applied to other groups of people, animals, spirits—their name is Legion. "Legion" originally designated the armies of Rome, which were organized into groups of 3,000 to 6,000 men. But the word is also used in the sense of an unorganized large gathering or multitude.

This phrase comes from the New Testament of the Bible, Mark, Chapter 5, often referred to as the story of the Gadarene swine. Jesus (having calmed the stormy Sea of Galilee in the previous chapter) arrives in the country of the Gadarenes, where he meets a man possessed by demons, who lives among the tombs, crying and cutting himself with stones. Attempts to capture and chain him have failed, but when the madman sees Jesus, he runs to him and worships him.

Jesus commands the demon possessing the man to come out, and asks his name; the demon answers, "My name is Legion, for we are many." At the command of Jesus, the devil enters a large herd of swine nearby; the animals rush into the sea and are drowned, and the man is restored to his right mind.

The term in use, by Bishop John Shelby Spong of the Episcopal Church, quoted by Larry B. Stammer in the *Los Angeles Times,* October 26, 1996:

People are turning from the church in great numbers, he said, in part because they cannot accept the literal truth of its stories. He said his daughter, who holds a doctorate in physics from Stanford University, is one of them. "She is never going to respond to the simple religion of her past," Spong told the *Times.* "And I think her name is Legion."

And by author Annie Dillard, quoted in the *Seattle Times,* September 24, 1996, when asked if she missed the Pacific Northwest:

The men were just wonderful, but the women out there had a kind of culture I couldn't share. They used chain saws and canned things and they breast-fed. . . . Out there I was suddenly a BLUE-STOCKING. And all of these men were following me around everywhere I went. . . . and every once in a while I'd turn around and say, "You guys, my name is Legion. I'm an Eastern woman; we're all this way." But their women were so dull, you know, that they would give up anything just to hear me for five minutes.

leitmotiv \\'līt-mō-₁tēf\\ A dominant recurring theme. Also a melodic phrase that accompanies the appearance of an idea, person, or situation. In German, it means "leading motive." The concept was developed by German composer Richard Wagner, who attached musical themes to the characters in his operas. Recurrence of the themes was used to heighten the dramatic effect.

The term in use, by Robert Sullivan profiling singer Tony Bennett in *Life,* February 1, 1995:

> There is a leitmotiv running through Bennett's narrative: Somebody told me. He never says, "I say this. . . . " He's careful not to sound egotistical. . . .

And by Michael Kinsley in the *New Republic,* October 10, 1994:

> The collapse of his health care reform has occasioned another round of advice to President Clinton that he needs to be more moderate, govern from the center, be bipartisan, repent his "paleoliberalism" and return to his "New Democrat" roots and so on. This directly contradicts, of course, the pundits' other favorite leitmotiv, on alternate days, that Clinton must show backbone, prove he stands for something, stop waffling and compromising and so on.

lemming A small, short, chubby, furry, and bobtailed rodent indigenous to cold regions of the Northern Hemisphere. The little creatures are famous for mass migrations when excess population drives them to search for food. Once moving, lemmings always travel in a straight line regardless of obstacles, including lakes and rivers, and vast numbers of them die. By extension, to be a lemming is to mindlessly follow the crowd, often to destruction.

The term in use, by Steven B. Kaufman in *Individual Investor,* December 1996:

> As the argument for or against a stock spreads through Wall Street, the lemmings pile on, creating a new path for the stock.

Another stock market reference, in *USA Today Magazine,* December 1, 1995:

> Many investors react to market conditions like lemmings—stampeding up the mountain when markets are rising and down into the cold sea when they are falling.

And by Neil Stebbins in *Ski,* December 1994:

> Most of the local powder puritans think Deer Valley is too flat, too ritzy or too expensive ($47 daily lift tickets at Deer Valley cost exactly $2 more than Park City and $7 more than Snow-

bird), so on powder mornings they all troop like lemmings to Park City and stand in long lines with all the other first-track zombies. Poor misguided souls.

lèse-majesté \‚lāz-'ma-jə-stē, ‚lez-, ‚lēz-\ A detraction from or affront to dignity or importance. It is French for "injured sovereignty." The expression originated in days when kings could be weakened by acts of high treason or rebellion, or by an insult. Now it has a lighter and more ironic meaning and is used to describe an act of impudence to a pompous or self-important figure, or an overblown reaction to an inoffensive act.

The term in use, by Charles Fenyvesi in *U.S. News & World Report,* March 1, 1993, describing an attempt by Mrs. Clinton to shop in a Washington supermarket:

> At first she and Chelsea were able to select several items without causing too much of a stir. However, when they reached the checkout counter, the supermarket manager, apparently worried that he might be committing lèse-majesté by accepting payment for the groceries, was unwilling to take the first lady's personal check.

Another example, from Michael Dirda, in the *Washington Post Book World,* August 27, 1989, reviewing Gary Taylor's *Reinventing Shakespeare:*

> No bardolater, Taylor maintains that Shakespeare's privileged status derives as much from social and political forces as from his virtuosity as a wordsmith, play doctor and theatrical jack of all trades. He hopes that his book-length work of lèse majesté will free readers from culturally conditioned responses of awe, humility, even downright sycophancy.

let a hundred flowers bloom An invitation to an outpouring of diverse opinion.

The invitation was extended by Mao Tse-tung in a speech in 1957, signaling that views that contradicted the party line would be acceptable in the power structure of the People's Republic of China. "Let a hundred flowers bloom," said Mao, "and a hundred schools of thought contend."

This is just what happened for a brief period after Mao's speech, but repression followed in the ensuing years of the Cultural Revolution. This revolution was a reign of terror in the 1960s in which those perceived to oppose it were subjected to public humiliation, mob action, imprisonment, exile to collective farms, and perhaps death.

The expression now is used to put the best face on embarrassing public disagreements among members of a group, or simply to suggest that a multitude of views is being expressed on a certain topic.

The term in use, by Kevin Maney in *USA Today,* August 7, 1997, on the alliance between computer rivals Apple and Microsoft:

> Keep in mind that in the early '80s, when Apple was the PC superpower, Jobs would summon Gates to Apple headquarters and

berate him for making non-Apple software. That was followed
by Gates working relentlessly for the next decade to crush
Apple. . . . The war is over. Let a hundred digital flowers bloom.
But will they?

And by this bank executive, quoted by Peter Nulty in *Fortune,* November 1, 1993:

Richard Huber, vice chairman of Continental, recounts the
bank's decision: "Our system wasn't bad broke, but we were like
a lot of companies. We developed highly centralized operations
in the Seventies and early Eighties. Then it was 'Let a thousand
flowers bloom,' and suddenly we had a crazy quilt of systems.
Some were pretty good, but they couldn't talk to each other."

And by Lance Morrow in *Time,* April 15, 1996, commenting on the
surge of conspiracy theories in the United States:

A hundred paranoias bloomed.

l'état, c'est moi \lä-tà-se-mwà\ Extreme interdependence of the head of
a government or institution and the health of that body, and his extreme
sense of entitlement. In French it means "The state, it is I." The statement
also expresses one's sense of grandeur—or, in most cases, makes fun of
someone else's sense of self-importance. It is attributed to Louis XIV
(1638–1717), called the Sun King and the Grand Monarch, who ruled
France for 72 years.

Whether he said it or not, Louis certainly acted the role. He was an
absolute monarch, in complete control of the French government and
armed forces. He expressed his sense of regal grandeur and entitlement
in constructing the ornate palace and gardens of Versailles and advanced
his policies for domination abroad with constant wars. Under his rule,
France was the strongest nation in Europe, and French art, literature, philosophy, fashion, and music dominated the cultural scene.

The term in use, by Melinda Henneberger in the *New York Times,* August
20, 1997, profiling Andrew Brimmer, head of the board put in place to
reform the government of the District of Columbia:

Even Dr. Brimmer's supporters seem to take an extreme view,
tagging him as the last hope for an unruly place where the timely distribution of parking tickets is widely regarded as the most
reliable city service. There are those who see him as a little too
regal—running through the streets shouting "L'état, c'est moi!"—
and those who feel reassured that he seems willing to do whatever is necessary to make the schools safe and fill the potholes.

And in a July 27, 1989, *Wall Street Journal* editorial on Congressional
perks:

. . . accustomed to the bowing and scraping of huge staffs, intimidated bureaucrats and favor-pleading lobbyists, many Congressmen assume an almost royal arrogance.... The egotism verges on: *l'état, c'est moi.*

let them eat cake A remark expressing heartless and flippant unconcern for the poor.

It is often used to describe the attitude—or economic theories—of one's political opponents by suggesting they lack compassion for the plight of the poor: What, the people lack bread? Let them eat cake.

The remark is often, incorrectly, attributed to Queen Marie Antoinette of France as an illustration of her selfish callousness toward her country's poor. But it actually comes from the writings of the ultra-Romantic Jean-Jacques Rousseau, composed before Marie Antoinette arrived in France:

> At length I recollected the thoughtless saying of a great princess, who on being informed that the country people had no bread, replied "Let them eat cake."

However, Marie Antoinette really was a wasteful, silly spendthrift. Indeed, her brother-in-law, the Duc de Provence, nicknamed her "Madame Deficit."

The term in use, in comments by Alvin Bessent of the *Newsday* editorial board, July 21, 1996:

> Still, with a steely resistance to taxes driving service cuts for people in need, it's tough to justify public subsidies for private sports teams that would probably thrive without a dime of tax money. That feels too much like "let them eat cake" for my taste.

Another example, from Matthew Miller in *Time,* July 21, 1996, on the views of Republican presidential candidate Steve Forbes:

> On social issues, where Forbes' views seem less fully formed, his instincts run from noblesse oblige to let-them-eat-cake.

leviathan \li-ˈvī-ə-thən\ The political state, especially a totalitarian state with a vast bureaucracy. It is from Hebrew, meaning "something large; a formidable monster." Sometimes the word is also used simply to mean something large or formidable.

In the Old Testament there are references to such a creature. For example, "Canst thou draw out Leviathan with a hook?" (Job 41:1). These references spring from an ancient myth in which God conquers a monster which represents chaos. Modern scholars speculate that it may have been a whale, or maybe a crocodile.

Leviathan is also the title of a treatise on government written in 1651 by Thomas Hobbes—a plea for a strong, controlling authority. (*See* HOBBESIAN; NASTY, BRUTISH, AND SHORT.) Thus Hobbes' Leviathan—government—was vast and powerful, and has become a favorite image of those who would like to shrink it.

The term in use, by George Will in the *Washington Post,* May 8, 1997, on the goals of the Republican congressional majority elected in 1994:

They would not just quibble about funding levels for the various tentacles of the federal Leviathan, they would shrink the government's reach, beginning with the abolition of entire Cabinet departments. . . .

And, in its "large and formidable" meaning, by Rick Telander in *Sports Illustrated,* January 23, 1995:

All season the 49ers and the Cowboys had moved relentlessly toward this showdown, a monumental grudge match between the NFL's leviathans.

libido \lə-'bē-(ˌ)dō *also* 'li-bə-ˌdō\ The sexual drive. The word was coined by Sigmund Freud to refer to pleasure-seeking as a motivating force in human activity, a source of psychic energy. The libido is one of the drives that all are born with, like hunger and thirst. (*See* ID.) Although the concept in psychoanalysis is more complex, the term commonly is used simply to mean sexual desire. Winifred Gallagher describes it as "the cranial software of sex," in "Sex and Hormones," in the *Atlantic,* March 1988.

The term in use, by David Briggs of the Associated Press, June 14, 1994, writing on the "True Love Waits" campaign:

Risking the ridicule of their peers, teens said abstinence gives them an opportunity for redemption in a culture that often expects them to give their libidos free rein.

And by Terry Wallace of the Associated Press, September 20, 1993, on the rapid expansion of "personals" ads in newspapers:

Those answering an ad dial up a "900" telephone voice-mail system at a cost of up to $2 per minute. Then the advertiser screens the responses by dialing the same number, also at a cost of up to $2 per minute.

"People don't want to pay for anything unless it's libido-driven. Then, the sky's the limit," said Richard Wallace, information service director for the *Village Voice*.

And in its adjectival form, by Greg Gardner in *Ward's Auto World,* May 1, 1996, reviewing the history of the automobile:

While Calvinists such as Henry Ford purposefully designed the Model T's seat so short as to discourage sexual intercourse, other manufacturers responded to young drivers' more libidinous tendencies.

The 1925 Jewett featured a fold-down bed. Nash introduced bed conversions in its 1937 models.

lilliputian \ˌli-lə-'pyü-shən\ *often capitalized* Small or miniature; petty.

The word derives from Lilliput, the name of the fictitious country in Jonathan Swift's satire, *Gulliver's Travels* (1726). The inhabitants, Lilliputians, are tiny, about one-twelfth human size, and small and petty in their lives, outlook, and politics. They are able to subdue Gulliver by tying him down in his sleep with hundreds of tiny ropes. Although he cooperates with his captors at first, he decides to make his escape when they begrudge him food and contemplate blinding him.

The term in use, by Rita Kempley, surveying love stories in contemporary movies in the *Washington Post,* August 3, 1997:

> Beauties, however, have become the beasts, which brings us back to Julia Roberts. What big hair she has, my dear, and what big teeth. These are Lilliputian, though, when compared with her cussedness as a green-eyed monster in *My Best Friend's Wedding.*

And from Anthony Dias Blue in *Wine Spectator,* June 30, 1995:

> Negotiating Bali, however, can be an adventure. The island feels like a lilliputian kingdom. Everything is very small in scale and tightly crammed together.

lily *See* GILD THE LILY.

lingua franca \\'liŋ-gwə-'fraŋ-kə\\ Any of various languages used as common tongues among different peoples; something resembling a common language. The term is also applied to the specialized jargon and terms of reference of particular professions, technical fields, or other subcultures. In Italian it means "Frankish language."

The original lingua franca was a hybrid language which developed in Mediterranean ports in the 17th century. A mixture of Italian, French, Spanish, Greek, Arabic, and maybe more, it became the language of commerce in the lively trade of the region.

Pidgin English is a similar sort of language; it originated in the English-Chinese trade in the 17th century.

The term in use, by Paul Farhi in the *Washington Post,* April 28, 1997:

> The Federal Communications Commission gave each of the nation's 1,600 TV stations a second channel over which to transmit programs in digital form, the computer language that has become the lingua franca of modern communications.

And in *Foundation News & Commentary,* January/February 1997:

> A current NCRP [National Center for Responsible Philanthropy] study reports that conservative foundations have been making extremely strategic grants over the past two decades, leading the way in making conservative ideas *lingua franca,* and paving the ground for the recent conservative takeover of Congress.

And by Gore Vidal in *American Heritage,* September 1992:

> Movies are the lingua franca of the twentieth century. The Tenth Muse, as they call the movies in Italy, has driven the other nine right off Olympus—or off the peak anyway.

lion *See* BEARD THE LION IN HIS DEN.

lion in winter A proud, prominent, strong man whose great strength and dignity have been eroded by age and adversity.

The quintessential example is England's King Henry II, portrayed in James Goldman's play *The Lion in Winter,* made into a successful film starring Peter O'Toole as Henry and Katherine Hepburn as Queen Eleanor.

Henry was an energetic king and bold soldier and had built a great empire in England and France. But at age 50—a venerable age in that violent era—the indomitable old lion was embattled. He faced threats from the king of France, the plots and rivalries of his three ambitious sons, and above all the formidable opposition of his imprisoned queen.

At the end of Goldman's story, nothing is decided; but Henry transcends his crises and defies his fate, still able to roar.

The title of the play combines the image of the British royal lion with the winter of old age and adversity—and the cold drafts of a medieval castle in December.

The term in use, by Walter Shapiro in *USA Today,* May 29, 1996:

> Four years after his marriage to the former Victoria Reggie, Kennedy has become, by all accounts, a man of modest habits. Yet the news stories that hail his lion-in-winter revival contrast this comeback with earlier tales of over-aged carousing.

Another example, quoted by Maureen Dowd, in the *New York Times,* February 1, 1996:

> Bill Kristol, the editor of the *Standard,* who has wooed Colin Powell and raised the Dole age issue, now says: "I hope he can play the lion-in-winter card. There's something moving about the guy's stoicism."

little cat feet *See* ON LITTLE CAT FEET.

loaves and fishes The feeding of the four thousand, one of the miracles of Jesus in the New Testament (Matt. 15:32; Mark 8:1).

Thousands of people followed Jesus into the wilderness to hear him preach. There was very little food for the great crowd, and the disciples nervously suggested that the people be sent away. But Jesus said to go ahead and feed them and blessed the few loaves of bread and the fish that they had among them. The food was miraculously multiplied and the multitudes were fed.

The phrase occurs in praise of resourceful and bountiful hosts or cooks who provide meals out of seemingly little. It is also seen in the phrase "having an eye to the loaves and fishes," that is, having an eye on physical and material needs rather than the spiritual. As Jesus said, "Ye seek me, not because ye saw the miracles, but because ye did eat of the loaves and were filled," and urged his followers to labor not for food which perishes, but for the spiritual nourishment which endures.

The term in use, by Phyllis Richman in the *Washington Post,* April 19, 1989:

> On April 27, the more you eat, the more there will be for the poor to eat. Call it the modern version of loaves and fishes—the miracle of the patés and mousses. It's the second annual Taste of the Nation, a 50-city feast organized by Share Our Strength, a nonprofit network of chefs and restauranteurs dedicated to fighting hunger.

And by Reagan Walker and Michelle Hiskey in the *Atlanta Journal and Constitution,* April 28, 1997, describing the meeting of the American Quilters Society in Paducah, Kentucky:

> And when it comes to feeding 30,000 quilters, it's loaves-and-fishes time. Restaurants alone can't handle the impact, so area clubs and churches pitch in. . . .

Lochinvar \'läk-in-ˌvär, ˌlȯk-in-'vär\ The hero of a ballad within the long narative poem *Marmion* by Sir Walter Scott (1771–1832), and hence a dashing young man who elopes with a young woman. Also, in a broader sense, a romantic suitor or a bold and handsome young man of action.
Lochinvar's lady love, the fair Ellen, enters a loveless marriage with another suitor ("a laggard in love, a dastard in war"). Lochinvar appears at the wedding feast and asks for one last dance with the bride. The young knight then sweeps her out the door and sets her on his horse ("through all the wide Border his steed was the best") and dashes away with her.
The term in use, by Charles Michener in *Time,* reviewing Mary Cantwell's *Manhattan, When I Was Young,* September 19, 1995:

> More fleshed out is the man she married and, after two children, divorced—a New York literary agent identified only as "B." Coming from a family of Jewish leftwing intellectuals, he was the perfect Lochinvar to take her out of Rhode Island. . . .

And by J. Anthony Lukas in the *New York Times Magazine,* March 12, 1989, on Harvard's Kennedy School of Government:

> What liberated Harvard's governmental studies from this cul de sac was the death of the university's young Lochinvar. Twenty-seven days after John F. Kennedy's assassination in 1963, his brothers convened a small group of present and former Harvard professors . . . to devise a "living memorial."

Lolita \lō-'lē-tə\ The title and central character of a 1955 novel (published in 1958 in the U.S.) by Vladimir Nabokov; a precociously seductive girl. Lolita is a 12-year-old girl, the sexual obsession of a middle-aged man, HUMBERT HUMBERT. To be close to her Humbert marries the girl's mother. She discovers his pedophilia but is run over by a Packard before she can unmask him. Humbert then clumsily attempts to seduce his stepdaughter; she is unwilling but less than naïve and seduces and enthralls him. The two then embark on an odyssey across the United States, from one third-rate motel to the next—and much, much more.

In a simplification of Nabokov's complex and shocking novel, Lolita is now generally applied to preadolescent girls who are knowingly seductive, or are displayed seductively in advertising or fashion, or who are the object of the sexual fantasies of older men.

The term in use, by the Associated Press, May 18, 1995:

> The ninth-grader who spent two months on the run with her gym teacher came home yesterday. . . . Mr. Harris has portrayed himself as a do-gooder who rescued Christina from a life of abuse at her parents' hands. Police believe they were involved in a "Lolita"-style love affair.

Another example, by Marylou Luther, in the *Christian Science Monitor,* November 18, 1993:

> The 18- to 34-year-old market is shrinking. It is also the one hardest hit by the economy. The 40- to 70-year-old market—the core group for designer merchandise—is growing. And yet many designers persisted this season in offering clothes patterned after the little girl/Lolita/nymphet model.

And also in the *Christian Science Monitor,* April 23, 1991, in Thomas D'Evelyn's review of *The Miracle Game* by Josef Skvorecky:

> Danny meets his avenging angel in one of his students. A blend of Lolita and wood nymph, Vixi is an orphan whose yellow T-shirt and dirty tennis shoes only emphasize her loveliness.

Loman, Willy \\'lō-mən\ The central character in Arthur Miller's 1949 play *Death of a Salesman,* which is a scathing indictment of the American value of material success over all else. The play won the New York Drama Critics Circle Award and the Pulitzer Prize.

Willy Loman is an aging salesman whose professional and family lives are crumbling. Neither he nor his two sons have achieved the financial gain and status he yearns for, despite his sacrifice of his principles to that end. As playwright Miller sardonically has noted, Willy had broken an unwritten law that says that a failure in society and business has no right to live. Says Miller: "The law of success is not administered by statute or church, but it is nearly as powerful in its grip upon men."

As the play ends, Willy loses his job and sees the emptiness of his life. His son Biff tells him, "Pop! I'm a dime a dozen and so are you!" Willy kills himself in the illusory belief that his life insurance money will enable Biff to finally become a success.

The term in use, by Bob Minzesheimer in *USA Today,* April 3, 1997, reviewing Don Snyder's book *The Cliff Walk:*

The Cliff Walk is about the arrogance of privilege and losing something bigger than a job or money. A professor without a classroom, Snyder becomes as lost as Willy Loman, the fictional salesman he once lectured about, the salesman with nothing left to sell.

And in an editorial in the *Philadelphia Inquirer,* November 30, 1994, on the death of Yippie leader Jerry Rubin:

> In Jerry Rubin, salesman, Brentwood resident, consciousness shopper, not so certain anymore, the anti-warriors of old had their own Willy Loman, the American dreamer at inglorious end.

long march A bitter or difficult period of trial from which an individual or an institution emerges stronger and ready to take power; a long and audacious journey. The expression comes from the 5,000-mile trek undertaken (1934–35) during the Chinese civil war by 90,000 embattled men and women who constituted the Red Army of the Chinese Communist Party under Mao Tse-tung.

Mao and his followers marched from southwest to central China, crossing 18 mountain ranges and 24 rivers in about a year. More than half of them perished, but the survivors who arrived in Shensi Province in 1935 were toughened and unified. From this crucible they emerged to take control of all China.

The term in use, by Mary McGrory, on House Speaker Newt Gingrich, in the *Washington Post,* January 9, 1997:

> There is no single figure in their political lives to whom they are more beholden. Gingrich was the grand marshal of their long march back to power, the Che Guevara of their revolution.

And by Yasser Arafat, quoted by Scheherezade Faramarzi of the Associated Press, February 12, 1996, at his inauguration as president of the Palestinian Authority:

> "I feel I have a very big responsibility on my shoulders, to carry on our long march, to continue in the peace process, to continue building our future," he told reporters after the ceremony, which closed with a band playing the Palestinian anthem. . . .

And by Walter Mossberg in the *Wall Street Journal,* July 7, 1994:

> It's the final leg in Microsoft's long march to give IBM-compatible computers the relative simplicity and ease of use of Apple's Macintosh machines, still the gold standard in user-friendly computing.

loose cannon A dangerously uncontrollable person or thing.

The expression comes from naval warfare and predates fixed-turret guns aboard ships. In earlier days, muzzle-loading cannons were mounted on wheeled carriages so they could be run in and out of gunports for loading and firing. When not in use they were lashed down. If a cannon came loose, that huge mass of metal careening hither and yon with every roll of the ship was a danger to everyone and everything in its path and to the ship itself.

The term in use, by Lt. Col. Oliver North in his testimony to the congressional committees investigating the Iran-contra affair, as reported in the *Washington Post,* July 8, 1987:

> I don't want you to think, counsel, that I went about this all on my own. I realized, there's a lot of folks around that think there's a loose cannon on the gun deck at the NSC. That wasn't what I heard while I worked there. I've only heard it since I left. People used to walk up to me and tell me what a great job I was doing.

And some variations on the theme, from Maureen Dowd in the *New York Times,* September 10, 1989, writing about Bush administration drug czar William Bennett:

> He rubbed other administration officials the wrong way, jumped too far out ahead on a couple of initiatives, and seemed about to fulfill predictions by White House advisors that he would be a black sheep, a bull in a china shop, a loose cannon, a Lone Ranger, "Mr. Aggressive Steam Roller," or, in a moniker Mr. Bennett was given when he was appointed to head the National Endowment for the Humanities, "a fat boy in a canoe."

And by Ron Fournier of the Associated Press, February 17, 1996, on the activities of political consultant Dick Morris:

> Dick Morris' secret overture to Bob Dole's campaign angered his boss the president and threatened Friday to widen a rift in the Clinton camp.
>
> Feeding his reputation as a loose cannon, Morris leaked internal poll results to a Dole adviser, arguing it would be in the Senate majority leader's political interest to cut a budget deal with President Clinton.

Lorelei \\'lōr-ə-ˌlī, 'lȯr-\\ A woman of irresistible allure. The name is taken from a crag in a gorge of the Rhine River near St. Goarshausen in Germany. Its shoals make it a hazard to navigation, and the promontory is famous also for its echo. The site was first associated with a woman in the early 19th century in a ballad by Clemens Brentano. Heinrich Heine's poem *Die Lorelei* (1827) established the idea of the supernatural siren who combs her blonde tresses and lures sailors to their doom with her song.

A modern comic incarnation is Lorelei Lee, the gold-digging heroine of Anita Loos' 1925 novel, *Gentleman Prefer Blondes.* The novel became a successful play and more successful musical with songs by Jule Styne and Leo Robin, the most famous being "Diamonds Are a Girl's Best

Friend." Carol Channing was a memorable stage Lorelei and Marilyn Monroe played the role in the 1953 film.

The term in use, by Thomas A. Stewart, *Fortune,* October 19, 1992:

> But beside the river of opportunity sits the Lorelei that seduced manufacturers: restructuring without investing in growth.

And by Liz Smith in *People,* November 3, 1986, profiling actress Kathleen Turner:

> In 1981 came her movie debut as the flesh-peddling Lorelei who lures William Hurt to his doom in *Body Heat.*

And by Ronnie Scheib in *Film Comment,* July-August 1990:

> In Wender's German films, the transpositions were explicit: heroes that wander in space because they cannot place themselves in time, seduced by the Lorelei call of Hollywood because they have no story or, being German, no story that can be told and lived with.

Lost Generation American and European writers and intellectuals who came of age during and after World War I. Disillusioned by their war experience and the social upheavals that followed, they rebelled against old values and ideals they considered discredited by the horrors of war and sank instead into cynicism and hedonism. By extension, usually not capitalized, any generation shaped by so jarring an experience.

"You are all a lost generation," American expatriate Gertrude Stein told Ernest Hemingway, one of the best known of the group. Others included F. Scott Fitzgerald, e.e. cummings, Ezra Pound, John Dos Passos, and Archibald MacLeish.

The term in use, by Michael J. Jordan in the *Christian Science Monitor,* October 24, 1996, on memories of the abortive Hungarian uprising against Soviet domination in 1956:

> Today, however as [Hungary] celebrates the uprising's 40th anniversary, most veterans wash their hands of the "lost generations"—the millions of Hungarians born after 1956 and taught to believe popular revolt against the Communists was, in fact, a counterrevolution perpetrated by the dregs of society.

Another example, also from the *Christian Science Monitor,* by James L. Tyson, December 21, 1988:

> During the past decade of economic reform, Zhang has seen communist leaders repudiate the Maoist ideals for which he sacrificed his education and risked his life. . . . Zhang is a member of what is known as China's "lost generation." As China races toward prosperity, he and other erstwhile Red Guards have been nudged into the slow lane by the older Chinese they persecuted and better-trained, younger Chinese. At first abused and now

neglected by the Communist Party, the group is a persistent source of social discontent.

lothario *often capitalized* A libertine, a careless or lighthearted seducer of women; a rake. The original was a character in a play, *The Fair Penitent* (1703) by English poet and playwright Nicholas Rowe. The term is often modified by the adjective gay, as in the play: "Is this that Haughty, Gallant and Gay Lothario?" There was a similar character in an even earlier play, *Cruel Brother* (1630) by Sir William Davenant.

The term in use, by Margaret Talbot in the *New Republic,* October 12, 1998:

> So what if one or two feminist leaders decided to try to reconcile their hard line on Republican Lotharios with their soft spot for Clinton not by turning on Clinton but by considering that maybe they were wrong in the past?

And by Don Aucoin in the *Boston Globe,* September 2, 1995:

> Once stigmatized as the province of desperate "losers" or fast-lane Lotharios, personal ads are becoming an accepted, even respectable, way to meet someone.

Lot's wife In a Biblical tale (Gen. 19:26), a disobedient woman who was turned into a pillar of salt as punishment for looking back to see the destruction of Sodom and Gomorrah as she and her family fled. Often evoked to remind us not to choose a worldly life, and never to look back.

According to Genesis, Lot was the nephew of Abraham. Lot and his wife and two daughters lived in the city of Sodom (*see* SODOM AND GOMOR-RAH), which was condemned to destruction for its wickedness. God sent angels disguised as men to look for ten righteous men in the city, but Lot was the only one found. As the host of these visitors, he had been gracious enough to offer them his virgin daughters, a form of righteousness not recognized today.

Lot was warned by angels to flee the city with his family, and not to look back as the city was destroyed. Lot's wife disobeyed, turned to look back, and was turned into a pillar of salt. Lot and his daughters escaped; since they were convinced that the rest of mankind had been destroyed, the daughters made their father drunk and copulated with him. Their children were the ancestors of the Moabites and Ammonites.

The sites of Sodom and Gomorrah are thought to be near the Dead Sea, where there are deposits of asphalt and bitumen which could have been ignited by the earthquakes to which the area is subject. There is also a salt mountain nearby and formations which could account for the legend of a woman turned to a pillar of salt.

The term in use, by George Will, in a column in the *Washington Post,* December 11, 1995:

> From afar, Phil Gramm's campaign resembles Lot's wife after God, who did not make a liberal's therapeutic response to trans-

gressions, turned her into a pillar of salt. Immobile, Gramm
seems.

And by Frank McConnell in *Commonweal,* February 11, 1994, describing his experience of the Northridge, California earthquake—when, of course, they all stayed closely tuned to television:

> It's a welcome palliative to anxiety: as long as the broadcast is
> on you know, at least, that L.A. hasn't been swallowed whole. It
> may not be McLuhan's idyllic GLOBAL VILLAGE, but it is something like the small-town thing where, when your house is struck
> by lightning, the neighbors come by just to let you know they're
> there. . . . And of course there's voyeurism involved: TV is, after
> all, a human medium, and since Lot's wife—the first TV junkie—
> that's been one of our best things.

Lotusland A dreamy, indolent, self-indulgent place where unreality prevails. In contemporary use in the United States it is applied to California. Canadians apply the same term to their beauteous western province, British Columbia, and for the same reasons—to mock its propensity for sometimes wacky political and social trends.

The term originates in the *Odyssey,* however. On their long voyage home from the Trojan War, Odysseus and his men come upon the land of the lotus-eaters. Some of the men eat the food, and forget their homes and wives; they want to stay in the land of the lotus eaters and abandon their hard life of fighting and pulling endlessly at their oars. Odysseus drags them all unwilling back to the boat and resumes his journey.

Alfred, Lord Tennyson describes the place in his 1832 poem *The Lotos-Eaters*—it was a place "In which it seemed always afternoon./All round the coast the languid air did swoon,/Breathing like one that hath a weary dream."

The lotus here is probably not the water lily, but the buckthorn, a shrubby plant with a sweet juice used for making candy. The plant is also known as the jujube, which has given its name to the extremely sticky candy often sold in movie theaters. There is no reference in Homer to wholesale destruction of ancient Greek dental work, however.

In American use, the name is frequently applied to Los Angeles, or southern California.

The term in use, by Lee Grove in the *Boston Globe,* May 9, 1982:

> It is a lotusland wholly unto itself, LA. Everywhere you sit, Butterfield's, Schwabb's, even the now very grubby Brown Derby,
> the men around you are talking movies, eating movies, sleeping
> with movies, divorcing movies.

And by Erik Heinrich in the *Toronto Star,* January 20, 1999:

> But take a walk down Hastings St. from Main to Richards Sts.—
> a distance of some seven blocks—and an entirely different picture of Vancouver [B.C.] emerges. Here you fnd the ugly

underbelly of Lotusland: skid row spreads out before you like a thoroughfare recently used by ATTILA and his Mongol hordes.

lounge lizard A ladies man; a fop; a social parasite. A cheap LOTHARIO. Lothario was himself a seducer of women in the 1703 play by Nicholas Rowe, *The Fair Penitent*. Picture him in a shiny suit, pointy-toed shoes, with every hair slicked into place above his leering visage.

Lounge lizard is a slang term from the early 20th century. William Safire says the expression was coined around 1912 to describe cheapskates who wanted to pet in a girl's parlor without first taking her out for a soda and movie.

The term in use, by Woody Baird of the Associated Press, January 8, 1993, on the Elvis Presley commemorative stamp:

> A nationwide election was held last summer to select artwork for the stamp, and more than 1 million ballots were cast. Fans went for a portrait of Presley as he looked in the 1950s, instead of the chubbier, lounge lizard look before his death.

And Alex Heard, writing in the *New Republic*, February 13, 1989, refers to "oilsoaked lounge iguana Julio Iglesias." Again, quoted by Lou Cannon in the *Washington Post*, November 5, 1987, on the rising star of General Colin Powell:

> He is similarly valued by former Pentagon colleagues. "He's not a guy who's come up as a Pentagon lounge lizard," an Army official said. "He's got a lot of field time."

loyal opposition *often capitalized L&O* In two-party systems such as those in the United States and Britain, the out-of-power political party.

The phrase suggests that the party not in power remains loyal to the country while disagreeing on policy matters with the party in power. In Britain, the outs have official status and are described as "His (or Her) Majesty's Loyal Opposition." The leader of the Opposition has a "shadow cabinet" of members with expertise who put forth the Opposition's views on matters relating to government policies. The public has the advantage of hearing what the other side would do on a given issue and knowing in advance who would hold key government positions should the Opposition win a majority and take over the government.

Wendell Wilkie, FDR's Republican opponent in 1940, helped to popularize the concept in this country. Following his defeat, he described the role of the GOP in the face of war in Europe: "A vital element in the balanced operation of democracy is a strong, alert and watchful opposition. . . . Let us not, therefore, fall into the partisan error of opposing things just for the sake of opposition."

The idea lacks official status in the United States, and doesn't work as well outside a parliamentary structure. Things become complicated in this country when one party controls the presidency and the other the Congress.

The term in use, by Calvin Woodward of the Associated Press, June 14, 1997:

> By comparison with the British parliamentary system, where a defeated party leader may lick wounds in the comfort of Her Majesty's Loyal Opposition, U.S. presidential politics are brutally efficient at the top. You lose, you're outta here.

And by James Pinkerton, in commentary in the *Philadelphia Inquirer,* October 6, 1997:

> Just as it took a Democratic-controlled Congress to get to the bottom of Republican executive branch misdeeds in Watergate and Iran-contra, so today a loyal opposition is needed as a watchdog over an over-reaching IRS.

And used figuratively by Francis Davis in the *Atlantic,* January 1990:

> Davis's reaction was typical of that of most young musicians in the 1940s. What thrilled them about bebop was its impossible combination of the breakneck and the BYZANTINE. It was all they wanted to hear and all they wanted to play. But an early mark of Davis's singularity was that soon after becoming Gillespie's protégé and Parker's sideman, he also became their loyal opposition.

Lucullan \lü-'kə-lən\ Rich, self-indulgent, opulent. It is an adjective fashioned from the name of a Roman general, Lucius Licinius Lucullus Ponticus (ca. 110 B.C.–56 B.C.). He was successful in war and brought home enough booty to live in great luxury when politics forced him out of his command.

The term in use, by Maya Angelou in *I Know Why the Caged Bird Sings* (1969):

> The needs of a society determine its ethics, and in the Black American ghettos the hero is that man who is offered only the crumbs from his country's table but by ingenuity and courage is able to take for himself a Lucullan feast.

And by Kevin Doyle in *Condé Nast Traveler,* Novmber 1994:

> For most, gaining a few easily shed pounds is a small price to pay for a week or two of Lucullan bliss. But others don't see it that way. "Some people feel so bad about gaining weight on vacation that they lose all their restraint when they return home," says Cathy Nonas, a registered dietitian at St. Luke's-Roosevelt Hospital in Manhattan.

And by Ted Levin in *Yankee,* May 1993:

> . . . and are geared for a nine-inning feeding frenzy: a Lucullan feast of hot dogs, peanuts, and melted ice-cream sandwiches. For them, the park is one of Boston's premier bird feeders.

Luddites A group of early 19th-century English workmen who destroyed laborsaving machines as a protest; hence, a person who is opposed to change, especially technological change.

The original Luddites date from 1811–16. They were bands of craftsmen in the days of Britain's Industrial Revolution, who smashed textile machines that were displacing them from their jobs. They were named after their semi-mythical leader, Ned Ludd.

The movement had its casualties: one band was shot in 1812 at the order of a manufacturer who felt threatened; he in turn was himself murdered. Twenty-four were hanged after a trial at York and others imprisoned or transported to Australia. At one point, Parliament debated the death penalty for the act of destroying textile machinery. A period of prosperity, laying the workers' worst fears to rest, put an end to the movement.

The term in use, by British author John Mortimer, quoted in *British Heritage,* April-May 1997:

> Mortimer on computers: "I'm a luddite. I think the whole thing should be abolished.... We bought something at Saks Fifth Avenue and it took half an hour for the person to do all this tick-tack typing. You used to go to hotels and they'd look on a list and you were in the room. All these machines slow up lives so incredibly."

And by John Gerstner and Phil Theibert in *Communication World,* June 16, 1996, in a profile of computer skeptic Clifford Stoll, author of *Silicon Snake Oil: Second Thoughts On The Information Superhighway* (1995):

> Stoll's attack on cyber-life would be easier to dismiss if he were simply another neo-Luddite smashing computers out of ignorance or fear. But Stoll is more reformed technogeek than technophobe.

lumpen proletariat \\'lùm-pən-ˌprō-lə-'ter-ē-ət, -'tar-, -ē-ˌat; 'ləm-\\ Dispossessed and uprooted individuals cut off from the lowest social and economic class. A German word coined by Marx to describe the poorest and most ignorant, the lowest class in society, even below the working-class proletariat.

It combines the German "lumpen"—"rags"—with the Latin-based "proletariat," from "proletarius," someone of the lowest class. It is often used now to suggest someone with lowbrow, anti-intellectual, or vulgar tastes, rather than an economic underclass.

The term in use, by Margo Howard, in the *New Republic,* May 18, 1987, reviewing *Vanna Speaks* by Vanna White, a sex object in television's vast wasteland:

> [S]he is the designated hostess of a television show called *Wheel of Fortune,* offering her life story because, presumably, millions of her fans are interested. The real answer is that Vanna White is the pinup girl of the lumpen proletariat, and this rambling col-

lection of you-name-it is an odd and strangely honest reply to
fan mail.

And by Frank Gaffney, in commentary in the *Washington Times,* October 9, 1995:

Americans, male and female, who listen to talk radio . . . are
affluent and well-educated. These Americans may not be the
"overclass" that so many gabble about these days, but they're
not exactly the lumpenproletariat.

And by J. Anthony Lukas in the *New York Times Book Review,* October
11, 1987:

As spy case after spy case bubbles to the surface in the 1980's, it
is clear that spies are the product less of a haughty elite than of
an American *lumpen* proletariat—rootless, bored, resentful and
mercenary.

*The trick of leadership is to project confidence. . . . The **man on horseback** has to look in control. Panic is contagious.*
—Jim Murray

Macbeth, Lady Wife of Macbeth, protagonist of Shakespeare's tragedy *Macbeth*. A woman of ruthless, unbridled ambition who influences and dominates her weaker-willed husband.

Lady Macbeth is instrumental in the events of Shakespeare's bloody tragedy. When she learns of the prophecy that her husband will be the future king of Scotland, she urges him to murder the king. When he reluctantly does so, it is she who steadies his nerves and places the bloody daggers next to the guards who are then blamed for the act. Ultimately she is driven insane by her guilty conscience and struggles to wash unseen blood from her hands ("Out, damned spot! out, I say!" *Macbeth* Act 5, Scene 1).

The term in use, quoted by Laura Blumenfeld, *Newsday,* April 9, 1996:

> "If Hillary is Lady Macbeth, Elizabeth Dole is Cinderella," says Kathleen Hall Jamieson, dean of the Annenberg School of Communications at the University of Pennsylvania.

Another example, by William Schneider in an editorial in the *Los Angeles Times,* May 28, 1995:

> Along came GOP strategist William Kristol, the Lady Macbeth of the fax machine: "Screw your courage to the sticking place, and we'll not fail."

And yet another reference to Mrs. Clinton, by Tom Teepen of Cox News Service, in the *Kansas City Star,* January 14, 1996:

> . . . Mrs. Clinton likely played First Lady Macbeth, though she had said she did not, in the stupid decision to fire the White House travel staff, presumably in favor of turning its duties over to old Clinton friends.

MacGuffin *or* **McGuffin** As defined by movie director Alfred Hitchcock, a MacGuffin is a catalyst that sets off the action in the story but which turns out to be otherwise of little importance.

Hitchcock said he took the word from a shaggy dog story in which train passengers asked a fellow passenger about the large, odd-shaped package he was carrying. He said it was a "MacGuffin" and explained that it was for catching tigers in the Scottish Highlands. They said that there were no tigers in the Highlands, and he responded that there were no MacGuffins either.

This nonstarter of a story nevertheless suggests what Hitchcock meant—what the characters in the story were chasing or worrying about was not really important, and what counted for the audience was the characters.

The term in use, by Michael McWilliams, television critic for the *Detroit News,* April 11, 1997:

> The Hitchcockian MacGuffin in *Gun* is the pearl-handled gun itself, which passes from hand to hand in each episode.

And by James Wolcott, reviewing an episode of *The X-Files* in the *New Yorker:*

> A recent two-parter, which began promisingly, with a Martian rock as a biohazardous McGuffin, broke down into a heap of head-scratching "Huh?"s. At one point, a Senate hearing is held to determine Mulder's whereabouts . . . , and when Mulder himself finally reappears— . . . having just made the world's fastest escape from a Russian GULAG—he isn't even questioned.

And from Kevin Ray, reviewing *Jackson's Dilemma* by Iris Murdoch in the *St. Louis Post-Dispatch,* April 14, 1996:

> What follows is a near-total reshuffling of alliances and affections, at the center of which is the late, mysterious Uncle Tim, a traveler, a misfit, a mystic, one of Murdoch's characteristic figures of romance and mystery, a kind of MacGuffin who, while absent, affects everyone's life and sets the novel's plot in motion.

Machiavellian \ˌma-kē-ə-ˈve-lē-ən, -ˈvel-yən\ Marked by cunning, duplicity, or bad faith. The word derives from the name of Niccolo Machiavelli (1469–1527), an Italian statesman and writer often considered a pioneer of modern political science because he attempted to report clearly and realistically what heads of state really do and why.

Machiavelli's most famous work is *The Prince* (1513), which closely analyzed the methods of the princes reigning over the warring city-states of Italy. Machiavelli concluded that human beings basically were corrupt, and that a successful ruler did what was necessary to keep this base nature under control.

In fairness, we should report that Machiavelli himself had ideals—he believed in a republican form of government, favored citizen armies rather than mercenaries, and opposed senseless cruelty. Historians acknowledge these virtuous sentiments, but nothing will shake Machiavelli's identification with ruthless, cold-blooded politics in which the end justifies the means.

The term in use, by Charles Trueheart in the *Washington Post,* June 14, 1992, revisiting the Watergate scandal:

But for sheer sanctimony and Machiavellian gall, nothing comes close to Nixon's quickly adding, after swaggering on at length about his ability to lay his hands on a million dollars of hush money, that it would be wrong: a sidelong whisper to his conscience, not to mention the whirring tape recorders reeling him down into history.

And by Elaine Ganley of the Associated Press, March 24, 1994, describing French president Francois Mitterand:

A consummate strategist, Mitterand did not shirk at Machiavellian tactics, but remained loyal to friends tainted by corruption scandals that plagued his administration.

madding crowd *See* FAR FROM THE MADDING CROWD.

magic bullet A substance or therapy able to destroy pathogenic agents—bacteria or cancer cells—without damaging side effects.

Sometimes the same properties are assigned to real silver bullets which have the legendary power to kill vampires. The Lone Ranger, a hero of radio and television, also had bullets made of silver; thus, like a magic bullet, a weapon to destroy the most fearsome foe.

The term in use, on the benefits of a high-fiber diet, quoted by Carole Sugarman in the *Washington Post,* August 1, 1989:

James Cleeman, a physician and coordinator of the National Cholesterol Education Program, is concerned about focusing too narrowly on psyllium and other soluble fibers. "They are not a magic bullet," he said.

Another example, from the *Arizona Republic,* February 21, 1990:

"We no longer have a magic bullet," said Dr. Marilyn Roberts, a pathologist at the University of Washington, where studies have found tetracycline-resistant bacteria prevalent even in women who have no recent exposure to the drug.

And by William Grimes in the *New York Times,* January 23, 1996:

No wonder that Americans frantically pick apart every new piece of scientific research on diet, looking for a magic bullet, a license to gorge.

Maginot Line \\'ma-zhə-ˌnō, 'ma-jə-\\ A line of fortifications built before World War II to protect France's eastern border, but easily outflanked by German invaders; thus also a defense easily overcome by innovative strategy.

In the First World War, heavily fortified positions played a decisive role and, after the slaughters of that war, such technology that could protect manpower had a powerful appeal. André Maginot, the French minister of war, conceived the Line as a foolproof protection against the power of a resurgent Germany—it had the thickest concrete walls, biggest guns, even air conditioning for the troops, who were moved about on underground railways.

It was a perfect strategy for winning World War I. Unfortunately, it was not right for World War II. The Maginot Line was rendered irrelevant by the new, highly mobile style of warfare adopted by the Germans. Instead of attacking France through the Maginot Line, the German army simply moved through the "impassable" Ardennes forest in southern Belgium and Luxembourg and swept south behind the helpless, fixed defenses.

The line has its defenders, however; they argue that it succeeded because the Germans were forced to go around it.

The term in use, by Marilyn Chase in the *Wall Street Journal,* October 3, 1994:

> "This plague epidemic shows us that we've been thinking in old-fashioned ways about the realities of disease in the modern world. It's the Maginot Line approach—create a barrier and stand behind it. That won't work," says Jonathan Mann, a professor at Harvard University's school of public health. Nor will it work to wait for disaster and then react too late.

And by Howard Rosenberg in the *Baltimore Sun,* February 14, 1988, discussing the heavy press coverage of the Iowa precinct caucuses:

> Major media are journalistic Maginot lines—rigid, immovable and unalterable once committed and in place. By the time TV began wondering aloud about this year's overcoverage, the major media had already spent so much energy and money on the coverage that they had a vested interest in the process. In fact, they had become part of the process.

And by Josef Joffe in the *New York Times Magazine,* June 8, 1997:

> Culturally, America's clout is so overwhelming that its oldest ally, France, is once more building Maginot lines—this time not against German panzers but against American movies and even words. You know you're on a roll when other governments threaten their own citizens with hefty fines for calling a *lavage voiture* a "car wash."

Main Street The principal street of a small town, and an environment of materialistic, complacent provincialism. Also the title of a novel by Sinclair Lewis published in 1920, a portrait of provincialism and boosterism at their least attractive.

Lewis's *Main Street* gives us the fictional town of Gopher Prairie, Minnesota, and tells of the efforts of Carol Kennicott, the spirited wife of the local doctor, to introduce culture to the townsfolk. She fails and leaves for a time to pursue her own life, but finally returns.

Gopher Prairie was modeled on Lewis's hometown of Sauk Centre, Minnesota, which knew it and didn't like it. In fact, it took many years for the town to forgive and honor Lewis for his famous portrayal of it as a dull, isolated, and inward-turning town.

Main Street has come to refer to the insular attitudes thought to be characteristic of smalltown America, a state of mind as well as a place, where conventionality reigns. The term is also sometimes used in a broader, nonpejorative sense to describe typical or ordinary American communities—*Middle America.*

The term in use, by author Michael Ranville in the *Detroit News,* April 22, 1997, recounting the story of Milo Radulovich, who was dismissed from the Air Force reserves at the height of the McCarthy era. Radulovich fought back and his story was investigated by Edward R. Murrow for his program *See It Now:*

> "This was MCCARTHYISM on Main Street," Ranville says. . . . [He] notes that a key event leading to McCarthy's fall from grace was the damning portrait Murrow's TV newsmagazine painted of McCarthy in March 1954. . . .

And, in its less pejorative sense, by presidential candidate Michael Dukakis, quoted in *Newsweek,* November 7, 1988:

> George Bush wants to help people on Easy Street. I want to help people on Main Street.

majordomo A butler or steward; also a person who speaks, makes arrangements, or takes charge for another. It comes from Latin where it meant "chief of the house."

The term in use, in "Dollars and Scents" by Stephanie Mansfield, in the *Washington Post Magazine,* March 6, 1988, in a profile of Ilona Domotor, longtime perfume saleswoman at a Washington department store:

> She is Ilona, the Ayacologna. The Major Domo of Aroma.

And by Peter Johnson in *USA Today,* June 6, 1997, describing CNN correspondent Wolf Blitzer:

> Blitzer is now the reigning majordomo in the White House press room, or as he put it Monday in a burst of repetition, "Among the senior of the seniors, I am the senior."

malaise speech A speech, negatively received, in which a politician suggests that the public's state of mind is apathetic at best and certainly less than positive and thus contributes to the problem being addressed. Conventional political wisdom generally agrees that the public does not like to be told such things by its political leaders.

The original was given by President Jimmy Carter on July 15, 1979, during a period of raging inflation and rising fuel costs, and of criticism of the Carter White House for ineptitude.

Carter decided to address a broad theme, the crisis of the American spirit. He went to Camp David, where he met with a wide range of American leaders. In the heat of the summer, speculation was rampant about the president's state of mind.

However, when the president returned to Washington and gave his speech, it was well received. Although he never used the word "malaise" (a French word meaning a vague sense of physical, mental, or moral ill-being), the word was quickly applied and became a catchword for his message. Negative reaction built rapidly when he purged several members of his Cabinet a few days later, reinforcing a sense of crisis and confusion in his administration.

The term in use, by Andrew J. Glass, in the *Atlanta Journal and Constitution,* September 26, 1995:

> Clinton backtracked on his use of the word "funk" to describe the mood of the country, saying it applied better to the America of a year ago, not today. The term was reminiscent of then-President Jimmy Carter's "malaise" speech, when Carter was criticized for implying that Americans had become pessimistic.

And from Mike Littwin in the *Baltimore Sun,* September 27, 1995, responding to the same Clinton remark:

> We were basically mentally and emotionally exhausted (the only possible explanation, by the way, for disco) from the '60s and Vietnam and Watergate and the Partridge Family. We elected Carter because he seemed so calm, although not quite so calm as Gerald Ford, who seemed possibly stuffed. One malaise speech, and he was gone.

And quoted in the *Charlotte Observer* by James Grieff, December 21, 1991:

> The national mood may have more to do with the sluggish economy than anything else. "I hate to give the Jimmy Carter malaise speech," said Kevin Kennelly, president of Charlotte-based Park Meridian Bank, "but we have a long-term economic problem that has to do with productivity, the work ethic and a lot intangible things."

And from David Warsh in the *Boston Globe,* February 2, 1992, on presidential candidate Paul Tsongas:

> If you like Jimmy Carter's malaise speech, you'll love this candidate. For Tsongas, the central metaphor for America is a bout with life-threatening cancer.

malaprop; malapropism The misuse or distortion of a word or phrase in which the speaker uses a word very much like, but ludicrously not, what is actually meant.

This term originates with Mrs. Malaprop, a character in Richard Brinsley Sheridan's 1775 comedy *The Rivals.* Mrs. Malaprop's name is actually from the French, *mal à propos,* or "inappropriate."

Sandy Reed of *InfoWorld,* June 10, 1996, offers a new breed of goofs—"technopropisms." These are mistakes that the human eye might catch, but which survive such technical aids as spelling checkers. Examples collected by readers include: "in the same vain," "mute point," and best of all, "baited breath."

The term in use, by Jeff Schultz, in the *Atlanta Journal and Constitution,* April 12, 1997:

> Reaffirming his tendency to speak before a thought is completely formed, Lou Duva blurted out at a news conference this week, "My guy can beat you with either hand. He's naturally amphibious." Then again, maybe Duva wasn't the victim of a malaprop. His fighter, Pernell Whitaker, believes he can beat Oscar De La Hoya with two hands or two fins.

And in the *New Republic,* December 5, 1994:

> The midterm elections have been variously characterized as the end of liberalism, the triumph of the religious right, the rebirth of Ronald Reagan, etc. But in the frenzy to make sense of the recent upheavals, one ominous resurgence has gone unnoticed: the SECOND COMING of Dan Quayle. These days, the prince of malaprop is biding his time within the confines of the Hudson Institute in his hometown of Indianapolis.

Malthusian \mal-'thü-zhən, mȯl-, -'thyü-\ Pertaining to the theory of Thomas Malthus holding that poverty and distress are unavoidable, barring moral restraint or disaster, because the population increases faster than its means of subsistence.

In 1798, Malthus (1766–1834), an English clergyman, economist, and pioneer in population studies, published *An Essay on the Principle of Population as it affects the Future Improvement of Society, with Remarks on the Speculation of Mr. Godwin, M. Condorcet, and other Writers,* setting forth his grim doctrine that since population grows in a geometric ratio while the food supply increases in an arithmetic ratio, population will always outstrip food production unless a change in behavior or a large-scale disaster interrupts the trend.

Malthus had so little faith in human nature that he could not imagine that men could solve the problem. Balance, he contended, would be imposed through inevitable war, famine, and disease. In an 1803 revision, Malthus offered self-imposed sexual restraint as another means of controlling population (in addition to his previous list of afflictions and catastrophes).

The term in use, by P.J. O'Rourke in his 1988 book, *Holidays in Hell:*

> This is the main thing the next quarter century will bring to the Third World—the same thing the last quarter century brought—lots and lots of colorful death. What with famine, war, genocide, sexually transmitted diseases and general dirty habits, we can

expect the next twenty-five years to be a veritable feast of Malthusianism.

And by CBS news anchor Dan Rather, reviewing *Between Marx and Muhammad: The Changing Face of Central Asia* by Dilip Hiro in the *Economist,* March 19, 1994:

> The supply of water is fixed but the population doubles every 20 years. How a Malthusian tragedy can be avoided, and how this looming crisis will affect relations between neighbours, is the central problem of Central Asia over the coming decades.

mandarin \'man-d(ə-)rən\ A person of position and influence; often traditionalist and reactionary, in literary and intellectual circles.

In imperial China, the mandarin class wielded great power throughout the government. Students aspiring to join had to follow a rigorous course of study and pass examinations to qualify.

Interestingly, the term is not Chinese but has a global origin, from Portuguese by way of Malay and Sanskrit words meaning "counsel."

The term in use, by Benedict Nightingale, describing British critic Kenneth Tynan in the *New York Times Book Review,* January 3, 1988:

> Tynan was an elitist egalitarian, a mandarin crusader for radical causes, a romantic realist, a libertine puritan and, as some unkindly said, a champagne socialist.

Another example, from Walter Russell Mead, reviewing *Archibald Cox: Conscience of a Nation* by Ken Gormley in the *Washington Post Book World,* November 9, 1997:

> Mass riots in the nation's inner cities mocked the hopes of the civil rights movement and the Great Society, and the nation's campuses were aflame as students rejected the values of their parents. Cox was one of the few mandarins to come through those years with his reputation unscathed.

man for all seasons, a A man of many talents who can handle any situation, stands by his convictions in all circumstances, and will not abandon his principles under pressure. (The reference to seasons also leads to much wordplay from sportswriters and garden columnists.)

A Man for All Seasons, a play by Robert Bolt, tells of the martyrdom of Sir Thomas More. More was a philosopher, poet, humanist, and statesman. His most famous work, *Utopia* [*q.v.*], describes an ideal place which is arranged according to More's principles and where social ills do not exist.

More was an active defender of the Catholic faith in a dangerous time: during the reign of King Henry VIII, shedder of wives and defier of popes. More was Henry's friend and Lord Chancellor in 1531 when Henry pronounced himself head of the Church of England. More resigned and two years later refused to take an oath acknowledging Henry as superior to all foreign rulers, including the pope—an oath which, no coincidence, allowed the king to divorce Catherine of Aragon and marry Anne Boleyn. More was singled out for revenge, imprisoned, and beheaded in 1535. He was canonized by the Catholic Church in 1935.

More's friend Desiderius Erasmus, a great Dutch humanist, described him as "omnium horarium homo," "a man for all seasons," an expression given currency by Bolt's play and the popular 1966 film based on it.

The term in use, by Leon Aron of the American Enterprise Institute, interviewed on National Public Radio's "All Things Considered," January 17, 1995:

> We thought—and my optimism was largely based on the belief that Yeltsin could prove to be the man for all seasons. He proved to be the man for the stormy season only.

And from a headline on a tribute to baseball's Jackie Robinson and Hank Greenberg, who together faced racial and religious bigotry, in the *Detroit News,* April 17, 1997:

> Robinson and Greenberg: MVPs for all seasons

And a play on the phrase by Lewis H. Lapham in *Harper's* magazine, March 1, 1995, describing House Speaker Newt Gingrich:

> Clearly a man for all grievances. . . .

And by Harold Meyerson in the *Los Angeles Times Magazine* profile of Congressman Henry Waxman, December 4, 1994:

> He is not liberalism's man for all seasons. He is only its legislative genius.

man Friday An efficient and devoted aide or employee; a right-hand man.

Friday is a character in Daniel Defoe's novel, *The Life and Strange Surprising Adventures of Robinson Crusoe, of York, Mariner,* published 1719–1720. Friday is the young native man rescued by Robinson Crusoe, certainly the best-known castaway in literature.

Crusoe is shipwrecked and lives alone on a desert island for 24 years, but one day is stunned to see a human footprint. Shortly thereafter he rescues the young man from cannibals, and calls him "man Friday" because he met him on a Friday. He instructs Friday in his own ways and faith and the two have many adventures. Ultimately they capture a mutinous ship and return to England.

Girl Friday is a term, now frowned upon, for a resourceful female assistant, made popular by the classic 1940 comedy adaptation of *The Front Page* starring Rosalind Russell as an ace reporter and Cary Grant as her cynical editor and ex-husband.

The term in use, by Larry Fine of Reuters, describing golfer Greg Norman, April 15, 1996:

A recent profile in *Sports Illustrated* magazine enumerated some of Norman's more expensive toys—two helicopters, a $28 million jet, five boats, six Chevy Suburban cars, one Mercedes and either six or seven Ferraris (neither Norman nor his man Friday were quite sure).

And by Peter Osterlund, in the *Christian Science Monitor,* December 15, 1986, describing Rep. Jim Wright of Texas as he prepared to take over as speaker of the House:

President Reagan and the Republican Senate took their places in 1981; the House of Representatives became the only Democratic stronghold in the government, and Wright became "Tip" O'Neill's man Friday while the Speaker led the opposition.

And by John Fairhall in the *Baltimore Sun,* August 20, 1995, on the First International Conference on Elvis Presley:

Musicians, impersonators, writers, cultural critics, Elvis' former cook, his one-time "man Friday," folk artist and minister Howard Finster and several "Elvis People"—those most devoted to his memory—enlightened through entertainment, lectures and testimonials.

manger *See* DOG IN THE MANGER.

Manichaean *or* **Manichean** \ˌma-nə-ˈkē-ən\ A dualistic viewpoint which sees things as black or white, good or bad, and caught in a struggle between absolutes.

It comes from a religion founded in the 3rd century A.D. in Persia by a prophet named Manes who saw the universe governed by a struggle between Good and Evil.

The term in use, by Andrew Ferguson in the *Weekly Standard,* April 25, 1997, discussing *Locked in the Cabinet,* the memoir of President Bill Clinton's first labor secretary, Robert Reich:

Thus in the Manichean struggle with the fat cats, Reich sides with the little people and the dogs. It's like, a moral obligation.

And by Randall Stross in the *New Republic,* April 22, 1996, on computer company rivalries:

When the IBM Personal Computer finally emerged in 1981, Apple responded by repackaging its image as countercultural chic and conjuring up a Manichean world. On the one side were arrayed the dark forces of mediocrity and sameness (IBM and its ilk); on the other—Apple, the creator of computers for the "rest of us"— i.e., everyone who was not an unthinking cipher. . . .

manifest destiny A future event accepted as inevitable; broadly, an arguably benevolent or necessary policy of imperialistic expansion. The slogan applied in American history to the drive for U.S. expansion across the North American continent to the Pacific Ocean: it was thought to be inevitable.

The expression appeared in 1845 in an editorial by John L. O'Sullivan in the *United States Magazine and Democratic Review,* which declared that it was America's

> manifest destiny to overspread and to possess the whole of the continent which Providence has given for the development of the great experiment of liberty and federated self-government entrusted to us.

That same year Texas was admitted to the Union; the United States settled a dispute with Britain, ending up with the part of the Oregon Territory below the 49th parallel; and war with Mexico in 1846 led to the acquisition of California and New Mexico. Manifest destiny so enthralled some Americans that President James Polk was criticized by more ardent jingoists for not seizing all of Mexico and a huge chunk of western Canada. For all that, the United States grew by more than a half million square miles during his presidency. (*See also* JINGOISM.)

The doctrine was revived in the late 19th century in response to a growing American appetite for status as a world power. As a result, Hawaii was annexed in 1897, and the U.S. Navy grew from the world's 12th largest to the third largest. The Spanish-American War, meanwhile, resulted in the acquisition of Puerto Rico, Guam, and the Philippines.

The term in use, by Todd Gitlin in commentary in the *Baltimore Sun,* March 12, 1995:

> The '60s broke the consensus on Cold War virtue, OZZIE AND HARRIET consumerism, white supremacy, America's manifest destiny, indeed, what it meant to be an American altogether.

And by Henry Allen in the *Washington Post,* June 15, 1988, describing a gathering of devotees of Harley-Davidson motorcycles:

> Instead of vaulting into the future, Harley is dedicated to preserving a past, manufacturing copies of old motorcycles with the great thick tires and mammoth mudguards like Spartan helmets, Wide Glides with Fat Bob gas tanks, that sense of inexorable heft, manifest destiny on wheels.

man in the gray flannel suit A conformist corporate employee, caught in the rat race. The expression is from the title of Sloan Wilson's 1955 novel which, along with William S. Whyte's *The Organization Man* (1956), created the 1950s image of the business-suited man on the corporate treadmill, head of a single-breadwinner suburban household. This vaguely discontented character has sacrificed his independence for the security of a corporate job and good income; he will conform rather than rock the boat at the office. At night the man travels home to his stay-at-home wife and his sweet baby-boom children transfixed by the new television set.

The protagonist of Wilson's novel is Tom Rath, who takes a job on Madison Avenue in order to make more money. Rath and his wife live in a modest home and he worries about his finances. But the new job presents new and uncomfortable dilemmas and discontents, and Rath must decide whether to tell his tycoon boss the truth, or what he wants to hear. Rath tells the truth and is rewarded with success, but he realizes that his family is more important.

The term in use, by Witold Rybczynski in *Wigwag,* November 1989:

> But in the 1950s the image of the commercial office building became so powerful that city halls, hospitals, courthouses—even museums—discarded their classical dress and adopted the anonymous steel-and-glass gray flannel suit of the business world.

And from Christopher J. Chipello, the *Wall Street Journal,* March 14, 1991:

> Yet Mr. Nishimura, a 48-year-old information-systems manager, is a typical salaryman, Japan's man in the gray flannel suit.

manner born *See* TO THE MANNER BORN.

man on horseback A figure, usually military, whose ambitions and popularity mark him as a potential dictator. Also, a dictator himself. The phrase comes from the nickname of Georges E.J.M. Boulanger (1837–1891), a French general who led an authoritarian movement in the 1880s that threatened to topple the government. He was called the "Man on Horseback" because he often appeared before the crowds in Paris mounted on a black horse. Ultimately, he was accused of conspiracy and fled the country.

There are exceptions to the rule that the man on horseback has to be or become a dictator; France's World War II hero Charles de Gaulle (whose height and sense of grandeur probably made the horse unnecessary) returned to power in the late 1950s to restore political order without jeopardizing democracy.

William Safire, in his *Political Dictionary,* notes that the expression was introduced to American politics by General Caleb Cushing in 1860, who expressed fear that an impending civil war could lead to danger for democracy—"a man on horseback with a drawn sword in his hand, some Atlantic Caesar, or Cromwell, or Napoleon."

The term in use, by Jim Murray in the *Los Angeles Times,* November 19, 1989:

> The trick of leadership is to project confidence, unflappability. The man on horseback has to look in control. Panic is contagious. Coach Shell is the least panic-stricken looking individual in the game.

And by Michael Barone, in *U.S. News & World Report,* June 1, 1992:

> In his office in a Dallas tower, Ross Perot keeps Frederic Remington sculptures of men on horseback—apt figures for one who

wants to be America's man on horseback, riding to rescue the nation from its problems.

man's reach should exceed his grasp, a To achieve excellence, one should aim at a goal beyond what is easily attainable. A poetic way of expressing a prosaic thought.

It is a line from a Robert Browning poem, "Andrea del Sarto." Andrea del Sarto was in fact a painter, a contemporary of Raphael and Michelangelo. Browning uses a dramatic monologue, spoken by the painter to his beautiful, discontented wife, which reveals the gnawing within him.

Del Sarto compares himself to Raphael and Michelangelo, who pour their souls into their work, as he does not; while he achieves technical perfection with his "low-pulsed forthright craftsman's hand," they achieve greatness even though they fall short of their aspirations. Andrea muses:

> Ah, but a man's reach should exceed his grasp
> Or what's a heaven for?

The term in use, by Patt Morrison in the *Los Angeles Times,* August 27, 1995, on the fad for exhuming the long-dead famous:

> For a time I thought "Apollo 13" might invert the digging impulse—space, the final frontier, a man's reach should exceed his grasp or what's a heaven for and all that. But no, we keep looking down, shoveling at the restless earth, exhuming. Graves are being opened up faster than Planet Hollywood restaurants. . . . Wayne Newton, who claims descent from Pocahontas, wants to have her dug up and shipped from England for reburial in Virginia. So relieved am I that he didn't propose bringing her to Las Vegas as the lobby display for an Indian-themed hotel-casino that I'm inclined to let him do it.

A playful turn, also from the *Los Angeles Times,* by Aaron Curtiss, October 27, 1995:

> However noble, the notion that a man's reach should exceed his grasp is anathema to Jim Ulrich. As an engineer who designs automobile interiors, Ulrich's philosophy is that nothing should be out of reach.

mantra \\'män-trə *also* 'man- *or* 'mən-\\ A mystical formula of invocation or incantation in Hinduism and elsewhere. Also, a watchword.

In Hinduism and Buddhism, a mantra is a sacred mystic word or verse chanted or sung repeatedly as part of devotions and meditation. "Om"—said over and over—is considered to be the greatest mantra, embodying the essence of the universe. By extension, the word has been applied to phrases, ideas, or slogans that appear often in a specific context.

The term in use, by Laura Meckler, of the Associated Press, September 8, 1997:

The mantra of welfare reform is work. But do welfare recipients in job-training slots deserve the same benefits and rights as other workers?

Another example, from the *Economist,* February 4, 1989:

It is an established routine: after every widely publicized gun massacre, gun-control advocates renew their call for legislation and the gun lobby repeats its mantra that if guns are made criminal only criminals will have guns.

And by J.D. Biersdorfer of *Close to the Machine* by Ellen Ullman in the *New York Times Book Review,* November 30, 1997:

Part memoir, part techie mantra, part observation of the ever-changing world of computer programming, *Close to the Machine* is the nicely-balanced story of a 46-year-old woman coming to terms with middle age in her personal life as well as in her chaotic profession as a software engineer.

man without a country, the A man in unhappy but self-inflicted exile from his country; often applied to a political exile.

The phrase is taken from the title of a story by American writer and minister Edward Everett Hale (1822–1909). The protagonist of the story is Philip Nolan, a young officer who is drawn into the treasonous plans of Aaron Burr. Burr is tried but acquitted; the fictional Nolan is convicted.

When he is given an opportunity to make a statement, he shocks the court by saying, "Damn the United States! I wish I may never hear of the United States again!" He is sentenced to sail the seas for the rest of his life—and never to hear his country spoken of again. Nolan at first is defiant, and treats his sentence as a joke, but as the years pass, he becomes withdrawn and unhappy—and dies a broken man in 1863. Many of the naval officers he encounters pity Nolan, and like him; but they uphold the sentence. And Nolan is a burden to every ship on which he is carried: when he is present, there can be no talk of home.

The term in use, by Alan Abrahamson and Tony Perry, writing in the *Los Angeles Times,* October 4, 1995, about prospects for O.J. Simpson after his acquittal for murder:

Simpson, in essence, faces the possibility of becoming, if not a man without a country, a man without the country he once knew—and something worse, a kind of exile in his own life.

And by John Niyo, in the *Detroit News,* July 10, 1997:

Hideki Irabu might be a man without a country, but he's got a heck of a fastball. And that can make a world of difference.

march to the beat of a different drummer To pursue an individualistic course; to act or think independently, without reference to, and often in conflict with, the habits, thoughts or actions of the majority. The image is that of a person who marches to a rhythm or cadence heard only by himself, rather than as part of a group. The term comes from that most individualistic American, Henry David Thoreau:

> If a man does not keep pace with his companions, perhaps it is because he hears a different drummer. Let him step to the music which he hears, however measured or far away.

The term in use, by Jeff Greenfield in the *New York Times Book Review*, June 18, 1995:

> With *Maverick*, Lowell Weicker has found a perfect title for his political memoir. Originally used to describe unbranded cattle, the word now defines a politician who wears no label, who marches to a distinctly different drummer and who generally drives members of his own party to apoplexy.

And in an advertisement for windows in *Sunset*, March 1992:

> There are those of us who march to the beat of a different drummer. And there are those within that group that insist they set the pace. A spirit of individuality guides their entire destiny. These individuals are finding their way to Weather Shield wood windows. It just happens.

And by Philip French in the *New York Times Book Review*, July 8, 1984:

> The popular image of [novelist James] Agee was that of a spiritual giant surrounded by pygmies, driven to booze because he despaired of ever realizing his ambitions in such a materialist society, corrupted by the security of Time Inc. and the lure of Hollywood, misunderstood by critics and publishers, marching ahead of his times to the beat of a different drummer.

Marquess of Queensberry rules Rules of boxing, and of fair play or behavior more generally.

Published in 1867, under the sponsorship of John Sholto Douglas, ninth marquess of Queensberry, they superseded the London Prize Ring Rules, adopted in 1838 to tame bare-knuckle boxing.

From these rules have come such basic tenets of good behavior as no butting, biting, gouging, kicking, hitting below the belt, or striking while down.

The term in use, by Martin Anderson, domestic policy advisor in the Reagan White House, in the *Washington Post Book World*, April 9, 1996:

> If effective, political writing will be attacked, and not necessarily by those abiding by Marquess of Queensberry rules.

In use again, by Jane Sumner of the *Dallas Morning News*, in the *Kansas City Star*, May 4, 1995, reviewing a book on tape by James Lee Burke about a tough-talking Cajun private eye:

Of course, the underbelly of New Orleans isn't for sensitive souls. Its denizens don't talk like nuns or play by the Marquess of Queensberry rules.

marriage of true minds The union of like-minded individuals, a relationship unshaken by change or adversity, and able to surmount all obstacles in its path.

The reference comes from Shakespeare's Sonnet 116:

> Let me not to the marriage of true minds
> Admit impediments. Love is not love
> Which alters when it alteration finds.
> Or bends with the remover to remove.

The term in use, by Martin Filler in *Harper's Bazaar,* August 1, 1994:

> "Let me not to the marriage of true minds/Admit impediments," wrote Shakespeare, and Laura Hartman and Richard Fernau have taken him at his word. Professional partners for the past 14 years, these two hugely talented San Francisco Bay area architects—and erstwhile lovers—are happily married to others. But so consuming is their unchanging mutual passion—architecture that responds to the needs of people—that it isn't always possible for them to sort out all the details of their long and fruitful relationship.

And by John Simon in the *New York Times Book Review,* June 23, 1996:

> It is now up to us to remember these two vital human beings by reading their letters, which are an action-packed tribute to a marriage of sometimes untrue bodies, but always true minds.

And again, with the emphasis on impediments, by Louise Sweeney in the *Christian Science Monitor,* October 24, 1989:

> When Shakespeare wrote "Let me not to the marriage of true minds admit impediments" (Sonnet 116), he may not have dreamed of impediments like Lucite-and-steel beds that rise to the ceiling like birds, rivers of silk banners that trap lovers, his and hers jodhpurs, or giggling intrigue in a royal court that looks like a rajah's fantasy.

martinet \ˌmär-tᵊn-ˈet\ A stickler for discipline. The Marquis de Martinet was a commander under King Louis XIV of France and a strict and demanding taskmaster. King Louis required that a young nobleman must learn to command a platoon in Martinet's regiment before he could take command of his own regiment. Martinet's system for training willful and privileged young aristocrats made his name synonymous with disciplinarian.

The term in use, by Klein & Reif in the *Village Voice,* December 10, 1991:

That he won three NCAA titles and a Stanley Cup while compiling an excellent record over all those years of coaching (he began at Warroad High School in 1956) is vivid proof that you don't have to be a drill sergeant, gym teacher, martinet, or robotic technocrat to win.

When Bob Johnson was around, it was always a good day for hockey.

And by Tom Mathews, et al. in *Newsweek,* March 11, 1991, describing General Norman Schwartzkopf:

At 56, and 240 pounds, he looked like a fatherly meat-packer, a dangerous man to annoy; but he came across as a warrior with a soul, not a dour martinet like William Westmoreland or a media slicker like Alexander Haig.

And by Cynthia Ozick in the *New Yorker,* February 24-March 3, 1997:

There is speculation that Dostoyevsky's father may have had a mild form of epilepsy himself: he was gloomy, moody, and unpredictably explosive, a martinet who drank too much and imposed his will on everyone around him.

Mather, Cotton An American clergyman and writer (1663–1728) often evoked, a bit unfairly, as the embodiment of extreme Puritanism with its rigid code of behavior.

Mather was a child prodigy who entered Harvard at age 12. He became a historian, folklorist, and writer on a broad range of subjects as well as an ardent Puritan. He was for a time inclined to believe in witchcraft, but he upheld the rational teachings of Isaac Newton, and he supported inoculation against smallpox when vaccination was the subject of great fear. Nevertheless, his name is now synonymous with devout, intolerant Puritanism.

Mather invoked, by Mary McGrory in the *Washington Post,* June 15, 1997, commenting on sex scandals in the military:

Not since Cotton Mather was terrorizing the Puritans of Boston has there been such a clamor about adultery.

And by Abigail Trafford in the *Washington Post* "Health" section, September 10, 1996:

What keeps the family going is this special, mostly subconscious, contract of mutual trust. It's not all gooey affection or selfless care-taking. Nor is it some Cotton Mather concept of duty.

maverick \'mav-rik, 'ma-və-\ An unbranded range animal, especially a motherless calf. Also, an independent person who does not go along with a group or party. From Samuel August Maverick (1803–1870), a Texas cattleman who did not brand the calves in his cattle herd and allowed them to roam. The term was then applied to any unbranded steer who strayed from the herd, and then transferred to independent and individualistic people. It is often applied to politicians who avoid affiliating themselves with a particular party.

The term in use, by James V. Grimaldi, in the *Seattle Times,* January 7, 1997:

> The maverick sophomore congresswoman from Hazel Dell, Clark County, stepped into a hallway and told dozens of reporters she would break from the GOP "family" and declined to support the Georgia Republican for speaker. "I don't care if he was my brother," Smith said. "He was getting in the way of what was best for America."

And from the *Baltimore Sun,* December 25, 1995, a *Boston Globe* story about archeologist Hanan Eshel's discovery of additional Dead Sea Scrolls:

> "He's the only one to have found texts near the Dead Sea since the 1960s," Mr. Broshi says, referring to the Jericho finds. "It's because he doesn't follow everyone's preconceptions. He's a maverick in the good sense of the word."

And from David Sterritt, in the *Christian Science Monitor,* January 17, 1992:

> Where there's a trend that bodes no good, however, there's often a maverick eager to move in precisely the opposite direction. In this case, the maverick is Lincoln Center, an elite cultural institution not usually associated with large quantities of derring-do.

Mc- A prefix, inspired by the immensely successful McDonald's restaurant chain, that suggests values associated with fast-food franchises: sameness, endless replication, homogeneity, simplicity, superficiality.

USA Today, the nationwide newspaper started by the Gannett Company in 1982, quickly was dubbed "McPaper," a jab by journalists for its initial shallowness and relentlessly upbeat tone. Surrendering to the inevitability of the nickname, Gannett adopted it, as reflected by the title of the paper's authorized biography by Gannett editor Peter Prichard: *The Making of McPaper: The Inside Story of USA Today.* The book quotes Jonathan Yardley of the *Washington Post* using the junk food theme to describe the paper:

> Like parents who take their children to a different fast-food joint every night and keep the refrigerator stocked with ice cream, *USA Today* gives its readers only what they want. No spinach, no bran, no liver.

The term in use, by Harry F. Waters in *Newsweek,* September 14, 1987, in a review of Bill Cosby's book, *Time Flies:*

> At 176 pages (for $15.95), it's two pages shorter (and $1 more) than its predecessor, which was not exactly a PROUSTIAN read

itself. *Time Flies* could easily be consumed by an airline passenger between the salted almonds and the after-dinner mints—even allowing for a trip to the lavatory. But if Cosby has cooked up a sort of McBook, he's also delivered exactly what his legions of admirers treasure. . . .

And in the *Washington Post Magazine,* April 30, 1989, in the headline over a piece by Richard Cohen decrying the loss of regional distinctions: "McAmerica the Beautiful."

McCarthyism A mid-20th-century political attitude of opposition to elements believed subversive or, just as likely, labeled subversive for purposes of political gain. Also the use of personal attacks on individuals through indiscriminate allegations based especially on unsubstantiated charges. "McCarthyism" is shorthand for both the tactics and the surrounding atmosphere of fear pervading the pursuit of Communists in the United States in the early 1950s. The word *witchhunt* [*q.v.*] is often used to describe the phenomenon. Today McCarthyism is also used as a counterattack: accuse your accusers of McCarthyism and put them on the defensive.

McCarthyism takes its name from the late Senator Joseph R. McCarthy, a Republican from Wisconsin; the ascendancy he achieved from 1950 to 1954 justifies the attachment of his name to this style of attack.

Individual rights received short shrift from investigative committees: guilt by association, persecution of dissenters and those who defended them, loyalty oaths, and anonymous informants were the order of the day. Differences of opinion became grounds for attacking patriotism, and many people—career diplomats, screenwriters, authors, teachers—lost their jobs and were blacklisted so they could not obtain work elsewhere.

McCarthy shot into the headlines with a speech in 1950: "I have here in my hand a list" (the phrase itself also appears as an allusion), 205 names of purported Communist spies in the State Department, working there with the knowledge of the secretary of state.

The charge was so shocking that a special Senate committee investigated. It concluded that the list was a hoax; McCarthy, in turn, implied that the committee chairman was a Communist sympathizer. When the chairman was defeated for reelection, McCarthy's colleagues became very careful about crossing him. In 1953 McCarthy became chairman of the Government Operations Committee and turned it into a tribunal for pursuit of alleged Communists and their sympathizers in government.

Some did speak out against McCarthyite tactics, Senator Margaret Chase Smith and broadcaster Edward R. Murrow among them. But McCarthy and his followers roared on. In 1954 McCarthy went after the U.S. Army in televised hearings—a first for the country, which was mesmerized.

Facing McCarthy at the witness table was Joseph Welch, a distinguished Boston lawyer serving as special counsel to the Army. Welch's dignified bearing was a telling counterpoint to McCarthy's grating voice, glowering countenance, and hectoring manner. When the senator attacked one of Welch's young associates, Welch responded, "Let us not assassinate this lad further, Senator. Have you no sense of decency, sir, at long last? Have you left no sense of decency?"

The spell was broken. The public was repelled by what it saw. That December, McCarthy was censured by the Senate, and he was no longer a political force, although the issues, accusations, and poisons remained.

The term in use, by former Colorado Governor Richard Lamm, quoted in the *Christian Science Monitor,* July 5, 1996:

> He [Lamm] calls the nation's current financial situation "like Greek tragedy. It's fiscal McCarthyism."

And from Bruce Feiler, writing in the *New York Times Magazine,* October 27, 1996:

> In the era of Michael Jackson, Americans have developed a near paranoia about men who interact with young people. Ultimately this is what chased my friend Buck from the ring: a climate of mistrust, a sexual McCarthyism that seems to be spreading across America.

And in a quotation cited by William Safire in the *New York Times Magazine,* May 5, 1991:

> "There is a new McCarthyism that has spread over American college campuses," writes Max Lerner, an old-line liberal. "We call it 'political correctness.' "

McCoys *See* HATFIELDS AND MCCOYS.

medium is the message, the The mode of communication affects both what is communicated and who receives it. The phrase was coined by Marshall McLuhan (1911–1980), a Canadian scholar of modern communications.

McLuhan coined other terms to characterize the effect of the medium: "GLOBAL VILLAGE," and "hot" (television) and "cold" (newspapers).

The term in use, by Jonathan Schell, in commentary in *Newsday,* January 21, 1996:

> The networks spent $140 million just on coverage of the Gulf War. It certainly would be an understatement in the face of this growth to repeat the old saying, "The medium is the message." Rather, the medium is, more and more, not just the message but the substance of the message.

And in extended use, by Bernard Schwarz, reviewing *Just As I Am,* the autobiography of Billy Graham in the *Los Angeles Times,* June 22, 1997:

> Graham himself hints at his regret at overstepping the line between politics and his calling as an evangelist, but he has often confused the worldly and the sacred, the medium and the

message. Such confusion is perhaps inevitable when evangelists promote the Gospel by promoting themselves.

Medusa \mi-'dü-sə, -'dyü-, -zə\ A mortal GORGON who is slain when decapitated by Perseus. The best known of the trio of gorgons of Greek myth, Medusa is said to have dallied with the sea god Poseidon in the temple of Athena; the outraged Athena then changed the offender's hair to snakes and made her so hideous that those who looked upon her were turned to stone. Her name, like that of the gorgons, describes someone who is ugly or frightening—either physically or spiritually.

Medusa was the only one of the three who was mortal, and she was eventually killed by the hero Perseus, who guided his sword by looking at the gorgon's reflection in Athena's shield. Interestingly enough, Renaissance artists portrayed her as very beautiful—but still dangerous, and still with bad hair.

The term in use, by J.A. Adande, in the *Washington Post,* May 23, 1997:

> Tonight, the Bulls shot 36 percent and the Heat shot 34 percent. Each team had a 12-point quarter. Each team endured a scoreless stretch of six minutes. "You never want to look ugly in the face," Michael Jordan said. This game was like staring at Medusa.

From Daniel B. Wood, in the *Christian Science Monitor,* November 19, 1995, in a story about theme parks:

> ... America's executors of escapism continue to adapt the latest technologies. ... And they include "virtual reality" devices, attractions where participants don Medusa-like headsets to enter and explore computer-generated fantasy worlds.

Another example, from Cindy Eberting, in the *Kansas City Star,* October 26, 1995:

> It won't be Marian Thomas, choir director, stepping up to the organ. Instead the audience will see Menacing Marian, wearing a black cape and an aluminum foil Medusa-like wig.

meltdown The accidental melting of the core of a nuclear reactor, and thus a rapid or disastrous decline or collapse. The original meaning, however, was more agreeable: the word was coined in 1937 by a writer for the *Ice Cream Trade Journal* to describe what happens to ice cream in the taster's mouth.

The word began to appear in the nuclear power industry in the 1960s to mean the melting of the core of a nuclear reactor, which occurs when the controlled use of nuclear reaction gets out of control, causing the release of radioactivity in dangerous amounts. The meltdown at the CHERNOBYL reactor in the Soviet Union underscored just how devastating such an event can be.

The term has come to be applied to other disasters, particularly the breakdown of systems or institutions.

The term in use, by Josh Meyer and Timothy Williams in the *Los Angeles Times,* April 4, 1997, on the Los Angeles County property tax system:

> But overhauling the system, which probably will cost more than $10 million, will have to wait. A much more urgent problem could send the entire property tax system into a "meltdown" if it is not addressed first.

And by David Segal, looking back on the week's turmoil on Wall Street, in the *Washington Post,* October 29, 1997:

> In addition to the well-known meltdowns of '29 and '87, October has hosted lesser-known nose-dives in 1937, 1978, 1979 and 1989, when the Dow lost 190 points, or 7 percent, in a single day.

ménage à trois \mä-'näzh-ä-'twä\ An arrangement in which three persons, often a married pair and a lover, have sexual relations especially while living together. A French phrase, meaning "a household for three." Now we also see the term applied to unusual alliances or cooperation among three individuals whose interests should not coincide.

The term in use, by Carl Schoettler in the *Baltimore Sun,* June 10, 1995:

> When Susan Eisenhower fell in love with the top Soviet space scientist Roald Sagdeev, she found herself involved in an unsettling ménage à trois: herself, Dr. Sagdeev and the KGB.

And by Martin Amis in his essay "Mr. Vidal: Unpatriotic Gore" from *The Moronic Inferno,* describing author Gore Vidal's years as a screenwriter in Hollywood in the 1950s:

> At one point there was surprising talk of a romance and engagement between Vidal and Joanne Woodward. They ended up living à trois for a time in California, the third member of this curious ménage being Paul Newman.

And by David Frickle, illustrating the "unusual alliance" meaning, in *Rolling Stone,* March 18, 1993:

> For a few brief moments in 1965 and '66, the Sons were the club band to beat in Los Angeles, tearing it up with a dynamic ménage à trois of ardent folk-blues scholarship, brassy Delta grind and Beatlesesque pop vigor.

mensch \'men(t)sh\ A person of integrity and honor. A Yiddish word for someone who is really admirable, noble, a good person. A mensch doesn't have to be important; the critical element is fine character.

Leo Rosten in *The Joys of Yiddish* (1968) says, "As a child, I often heard it said: 'The finest thing you can say about a man is that he is a mensch' or 'Be a mensch!' This use of the word is uniquely Yiddish in its overtones."

A cross-cultural application of the term from writer Nat Hentoff, self-described Jewish atheist and author of a biography of Cardinal John O'Connor, quoted in the *New York Times Book Review,* July 10, 1988:

Yeah, I like him. . . . Whatever disagreements I have with him, I
guess what I like most about O'Connor is that he is a mens[c]h.

And from syndicated columnist Charles Krauthammer, appearing in
the *Deseret News,* April 20, 1997, in praise of golf phenomenon Tiger
Woods:

Americans are simply overcome with relief to find, rising out of
this swamp of bad-boy athletes, a mensch like Woods.

And by David Everitt, in the *New York Times,* October 26, 1997, describing the comic character Mr. Bean created by Rowan Atkinson:

Mr. Bean's selfishness is tempered somewhat, although he's not
likely to be mistaken for a CAPRAESQUE mensch.

mentor A wise and trusted counselor. The original Mentor was a character in the *Odyssey* [*q.v.*] who serves as the advisor of young Telemachus,
the son of Odysseus. Mentor is especially helpful because much of the
time he is actually the goddess Athena, who assumes Mentor's identity in
order to give Telemachus advice and information.

Today, the term is applied to a senior person, often in an organization,
who assists a less-experienced and usually younger person to succeed. The
concept is so familiar that it has turned into a verb.

The term in use, by Evgenia Peretz, the *New Republic,* November 13,
1995:

There was a time, not too long ago, when the best an unmarried
woman could hope for was a respectable old-maidenhood, a life
of fine embroidery, charity work and the satisfaction of serving
as confidante and mentor to younger women worrying about
their own chances.

And by Darryl Van Duch in the *National Law Journal,* September 1,
1997:

And stay tuned, say the politicos of Chicago, where Ms. Sher, 49,
was the city's first female corporate counsel. . . . Her ex-boss and
mentor, Mayor Richard M. Daley, was widely believed to be a
shoo-in for election to a third term in 1999, and is rumored to
be interested in becoming Illinois' governor one day.

And by James Shapiro, the *New York Times Book Review,* January 4,
1998:

Much has been written about academic freedom, little about academic responsibility. Kennedy's account of the multiple demands
on scholars to publish, to teach well, to mentor, to serve the university, to reach beyond the walls of academe and to risk change
captures both the pleasures and pitfalls awaiting those entering
the profession.

Mephistophelean \ˌmef-ə-stə-ˈfēl-yən, mə-ˌfis-tə-, ˌme-fə-ˌstä-fə-ˈlē-ən\ Having to do with Mephistopheles, a chief devil in the Faust legend, who tempts Faust to sell his soul. (*See* FAUSTIAN BARGAIN.) The origin of the name may be Greek "not loving the light," or Hebrew, "destroyer and liar." Both seem apt.

In legends, Mephistopheles appears in various forms: as one of the chief devils, or as a mischievous spirit, or as an urbane demon who sneers at virtue. He is not the highest-level devil himself but clearly is devilish in actions and intent.

The term in use, by Phil Kloer in the *Atlanta Journal and Constitution,* February 7, 1997, reviewing the latest installment of the British police series *Prime Suspect:*

> And there's "The Street" (Steven Mackintosh in a mesmerizing performance), the nickname of the most charismatic and one of the smartest baddies Tennison has battled. A Mephistophelean gang leader and drug pusher, he so slick that his neighborhood and even some of the cops think he's God's gift.

And by S.L. Wykes in the *San Jose Mercury News,* October 16, 1993, on the image problem of snakes:

> The lure of the venomous snake, said Chiszar, is the "Mephistophelean ambiance of intimidation." Said Madge Minton, people who keep poisonous snakes "are mostly between the ages of 12 and 17 and have something against their mother."

Merriwell, Frank The beau ideal, the All-American boy, the gentleman-amateur, athlete-hero of Yale, chivalrous scion of the now-vanishing WASP ascendancy; a fictional hero created by William Gilbert Patten in 1896. The weekly stories were immensely popular and ran for years, one of the most successful series of juvenile literature in history.

Frank was so virtuous that he became a caricature, but as WASP historian E. Digby Baltzell put it, in *Sporting Gentlemen: Men's Tennis from the Age of Honor to the Cult of the Superstar* (1995), he "made for far more interesting reading than the Horatio ALGER sagas of the dull, boot-licking bores from the hinterland who rose to wealth through keeping their eyes on the cash register and the boss's daughter."

The term in use, by John Hunt, in *Baseball Weekly,* May 17, 1995:

> Shades of Frank Merriwell: Wake Forest junior Rusty LaRue became the first athlete in the 42-year history of the Atlantic Coast Conference to play in football, basketball and baseball in the same season. . . .

And from Jim Murray, in the *Los Angeles Times,* November 14, 1996, describing professional golfer Greg Norman:

> The shock of cotton hair, the flashing blue eyes, out-thrust jaw, he was a combination of Fearless Fosdick (*see* DOGPATCH) and Frank Merriwell.

And finally, by George Weigel in *Commentary,* November 1, 1994, reviewing Ken Burns' documentary *Baseball:*

> Among the best of his sketches of the pastime's greats—themselves an entire gallery of Americana—are those of Cap Anson, a magnificent player and an unreconstructed racist who drew the "color line" in 1888; Christy Mathewson, the "Christian gentleman" from Bucknell who was a nonfiction Frank Merriwell. . . .

messenger *See* KILL/SHOOT THE MESSENGER.

mess of pottage Something valueless or trivial or a transitory comfort or advantage, especially when accepted instead of a rightful thing or one of far greater value. The term is often used in the context "sell one's birthright for a mess of pottage." "Mess" means a prepared dish of food; "pottage" is a thick soup or stew of vegetables and perhaps meat.

The allusion is from Genesis 25:33–34 in the story of brothers Esau and Jacob. Esau returns from hunting, faint with hunger. Jacob, his younger brother, is cooking but will not give Esau anything to eat until he agrees to give up his right of inheritance as the oldest son. Thus Esau sells his heritage for something temporary and of little value.

The term in use, quoted by Jill Dutt in *Newsday,* November 18, 1993, reporting on debate on the North American Free Trade Agreement in the House of Representatives:

> [Rep. John] Lewis called the frenzy of last-minute deals cut by the White House to win votes "obscene," and even lapsed into Biblical references: "The people of the Fifth Congressional District of Georgia did not send me here to sell them out for a mess of pottage and THIRTY PIECES OF SILVER."

And by Ellen Willis, in the *New York Times Book Review,* June 15, 1997, reviewing *Without a Doubt* by O.J. Simpson prosecutor Marcia Clark and Teresa Carpenter:

> Marcia Clark is still furious. By the end of *Without a Doubt,* her rage and contempt have seared almost everyone involved with the O.J. Simpson trial, from Mr. Simpson himself to . . . various witnesses who sold their credibility for a mess of tabloid pottage. . . .

Micawber, Mr. \mi-'kȯ-bər, -'kä-\; **Micawberesque** A kindhearted, incurable optimist.

Mr. Wilkins Micawber was a character created by English novelist Charles Dickens (*see* DICKENSIAN) in his semi-autobiographical novel *David Copperfield* (1849–1850).

Mr. Micawber, who is thought to be based on Dickens' own ne'er-do-well father, is always impoverished and frequently unemployed, cherishing schemes that promise wealth but always fall apart. Nevertheless, Mr. Micawber is always certain that "something will turn up" to help him out

of his pecuniary difficulties. He is feckless but kind, and eventually helps
to defeat the schemes of the villain Uriah HEEP.

The term in use, by syndicated columnist Donald Kaul, appearing in
the *Philadelphia Daily News,* presenting his annual Incredible Awards, January 2, 1992:

> The Mr. Micawber Award for Economic Development—To
> George Bush, who, in an attempt to bolster consumer confi-
> dence, stopped off at a J.C. Penney's and bought four pairs of
> socks.

And by Bill Hirschman in the *Wichita Eagle,* August 26, 1990, reviewing Kirk Douglas' novel *Dance With the Devil:*

> When I started reviewing books and plays in 1971, I promised
> never to walk out on a show and always to finish a novel no mat-
> ter how bad. Like Dickens' Mr. Micawber, I'd keep hoping that
> something good would turn up.

And by Jack Beatty in the *Atlantic,* February 1989, on the legacy of
Ronald Reagan in arms control:

> Events might thrust crises before President Bush from which he
> could try to extract a "win." But this Micawberesque vision of
> foreign policy—something might turn up—is a formula for drift,
> not mastery.

Mickey Finn A drink of liquor doctored with a purgative or a drug. The
term is gangster slang from the 19th century. A customer in a bar might
wake up hours later with a thumping headache and an empty wallet
because he was drugged by thieves who slipped him a Mickey Finn. The
term now refers to a surreptitious, unscrupulous tactic to disable a victim, or an opponent in competition; or to administer a blow so strong that
its effect is the same as a drug.

The term in use, by Jane Bryant Quinn, writing on the bond market in
Newsweek, February 23, 1981:

> The Mickey Finns: Companies leave you alone with your folly
> when interest rates rise. But they hate to see you collecting high
> payments on older bonds when interest rates fall. So they're
> pouring Mickey Finns into the sub-clauses, to knock out high-
> yielding issues as soon as it suits them.

And by Mike Lopresti, Gannett News Service, November 6, 1994:

> Let us all raise a double-cheeseburger in a toast today to George
> Foreman. . . . Hero of the middle-aged, and middle-spreaded.
> When he dropped Michael Moorer in the 10th round Saturday
> night with a two-punch Mickey Finn, the momentous nature of
> the occasion struck me immediately. It is rare to be able to root
> for a victorious athlete whose pants I can fit into.

Midas touch An uncanny ability for making money in every venture. A golden touch.

The expression comes from the legend of King Midas, a cautionary tale: be careful of what you wish for, because you may get it.

King Midas asked the gods that everything he touched be turned to gold. Once granted, his request turned out to be a curse: his food and wine turned to gold and he nearly starved. (In one version of the story, he embraced his daughter and she too turned to gold.) He prayed for relief, and was told to bathe in the Pactolus River. He did, and ever after the river's sands were golden.

Despite Midas's experiences, current use is positive: the Midas touch is thought to be a great thing to have, the ticket to prosperity.

The term in use, by Bill Reel in *Newsday,* February 9, 1996:

> The truth is the Archdiocese of New York, headed by O'Connor since 1984, is going to be so broke by the time he retires that a man with a Midas touch will be required to restore it to financial health.

And by Ross Atkin, in the *Christian Science Monitor,* February 14, 1995, on the 1995 National Figure Skating Championships:

> Todd Eldredge, a fisherman's son, regained the men's title that he held in 1990 and '91. His coach, Richard Callaghan, apparently has the Midas touch, since he also teaches the new women's champion, Nicole Bobek. . . .

millstone; to carry a millstone around one's neck A heavy burden which weighs one down. A millstone is one of a pair of large, circular stones used in a mill to grind grain. In old-fashioned mills, the upper stone is turned by a shaft and grinds the grain against the lower, or nether stone, which is chosen for its hardness, the source of another old saying, "hard as the nether millstone."

The term in use, by Mike O'Hara, in the *Detroit News,* December 26, 1996:

> But the Lions' offensive failures only heightened and exposed the defensive weaknesses. The offense was supposed to carry the team. Instead it was a millstone.

And from Martin Sieff, in the *Washington Times,* January 16, 1995:

> The North American Free Trade Agreement, even more than support of Mr. Yeltsin, was seen as a Clinton policy success and the object of bipartisan support. But with the crash of Mexico's currency and new fears about stability south of the border, even this may become a millstone around Mr. Clinton's neck.

Milquetoast, Caspar A timid, meek, or unassertive person. The name of the main character in a newspaper cartoon "The Timid Soul," created by H.T. Webster in 1924. Caspar is probably descended from a much older insult *milktoast* or *milksop,* both referring to a dish of bread soaked in milk and both used to describe a spiritless, weak person.

The term in use, quoted in the *Seattle Times,* August 18, 1996, in a piece on voter sentiment:

> Politicians don't provide straight answers, said Tim Selden: "They're wishy-washy. . . . They give a milquetoast answer."

And by Scott Ostler, in the *San Francisco Chronicle,* April 18, 1995, on quarterback great Joe Montana:

> Montana off the field, especially in the early years, didn't seem driven, angry, fiery, tough, flamboyant. Didn't say much. He just showed up and played football good. How that off-field milquetoast mien transformed itself into inspirational leadership and clutch performance on the field is anybody's guess.

And again, by Peter Stack, reviewing *The Cable Guy* in the *San Francisco Chronicle,* June 14, 1996:

> [Jim] Carrey makes co-star Matthew Broderick, playing mild-mannered architect Steven Kovacs, come across as a saintly milquetoast.

Milton *See* MUTE INGLORIOUS MILTON, A.

mine shaft *See* CANARY IN A MINE SHAFT/COAL MINE.

mise-en-scène \ˌmē-ˌzäⁿ-ˈsen, -ˈsän\ The physical setting of an action; the context, environment, or milieu. A French phrase originally used in the theater to refer to the arrangement of actors and scenery on the stage.

The term in use, by Mary Williams Walsh, describing the reconstruction of Berlin's famous Adlon Hotel, in the *Los Angeles Times,* July 7, 1997:

> During the Third Reich, the hotel was a preferred mise-en-scène for top Nazis; Adolf Hitler's chancellery and Gestapo headquarters were just a few goose steps down the street. . . . Famed journalist-historian William L. Shirer filed his war correspondence from the hotel.

And by Thomas Matthews in *Wine Spectator,* October 15, 1995:

> Peppone, a lively ristorante in a Brentwood shopping center has been open for 20 years, and only cigarette smoke and Frank Sinatra's Rat Pack are missing from the 1970s mise-en-scéne.

Mitty, Walter A mild-mannered, henpecked daydreamer who escapes humdrum reality by imagining himself in heroic adventures. Walter is a character created by humorist James Thurber in his famous short story, "The Secret Life of Walter Mitty." He has since become the eponym for dreamers who imagine themselves in dramatic or heroic situations.

The term in use, by Jon Krakauer, author of *Into Thin Air,* an account of deaths on an Everest expedition, reviewed by Alastair Scott in the *New York Times Book Review,* May 18, 1997:

> Mr. Krakauer calls the amateur climbers "Walter Mittys with Everest dreams" who "need to bear in mind that when things go wrong up in the Death Zone—and sooner or later they always do—the strongest guides in the world may be powerless to save a client's life. . . . "

And by Walter Shapiro, in *USA Today,* April 30, 1997:

> Donning my green eyeshade, I selflessly pored over the federal budget in quest of painless cuts. . . . I don't want to exaggerate my altruism, since in my Walter Mitty moments I fancy myself as Shapiro the Auditor, who can sniff out budgetary savings that elude mere mortals.

Again, from George Lang, in *Town & Country,* August 1, 1995:

> Of all the thousands of people I have met, Gilbert E. Kaplan, 54, certainly is one of the most extraordinary. He is a real-life Walter Mitty—but with a major refinement: unlike Mitty, he has realized his dream—and more. A few weeks ago, Kaplan joined a select handful of amateur conductors who have led the Los Angeles Philharmonic (at the Hollywood Bowl). . . .

And by William E. Leuchtenburg in *American Heritage,* May/June 1990:

> On September 22 I experienced a Walter Mitty day as uniformed officers waved me past the White House guard post and a sleek black limousine whisked me out of the White House gates up to Capitol Hill and down again.

Möbius strip \\'mȫ-bē-əs, 'mə(r)-, 'mō-\\ A one-sided surface constructed from a rectangle by holding one end fixed, rotating the opposite end 180°, and joining the two. Named for the German mathematician and astronomer who discovered it, August Ferdinand Möbius (1790–1868), the discovery was made virtually simultaneously by Johann Benedict Listing, in 1858.

The strip is a "topological space" that looks as if it has two edges, just as it did before the ends were connected, but if you trace one edge with a pencil, you find there is only one. The strip retains the same property when cut down the middle. In nonliteral uses, the term usually applies to things that look simple but are also mysterious and fascinating.

The term in use, by critic David Sterritt, reviewing the film *The Never Ending Story* in the *Christian Science Monitor,* July 19, 1984:

> The symbol of the book (and also the movie) is a snake eating its own tail. . . . In the spirit of that unusual reptile, the film tries to become a Möbius strip, an endless loop dipping into both the real and the imaginary.

And by Jay Fernandez in the *Washington Post Book World,* June 29, 1997, reviewing *Time on My Hands* by Peter Delacorte:

> With his third novel, *Time on My Hands,* he takes a slight left turn, both creatively and ideologically, in creating a four-dimensional Möbius strip of a story his narrator calls an "ante-memoir."

And by Vic Sussman, in the *Washington Post Magazine,* January 22, 1989:

> And when I turn the page again I see a picture that directly confronts my existential Tupperware questions: here are Tupperware containers designed to hold Tupperware containers! A Möbius strip of endlessly compulsive neatness—Tupperware nestled inside Tupperware nestled inside Tupperware.

Moby Dick The fictional great white whale pursued by the fanatical Captain AHAB and his ship *Pequod* in Herman Melville's 1851 novel *Moby-Dick;* also, a monster or the object of a mystical quest.

Melville's complex work is viewed as one of the greatest novels of American literature. Many theories of the whale's symbolism are offered—Moby Dick is the incarnation of evil, or the victim of modern man's destruction of nature, or the embodiment of the knowledge and understanding of reality.

Ahab, maimed by the creature, pursues the whale with an obsessive hatred, sweeping along to their deaths all the crew except the narrator Ishmael.

The whale, evoked by James M. Markham in the *New York Times,* May 1, 1989, writing from Paris on the architecturally controversial Bastille Opera:

> "It's surprising looking," said Maurice Solignac, the owner of the Tour d'Argent restaurant, which flanks the new opera, melding into its mass. The gentle, 68-year-old Mr. Solignac was doing his best to sound polite about the architectural Moby Dick beached on his doorstep.

Another example, by William L. Vance, author of *America's Rome,* (1989), describing the widely varying responses of American visitors to the Colosseum:

> The Moby Dick of architecture, a sublimely multivalent symbol, ravaged and enduring.

And by Scott Armstrong in the *Christian Science Monitor,* June 21, 1994, writing about an airport that had all kinds of trouble being completed:

> Called simply DIA—short for Denver International Airport, the monolith sits, unopened, amid the prairie and pronghorn northeast of town. But to critics, DIA stands for Done in Awhile, or Done in August (you pick the year), or just plain Moby Dick.

modest proposal, a A proposition that would solve a problem with an outrageous cure.

The expression is the shortened title of *A Modest Proposal for Preventing the Children of Poor People from being a Burthen to their Parents, Or the Country, and For Making Them Beneficial to the Publick,* a satiric pamphlet written by Jonathan Swift in 1729. He suggested that the answer to the grinding poverty of Irish peasants was for them to raise their children as livestock and sell them as food to wealthy English landlords. Just to make sure you got the idea, Swift helpfully included recipes.

The proposal was a classic example of Swift's bitter satire, an attack on the wrongheadedness of British governmental policy toward the Irish. And ever since, "a modest proposal" has been one which carries a shocking idea to ridiculous extremes to make a point.

The term in use, by Nancy Watzman in an essay in the *Christian Science Monitor,* September 6, 1996:

> When stock-car racer Dale Earnhardt climbs into his Chevrolet Monte Carlo, he wears his corporate sponsors on his sleeves. Sprinter Michael Johnson and basketball star Cheryl Swoopes both won their Olympic events in specially designed Nike shoes, complete with the company's characteristic "swoosh" logo. Bob Dole and Bill Clinton, however, prefer plain blue business suits.
>
> Here is a modest proposal. Starting now, all candidates for president and Congress should wear the corporate logos of their campaign contributors on their power suits.

And by columnist Ron Shaffer, who writes on traffic woes under the sobriquet "Dr. Gridlock," in the *Washington Post,* September 9, 1988. Under the heading "A Modest Proposal," Shaffer printed a letter from a pothole-weary reader proposing that the armed forces be called out to complete a long-delayed freeway segment through the District of Columbia, and that highway construction firms be sent overseas to defend the country against a Soviet invasion: "All they'd have to do is work on their roads."

mojo A magic spell, hex, or charm; magical power.

The word is probably of African origin, and was an African-American expression before being incorporated into the slang of the hippies in the 1960s.

The term in use, by Henry Allen, in the *Washington Post,* January 16, 1997, on our obsession with measurements and numbers:

> Dress size becomes a holy number—there are women who find a dress they love in a size 8, which proves too small, but they refuse to buy the same dress in size 10, because They Are an Eight, by God, though they'll buy a European 42, the metric numbers having yet to acquire the same terrible mojo as 2, 4, 6, 8, 10, 12 and 14 (where you can still say you're big-boned, though 16 means you're just fat).

And from Jacki Lyden, on National Public Radio's *All Things Considered,* February 27, 1994:

> The guitar twang of an old cotton-pickin' blues man down at the crossroads who's got his mojo workin' may beckon the blues, but supposing one of those blues men met the guitar twang of an old cotton-pickin' good ole boy down at the crossroads and he was playing country?

Mommie dearest A terrifying, abusive mother; alternatively, a vengeful style of autobiography, in which a famous parent (often dead, not a good defensive position) is portrayed as a monster of cruelty by an adult child.

The phrase is taken from the title of Christina Crawford's tell-all tale of life as the adopted child of Hollywood diva Joan Crawford. Crawford's long career took her from roles as a brassy flapper in the 1920s to a haggard horror in the 1960s. In her heydey she was an imposing figure on the screen with her commanding eyes, scarlet lipstick and famous shoulder pads. She even strapped on a six-gun for a shootout with Mercedes McCambridge in the kinky Western classic *Johnny Guitar* (1954).

According to Christina's account, Joan required her children to address her as "Mommie Dearest." Published in 1978, after the actress's death, the book remained a bestseller for weeks. In a fashion which would become typical of this genre, Christina Crawford's siblings disagreed over the truthfulness of the book.

The term in use, by A. Scott Walton in the *Atlanta Journal and Constitution,* June 27, 1996:

> Children of famous parents are famous for writing "Mommie Dearest" books blaming their mothers and fathers for all their problems. Not Sharon Robinson. The daughter of color-barrier-breaker Jackie Robinson has nothing but praise for the baseball great in her memoir *Stealing Home.*

And a play on the term by A.J. Jacobs in *Entertainment Weekly,* June 27, 1997, reviewing Jerry Oppenheimer's biography of Martha Stewart, *Just Desserts:*

> She's "the PMS poster girl from hell," "a control freak," "Captain QUEEG in drag," "Martha Dearest."

Mona Lisa Portrait of a woman with an enigmatic smile. Arguably the most famous painting in the Western world. The term is used to suggest an enigmatic person, expression, or situation, or a mystery into which individuals read whatever they choose.

The painting is by Leonardo Da Vinci, and is of the Madonna (Mona) Lisa del Giocondo, sometimes called La Gioconda, painted by the master ca. 1503–1506. While experts contend that undecipherable smiles were characteristic of portraits of the period, much speculation has been expended about the reason for the lady's expression.

The Mona Lisa, evoked by Rick Reilly, *Sports Illustrated,* September 23, 1996:

> This is what NBC's John Dockery said as part of a violin-accompanied, soft-filtered five-minute tribute before Powlus's first snap at Notre Dame Stadium, in September 1994: "We're unveiling a very special painting today, like a Mona Lisa."

And from Richard Martin in *Out* magazine, quoted by Ted Anthony of the Associated Press, October 7, 1996:

> He calls [actor James] Dean "the gay man's Mona Lisa."

From Inga Saffron, Knight-Ridder Newspapers, in the *Seattle Times,* December 26, 1996, on the wife of President Slobodan Milosevic of Serbia:

> With a purple flower tucked in her hair, a cascade of black bangs and her Mona Lisa smile, Markovic is certainly difficult to ignore.

Montagues and Capulets The feuding clans of William Shakespeare's *Romeo and Juliet.* Now used to describe opposing sides in similar long-standing, destructive feuds. (*See* HATFIELDS AND MCCOYS.)

The names are actually Anglicized versions of the Capelletti and the Montecchi, two noble families of Verona, Italy, in the 14th century.

The term in use, by Bob Hicks, in the *Portland Oregonian,* January 26, 1996:

> Move over, Hatfields and McCoys. Step aside, Montagues and Capulets. Sign a cease-fire, Bill and Newt. In the ongoing culture wars, one of the biggest chasms is between those curious creatures called The Critics and the readers who love to hate them.

And by Thomas Oliphant in the *Boston Globe,* August 1, 1993:

> What the Montagues and the Capulets did to each other, and above all to Romeo and Juliet, is at least understandably destructive compared with the multifaceted mess the country's politicians have made of this year's post-election opportunity to end a decade of debilitating gridlock.

morality play A situation that involves a direct conflict between right and wrong or good and evil and from which a moral lesson may be drawn. Allegorical plays were a popular form of entertainment in medieval Europe. They were sermons presented as drama in a simple form for illiterate audiences. The characters were not real people but rather personifications of abstract ideas, such as EVERYMAN, Mercy, Vanity, or Truth.

The term in use, by John Elson, *Time,* November 25, 1996, writing about Alger Hiss:

His 1949 trial and retrial in a Soviet-espionage case personified the explosive political and class conflicts of the time, serving as the first morality play of the red-baiting era.

Another example, by Deborah Sharp, *USA Today,* January 13, 1997:

On the Sunday after money rained down upon Miami from on high—or at least from the interstate—the tale of the overturned Brink's truck echoed from pulpits as morality play.

And finally, from Gus Tyler, *Forward,* August 4, 1995:

Brian and Quentin, however, may be more than just two children caught up in the mindless violence of the young. They may be classic characters in a morality play about a growing global inhumanity of human to human.

morph To change shape or form. Morphing is the process (using computer technology) by which one visual image is transformed seamlessly into another. By extension, morphing also refers to the process through which persons or organizations may transform their public image.

"Morph" is short for "metamorphose"—a verb meaning to change or transform. Morphing originates with the entertainment and toy industries and was popularized by the hit children's show (and movie and toys), "Mighty Morphin Power Rangers." The Rangers are high school students who transform themselves into super beings to fight the forces of evil. They drive fantastic vehicles which change into weapons. The visual tricks of the series became popular in television advertising as well.

The term in use, by Peter Appelbome in his book *Dixie Rising: How the South Is Shaping American Values, Politics and Culture* (1996):

Furthermore, in a way that once would have seemed a contradiction in terms, Southern Baptists were no longer geographically Southern Baptists. Beginning in 1942, when they spread to California, Southern Baptist congregations have set up shop in every state in the Union; now there are 1,900 black congregations, 3,000 Hispanic ones, and 800 Korean ones, a denomination speaking 101 languages endlessly morphing and reproducing itself across the country.

And Larry Powell longs for transformation of baseball's Texas Rangers in the *Dallas Morning News,* October 27, 1995:

I have kicked over a container of Ballpark Fortune-Telling Nachos and seen the future in the oozing cheese. The Specter of Perpetual Loss that has reigned for 24 seasons over any ballpark in Arlington soon will morph into the Mighty Marketing-Powered Rangers. . . . I love the Texas Rangers. I feel their pain. But I know the truth: the pennant-free Texas Rangers are the unpopped kernels of big league baseball.

mother of all . . . The ultimate; the biggest of something, of anything, the standard by which all others are gauged. Used frequently with a tone of irony or mockery.

It's a phrase brought into the American language by Iraqi dictator Saddam Hussein. He used it in a 25-minute speech to his nation on January 6, 1991, on the eve of what would become the Gulf War between Iraq and a U.S.-led coalition. The war forced Iraq to retreat from Kuwait, which Saddam's forces had invaded the previous August.

Saddam told his army that it was fighting against social and economic oppression, against discrimination, and against the oppression of foreign powers, "against double standards, corruption and hegemony. For these reasons," he said, "the battle in which you are locked today is the mother of all battles." In his use of the term he was hearkening back to the original mother of all battles in Arabic history, the battle of Qadisiya in A.D. 637 in which a united Islamic Arab force defeated Persia.

The term in use, by Jon Anderson, in the *Chicago Tribune,* December 31, 1996:

> Fact is, in these waning years of the 20th Century, all remaining New Year's Eves are but pale warmups for what is coming to a time zone near you. Call it the Night of the Millennium. Or simply the big one.
>
> Three years before the onslaught of the Mother of All New Year's Eves, a startling 183 rooms have been booked at the Drake Hotel for the historic night of the big change.

And by Alan Abelson in *Barron's,* May 12, 1997:

> With the little stocks beginning to come to life and word out that their big brothers, despite their awesome runs, are still "underowned" by the underperforming institutions, what's manifestly in the offing is not just a summer rally, but the mother of all summer rallies.

And an oddity, demonstrating that Saddam wasn't the mother of all phrasemakers, from the 1958 big-screen Western, *The Big Country*—Burl Ives, playing the patriarch of one of two families embroiled in a bitter feud, addressing his sniveling, bullying son: "Well, if you ain't the mother and father of all liars!"

mousetrap *See* BUILD A BETTER MOUSETRAP.

moving the goal posts Changing the rules in the middle of the game; changing what is required to score and win. It is a sports analogy suggesting unfairness that assumes that nonsports situations are, like sports, played by established rules known to everyone and enforced by referees.

The term in use, by William H. Carlile in the *Arizona Republic,* April 17, 1996:

Vietnam has received a reputation among some investors and business people as the "land of the moving goal posts," making it difficult for businesses to score successes.

And from Anthony Lake's letter to President Clinton asking that his name be withdrawn from nomination as director of the Central Intelligence Agency, after a prolonged confirmation struggle in the Senate, quoted in the *Washington Post,* March 18, 1997:

While we have made great progress in the nomination process over the past month and during last week's hearings, I have learned over the weekend that the process is once again faced by endless delay. It is a political football in a game with constantly moving goal posts.

Another example, by Ron Arnold, of the Center for the Defense of Free Enterprise, quoted in the *San Francisco Chronicle,* June 4, 1995:

The environmentalists kept moving the goal posts farther and farther back. Nothing was ever good enough for them.

Mrs. Grundy *See* GRUNDY, MRS.

Mrs. O'Leary's cow An unwitting agent of disaster.
According to popular myth, the cause of the Great Chicago Fire of 1871 was the cow kicking over a kerosene lantern in Mrs. Catherine O'Leary's barn on DeKoven Street. Old Chicago was a wooden firetrap, and there had been a long drought. The fire destroyed over 17,000 buildings, left almost 100,000 people homeless, and killed an estimated 250. It was finally contained by explosive demolition of buildings in its path.
The widow O'Leary denied the story, and said that the fire had been started by someone else. And in January 1997, Chicago lawyer and historian Dick Bales published an article suggesting that the culprit was Daniel "Peg Leg" Sullivan, who lived across the street.
In any case, the cow is frequently evoked as the immediate cause of catastrophe—particularly in matters affecting Chicago.
The term in use, by Lee Benson, sports columnist of the *Deseret News,* June 2, 1997, on the woes of Karl Malone, who missed two free throws at the end of a 1997 NBA Finals game between the Chicago Bulls and the Utah Jazz:

Man oh man, what's an MVP to do? You dominate the regular season, you finally beat Jordan out for the best-player-on-the-planet trophy, you haul your team into the NBA Finals for the first time ever, you nail a couple of timely fourth quarter jumpers so you're in a position to win, and then suddenly, just like that, you're that Buffalo Bills field goal kicker who was wide right, you're the guy who left the iron on, you're Mrs. O'Leary's cow.

That Bulls-Jazz Finals series inspired another reference, this by Shaun Powell in *Newsday,* June 12, 1997, when Michael Jordan came down with the flu:

> Jordan missed the morning shootaround and the news hit Chicago almost as hard as Mrs. O'Leary's cow kicked that lantern.

And in the *Los Angeles Times,* December 31, 1994:

> It wasn't as bad as the time Mrs. O'Leary's cow kicked over the lantern and started the Great Chicago Fire, but a large Valley puppy nonetheless created a stir Friday when its antics ignited a small home fire.

muckrake To search out and expose real or apparent misconduct of prominent individuals or businesses.

A muckrake is, well, just that—an implement for cleaning stables and the like. That great 17th-century moralist John Bunyan gets credit for the first figurative use in *Pilgrim's Progress,* in which he spoke of the man with a "Muck-rake in his hand" who raked filth rather than look up to nobler things. The term was applied later to someone interested in trashy affairs, including trashy scandals.

But the reform impulse in the Progressive Era in the United States, roughly the first 15 years of the 20th century, gave the term a positive twist, thanks to Theodore Roosevelt. A new breed of reformist journalists, seeing themselves as scientifically exposing the ills of modern industrial society, took aim at business and political corruption. They were still raking scandal, but in a good cause.

Their exposés touched the conscience of the middle class, and the resulting indignation at the callousness and ruthlessness of the rich and powerful led to a wide range of regulatory legislation, including anti-trust laws, pure food and drug laws, regulation of railroads, and child labor laws. From 1902 to 1912, more than a thousand muckraking articles ran in such magazines as *McClure's, Everybody's,* and *Collier's.*

As TR said in 1906: "The men with the muckrakes are often indispensable to the well-being of society, but only if they know when to stop raking the muck"—and therein lies the debate about the press that continues today. (*See* BLOOD IN THE WATER, FEEDING FRENZY.)

The term in use, by columnist Jack Anderson's cohort Jan Moller, lamenting the decision by the *Washington Post* to drop the column, quoted by the Associated Press, January 24, 1997:

> We are disappointed to lose the *Post,* naturally, but we're not planning on going anywhere. There's still muck to be raked in Washington, and we're going to do it.

By David Remnick in the *New Yorker,* January 20, 1997, writing about Katharine Graham's autobiography *Personal History:*

If there was one journalist she admired more than any other, it was James Reston, and it was Reston who, despite his many virtues, had famously said, "I will not have the *New York Times* muckraking the president of the United States."

Mudville *See* NO JOY IN MUDVILLE.

Mugwump A bolter from the Republican party in 1884; also, an independent in politics. The Blue Earth, Minn., *Post* once described a mugwump as "a sort of bird that sits on a fence with his mug on one side and his wump on the other." The term originated in the language of the Massachuset tribe, where it meant "war leader."

The Mugwumps were intellectual, reformist Republicans who opposed the spoils system in government employment. They bolted from the GOP during the election of 1884 when they could not stomach the Republican nominee James G. Blaine, whom they believed (with cause) to be corrupt. Instead, they backed the Democrat, Grover Cleveland. The *New York Sun* called them "Little Mugwumps"—little men attempting to be chiefs.

The campaign of 1884 still stands among America's dirtiest. Cleveland had earned a reputation for hard work and honesty as governor of New York, but he was attacked for having fathered an illegitimate child and for dodging military service during the Civil War. Chanted the Republicans, "Ma, Ma, where's my Pa? Gone to the White House, hah, hah, hah." Democrats retorted with a jingle about "Blaine, Blaine, James G. Blaine, the monumental liar from the state of Maine."

A week before the election, a dinner in Blaine's honor was attended by the richest ROBBER BARONS in the country. The same day a clergyman denounced the Democrats as the party of "Rum, Romanism and Rebellion." The Democratic press seized its opportunity. A *New York World* cartoon showed the fatcats feasting with labor shivering outside. Cleveland won, narrowly. Triumphant Democrats were able to taunt their foes thus: "Hurrah for Maria, hurrah for the kid; we voted for Grover and we're glad we did!"

Cleveland was not as reformist a president as the Mugwumps wanted, and they did not support him in 1888. He lost, but was returned to office with Mugwump support in 1892, becoming the only president to serve two nonconsecutive terms.

The term in use, by Sidney Blumenthal in the *New Republic,* August 10, 1992:

> He [Gary Hart] left the field to be occupied by Michael Dukakis who tried to use the "Massachusetts Miracle" as a postindustrial model; but its political dimensions were beyond the grasp of his narrow, linear mind. His view of the party remained stunted; it was that of a horrified mugwump.

And by Mark Feeney in the *Boston Globe,* March 16, 1986, on the work of MUCKRAKE Dwight Macdonald (1906–1982):

A WASP among the predominantly Jewish New York intellectuals, a movie columnist who loathed popular culture, an anti-Fascist who advocated pacificism during World War II, a political writer who bragged about how rarely he voted, a Marxist who ended up a self-proclaimed "Mugwump," Dwight Macdonald (to avoid the cliché evades the truth) was one of a kind.

mullah \\'mə-lə, 'mü-\\ An educated Muslim trained in religious law and teaching and usually holding an official post. In Arabic, literally, "master."

In the United States, after the crisis in which Iranians held 52 Americans hostage in their embassy in Teheran for 444 days, from November 1979 to January 1981, the term came to connote a person who encourages religious fanaticism or extreme, intolerant political views.

The term in use, by Sean Wilentz, in the *New Republic,* April 25, 1988, on fundamentalist Christian Reverend Jerry Falwell:

> Not too long ago, after all, many people thought of Falwell as an American mullah in the making, a clear and present danger to democracy—fears that Falwell fed with his fiery rhetoric about putting the nation back on a biblical footing.

And by Martin F. Nolan of the *Boston Globe,* commenting on the 1992 Republican national convention, in the *St. Paul Pioneer Press,* August 21, 1992:

> With the Democratic platform matching it bromide for bromide in welfare-bashing and cooing about family values, the mullahs of the GOP have begun to panic. Economics and other secular issues have slipped from their grasp, so they have launched a JIHAD against alternative lifestyles and deviant behavior.

munchkin A person who is notably small and often endearing. Also, a minor player, someone who is eccentric, weak, or unimportant.

The munchkins were small, kind, elflike people in Frank L. Baum's *The Wonderful Wizard of Oz* (1900). As Dorothy's adventures begin, her house falls on the wicked witch who had ruled over the Land of the Munchkins, and they are very grateful to her for liberating them. They set Dorothy on her way, following the YELLOW BRICK ROAD, and the rest is history.

The term in use, by Thomas V. DiBacco in *USA Today,* August 16, 1994, on the organization of professional baseball:

> Each time the owners have appointed a permanent commissioner, the occupant has lost sight of his appropriately Munchkin-like authority, which is to oversee the sport only in the owners' interests.

And by Jeff Franks, reporting on, as they say, a different breed of cat, for Reuters, July 31, 1995:

> Cat breeders have finally succeeded in producing a cat that even self-proclaimed cat lovers do not like: the munchkin.
> Munchkins come in all colors and coats, but their back legs are about half as long as those of a normal cat, and the front legs are even shorter.

Munich Shortsighted and often dishonorable appeasement of a tyrant.

On September 30, 1938, British Prime Minister Neville Chamberlain, French Premier Edouard Daladier, German chancellor Adolf Hitler, and Italian dictator Benito Mussolini met at the German city of Munich and signed an agreement ceding to Germany the Sudetenland, an area in western Czechoslovakia inhabited by ethnic Germans. This was an attempt to satisfy once and for all Hitler's demands for more territory. The Czechs were there only to sign, not to negotiate; they signed "to register their protest before the world against a decision in which they had no part."

Chamberlain returned to London and read to an enthusiastic crowd a pledge of everlasting Anglo-German friendship signed by himself and Hitler. With his familiar umbrella (now itself a symbol of appeasement) in one hand, waving the document in the other, he uttered a phrase that has become famous for its historic misreading of a situation, declaring that the accord meant "PEACE FOR OUR TIME."

Thus Munich has come to stand for a policy that seeks to appease an aggressor nation, particularly at the expense of small or weak nations, a policy that can lead only to failure and ultimately to war.

The term in use, by Daniel Schorr in the *New Leader,* January 13, 1997:

> The transition reflects a pendulum swing between the "no more Munichs" syndrome—no more appeasement of aggressors and dictators—and the "no more Vietnams" syndrome—no more plunging America into Third World quagmires. President Clinton was part of the "no more Vietnams" generation, but now "no more Munichs" may be making a comeback with Secretary of State Madeleine K. Albright. . . .

And by David Warsh in the *Boston Globe,* in a profile of the late newspaper pundit, Joseph Alsop, August 30, 1989:

> The extreme rhetoric of Alsop's position on Vietnam—that the loss of Saigon would be "another Munich"— has not been proven out in recent years, to say the least.

Murderers' Row A formidable, deadly array, poised for action. A group of heavy hitters.

The expression is thought to come from the row of cells set aside for the most dangerous criminals in the Tombs prison in New York. The nickname quickly migrated into baseball to be applied to a roster of power-ful batters.

The accolade was most famously given to the batting order of the 1927 New York Yankees, thought to be one of the greatest baseball teams in history. Babe Ruth, batting third, hit 60 home runs in 1927, and Lou Gehrig, batting fourth, led the league with 175 RBIs and finished the season with 47 home runs. The lineup also included Earl Combs (who led the league in hits, singles and triples), Bob Meusel, and Tony Lazzeri.

The term is used on a caption of a famous photograph in *US Navy Photographs: Pearl Harbor to Tokyo Harbor.* Taken December 8, 1944, it is an aerial shot of six great aircraft carriers (*Wasp, Yorktown, Hornet, Hancock, Ticonderoga* and *Lexington*) anchored in a row at Ulithi, then a major reprovisioning point. These fast carriers had been grouped together to provide a swift strike force of crushing power. In the photograph, the carriers lie at rest in perfect symmetry, the biggest hitters in the park.

Another example, by Rick Reilly in *Sports Illustrated,* October 5, 1998:

> The trio—one gray-templed veteran near the omega of his career (*see* ALPHA AND OMEGA) and two Davis Cup neophytes ranked 50th and 100th, respectively—was something other than a mur-derers' row.

And by Rick Reilly in *Sports Illustrated,* April 5, 1993:

> And so when he had fashioned a one-shot lead through last Sat-urday in The Players Championship . . . somebody asked him if he was scared by the all-star leader-board lurking behind him— Greg Norman, Mark O'Meara and Bernhard Langer one shot back; Paul Azinger, two; Payne Stewart and Ken Green, three; Corey Pavin, five—a Murderers' Row in pleats.

And by Richard Zoglin in *Time,* April 3, 1989:

> A new round of star wars is in full swing at the network news divisions. CBS, in desperate need of a female power hitter, last week grabbed one of the league's best, Connie Chung, from NBC. She will fill a gap in the CBS line-up opened last month when Diane Sawyer left to join the burgeoning Murderers' Row at ABC.

mustard gas An irritant; a blistering, oily liquid used as a chemical weapon. Hence, a treacherous, poisonous tactic, in war and by extension in other activities such as politics, but one that is hard to control.

In World War I, the Germans used this poison gas, given its name because of its blistering effect on skin, eyes, and lungs. It destroys the respiratory systems of its victims, causing death or terrible injury. (The British responded with chlorine gas.)

The term in use, by Jon Greenburg on National Public Radio's "Morning Edition," July 15, 1996:

> The independent counsel law is the mustard gas of politics— effective on the enemy, but a change in the political wind can cause it to drift back on friends.

Another example, from the *Los Angeles Times,* August 2, 1990, describing the drug and perjury trial of Marion Barry, mayor of Washington, D.C.:

> A defense attorney acknowledged that Washington mayor Barry has used cocaine but he likened the FBI sting operation in which Barry was ensnared to an attack of mustard gas that cannot be contained.

mute inglorious Milton, a A potential genius of promise unfulfilled through lack of opportunity.

Another memorable phrase from Thomas Gray's "Elegy Written in a Country Church Yard." (*See* FAR FROM THE MADDING CROWD.) Gray meditates on the churchyard burying ground in a country town:

> Some mute inglorious Milton here may rest,
>   Some Cromwell guiltless of his country's blood.

John Milton (1608–74) was one of the greatest poets of the English language. (*See* PARADISE LOST.) Oliver Cromwell (1599–1698) was a country gentleman and a member of Parliament whose great military abilities emerged in the English Civil War, and he became Lord Protector of England. Thus, Gray speculates that in this obscure graveyard may lie someone of similar but untapped genius, whose abilities were never sparked into being by events.

H.L. Mencken had a retort for this; in *Prejudices, Third Series* (1922) he observed, "There are no mute inglorious Miltons, save in the hallucinations of poets. The one sound test of a Milton is that he functions as a Milton."

The term in use, by Diane Roberts in a review of *The Brontës* by Juliet Barker, in the *Atlanta Journal and Constitution,* October 29, 1995, describing Branwell, the ne'er-do-well brother of Charlotte, Emily, and Anne:

> She [Barker] suggests that Branwell was an artist of immense talent, underappreciated by the Brontë establishment. But Branwell did not produce the novels and poems his sisters did. Perhaps

he was a sort of "mute, inglorious Milton," but the fact remains that he was an alcoholic and an opium addict, who could not or would not bring his genius to flower and who died in his early 30s.

And again, in Frederic Morton's review of *Extraordinary Minds: Portraits of Exceptional Individuals and an Examination of Our Extraordinariness* by Howard Gardner, in the *Los Angeles Times,* July 20, 1997:

Gardner tries to tease out dimensions in singularity (unique excellence) that can be tapped by us all, so that the mute, inglorious can flower, to some degree, into Miltons.

mystery *See* RIDDLE WRAPPED IN A MYSTERY INSIDE AN ENIGMA.

For legions of aspiring writers, the Web was **nirvana,** *a magical place where everyone could become a publisher. . . .*

—Howard Kurtz

nabob \'nā-ˌbäb\ A person of great wealth or prominence. It comes from the Hindi word, "nawwab," which was used to refer to a provincial governor in the Mogul Empire (in India, 1526–1817). These men usually became wealthy and powerful. Today, the word has a mocking tone, suggesting self-importance and/or vulgar wealth.

The word worked its way into English in the early days of British occupation of India. English merchant adventurers who made their fortunes there and returned home to enjoy their wealth were derided as "nabobs," "nouveau riches."

Journalist William Safire admits to rejuvenating the word when he was a speech writer for Vice President Spiro T. Agnew. On September 11, 1970, Agnew attacked the press (in a Safire-written speech) as "nattering nabobs of negativism." The speech's notoriety propelled Agnew along an alley of alliterative allusions.

The term in use, by James W. Scott in the *Kansas City Star,* May 19, 1992, paying tribute to Kansan Bill Koch's success in winning the America's Cup:

> For years the America's Cup was monopolized by the New York club which held the event off Newport. A Kansan entering the fray probably was received by the coastal nabobs of yachting about the way the British saw the original *America* entering the Race of All Nations Aug. 22, 1851. . . .

And by Thomas S. Mulligan in the *Los Angeles Times,* April 15, 1997, describing Martha Stewart and illustrating, as do all of the following quotations, the tendency for *nabob* to bring out an alliterative streak in writers:

> The Contessa of Cuisine, the DOYENNE of Decor, the Nabob of Nesting.

And by Melanie Warner in *Fortune,* September 8, 1997, on the *New York Observer:*

> The ten-year-old *Observer* has evolved into an eagerly awaited must-read among New York's chattering cognoscenti. . . . The weekly salmon-colored paper chronicles the lives and loves of New York's nabobs in media, society, business, show business, real estate and local politics.

And by Thomas A. Stewart in *Fortune,* July 11, 1994:

> Network nabobs have begun to distill the wisdom of managing
> in a wired organization—the dos and don'ts, the predictable sur-
> prises and conflicts.

naked city The unvarnished, gritty harshness of life in the city, where
every person has an interesting tale to tell or to hide. Now often used in
a jocular way to refer to the complexities—humorous and otherwise—of
urban life. A reference to the trendsetting 1948 cop-thriller movie of the
same title. The famous voice-over at the end says: "There are eight million stories in the naked city. This . . . has been one of them."
The film was shot on location in New York City and followed a squad
of homicide detectives through the seamy parts of the city as they investigate a young woman's murder. It led to a highly successful television
series in the 1960s.
The term in use, by David Wharton, in the *Los Angeles Times,* January
26, 1997:

> There are what seems like a million sports bars in the naked city.

And by Craig Crossman, Knight-Ridder News Services, in the *Washington Post,* "Business," September 16, 1996:

> There are now more than 8,000 known computer viruses in the
> Naked City, and just one of them can corrupt data, give you
> weird messages or spread to a friend's computer.

namby-pamby Wishy-washy, weak, insipid; affectedly sentimental, cutesy,
childish. The term began as a literary insult, denigrating the work of English poet Ambrose Philips (ca. 1675-1749). Philips got into a literary quarrel with Alexander Pope, and got the worst of it (as did everyone who
took on Pope, "the Wasp of Twickenham").
Namby-Pamby is a baby-talk play on the name Ambrose. Henry Carey
(ca. 1687-1743), a poet, musician and playwright—and ally of Pope—sent
up Ambrose in a 1726 poem, "Namby Pamby":

> Namby Pamby's little rhymes,
> Little jingle, little chimes.

The term in use, by Robert Wright as TRB in the *New Republic,* October 9, 1995:

> A derisive hostility toward environmentalism is common among
> congressional Republicans. One thing that especially galls them
> is all this globaloney about the greenhouse effect and the thin-
> ning of the ozone layer. It combines namby-pamby liberal nature-
> loving with a namby-pamby liberal concern about matters
> beyond our borders.

And by Anatole Broyard in the *New York Times Book Review,* June 21,
1987:

Anyway, who wants to read a compassionate book? Is the Bible compassionate? Is Shakespeare? There's something sticky, pious or namby-pamby about the work. A good character doesn't need all that compassion—he can stand on his own.

And by Adam Goodheart in *Civilization,* August/September 1997:

Just imagine them lisping this noble verse: rank upon rank of stout-hearted Victorian toddlers, already prepared to die for Queen and Country! Theirs was a nation that knew what was what, what? Back then, one heard no namby-pamby bleating about the right to self-determination of the territories of the nawab of Oudh. Empire meant spending the morning racking up new colonies like runs on the cricket pitch, and then white linen and gin fizzes on the veranda all afternoon long.

nasty, brutish, and short Life is basically and fundamentally unpleasant, and leads only to death. A bleak assessment of the human condition from a bleak assessor.

The phrase refers to the best known passage in Thomas Hobbes' book *Leviathan* [*q.v.*], (*see also* HOBBESIAN). It describes the state of man when there is no strong governing power and men pursue their selfish interests with no constraint on their worst impulses. The result:

No arts; no letters; no society; and which is worst of all, continual fear, and danger of violent death; And the life of man, solitary, poor, nasty, brutish, and short.

The term in use, by Lewis H. Lapham, *Harper's* magazine, March 1, 1995:

Like so much else about the Republican risorgimento, the political passion was attached to a preferred image rather than a plain or ambiguous fact, not to the Gingrich who had just delivered a conciliatory speech but to the Gingrich renowned for being nasty and brutish and short—the militant Gingrich blessed with a boll weevil's appetite for destruction. . . .

And from Brad Darrach, in *Life* magazine, December 1, 1995:

Since life in pro sports is apt to be nasty, brutish and short, superstars are expected to grab while the grabbing's good.

And from Anthony Lake, in a letter to President Clinton withdrawing his name from nomination as director of the Central Intelligence Agency, after a bruising confirmation battle, quoted in the *Washington Post,* March 18, 1997:

It [the confirmation process] is nasty and brutish without being short.

native *See* GO NATIVE.

neighbor *See* BEGGAR-THY-NEIGHBOR.

nemesis \'ne-mə-səs\ One who inflicts retribution or vengeance; also a formidable and usually victorious rival or opponent. The word comes from the name of the Greek goddess of retributive justice, Nemesis.
The term in use, by Thomas Maier in *Newsday,* September 8, 1996:

> In the swirl of controversy surrounding Jack KEVORKIAN, perhaps his biggest nemesis has been [Dr. L.J.] Dragovic, the county's 46-year-old medical examiner. He's testified as a government witness in the three trials that eventually acquitted Kevorkian.

And by Laurie Goodstein in the *Washington Post,* December 23, 1996:

> The man whose lawsuit has pushed the Cult Awareness Network into bankruptcy has done an about-face and is no longer moving toward putting the group out of business.
> He has abruptly dismissed his lawyer, a prominent member of the Church of Scientology, the anti-cult group's nemesis, and hired an attorney who has battled the church in the past.

And again, by Mike Delnagro of Gannett News Service, April 24, 1994:

> The Knicks, with the Eastern Conference No. 2 seed, will face their current nemesis, the seventh-seeded New Jersey Nets, in the best-of-five first round of the NBA playoffs, starting Thursday or Friday in New York.

never-never land A fantastical place where no child has to grow up. It was created by Scottish playwright J.M. Barrie in his beloved classic *Peter Pan, or The Boy Who Wouldn't Grow Up*, first staged in 1904. It is here that Peter, with the assistance of the fairy Tinkerbelle, does battle with his enemy Captain Hook and his pirates. (*See also* PETER PAN.*)*
The term in use, by Jay Cocks in *Time,* September 4, 1989:

> The Grateful Dead persisted, a whole band of Peter Pans camping out in a hippie never-never land.

And by Charles Lane in *Newsweek,* August 13, 1990:

> A futuristic glass-and-steel capital rose from the desert sand, complete with a Disneyesque amusement park named Entertainment City. At a vast shopping mall called Sultan Center, where the supermarkets stayed open 24 hours, the people browsed among French fashions by day and sampled Norwegian salmon at night. At the ice-skating rink, robed men glided on a spot where camels used to roam. . . . This place was called Kuwait. Oil money built it. The Kuwaitis thought they would live happily ever after—until Iraq came and took Never-Never Land away.

And from Rick Sylvain in the *Pittsburgh Press,* October 25, 1987:

Cancun's actually an island shaped like a 7. A nicely landscaped
boulevard called Paseo Kukulcan runs its length.

At least across the bridge on the mainland, in Cancun City,
you get a sense of being in Mexico and not in the never-never
land of the resort area.

Newcastle *See* COALS TO NEWCASTLE, CARRY.

Newspeak The artificial, abbreviated-style official language of the state
in George Orwell's novel *Nineteen Eighty-four*. The name is now applied
to obfuscatory or misleading language, especially terminology used by
politicians, bureaucrats, or ideologues.

The novel's protagonist, Winston Smith, works in the Ministry of Truth,
where his job is rewriting works of literature and history into Newspeak.
Literature has the power to inspire unorthodox thought, which is a threat
to authority. The government therefore destroys literature and history by
destroying language.

The term in use, by Strobe Talbott in *Time,* February 19, 1990:

> The [Communist] party has called itself the "dictatorship of the
> proletariat" and the "vanguard of the toilers." It has operated on
> the principle of "democratic centralism," a brazen contradiction
> in terms. Everyone knew which words in the Newspeak were
> camouflage and which meant what they said. The party was boss,
> and there was no other boss.

And by Neal Ascherson, reviewing *King Leopold's Ghost: A Story of
Greed, Terror, and Heroism in Colonial Africa* in the *Los Angeles Times,*
January 10, 1999:

> It was the first ORWELLIAN big lie, which sold a gigantic mech-
> anism of greed and terror to the world as a crusade for human-
> itarian values. A Newspeak was devised in which everything
> became its opposite—until Free State officials could write unself-
> consciously in their official reports about "volunteers in chains"
> and "liberated men chained by the neck."

night of the long knives June 30, 1934, when Hitler's henchmen assassinated possible rivals to his recently acquired power in Germany. Hundreds of real or suspected adversaries, including old friends and
collaborators, were brutally murdered.

The term is used to describe ruthless struggles among rival political factions, including non-bloody power struggles among bureaucrats, corporate executives, or ideologues in a movement; or purges in organizations.
In all cases, jobs are lost as real or suspected opponents are ousted.

The term in use, by Tom Kenworthy and Don Phillips in the *Washington Post,* March 20, 1989, describing turmoil in the House of Representatives over ethics charges against the Speaker of the House, Jim
Wright:

Speculation is mounting that Wright will not survive as speaker. The corridors are full of the sound of long knives being sharpened.

And eight years later, more knives, different Speaker—by Nancy Gibbs in *Time,* April 7, 1997:

In all quarters of the Capitol the question is not if Gingrich will fall but when. "This is the night of the long knives," says a Republican House member.

And by Marty Goldensohn in *Newsday,* February 14, 1995:

It looks like we are in for night after night of the long knives in the palace of Rudy Giuliani. Watch your back, especially if you're a public relations officer. A number of city flacks have been sacked already, basically for the same reason: They forgot that Job One was to make the mayor look good.

Nimrod \\'nim-ˌräd\\ A mighty hunter.

He is a figure in the Book of Genesis, described as "a mighty one in the earth" and a "mighty hunter before the Lord." While today the term is applied to someone who hunts animals, Alexander Pope interpreted the Scripture to mean that "his prey was man." According to the Bible, Nimrod established a great kingdom, Shinar, and he is credited for building the Tower of BABEL with the disastrous idea of reaching heaven. Thus a nimrod can also be a tyrant or a stupid fellow. This last is how he shows up in Dante's *Inferno.*

The term in use, by C.W. Gusewelle in the *Kansas City Star,* January 29, 1996, disapproving of high-tech hunting equipment for wild turkeys:

A laser sight will display the target—otherwise known as the turkey—in an aiming display somewhat like the one jet pilots use when engaging an enemy plane or releasing their smart bombs. Even after the bird is locked in, so to speak, and the fearless nimrod has squeezed the trigger, his wundermachine will continue working on his behalf.

And by Douglas Starr in *International Wildlife,* November-December, 1989:

Italy has the world's second highest concentration of hunters, after the tiny island-nation of Malta, with each Italian nimrod stalking an average hunting area about the size of two football fields.

And here as a verb, by John Gould in the *Christian Science Monitor* on moosehunting in Maine, August 7, 1992:

Back in the 1930s and earlier, the vast moose on our Great Seal of the State of Maine had been reduced by the sporty hunters until just a tax-gatherer's handful remained in our wilds. Much,

much too late our legislators rallied to enact a perpetual closed season—never again would a Maine moose be nimrodded.

Ninety-five Theses The fundamental document of the Protestant Reformation, nailed by Martin Luther (1483–1546) to the door of the castle church in Wittenberg, Germany, in 1517. The term is now used of any set of controversial ideas boldly set forth. The expression "nailing a message to the church door" is also drawn from this incident.

Luther, a professor at the University of Wittenberg, had been provoked to rebel against the Roman Catholic Church by a visit to the area of a monk selling indulgences to finance the construction of St. Peter's in Rome. (In the Roman Catholic Church, an indulgence is a remission of punishment for sins and is supposed to save the sinner from having to spend time in purgatory.) Luther believed that a soul could not be saved in such a way. His theses contended that the sinner was freed of his burden by faith, not by confession, and that the priest was not a necessary intermediary between man and God.

The term in use, by automobile columnist Brock Yates, having set forth his program as imaginary czar of the auto industry in the *Washington Post Magazine,* November 6, 1988:

> There you have it. You will recall that Martin Luther nailed 95 theses to the door of the Wittenberg Cathedral, but I have managed a certain triumph of brevity by limiting mine to 58.

Another example, from B. Drummond Ayres Jr., in the *New York Times,* July 9, 1989:

> The Rev. George Augustus Stallings, Jr., says he is no Martin Luther, no renegade Roman Catholic with a fistful of heretical theses to nail to a church door.
> But if he is no Luther, this maverick among Catholic priests has nevertheless defiantly embarked on a course that is forcing the 53-million-member church to consider anew whether it is adequately addressing the needs of its 1.5 million black parishioners.

And by Robert Reno, in *Newsday,* April 16, 1997:

> Not since the Reformation itself have we witnessed such an obsession with the idea, if not the substance of reform. . . . The problem is we have devalued the word. It's as if Ralph Reed and the Christian Coalition were mistaken for Luther and his Ninety-Five Theses.

nirvana \nir-'vä-nə, (ˌ)nər-\ *often capitalized* The final beatitude that is sought especially in Buddhism through the extinction of desire and individual consciousness. A state of bliss, of oblivion. Paradise, heaven. The Western idea seems to be a version of heaven where all one's needs are met, as opposed to the Eastern vision of having no needs.

It is a Sanskrit word meaning "extinction," as in the extinguishing of a light. Among Buddhists, it is a state to be wished for, a union with the Buddha following the destruction of one's KARMA.

The term in use, by Howard Kurtz in the *Washington Post,* May 28, 1997:

> For legions of aspiring writers, the Web was nirvana, a magical place where anyone could become a publisher without having to shell out for printing presses or delivery trucks.

And by Randy Tucker in the *Christian Science Monitor,* July 2, 1997:

> Welcome to employment nirvana on the Great Plains. While the national jobless rate has sunk to its lowest level in a quarter of a century, workers in Nebraska are reveling in an unemployment rate that's half as much: 2.3 percent, the lowest in the U.S.

noble savage A mythic conception developed in European literature and philosophy of primitive non-European cultures living in a state of unspoiled virtue and simplicity, uncorrupted by European civilization.

The age of exploration in Europe, particularly the discovery of America, led many European writers to embrace this idea. The earliest known use of the phrase is by John Dryden, in his 1672 play *The Conquest of Granada:*

> I am as free as Nature first made man,
> Ere the base laws of servitude began,
> When wild in woods the noble savage ran.

The idea must have had powerful appeal in a century in which Europe was torn by war and religious persecution.

Jean-Jacques Rousseau (1712-1778) is frequently associated with the concept; in his writings he disputed the prevailing view in the 18th century that progress in science and the arts would advance the welfare of all. Instead, he rebelled against social and political authority, foreshadowing the Romantic movement.

The term in use, by Fernando Gonzalez in the *Boston Globe,* October 28, 1988, reviewing *Bird,* a film about jazz musician Charlie Parker:

> Also disturbing is the movie's "noble savage" approach to Parker's work. In "Bird," things just happen. Whether intended or not, isn't this another instance of the misconceived notion of a black person blessed with "natural ability"?

And by Lorrie Moore in the *New York Times Book Review,* January 25, 1987:

> Mr. Pattison establishes a literary backlighting to reveal how rock music belongs to a tradition of Romantic counterfeits, of bogus "noble savage" folk culture. . . .

Also from Lewis H. Lapham in *Harper's,* August 1984:

Their belief in the transfiguring power of personality derives its egalitarian bona fides from Jean Jacques Rousseau's panorama of man as a noble savage at play in the fields of the ID, of man set free from laws and schools and institutions, free to constitute himself his own government, free to declare himself a God.

noir *See* FILM NOIR.

no joy in Mudville A sense of pervasive and shared disappointment. In the fictitious community immortalized by Ernest Lawrence Thayer in his 1888 poem *Casey at the Bat,* Mighty Casey meets his WATERLOO, and gloom reigns:

> Oh, somewhere in this favored land the sun is shining bright,
> The band is playing somewhere, and somewhere hearts are
>   light;
> And somewhere men are laughing, and somewhere children
>   shout,
> But there is no joy in Mudville; Mighty Casey has struck out.

The last line has stuck; we are all Mudvillians, and the fate of the home team or local hero can mean joy all around or ubiquitous despair.

The term, indeed the whole final stanza, in use by Langdon Winner in *Technology Review,* May 15, 1996, describing the duel between chess champion Garry Kasparov and IBM's Deep Blue:

> Somewhere in this favored land, monitors are shining bright. Soundboards are playing somewhere, bits travel at the speed of light. Somewhere nerds are laughing, somewhere programmers shout. But there's still some joy in Mudville: mighty Kasparov did not strike out.

And by Erik Brady in *USA Today,* January 31, 1994:

> And you thought there was no joy in Mudville? Mighty Casey only struck out once.
>   The Buffalo Bills lost the Super Bowl Sunday. Again. For the fourth time in a row.

And by Robert P. Hey, in the *Christian Science Monitor,* April 9, 1991:

> As baseball undergoes its annual metamorphosis from spring training to regular season, the sport brings its yearly two games to the nation's capital—outside of Mudville the most famous American baseball town not to have a major league team.

nom de guerre \,näm-di-'ger\ An assumed name under which one paints, performs, or fights; a pseudonym. It's French and means "war name." The term dates from the days of chivalry, when knights were known by the symbols on their shields. "Nom de plume," or "pen name," is specifically a writer's pseudonym.

The term in use, by Loren Jenkins in the *Washington Post,* April 17, 1988, discussing the assassination of Khalid Wazir, the military chief of the Palestine Liberation Organization:

> Wazir, better known by his nom de guerre, Abu Jihad, was known to be responsible for coordinating the continuing Palestinian uprising in the Israeli-occupied West Bank and Gaza Strip.

And by Richard Wolkomir in *Smithsonian,* August 1992:

> . . . "Captain Nabber" pushes his kayak into the water. He is tall, fortyish and mild-mannered. His nom de guerre is used here to protect his job; he's an engineer working for an industry Bay-Keeper watches. In his spare time, he is one of BayKeeper's most tigerish volunteers.

And by Bill Iezzi, in the *Philadelphia Inquirer,* June 8, 1997, on watching a women's boxing match:

> So if "Joltin' Janaki," a bomber of another sort, wants to wing it with another female in what they call executive boxing, why not? Her nom de guerre was bestowed by David Paul, a self-described certified personal trainer, hypnotherapist and white-collar boxing innovator, who has his clients engage in pugilism as a way of centering themselves mentally.

non-denial denial A carefully worded official statement which ostensibly rejects allegations of wrongdoing but does not quite say they are false. A statement of equivocation.

It's a term we owe to the Watergate era and was used to describe the responses issued by the Nixon administration and the Committee to Re-elect the President to newspaper reports of the unfolding scandal.

The term in use, by Peter H. King in the *Los Angeles Times,* February 22, 1995, on whether California Governor Pete Wilson would seek the presidency in 1996:

> Campaign promises and subsequent non-denial denials to the contrary, Wilson has left subtle clues he intends to run. For instance, last month he dragged his poor wife to a tedious news conference on the state budget.

And by Tim Sullivan, Gannett News Service, January 26, 1996, describing National Football League chief Paul Tagliabue:

> Tagliabue is a master of the artful evasion, and the non-denial denial.
> He may mean exactly what he says, but sometimes it is only in the narrowest sense of his words. This reflects a wealth of legal knowledge and a certain lack of conviction.

And by Dave Skidmore of the Associated Press, June 23, 1994:

If this were the Watergate era, Federal Reserve Chairman Alan Greenspan's answer might have been called a non-denial denial. He pooh-poohed the suggestion, raised by *Washington Post* reporter Bob Woodward, that he worked so closely with the Clinton administration last year that he "in some ways was a ghost-writer" of its economic policy.

normalcy The state or fact of being normal or regular. A word made current in our time by Warren G. Harding, 29th president of the United States. Harding was picked for the office in the original smoke-filled room when the Republican convention of 1920 deadlocked. Harding promised, popularized and epitomized "normalcy"—a time of retrenchment and consolidation at the end of a period of great endeavor, sacrifice, controversy and turmoil. In Harding's case, blissful normality followed the upheavals of World War I, the bitter national debate over participation in the League of Nations, and domestic social conflict.

Harding was mocked for creating the word, but he claimed he found it in the dictionary, and it does turn up as far back as the mid-19th century.

Harding used the term in accepting the Republican nomination on July 22, 1920: "We must stabilize and strive for normalcy." But he used it even earlier, on May 20 of that year, in a speech in Boston, when he made his case this way:

> America's present need is not heroics, but healing; not nostrums, but normalcy; not revolution, but restoration; not experimentation but equipoise.

And by Mike Evans in *Industry Week,* February 7, 1994:

> The 1970 recession was clearly an attempt to return the economy from the superheated growth of the Vietnam War era to normalcy.

And by Ronald Powers of the Associated Press, July 7, 1997, on Rep. Carolyn McCarthy of New York:

> Mrs. McCarthy is what some consider an ideal member of Congress—a citizen lawmaker, an everywoman (*see* EVERYMAN) with more common sense than political savvy, someone who reluctantly waded into the fray to right what she saw as a terrible wrong.
>
> And for the former nurse and suburban housewife, her new career is providing a path back to normalcy from a horrific family tragedy.

not with a bang but a whimper A half-hearted, ignominious, or anticlimactic end, a fizzle rather than an explosion.

The phrase is the closing of T.S. Eliot's "The Hollow Men"—the poet's gloomy view of the 20th century: "This is the way the world ends/ Not with a bang but a whimper."

The term in use, by *Washington Post* television critic Tom Shales, April 20, 1997:

> *Hallmark Hall of Fame* ends its season on CBS tonight with more of a whimper than a bang, but it's a sweet sort of whimper, a winsome whimper.

And by Peter Baker in the *Baltimore Sun,* September 3, 1995:

> Fall rockfish season opened Friday, the earliest late-season period for striper fishing for recreational and charterboat anglers since the fishery was closed for five years starting in January of 1985. And according to several accounts, opening day was somewhere between a bang and a whimper.

And by Patricia Ward Biederman in the *Los Angeles Times,* July 21, 1995, in a profile of the Kingston Trio, a popular folksinging group formed in 1957:

> The trio's heyday ended not with a bang, nor a whimper, but with a yeah, yeah, yeah. In 1962 they headlined a series of concerts in London. One of the opening acts was a quartet called the Beatles. "We came back to California and told people about this great group," recalls Shane. "We should have shut up."

Nuremberg defense \\'nùr-əm-ˌbərg, 'nyùr-\\ The defense—"I was just following orders"—which was unsuccessfully offered by Nazis who were put on trial for war crimes following World War II at Nuremberg, Germany. Now the term is used to contemptuously characterize the excuse when offered by someone who has carried out orders to perform what he knows to be a criminal or reprehensible act.

The term in use, by columnist George Will, in the *Washington Post,* February 20, 1997:

> Pity the poor fellow who was working at the Blockbuster store when John Kasich spotted a cassette of *Fargo*. The people who distribute Academy Award nominations like that movie, but the congressman from Columbus, Ohio, emphatically—all his judgments are emphatic—does not. The Blockbuster fellow tried a Nuremberg defense—"I'm just the store manager"— but Kasich would have none of it. . . .

And Christopher Buckley, quoted by Jonathan Foreman in the *National Review,* March 24, 1997, in a review of Buckley's book *Wry Martinis:*

> Nor does his Republicanism make him unwilling to skewer Big Business. When a tobacco-company flack defends her work to him, he comes back with, "Of course: the Yuppie Nuremberg defense: I vas only paying ze mortgage."

*It is those **Ozymandian** budget deficits that are soaking up private capital. . . .*

—Time

October surprise A last-minute political statement or act by a politician— a bombshell—timed to affect the outcome of an election.

The Ronald Reagan camp injected the term into the political lexicon during the 1980 presidential campaign by talking ceaselessly of its expectation that President Jimmy Carter would exercise the power of his office to produce an event—perhaps the release of the American hostages in Iran—timed to derive maximum political benefit for the Democratic ticket. The Reagan managers hoped to undercut the impact of such a surprise by warning of it in advance and calling into question the motives behind it. No surprise materialized.

The term in use, by Jack Nelson in the *Los Angeles Times,* September 12, 1996:

> Some Republican and conservative commentators have suggested that President Clinton's chances of reelection might be damaged by an "October surprise" in the form of election-eve indictments or a public report on the investigations.

And by Walter Mears, of the Associated Press, October 13, 1988, on the Democrats' use of Social Security as an issue in the presidential campaign:

> The issue is back, with the volume relatively low so far but with the Democrats likely to turn it up in the waning days of the campaign. A push on Social Security hardly would qualify as an October surprise. It has become an October habit.

odyssey \'ä-də-sē\ A great journey, especially a long and complicated one. Such a journey may be physical, but this word is often applied to mental, emotional, or spiritual searches. The word comes from the title of the second epic poem of Homer. The *Odyssey* is the story of the 10-year wandering of Odysseus, king of Ithaca, in his effort to return home after the Trojan War. Odysseus has to contend with many obstacles, some of which are allusions the reader will find in this volume: CYCLOPS, the land of the Lotus Eaters (*see* LOTUSLAND), SCYLLA AND CHARYBDIS. There are the tribes who imprison him, and the cannibals. Then there are the women, Nausicaa, the princess, and Circe, the enchantress.

Of course, when Odysseus finally arrives home, he finds his palace overrun with greedy suitors who hope to marry his wife, Penelope. Penelope has been stalling them for years, but the situation is getting very dif-

Oedipal

ficult, with the unwanted guests eating her out of house and home. Odysseus kills them all and is happily reunited with his wife and son. (*See* MENTOR.)

The term in use, by Anthony Dias Blue in *Wine Spectator,* March 15, 1994:

> Necker Island is a rocky land mass of 74 acres located at the northeastern limit of the Virgin Islands chain. Just across the narrow channel is the promontory of Pajaros Point, one of the many places that claims it was Christopher Columbus' first landing place on his odyssey to the New World.

And by Joseph Heller, in *Picture This* (1988):

> For on this parcel, in time, would rise the Metropolitan Museum of Art in the City of New York, a building of deplorable look, in which the painting *Aristotle Contemplating the Bust of Homer* would come to rest after a journey of three hundred seven years, an odyssey much longer in time and miles than Homer's original and one richly provided with chapters of danger, adventure, mystery, and treasure, and with comical episodes of mistaken identity.

And by Rick DeMarinis in *Harper's,* April 1991:

> The doctor who put my nose back, after hearing about my life odyssey from highly respected engineer to bottom-feeding drunk, said, "You know, Bud, if I were a writer, I'd write about you."

Oedipal \\'e-də-pəl, 'ē-\\ Relating to a child's positive sexual feelings toward the parent of the opposite sex and jealous or hostile feelings toward the parent of the same sex. Freud originated the concept and gave it the name "Oedipus complex."

The term springs from Greek legend. When Oedipus was born to King Laius and Queen Jocasta of Thebes, an oracle warned that the child would kill his father and marry his mother. To avert such a tragedy, the parents left him on a mountain to die. He was rescued by a shepherd, who gave the child to the king of Corinth. Oedipus was raised believing that this king and his wife were his true parents. When he learned of the prophecy, he left Corinth seeking to avoid fulfilling it. On the road he unknowingly met and quarreled with Laius, his true father, and killed him. Oedipus then went to Thebes, saved the city from the Sphinx by solving her riddle, and was offered the throne of the city and the hand of Laius' widow, Jocasta. He accepted both, not knowing, of course, that Jocasta was his mother. After many years, he learned the truth and, in horror, blinded himself; Jocasta killed herself.

The story has been the basis for works of literature, music, and psychology, most notably the Greek tragedian Sophocles' *Oedipus Rex.* Freud chose the name well for the complex he claims arises in the psychosocial development of the personality around ages 3 to 5.

The term in use, by Timothy Noah in the *New Republic,* April 3, 1989, on the career of the late Senator Prescott Bush, father of President George Bush:

> And most puzzling of all is that the leader of the free world should have such a diminished view of himself in comparison to this particular father. In the great Oedipal footrace, George Bush has lapped Prescott Bush several times over.

And by Marshall Fine in *Newsday,* February 21, 1997, reviewing the reissued *The Empire Strikes Back,* part of the *Star Wars* trilogy:

> *The Empire Strikes Back: The Special Edition* still packs the same power as it did the first time around, with its wonderfully imaginative action story . . . and its fairy-tale-like plot about a warrior's coming-of-age, with Luke being trained by Yoda before his Oedipal confrontation with Darth Vader.

And by Lance Morrow in *Time,* August 26, 1996:

> The baby boomers' rites of passage turned into a huge Oedipal overtoppling of authority, an assault on Dad that was disorientingly successful.

offending Adam *See* WHIP THE OFFENDING ADAM.

O.K. Corral, the The site of a showdown or of a dramatic, probably violent confrontation. Also, the confrontation itself.

The real O.K. Corral is the scene of one of the fabled events in the history of the American frontier, the gunfight between the Clanton gang and the Earp brothers, Virgil, Wyatt, and Morgan, and Doc.Holliday on October 26, 1881, in Tombstone, Arizona.

Thanks to multiple cinematic renditions of the story, the O.K. Corral is known throughout the world. We won't settle here whether the gunfight was a noble effort to protect the town against a violent gang or closer to a turf war between two heavily armed groups that wanted to control the town for their own gain.

The term in use, by racehorse trainer Bob Baffert, describing his experience in his first Kentucky Derby, quoted by Bill Christine in the *Los Angeles Times,* May 11, 1996:

> Reality slapped Baffert in the face on Derby day, when he led his two horses—Cavonnier and Semoran, who would finish 14th—on that long walk from the barn to the paddock in front of more than 140,000 people.
>
> "I felt like Wyatt Earp," said the trainer who grew up with cattle and chickens on a ranch in Nogales, Ariz. "I thought I was going to the O.K. Corral."

And by Ross Atkin in the *Christian Science Monitor,* March 28, 1986:

> The Final Four, college basketball's answer to "Gunfight at the O.K. Corral," features a classic confrontation of the nation's top two teams, Duke and Kansas, in Saturday's NCAA semifinal action at Reunion Arena.

old guard *often capitalized O&G* A group of established prestige and influence. The conservative members of an organization, particularly a political party. (*For the opposite of Old Guard, see* YOUNG TURKS.)

The term comes from the elite imperial guard of Napoleon, a unit of towering prestige. Their imposing presence was enhanced by long coats with broad epaulets at the shoulder and tall bearskin hats. They were devoted to their emperor, who always relied upon them in the most desperate circumstances. But not even they could save Napoleon at WATERLOO. Late in the day the Emperor hurled them at the Duke of Wellington's battered formations. The Old Guard charged valiantly, but for the first time in their history they were broken.

The term in use, by Tom Kenworthy and Don Phillips in the *Washington Post,* March 20, 1989, describing the race for the Republican whip position in the House of Representatives:

> Gingrich's reputation as a bombthrower so bothers some old-guard Republicans that there has been an extraordinary effort to defeat him.

And by Misha Berson, *Seattle Times* theater critic, reporting on the Tony Awards, June 3, 1996:

> But if the upstart generation clocked the most airtime on this year's tightly paced Tony telecast, the old guard were also much in evidence.

old school tie A necktie displaying the colors of an English public school; by extension, the attitude of aplomb and conservativism associated with graduates of elite public schools. Also the upper-class solidarity and bonds established at such institutions. (This is similar to the "old-boy network"— old boys, and old girls, in this sense being former students at a particular school. The old-boy network is often credited with accomplishing goals outside regular channels by instead relying on old friendships and—old school ties). Also applied to graduates of elite prep schools and colleges in the United States.

A conservative, traditional point of view thought to be shared by such individuals. More generally, a clannishess among members of an established clique.

The term in use, in the *St. Louis Post-Dispatch,* October 12, 1998, on criticism of Supreme Court justices' practices in hiring their clerks:

But no law firm could defend the hiring practices that the justices use—practices that are long on old-boy networks and old school ties and short on outreach and recruitment.

And by James Fallows in the *Atlantic,* March 1987:

> Then comes the struggle for college admission, which for the white-collar part of the populace is the most important hurdle they will ever have to jump. Americans sometimes grumble that standardized tests are too important and that the Old School Tie counts for too much.

And from Jack Fincher in *Smithsonian,* November 1985:

> Trippe came equipped with stratospheric ambition and the Old School ties to match. The Army and Navy Departments were stacked with the sons of Eli [that's Yale, for the un- or non-old-tied], and his brother-in-law Edward R. Stettinius Jr. was a future Secretary of State.

omega *See* ALPHA AND OMEGA.

on little cat feet Silently, delicately, almost undetectably. The phrase is taken from "Fog," a poem by American Carl Sandburg (1878–1967). Sandburg famously compares the silent movement of fog with the noiseless padding of a cat: "The fog comes in/on little cat feet."

The term in use, by columnist Donald Kaul in the *Des Moines Register,* November 29, 1996:

> The entries to the "Do-It-Yourself" Constitution Contest, have come rolling in; some have rolled, some have come in like fog, on little cat's feet.

And by Joseph Spiers in *Fortune,* June 13, 1994, describing Federal Reserve policies:

> The Fed is trying to keep growth within the 2.5% range by raising short-term interest rates to the point where monetary policy is "neutral." That is, it neither stimulates the economy nor holds it back. Nobody knows where that point is, so the Fed is endeavoring to creep along on little cat feet.

And by columnist Tony Snow, Gannett News Service, January 27, 1997:

> We have become so accustomed to crisis that we have forgotten the art of everyday life. We expect stimulation and gratification, not complacency and reflection. Reformers can't stir anyone to anger, so change moves on little cat feet.

opera's not over till the fat lady sings, the Victory in a game or contest is not conceded until all possible efforts are exhausted or all time expired. It is generally credited to sports commentator Dan Cook in April 1978.

Dick Motta, coach of the NBA's Washington Bullets adopted the expression during the Bullets' drive to the NBA championship in 1978.

As Motta described it in the *Washington Post,* June 11, 1978, he turned on the television set in his hotel room in San Antonio:

> Some television announcer, a guy by the name of Cook, I think, said something about how the series between the Spurs and us was like an opera. It wouldn't be over until the fat lady sang.

It is drawn from the idea of a spectacular final aria sung by the stout female opera singer of cartoon caricature. It is applied particularly in sports, usually uttered by the side which is behind and determined to fight through the last second. And, it is akin to Yogi Berra's immortal: "It's never over till it's over."

The term in use, by Peter Nulty in *Fortune,* May 16, 1994:

> The dramatic restructuring of U.S. industry won't be over, as the saying goes, until the fat lady sings. Hundreds of companies have performed massive renovations—Ford, Chrysler, Texaco, Xerox, IBM. But now the diva enters. She is the last of the great, corpulent, 20th century American enterprises to sing the rejuvenation aria. She walks to center stage. She turns to the audience. She is Eastman Kodak.

And quoted by the *Washington Post,* February 9, 1999:

> Money may keep Dennis Rodman from playing for the Lakers, who can offer him only the prorated portion of the veteran minimum of $1 million.
>
> "I just don't imagine Dennis playing for that kind of money," Lakers owner Jerry Buss said. "But it's not over until the fat lady sings. I know he wants to play here."

original sin The state of sin that, according to Christian teaching, characterizes all humans as a result of Adam's fall. The idea is this: humankind is inherently corrupt, from the moment of conception, because we are all descended from Adam and therefore tainted with his sin. Redemption is possible only through baptism, the ceremonial initiation into Christianity through purification by water.

The expression is used to describe actions viewed as heresies or gross ideological errors by the political and social powers that be.

The doctrine is largely the work of St. Augustine (354–430 A.D.), who argued it out with his theological foe Pelagius, a rival writer who maintained that human beings could perfect themselves by their own actions. These were life and death issues as Christians branded and persecuted each other as heretics.

The term in use, by political columnist Tony Snow in the *Detroit News,* April 18, 1996:

If slavery was America's original sin, race-baiting has become its grotesque progeny.

And by Ron C. Judd in the *Seattle Times,* October 11, 1997:

In the world of modern sport, boredom is the original sin.

And from Irving Kristol in *Insight,* February 23, 1987:

Again and again, Wills commits the original sin of the intellectual: the failure to distinguish the realm of reality from the realm of ideas, of life from literature.

Orwellian \òr-ˈwe-lē-ən\ Characterized by oppressive bureaucracies and spying governments ("BIG BROTHER is watching" comes from Orwell); propaganda campaigns in which truths are twisted to mean their opposite; language is redefined (*see* -SPEAK); history is edited to serve the state; and truth is blotted out. An adjective drawn from the name and works of British novelist George Orwell (real name Eric Arthur Blair, 1903–1950), and most particularly his 1949 novel *Nineteen Eighty-four.* Orwell fought on the Republican side during the Spanish Civil War but came away disillusioned by communism. His books depict the horrors of a totalitarian society in which individuality counts for nothing and, indeed, is viewed as a detriment to the overall good. In Orwell's tale, truth is turned on its head by a pervasive, intrusive government and its relentless propaganda machine.

The term in use, by Austin Murphy in *Sports Illustrated,* August 11, 1997:

To better enforce curfew at training camp, and to monitor the comings and goings of the players and their guests, Jones took the Orwellian measure of installing video cameras in the hallways of the players' dorms.

And by David Wild in *Rolling Stone,* November 30, 1995:

The *X-Files* and its spooky televised brethren dwell in that political twilight zone where left and right meet and greet—an Orwellian, KAFKAESQUE alien nation that's populated with suspicious folks who have too much time on their hands and a deep sense that something is horribly, horribly wrong.

And in the *Toronto Globe and Mail,* June 28, 1995:

The EU aggravates its image problem by doing some truly Orwellian things. For example, Brussels really does classify carrots as fruit. The regulation was adopted so that Portugal's carrot jam could continue to be sold.

Out, damned spot! The exclamation of Shakespeare's Lady MACBETH, in Act 5, Scene 1. Tortured by her guilt in the murders she has incited, she hallucinates blood on her hands and struggles to wash it off; but she cannot. "What, will these hands ne'er be clean?" she moans. Despite the identification of the phrase with ghastly crimes and the tortures of conscience, it is usually used today in humorous references to such matters as drycleaning or misbehaving Dalmations.

In the first example, however, the expression is applied in its original sense, by former Prime Minister Benazir Bhutto of Pakistan, quoted by Barry Bearak in the *Los Angeles Times,* November 7, 1996. Bhutto had these words for the president of Pakistan, accusing him of killing her brother and kidnapping her husband before he dismissed her from office:

> "All his life," she said, "he will be like Lady Macbeth, saying, 'Out, damned spot.' "
> The spot that allegedly made its indelible stain on him came a day earlier, when Leghari used his presidential powers to dismiss Bhutto as prime minister. . . .

And by Eileen Smith, Gannett News Service, November 27, 1995:

> Joann Cicinato mops up misery, she outs the most damned spots left after murder, suicide and serious accidents in the home. Some people think the professional cleaner is gruesome. And some, like the father who can't bear to enter the basement after his teenager shoots himself, call Cicinato an angel for hire.

Ozzie and Harriet The paradigm of the 1950s white-bread nuclear family; the norm of NORMALCY. They are evoked most often by critics of '50s nostalgia to sum up an oversimplified, idealized view of the era.

Ozzie and Harriet Nelson played Ozzie and Harriet Nelson and their sons David and Rick played themselves in the fondly remembered family television comedy, *The Adventures of Ozzie and Harriet*. The series began in 1952 and ran until 1966. The program was never a hit, but was a dependable draw, one with which audiences felt comfortable.

Mom was always at home, Dad an amiable presence, although nobody really knew what he did for a living. Of course, what he actually did for a living was write and produce the television show. What viewers saw was not just a working couple but an entire working family.

The term in use, by Roger Simon, commenting in the *Baltimore Sun,* August 30, 1995, on the veracity of presidential candidates' biographies:

> So if Phil Gramm paints an "Ozzie and Harriet" portrait of his childhood and the truth seems somewhat closer to a Tennessee Williams play, that is going to be revealed.

And from Timothy Egan of the New York Times News Service, in the *Deseret News,* August 25, 1996:

The case against them reads, in part, like Ozzie and Harriet go to terrorism school. Pipe bombs capable of shattering a court-room were stashed in barbecues and transported by bicycle, according to the indictment.

Also, from Christopher Johns, in the *Arizona Republic,* September 10, 1995:

Remember Ozzie and Harriet, and when there was no crime, racial tension and just carefree Americans barbecuing burgers in cozy backyards? Myth.

Ozymandian \ˌäz-ē-ʹman-dē-ən\ Something huge or grandiose but ulti-mately devoid of meaning. An ironic commentary on the fleeting nature of power and the enduring power of human egotism. "Ozymandias" is a sonnet, published in 1818, by English poet Percy Bysshe Shelley. The poem describes the colossal ruined statue of an ancient king in a barren desert, like the monuments of Egyptian pharaohs. ("Ozymandias" is the Greek name for the Egyptian pharaoh Ramses II.) Shelley was com-menting on the foolish arrogance of tyrants who believe that their grandeur will never fade. Its line "Look on my works, ye Mighty, and despair" is often put to use in other works, mighty and otherwise, to mock self-aggrandizement.

The term in use by columnist William Safire in the *Springfield (Mass.) Union-News,* November 16, 1990:

Radio Free Iraq broadcasters should be taping interviews with Italian sculptors near the quarry and foundry of Carrara, who are busy on assignments to create huge new marble and bronze statues of the egomaniacal Saddam Hussein and his latest gen-erals—Ozymandian objects that impoverished Iraqis are forced to pay for and worship.

And in *Time,* February 8, 1982:

Federal Reserve Board Chairman Paul Volcker charges that by letting the deficit run up toward $100 billion, the White House has all but abandoned its fight against inflation. This has left the struggle to be waged singlehanded by the Federal Reserve, and that, Volcker feels, is asking too much of the American central bank. It is those Ozymandian budget deficits that are soaking up private capital, depriving the economy of productive invest-ment.

And a play on the sonnet by Martin Amis, in his essay "Norman Mailer: The Avenger and the Bitch" in the *Moronic Inferno* (1987):

His name is Norman Mailer, king of kings: look on his works, ye Mighty, and—what? Despair? Burst out laughing? In secure retrospect, Mailer's life and times seem mostly ridiculous . . . only towards the end, perhaps—with no more drink and "no more stunts," dedicated to his work and to a noncombatant sixth wife—has he struck a human balance. As for the past, nothing beside remains.

*. . . look back upon the 20th as the century in which their forebears had the amazing confidence, the **Promethean** hubris, to defy the gods. . . .*

—Tom Wolfe

pale *See* BEYOND THE PALE.

palooka \pə-'lü-kə\ An inexperienced or incompetent boxer. An oaf or lout. A slang term.

Joe Palooka was a comic strip named for its hero, a big, kindhearted fighter who was honest but simpleminded. The strip was created by Ham Fisher in 1928. Unlike the generic palooka, Joe was a champion and a gentleman, too.

The term in use, by Dan Rodricks in the *Baltimore Sun,* September 1, 1995:

> And in Kennedyville, down on the Eastern Shore, there was the burglar who locked himself out of his getaway car. . . . So you know what this fellow did? Did he get a coat hanger and try to jig open the lock? Did he bust the window and make a quick getaway? No. HE CALLED THE POLICE! TO HELP HIM UNLOCK THE CAR! And Cpl. Bill Dwyer came. He's no dummy, he figured out what had happened. He took this palooka to jail.

And by Ronald Grover, with Jennifer Reingold in *Business Week,* November 18, 1996:

> Flash, dash, and a pile of cash. That's Don King, arguably the most powerful fight promoter in history. Counted out more times than a palooka from Nowheresville, King today sits atop a boxing empire of nearly 80 fighters. . . .

And again, from Norman Mailer, quoting himself, in his interview with presidential candidate Patrick Buchanan in *Esquire,* August 1, 1996:

> The Soviets were a wornout palooka by 1970. They knew in their bones it wasn't working anymore.

Penates *See* LARES AND PENATES.

Pandora's box \pan-'dōr-əz, -'dȯr-\ A prolific source of troubles.

The story comes from Greek myth; it tells their version of the creation of the first woman and how the ills of mankind resulted.

To punish Prometheus (*see* PROMETHEAN), who had stolen fire from him, Zeus ordered Hephaestus, the god of the forge, to create the first mortal woman, who was irresistibly beautiful and to whom each of the gods gave a power to insure the ruin of man.

Zeus sent her to Prometheus' brother, carrying a lidded vessel as a gift. He opened it, and out flew all the evils of mankind. In some versions of the story it is Pandora's doing, because she cannot contain her curiosity. And sometimes hope remains in the jar.

The term in use, by Sherri Eisenberg in *Washington Monthly,* June 1997:

> Given these statistics, you'd think both the government and the media would be doing everything in their power to help parents understand the impact of day care on children. They're not. Politicians have shied away from this politically charged Pandora's Box for years, resulting in a pathetic absence of public policy.

And by the Associated Press, September 30, 1996:

> After four deadly days, Jews and Arabs have forced down the lid on Pandora's Box, but few Palestinians now speak of the "peace process" without a sneer or a sigh.

And by John F. Ross in the *Smithsonian,* January 10, 1993:

> Scientists in New York and California respectively have isolated and sequenced pieces of DNA from them. These earlier studies have opened a Pandora's box of speculation, energizing that netherworld where science meets the imagination.

Panglossian \pan-'glä-sē-ən, paŋ-, -glȯ-\ Marked by the view that all is for the best in this best of all possible worlds. Excessively optimistic. Taken from Dr. Pangloss, a character in Voltaire's *Candide.* Dr. Pangloss is notable for his incurable, absurd optimism, regardless of circumstance, and his constant refrain, "All is for the best in this BEST OF ALL POSSIBLE WORLDS".

The term in use, in the *Economist,* January 14, 1989, on Ronald Reagan's farewell address:

> It would be churlish, while pausing on Mr. Reagan's Panglossian cloud, to question whether government has grown less greedy in the past eight years. For while the president is modest in his way of putting things . . . his views of his political achievements are wonderfully immodest.

And by Ron Fimrite in the *Washington Post Book World,* November 2, 1997, reviewing Doris Kearns Goodwin's memoir, *Wait Till Next Year* (1997):

> Her title is borrowed from the Panglossian headline that ran in the Brooklyn Eagle after the Dodgers lost the 1941 World Series to the Yankees.

Panza, Sancho A loyal assistant or subordinate to a colorful, quixotic leader. One of literature's great sidekicks, Sancho Panza was the earthy, commonsensical squire of the romantic idealist Don QUIXOTE in Miguel de Cervantes' classic. And since Panza means "paunch" in Spanish, the expression may note a physical difference between leader and assistant. (*See also* TILTING AT WINDMILLS.)

The term in use, by Jim Hoagland in a commentary in the *Phoenix Gazette*, November 7, 1995:

> Haber eagerly played Sancho Panza to [Israeli Prime Minister] Rabin's Don Quixote through times hugely thick and spectacularly thin.

And from Jay Boyar, in the *Phoenix Gazette*, April 14, 1995:

> Along with Sancho Panza, Dr. Watson and Ed Norton, Robin is one of the world's great sidekicks. But as all bat-fans know, the Dark Knight's spunky squire has been conspicuously absent from the first two installments of the popular film series.

And from Martin Walker of Britain's *The Guardian*, writing in the *Los Angeles Times*, July 17, 1994:

> The most compelling image, however, has always been of the Americans as Don Quixote, with Britain as plump little Sancho Panza, trotting loyally alongside, occasionally plucking fretfully at his master's sleeve to suggest that some windmills are not for tilting.

Peoria *See* PLAY IN PEORIA.

papal bull A solemn letter issued by the pope and sealed with a bulla (seal) or red-ink imprint of the device on the bulla; an edict or decree issued by the pope. In nonecclesiastic usage, an authoritative statement: the law, as laid down by someone on high; also, when used ironically, pretentious nonsense.

The term in use, by Garry Ray in *PC Week*, March 15, 1988:

> It is an ICON in the company's theology, a step into the world of tomorrow, a fundamental change from the way things are to the way they will be. It is one more step in Microsoft's journey to its highest vision: The Automated Office.
> You may think this is a spoof, but it is precisely the papal bull issued by Mr. Letwin in the first two chapters of his entertaining encyclical on OS/2.

And by Frank Deford in *Sports Illustrated*, April 17, 1989, paying tribute to Bart Giamatti, the new commissioner of baseball and former president of Yale. At Yale, Giamatti had issued a tongue-in-cheek decree: "I wish to announce henceforth that as a matter of University policy, evil is abolished and paradise restored." Deford continues:

> Baseball isn't about memos, thank God. It's about lineups, and should the new commissioner issue any such papal bull as he did

during his tenure at Yale, it ought to be in the form of a lineup card, to be posted in hearts and dugouts everywhere.

Paradise Lost A lost or ruined EDEN or UTOPIA, a place of bliss, felicity, or delight destroyed by human greed or foolishness; the title of John Milton's 1667 poem. One of the greatest works in the English language, it tells the story of Adam and Eve's loss of Eden through their disobedience to God.

> Of man's first disobedience and the fruit
> Of that forbidden tree whose mortal taste
> Brought death into the World, and all our woe,
> With loss of Eden.

Much of the poem tells of the rebellion of the angels led by Satan. He is defeated and expelled from Heaven but returns to Eden to enter the serpent to tempt Eve; she eats the forbidden fruit. Adam, "fondly overcome with female charm," eats so that he may perish with the woman he loves.

Satan returns to Hell in triumph and the archangel Michael leads a chagrined Adam and Eve from the garden, telling them that Jesus Christ has offered himself as ransom for man and that Satan will ultimately be defeated.

The term in use, by Paul de Barros, in the *Seattle Times,* April 24, 1997:

> Some slack key songs are laments for a paradise lost, reflecting the Hawaiian sovereignty movement, which seeks recompense for lands appropriated in 1893, when Queen Lili'uokalani, Hawaii's last monarch and a composer herself, was overthrown by the United States.

Another example, from Brad Knickerbocker, in the *Christian Science Monitor,* May 21, 1996:

> In 1929, the Coeur d'Alene Press ran a series of articles on mining pollution. Wrote city editor John Knox Coe: "It is a veritable 'Valley of Death' in a 'Paradise Lost.' "

And from Margaret Putnam, in the *Dallas Morning News,* October 13, 1995, reviewing a ballet about baseball by Moses Pendleton:

> Mr. Pendleton says the strike provided a creative spark, suggesting a dramatic structure.
> "I had started with baseball as a kind of paradise, and the strike gave me a curve to the work. I developed the idea of Paradise Lost, and then hope of a return."

pariah \pə-'rī-ə\ An outcast; that which is base, despised. The word comes from the caste system in India; the Pariahs—an Anglicized version of a Tamil word—are a numerous and low caste in southern India. Europeans extended the word to any lower-caste person, or someone without caste.

("Caste"—from a Portuguese word meaning race—is the name applied to the hereditary class system of India. The word is used in a larger sense to describe rigid social barriers in general.)

Pariah has been applied in the arena of world politics to nations engaged in activities deplored by the world community, such as chemical and biological warfare and genocide.

The term in use, from *People,* September 18, 1995, on the death of radical lawyer William Kunstler:

> To detractors, Kunstler was an egotistical headline grabber, playing to the cameras decades before Court TV. But to admirers he was a zealous believer in justice. "He embraced society's pariahs while they were still society's pariahs," says Ron Kuby, his partner.

And by Jennifer Steinhauer, in the *New York Times,* October 1, 1997:

> Fashion is once again placing its bets on fur, so recently a pariah in the industry.

And by President Bill Clinton, in a statement urging ratification of the Chemical Weapons Convention, April 18, 1997:

> The bottom line is this: Will the United States join a treaty we helped to shape, or will we go from leading the fight against poison gas to joining the company of pariah nations this treaty seeks to isolate?

Paris is well worth a mass A statement of political pragmatism, a willingness to compromise principle in order to gain an end. The phrase is invoked today to sneer at a cynical switch of sides. But it's worthwhile to take a look at the context.

The statement was made by Henry of Navarre (1553–1610) as he embraced the Catholic faith for the second time in order to win the throne of France. In Roman Catholicism, the service of holy communion is called a mass.

Henry was the Protestant king of Navarre, an area in what is now southern France. He was, however, in line to become king of all France; the three sons of the reigning Valois dynasty had come to the throne in rapid succession without heirs. Nevertheless the Valois adherents (not the least of whom was the Queen Mother, Catherine de Medici, a MEDUSA for the ages) were ferociously opposed to having a Protestant on the throne and reluctant to give up their political power. The result was a succession of horrendous political and religious wars that lasted for more than 30 years.

In 1572 Henry married the Catholic princess Margaret, sister of the king of France and daughter of Catherine de Medici. Catherine was in favor of the marriage but nevertheless engineered the Massacre of St. Bartholomew, when Valois adherents slaughtered thousands of Protestants in Paris and throughout the country. Henry saved himself by pretending to convert to Catholicism. More warfare ensued—culminating in the War of the Three Henrys (Henry of Navarre, Henry of Guise, a powerful Catholic nobleman, and King Henry of France, the cross-dressing last of the Valois).

Henry of Navarre won on the battlefield, recanted his Catholic conversion, and beseiged Paris. The city held out well past the rat-eating stage; the bones of animals and human dead were ground for flour. Thousands died of starvation and disease. It was then that Henry observed, "Paris is well worth a mass." He once again gave up the Protestant faith, and was admitted to the city without further bloodshed. He took up the government of a shattered France, and ruled wisely and well as Henry IV. (*See also* CHICKEN IN EVERY POT.) Among other things, he promulgated the Edict of Nantes, which decreed freedom of worship. He is still revered for his boldness in the field, generosity in victory, and his delighted pursuit of the ladies. He was assassinated by a fanatical Catholic priest in 1610.

The term in use, by columnist George Will, appearing in the *Detroit News,* May 13, 1996:

> It is not news that Clinton is our Henry of Navarre, the French king who was raised a Protestant but twice converted to Catholicism for political convenience, saying "Paris is well worth a Mass."

And by Robert G. Lopez, in a letter to the editor of the *San Francisco Chronicle,* December 9, 1996, commenting on the hypocrisy of Cuban dictator Fidel Castro's visit to the Vatican:

> Should one laugh or cry at the spectacle in Rome? The Che Guevara fatigues traded for the conservative blue suit. The reverential inclination. The murmured "Your Holiness." Hypocrisy endures. One is reminded of Henri IV: "Paris is worth a Mass."

And by Congressman John Dingell (D-Mich.), quoted in the *Washington Times,* August 13, 1994, on deals made on health legislation:

> Asked if it is appropriate for the leadership to craft provisions in the bill in order to get the backing of lawmakers, Mr. Dingell quoted Henry IV of France . . . : "Paris is worth the mass."

Parkinson's Law An observation laid down in 1955 by British historian C. Northcote Parkinson (1910–1993) in his book of the same title. It holds: "Work expands so as to fill the time available for its completion." Its corollary is: the number of subordinates increases at a fixed rate regardless of the amount of work produced.

Following the enunciation of his law, writes Paul Dickson, author of *The Official Rules* (1978), "Parkinson became famous and his law has become a permanent tenet of organizational life." (*See also* PETER PRINCIPLE.)

The term in use, by syndicated columnist Richard Reeves in commentary in the *Philadelphia Inquirer,* May 16, 1992:

That kind of legislative overload, I must hasten to say, is the product of the legislators themselves. Long hours justify more perks and more staff to make even more work. There's a Parkinson's law in there someplace: Elected officials' work expands to fill the amount of staff allotted to each.

And by John Carman, commenting on media coverage of political conventions in the *Lexington Herald-Leader,* July 16, 1992:

What CNN wasn't providing, of course, was news with a SHELF LIFE of more than a minute or two. You could watch CNN for hours at a time, and I did, without learning anything of practical or lasting value.
It's Parkinson's Law of television: Nonsense will expand to fit the allotted time, regardless of its gaseous composition.

And by Richard Zoglin, expressing a similar thought in *Time,* February 29, 1988:

It was another of those weeks when TV seems to have a bear hug on the nation's attention. And another week that illustrated the video corollary of Parkinson's Law: the significance of an event expands according to the TV time allotted for it.

Parnassian \pär-'na-sē-ən\ Pertaining to Mt. Parnassus, a mountain in central Greece which was sacred to Apollo and the Muses; by extension, relating to literature, especially poetry. Sometimes the noun form *Parnassus* is used in the same sense.

The name was particularly applied to a school of French poets active in the second half of the 19th century. The Parnassians rejected the emotionalism of the Romantic poets and embraced calm objectivity and technical perfection.

The term in use, by John Heminway in *Town & Country,* August 1, 1997:

Charles, PROTEAN conversationalist, brilliant strategist (but never cunning), secretly generous and probably secretly shy, was most at ease on safari, or fishing, or with backgammon buddies and golden retrievers. He, too, suffered fools little, but, childlike at times, he mixed with his children—especially when they challenged him on his high Parnassian ground.

And by Michael Ignatieff in the *New Yorker,* September 28, 1998:

Isaiah Berlin thought himself unprepossessing, even ugly. In his usual deflationary style, he always said that he was just a typical Oxford don. Yet he was not typical. A Russian exile, in 1932, when he was only twenty-three, he became the first Jew elected to All Souls College, the Mt. Parnassus of Oxford.

And from Justin Kaplan, in the *New York Times Book Review,* March 10, 1996:

She sees this as part of a long-standing cultism that assigns a dominant position to "white, Protestant, middle-class male authors"—Emerson, Hawthorne and Melville, for example— while relegating women authors, especially authors of best-selling novels, to the kitchen middens of Parnassus.

pas de deux \ˌpä-də-ˈdə(r), -ˈdü\ A dance or figure for two performers. An intricate relationship or activity involving two parties. In French, it means "step for two," or a dance for two. In ballet, a pas de deux is performed by a ballerina and her male partner.

The term in use, by Tom Carter in the December 1988 *Bicycle Guide,* describing the neck-and-neck competition of two cyclists in the 1988 Race Across America:

> With about 700 miles to the finish line, Fedrigon and Templin were still engaged in their pas de deux.

And by John Powers in *Vogue,* September 1995:

> For this is a story about the allure of success and the ease with which good men sell themselves to bad ones. It's a story about the tortuous pas de deux between WASPs and Jews, and the effortless way corporations seized control of what we see on television.

And by Anna Quindlen for the New York Times News Service, appearing in the *Kansas City Star,* October 11, 1994:

> When members of the arts communities were asked recently about one of their biggest benefactors, Philip Morris, and its requests that they lobby the New York City council on the company's behalf, the pas de deux of self-justification was so painstakingly choreographed that it constituted a performance all by itself.

paths of glory Life as a journey or movement to greatness. This phrase is a line from Thomas Gray's famous *Elegy Written in a Country Churchyard* (published 1751). Often referred to simply as "Gray's Elegy" and one of the most quoted poems in the English language, it is a meditation on the graves of simple, unknown people in a country churchyard—what they might have been, what unrecognized or unexpressed talents they possessed. (*See* FAR FROM THE MADDING CROWD; MUTE INGLORIOUS MILTON.) And yet, the poet also recognizes, "the paths of glory lead but to the grave;" many users of the phrase forget the warning note.

It is also the title of Humphrey Cobb's novel of World War I, made into an acclaimed film in 1957, on the madness of war.

The phrase in use, by Al Carter, in the *Dallas Morning News,* October 21, 1995, on the success of Texas Christian University football in the 1930s:

> From 1974 to 1983, TCU won a grand total of 15 games, just three more than the Horned Frogs won in the winningest season

ever. That was in 1935, the year when college football's paths of glory found a crossroads in Fort Worth.

Patient Griselda The archetypal, stereotypical long-suffering and obedient wife who stays with her husband no matter how abusive he is.

Her story is one of Boccaccio's tales in *The Decameron* (1351–1353) and was later told by Geoffrey Chaucer in *The Canterbury Tales.*

Griselda is a poor but beautiful girl who marries a nobleman, a great marquis. He decides to test her love in terrible ways, including taking away her children and telling her that they are dead and that he is sending her away so he can marry another. Through it all she is obedient, submissive, and loving. Finally he is convinced of her devotion, embraces her, and they live happily ever after.

The term in use, by A.N. Wilson, author of *The Rise and Fall of the House of Windsor,* in commentary on the death of Diana, Princess of Wales in the *New York Times,* September 3, 1997:

> If she had not rocked the boat by talking to journalists (above all, to Andrew Morton, author of *Diana: Her True Story*) about her husband's love for Camilla Parker Bowles, the royal marriage or an appearance of a royal marriage could have survived. So it is argued and believed in conservative establishment circles.
>
> If the marriage had survived, and if she had been a Patient Griselda, the ancient and indissoluble links between church and state could have continued unquestioned.

And by Merle Rubin, reviewing *Eleanor Roosevelt: Volume One 1884–1933* by Blanche Wiesen Cook in the *Christian Science Monitor,* May 19, 1992:

> She [Cook] applauds Eleanor for acting affirmatively and deplores her lapses into the passive role of long-suffering "patient Griselda."

Pavlovian \pav-'lȯ-vē-ən, -lō-; -'lȯ-fē-\ Being or expressing a conditioned or predictable reaction. The word comes from the name of Russian physiologist Ivan Petrovich Pavlov (1849–1936, winner of the 1904 Nobel Prize), who rang a bell when he fed dogs. After a while, he found that the dogs would salivate when the bell rang, even though there was no food in sight. He had discovered the "conditioned reflex."

Thus someone who acts like Pavlov's dog, or who shows a Pavlovian response, is reacting in a completely predictable, automatic fashion to a particular stimulus.

The term in use, by Bill Rodgers in *Marathoning* (1980). The runner/author characterizes press reaction when runners drop dead of heart attacks: "The automatic Pavlovian response was to call me."

And by Colbert King, in commentary in the *Washington Post,* June 14, 1997, reminiscing about his father:

At five sharp, my father's whistle pierced the air for blocks. The King kids, in a response that would have made Pavlov proud, could be seen abandoning marbles, cards, third base—everything—to make a beeline for home. That's when the real fun began anyway.

And by Jaime Diaz in *Sports Illustrated,* June 10, 1996:

Sure, he holed a few unlikely putts and a couple of sand shots on Friday and Saturday. But on Sunday, the day that has induced a Pavlovian freeze in Watson almost every time he has been in contention during the last five years, the flinty and determined yet vulnerable hero had to overcome an assortment of challenges, from an early case of the yips to the pressure of a tightrope finish.

Pax Americana A period of general stability in international affairs under the dominant influence of U.S. power. The "American Peace," from the Latin "pax," meaning "peace," modified by the Latinized adjective "Americana." The expression is the etymological grandchild of "Pax Romana" and the child of "Pax Britannica."

The Pax Romana refers to the period of peace and civil order that prevailed within the Roman Empire under Augustus Caesar. In the 19th century, many British likened their colonial rule and the worldwide economic and political power they wielded to those of Rome, and the term Pax Britannica gained currency.

After World War II, with British power diminished and the empire breaking up, many Americans thought the United States should step into the role of world banker and policeman.

The term in use, by Leonard Silk in the *New York Times,* January 27, 1987, referring to the effect of the federal deficit on the fluctuating value of the American dollar:

But this indirect method of financing the Pax Americana makes an extremely volatile dollar inevitable, with dangerous consequences for the United States and the world economy.

And in *Harper's,* January 1994:

A year ago, when President Clinton took office, the job of directing "the world's only superpower" seemed an easy one. The phrase promised a global Pax Americana: history was at an end, what remained to be done was routine police work.

The *Oxford English Dictionary* notes that a variety of similar constructions have been fashioned on this model (including "pax atomica") to refer to the peace imposed by a great power. An example in *Time,* September 25, 1989, by Charles Krauthammer:

Germany was conquered, then divided into two states designed
to remain forever in a state of permanent, if cold antagonism.
Pax Americana and Pax Sovietica solved the German problem.

peace for our time A false peace; an appeasement which will lead to disaster; another MUNICH. British Prime Minister Neville Chamberlain used
this phrase to describe the agreement made with Hitler at Munich in September 1938 to give Germany part of Czechoslovakia. Referring to the
agreement as "peace with honour," Chamberlain said, "I believe it is peace
for our time."

Hitler was not appeased; World War II began less than a year later.

Chamberlain is often misquoted as having said "peace in our time,"
which is from the Church of England's *Book of Common Prayer.*

The term in use, by Ariel Cohen of the Heritage Foundation in a letter
to the editor of the *Jerusalem Post,* April 7, 1996:

> Shimon Peres proclaimed worldwide from Tel Aviv that Presi-
> dent Clinton is striving to "bring peace in our time" to the Mid-
> dle East. . . .
> Shimon Peres's FREUDIAN SLIP gave out what the people of
> Israel know—and what Shimon Peres realizes in his subcon-
> sciousness: the "processed" peace with Arafat is Munich-style
> capitulation fraught with mortal danger for Israel.

And by Tim Sullivan, for Gannett News Service, November 27, 1996:

> Peace in our time. Peace, and it's about time. Peace unto the
> wicked. Peace for battered baseball.
> Can it be true? Have the senseless stewards of the Grand Old
> Game really achieved an armistice after so many seasons of labor
> strife?

pecking order The basic pattern of organization within a flock of birds
in which each pecks a bird lower in the scale and is pecked by one
higher. A dominance hierarchy in a group of social animals. A social hierarchy.

The term in use, in a story by the Associated Press in the *Dallas Morning News,* on the financial troubles of a New Orleans casino, December
7, 1995:

> Under the Chapter 11 filing, Harrah's Jazz will get at least 120
> days to reorganize its finances. During that time, the company
> is shielded from creditors.
> Bankruptcy law creates a major problem for contractors and
> vendors: they are unsecured creditors, which means they are far-
> ther down the bankruptcy pecking order than bondholders, who
> are owed $435 million.

And by Catherine Field for the London Observer Service, in the *Deseret
News,* February 4, 1996:

So aloof are China's rulers that analysts often resort to the tactics of Brezhnev-era Kremlinology to gain an inkling of any changes. Some pore over protocol lists; others time the evening news and count the seconds allotted to each politician to get an idea of the pecking order.

And by Lester C. Thurow in *Harper's,* March 1992:

The lack of importance attached to human-resource management can be seen in the corporate pecking order. In an American firm the chief financial officer is almost always second in command. The post of head of human-resource management is usually a specialized job, off at the edge of the corporate hierarchy.

Peck's bad boy One whose bad, mischievous, or tasteless behavior is a source of embarrassment or annoyance. It comes from the 1883 novel *Peck's Bad Boy and His Pa* and years of humorous sketches by George Wilbur Peck, an American journalist and aphorist who served twice as governor of Wisconsin. Hennery, the bad boy in question, was given to playing tricks on his boozy father, such as lining his pa's hatband with limburger cheese.

The term in use, by Tom Shales, in a profile of Ted Turner in the *Washington Post,* April 13, 1989:

He's a major player and a legend among oddballs, and never too busy to become Peck's Bad Boy. He's a MAVERICK, an upstart, a rogue and a swashbuckler. The last of the red-hot moguls. A Frank Capra hero.(*See* CAPRAESQUE.)

And by Stephen Hunter, film critic of the *Baltimore Sun,* September 2, 1995, describing Andy HARDY, as played by Mickey Rooney:

Befreckled under a thatch of strawberry blond hair, he was Huck and Tom, he was Peck's not-so-bad boy, he was apple-cheeked innocence and the spirit of can-do smelted down into one archetypical figure.

And by Gore Vidal in *Newsweek,* July 13, 1987:

Lt. Colonel Oliver L. North (USMC) has now metastasized in the national psyche rather the way that Tom Sawyer did more than a centruy ago. Like Tom, Ollie is essentially fictional; like Tom, Ollie is an American archetype: the conman as Peck's Bad Boy.

Pecksniffian \pek-'sni-fē-ən\ One who is unctuously hypocritical.

The term is taken from the character Seth Pecksniff in Charles Dickens' 1844 novel *Martin Chuzzlewit.* Pecksniff is notable for uttering pious moral statements while acting heartlessly.

The term in use, by Leo Rosten, in *The Joys of Yiddish* (1968):

In the United States, the social prestige scale was sensitive and exact: first-generation Jews envied second-generation Jews; and

> German Jewish families . . . became an elite of remarkable influence and social cohesiveness. The "PECKING ORDER" of this Establishment, its pride, philanthropy, snobbery, and Pecksniffian patronage of Russian and Polish Jews—all this is described by Stephen Birmingham in *Our Crowd: The Great Jewish Families of New York.*

And by Michael Pterniti in *Harper's* magazine, October 1997:

> If we've incorporated the theory of relativity into our scientific view of the universe, it's Einstein's attempt to devise a kind of personal religion—an intimate spiritual and political manifesto—that still stands in stark, almost sacred contrast to the Pecksniffian systems of salvation offered by the modern world.

And by William Grimes in a profile of Jack Paar in the *New York Times,* December 19, 1991:

> His face still has the Pecksniffian glow that makes him seem like an evangelist with a few dark secrets. His hands moved wildly in the Jack Benny mannner. Nothing, it seems, has changed, although Mr. Paar now wears glasses.

Pentagon Papers A secret history of United States involvement in Indochina commissioned in 1967 by Secretary of Defense Robert McNamara. The papers, classified "top secret," were leaked and their publication gave rise to a historic legal battle between government and the press. By extension, "Pentagon Papers" refers to politically charged revelations from secret documents through unofficial channels.

Daniel Ellsberg, a military analyst who had become disaffected by the war, leaked the papers to the *New York Times.* The *Times* began publishing them on June 13, 1971.

The government went into court to prevent further publication by the *Times* and the *Washington Post,* which had also obtained the documents. An injunction was requested based on a claimed threat to national security. This was the first attempt at "prior restraint" of the press by the government in the history of the United States, and it took place in a time of profound conflict within the country over the Vietnam War. A few frenzied days of court arguments and appeals led to a landmark Supreme Court decision on freedom of the press on June 30. The court held 6–3 that the government had failed to justify restraint of publication. However, the justices were sharply divided among themselves on the reasons for their decision.

The Nixon Administration's efforts to prevent further leaks, and to gather information to discredit Ellsberg, led to the creation of the White House "plumbers" unit (to stop leaks) and to many of the abuses later revealed in the Watergate scandals. Among other things, Nixon White House operatives led by G. Gordon Liddy broke into the office of Ellsberg's psychiatrist in order to examine Ellsberg's records.

The term in use, in *Publishers Weekly,* April 29, 1996:

> *FYI*: University of California is also publishing *The Cigarette Papers,* a collection of internal documents from cigarette manufacturer Brown & Williamson, which many are calling "the Pentagon Papers of tobacco."

And from John Stewart, in the *San Francisco Chronicle,* December 31, 1995, writing about the imprisonment of Mordechai Vanunu, an Israeli nuclear worker who had leaked information on Israel's nuclear capability to the *London Times:*

> He was secretly tried and convicted of treason and espionage and sentenced to 18 years in isolation—all for a crime roughly equivalent to Dan Ellsberg's copying and publication of the Pentagon Papers, except that Ellsberg was revealing facts that few people knew, whereas Vanunu was merely blowing a hole in the world's worst-kept secret.

Perfidious Albion Treacherous England.

Albion is an ancient name for England, possibly from Greek through the Latin word for white, *albus,* in reference to the white cliffs of the English south coast. Another possibility is that it is derived from an ancient Irish Celtic word for the island of Britain. *Perfidious* means unreliable, faithless.

The French are given credit for coining the phrase; it was certainly in use during the Napoleonic era. The term is now applied by critics when the British government appears to back out of obligations.

The term in use, by James Walsh in *Time International,* June 9, 1997, writing about Christopher Patten, last Governor General of Hong Kong:

> By his defenders' lights, the Governor proved to be a brilliant, principled politician who opened up the government and civil service to an extent no preceding viceroy ever considered. Such champions are convinced that, by standing up to China, he not only redeemed his country's sometime reputation as perfidious Albion but gave Hong Kong a reasonable measure of confidence to protect its own interests in the future.

And in the *Economist,* September 10, 1994, on the political situation in Northern Ireland:

> Protestant suspicion of secret deals is also understandable. Last year it emerged that the government had been chatting to the IRA at a time when John Major said it would "turn my stomach" to meet them. So the notion of a perfidious Albion, seduced by silver-tongued nationalists into betraying the loyalists, appeals to many. . . .

And by Arthur Hoppe, in the *San Francisco Chronicle*, January 20, 1995, on cutting funds for the National Endowment for the Arts and the Public Broadcasting System:

> Would ATTILA THE HUN have conquered mighty Rome had he lollygagged around in the evenings, watching cockroaches copulate on PBS? And if Hitler hadn't been a Sunday painter, there's no doubt he would have conquered both Red Russia and perfidious Albion.
>
> No, the Republicans are on the right track. If it weren't for the munificence of governments and wealthy patrons, we wouldn't be in the mess we're in today.

Periclean \ˌper-ə-ˈklē-ən\ Wise and eloquent; or, characteristic of an era in which governance is in the hands of those who are. Pertaining to the Athenian statesman Pericles, his eloquence, his accomplishments, or his times.

Pericles (ca. 500–429 B.C.) was leader of Athens from 460 B.C. until his death, a time of great achievements in the arts and in building, and in democratic reforms. Under his leadership the Parthenon and the Long Walls of Piraeus were built, as were many other temples. It was a period of peace, prosperity, and progress.

It had to come to an end, of course: the Peloponnesian War began in 431 B.C.; a conflict with Sparta ended in the defeat of Athens in 404; and there was a disastrous plague. Pericles also had domestic political problems: his mistress, the courtesan Aspasia, beautiful and learned, helped him in his work, and that was not well received in some quarters. More awkward was Pericles' ward Alcibiades, a brilliant general but arrogant, dissolute, and a traitor to Athens.

The term in use, by Franklin Foer, in the *New Republic*, November 4, 1996, on the phenomenon of the frequently quoted media resource, in this case, Kathleen Hall Jamieson:

> She pontificates with Periclean authority and has the poise of a Fortune 500 executive.

And by Garry Wills in *Lincoln at Gettysburg* (1992):

> True, his sense of style in words was far greater than his feel for the ornaments on his Greek Revival house; but he was not aiming at Periclean effect. Yet his speech is now at least as famous as the Athenian's. That is because Lincoln was an artist, not just a scholar.

The word is often used for unfavorable comparison: the speeches we hear and the leadership we see are usually less than Periclean. An example, from Robert Reno in *Newsday*, July 31, 1996:

> The latest idea is that a nation which shares common federal citizenship, a common Army, Navy and Air Force, common water

and air quality standards, even common regulation of the flammability of pajamas, can somehow be better served by 50 different standards for dealing with the impoverished. . . . This, of course, will tempt some future Congress to come to a very logical conclusion: If the states are such fountains of Periclean wisdom, let them also figure out a way to pay for their 50 different welfare schemes. The result will be a contest of states to abandon the poor.

petard *See* HOIST WITH ONE'S OWN PETARD.

Peter Pan A young man who resists adult responsibilities; a perpetual adolescent. Taken from the name of the hero of J.M. Barrie's classic fantasy *Peter Pan, or The Boy Who Wouldn't Grow Up,* first produced in 1904 but drawn from earlier Barrie books. Peter has run away to NEVER-NEVER LAND in order to escape adulthood, and there he leads the band of Lost Boys in battles with the pirates.

Peter befriends the Darling children, Wendy, Michael, and John and teaches them to fly. He takes them to Never-Never Land with him where they have many adventures. The Darlings eventually become homesick and return.

The story was made popular in the United States by the Walt Disney animated feature released in 1953 and by a Broadway musical version starring Mary Martin, which opened in 1954. This award-winning production was televised in 1955.

Peter Pan made his appearance in the pop-psychology field with *The Peter Pan Syndrome: Men Who Have Never Grown Up* by Dan Kiley in 1983. Kiley followed his best-seller with *The Wendy Dilemma* in 1984, to counsel the wives and girlfriends afflicted by Peter Pannish men.

The term in use, by Sadie Van Gelder in *Seventeen,* July 1994:

> On the cross-country trek I made with just one other friend, he drove while I got to check out the scenery for all 3,000 miles. Yes, it could quite easily have turned into a guilt trip, but I squeegeed the front and back windshields at service stations and made sure to stay awake in solidarity. For me, cars have always signified cruising. Since I can stare out the window and not worry about anything, I'm a passenger-seat Peter Pan

And from Bill Flanagan in *GQ,* April 1997:

> If you're more than 25 years old, it's almost embarrassing to fall in love with a rock-and-roll album. Rock music means the world to teenagers and young adults during the difficult years when they stop being someone's children and begin being someone's parents. When the same music that helped you struggle through adolescence continues to possess you into middle life, however, people figure you have a Peter Pan complex.

And by Jody Shields in *Elle,* September 1988:

Elsa Schiaparelli had a Peter Pan quality. Her clothes looked like
a child's giddy vision of what a grown-up lady would wear. . . .
In the 1930s, she was the reigning queen of fashion, wooing clients
with chic, theatrical, humorous clothing and accessories.

Peter Principle An observation: in a hierarchy employees tend to rise to
the level of their incompetence. Named for educator and author Laurence J. Peter; it was proclaimed in Peter's 1969 book, *The Peter Principle: Why Things Always Go Wrong.*

Do a good job, contended Peter, and you'll be promoted; keep doing
well and you'll move up until you're finally assigned to work you can't
do, and there you'll stay. The principle explains why so many supervisors
are in over their heads. (If you don't think so, ask their underlings.)

The term in use, by commentator Frank Deford on National Public
Radio's "Morning Edition," September 21, 1994:

By an embarrassing score of zero to 31, the Arizona Cardinals
lost their third straight game Sunday under their cantankerous
new coach Buddy Ryan. The high hopes in the desert for Buddy
Ball, so-called, have been utterly turned to Batty Ball. Ryan
appears to be the clearest example of the Peter Principle, which
is nowhere in sport more classically visible than with assistant
football coaches who get promoted to the head position.

And another example from the sports world, by Jerry Tipton, quoting
Boston Globe sportswriter Bob Ryan, in the *Lexington Herald-Leader,*
March 30, 1997:

They [the Boston Celtics] don't have a coach. They have a nice
fellow who is a glowing example of the Peter Principle.

Peyton Place \'pā-tən\ A town that appears quiet and innocent but turns
out to have lots of steamy goings-on and dark secrets beneath the surface.

It comes from *Peyton Place,* a 1956 bestselling novel by Grace Metal-
ious (1924–1964) about a small New England town (actually Gilmanton
Iron Works, New Hampshire). Prepublication stories alleged that the
author's husband had lost his job because of the beans she spilled in the
novel, and that sent hordes of tourists and reporters to Gilmanton Iron
Works. The novel purported to represent the secret life of violence and
illicit sex lurking behind the respectable facade.

In its day, the racy sex scenes shocked and outraged many readers and
assured the success of the novel. "A horny book," says Grace Slick, ICON
of rock, who read it as an 18-year-old college student.

The term in use, by a resident of tony Southampton, Long Island,
quoted in the *New York Times,* November 5, 1989, on the arrest and conviction for prostitution of a local doctor and his wife:

"There's a lot of curiosity, quite frankly, about someone who is
a doctor and has another life," said Trudy Kramer, director of

the Parrish Art Museum. "This is a small town and, like any small town, sort of a Peyton Place."

And by Susan Baer in the *Baltimore Sun,* August 8, 1995, on hearings on the Whitewater scandal:

Republicans insisted that the Clintons presided over a "financial Peyton Place" and were part of the 1980s decade of greed even as they postured in public as "defenders of the little guy."

Pharisee \'far-ə-(ˌ)sē\ A sanctimonious, hypocritical person who observes the letter, but not the spirit, of the rules. The word originally referred to a member of a strict Jewish sect from the period between the Old and New Testaments who were noted for strict observance of the rites and ceremonies of the written law and for insistence on their interpretation of the law.

The Pharisees were first noted in the first century B.C. and are known to us chiefly through the writings of the historian Josephus, the collection of Jewish law and tradition known as the Talmud, and the New Testament.

In the New Testament, the Pharisees appear as the chief opponents of Jesus, whom they attacked for such violations of religious law as breaking the Sabbath and consorting with sinners.

Jesus rebuked the Pharisees for their self-righteousness and their merely outward conformance with the letter of the law. This view led to the contemporary meaning: hypocrites, outwardly pious but lacking compassion.

The term in use, by Cynthia Tucker in a commentary in the *Atlanta Journal and Constitution,* April 13, 1997:

Here we go again. The Pharisees of American public life are once again proposing to cure all that ails the country by legalizing prayer in the public square—schools, ballgames, courtrooms and so on.

And by columnist Tony Snow, Gannett News Service, January 30, 1997, on calls for special prosecutors to investigate the Clinton administration:

Republicans would love to put the president and his wife on a political spit and roast them indefinitely. . . . But a healthy proportion of the people who demand special prosecutors seem more concerned with moral showmanship than morality. Like Pharisees, they try to enhance their standing by sullying other people's reputations, saying, "This looks bad to me, so it must be illegal."

Philadelphia lawyer An exceptionally able, clever lawyer, but one given to shrewd and perhaps unscrupulous manipulation of the law. It's an expression that started out as a compliment early in American history but has since taken on a negative cast.

Philadelphia was one of the largest cities in the developing American nation and was bound to attract the most learned practitioners of the law. A Philadelphia lawyer, for example, won the acquittal of John Peter Zenger in 1735. Zenger had published attacks on the government and had been imprisoned for seditious libel. Attorney Andrew Hamilton came from Philadelphia to defend Zenger after the judge had barred two New York lawyers from representing him. Hamilton argued successfully that if Zenger's statements were true, they were not libel. It was a landmark case and undoubtedly made a big impression on both sides of the Atlantic.

However, since we are a country which both reveres and despises practitioners of the law, the expression has also come to mean a smart but slightly shady lawyer—an ambulance-chaser, a shyster too clever for his own good.

The term in use, by shrimp fisherman C.L. Standley, quoted by the *Christian Science Monitor,* June 29, 1990:

> Government regulation, indeed, is one of Standley's pet peeves. "There are so many regulations that, if he isn't a Philadelphia lawyer, a fisherman gets violations and doesn't even know it," he observes.

And by John H. Lenear, in the *Cleveland Call and Post,* January 26, 1995, on the NFL expansion draft:

> Each of the 28 NFL teams contributed a list of six players to the pool. . . . As expected the list was filled with the aged, the infirm, and the financially bloated. It also contains some underachievers, locker room advocates and Philadelphia lawyers.

philippic \fə-ʹli-pik\ A discourse or speech full of bitter condemnation. A tirade.

Specifically (and capitalized), the term refers to the speeches (Philippics) in which the orator Demosthenes tried to rouse the Athenians to resist the advancing power of King Philip of Macedon. (Rhetoric failed; King Philip completed his conquest of Greece in 338 B.C.) The orations of Cicero against Mark Antony are also called "Philippics" for their similarity to Demosthenes's declamations.

The term in use, by Holly Wheelwright in *Money,* November 8, 1989, describing the newsletter published by retiree/activist Leonard Shapiro:

> As he dug deeper into the city's bureaucracy, Shapiro says he got angrier about "how few people were at public meetings to see these officials getting away with murder. Then it occurred to me that a newsletter reporting everything I was finding out would goad the press to cover these things better." Almost nine years later, 5,000 copies of the eight-page philippic are fired off each month. . . .

And by Jonathan Yardley of the *Washington Post,* November 20, 1988, reviewing *At Home,* a volume of essays by Gore Vidal:

Ronald Reagan, the Israel lobby, fundamentalist rightwingers, Hollywood, Oliver North—on these and other subjects of public interest Vidal writes sardonically, if not as crisply as his previous philippics have led us to expect.

And by Alexander Wolff in *Sports Illustrated,* April 17, 1996, reporting on the University of Kentucky basketball team's victory in the NCAA finals:

> The foundation of Kentucky's 76–67 title-game victory was laid a year ago, after that loss to the Tar Heels, when Pitino took his players one by one into a darkened hotel banquet room in Birmingham and lashed into each with a personalized 20-minute philippic so harsh that the players hated him for weeks afterward.

philistine \\'fi-lə-ˌstēn; fə-'lis-tən, -tēn; 'fi-lə-stən\\ The term originally applied to a native or inhabitant of ancient Philistia. One who is guided by materialism and is usually disdainful of intellectual or cultural values; also, one who is uninformed in an area of knowledge.

How did the definition move from neutral to negative? The Philistines of the Old Testament lived in Palestine and fought the Israelites, who naturally took a dim view of them, as reported in the Bible. From them came the giant Goliath and Samson's seductress Delilah. Archaeologists say they had a significant culture and valued hard work: the Philistines were no philistines.

But the story doesn't stop there. As *Brewers Dictionary of Phrase and Fable* elaborates, the term came to be used as an epithet in Germany. It seems there was a dispute between the townspeople and university students at Jena in 1693 in which a number of people died. The university preacher took for his text "The Philistines be upon thee" from Judges, using it as a play on "philister," a German term for outsiders. Matthew Arnold used the term in *Culture and Anarchy* (1869), to criticize those whose sole interest was the accumulation of wealth.

The term in use, by George Will, in the *Washington Post,* November 27, 1988, on the retirement of Senator William Proxmire:

> Proxmire knows how to get noticed, as with his monthly Golden Fleece award, ridiculing what he considers foolish government spending. Some of his awards have been philistine, but populism often is.

And by Benedict Nightingale, reviewing the play *Amy's View,* playing in London, for the *New York Times,* June 29, 1997:

> For Esme, Dominic is a philistine whose career is a moral disgrace, consisting as it variously does of making slick, violent movies and sleazy, sneering television programs that poke fun at anything vaguely artistic.

And by David Cannadine in the *New York Times Book Review,* May 26, 1996:

> The decisions concerning the education of her children were taken by Prince Philip—including the disastrous choice of Gordonstoun as a school for the Prince of Wales, a remote and philistine institution to which he was completely unsuited.

phoenix rising from the ashes A person or thing that makes a dramatic recovery from defeat or adversity.

The phoenix, a bird the size of an eagle with scarlet and gold feathers, was a mythological creature in the legends of ancient Egypt, Greece, and the early Christian era. Only one lived at a time; its life span was about five hundred years. When it was about to die, the bird would build a pyre and set it on fire. The phoenix would be consumed by the flames but would rise anew and alive from the ashes to live another five hundred years.

The bird thus was associated with immortality and was an allegory for resurrection and life after death.

The term in use, by Jay Parini in *Elle,* October 1990:

> One sensed vividly that Jong, in the vein of her phoenixlike heroine, Ms. Wing, had been reborn, that she had come to terms with painful issues that have been nagging at her for a long time.

And in a *Newsday* editorial, April 19, 1993, on Los Angeles after the 1992 riots:

> Despite the fanfare and energy that accompanied the founding of the nonprofit Rebuild L.A., there is no 21st-century phoenix rising from the ashes and rubble of South Central Los Angeles and Koreatown.

And by Michelle Locke, for the Associated Press, June 29, 1996, describing a Tibetan Buddhist temple in California:

> Those who helped create the fabulous temple see more than a piece of the Far East imported to the stunning vistas of the California coast.
>
> "It's the phoenix rising from the ashes of the destruction of Tibetan Buddhism," says Sylvia Gretchen, who has been involved in the 21-year project since its inception.

Pickett's charge A dramatic, even romantic, but doomed, effort or gesture.

Pickett's charge was the climax of the battle of Gettysburg, fought July 1–3, 1863. After two days of unsuccessful assaults on Union positions, Confederate commander Robert E. Lee made a last desperate gamble. On July 3, Major General George Pickett was ordered to lead his 15,000 troops against the center of the Union line. Witnesses said it was an unforgettable sight as the Confederate troops emerged from the cover of woods and marched in battle order across open fields under the deadly fire of Union forces. The attack failed, with terrible losses; Lee, forced to withdraw, never again came close to administering a decisive blow to the Union army.

The term in use, by Patrick Buchanan, on his possible candidacy for president in 1988, as quoted in the *Washington Post,* January 21, 1987:

> Some of the oldest friends I have in politics have said pointedly that a Buchanan campaign would be the Pickett's charge of the American Right. . . .

And by Curtis Wilkie in the *Boston Globe,* September 8, 1991, describing a meeting of Democratic loyalists in Sioux City, Iowa:

> McGovern is an unflinching liberal who treasures principle over victory. He exhorted the Democrats to make a Pickett's charge against superior Republican forces.

pick up the gauntlet *See* GAUNTLET, THROW DOWN/PICK UP THE.

Pickwickian \(ˌ)pik-ˈwi-kē-ən\ Someone resembling in character, manner, or appearance Samuel Pickwick, a character created by Charles Dickens in his humorous novel *Pickwick Papers,* first published serially 1836–1837 as *The Posthumous Papers of the Pickwick Club.* Mr. Pickwick is a naive, kindly, and rotund old gentleman.

The expression "in a Pickwickian sense" refers to the unusual or peculiar meaning given to words, usually epithets, at variance with their commonly understood meaning. This comes from an incident in which Pickwick accuses Mr. Blotton of behaving in a "vile and calumnious" manner; Mr. Blotton calls Pickwick a "humbug." Eventually it is understood that both men used the words not in their common senses, but in their Pickwickian sense and in fact have great mutual regard.

Medical science memorializes Mr. Pickwick through the Pickwickian syndrome, another name for sleep apnea, which afflicts mostly older, overweight men.

The term in use, by Robert F. Jones in *Sports Illustrated,* December, 24-31, 1984:

> Tom Burnside, the jolly, almost Pickwickian computer consultant who wooed me to the game. . . .

And from Ted Loos in *Wine Spectator,* February 28, 1997:

> "We went to Bordeaux for a long weekend and drank claret," says [David] Parker of the grim necessities of research. "It was hell, but when duty calls, obey." It's a Pickwickian sentiment that Dickens—an enophile and journalist himself—would have appreciated.

And by Jack Thomas in the *Boston Globe,* November 30, 1985, previewing the public television dramatization of Dickens' *Bleak House:*

I . . . beg the indulgence of those dear readers of this journal, meager as it is, and to implore them to direct their attention tomorrow night to Masterpiece Theatre, a series infinitely preferable to the hash on network television, which even the ARTFUL DODGER can see is a smattering of everything and a knowledge of nothing, and which, in a Pickwickian sense, is as dumb as a drum with a hole in it.

Pied Piper One who offers strong but delusive enticement. A leader who makes irresponsible promises. A charismatic leader who attracts followers.

The term comes from a German folktale: in 1284, the town of Hamelin was plagued with rats. A mysterious stranger in a multi-colored costume (*pied* means patches of different colors) came to town and offered to get rid of the rats for a price. The town agreed, and the stranger played his pipe and led the rats to drown in the river.

But the town reneged, and the stranger returned for revenge. This time he charmed away all the children. They disappeared into a cave, and only two returned.

The story is thought to have its roots in the tragedy of the CHILDREN'S CRUSADE, which cost the lives of thousands of children. The legend was memorably told by Robert Browning in his 1842 poem, *The Pied Piper of Hamelin*.

The term in use, by Erin Riley in the Portland *Oregonian,* February 10, 1996:

> The state Examining board of Psychology has dismissed allegations that James Goodwin, known as the "Pied Piper of Prozac," is mentally impaired and should be barred from practicing psychology.

In use again, by Tovah Redwood in the *Kansas City Star,* March 6, 1997, writing about Kansas City Symphony conductor William McLaughlin:

> McLaughlin is known as a Pied Piper in the music world, eager to spread the word about the joys of music to a wide audience.

And by John Weyler in the *Los Angeles Times,* November 6, 1994, writing about a participant in the Ironman Triathalon:

> By the time Piper had made the final turn in downtown Kailua-Kona and was about a half-mile short of the finish, he began to feel his age, and then some. Within seconds, a slight twinge had erupted into a full-fledged back spasm and the Pied Piper of sexagenarians had become the hunchback of Notre Dame.

Pilgrim's Progress The struggle of a simple person to reach salvation, as told in the prose allegory by English writer and preacher John Bunyan. Published in the late 1600s, its longer title is *The Pilgrim's Progress from This World to That Which Is to Come.*

In *Pilgrim's Progress* Bunyan, a Puritan, tells the tale of Christian, who goes on a pilgrimage and eventually reaches the Celestial City after overcoming many dangers, hardships, and temptations, representative of the journey through life. Along the way he is helped by such persons as Evangelist, Mr. Goodwill, Hopeful, and Faithful; and is distracted and tempted by Mr. Legality, Mr. Worldly-Wiseman, Simple, Sloth, and Presumption. The book contributed many expressions to the language, including Vanity Fair, the SLOUGH OF DESPOND, Doubting Castle, and House Beautiful.

The term in use, by Carey Harrison, reviewing *Spinsters* by Pagan Kennedy in the *San Francisco Chronicle,* July 16, 1995:

> Throughout Frannie and Doris' stumbling but joyous odyssey, home, with its New England townscape, is never far away, never less than luminous. It's one of the magical, unexpected strokes in Kennedy's latter-day pilgrims' progress, that whatever the roller-coaster ride of the present may bring, it's a reconciliation with the past that its protagonists seek.

Another example, from director Robert M. Young on his film *Triumph of the Spirit,* based on the true story of a Jewish boxing champion who survived the Auschwitz concentration camp by winning matches against Nazi opponents, in the *Washington Post,* August 20, 1989:

> "There are moral choices involved," said Young, who described *Triumph* as "kind of a pilgrim's progress. By that I mean a journey that a man takes where he becomes witness to the human spirit in torment—where people become more than they ever were and people become less than they ever imagined they could be."

And by Genelle Pugmire in the *Deseret News,* November 12, 1997, reviewing a dramatization of Louisa May Alcott's *Little Women:*

> Themes from *Pilgrim's Progress* are woven into the lives of the March girls, who take their mother's challenge to be pilgrims in their world. . . . the young women are challenged to take on a new voyage of improving their strengths and shunning their weaknesses.

pillar of fire An inspired sign which clearly shows the way.

It is a reference to the sign sent by God to lead the children of Israel through the wilderness after they marched out of Egypt (Ex. 13:21–22; 14:19, 24; 40:38). A pillar of cloud guided them by day and a pillar of fire by night so that they could not mistake their path.

The term in use, by Noa Ben-Artzi, eulogizing her grandfather, assassinated Israeli Prime Minister Yitzhak Rabin, reported on National Public Radio's "All Things Considered," November 6, 1995:

Grandpa, you were the pillar of fire before the camp and now we are just a camp shrouded in lonely darkness. . . .

And by Richard T. Cooper, in the *Los Angeles Times,* December 31, 1995:

Back in January, they swept into the Capitol like a conquering army.

With Republican majorities controlling both houses of Congress for the first time since 1955 and the "Contract With America" before them like a pillar of fire, House Speaker Newt Gingrich and his fellow Republicans looked like the vanguard of an unstoppable revolution.

Pinocchio's nose An indicator of falsehood.

In the children's story *The Adventures of Pinocchio,* by Carlo Collodi, published in 1883, Pinocchio—as the world knows, thanks to the 1943 feature-length Disney cartoon—was a puppet who came to life. His most memorable feature was his nose, which grew longer when he lied.

The term in use, quoted by political columnists Jack Germond and Jules Witcover in the *Baltimore Sun,* July 25, 1995, commenting on developments since President Clinton and House Speaker Newt Gingrich shook hands at a town meeting on a proposal to create a bipartisan commission on campaign finance reform:

His [Gingrich's] press aide, Tony Blankley, who often speaks as if he is Gingrich, called Clinton "the Pinocchio president" who "can't resist taking the political angle rather than the high road. . . . "

And from William M. Welch, in *USA Today,* July 3, 1996:

Before he became President Clinton's personnel security chief, Craig Livingstone outfitted hecklers with chicken costumes and Pinocchio noses to taunt President Bush during the 1992 campaign.

plague on both your houses, a A curse on or an expression of disgust with the parties to a quarrel, a statement that implies that the selfish cruelty of all involved is at fault and all parties share the blame.

The phrase is a coinage by Shakespeare. In *Romeo and Juliet,* Act 3, Scene 1, Mercutio, Romeo's friend, is mortally wounded when Romeo intervenes in a sword fight between Mercutio and Tybalt of the House of Capulet. Romeo tries to break up the fight, but his intervention allows Tybalt's sword to find its mark.

The dying Mercutio cries bitterly, "I am hurt. A plague o' both your houses!"

The term in use, by Richard Eder in *Newsday,* reviewing *The Name of a Bullfighter,* by Luis Sepulveda, October 24, 1996:

It is in the bleak political dialogues and portraits that the book is at its acerbic best. The author invokes a plague on all the houses of recent history.

And by John Leo, writing on apathy among young voters in *U.S. News & World Report,* July 20, 1992:

> ... the young have a lot to be disaffected about—an unresponsive system filled with appalling politicians who refuse to discuss issues honestly. Staying home doesn't do much to reform the system, but "a plague on both your houses" (or this year "a plague on all three of your houses") is a political statement too.

And in a variation by James Baldwin, quoted in the *New York Times Book Review,* May 27, 1984:

> I was a maverick, a maverick in the sense that I depended on neither the white world nor the black world. That was the only way I could've played it. I would've been broken otherwise. I had to say, "A curse on both your houses." The fact that I went to Europe so early is probably what saved me. It gave me another touchstone—myself.

Plato's cave An allegory used by Plato (ca. 427–ca. 348 B.C.), the Greek philosopher, to illustrate how perceptions can be false, misleading, and completely out of touch with reality.

In the allegory, men chained in a cave are held in a way that permits them to see only the back of the cave by the light of a fire burning behind them. They can see only their own shadows and those of other men as they go by. Knowing nothing else, the men in the cave assume the shadows they see are reality.

The term in use, by Anthony Lewis, in the *New York Times,* November 10, 1988:

> Madison's vision was of an informed electorate "examining public characters and measures": the voters would be active participants in a public policy debate. Today the voters are passive figures in a process utterly removed from public policy, watching shadows on the wall of Plato's cave.

And by M. Delal Baer, in commentary in the *Los Angeles Times,* December 10, 1995:

> Mexican politics have long resembled Plato's cave, where shadowy hands holding jewels and daggers flickered on cave walls but the truth remained elusive.

play in Peoria Be acceptable to the uncritical masses of ordinary people. A term which probably originated in VAUDEVILLE when acts were tried out on audiences in cities like Peoria before going on to Chicago or St. Louis. It's usually used as a question posed by a political operative or observer: "Will it play in Peoria?" meaning, "Will ordinary folks buy it?"

The expression gained currency in the Nixon administration, which claimed to be in touch with the heartland, or, another Nixonian term, "the silent majority," the people who don't picket or protest—as distinct from the media centers on each coast, or the supercilious elites inside the Beltway—but who hold the country together.

The term in use, by Janet Maslin in the *New York Times* reviewing the film *A Thousand Acres,* September 19, 1997:

> Shakespeare doesn't play in Peoria, at least not in the screen adaptation of *A Thousand Acres* by Jane Smiley. Or even in Iowa, which is no closer to home for *King Lear.* That was the underlying inspiration for Ms. Smiley's literary experiment.

And by Michael Fleeman for the Associated Press, November 25, 1995:

> It could have been a three-way marriage made in fashion heaven: TV star Roseanne and then-husband Tom Arnold united with a maker of a line of clothes for big people.
> Then came that other three-way marriage. And the lesbian revelations. And the 21 personalities. . . .
> And all of a sudden, the clothes maker feared, the Arnolds' peccadilloes wouldn't play in Peoria.

playing fields of Eton English public (meaning private) school, said to be the source of British leadership, character, and competitiveness which prevailed at the battle of WATERLOO. That's what the Duke of Wellington is said to have said. The implication is that British officers had acquired all important traits through their elite education.

The expression is attributed to the Duke of Wellington and is used today not only to suggest the character-building virtues of sports but to describe the privileged environment of elite private schools both in Britain and the United States.

It is doubtful that Wellington ever actually said these words. Elizabeth Longford, one of his biographers, says there were no organized games at Eton during his three unhappy years there. She also notes that the quotation did not make its appearance until three years after the duke died. A French writer quoted Wellington as saying during a visit to the school, "It is here that the battle of Waterloo was won." No mention of playing fields; that was added by later writers. (Eton's headmaster, Robert Birley, made a gallant attempt to recover the situation for the academic side, saying "here" meant the classroom.)

The term in use, by Rebecca Smith in the *San Jose Mercury News,* May 29, 1995, on military application of computer technology:

> The young soldiers are often the quickest to embrace the new technology, officers say. They weren't exactly trained on the

playing fields of Eton, but in the "video arcades of America's shopping malls," says Stinnett, spokesman for the Army's training command.

"They've grown up in the information age and are completely comfortable with computers."

And a play on the expression, by Jonathan Yardley, in the *Washington Post,* November 14, 1988, referring to Andover, the prep school attended by George Bush:

What, if anything, does it mean that for the first time since 1945 the country is to be led by a man whose "values," as he insists on calling them, were shaped in the playing fields of Andover and in the sanctuary of the Episcopal Church?

pleasure dome A place of pleasurable entertainment or recreation; a resort.

It's a reference to Samuel Taylor Coleridge's poem "Kubla Khan." (*See* XANADU.) The Great Khan did "a stately pleasure dome decree," and quite spectacular it was, with walls and towers and gardens "where blossomed many an incense-bearing tree" and fountains and caves of ice.

The term in use, by Linda Grant in *Fortune,* February 5, 1995, on the plans of Federated Department Stores CEO Allen Questrom:

He is further convinced that the department store continues to be a pleasure dome in which glittery style can be displayed and sold by the billions of dollars.

And by Ike Flores of the Associated Press, December 1, 1995:

Behind closed doors, the quiet white house in an exclusive neighborhood becomes a "Pleasure Dome"— teeming with group sex, bondage and fantasy nights.

Long aware that a sex club has been operating in their midst, outraged neighbors in this leafy Orlando suburb have waged a battle to throw a little cold water on what they see as wantonness.

plowshares *See* BEAT SWORDS INTO PLOWSHARES.

poetic justice An outcome in which vice is punished and virtue rewarded, usually in a manner ironically appropriate. It is a convention that literature should see that justice is done—that evildoers are punished and the virtuous rewarded. The expression is often used in situations in which someone who has done wrong has the tables turned in a way which deliciously mirrors the crime or hits at a particularly sensitive spot.

The term was coined by Thomas Rymer in England in 1678, at a time when the idea that literature should reflect a moral point of view was going out of fashion, perhaps as a result of the bitter civil war and religious conflicts of that century. The argument goes on today; audiences still love to see the bad guys get their comeuppance, although their sympathies certainly can be manipulated.

The term in use, by Rodger L. Hardy in the *Deseret News,* February 4, 1997, reporting on fan misbehavior at high school basketball games:

> True to tradition, Springville fans threw tortillas on the floor when their team scored its first basket. Referees called a technical foul, and the Spanish Fork Dons made the two 1-point baskets.
>
> In the end they beat Springville 53–52. That may be considered poetic justice. . . .

And in the *Baltimore Sun,* July 19, 1995, on the decision to place a statue of African-American tennis champion Arthur Ashe on a Richmond boulevard lined with statues of Confederate war heroes:

> The vote of 7–0 came at 1 a.m. after a seven-hour hearing televised on several stations. Some speakers contended the placement amounted to poetic justice, while others saw it as the final insult.

And in an editorial in the *Springfield (Ohio) News-Sun,* March 13, 1997, on the death of a rapper:

> Many will dismiss the shooting of Notorious B.I.G. . . . as poetic justice: A man who lived (at least metaphorically) by the code of the streets has died by it.

Pogo A gentle, whimsical comics-page opossum known for pithy comments on contemporary events. The most famous is: "We have met the enemy and he is us," from an Earth Day strip in 1971, as he and his friend Porkypine look at a swamp choked with rubbish.

Pogo was paraphrasing American naval hero Oliver Hazard Perry, reporting on his victory over a British squadron on Lake Erie during the War of 1812. In a letter dated September 10, 1813, Perry wrote, "We have met the enemy, and they are ours." It was one of the great naval victories in American history.

Pogo was invented by Walt Kelly for a daily comic strip in 1948 and became tremendously popular. Pogo and his many animal friends lived in Okefenokee Swamp, and their experiences had a remarkable way of mirroring human nature as well as current events. In the 1950s Pogo was boosted for president; his slogan was "I Go Pogo," not unlike "I Like Ike." The swamp was visited by a scowling beast named Simple J. Malarkey, who bore a marked resemblance to Senator Joseph McCarthy. (*See* MCCARTHYISM.)

Pogo quoted, by Marie Cocco in *Newsday,* May 2, 1996:

> We have, again, met the enemy. And it is still us.
>
> A glance at the parking lot of any suburban ballfield or shopping mall this weekend will reveal more truth about the long-

term trend in gas consumption—and future prices—than all the hot air Washington can produce. . . . Weaned for a time off gas-guzzlers . . . Americans have fallen off the wagon—and into big, ugly trucks and vans.

And from Richard Corliss in *Time,* July 8, 1996, on the popularity of government conspiracy as a theme in television programming:

It isn't only the Montana Freemen who believe that we have met the enemy and he is U.S. "We know we've been lied to," says Bryce Zabel, *Dark Skies* co-creator, "about Vietnam, Watergate, Iran-contra."

pogrom \'pō-grəm\ An organized massacre of helpless people; specifically, such a massacre of Jews.

The word is Yiddish, from the Russian for "devastation."

The term in use, by Robert Leckie in *Delivered from Evil: The Saga of World War II* (1987), in which he writes of the days in Germany that were a precursor to the Holocaust:

Gradually the pogrom against the German Jews escalated, culminating on November 9, 1938, in KRISTALLNACHT, or Night of Broken Glass, so called because of the shattering of thousands of Jewish shops across the country.

And by Daniel Bauder in the *Miami Herald,* October 26, 1993, on the celebration of corporate executives who downsize their companies:

In a recent issue, *Business Week* also celebrated corporate pogroms and the head-choppers who carry them out.

And from *Sports Illustrated,* in an article about professional football's equivalent to downsizing, September 6, 1993:

Around the league there's a feeling that the Niners, well over the salary cap projected for next year, must trade now—before the great financial pogrom of '94. Maybe this Niner team doesn't compare with those of yesteryear—but it doesn't have to play them.

point man In politics or any area of controversy, the individual who is in the forefront. It's originally a military term for a soldier who goes ahead of a patrol—a dangerous position, where a man is most likely to get shot. The political point man often draws fire, too.

The term in use, by B. Drummond Ayres Jr. in the *New York Times,* August 8, 1995:

Gov. Pete Wilson of California is now the point man in the fight to eliminate affirmative-action programs based on race and sex.

Another example, from David Goldstein in the *Kansas City Star,* August 29, 1996: "Gore was the point man for federal downsizing."

The terms *point woman* and *point person* are also used, as illustrated by this example from Andy Meister in a profile of actress Diahann Carroll in *TV Guide,* March 23, 1985:

> It was important. A white man named Hal Kanter was determined to make a point about integration, and Carroll was his point woman.

And this example from *Ms,* May-June, 1994:

> As the Clinton administration's point person on disability and education, she has been especially outspoken about girls and women.

poison pill A financial tactic (such as increasing indebtedness) used by a company to deter an unwanted takeover.

If you swallow a poison pill, you will also poison whoever swallows you. That's the theory behind such corporate ploys as requiring that shareholders receive special shares at one price which a successful corporate raider must instantly buy back at twice the price. The goal is to make a company unpalatable, too difficult or expensive to gobble up. The term has expanded beyond the business world to describe similar tactics in other arenas. In legislation, for example, an amendment which alters a bill in a way to make it noxious to its proponents is called a poison pill.

The term in use, in a press release by Common Cause on pending campaign finance reform legislation, October 1, 1997:

> The three ways to judge which senators are serious about reform are whether they will vote against any poison pill amendments designed to kill reform, whether they will vote to end a filibuster, and whether they will end the soft money system.

And by the *Economist,* March 11, 1989:

> The budget deficit looms over and paralyses most conceivable policy initiatives. Some cynical Democrats think this is why it was created: Ronald Reagan's poison pill that for years to come guarantees a welcome inertia in Washington.

Pollyanna An irrepressible optimist with a tendency to find good in everything.

The original Pollyanna was the creation of Eleanor Hodgman Porter (1868–1920), who wrote *Pollyanna* in 1913 about a young girl who always, *always* looks on the bright side and brightens up everyone else in the process.

The book was an enormous success, and was followed with successful sequels. *Pollyanna* became a Broadway play starring Helen Hayes in 1916 and a movie starring Mary Pickford in 1920, remade starring Hayley Mills in 1960. The name entered the language, but all that relentless sunshine was just a little too much, and there is now a pejorative twist—

Pollyanna is an optimist, but an unrealistic one, someone who lives in a fool's paradise.

The term in use, by Charles C. Mann in the *Atlantic,* February 1993:

> On one side, according to Garrett Hardin, an ecologist at the University of California at Santa Barbara, are the CASSANDRAS, who believe that continued population growth at the current rate will inevitably lead to catastrophe. On the other are the Pollyannas, who believe that humanity faces problems but has a good shot at coming out okay in the end.

And in a *Christian Science Monitor* editorial, March 23, 1994, on the British Broadcasting Corporation's plan to present a one-hour-per-week "good news" program:

> On the basis of a 24-hour day and a seven-day news week, the BBC's new token hour of optimism will still leave 99.4 percent of its airtime available to politics, fires, floods, earthquakes, famines, and man's inhumanity to man, including the usual news quotas of wars, massacres, and serial killers. So there's no need to worry about journalists turning into Pollyannas.

Polonius \pə-'lō-nē-əs\ A garrulous old man; the courtier and father of Ophelia and Laertes in Shakespeare's *Hamlet.*

Polonius is a talkative old fellow famous for his endless maxims. He spies on Hamlet, who kills him by running his sword through the arras (tapestry) behind which the old man is hiding.

Pomposity aside, one of the most famous speeches in Shakespeare is the final advice Polonius gives to his son:

> This above all: to thine own self be true,
> And it must follow, as the night the day,
> Thou canst not then be false to any man.

The term in use, by Lewis H. Lapham in *Harper's* magazine, June 1997:

> Gingrich administered the restorative bombast (balanced budget, destruction of the I.R.S., etc.) with the verve of a latter-day Polonius or Dr. Pangloss, and although he declined to answer questions about how and when he would pay the $300,000 fine imposed on him by the Ethics Committee, on the matters of state he was happy to say that everything was for the best in this BEST OF ALL POSSIBLE WORLDS. [*See also* PANGLOSSIAN.]

And by actor Michael Moriarity, objecting to the efforts of politicians to control content on television programs, quoted by Jonathan Storm in the *Philadelphia Inquirer,* February 12, 1994:

> He compares [Attorney General] Reno to *The Caine Mutiny*'s Captain QUEEG, a person "elevated roughly five notches beyond

his capabilities," and to Joseph McCarthy. He calls [Illinois Sen. Paul] Simon "Polonius with a bow tie."

Ponzi scheme An investment swindle in which some early investors are paid off with money put up by later ones to encourage more, bigger risks. A financial fraud; a pyramid scheme. If investors stop paying in, the pyramid collapses. The scheme takes its name from Charles Ponzi, an enterprising immigrant who perpetrated such a fraud in the United States in 1919–1920. He was not the first, and certainly not the last, but he was a big success in his time.

He offered investors a return of 50 percent interest in 90 days, or an annual rate of 400 percent on arbitrage of international postal coupons. A lot of people believed him, and soon he had over 30,000 investors who had put in almost $15 million. He was exposed by the *Boston Post* newspaper, which won a Pulitzer Prize for its reporting. Public confidence was shaken by the exposure, investing stopped, and that was that. Ponzi was sent to prison, but swore to the end of his days that the operation was legit and that it was only government interference that kept him from paying off his investors.

The term in use, by commentator Matt Miller on National Public Radio's "Morning Edition," August 14, 1996, on federally subsidized housing:

> But as a new Brookings Institution report points out, there was a kind of Ponzi scheme at work. Government could avoid becoming liable on its mortgage guarantees only as long as the rental subsidies continued. If they were cut, the whole scheme would collapse.

And by Genevieve Stuttaford in *Publishers Weekly,* July 29, 1996:

> Whether one accepts Peterson's apodictic pronouncement that "Social Security is a vast Ponzi scheme in which only the first people in are big winners," his proposals for a graying America to return to an earlier generation's collective restraint are worthy advisories to which attention should be paid.

pooh–bah A person in high position or of great influence. Somebody important, or at least pompous, or who holds many jobs at the same time.

In Gilbert and Sullivan's *The Mikado* (1885), the original Pooh-Bah was the Lord High Everything Else, a self-important bureaucrat.

The term in use, by Paul Gray in *Time,* September 26, 1988:

> Many sports fans believe the Pooh-Bahs of professional athletics—the commissioners, presidents, team owners, the whole briefcase brigade—should play a role similar to background music at the movies. They are doing their jobs most successfully when no one notices them at all.

And by Howard Kurtz in the *Washington Post,* October 25, 1997, reporting a flap on invitations to White House press dinners:

A strict reading of the rules means plenty of journalistic BIGFEET will be barred. . . .

[Presidential press secretary] McCurry left himself some wiggle room. "We'll have to take care of people who consider themselves media pooh-bahs."

Poppins, Mary A magical, good-hearted, and exceedingly efficient nanny, created by Australian writer P.L. Travers in a series of stories starting in 1934. Mary Poppins has all the nanny virtues, although she is not the cutesy figure created by Julie Andrews in the 1964 Disney film. Travers' Mary Poppins was, according to critic Mimi Kramer (*Time,* May 6, 1996, at the time of Travers' death)

. . . somewhat fierce, somewhat formidable and perennially unfair. The point about the Mary Poppins of the books is that although wonderful things begin to happen when she arrives, she's not very nice to be around.

The live-in care provided by nannies in upper-income homes has been a feature of English life and fiction for generations. Some nannies are fearsome, others kind. Winston Churchill, for instance was devoted to his nanny, who filled the void left by glamorous but distant parents. And in the United States today, Mary Poppins surely must be the heart's desire of working parents worrying about day care for their children.

The term in use, by Jeff Wilson of the Associated Press, October 28, 1994:

Walt Disney's housekeeper was a crusty, chain-smoking character who was more Hazel than Mary Poppins. In the end Thelma Howard proved to be a fairy godmother.

Another example, from Karen Williams, in the *Christian Science Monitor,* March 27, 1997:

Everyone agrees that reading aloud to children is good. But many families are hard-pressed to find enough time to do much of it. That's when books on audiocassettes can come to the rescue like a high-tech Mary Poppins.

portmanteau word \pȯrt-'man-(ˌ)tō, pȯrt-\ A term used by Lewis Carroll for a word made up from the parts of others. It comes from *portmanteau,* the word for a kind of large suitcase, especially one that opens into two compartments. "Smog"—a combination of smoke and fog—is a portmanteau word; "brunch" is another.

In *Through the Looking Glass,* Alice has a conversation with HUMPTY DUMPTY and asks him the meaning of the poem "Jabberwocky," which is filled with strange words like "slithy." Humpty explains that slithy is a combination of "slime" and "lithe": "You see, it's like a portmanteau—there are two meanings packed up into one word."

The term in use, by Amby Burfoot in *Runner's World,* April 1, 1994:

Not that long ago, I fancied myself a veritable Ironman among
runners. I ran 100 miles every week, I finished every race, and
I called myself a "stotan"—Percy Cerutty's portmanteau word
for someone who combines the qualities of a stoic and a
spartan.

By extension, *portmanteau word* has also come to mean "a word that
suggests two meanings" or "a word that has a broad and vague range of
meanings."

An example of this meaning of the term, by Mel Gussow in the *New
York Times,* January 30, 1991:

> In several cases, including that of his new book, Mr. Naipul's
> work has been categorized as travel writing, a label that he
> accepts as "a portmanteau word." But in no sense is it a book
> for travelers; it is a book by a traveler.

And by Maureen Johnson of the Associated Press, March 5, 1990, on
British conservatives' attacks on the British Broadcasting Corp.:

> Norman Tebbit, who as governing Conservative Party chairman
> from 1985 to 1987 spearheaded battles with the BBC, alleges the
> corporation is permanently in the thrall of the left.
> "The word "conservative" is now used by the BBC as a port-
> manteau word of abuse for anyone whose political views differ
> from the insufferable, smug, sanctimonious, naive, guilt-ridden,
> wet, pink orthodoxy of . . . the 1960s," Tebbit declared in a recent
> address at Oxford University.

Potemkin village \pə-'tem(p)-kən\ An impressive facade or show designed
to hide an undesirable fact or condition. Such places created by Prince
Grigori Aleksandrovich Potemkin, chief minister (and lover) of Catherine the Great, who ruled Russia from 1762 to 1774.

Catherine invited Emperor Joseph II of Austria to join her in 1774 on
a tour of Russia's newly acquired Black Sea provinces. Potemkin arranged
for the construction of artificial, one-street villages along the route, complete with cheering crowds of happy peasants. He thus qualifies as one of
the most creative political advance men in history.

The term has come to stand for a phony, bogus image, a false front that
is used to fool people into thinking a fake proposition or situation is real.

The term in use, by Daniel Williams in the *Washington Post,* July 22,
1997, reporting on efforts to clean up Moscow for its 850th anniversary:

> The assault on the prostitutes—there's no law against prostitu-
> tion in Russia—is emblematic of how the city's current makeover
> is turning Moscow into a Potemkin village. Of course, Russia
> invented the Potemkin village.

And by Martin Schram in *Newsday,* August 15, 1996, describing the
Republican convention:

The journalists and the delegates are but a Potemkin village, a poster backdrop that more than served the propaganda purposes of the most skillful bunch of political strategists that ever put one over on the media.

Potiphar's wife \'pä-tə-ˌfär\ A woman scorned who seeks revenge against the man rejecting her by falsely accusing him of rape.

The reference is taken from Genesis 37:36, 39:6–18, in the story of Joseph. Joseph is the favorite son of Jacob, and his jealous brothers sell him into slavery in Egypt. As a slave he becomes the overseer of the household of Potiphar, an important official. Potiphar's wife "cast her eyes upon Joseph; and she said, Lie with me." But Joseph refuses. When she propositions him again, he flees, leaving his clothing in her hand.

She retaliates by telling her husband that he has attacked her, displaying his garment as proof. As a result, Joseph is imprisoned.

The term in use, by Stanley Kauffmann in a review of the film *Disclosure* in the *New Republic,* January 9, 1995:

Her vengeance then follows the ancient principle of Potiphar's wife: a spurned woman accuses the man she wanted of sexual aggression.

And by columnist Ellen Goodman in the *Boston Globe,* May 16, 1985, commenting on the case of a woman who had recanted her testimony in a rape case after the man involved had been jailed for several years:

But since her rape-and-recant, Webb has become more famous than Potiphar's wife, the Old Testament woman who cried rape against Joseph.

pound of flesh Infliction to the exact letter of the law, without mercy, of a punishment that is cruelly painful. Exaction of precise payment due.

The expression comes from Shakespeare's *The Merchant of Venice.* The merchant Antonio borrows money from Shylock the Jew. Shylock reminds him of the contempt Antonio has shown him in the past, but agrees to lend the money on the condition that Antonio sign a bond stating that if the money is not paid back when due, Shylock is entitled to "an equal pound" of Antonio's flesh, to be cut "[i]n what part of your body pleaseth me."

Antonio needs the money to finance his friend Bassanio's voyage to woo and so marry Portia. But the ships which would have brought Antonio the money to repay the debt are reported lost, Antonio cannot pay, and Shylock demands the fulfillment of the agreement.

Portia hastens to the court disguised as a lawyer, and intervenes to save Antonio. She urges mercy, but Shylock demands instead the letter of the law. The bond is forfeit, says Portia, but the agreement makes no mention of blood. Shylock may have his pound of flesh, but if one drop of blood is shed, or if he takes more or less than an exact pound, his property and life are forfeited to the state. The letter of the law thus is turned on Shylock, who now faces punishment for threatening the life of a citizen.

The term in use, quoted by the Associated Press, January 22, 1997:

> During the plea bargaining over Newt Gingrich's punishment for admitted misdeeds, the ethics committee's special counsel sought a financial penalty that would have nearly tripled the $300,000 assessed against the House speaker, Gingrich's lawyer says.
> "They wanted to make sure they got their pound of flesh," attorney J. Randolph Evans said yesterday.

And by J. Clark and S. Buri, in *Kiplinger's Personal Finance* magazine, June 1, 1992:

> Fitness buffs looking for supervised workouts and a little extra motivation are getting custom service from personal trainers— and they aren't paying a pound of flesh for the privilege. As the number of trainers has grown, costs have dropped.

pour encourager les autres \pür-ä^n-kù-rä-zhā-lāz-ō-trə\ Going to extremes to make an example of another. Used pointedly and ironically—the intent is to discourage others from similar behavior. In French, "to encourage the others." The expression comes from a reference in Voltaire's *Candide* to the execution of Admiral Byng in 1757: "In this country [England], it is well from time to time to kill an admiral to encourage the others."

During the Seven Years' War (1750–1757) between Britain and France, Byng was sent with a naval force to break a French siege of the island of Minorca. His force was inadequate, so he made only a half-hearted attempt before withdrawing. In the ensuing political uproar at home, the prime minister, the Duke of Newcastle, promised that the errant admiral would be "tried immediately and hanged directly." Byng was tried and found guilty of neglect of duty, but he was spared a hanging; he was executed by firing squad instead.

The term in use, in the *Economist,* March 31, 1984:

> Should Miss Sarah Tisdall, leaker of one Whitehall document that plainly did not concern national security and another that conceivably did, have been given six months in prison pour encourager les autres? That, Mr. Justice Cantly last Friday made clear, was the reason for the jail sentence. . . .

And by John Laughland in the *National Review,* May 1, 1995, characterizing the record of French President François Mitterand:

> Whenever faced with the failure of policies which he had instructed the government to conduct through parliament, he tended merely to dispose of his prime minister, pour encourager les autres, and to press on, rather like a snake shedding its skin.

praetorian guard; praetorians *often capitalized* The imperial bodyguards of Roman emperors, from Augustus to Constantine, who acquired great political power and sometimes were able to make (and unmake) emperors. Nowadays, these are powerful, protective aides or close associates of those in power.

One example of an emperor who was manipulated into office by his guards was Claudius, who ruled from 41 to 54 A.D. Following the assassination of Caligula, the Praetorian Guards, knowing that without an emperor they'd be out of work, squelched an effort in the Roman Senate to restore the republic. The Praetorians discovered Claudius, a neglected grandson of Augustus who was regarded as mentally defective, and declared him to be the emperor. (Claudius surprised everyone by doing a decent job.) The guards were dispersed in 312; by that time generals were using the legions at their command to install themselves as emperors, and the praetorians were superfluous.

The term is applied to functionaries who surround and serve, and sometimes manipulate, powerful officeholders.

The term in use, by William R. Doerner in *Time,* January 8, 1990:

> According to Ion Pacepa, a Rumanian lieutenant general who defected to the U.S. in 1978, the Securiatate under Ceausescu had various functions. One was to serve as a kind of Praetorian Guard for members of the Communist Party's Central Committee and specifically the Ceausescu family.

And in an editorial in the *Christian Science Monitor,* March 16, 1992:

> When savings-and-loan buccaneer Charles Keating was busy defrauding investors and costing American taxpayers some $2.6 billion in government insurance, he got a lot of help. . . . Surrounding Keating like a praetorian guard were phalanxes of lawyers and accountants who assured both investors and regulators that their client's Lincoln Savings and Loan was sound.

primal scream A gut-wrenching, infantile, and therapeutic scream of emotional release. The term comes from a type of psychotherapy known as primal scream therapy in which the patient is brought to focus on repressed pain from infancy or childhood. The primal scream is made when a patient makes contact with the primal trauma thought to lie at the core of neurosis.

In popular use, it refers to a deeply felt cry of rage or pain.

A famous example comes from the account of the Watergate scandal, *All The President's Men* (1974) by *Washington Post* reporters Carl Bernstein and Bob Woodward. Bernstein had called former Nixon campaign manager John Mitchell for comment on a story claiming that Mitchell controlled a secret political fund while attorney general:

> For Bernstein, the only constant had been an adrenal feeling that began with Mitchell's first JEEEEEEESUS—some sort of primal scream.

Another example, from Rob Kasper, in the *Baltimore Sun,* January 21, 1995, on coping with a rogue car alarm:

> The way to solve the problem, the car-alarm guy said, was to let it rip with a good holler. He told me to set off the car alarm, letting it wail until it had a good yell, about one minute. Usually this primal scream "completes the cycle" and clears the car alarm's brain, he said.

And from Kevin Phillips in the *New York Times Magazine,* April 12, 1992:

> Frustration politics, even in its more extreme forms, represents a sort of primal scream by the electorate that major party politics must heed if the center is to hold. [*See* CENTER CANNOT HOLD, THE.]

primrose path A path of ease, or of least resistance, or pleasure—especially sensual pleasure—which leads to probable downfall or ruin.

Another expression from Shakespeare's plays. It appears in *Hamlet,* Act 1, Scene 3, in which Laertes gives brotherly advice to his sister Ophelia and warns her to be wary of the attentions of Hamlet. She responds, as any little sister would:

> Do not, as some ungracious pastors do,
> Show me the steep and thorny way to heaven,
> Whiles, like a puffed and reckless libertine,
> Himself the primrose path of dalliance treads. . . .

There is also a reference in *Macbeth,* Act 2, Scene 3, in which the drunken porter responds to knocking at the door, pretending to be the keeper of hell-gate: "I had thought to have let in some of all professions that go the primrose way to th' everlasting bonfire."

The term in use, by conservative activist Gary L. Bauer in the *National Review,* December 9, 1996, on why Bob Dole lost the presidential election:

> What was taken seriously in this campaign was the high-priced counsel of pollsters and consultants who urged Dole along the primrose path of "moderation."

And in a *Los Angeles Times* editorial, December 10, 1994, on the causes of the financial collapse of the Orange County government:

> Did investment houses exploit cozy relationships with municipalities to lure them into unwise investments? A 1993 Orange County ordinance was broadly aimed at curbing gifts to county officials not just from bankers but from developers and the like, precisely to discourage the luring of officials down the primrose path. But a few Lakers tickets or other small gifts do not make for the kind of colossal failure in oversight now evident in Orange County.

And again, from Richard des Ruisseaux, Gannett News Service, April 5, 1994:

> Those familiar walking fingers are leading some businesses down the primrose path, getting them to pay for listings they don't really want in specialized phone directories.

procrustean \prə-'krəs-tē-ən, prō-\ *often capitalized* Marked by arbitrary often ruthless disregard of individual differences or special circumstances.

The term comes from the robber Procrustes who, according to ancient Greek legend, would take prisoners and place them on an iron bed. If they didn't fit, he would either stretch them or amputate parts until they did. From this story, we also get the term *procrustean bed* for a scheme or pattern into which someone or something is arbitrarily forced.

The term in use, by Florence King in the *National Review,* July 1, 1996, on the controversy about whether the memorial to Franklin D. Roosevelt should show him in a wheelchair:

> The memorial flap is an attempt to diminish FDR's legacy of noble stoicism until he fits the mold prescribed by Hillary Clinton's ex-guru, Michael Lerner, in *The Politics of Meaning:* "If the world needs to be healed, it will be done by 'wounded healers,' people who themselves are in need of healing."
>
> Now the Procrustean banditti are after Bob Dole, urging him to talk about his arm, and he, poor fool, is going along with it.

And by Gary Hector writing in *Fortune,* December 3, 1990:

> Based on what we learned, we developed a somewhat Procrustean formula to be applied across the board to the balance sheets of every bank we looked at, whatever the actual quality of its portfolio. . . .

And by Allen Ramsey, giving his views on charges of liberal bias in the news media, in commentary in the *Kansas City Star,* October 9, 1992:

> There may be a place for such Procrustean beds in the house of journalism, but they do nothing for the integrity of the profession. . . . And, better to have journalists with the courage to cross ideological lines when the truth demands it rather than denying we have a truly terrible president, whether that person be a peanut farmer from Georgia or a Yale preppie from Maine.

prodigal son \'prä-di-gəl\ The biblical character who squandered his patrimony and returned to his father's home in poverty. It is from the New Testament, Luke 15:11–32. A son who "wasted his substance with riotous living" in a faraway place returns to his father's house. His father, rather than scolding him, forgives him and rejoices at his return. Although the good brother who had stayed at home is jealous and reproachful, his father tells him that celebration over the return of a son thought lost or dead is entirely fitting.

The term in use, by Hugh Dellios for the *Chicago Tribune,* in the *Seattle Times,* March 23, 1997, writing on Zairean rebel Laurent Kabila:

> Three months and hundreds of miles of occupied territory later, Kabila stood before 10,000 fellow residents of Shaba Province and received a homecoming worthy of a prodigal son.

By Jason DeParle, in the *New York Times Magazine,* July 14, 1996, quoting Bay Buchanan, manager of the presidential campaign of her brother Patrick:

> Bay Buchanan puts it differently: "That prodigal son didn't get to the end of the block."

And from Hilary DeVries, in the *Christian Science Monitor,* April 10, 1987:

> If there is anything redemptive about the current "prodigal son" wrinkle in his career, it is not lost on Anthony Hopkins. . . .
> Like the prodigal, Hopkins has returned from a decade spent in Tinsel Town to resume his rightful career on the London stage.

Promethean \prə-ˈmē-thē-ən\ Of, relating to, or resembling the Greek Titan Prometheus, his bold creativity, his art, his defiance of authority, and the dreadful punishment he suffered.

As the story goes in Greek mythology, Prometheus modeled man from clay and then taught him agriculture and all the arts of civilization. He also stole fire from the gods and gave it to man. As punishment, Zeus chained Prometheus to a rock where an eagle tore out his liver by day; by night, it was restored so the torture could begin again.

The Greek dramatist Aeschylus (525–456 B.C.) treated Prometheus as a hero. So did the 19th century Romantics, who liked his anti-establishment rebelliousness. Prometheus is variously portrayed as a rebel against tyrannical power, a Christ-like figure who sacrificed himself for man, and a symbol of man's creativity and independence.

Prometheus invoked, by Tom Wolfe, in the *American Spectator,* December 1987:

> But above all they will look back upon the 20th as the century in which their forebears had the amazing confidence, the Promethean HUBRIS, to defy the gods and try to push man's power and freedom to limitless, godlike extremes.

And by George Gurley, reviewing Neil Levine's *The Architecture of Frank Lloyd Wright* in the *Kansas City Star,* July 28, 1996:

> Wright was Promethean in his ambition and imagination. He attempted to relate his buildings to time as well as space. He incorporated earth, fire, water and air symbolically into his conceptions.

And, a reference to the Titan himself, by Jon Pareles on Elvis Presley in the *New York Times,* August 18, 1997:

> He was a Prometheus who stole the fire of the blues for popular music and ended up as a feast for vultures. He was a rebel who won his battle, then lost his way.

promised land Something, especially a place or condition believed to promise final satisfaction or realization of hopes. In Genesis, where it is usually capitalized, it is the land of Canaan, which God promised Abraham, Isaac, and Jacob that their descendants would inhabit. The Israelites finally arrived after the flight from Egypt and forty years of wandering in the WILDERNESS. Moses, who led his people on their wanderings, was forbidden to enter the promised land; he viewed the land from the top of a mountain, traditionally believed to be Mt. Nebo, also known as Mt. Pisgah, where he died.

The term in use, by Frank Rich in the *New York Times,* May 15, 1997:

> My first brush with organized religion was as part of a hopelessly disorganized Sunday kindergarten class, praying in a makeshift sanctuary in a Jewish Community Center in downtown Washington. . . . By 1969, a year after the post-King-assassination riots nearby, the J.C.C. itself fled 16th Street for the sylvan promised land of Rockville, Maryland.

And Interior Secretary Bruce Babbitt, quoted in the *Christian Science Monitor,* August 23, 1993:

> "In Alaska, unlike most of the US, there is enough time and unspoiled ecosystem left to [improve resource management], instead of struggling to correct past environmental mistakes," he said. "I know we're all a little crazy when we come up here, because we're coming from the desert to the Promised Land."

And by Norma Rosen, in an essay in the *New York Times Magazine,* August 3, 1997:

> A few months before my grandson arrived, my mother died. She lived, as the saying goes, for the grandchildren. She knew they were expecting . . . and she fought hard, at nearly 95, to hang onto life till then. In imagination, she looked into the promised land. But she could not get there.

And a famous, deeply poignant, example from the last speech of Dr. Martin Luther King, given April 3, 1968, one day before he was assassinated in Memphis, Tennessee. King spoke extemporaneously, referring to the threats against his life:

> Well, I don't know what will happen now. We've got some difficult days ahead. But it doesn't matter with me now. Because I've been to the mountaintop. And I don't mind. Like anybody, I

would like to live a long life. Longevity has its place. But I'm not concerned about that now. I just want to do God's will. And He's allowed me to go up to the mountain. And I've looked over. And I've seen the promised land. I may not get there with you. But I want you to know tonight, that we, as a people will get to the promised land.

Prospero \\'präs-pə-ˌrō\ The rightful duke of Milan in Shakespeare's *The Tempest,* a sage and a magician and a wise older man of great intellect and moral force.

Prospero is in exile, having been overthrown by his brother and the king of Naples. He uses his magic to cause a tempest that wrecks a ship carrying his enemies on the shore of his enchanted island. Prospero's daughter Miranda (*see* BRAVE NEW WORLD) falls in love with the son of the king of Naples, and all ends happily.

As the play ends, Prospero frees his servants Ariel and Caliban, gives up his magic and prepares to return to Milan and his duties as duke.

The term in use, by David Gates in his review of *Private Confessions* by Ingmar Bergman in the *New York Times Book Review,* January 12, 1997:

> Ingmar Bergman retired from film making 10 years ago. Since then, he's written two volumes of autobiography and three novels, and has been living on the island of Faro in Sweden, like a Prospero who has broken his staff but not drowned his book.

And again, by novelist John Updike, quoted by Maturity News Service, July 7, 1996:

> Shakespeare's Prospero, upon taking his retirement, promised that "every third thought shall be my grave," Updike went on, adding: "That leaves two thoughts, however, to entertain above the ground, and you have in your colorful pilgrimage long rehearsed what these thoughts might be: love one another, and seize the day."

protean \\'prō-tē-ən, prō-'tē-\ Displaying great diversity or variety; versatile. Like Proteus, with a varied nature or the ability to assume different forms. Proteus was a figure in Greek mythology, the herdsman of Poseidon, the god of the sea. Proteus' claim to fame was his ability to change himself into different forms at will.

The term in use, by David Hoffman in the *Washington Post,* August 13, 1989:

> Bush is a protean figure. . . . He adapts readily to the shifting demands of politics and public opinion; he transformed himself from last year to this and will evolve again.

And by Pat Dowell, reviewing David Thomson's *Rosebud: The Story of Orson Welles* in the *Washington Post Book World,* August 18, 1996:

So does the world need another book about George Orson Welles, the unfathomable conjurer, the Protean actor, the martyr to crass commerce, the eternal rebuke to mediocrity?

And by Kim Levin in *Travel & Leisure,* March 1997:

Our appetite for Spain's protean, prolific 20th-century master seems to be insatiable: as soon as one Picasso show closes, another opens.

Proustian \\'prü-stē-ən\\ Marcel Proust (1871–1922) was a 20th-century French novelist, one of the great literary figures of modern times. His name became an adjective synonymous with complexities of style as well as with elements of his life's work, *Remembrance of Things Past,* a gigantic novel in seven volumes.

The difficulty of reading Proust's work is legendary. The 3,000-page novel is filled with long, complicated sentences, digressions, metaphors, imagery, and analyses packed into dense paragraphs. He frequently employs a stream-of-consciousness technique. For example, the taste of tea and a madeleine (a feather-light French tea cake in an elongated petal shape, perhaps the most important cookie in world literature) stimulates a recollection of his childhood and memories of holidays spent by the sea in the village of Combray.

The term in use, by David Denby in the *New Republic,* May 22, 1989, reviewing John Updike's autobiography *Self-Consciousness:*

The reminiscing sidewalk tour which turns, by degrees, into an interior journey, marvelously combines a Proustian caressing of the frayed crib-coverlets of childhood with flinty O'Hara-like Pennsylvania class distinctions.

And by Sven Birkerts, reviewing *The Portable Jack Kerouac* in the *New Republic,* April 24, 1995:

[Kerouac] went so far as to view his ongoing endeavor as making up a kind of Proustian remembrance, and believed that this could be clarified by judicious excerpting from the books. Alas, the Proustian has here met the PROCRUSTEAN, and while the volume does serve as a handy overview . . . it does not finally serve Kerouac's cause of being seen as a major writer.

Prynne, Hester A publicly labeled adulterous woman. She is the heroine of Nathaniel Hawthorne's classic novel of 17th-century Puritan Massachusetts, *The Scarlet Letter* (1850). Hester is a young married woman who has given birth to an illegitimate child. She is punished for her adultery by being required to wear a scarlet A on her breast.

Hester shows courage in the face of her public shame; she refuses to reveal the name of the father of her child, and richly embroiders the letter, turning it into something beautiful. By contrast, the father of her child, the Reverend Arthur Dimmesdale, lacks the courage to acknowledge his sin. Her husband, Roger Chillingworth, who arrives on the scene from England, becomes the worst of all; he suspects Dimmesdale and cruelly torments him.

Thus, while Hester is publicly condemned as a sinner, she really is the best of the lot.

The term in use, by columnist Charles Krauthammer of the *Washington Post,* in the *Deseret News,* January 19, 1997:

> I particularly recommend the section on regulation, where Murray comes up with an ingenious idea: That government allow any business, any product, any service to be marketed without any regulation whatsoever, so long as the product or service is stamped, Hester Prynne-like, "UNREGULATED."

And from Maureen Dowd, in the *New York Times,* May 21, 1997, on the case of a female Air Force pilot forced from the service over accusations of adultery and lying to superiors:

> But it is hard to believe that there wasn't something this side of Hester Prynne to resolve a case with someone who had been showcased as the first female B-52 bomber pilot.

Ptolemaic universe \ˌtä-lə-'mā-ik\ The theory of planetary motions that holds that the earth is at the center with the sun, moon, and planets revolving around it. The theory was devised by the astronomer-mathematician-geographer Ptolemy (Claudius Ptolemaeus, ca. 85–165) and his idea was accepted until the 16th century when Polish astronomer Nicholas Copernicus disproved it, laying the foundation for modern astronomy.

The term in use, by Lance Morrow in *Time,* October 24, 1988, on the presidential campaign of 1960:

> One man who helped transform that election campaign into instantaneous myth was Theodore H. White. . . . The premise that gives his narrative its dramatic drive is a broad foundation of certitude about the rightness and preeminence of American power and, therefore, the absolute centrality of the presidential race in the drama of the world. It was then a Ptolemaic universe, revolving around the White House. What higher story to tell? Americans did not then lose wars. Presidents did not get assassinated, or lie, or have to barricade themselves in the White House.

And by mystery writer Robert Parker in the *Boston Globe Magazine,* April 6, 1980, fondly recounting his childhood baseball memories:

> The Braves went to Milwaukee before the 1953 season. Childhood's end. For fifty years it had been as fixed as the Ptolemaic universe: two leagues, sixteen teams in ten cities, none farther south than Washington, none farther west than St. Louis. Fifty years. Always. And then they were gone.

pumpkin papers Secret documents or pieces of information which trigger a political scandal.

The pumpkin papers were microfilmed documents hidden in a pumpkin patch in a celebrated incident during the Red-hunting days of the Cold War—and opened a door to bigger things for one Richard M. Nixon, novice congressman.

Whittaker Chambers, a former communist and an editor of *Time,* alleged in August 1948 before the House Un-American Activities Committee that he had known State Department official Alger Hiss in the 1930s as a fellow communist. Hiss denied it; the case turned on whether or not Hiss perjured himself.

Young Congressman Nixon, whose frettings about the role he should play in the case became one of the crises in his memoir *Six Crises,* decided to subpoenae papers that Chambers told him would be a "bombshell." Chambers led HUAC investigators into the pumpkin patch on his farm in Westminster, Maryland, and pulled some microfilm from a hollowed-out pumpkin. When examined, it showed classified documents, which Chambers alleged he got from Hiss.

Bombshell it was. Hiss was indicted for perjury. His first trial ended in a hung jury; he was found guilty in a second trial in January 1950 and served a term in prison. He then spent the rest of his life seeking to restore his reputation, which is still being debated. Nixon went on to other things.

The term in use, by Victor S. Navasky, in a review of David Halberstam's *The Best and the Brightest,* in the *New York Times Book Review,* November 12, 1972:

> It [U.S. involvement in the Vietnam war] happened, Halberstam concludes, because "they had, for all their brilliance and HUBRIS and sense of themselves, been unwilling to look and learn from the past. They ignored Hanoi history and misunderstood MUNICH history. And they had been swept forward by their belief in the importance of anti-Communism (and the dangers of not paying sufficient homage to it)." The Age of the PENTAGON PAPERS is, in reality, the Age of the Pumpkin Papers.

And by Martin Nolan of the *Boston Globe* reporting on the convention of the California Republican Party, October 1, 1997:

> For a breakfast on "Pride in Diversity," the convention imported Helen Chenoweth, the Idaho representative who once opined that white males are an endangered species. Speaking of the Civil War and of liberty, she delighted grateful males and females, too, several in elaborate beehives of a russet hue favored by women who saw too many Maureen O'Hara movies in the 1950s. One impressive coif could have camouflaged those precious Nixonian artifacts, "the pumpkin papers."

pushing the envelope Testing the very outermost limits. A technological phrase popularized by Tom Wolfe in his look at the development of the U.S. space program in the 1979 bestseller *The Right Stuff.* (*See also* RIGHT STUFF, THE.)

In *The Right Stuff,* this was a term used by test pilots and engineers as they tested the performance of aircraft. Interestingly, "envelope" is a term used in many mathematical, technical, and medical areas, and refers to a three-dimensional conception of a range of motion, or the effective range of a weapon, for example.

The phrase has generally come to mean testing the limits of anything, from mechanics to morals to public standards of civility.

The term in use, in *Time,* March 4, 1996, on the presidential campaign of columnist/polemicist Patrick Buchanan:

> When he derides "the worship of democracy" or calls Martin Luther King "immoral, evil and a demagogue," is Buchanan just pushing the edge of the envelope, or is he tearing it to shreds?

Another example, from *USA Today,* November 8, 1996:

> "The marketers are pushing the edge of the envelope," says Sean Kelly, an American writer living in London. "Now all's fair in love, war and the marketing of distilled drinks."

Another example, quoted by Albert B. Crenshaw, in the *Washington Post,* April 12, 1997:

> The strategy, coupled with earlier disclosure of Freddie Mac's use of a tax-avoidance device known as fast-pay preferred stock, suggests the company has adopted a "push-envelope culture," said Rep. Jim Leach (R-Iowa), chairman of the House banking committee.

putsch \'pùch\ A secretly plotted and suddenly executed attempt to overthrow a government. In German, the word means "a revolutionary attempt."

History's most famous putsch took place in 1923, when Adolph Hitler and sixty of his storm troopers tried to overthrow the government of the state of Bavaria and install Hitler at the top—the so-called Beer Hall Putsch. Learning that the state's ruling triumvirate in Munich had called a meeting of 3,000 officials at a hall known as the Burgerbraukeller, Hitler and his thugs stormed the gathering.

The attempt failed. Hitler was imprisoned and used the time to write *Mein Kampf* (in English, *My Struggle*). Although sentenced to five years, he was released in less than one and was able to resume his career with his reputation enhanced.

The term today is applied more generously to rebellious activities, such as attempts to take over organizations, clubs, companies, and the like, as well as governments.

The term in use, by James M. Markham in the *New York Times,* March 19, 1989, describing a walking tour of Paris landmarks of the French Revolution:

> At No. 286 (Rue St. Honoré) is the church of St.-Roch, where on October 5, 1795, Napoleon massacred more than 200 royalists who had hoped to stage a putsch against the Convention installed in the nearby Tuileries; it was a turning point in his fast-rising career.

And by *Washington Post* columnist Steve Twomey, August 14, 1997, after Congress passed legislation stripping the mayor of the District of Columbia of much authority but leaving him in charge of the tourism office:

> Let's pause here. Does it make sense that Congress, staging a beer hall putsch in the name of cleansing Washington of 15 years of Barryism, would strip him of his most visible powers but leave him the job of singing the city's glories?

puzzle palace A large, often secretive, bureaucratic governmental institution. Specifically, the nickname given the National Security Agency, a little-known federal agency possessing the most sophisticated technology in the world for communications spying. The name is now applied to other complex, BYZANTINE government agencies as well.

The Puzzle Palace (1988) by James Bamford is about the NSA, an agency so secret that the government used to deny its existence (leading knowing Washingtonians to say that NSA stood for "No Such Agency"). The NSA's budget is considerably larger than that of the CIA, also sometimes referred to as "the puzzle palace."

The term in use, by pundit-without-portfolio Norman Ornstein, speaking on National Public Radio's *Weekend Edition,* May 18, 1996: "Ronald Reagan got out there and decried the puzzle palaces along the Potomac."

Another example, capitalized, from Rachel Shuster in *USA Today,* September 20, 1996:

> But amazingly, no one made the connection between Kamisiyah [Iraq]'s bunkers of chemical weapons and the U.S. troops who destroyed them until the memo was "re-found" by the Pentagon this year.
>
> Even in the LABYRINTH called the Puzzle Palace, that's a hard sell.

Pygmalion \pig-'māl-yən, -'mā-lē-ən\ One who creates or remakes another person by teaching skills or accomplishments and then falls in love with his or her protégé.

Pygmalion, in Greek myth, was a sculptor who spurned the love of all women and instead created a statue of the ideal woman. The goddess of love, Aphrodite, was offended, and punished him by causing him to fall in love with his own cold and lifeless creation. Pygmalion prayed for the statue to be brought to life; the goddess relented and transformed the sculpture into a living woman, Galatea. A frequent mistake applies the name "Pygmalion" to Galatea, the pupil or protégé, rather than to the teacher/creator.

The story has been retold in various forms, the most famous being George Bernard Shaw's 1912 play, *Pygmalion,* which was in turn the basis for the 1956 musical *My Fair Lady,* by Alan Jay Lerner and Frederick Loewe. In Shaw's play the Cockney flower girl Eliza Doolittle is taught to speak English properly by the irascible Professor Henry Higgins. Shaw shaped the story to make his own comment on society, of course—Higgins transforms the guttersnipe into a lady, but she cannot return to her old life and he does not marry her.

The legend is also understandable as a cautionary tale against the single-minded pursuit of an ideal; such an obsession can leave the seeker caring only for a cold and lifeless work of art.

The term in use, by Karin Lipson, on the continuing fascination with the "wild child" as in the 1995 film *Nell* and other works, in *Newsday,* December 14, 1994:

> The issue of written language figures in Alice Hoffman's best-seller *Second Nature,* a novel that's been described as part Pygmalion story, part wild-child comes to Long Island.

And by syndicated columnist Ellen Goodman, appearing in *Newsday,* December 29, 1996:

> What would Henry Higgins make of this? What if he went to teach a flower girl the King's English only to discover that her local school board had declared Cockney another language?
>
> In Oakland, Calif., they are involved in a modern remake of the Pygmalion story. A school board . . . has now decreed slang to be a valid and different language.

And by Rick Reilly in *Sports Illustrated,* December 16, 1991, on the varied married life of Washington Redskins owner and tycoon Jack Kent Cooke:

> Cooke told [third wife] Suzanne what kind of clothes to wear, what books to read, how to speak at parties. . . . Pygmalion? Cooke doesn't wear that Rex Harrison hat for nothing.

Pyrrhic victory \\'pir-ik\\ A hollow victory, won at excessive cost, a cost that outweighs or negates expected benefits.

Pyrrhus, king of Epirus, defeated the Romans in battle in 279 B.C. but with such heavy losses that he said, "One more such victory and we are lost." The expression is now applied to quarrels or contests in which the damage inflicted on the winner is greater than the fruits of victory.

The term in use, by Sarah Lyall in the *New York Times,* June 22, 1997, in the "McLibel" trial in Britain, in which McDonald's had sued two people, claiming they had libeled the company by asserting the company was cruel to animals, exploited children through advertising, and depressed wages:

> So the trial—the longest ever in Britain—proved a Pyrrhic victory for McDonald's, not only because it was a multi-million-dollar public relations nightmare but also because nobody expects the hard-up defendants to pay.

And by *Washington Post* columnist Tony Kornheiser commenting April 29, 1997, on the Washington Bullets' straight-game defeat in a playoff series, hyped as a "learning experience":

> But getting swept doesn't automatically make you smarter. The only thing it automatically makes you is out of the playoffs. Enough Pyrrhic victories.

Pythias *See* DAMON AND PYTHIAS.

*. . . has developed a Don **Quixote** reputation for dogged pursuit of wrong-headed causes.*
—Jay Mathews

quantum leap *or* **quantum jump** An abrupt transition (as of an electron, an atom, or a molecule) from one distinct energy state to another. Commonly used to describe a dramatic change that is very clear and great in scale. "Quantum" comes from Latin, meaning "how much."

In quantum mechanics the smallest change that can occur in the energy of an electron or atom or molecule is a jump to the nearest neighboring allowed energy value. In going from one value or level to another the particle cannot take on intermediate values. This full switch directly from one level to the next is the quantum jump. The jump is always abrupt, but in physics it is not necessarily large.

Popularly, the expression is almost invariably used to suggest a mammoth change.

The term in use, quoted by Greg Sarra in *Newsday,* July 26, 1993:

> "We expect Rob to have a tremendous season," said Jets head coach Bruce Coslet. "We expect this year to be a quantum jump for him."

And by the gossip columnist "Suzy" in the *New York Post,* May 8, 1989:

> Wozencraft, who at one time thought of becoming a nun, took instead a quantum leap and became an undercover narcotics agent in Texas.

And from Ron C. Judd in the *Seattle Times,* June 5, 1997:

> Our friend Kit Boss, a former journalist who several years ago went south to become a Mr. Bigshot Emmy-Award-winning Hollywood TV writer, alerts us via e-mail that the Golden State of California has discovered "Glide," the official, ultra-smooth Gore-tex dental floss. Kit calls it "a quantum leap in floss technology."

Quasimodo Title character, the deaf, pitiably ugly protagonist of Victor Hugo's *The Hunchback of Notre Dame* (1831). Hugo's tale is set in medieval Paris, where Quasimodo is the bellringer of the cathedral of Notre Dame. He is a human gargoyle, and his name is now associated with a courageous heart beneath a grotesque exterior—and with ringing bells.

Despite his outward deformity, Quasimodo is devoted and faithful. He loves the beautiful gypsy Esmeralda who was kind to him when he was tortured by a mob for his ugliness. The mob later turns on Esmeralda; Quasimodo hides her in the cathedral and fights, tragically and unsuccessfully, to protect her.

The term in use, by Laura Zigman, in the *New York Times,* December 12, 1996:

> I hadn't drooled this much since I'd basked, Quasimodo-like, in the resident manager's kindness a few months before.

Another example, from the Associated Press, December 16, 1996, that focuses on his bell-ringing skills:

> Needed: Quasimodo. Or anyone with stamina and a good sense of rhythm. Britain wants to ring in the millennium with a national peal of bells on January 1, 2000.

And from Hal Hinson, quoting film director Oliver Stone on Richard Nixon in the *Washington Post,* December 20, 1995. Here, ugliness and the need to be loved are the issues:

> "He is many things," Stone says, "but primarily, at his heart, the tortured protagonist is a sort of political Quasimodo, an ugly troll, who sold his soul for high office in hopes that the people would love him."

Queeg, Captain The unstable skipper of a minesweeper in Herman Wouk's novel *The Caine Mutiny* (1951), about the American navy in World War II. Queeg, a solitary, querulous, suspicious man, commands the *Caine*. He compulsively pursues small issues such as the theft of strawberries from the officers' mess but is unable to lead effectively or to gain the trust of his men. He blames his failures on the incompetence and conspiracies of others. A famous Queegian quirk is that in moments of stress he rolls two ball bearings in his hand, making a tense clicking sound.

Thus, a Captain Queeg is someone in authority who is a MARTINET about petty rules, small-minded, arbitrary, defensive, even slightly paranoid.

The term in use, by Tom Shales, the *Washington Post,* January 12, 1988, in a profile of CBS News anchorman Dan Rather:

> It was bandied about in New York media circles that Rather was taking medication for clinical depression, and was holed up in his office like some sort of Captain Queeg waiting for the *Caine* to founder.

And by Nick Coleman, in commentary in the *St. Paul Pioneer Press,* August 9, 1994:

> With the Sept. 13 primary election only 35 days away . . . this is an opportune occasion to handicap the candidates for governor and make odds on which of these beasts is most likely slouching toward election. . . . [*See also* SLOUCHING TOWARD BETHLEHEM.]

Allen Quist. Still sounds like he is receiving messages through the fillings in his teeth. Quist quickly needs to shed the Capt. Queeg image of a guy who is out of the reality loop.

And by Joseph Dolman in *Newsday,* October 23, 1997:

Aw, what a disappointment. I was hoping to see Rudolph Giuliani in all his maniacal glory—you know, maybe catch a glimpse of the Captain Queeg routine as he nervously clicks the ball bearings despite a double-digit lead in the polls.

Queen of Hearts *See* SENTENCE FIRST, VERDICT AFTERWARDS.

Queensberry *See* MARQUESS OF QUEENSBERRY RULES.

quick and the dead, the The living and those already dead. A New Testament phrase referring to the Day of Judgment, when Jesus Christ will return from heaven to judge everyone, both the quick and the dead, and will determine who will have eternal life and who will be damned.

The phrase was used memorably by financier-statesman Bernard Baruch at a meeting of the United Nations on June 14, 1946. Less than a year had passed since the atomic bomb had been dropped on Hiroshima and Nagasaki, and that apocalyptic vision filled the postwar atmosphere with urgent concern about control of the atom.

Baruch proposed his plan for an international atomic inspection authority, and his phrasing deliberately invoked Judgment Day:

My fellow citizens of the world, we are here to make a choice between the quick and the dead. . . . That is our business. Behind the black portent of the new atomic age lies a hope which, seized upon with faith, can work our salvation. . . . We must elect World Peace or World Destruction.

And from David Sterritt, in the *Christian Science Monitor,* February 13, 1995:

The Quick and the Dead, about a sheriff who keeps order by holding nonstop shootouts in the town square, is the liveliest western I've seen in ages. But many moviegoers will be slow to see it, since the western genre has been more dead than quick at the box office in recent years.

From Joan Kirchner, in the *Washington Times,* July 19, 1994:

An earthen dam spilled more water into the swollen Flint River yesterday as volunteers worked frantically to gather up the quick and the dead—residents cut off by rising floodwaters, drowning victims and long-dead corpses that popped out of floating coffins.

Of course, many plays have been made on "quick," as in speedy; a notable observation was made by Lord Dewar in 1933, grumbling that there are "only two classes of pedestrians in these days of reckless motor traffic—the quick, and the dead."

And quoted by Daniel Howes, in the *Detroit News,* August 9, 1996:

> Pressure is mounting on GM to react faster to competitors and changing market whims.
>
> "In the future, there will be only two kinds of business competitors—the quick and the dead," said Kenneth Baker, GM's vice-president of research and development.

quis custodiet ipsos custodes? \ˌkwis-kủs-'tō-dē-ˌet-ˌip-ˌsōs-kủs-tō-ˌdās\ A Latin phrase meaning "who will guard the guards themselves?" It's a question asked by the Roman satirist Juvenal, a sharp observer of his fellow-man who made telling comments on their weaknesses and foibles. He asked the question of men who hired guards to police the chastity of their wives, but it is relevant whenever anyone is set in a position of watchful authority over others: Who will keep *them* on the straight and narrow?

The term in use, by Michael Kinsley, in the *Washington Post,* April 16, 1997:

> This anti-Internet alarmism is a heavy-handed attempt to distract attention from the really dangerous medium: paper. *J'accuse* [*q.v.*]. *Quis custodiet ipsos custodes? Et cetera.*

And as reported by music critic Lesley Valdes in the *Philadelphia Inquirer,* January 15, 1994:

> Composer Alvin Singleton has often used music to make comments on the circumstances of our troubled times. His latest work, "56 Blows (Quis Custodiet Custodes?"), is his response to the Rodney King beating and the initial acquittals of Los Angeles police officers charged in the assault.

quisling \'kwiz-liŋ\ A collaborator with the enemy, a traitor.

Vidkun Quisling was a Norwegian fascist leader whose name became a synonym for traitor. Quisling, founder of the fascist Nasjonal Samling (National Unity) Party, served as the advance agent for Hitler's invasion of his country in 1940. After the invasion, he was installed by the Nazis as the puppet premier and lasted until the German defeat in 1945. After the war he was tried for high treason and shot.

The term in use, quoted in *USA Today,* March 3, 1996:

> Israeli leaders are calling for an end to the peace process until Arafat does what Israel has been unable to do—destroy Hamas.
>
> On one hand, it "obliges Israel to become more repressive," says terrorism expert Jenkins of Kroll Associates. On the other, it "demonstrates Arafat's impotence if he does nothing" to stop the bombings. And if he cooperates further with Israel "it makes him look like a quisling."

And quoted by the *Philadelphia Daily News* August 22, 1992:

A day after President Bush sought to rally support with a rousing convention speech, a group of prominent Republicans in the conservative stronghold of Orange County deserted him and backed Democrat Bill Clinton. . . .

Outside the plush Newport Beach club where the group made its announcement, a dozen Republican loyalists led by U.S. Rep. Dana Rohrabacher accused the eight of being rich, elitist "pretend Republicans" and "quislings."

Quixote, Don \\'kwik-sət, kē-'hō-tē, -ō-\\; **quixotic** \\kwik-sä-tik\\ Don Quixote is the central figure of *Don Quixote,* the 17th-century novel by Miguel de Cervantes whose character is so memorable that his name gave birth to an adjective: *quixotic.* The word means "romantically impractical," "unrealistically idealistic," and often "extravagantly chivalrous."

All of which Don Quixote is. He is Alonso Quijano, a kindly country gentleman who becomes convinced by reading chivalric romances that he must redress the wrongs of the whole world. He takes the name of Don Quixote de la Mancha and is knighted by an innkeeper. After a series of misadventures (*see* TILTING AT WINDMILLS), he wearily returns home and gives up chivalric novels. (*See also* PANZA, SANCHO.)

The term in use, by Jay Mathews in the *Washington Post,* November 19, 1988:

> Over the years, however, [Ralph] Nader has developed a Don Quixote reputation for dogged pursuit of wrong-headed causes, the staff member said.

And use of the adjective by Marianne Means of Hearst Newspapers, in the *Deseret News,* September 1, 1997, on the possibility that House Speaker Newt Gingrich might run for president:

> Former Massachusetts Gov. William Weld may be quixotic to crusade for an ambassadorship, but a Gingrich campaign would be downright nutty.

And by Bill Hunt in the *Anchorage (Alaska) Daily News Magazine,* March 19, 1995:

> In reading "Polar Dream," I recalled newspaper stories in 1988 about the quest for polar glory by a 50-year-old woman who skied alone to the north magnetic pole. Helen Thayer's purpose in making such a dangerous voyage seemed quixotic—if not absurd. But this personal narrative of the journey contributes to a better appreciation of her background, ambitions and capabilities.

*The first thing a party does after it loses an election is to **round up the usual suspects.***
—Charles Krauthammer

rabbi \'ra-ˌbī\ A Jewish clergyman or clergywoman; by extension, a protector or MENTOR.

In Hebrew, *rabbi* means "my teacher" or "my master." A rabbi, an ordained teacher of Jewish law, fulfills many of the same functions as other clergy, performing the ceremonies that attend birth, confirmation, marriage, and death; teaching the tenets of Judaism; and serving as counselors. But the origins of the role are different from those of Protestant or Catholic clergy. Rabbis were traditionally primarily scholars; Leo Rosten, author of *The Joys of Yiddish* (1968), says rabbis had no hierarchical status or power other than the authority which rested on their character and learning.

In contemporary life, especially politics and business, *rabbi* has come to mean a mentor or patron, someone in a position of power and seniority who takes a junior person under his or her wing and helps to advance the junior person's interests. The employee with a rabbi upstairs will enjoy a big advantage.

The term in use, by Andrew J. Glass in his review of *Guts and Glory: The Rise and Fall of Oliver North* by Ben Bradlee Jr., in the *New York Times,* July 3, 1988:

> Over the years, Mr. North invariably has had such a rabbi at hand. At Annapolis, it was Emerson Smith, the Naval Academy's famous boxing coach.... For most of his years at the White House, Mr. North's rabbi was Robert (Bud) McFarlane....

And from David Stockman's book *The Triumph of Politics: How the Reagan Revolution Failed* (1986), on his tenure as director of the Office of Management and Budget in the Reagan administration:

> All my mentors and rabbis had been intellectual powerhouses: Morrison, Moynihan, Anderson, Kemp. Even Grampa Bartz. They had all burned with ideas, curiosity.
>
> Now my greatest rabbi of all, the President-elect of the United States, seemed so serene and passive.

rabbit hole *See* DOWN THE RABBIT HOLE.

race to the bottom A competition in which the parties seek to win by lowering standards rather than raising them.

The image is striking; competition is usually thought of as an uplifting force—to fly higher, to run faster, to create something new and better. In economic terms it is touted as the incentive and the means to offer the best product and achieve the greatest efficiencies.

But a race bottomward is a competition that many deplore. It is competition among nations, states, or communities to reduce welfare benefits so as to encourage recipients to go elsewhere or to grant overly generous regulatory or tax concessions to attract business investment. Opponents argue that these concessions are harmful to the larger community.

The term in use, by Michael Lind in the *New Republic,* March 11, 1996:

> Kemp wants inner cities to get in on this race-to-the-bottom strategy, potentially by waiving minimum wage laws and health standards. In other words, he would relegate the poor he wants to help to the status of second-class citizens as a matter of public policy.

And by labor activist Charles Kernaghan, quoted in the *Christian Science Monitor,* July 3, 1996:

> In a 13-page letter sent to Disney president Michael Eisner on May 29, Kernaghan objects to a global economy that he says pits US against Haitian workers. "It is a race to the bottom over who will accept the lowest wages and the most miserable working conditions."

And reported in *Newsday,* December 1, 1995, in a story on construction site safety by Andrea Bernstein:

> Added Richard Schrader, director of the Alliance for Consumer Rights, which studies workplace safety issues: "Deep economic changes in Long Island have produced substantial weakening of government's ability to police the work site and in unions' ability to force employers to abide by the law. There has been an ongoing race to the bottom as far as construction safety is concerned."

And by Howard Kurtz in the *New Republic,* February 12, 1996:

> In the end, Phil Donahue, who invented the genre that kept sinking ever lower into a miasma of tawdriness and sleaze, was simply outpaced in the race to the bottom.

radical chic \'shēk\ A fashionable practice among socially prominent people of associating with radicals or members of minority groups. *Chic* is a French word meaning "stylish elegance" that has entered the English language in its own right.

The term *radical chic* was first used by Seymour Krim in an essay blasting the *New Yorker* (where he had worked) for "stretching its now rubber conscience to include tokens of radical chic and impressiveness on top but not on the bottom where it counts—it will finally become indistinguishable from any other superslick magazine." The essay appeared in January 1970. The expression was popularized by Tom Wolfe's acid essay on fund-raising for the revolutionary Black Panthers in the Manhattan home of composer-conductor Leonard Bernstein, which appeared in the June 1970 issue of *New York:*

> The very idea of them, these real revolutionaries, who actually put their lives on the line, runs through Lenny's duplex like a rogue hormone. Everyone casts a glance, or stares, or tries a smile, and then sizes up the house for the somehow delicious counterpoint. . . . Deny it if you want to! but one does end up making such sweet furtive comparisons in this season of Radical Chic. . . .

Wolfe's term has become a standard sneer at leftish political trends taken up by the faddish and shallow for whom fashion is conviction.

The term in use, by Owen Geliberman in *Entertainment Weekly,* August 16, 1996, reviewing the movie *Basquiat,* on the life of the artist Jean-Michel Basquiat:

> For some, he was a visionary culture-zone smasher; for others, a radical-chic opportunist.

And by the *Economist,* October 11, 1997, on the popularity of Cuban revolutionary Che Guevara:

> Che may be radical chic in Europe and the United States, but Latin culture has turned him into a saint. Locals have discovered memories and a plethora of "San Ernestos."

rainmaker Someone who brings clients or business to a firm, especially a law firm; in a larger sense, someone who makes things happen.

Originally, a rainmaker was someone who was thought to have the power to make it rain, a SHAMAN or aboriginal holy man who could conjure rain or a scientist armed with the latest cloud-seeding techniques.

The term in use, by Christopher Byron, in the *American Spectator,* August 1, 1994:

> Last year the Republican-rooted firm picked up a Democratic "living legend" who was expected to lure clients to the company, especially its struggling Washington, D.C., office. The would-be rainmaker? Mr. Pierre Salinger, global super-journalist extraordinaire (so to speak).

In use again, by Bernie Ward, a San Francisco talk show host, quoted in the *San Francisco Chronicle,* November 5, 1995, about Duane Garrett, another popular radio host and political power broker:

> He was a real rainmaker. He could go through a room and know everybody in it, a whole room full of clients or potential clients.

And by Pascal Zachary in the *Wall Street Journal,* April 29, 1994:

> Appointed chairman of the department of molecular biology and immunology, Dr. So has been a rainmaker, with grants to her department nearly tripling since her arrival three years ago. She has attracted 20 postdoctoral researchers to her program, up from one when she arrived.

Rashomon \rä-'shō-mōn\ The same set of events as perceived from several different points of view. A classic 1951 Japanese film that teaches that absolute truth in human experience is impossible to attain, that the truth lies in the perceptions of each individual.

The film was directed by the Japanese director Akira Kurosawa and based on a short story by Akutagawa Ryunosuke. The story takes place in 12th-century Japan and recounts the varying recollections of a crime— a rape and murder—by the characters: a samurai, his wife, a woodcutter, and a bandit (and the victim, through a medium). Each has a distinctly different version.

The term in use, by David A. Koplan in the *New York Times,* July 16, 1989, reviewing a television program on the murder of a Chinese-American in Detroit:

> Two New York film makers, Christille Choy and Renee Tajima, subsequently made a *Rashomon*-style documentary that explores the legal and social ambiguities of the case. *Who Killed Vincent Chin?* . . . allows the real-life characters—the killers, the witnesses, the lawyers, the Asian-American activists and relatives of Vincent Chin—to tell their stories in a way that proves reality is not a fixed point.

And in the *Wichita Eagle* "TV Week," April 27, 1997 previewing the film *Riot,* portraying the 1992 Los Angeles riots:

> *Riot* is an ambitious and unique film with four directors and four different views of the same event. It's similar to the classic *Rashomon* in pointing out that different people perceive the same thing differently.

Raskolnikov \ˌrə-'skȯlʸ-nʸi-kəf\ The protagonist and murderer in Fyodor Dostoyevsky's *Crime and Punishment;* by extension, a murderer who believes he is above morality and the law but then is tortured by his conscience.

In Dostoyevsky's 1866 novel, Raskolnikov is an impoverished student whose brooding over his predicament leads him to kill an old woman pawnbroker and steal her money. His rationalization is that this act will enable him to improve himself and to rise to a position to benefit humanity.

He murders the old woman, and kills her deranged sister when she discovers him in the act. Despite his attempts to justify his crime to himself, he is burdened by guilt and is pursued by the wily and thoughtful

Porfiry Petrovich, a police inspector who waits for his quarry to break down. Raskolnikov does finally crack, although he does not admit to remorse. Sentenced to Siberia, he eventually achieves peace and repentence.

The term in use, by Michael Dirda in the *Washington Post Book World,* June 22, 1997, reviewing Donald E. Westlake's *The Ax,* a tale of a downsized manager who finally lands a job by killing his competition:

> Satirical, savage, fast-paced, *The Ax* filters everything through the consciousness of an out-of-shape Raskolnikov with bifocals. Burke Devore could be the unemployed guy next door, even the former colleague from down the hall.

And by Glenn Lovell, film writer for the *San Jose Mercury News,* April 24, 1992, reviewing the inside-Hollywood satire *The Player:*

> [Tim] Robbins gives his richest performance to date as the Raskolnikov of the back lot, a self-obsessed jerk who's a genius at stringing people along while paying lip service to the "real movies" of Capra and Welles.

Rasputin \ra-'spyü-t°n, -'spü-, -'spu̇-\ One who has a powerful, corrupting, and damaging influence over another in power. Grigory Yefimovitch Rasputin (1872-1916), a Siberian monk, was just that. He is notorious for his controlling, destructive influence over the Russian Imperial family in its last years.

Rasputin means "licentious," a sobriquet bestowed on young Grigory by his neighbors in the village where he grew up. He turned to religion when he was about 30, and gained a reputation as a holy man with the gift of prophecy. He turned up in St. Petersburg in 1904 and gained entry to the czar's inner circle through his success in relieving the suffering of the czar's young son, who was afflicted with hemophilia.

This won him the support and indulgence of the czarina but his interference in the government damaged the standing of the monarchy with the public. He was dissolute in the extreme, and filthy and coarse in his habits.

Rasputin's death is legendary. A group of aristocrats plotted to assassinate him, but it wasn't easy. They invited him to dinner and administered an enormous dose of poison with no effect. They shot him three times but still he lived. Finally they beat him and threw him off a bridge into the icy waters of the Neva River.

In use, by Martin Sieff, in the *Washington Times,* May 29, 1995:

> It is as though Rasputin had joined the KGB: A former Soviet secret police officer with a penchant for the occult has become a top general for Boris Yeltsin and is said to be terrorizing Kremlin bureaucrats.

And from Ruth Coughlin, reviewing John Grisham's *The Runaway Jury,* in the *Detroit News,* May 17, 1996:

Not only are the plaintiff and the defense backed by millions of dollars, now both sides have upped the ante on who can play dirty pool the best, with the defense team's gun-for-hire security specialist Rankin Fitch making Rasputin look like a choir boy.

And from syndicated political columnist Tony Snow, in the *Detroit News*, December 7, 1995:

Carter developed the concept [fiscal conservatism combined with social liberalism] during his 1976 campaign, possibly at the urging of his Rasputin, Patrick Caddell.

reach *See* MAN'S REACH SHOULD EXCEED HIS GRASP, A.

read the riot act Deliver a rigorous reprimand or warning. The context could range from an exasperated teacher telling noisy children to sit down and be quiet to a head of state reprimanding a foreign ambassador for the actions of the ambassador's government.

The original Riot Act was passed by the British Parliament in 1715 to deal with noisy street gatherings held to object to the unpopular new king, the brusque, domineering, and very German George I, who hadn't bothered to learn English. Under the act, if a dozen or more persons assembled unlawfully, a sheriff or magistrate could order them to disperse by reading this proclamation: "Our Sovereign Lord the King chargeth and commandeth all persons assembled immediately to disperse themselves and peacefully to depart to their habitations or to their lawful business." If they had not done so within an hour, they would be guilty of a felony and find themselves in jail.

The term in use, by Blake Green in *Newsday,* May 9, 1995:

No matter how many times you return to the bedroom to read the riot act, a group of young children in a common room in sleeping bags will not settle down until midnight—if you're lucky.

And by Ciro Scotti in *Business Week,* October 14, 1996:

What would Bart Giamatti have done? Well, if history is any guide, the late commissioner of Major League Baseball, a gentle-spoken, erudite student of the game, would have pulled Baltimore Orioles second baseman Roberto Alomar into his office by the ear, read him the riot act, and suspended him on the spot. Spitting in an umpire's face, as Alomar did in a Sept. 27 game against Toronto, would not have been tolerated in Bart Giamatti's baseball.

And by Tom Teepen in the *Atlanta Journal and Constitution,* January 14, 1997:

In particular, party heavies are strong-arming the 200 CEOs of the Business Roundtable, the gilt-edged elite of American business. GOP congressional leaders have read the executives the political riot act, and retiring party chairman Haley Barbour has been especially blunt.

Realpolitik \rā-'äl-ˌpō-li-ˌtēk\ Politics based on practical and material factors rather than on theoretical or ethical objectives.

This German word came into use in the years after the failed revolutions of Europe in 1848. It was coined by Ludwig von Rochau in 1853 in criticizing the lack of realism on the part of German liberals during this period.

The term was subsequently applied to the policies of Otto von Bismarck as he worked toward unifying many small states into a unified Germany. Bismarck's actions were based on "a scrupulous attention to what is possible, a shrewd estimation of what one's opponent really wants, rather than what he says he wants, and a preparedness to assert force when necessary," says Roger Scruton in *A Dictionary of Political Thought*.

In pursuit of his goal Bismarck made and broke political alliances, made war or insisted on peace as it suited his needs. As he said: "Not by speeches and majority votes are the great questions of the day decided . . . but by blood and iron."

The term in use, by R.W. Apple Jr., in the *New York Times,* May 24, 1989, on American response to the suppression of the pro-democracy movement in China:

> Ever since Richard M. Nixon's opening to China, Washington has asked less of the leaders in Beijing on human rights than it has asked of others. That point was noted forcefully this week by Chinese students attending American universities in asking for more palpable signals of support for their brethren at home. Perhaps they are wrong. Perhaps Realpolitik dictates that the Chinese regime be treated with kid gloves, lest the advances of two decades be lost.

Another example, from a *Wall Street Journal* editorial, December 12, 1989:

> We agree that the Nixon-Kissinger opening to China was a triumph of Realpolitik.

And from the *New Yorker,* May 30, 1994, illustrating an extended use of the term:

> If America was killing Kennedys, she exclaimed, she wanted to leave the country. Four months after Robert's death, she married her husband's antithesis, Aristotle Onassis. By pulling herself down from the pedestal, she could begin living as a human being again. One might say that in both her marriages she was a master of Realpolitik.

rebel without a cause A moody delinquent who rebels more for the sake of rebellion than for any comprehensible reason. The phrasing is often changed to the opposite—someone who is a "rebel with a cause" is troublesome for a clear reason.

The phrase is the title of a 1955 film and inseparable from the persona of 24-year-old James Dean, who died in a car crash shortly before the film was released. Dean made only three major movies in his career but created an indelible image of youthful defiance of adult norms of behavior: rebellious, handsome, unutterably cool.

Rebel Without a Cause was not the first of the burgeoning film genre of youth rebellion—it was preceded by *The Wild One,* starring Marlon Brando, in 1954, and *The Blackboard Jungle* in 1955. But unlike the motorcycle hooligans of *The Wild One,* the *Rebel Without a Cause* delinquents came from comfortable middle-class homes. Andy HARDY they were not. The film established another youth-rebellion cliché: the parents were shown as less sensitive and less moral than their delinquent children.

The term in use, by Marion Winik in *Cosmopolitan,* April 1, 1994, musing on "women who love men who don't pay their parking tickets":

> The easiest way to rebel is to date an established rebel. Without a cause, without a credit card, without the keys to the family car, rebels are sexy in ways that acceptable young men are not. And there they are, right out in the high school parking lot.

And by James Pinkerton, using the inverted form in reminiscing about the year 1955 in commentary in *Newsday,* November 16, 1995:

> Yet for all the preoccupation with aimless youth, another rebellion was launched that year, one that continues to reverberate four decades later: November 19, 1955, was the date of the first issue of William F. Buckley's *National Review.*
>
> Buckley, then all of 30 years old, was a rebel with a cause. His magazine, he declared in that premiere edition, "stands athwart history, yelling Stop."

reboot To restart a computer system after a power failure or breakdown. The word is now used to describe the restarting of institutions or processes that have broken down.

Boot means to start a computer initially, or to load a program into a computer.

Of course, LUDDITES might prefer to give computers the boot rather than booting or rebooting them.

The term in use, by Julie Wakefield in the Washington, D.C., *City Paper,* November 15, 1996, on the crisis in the District of Columbia government:

> From his perch in FCC's [Federal City Council] leather chair, [former House Speaker Thomas] Foley recently called for rebooting the home rule charter, the 1974 document that by most accounts has saddled the city with an unworkable relationship with Congress.

And from A.J. Cook, Scripps Howard News Service, in the *Detroit News,* February 19, 1996:

> The Internal Revenue Service refused to allow a psychology professor to deduct a computer he bought for a massive research project when his university had no computer.
> But the court rebooted the deduction, ruling for the professor.

And from Bernie Miklasz, in the *St. Louis Post-Dispatch,* March 9, 1997, describing University of Missouri basketball coach Norm Stewart:

> Missouri has reinvented itself. Stewart has rebooted himself, and his circuit boards are wired and charged properly.

redbrick Not simply a building material but a British coinage to refer to those universities in Britain other than Oxford and Cambridge (and sometimes the ancient universities of Scotland). The term is often used as a journalistic (and sometimes snobbish) shortcut to categorize these lower-order institutions and their graduates. These universities were typically founded in major industrial cities such as Liverpool in the late 19th and early 20th centuries, and their buildings were constructed of brick.

The term in use, by Martin Amis in the *New Yorker,* January 8, 1996:

> In David Lodge's novel *Changing Places,* a tweedy little British academic goes to teach at Euphoric State University, on the West Coast, while a big brash American academic goes to teach at a rain-sodden redbrick called Rummidge.

And by Peter Koenig in the *Independent on Sunday,* December 21, 1997:

> In many ways it was the British success story of the year. Unheralded redbrick university graduate (Leicester) finds her way to the City. Lands a job as a librarian at the renowned merchant bank SG Warburg. Begins to read the company research reports and is asked to look out for bankers. Starts offering her views.... Gets noticed. Gets her break.

Andy by Pico Iyer, in the *New York Times Book Review,* August 10, 1997:

> At Elphinstone College, in the redbrick Victorian heart of the University of Bombay, I was greeted by an "Institute of Distance Education" just down the corridor from a "Backward Class Cell."

Red Queen's race Running very hard to stay in the same place. The Red Queen is a chess piece come to life in Lewis Carroll's *Through the Looking-Glass* (1872), and she follows few of the rules of logic and none of the rules of chess. Alice and the Red Queen set off running as fast as they can. After a while, they find themselves at exactly the place where they were before. "Well, in our country," says Alice, "you'd generally get to somewhere else—if you ran very fast for a long time as we've been doing."

"A slow sort of country!" responds the Queen "Now, here, you see, it takes all the running you can do, to keep in the same place. If you want to get somewhere else, you must run at least twice as fast as that."

(The Red Queen should not be confused with the irritable denier of due process, the Queen of Hearts, of *Alice's Adventures in Wonderland*.) (*See* SENTENCE FIRST, VERDICT AFTERWARDS.)

The term in use, by David Streitfeld in the *Washington Post,* September 24, 1997:

> The publishers—who actually own all those books in the stores— are running the Red Queen's race, producing ever more copies to fill these new stores and getting ever more returned when they don't sell.

And by Lynn Yarris, in the *San Jose Mercury News,* July 6, 1997, on the ongoing struggle to maintain computer security:

> Freedman and Mann see the future as "a Red Queen's race, a constantly escalating conflict between a small squad of . . . hackers and their opponents, a much larger army of crackers, many armed with the newest techniques. . . . The good guys— the hackers—are shrewd, able, and dedicated. But the cardinal attribute of a Red Queen's race is that it has no final winner."

redux \(ˌ)rē-ˈdəks, ˈrē-ˌ\ Brought back. A Latin word.

The word has been popularized by John Updike in his 1971 novel, *Rabbit Redux,* part of the saga of Harry "Rabbit" Angstrom. In the 19th century, Anthony Trollope chronicled the revitalized parliamentary career of his hero, Phineas Finn, in *Phineas Redux.*

The term in use, by the *Washington Post* in a January 15, 1989, headline on the return to power of old line elites in the Bush administration: "Establishment Redux: New Jobs for the OLD GUARD."

And by Sandy Grady in the *San Jose Mercury News,* December 18, 1994, on the Strategic Defense Initiative ("Star Wars"):

> Funny, the more Gingrich prattles about tax cuts, orphanages and Star Wars, the more he sounds like Reagan Redux.
>
> We're back in the Land of the Gipper, kiddies—a fairy-tale world where you pay for a space umbrella with your daddy's credit card. [*See* WIN ONE FOR THE GIPPER.]

And by *New York Times* columnist Maureen Dowd, appearing in the *Kansas City Star,* August 20, 1997, decrying Hollywood movies based on '50s and '60s television programs:

> This isn't just commerce, it's also narcissism. The childhood of the boomers was by definition the greatest childhood ever lived, and so they see no reason not to immortalize it. But why should the Cleavers mean anything to anybody born after, well, *Leave*

It to Beaver? Once Hollywood gave children the magical *The Wizard of Oz.* Now it offers *Flubber,* redux.

regency The period of rule by one who governs a kingdom during the minority, absence, or disability of the sovereign. With a capital "R," the word refers to the period in the reign of King George III of Great Britain when his son George, the Prince of Wales, served as regent during his father's spells of mental disability between 1811 and 1820. The period is noted for its distinctive styles in architecture, decoration, and fashion and also for its naughtiness—Lord Byron (*see* BYRONIC), Lady Caroline Lamb, Beau BRUMMELL, gambling clubs, and all that. Perhaps society relaxed in the aftermath of the Napoleonic wars, or the influence of the French Revolution took hold, or perhaps the period simply looks racier in contrast to the Victorian era that succeeded it.

The Regency has since inspired a subgenre of romance novels in which rakes are regularly reduced to romantic gelatin by perky and virtuous heroines. (*See* GOTHIC.)

The term in use, by Henry Allen in the *Washington Post,* November 22, 1988, writing about President John F. Kennedy on the 25th anniversary of his assassination:

> Much has been made of authenticity, CAMELOT, Weberian concepts of charisma and so on: the wit, the cool, the Irishness, the aristocracy, the family man, the Regency rake, the war hero, the media manipulator, and our nostalgia for an era when everything was possible and nothing was quite real.

And by Richard Alleva, commenting on recent film and television productions of Jane Austen novels in *Commonweal,* March 8, 1996:

> If the film *Persuasion* steers Austen close to Brontë country, this *Pride and Prejudice* dumped her right into the land of Regency Romance paperbacks.

reign in hell *See* BETTER TO REIGN IN HELL THAN SERVE IN HEAVEN.

reign of terror A time when a society, institution, or community lives in fear of extreme violence by those in control. The phrase comes from the French Revolution, and capitalized, specifically refers to the period in 1793–94 when France was ruled by the dictatorship of the Committee of Public Safety.

The committee had been established to protect the revolution from both external and internal threats. Revolutionary France was at war with royalist armies on several fronts, civil insurrections were breaking out in the provinces, and the Paris SANSCULOTTES were growing ever more restless in the face of food shortages, high prices and cries of betrayal. On July 27, 1793, ROBESPIERRE joined the committee and immediately dominated it.

In September, the Convention adopted a JACOBIN Club resolution proposing that "Terror be the order of the day," and the tempo of executions increased, led by that of Marie Antoinette on October 6. Definitions of guilt were expanded and trials became utterly arbitrary.

The Terror was used to eliminate fellow revolutionaries in rival factions: the Girondists in October, Madame Roland in November, Hebert in March 1794, and Danton and his allies in April. But prominent political figures constituted only a small percentage of the casualties. A person could be seized, tried and executed for a casual remark or for weeping at the execution of a relative—or, in the case of a publican, for selling sour wine to soldiers. About 3,000 people were executed in Paris; many more thousands in the provinces, especially where resistance movements were suppressed.

The Terror came to a sudden conclusion. Robespierre planned further deaths, speaking of "purifying" the Committee on Public Safety. In the convention, deputies who realized they would be next accused Robespierre of aggravating the nation's ills and shouted, "Down with the tyrant!" His arrest was proposed and immediately adopted on July 27, and he was executed the following day. In the counter-revolutionary reaction which followed, a White Terror was instituted against the sansculottes, and the Jacobin Club was closed. (*See also* GILDED YOUTH; THERMIDOR.)

The term in use, by James Neuchterlein in the *American Scholar,* Summer 1988:

> The University is a long way from establishing the publish-or-perish reign of terror under which professors at high-prestige institutions operate (at least until safely tenured), but those who do not publish have in recent years found the promotion ladder cut off at the rank of associate professor.

And by Nina Darnton in *Newsweek,* September 10, 1990:

> The author, Charles Pekow, 36, spent from 1965 to 1975 at Bettelheim's Sonia Shankman Orthogenic School, a residential institution for emotionally disturbed children at the University of Chicago. Pekow bitterly accused Bettelheim of instituting a reign of terror in which he bullied, publicly humiliated and physically abused the children in his care.

And by Genevieve Stuttaford in *Publishers Weekly,* May 1, 1995:

> Taking full advantage of the federal government's postwar leniency toward their rebellion, unreconstructed Confederates instituted a reign of terror against blacks and their few white supporters. Kennedy documents his case largely with testimonials taken by a congressional committee in 1871-72. They describe a pattern of brutality essentially unchecked by the Union occupying forces.

rich are different from you and me, the A slightly cynical analysis of the qualitative distinctions between the behavior of the rich and that of ordinary folk. A paraphrasing of F. Scott Fitzgerald, in his story *The Rich Boy*

(1926). The statement is almost always linked with Ernest Hemingway's famous riposte. We offer both:
  Fitzgerald:

> Let me tell you about the very rich. They are different from you and me. They possess and enjoy early, and it does something to them, makes them soft where we are hard, and cynical where we are trustful.

And from Hemingway, *The Snows of Kilimanjaro* (1938):

> The rich were dull and they drank too much. . . . He remembered poor Julian [in original publication in *Esquire,* August 1936, it was "poor Scott Fitzgerald"] and his romantic awe of them and how he had started a story once that began, "The very rich are different from you and me." And how someone had said to Julian, Yes, they have more money.

Maxwell Perkins, who edited both Fitzgerald and Hemingway, lunched with Hemingway and critic Mary Colum and attributes the remarks differently. In response to Hemingway's remark, "I am getting to know the rich," it was Colum that said, "The only difference between the rich and other people is that the rich have more money." This version is from Matthew J. Bruccoli, *Scott and Ernest* (1978).
  The phrases in play, from Lee Krenis More, Gannett News Service, October 10, 1996, describing photographs in the 150th anniversary edition of *Town & Country:*

> Here are ROBBER BARON Jay Gould's grandchildren, in the specially built kiddie motor cars, circa 1900. Here are F. Scott Fitzgerald and Zelda in 1923, before the fall. Here are Clark Gable, Van Heflin, Gary Cooper and Jimmy Stewart, dressed in tuxedos and laughing over champagne.
>
>   Yes, the rich are different from you and me: They can afford much better bubbly.

And from Lynn Brenner in *Newsday,* April 2, 1995:

> The rich are different from you and me; for one thing, they cheat more on their taxes. A new Harris poll of 1,000 people, conducted for the Lutheran Brotherhood, found 95 percent professing to file honestly. . . . As for the rich, 9 percent admit to chiseling Uncle Sam. That's three times more often than people on the bottom rungs.

And by Mike Littwin, in the *Baltimore Sun,* January 1, 1995, describing his luxury flight aboard MGM Grand Air:

> Turns out, the rich are different from you and me. They fly better. Much better.

riddle wrapped in a mystery inside an enigma Russia, as described by Sir
Winston Churchill in a radio broadcast October 1, 1939. The phrase is
used often to describe Russia and things Russian, often baffling to Western observers.

By extension, the phrase is applied to puzzling, hard-to-read people and
institutions. By further extension the phrase is imitated, with other nouns
inserted.

The Soviet Union under Joseph Stalin at the time of Churchill's coinage
was absolutist, closed, suspicious, dangerous, driven by ancient imperatives and fears. Those imperatives were never more shocking to the West
than when Stalin made a nonaggression pact with Hitler on August 23,
1939. Throughout that summer the British and the French had tried to
form an alliance with the Soviets, but to no avail. Instead, Communism
and Nazism, thought to be ideological opposites, bound themselves in an
agreement not to attack each other and to divide Poland and the Baltic
states between them. Thus fortified, Hitler invaded Poland on September 1.

The term in use, by Michael Farber in *Sports Illustrated,* May 29, 1995,
on a contingent of Russian emigrés playing in the National Hockey
League:

> Kovalev is the Churchillian Russian, a riddle wrapped in a mys-
> tery inside an enigma, a dancing master on skates who heeds an
> internal rhythm.

And by Patt Morrison, in the *Los Angeles Times,* January 1, 1996, describing the Los Angeles landfill at Lopez Canyon:

> Russia, said Churchill, is a riddle wrapped in a mystery inside an
> enigma. America is plastic within paper inside shrink-wrap, as
> lavish in its waste as in its consumption.

And by Laura Jacobs, in the *Washington Post,* April 20, 1997, reviewing ballerina Allegra Kent's autobiography *Once a Dancer. . . :*

> It captures her twilight vibration, the "unrealizable" aura that
> made her the favorite of artist Joseph Cornell, who often worked
> pictures of her into his famous shadow boxes. She was an Al-
> legra wrapped in an enigma.

riff A musical phrase repeated persistently and typically supporting a solo
improvisation; also, a piece based on such a phrase. *Riff* is a jazz term. By
extension, a riff is also an oft-repeated story or theme or a routine, as in
a comedy routine. The term can also be used to mean a takeoff on a more
serious subject.

The term in use, by Hap Erstein of Cox News Service in the *Baltimore
Sun,* November 12, 1995, in a review of the performance of Eric Bogosian:

> The mention of Andrew Lloyd Webber's feline pageant—about
> as far removed from a Bogosian performance as you could get—

launches him into a riff about audiences and the woeful state of Broadway.

And by Mike Duffy in the *Detroit Free Press,* December 20, 1993, on comic George Carlin:

> For more than 30 years, Carlin has honed his craft in clubs, concerts and on TV. Back in the 1960s, when he first broke through, he was known for his off-center comic riffs with such characters as the Wonderful Wino and Al Sleet, the Hippy-Dippy Weatherman.

right stuff, the A combination of courage, intelligence, daring, and discipline enabling a person to function at the highest level in dangerous and complicated circumstances. The expression is from the title of Tom Wolfe's 1979 book about the first American astronauts and was a description of the qualities of the most successful American military pilots.

As Wolfe put it in his introduction, "the ability to go up in a hurtling piece of machinery and put his hide on the line and then have the moxie, the reflexes, the experience, the coolness, to pull it back in the last yawning moment." And, as Wolfe points out, this test is met routinely, day after day.

The term in use, quoted by Kim Heacox in *National Wildlife,* June–July 1990:

> Though they risk their necks every day and have some remarkable stories to tell, few of these pilots think of themselves as heroes or waste time bragging. "They don't have that cocky 'Top Gun' attitude," says Batten. "They tend to be extremely competent but also soft-spoken, humble and levelheaded. It's the right stuff for flying in Alaska."

And by Adele Conover in *Science 84,* March 1984:

> Like biblical sinners, field biologists become afflicted with boils and fevers, agues and warbles—evidence that while they toil, their parasitic passengers are browsing in their bodies. But as most are quick to tell you, it all goes with the territory. It's part of their dues, proof of the Right Stuff, and they talk about their medical misadventures with wry and often ribald humor.

And by veteran football player Ronnie Lott, quoted by Michael Knisley in *Sporting News,* September 4, 1995:

> Still, theoretical analysis of the proper approach to a football hit doesn't amount to anything, Lott says, if the hitter doesn't have "the right stuff." Loosely defined, the "right stuff" in this case is the ability to quell any natural concern for one's health and welfare.

riot act *See* READ THE RIOT ACT.

Rip van Winkle *See* VAN WINKLE, RIP.

River City *See* TROUBLE IN RIVER CITY.

road less traveled, the A phrase taken from "The Road Not Taken," by New England poet Robert Frost (and also the title of a best-selling self-help book in the 1990s).

The poem is a meditation on the choice of a path in the woods: the narrator paused where the paths diverged, and then, "I took the one less traveled by." While many consider the choice emblematic of the career of Frost himself, the final lines suggest self-mockery: "And that has made all the difference."

The term in use, by the Associated Press, February 6, 1996:

> Two roads diverge in Kobe Bryant's future, and both are paved with hardwood.
> The 6-foot-6 suburban Philadelphia high school star can choose the well-worn path and play for any college in the nation next year, or he may select the road less traveled and jump straight to pro basketball.

And by Melissa A. Trainer in the *Seattle Times,* June 18, 1997:

> "Selling top-notch certified organic vegetables has been a fairly easy market to get into with so many up-and-coming restaurants here in Seattle," says Andrew Stout of Full Circle Farm in North Bend.
> While many recent college grads may choose to head into the corporate whirlwind, the three twentysomething farmers at this Eastside farm have found a successful way to take the road less traveled.

road to Damascus \də-'mas-kəs\ The point at which a dramatic change in viewpoint occurs, owing to some miraculous intervention, or someone is converted by sudden insight to a sharply different opinion.

Saul of Tarsus was a young rabbi on his way to Damascus to persecute Christians there. As described in the New Testament (Acts 9:1–19, 22:1–21, 26:1–23), Saul suddenly saw a great light, and Jesus spoke to him, saying, "Saul, Saul, why persecutest thou me?" Saul was converted on the spot, and, as Paul, became the great apostle and missionary of Christianity. He traveled throughout the Roman world, and his writings, the Epistles, are the most influential of early Christian documents.

The term in use, by Peter Carlson in the *Washington Post Magazine,* March 20, 1988, in a profile of antiabortion activist ChristyAnne Collins:

> One day, a friend invited her to an Episcopal church service. Collins, a lapsed Catholic and a confirmed skeptic, went reluctantly. It turned out to be her road to Damascus.

By Rep. Henry Hyde, R–Ill., quoted by Margaret Carlson in *Time,* May 16, 1994, on his conversion from an opponent of a federal ban on the sale of assault weapons:

> At the end of reading this list of bloody crimes, I had to conclude these guns have no purpose but to kill a lot of people very rapidly. It wasn't like falling off a horse on the road to Damascus. But like many things complicated and emotional, you don't dwell on them unless forced to.

And by Herb Greer, reviewing John Charmley's *Churchill's Grand Alliance* in *The World & I,* February 1, 1996:

> John Charmley is a historian of some reputation who, on his own rather smug account, underwent a sort of road-to-Damascus conversion over prewar British appeasement of Hitler.

robber barons American capitalists of the latter part of the 19th century who became wealthy through exploitation of resources or workers. The term is used generically to describe unscrupulous and ruthless business tycoons.

The robber barons were a feature of the economic landscape of the time. Economic growth and industrialization led to the creation of great fortunes through economic buccaneering unrestrained by government regulation. The period saw the rise of business empires, especially in railroading, steel, banking, and oil.

The reference is undoubtedly inspired by the rogue noblemen of medieval times who defied the authority of kings and took plunder as they saw fit. The image was a natural fit for reformers who decried the evils of untrammeled economic power in America during the GILDED AGE.

Matthew Josephson's 1934 book *The Robber Barons: The Great American Capitalists 1861–1901* popularized the expression in the 20th century.

The term in use, by Craig Mellow in *Fortune,* March 3, 1997:

> After getting their start running rings around the lumbering Soviet state, these latter-day robber barons are now inheriting it. They are forming new power centers, built mostly around commercial banks and natural-resources companies.

And in *Vanity Fair,* October 1995, describing Bill Gates:

> The rap on the Seattle-born Harvard dropout is that he's a 13-year-old trapped in a billionaire robber baron's body. Competitors complain that Microsoft routinely steamrollers, mugs, robs, disses, irks, ignores, and generally enrages everyone else in the industry, where it's known simply as "the EVIL EMPIRE."

Robespierre \\'rōbz-ˌpir, -ˌpyer; ˌrō-bes-'pyer\ A zealous leader of the French Revolution whose name is synonymous with ruthlessness and extremism.

Maximilien Francois Marie Isidore de Robespierre (1758–1794) was one of the most radical of the radical JACOBINS and virtual dictator of France during the Reign of Terror, 1793–1794. An icy, priggish intellectual with considerable powers of oratory and a reputation for incorruptibility, Robespierre was fanatically dedicated to the revolution. He instigated the executions of fellow revolutionaries, most notably Danton, who predicted on the way to the guillotine that Robespierre would soon follow.

Danton was right; the Terror ultimately consumed itself. Robespierre was overthrown on July 27, 1794, by deputies who disagreed with his policies and who feared they might be next to be shaved by the "national razor." Robespierre was guillotined the next day with several associates.

The term in use, by Nat Hentoff in the *Washington Post,* September 10, 1997:

> Some years ago, as the Robespierre-like "political correctness" movement was taking root in colleges across the country, my son Tom was the editor of the student newspaper at Wesleyan. He was being pressured by his staff to mandate that the term "freshperson" be used henceforth to identify all incoming students.

And by syndicated columnist Charles Krauthammer, appearing in the *Philadelphia Inquirer,* October 3, 1995, on the enthusiasm for Gen. Colin Powell as a presidential candidate:

> Conservatives are also seeing in Powell what they want. The more optimistic see President Powell as a passive monarch, reigning with dignity while the country is run by Congress' grubby revolutionaries and their two Robespierres, Newt Gingrich and Trent Lott.

Rogers, Buck Futuristic technology or the person using it.

Buck was the central character of a science-fiction film serial produced by Universal in 1939. He was played by Buster Crabbe, a former Olympic swimming star who parlayed his physique into roles as Tarzan and Flash Gordon. In the serial, Buck Rogers awakens 500 years in the future and finds that the world has been conquered by Killer Kane. "Buck Rogers" was also a comic strip between 1929–1967.

The term in use, in a *Sacramento Bee* editorial, January 13, 1996:

> But the political will for continued exploration [of space]—the bucks required to fuel Buck Rogers—is vastly diminished.

In use again by Julian L. Simon of the Cato Institute in a *Wall Street Journal* essay November 18, 1996, discussing genetic manipulation of plants and other means of feeding a crowded world:

> This is not Buck Rogers futurism and not a desperate last resort. The technology is already in commercial use without government subsidies.

Rogers, Will American humorist (1879–1935) whose salty, trenchant observations have become part of American national folklore.

Will Rogers was born in Oklahoma (then Indian Territory) with Cherokee ancestry on both sides. His act, as he developed it over the years, consisted of doing tricks with a lariat and making comments about society and politics, just a simple cowboy who nevertheless came up with shrewd observations about the issues of the day. He appeared in films, wrote books and a daily newspaper column, and broadcast a Sunday morning radio talk. His fame and popularity were enormous. His humor was so infectious that he was able to make people laugh at themselves even as he offered penetrating commentary on their foibles. For instance, he got away with addressing a convention of bankers as "loan sharks and interest hounds."

In 1927, the National Press Club named him "congressman at large" and he responded:

> I certainly regret the disgrace that's been thrust on me here tonight. . . . I certainly have lived, or tried to live, my life so that I would never be a congressman, and I am just as ashamed of the fact I have failed as you are.

Before the stock market crash of 1929, he warned,

> You will try to show us that we are prosperous, because we have more. I will show you where we are not prosperous, because we haven't paid for it yet.

During the Depression he performed at benefits and donated large sums to relief. He kidded his countrymen: "You hold the distinction of being the only nation ever to go to the poorhouse in an automobile."

His sayings have become clichés. No political season can pass without a pundit quoting him, "I belong to no organized political party; I'm a Democrat."

Will Rogers died in a plane crash in Alaska with aviator Wiley Post in 1935.

Another famous Will Rogers statement invoked, by Richard Cohen, in the *Washington Post,* October 31, 1989:

> The president is a parody of Will Rogers. The late humorist said he never met a man he didn't like. Bush feels the same way about constitutional amendments.

And by Paul Andrews in the *Seattle Times,* September 22, 1996:

> A typical techhead would be happy with these small accomplishments. But Eppley, although a consummate tinkerer and wirehead, had more humanistic ambitions. The man's affection for his fellow species makes Will Rogers look like a TROGLODYTE; Eppley wanted each and every person we encountered to be part of the Web experience.

room of one's own, a A private place, away from external distractions and demands, in which an individual has the solitude required for thinking and working. The phrase is the title of a 1929 essay by British author Virginia Woolf on the difficulties faced by women artists and the status of women in society.

The term in use, by Lauren Picker in *Newsday,* July 23, 1995, in a profile of mystery writer Mirissa Piesman:

> She writes her mysteries aboard the A train that transports her from her Washington Heights home to her Wall Street law office. It's no room of one's own but, hey, it works for her. "It's like the Pavlov's dog thing," explains the moonlighting real-estate attorney . . . "I just do the same thing every morning."(*See* PAVLOVIAN.)

And by Colin Campbell in the *Atlanta Journal and Constitution,* November 9, 1995, describing a lecture he'd given at a homeless shelter:

> I summarized what I'd been writing about the homeless: about how lots of us are fed up with aggressive panhandling and urinating in doorways, and about how it's more important to give the homeless real help (and stop yammering about them) than to insist upon their constitutional right to take over our streets and parks.
>
> After that, everybody talked. And the topics were justice, drugs, a room of one's own, labor pools, anger, personal responsibility, alcohol, bathing, power, faith and more.

And by essayist Edward Hoagland, quoted by Brad Knickerbocker in the *Christian Science Monitor,* December 3, 1992:

> Honesty is a key to essay writing: not just a "room of one's own." The lack of it sinks more talented people into chatterbox hackwork than anything else.

Rorschach test \\'ròr-ˌshäk, 'rōr-, -shäk\\ A personality and intelligence test in which a subject interprets inkblot designs. The hypothesis is that as subjects describe and interpret the blots, they reveal emotional and intellectual factors. In other words, an individual's experience and personality colors what he or she sees. Named after its creator, Hermann R. Rorschach, the test has been questioned as an accurate device for many years.

In recent years, the term has been used to refer to something—often a person or event—about which people will have varying reactions depending on their background or attitudes.

The term in use, by Matthew Purdy, in the *New York Times,* April 13, 1997, on the crash of TWA flight 800:

> With the cause of the crash still undetermined, the investigation has become a Rorschach test, an inkblot of facts and evidence in which conspiracy theorists find proof of a government plot, millennialists imagine the hand of God hurling a piece of space junk and engineers come up with Rube GOLDBERG explanations, odd arrangements of circumstances that could have downed the plane.

And by Richard Jerome, *People,* December 2, 1996:

> Alger Hiss, who died of emphysema in New York City on Nov. 15, was many things in his 92 years—lawyer, diplomat, architect of the United Nations. But after 1948, when a *Time* magazine editor named Whittaker Chambers accused him of espionage, Hiss became a national Rorschach test. He was seen by some as a betrayer of his country . . . by others as a selfless public servant who was himself betrayed by self-serving scare-mongers.

And from First Lady Hillary Rodham Clinton, quoted in *Newsday* by Marie Cocco, August 27, 1996:

> Hillary Clinton once sent up one of the many flares surrounding her tenure in the White House when she said she believes she is a controversial figure because she is a "Rorschach test" for our times. People experiencing the upheaval of changing gender roles, Hillary Clinton said, project onto her whatever it is they are feeling in their own lives.

Rosebud The key to a personality; the talisman that embodies a heart's desire and drives one to achieve and act.

It is a word from cinematic history, the dying whisper of Charles Foster Kane, in Orson Welles' 1941 masterpiece *Citizen Kane.* Often designated the greatest film of all time, *Citizen Kane* parallels the career of newspaper magnate William Randolph Hearst. Kane's story is told in flashback as a reporter interviews people from Kane's past to discover the meaning of "Rosebud." At the end of his apparently fruitless search, the reporter tells colleagues it must have been "something he couldn't get or he lost."

But as the unwanted remnants of Kane's possessions are burned, a battered sled is thrown on the fire, and the audience sees "Rosebud" across the front. The sled was abandoned when Kane was a small boy: the family achieved sudden wealth, and he was sent away to school when a bank became his guardian. He grieved bitterly but in secret when he left his mother and his beloved toy behind.

The term in use, quoted by Deborah Stead, in the *New York Times,* October 6, 1996:

> Fat tires, gleaming chrome, coaster brakes, a clunky kickstand. A lot of us can conjure up the look and feel of our first Schwinn. A "Rosebud for the middle class," suggest Judith Crown and Glenn Coleman, in their book about the company behind the bicycle.

And from Delia Ephron, in the *New York Times Book Review,* November 5, 1995, reviewing Shana Alexander's memoir *Happy Days: My Mother, My Father, My Sister & Me:*

> This gigantic question mark—why did their family life suddenly cease?—is the "rosebud" of Cecelia Ager's life, the mystery that plagues her daughter and drives the plot, so to speak, of this memoir.

And from Terry Teachout, in the *New York Times Book Review,* November 5, 1995, reviewing biographies of Frank Sinatra:

> Kitty Kelley, the author of *His Way: The Unauthorized Biography of Frank Sinatra* (1986), rummaged through steaming heaps of Las Vegas garbage and found everything—except the sled called Rosebud.

Rosetta stone \rō-ˈze-tə\ The key to a mystery. Originally, a black basalt stone found in 1799 in Egypt that provided the first clue to the decipherment of Egyptian hieroglyphics.

The stone was found near Rosetta in northern Egypt by Napoleon's troops. The inscriptions on the stone in hieroglyphics, demotic characters (a simplified form of ancient Egyptian writing), and Greek provided scholars with the key to Egyptian hieroglyphics.

Dr. Thomas Young, using the Greek version, translated the demotic text in 1819; French Egyptologist J.F. Champollion was then able to construct a hieroglyphic alphabet (1821–1822), enabling us to understand ancient Egyptian writings for the first time. The stone, one of the great archaeological finds of history, is now in the British Museum.

The term in use, by Stephen Braun, in the *Los Angeles Times,* May 14, 1996, reporting on a political scandal in the Chicago City Council:

> Streeter's 250 taped conversations were distilled into a plea argument that has become the Rosetta Stone of the council's behind-the-scenes braggadocio—a document showing how "Chicago's time-honored tradition of political corruption has not vanished," said U.S. Atty. James B. Burns, who is overseeing the probe.

And by Albert Crenshaw, in the *Contra Costa Times,* September 23, 1996:

The Federal Reserve Board last week handed consumers what it hopes will be the Rosetta stone of car leases: a set of rules requiring leasing companies to spell out in writing all the charges associated with a lease and where they come from.

And by syndicated columnist Anna Quindlen, appearing in the *Detroit Free Press,* December 14, 1993:

When initial reports suggested that Colin Ferguson, accused of blowing away a car full of commuters on the Long Island Rail Road, was a black man who hated whites, race rage was seized upon as the Rosetta stone of an unfathomable act.

Rosy Scenario An optimistic economic forecast based on questionable assumptions. The expression comes from David Stockman, budget director for President Ronald Reagan in the early 1980s. (*See also* WOODSHED.) As Stockman put it in his book *The Triumph of Politics: How the Reagan Revolution Failed,* "The February 1981 economic forecast eventually became known as 'Rosy Scenario.' " Rosy began to be referred to as a person—as Stockman said, ". . . Rosy Scenario, why, she was an economic heart-throb."

This expression has, like the deficit, shown considerable staying power. The public has learned that budget-making is not an exact process, and that income and expenditure projections reflect the agendas of those making them. So you can continue to count on one side accusing the other of presenting a "rosy scenario" based on unwarranted assumptions.

The term in use, by Rep. Dick Armey (R-Texas), quoted by Robert Dodge of the *Dallas Morning News,* November 23, 1995:

We have no need for smoke and mirrors, we have no use for econo-magicians, and we don't date "Rosy Scenario."

The expression shows up in other contexts to describe any excessively optimistic analysis tailored to justify a dubious decision.

An example, from John Omicinski, Gannett News Service, February 16, 1997:

A rosy scenario of China as a democracy in the making—the so-called "Berlin Wall" theory—appears to have become the core of President Clinton's doctrine.

And from correspondent Dennis Moore of public television's *Nightly Business Report,* May 1, 1997:

And what used to be the rosy scenario economic assumptions gimmick in budget balancing has become the surprising reality this year.

round up the usual suspects To gather up and blame the customary people or circumstances for what's gone wrong and to do so perfunctorily and without expectation of finding a real solution.

The phrase was popularized by the 1942 movie classic *Casablanca.* After two appearances early in the film, this phrase returns memorably at the conclusion. The elegantly cynical French policeman, Captain Reynaud, deflects the police from arresting the obviously guilty Rick for murder by instructing his men, "Major Strasser has been shot. Round up the usual suspects." Never mind that Rick (with a gun), Reynaud, and the very dead Nazi Strasser are the only ones on the scene. And off the police go, allowing Rick and Reynaud to escape.

The term in use, by Charles Krauthammer in *Time,* December 5, 1988:

> The first thing a party does after it loses an election is to round up the usual suspects. The Democrats' post mortem of the Dukakis debacle has produced a fairly standard list of fall guys.

And by Bruce Meyerson of the Associated Press, October 31, 1997, on volatility in the stock market:

> "People are having a difficult time getting a clear idea about each company's specific exposure in Asia," said Robert Streed, senior investment advisor at Northern Trust in Chicago. "We know technology companies have more exposure, so technology companies are being painted with a broad brush. They rounded up the usual suspects and took them out to shoot them (Thursday) morning."

And in *Wilson Quarterly,* Autumn 1990:

> The authors line up the usual suspects to explain the small number of serious readers: the declining quality of education, television, and even the inaccessibility of writers.

Rube Goldberg *See* GOLDBERG, RUBE.

Rubicon \'rü-bi-ˌkän\ A boundary or limit, which when crossed commits a person irrevocably.

In 49 B.C., Julius Caesar led his army to the banks of the Rubicon, a small river that marked the boundary between Italy and Gaul and which the Roman Senate had forbidden him to cross. "The die is cast," said Caesar, wading in, knowing full well that this step would mean civil war.

The term in use, by Mike Littwin in the *Baltimore Sun,* November 18, 1995, on the social significance of the Beatles:

> But would there have been the counterculture that still divides America, that Newt Gingrich and others still rail against? And would there have been that Rubicon we crossed when the '50s ended and that we've never been able to get back over again?

And in an editorial in the Columbia (S.C.) *State,* November 17, 1996, on the governor's decision to act to remove the Confederate battle flag from the state capitol building:

It took courage—and a deep sense of moral conviction—for the governor to make this turnaround. Now he has crossed his Rubicon, and there will be no going back. He will either succeed in resolving the festering flag issue or fail in a way that could end his political career.

And by conservative Patrick Buchanan, quoted in *Newsweek,* March 1, 1999, on whether to seek the Republican presidential nomination for 2000:

"I haven't crossed the Rubicon yet. I'm up in the trees looking down at the river."

ruby slippers Magic footwear with the ability to transport the wearer to another, better place. They are the preternatural pumps worn by Dorothy in the 1939 film of L. Frank Baum's children's fable, *The Wonderful Wizard of Oz* (1900).

When Dorothy's house is transported to Oz by the tornado, it drops on the wicked witch who rules the land of the MUNCHKINS. Dorothy puts on the witch's sparkling ruby slippers (a perfect fit) to wear on her tour of Oz. (In Baum's book, the ruby slippers were silver shoes, but their powers are the same.)

After Dorothy's adventures in her quest to return home, she learns that the slippers can transport her there: she need only click her heels together three times and say out loud where she wishes to go. "There's no place like home," she says, and returns to her aunt and uncle's Kansas farm, filled with love and appreciation for that humble, ordinary place and its inhabitants.

The term in use, by Mike Phillips in the *Miami Herald,* September 30, 1993, on a local high school football game:

Let's talk defense. . . .

Springs (4–0) and the West (2–1) might play all night without giving up a point. Honest, this game could go to Kansas (that's OT, to those who don't follow high school football) in a scoreless tie. Both teams will be clicking their ruby slippers, chanting: "There's no place like the end zone." That man behind the scoreboard isn't a wizard at all, just the scoreboard operator who will be dozing off as he counts the 0's.

And by Mary Ellen Snodgrass in the *Charlotte Observer,* April 4, 1993:

Gradually, a man-type fact of life dawned on me—shoe shining may do wonders for leather, but Oh!, what it does for the soul. . . .

As the day took shape, I found moments to glance down at my glittering tootsies, which surpassed even ruby slippers.

I think my Virginia convention experience taught me more about self-esteem than about selling books.

Little things, especially the ones that affect the body, can resurrect a flagging outlook.

ruined choirs *See* BARE RUINED CHOIRS.

run and gun A fast, aggressive style of basketball in which a team runs hard and shoots at the basket often. Outside the world of sports, it means a fast-moving, hard-charging offensive strategy or style.

The term in use, by John Nolen, in the *Portland Oregonian,* March 16, 1996:

> Tillamook's run-and-gun offense mowed down Marist on Friday night, giving the Cheesemakers a shot at their first Class 3A boys state basketball title.

Another example, from a profile of television personality Kathie Lee Gifford (wife of football legend and television sportscaster Frank Gifford) in *Redbook,* by Christina Boyle, Gail Hoch, Elizabeth Johnson, Susan Schulz, and Ellen Seidman, August 1, 1994:

> "She just goes nine thousand miles an hour, and then she just collapses," says Frank of Kathie Lee's run-and-gun style. "She's cute that way."

And by Terence Rafferty in the *New Yorker,* January 22, 1996:

> If you're in the mood, you could find some entertainment value in this picture's evenly matched battle for coherence: [director] Gilliam's relentless run-and-gun offense against the script's alert, intelligent defense.

run the gauntlet *See* GAUNTLET, RUN THE.

Runyon, Damon; Runyonesque; Runyonese Alfred Damon Runyon (1884–1946) was an American journalist and short-story writer who wrote colorful tales of streetwise New Yorkers—bookies, gamblers, fight promoters, and other lovable rogues. Among the characters he created were Apple Annie, Joe the Joker, and Regret the Horseplayer. Runyon so distinctively used the slang and underworld jargon of the period in his stories that the language became known as "Runyonese." Even today vivid underworld or police personalities are often called "Runyonesque."

The term in use, by Shirley Povich, sports editor emeritus of the *Washington Post,* reminiscing on his career in an article for the *Washington Post Magazine,* October 29, 1989:

> And how many can truthfully say they actually heard a to-be-famous phrase actually enter the language? I did. This was during the 1934 World Series on a cold, blustery day in Detroit. Standing behind me in the upstairs press box was Joe Jacobs, a Damon Runyon character and manager of boxer Max Schmeling. He didn't like baseball much, but the World Series was a place to be seen. Now he was stomping his feet in the chill and drawing his topcoat tighter about him, shivering and unhappy. That's when he muttered to me and my pressbox neighbor Paul Gallico, "I shoulda stood in bed."

Another example, from *Village Voice* movie critic Georgia Brown, reviewing *Bloodhounds of Broadway,* December 19, 1989:

> Anorexic society matron (Julie Hagerty) has a yen for babyfaced gunmen. The door to her mansion is tended by an ancient butler (William Burroughs), whose line, "Your coat, Sir," receives the Runyonesque comeback, "What about it?"

And by Paul Duggan and Manuel Perez-Rivas, in the *Washington Post,* June 15, 1997, describing a diner:

> Dave's was five miles up Route 40 from Monticello Raceway, so it served a Runyonesque railbird clientele, plus many of the thousands of working-class New Yorkers who fled summer in the city. . . .

*. . . these essays . . . were circulated more widely through the **samizdat** of the photo-copier. . . .*
—Henry Louis Gates Jr.

Sadie Hawkins day A day on which the women can propose marriage to men, demand dates or favors, or determine events and generally take charge.

The day, widely observed by high school and college students, is the invention of cartoonist Al Capp, creator of the comic strip "L'il Abner." On October 16, 1939, the mayor of Capp's fictional hillbilly community of DOGPATCH issued a proclamation that Saturday, November 4, would be Sadie Hawkins Day. A footrace would be held, "the unmarried gals to chase the unmarried men and if they ketch them, the men by law must marry the gals and no two ways about it." (Sadie Hawkins was the mayor's daughter, strapping, fleet of foot, and without a mate.)

The term in use, by then-U.N. Ambassador Madeleine Albright, quoted in *Time,* February 17, 1997:

> And during one tense round of negotiations over Haiti, Albright turned to the Chinese ambassador, who was being obstreperous, and pleaded, "It's Sadie Hawkins Day, and on that day men are supposed to do something nice for women."

And by Dell Poncet, in the *Philadelphia Business Journal,* July 28, 1995:

> But a look-see doesn't mean a done deal—especially with the Sadie Hawkins-like Bank of Boston.

And again, from A. Scott Walton, in the *Atlanta Journal and Constitution,* February 28, 1997:

> In my decade's worth of nightclubbing, I've never observed so much attention being lavished on men as I did the night I visited American Pie. Beer-bellied? Bookwormy? Brawny? Didn't matter. All men had a chance to be Sadie Hawkins-ed onto the dance floor.

St. Helena A place of exile from which there is no escape.

St. Helena is a small island in the South Atlantic about 1,200 miles west of Africa. It is a British possession and it was the site of Napoleon's second, permanent exile.

Napoleon abdicated as emperor of the French on April 4, 1814, as the allies converged on Paris. The Bourbon monarchy was restored, and Napoleon was sent into exile on the island of Elba, off the Italian coast.

But Elba did not hold him long. On March 1, 1815, he landed in the south of France with a small army and began a march to Paris, gathering forces as he went. The Bourbons fled, and he took over the government once again.

He moved swiftly to attack his enemies before they could unite effectively against him, but was defeated in Belgium at WATERLOO. He abdicated once again, and was sent to St. Helena, where he died May 5, 1821. He had expected better treatment from the British government and was furious over the indignities and discomforts of his situation there. Nevertheless, he worked steadily, writing his memoirs and commentaries.

The term in use, by Stanley J. Kutler, in his book *The Wars of Watergate* (1990) on President Nixon's resignation speech, August 8, 1974:

> The rest of the talk focused on his achievements. . . . Nothing was said of any gains toward that domestic peace which Nixon had promised more than five years earlier. Finally, he insisted that resignation would not be his St. Helena; rather, he promised that the nation would see more of him in the years to come.

And by Peter Gammons in the *Boston Globe,* June 16, 1996, on the positive effect of sanctions against Cincinnati Reds baseball team owner Marge Schott:

> Two and a half years from now, Marge Schott may come back from St. Helena and find the Reds in a new ballpark, with an energized fan base and development system.

salad days Time of youthful inexperience or indiscretion; an early flourishing period.

The expression goes back a ways. This is from Shakespeare's *Antony and Cleopatra* Act 1, Scene 5:

> My salad days,
> When I was green in judgment.

The term in use in more recent times, from Brad Hooper in *Booklist,* April 1, 1995:

> We forget that in the salad days of the U.S. automotive industry there were far more companies than exist today, most of them coming to horseless-carriage making from horse-drawn carriage making, and certainly not all were located in Detroit—cars "were made everywhere."

And by former New York City Mayor Ed Koch, quoted by the Associated Press, March 17, 1997:

> "Back in my salad days, I told people, 'Go ahead, don't vote for me. I'll get a better job, but you won't get a better mayor,' " Koch said during a break at his Rockefeller Center law office. "I think I was right on both counts."

salt *See* BELOW THE SALT.

Samaritan *See* GOOD SAMARITAN.

samizdat \'sä-mēz-ˌdät\ An informal, underground system in the former U.S.S.R. and countries within its orbit by which government-supressed literature was clandestinely printed and distributed. Also, such literature. A Russian word, it was applied particularly to the methods used, often simply producing carbon copies and passing them around.

The term in use, by Richard I. Kirkland Jr., in *Fortune,* February 6, 1995, on the growing influence of small business and religious and anti-government conservatives in the Republican Party:

> Sample the various TV and radio broadcasts of the large and growing Christian media samizdat, and at some point you stumble . . . across folks earnestly debating whether Russian fascist Vladimir Zhirinovsky is the Beast 666 from the Book of Revelations.

And by Henry Louis Gates Jr. in the *New Republic,* September 20 & 27, 1993:

> Gathered together for the first time, these essays—which originally appeared in law reviews over the past several years, and were circulated more widely through the samizdat of the photocopier—complement each other surprisingly well.

And by Stephanie Gutmann in the *New Republic,* February 24, 1997:

> In general, the military has maintained a virtual silence about problems with the new influx of female soldiers, and, in the ranks, negative comments about integration are considered "career killers." Those who don't "get it" talk about it in the barracks and on the Internet, which has become a haven for military samizdat about sex and other dicey matters.

sansculottes \sanz-kù-'lät, -kyü-\ Extreme radical Republicans in France at the time of the Revolution. More generally, a sansculotte is a radical or violent extremist in politics. In French, it means "without knee breeches," from the description of the poor, who did not wear knee breeches, the fashion for men of the middle and upper classes; instead they wore trousers, or pantaloons.

This difference emerged as a symbol, and the most radical elements of the Paris mob came to be called the sansculottes. Their power in the Revolution reached its peak during the REIGN OF TERROR (1793–1794) in which thousands of people were executed. As a sign of the mob's power, politicians also proclaimed themselves sansculottes, even though they were middle-class lawyers and intellectuals. Certainly their leader, the ruthless ROBESPIERRE, did not forego his dandified dress. The power of the sansculottes ended with the overthrow and execution of Robespierre in July 1794. (*See* THERMIDOR.)

The term in use, by Mark Leyner in the *New Republic,* November 21, 1994:

> We live in an era of rampant debunking and giddy tabloid iconoclasm.... We want the genius mainstreamed, the sui generis homogenized.
>
> And so, with the guillotine of egalité beheading icon after icon, it should come as no surprise that Albert Einstein, that paragon of genius and intellectual heroism, would finally be ushered from the pantheon and carted off in a TUMBREL to the delirious approbation of sansculottes everywhere.

And by Anne Fadiman in *Harper's,* April 1994, discussing a meeting of right-to-die proponents:

> I had expected a cell of wide-eyed sansculottes and had found, instead, a genteel sorority of senior citizens. I was sure they would never let their movement go anywhere untoward.

satanic mills *See* DARK SATANIC MILLS.

Savonarola \,sa-və-nə-ʹrō-lə, sə-,vä-nə-ʹrō-\ A name that has become synonymous with fanatical religious zealotry or puritanical extremism, especially regarding the arts.

Girolamo Savonarola (1452–1498) was a monk who came to Florence to preach repentance, denouncing the corruption of the city and of the Papacy (the pope was Rodrigo BORGIA, so there were some serious issues to discuss). He is regarded as one of the forerunners of the Protestant Reformation.

Savonarola's powerful sermons aroused tremendous emotion and religious fervor, and led to the burning of books and art—the "bonfire of the vanities"—and attacks on other influences deemed to be corrupting. He held tremendous power in Florence for a brief period; the city became a battleground between his supporters and opponents. He was excommunicated but continued to challenge the authorities. The mob turned on him; the civil authorities arrested him. He was tortured, sentenced to death, and hanged and burned.

The term in use, by columnist Tony Snow in the *Detroit News,* January 30, 1997, on campaign finance scandals:

> If Democratic Party officials broke the law, the Department of Justice can investigate without having to appoint an outside (and presumably Republican) Savonarola.

Another example, from Donald Kaul, in the *Des Moines Register,* July 16, 1989:

> Mr. Fillmore objected to my calling Newt Gingrich "the Republican Savonarola," on the grounds that the priest was better than that. He wrote: "Savonarola was a sort of 15th-century Ralph Nader who preached against the vanities and excesses of his

age. . . . " and was a good guy. Sure, and all Gengis Khan wanted to do was rearrange the furniture.

scarlet letter A scarlet "A" worn as a punitive mark of adultery. A symbol or mark of shame. It is a reference to the 1850 novel *The Scarlet Letter* by Nathaniel Hawthorne, about 17th-century Puritan Massachusetts.
The novel's heroine, Hester PRYNNE, is condemned to wear the scarlet
letter "A" so that all will know of her adultery; she had borne an illegitimate child while her husband was absent in England.

As Hawthorne tells the story, Hester defies the powers of the colony by
refusing to divulge the name of the father. Further, she richly embroiders
the scarlet badge and turns it into a thing of beauty. Thus, while submitting to her fate, she refuses to let it destroy her.

The term in use, by Sam Fulwood III, in the *Los Angeles Times,* February 13, 1997:

> U.S. Term Limits had successfully persuaded nine states to vote
> on ballot initiatives to force their representatives to vote for term
> limits or risk a "scarlet letter"—a voter notification reading "Dis-
> regarded Voters' Instructions on Term Limits"—attached to their
> name on the next ballot.

And from the Associated Press, July 20, 1996, recounting the prosecution of a Utah teenager under a 75-year-old fornication law:

> The prosecutor's critics decry his crusade as nothing more than
> an attempt to resurrect the scarlet letter in the 1990s, and to
> inflict needless trauma on teens already saddled with the over-
> whelming responsibility of parenthood.

And quoted by Kenneth Cole, in the *Detroit News,* March 27, 1997, on
making public a list of sex offenders:

> "There should be a scarlet letter put on their forehead," he said.
> "These people will never be cured. So we should reveal who they
> are to protect the innocent people."

Scarlet Pimpernel A swashbuckling hero and elusive master of disguise,
who rescues those in perilous circumstances.

The Scarlet Pimpernel, in Baroness Emuska Orczy's 1905 novel by that
name, was an English nobleman who pretended to be a frivolous fop to
disguise his true identity as the daring rescuer of doomed French aristocrats during the French Revolution. The pimpernel, a tiny flower of the
primrose family, was the hero's emblem.

The novel has made it to the large and small screen, memorably so in
1934 with Leslie Howard as that "demmed elusive Pimpernel." Howard
reprised the role in 1941 in *Pimpernel Smith,* about a mild-mannered
professor smuggling fugitives out of Nazi Germany. The character was
also brought to the screen by Daffy Duck as *The Scarlet Pumpernickel*
(1950).

The term in use, by H.D.S. Greenway, in the *Des Moines Register,* October 23, 1989, describing the heroic Swedish diplomat Raoul Wallenberg:

> A modern Scarlet Pimpernel, Wallenberg used his diplomatic immunity and the neutrality of Sweden in the last months of World War II to save tens of thousands of Hungarian Jews from death at the hands of the Nazis.

A play on the name, from *Higher Than Hope: A Biography of Nelson Mandela* (1990) by Fatima Meer, describing Mandela's underground campaign against apartheid in South Africa:

> Nelson planned a strategy whereby he would keep the government constantly engaged but himself disguised, secret and inaccessible. The black public thrilled at the adventure that Mandela created. . . .
> The Black Pimpernel was everywhere.

scorched earth A policy of total destruction or all-out war. It refers to a tactic used against or by an invading army in which the defenders retreat, destroying all crops and supplies that might be of use to the aggressor, hoping to starve the foe as he moves farther from his source of supply. Or the invader may himself destroy food supplies and means of production in order to break down civilian resistance. Such a tactic leaves little in the way of spoils for the victor.

The term apparently comes from a translation of a Chinese phrase. The *Oxford English Dictionary* reports a use in the December 6, 1937, *Times* of London, describing the Japanese advance into China:

> The populace are still disturbed, in spite of official denials, by wild rumours of a "scorched earth policy" of burning the city before the Japanese enter.

Edgar Snow's 1941 book *Scorched Earth* attributes the policy to a general on the staff of Chiang Kai-shek, leader of the Nationalists in China's civil war against Mao Tse-tung's Communist forces.

The term in use, by Adam Clymer in the *New York Times,* July 27, 1997:

> Mr. Gingrich, after years as a scorched-earth outsider who condemned Democrats personally and rudely, has figured out that since a Democrat is President, he has to work with him. . . . But to some of the junior Republicans who enlisted to follow the old Newt, such a shift seems sinful, and they assume, as their fathers did about any deal with the Soviet Union, that they are bound to be out-slicked in any negotiation.

And by Gary H. Anthes in *Computerworld,* December 19, 1994, on junk E-mail:

> "Delete all" does just what you would expect. It is MCI Mail's digital neutron bomb, a scorched earth command for cyberspace.

Scotty *See* BEAM ME UP, SCOTTY.

Scrivener *See* BARTLEBY THE SCRIVENER.

Scrooge A miser, a skinflint. Taken from Ebenezer Scrooge, the rich tightwad of Charles Dickens' *A Christmas Carol,* famed for his exclamations of "Bah, humbug." Scrooge is redeemed through visions of Christmas past, present, and future; he comes to understand and appreciate the values of generosity, love, and friendship, and he begins to spend his money accordingly. Nevertheless, it is the pre-redemption Scrooge who lives on as an allusion.

The term in use, by Anita Diamant in *Parenting,* September 1994:

> In theory, it sounds like a good balance: He keeps me from turning into Mrs. Scrooge; I keep him out of bankruptcy court. But it's not that cut and dried.

And by Steve Rushin in *Sports Illustrated,* June 22, 1992:

> The tall, white-haired, 76-year-old Minneapolis banker has been prortrayed by at least one local scribe as a farm-foreclosing Scrooge. Another recently referred to Pohlad—eight times in one column—as an "arrogant butthead."

Also from Terry Weeks in *Gourmet,* December 1987:

> Ebenezer Scrooge would never have been able to remain true to his nasty character during a Christmas season in Nantucket.

Scylla and Charybdis \'si-lə . . . kə-'rib-dəs *also* -shə- *or* -chə-\ Two equally hazardous alternatives.

Scylla and Charybdis are hazards that figure prominently in the Greek legend of Jason and the golden fleece and in Homer's *Odyssey* [*q.v.*]. Some would locate them at the north end of the Strait of Messina, which separates the coast of Sicily and the mainland of Italy. Scylla is a huge promontory; Charybdis is a whirlpool. Waters in this part of the strait have been dangerous to shipping through the ages.

The Greeks turned the hazards into mythical sea monsters. Scylla had six heads, each with three rows of sharp teeth; she seized and devoured unwary sailors. Charybdis gulped down seawater and spewed it forth again three times a day. Vessels which managed to evade Scylla would fall prey to Charybdis and vice versa. (Odysseus, hero of the *Odyssey,* and Jason managed to pass with help through the strait in their wanderings; mythological heroes can sometimes escape mythological monsters with the aid of a friendly god.)

The term in use, in a *San Francisco Chronicle* editorial, May 21, 1997:

> Caught between the Scylla and Charybdis of trade and human rights, the administration has little choice but to engage China as a full-fledged trading partner and hope that eventually—

through economic, cultural and political interaction—the principles of democracy and decency will prove contagious.

And by Victor Gold in the *American Spectator,* March 1988, describing the hazards of a presidential campaign:

Find the candidate who can slip his presidential aspirations past the Scylla of Ames [Iowa]—then, two weeks later, the Charybdis of Concord [New Hampshire]—and you may have a winner.

sea change A marked change; a transformation. Originally the term referred to change brought about by the sea. The phrase appears first in Shakespeare's *The Tempest* (1610), Act 1, Scene 2:

Full fathom five thy father lies,
Of his bones are coral made:
Those are pearls that were his eyes:
Nothing of him that doth fade,
But doth suffer a Sea-change
Into something rich, & strange.

The term in use, by Wendy Smith, quoting a biography of Mary Pickford, *Pickford: The Woman Who Made Hollywood* by Eileen Whitfield, in the *Washington Post,* August 21, 1997:

Pickford liked to be excellent . . . [she sensed] that translating stage acting onto celluloid demanded a sea change in technique.

And from a *Washington Post* editorial, December 20, 1997:

Both sides in the contentious debate over gay rights will be tempted to treat as a sea change the decision by the state of New Jersey to allow gay and unmarried couples to adopt children.

And by Jon Wiener in *Nation,* November 7, 1994:

Poor writing skills are part of a cultural sea change in which reading and writing have long since lost out to MTV and video games on the one hand and to the need to learn a marketable skill on the other.

Second Coming The coming of Christ as judge on the last day. As foretold in the book of Revelation in the New Testament of the Bible, after Armageddon comes the Day of Judgment, when Christ is to return to earth to judge the QUICK AND THE DEAD. The righteous are to be rewarded in heaven and sinners sent to eternal damnation.

The term, without capitals, is now used to refer to a victorious return from obscurity or defeat, or to an event not likely to happen in the foreseeable future (as in, "We'll see the second coming first. . . . ").

The term in use, by Walter Shapiro in *Esquire,* December 1, 1994:

What's going on here? When did we start rollin' with Colin, instead of hoping for a thrill with Bill? How in a few short weeks, was General Powell transformed from a bit player in the Carter peace-pipe playlet in Port-au-Prince into the second coming of Dwight Eisenhower?

And in *Maclean's,* January 25, 1988, on Apple Computer cofounder Steven Jobs:

Clearly it is too soon to rule out a second coming for Steven Jobs.

And by Stanley Weintraub in the *New York Times Book Review,* April 27, 1997, writing about U.S. president Woodrow Wilson:

When Wilson, popularly acclaimed with Second Coming ecstasy, arrived in France that December for preliminary discussions on a treaty, he had already been outmaneuvered by the British and French military commanders. . . .

second law of thermodynamics A principle of physics that states that the total entropy or level of disorder of the universe does not change when a reversible process occurs and always increases when an irreversible process occurs. And this increase will continue into chaos. In other words, the universe is moving inexorably toward chaos. This concept, grossly simplified, is applied by pessimists to the social order, to explain why everything falls apart, society collapses, love ends, coffee gets cold, nothing is as good as when you were a kid.

The term in use, by Tom Siegfried in the *Dallas Morning News,* September 25, 1995:

It's a law of nature that things get messy. It's the second law of thermodynamics and it applies to molecules, living rooms and desks.

And by David Gergen, in *U.S. News & World Report,* July 15, 1996:

In his provocative new book *The End of Science,* John Horgan notes that under the second law of thermodynamics, everything in the universe is drifting inexorably toward disorder—or "heat death." Judging from today's Washington, that law applies as much to politics as it does to physics.

seed corn *See* EAT THE SEED CORN.

see through a glass darkly To have an unclear or inaccurate vision of reality obscured by one's own innate or acquired limitations.

The phrase comes from the New Testament. Paul, in Corinthians 13:12, explains that man's knowledge is as imperfect as the image in a dull mirror that gives a poor reflection compared with the clarity that will prevail when God's purpose is revealed. He says:

Now we see through a glass, darkly; but then face to face: now I know in part; but then I shall know even as also I am known.

The term in use, by President Clinton in his 1996 election night victory speech, reported by the Associated Press, November 6, 1996:

> When the times were good, they reminded me that humility is always in order in the presidency, for in this life we see through a glass darkly and we cannot know the whole truth of our circumstances or the motives of those who oppose us.

And by television critic Tom Shales, playing with the term, in a review in the *Washington Post,* October 25, 1988:

> That's a lot of gloom and doom for one night on one network. A look at prime-time tubal 1988 could almost be called "Through a Glass Darkly."

sentence first, verdict afterwards A famous pronouncement by the Queen of Hearts in Lewis Carroll's *Alice's Adventures in Wonderland* (1865). She is best known for her screams of "Off with his [or her] head!" when anyone crosses her. During the trial of the Knave of Hearts (for stealing tarts), she demands: "Sentence first—verdict afterwards." (Not to be confused with Carroll's Red Queen) Given her impatience with due process, the Queen of Hearts is often invoked by those complaining of arbitrary treatment at the hands of authority. (*See also* ALICE IN WONDERLAND; RED QUEEN'S RACE.)

The term in use, by Paul Perito and Robert Plotkin, writing in the *New York Times,* October 15, 1989, decrying the treatment of their client by a congressional subcommittee:

> The subcommittee has, while piously declaring its respect for the Fifth Amendment, linked Mr. Pierce to the infamous TEAPOT DOME scandal and dared him to return Oct. 27 to play the same game by the same rules. As the Queen of Hearts in *Alice in Wonderland* bellowed at her topsy-turvy courtroom: "Sentence first; verdict afterwards."

And reported by Gene Emery of Reuters, April 16, 1997, on reaction to recommendations by a federal advisory panel on mammograms:

> "The panel was accused of condemning American women to death and its report was described as fraudulent," Fletcher wrote, quoting the Queen of Hearts in *Alice's Adventures in Wonderland* in saying, "Sentence first—verdict afterwards."

And by Mike McCurry, when he was press secretary for President Clinton. McCurry, quoted by Tom Raum of the Associated Press on July 14, 1998, was speaking of Senate Republican leader Trent Lott:

> "Mr. Lott said they had reached no final conclusions but they had reached five major interim judgments, which struck me as a little bit like Alice in Wonderland time," McCurry said. "You know . . . sentence first, verdict afterwards, facts sooner or later forgotten."

serve in heaven *See* BETTER TO REIGN IN HELL THAN SERVE IN HEAVEN.

shaman \\'shä-mən, 'shä- *also* shə-'män\ A priest or priestess who uses magic for the purpose of curing the sick, divining the hidden, and controlling events. A high priest. By extension, the word is applied to wonderworkers and fixers on Wall Street and to others with inexplicable abilities to work change in difficult situations.

The word originated with the peoples of northern Europe and Siberia, where shamanism was a belief in an unseen world of gods, demons, and ancestral spirits responsive only to shamans.

By extension, the word generally means a medicine man, a practitioner of primitive spiritual and physical arts, as opposed to medicine as we know it.

The term in use, by Diego Ribadeneira, in the *Boston Globe,* quoted in the *Baltimore Sun,* October 8, 1995:

> Elsewhere in *Esquire,* Chip Brown provides an expose of Deepak Chopra, high shaman or charlatan, depending on whom you believe, of Eastern-style medicine.

And by Scott Burns, in the *Dallas Morning News,* December 10, 1995, quoting money manager Morgan White:

> "But many people are money phobic. It's a mystery to them. And managing it is exalted. It's almost as if the magazines were holding up managers as a shaman class—people who have wisdom others don't possess."

And by Lewis H. Lapham in *Harper's,* September 1995:

> In the meantime, we wait for Godot or the millennium, equipped with increasingly improved means toward increasingly incomprehensible ends, bereft of history but surrounded by a collection of marvelous toys, beset by shamans and stock market touts selling maps of the pilgrim road to the land of virtual reality. [*See also* WAITING FOR GODOT.]

shanghai \shaŋ-'hī\ To use trickery to put someone into an undesirable position. To put aboard a ship by force, often with the help of liquor or a drug. In the 19th-century days of the China trade, ship captains sometimes obtained the additional hands they needed by drugging men on shore, carrying them aboard ship, and sailing before they regained consciousness.

Contrary to common belief, the origin of the term may have had little to do with unsavory doings in the great Chinese seaport of Shanghai. Instead, *Brewer's Dictionary of Phrase and Fable* suggests it stems from the phrase "ship him to Shanghai," meaning to send someone on a long voyage, often to the Orient.

The term in use, by R. Emmett Tyrell, in the *American Spectator,* August, 1989:

The Hon. Thomas Stephen Foley was shanghaied by fellow Democrats to become Forty-ninth Speaker of the House of Representatives.

And by Doreen Iudica Vigue, in the *Boston Globe,* December 7, 1996, quoting a husband who waits while his wife Christmas shops:

> "She knows what she's doing in there, in that jungle. I don't. . . . I would imagine there will be more guys in their cars in the coming weeks, as more of us get shanghaied into coming here."

And by Russ W. Baker in the *Village Voice,* September 4-10, 1991, in an article about the CIA:

> The latest step in the shanghaiing of Congress occurred last November 30, in a rather daring move by President Bush that stunned the Hill but received little press coverage.

Shangri-La \ˌshaŋ-gri-ˈlä\ A remote, beautiful, imaginary place where life approaches perfection; UTOPIA. More broadly, a remote, idyllic hideaway. In James Hilton's 1933 novel *Lost Horizon,* made into a popular movie in 1937, Shangri-La was ostensibly located in Tibet.

Franklin D. Roosevelt had some fun with the name. In April 1942, he dodged questions about the launching site (actually the carrier *Hornet*) of the bombers used in the Doolittle Raid over Tokyo, saying they came "from Shangri-La." Similarly he once announced that two battleships had gone to Shangri-La, a place, Berlin Radio said in a subsequent broadcast, that German authorities had not been able to locate on a map.

Shangri-La was also the name Roosevelt gave to the rustic presidential hideaway established at an old Civilian Conservation Corps camp in the Catoctin Mountains of Maryland. The presidential retreat was renamed "Camp David" by Dwight Eisenhower, after his grandson.

And ultimately, the name of this fictitious land of peace was given to an American warship. In tribute to Roosevelt, the aircraft carrier *Shangri-La* was commissioned in 1944. The ship was decommissioned in 1971.

The term in use, by Pico Iyer, in *Time,* June 9, 1986:

> Sometimes an EDEN is brought down by the quite literal invasion of the real world, as even the most faraway places get placed in the sights of the superpowers. Tibet was stormed by the Chinese, and now the dreamed-of Shangri-La is vanished forever. . . . Afghanistan was overrun by Soviet tanks, and now a book of photographs remembering its fugitive beauties is subtitled, mournfully, PARADISE LOST.

Another example, from Nancy Shute in the *New Republic,* May 2, 1994, on life in Kamchatka, Russia:

> When I first arrived in 1991 it was innocent and chaste—a Soviet Shangri-La that lured residents with fat government pay-

checks and a spectacular landscape inhabited by giant grizzly bears and trophy-sized trout.

And by Larry Light in *Business Week,* July 29, 1991:

> The half-finished $1.25 billion luxury condominium development, located off the southern tip of Miami Beach, is meant for the big-money crowd. Units are priced as high as $7 million. This Shangri-la has two docks that can accomodate 200-foot yachts, seven gourmet restaurants, a spa, and sand imported from the Bahamas.

shelf life The period of time during which a material may be stored and remain suitable for use; the period during which something lasts or remains popular.

The term in use, in the *Baltimore Sun,* November 27, 1995:

> But contrary to another joke, fruitcake does not have a shelf life of 16 years.

And also from the *Sun,* July 30, 1995:

> "No matter how good your education was, its shelf life is probably not as long as your career," said Charles W. Hickman, director of projects and services for the St. Louis-based American Association of Collegiate Schools of Business.

And by David Rieff in *Vanity Fair,* December 1994, writing about the crisis in Rwanda:

> But more predictable than the foreigners' indignation over this was the certainty that they would soon leave. Disasters are compelling for only so long. The CNN effect has a short shelf life.

shell game A swindling trick in which a small ball or pea is quickly shifted from under one to another of three small cups to fool the one guessing its location. Fraud, especially where a worthless item is substituted for a valuable one.

In the game, the operator places a pea or pebble under three inverted nutshells or cups. The shells are then moved rapidly in and out of position before the fascinated gaze of the rube who has been enticed to play. The mark then chooses the shell under which he thinks the pea is hidden, and wins or loses according to the strategy (and sleight of hand) of the operator.

The term in use, by Matthew Miller in a commentary in *U.S. News & World Report,* May 19, 1997:

> Ultraconservative Sen. Phil Gramm of Texas laments that his party has assented to a Medicare shell game that extends the solvency of the program's trust fund only by moving expenses for home health care from one Medicare account to another....

And again by John U. Bacon in the *Detroit News,* January 19, 1997:

> Against a backdrop of NFL players padding their police records like resumes and NFL owners moving their teams back and forth in a cynical shell game, the scene at Lambeau Field provided a stark contrast. Visiting Green Bay is like taking a time-machine back to an era when fans loved their teams without reservation and the teams returned that devotion just as completely—in other words, an era most cities said good-bye to decades ago.

Sherlock Holmes *See* HOLMES, SHERLOCK.

Shermanesque Of or referring to an absolute, unequivocal refusal to run for office. In 1884, some 20 years after his SCORCHED EARTH destruction of Atlanta and march to the sea, General William Tecumseh Sherman squelched a movement to draft him as the Republican presidential nominee. Justly famed for his terse, direct style (*see* HOLD THE FORT), Sherman enunciated what has become the standard for forthright refusal. He informed the GOP national convention: "I will not accept if nominated, and will not serve if elected." He wasn't and didn't.

The term in use, by Donald Lambro in the *Washington Times,* May 5, 1995:

> Sen. John McCain of Arizona says he is "not interested" in the Republican nomination for vice president but would have to reconsider it if Sen. Bob Dole said he needs him on the ticket. . . .
> "The only reason why I cannot be totally Shermanesque is because, if the nominee of our party said 'Uncle Sam needs you,' then you would have to go through a decision-making process" to consider it, he said.

And by Bob Minzesheimer in *USA Today,* November 9, 1995:

> The rise and fall of the Colin Powell non-candidacy, ended in a Shermanesque statement by the general Wednesday, says little new about Powell. But is says much about the American people.

Sherpa A member of a Tibetan people living on the high southern slopes of the Himalayas who provide support for foreign trekkers and mountain climbers. The most famous Sherpa is Tenzing Norgay, who accompanied Sir Edmund Hillary on the first ascent of Mt. Everest in 1953.

The term has come to be part of the diplomatic lexicon. Diplomats who do the necessary preparations for international meetings of heads of governments are sometimes called sherpas—in lower case—by their colleagues and the media, apt for those who act as guides for successful "summit meetings." This usage appeared after Hillary's achievement and as the era of meetings of U.S. presidents and Soviet leaders began in the mid-1950s. The word is also used, more generally, to describe a local guide, wise to the ways of the neighborhood.

The term in use, by the Associated Press, June 22, 1997:

Discussing issues for the century ahead, summit "sherpas" fashioned a policy against human cloning at the urging of French President Jacques Chirac.

And by Leonard Garment in his memoir *Crazy Rhythm* (1997):

No doubt there were fair-minded, judicious men and women among the vast teams of Watergate sherpas who gathered in Washington in 1973 for the assault on Mount Nixon. I knew one, maybe two, myself.

shocked, shocked An exclamation of hypocritical or mock outrage and surprise. The phrase comes from the film *Casablanca* in which the German Major Strasser, outraged by the patrons' singing of "La Marseillaise," storms out after ordering police Captain Renaud to close down Rick's cafe. When Rick (Humphrey Bogart) demands to know the grounds for this action, Renaud (Claude Rains) announces that he is "shocked, shocked to find that gambling is going on here!" A croupier then appears at his side, murmurs, "Your winnings, sir," and presents Renaud with a wad of bills.

This expression conveys the recognition of the hypocrisy or self-mockery of someone's indignation at a fault or vice or act in which they no doubt share or which is hardly worthy of acknowledgement.

The term in use, from an editorial by Lucian K. Truscott 4th in the *New York Times,* November 17, 1996, on sex in the military:

The regulations are routinely violated, and everyone in the army knows this is so, despite the Casablancaesque "I'm shocked—shocked!" protestations of army commanders in reaction to the sexual harassment scandals.

And from Cynthia Tucker, in the *Atlanta Journal and Constitution,* March 9, 1997:

So nobody but members of the opposition party pretends to be shocked—shocked—to learn the president is selling his soul, not to mention his influence, to wealthy campaign contributors.

shock troops Troops especially suited and chosen for offensive work because of their high morale, training, and discipline. Also, a group militant in pressing a cause.

The term originated in the Spanish Civil War with the "shock police" used by the Republic. This war (1936–1939) served as a laboratory for military methods later used in World War II. (*See* FIFTH COLUMN.) The term is also used to refer to highly motivated activists in the vanguard of aggressive political movements.

The term in use, in the *Los Angeles Times,* November 2, 1995:

Indeed, if religious broadcaster Pat Robertson's Christian Coalition—with arguably the best organized precinct organization in the country—forms the political shock troops of the religious right, then some see [broadcaster James] Dobson as a minister of ideology, a defender and definer of biblical morality.

Another example, from the *Christian Science Monitor,* June 13, 1996:

In 1991, striking coal miners in Kemerovo Russia were Boris Yeltsin's shock troops, the vanguard of his anti-communist revolution that swept away the USSR.

And by Gloria Borger in *U.S. News & World Report,* August 31– September 7, 1992:

What they want most of all is more Republican seats on key committees. And they hope to mold incoming Republicans into conservative shock troops with an orientation session separate from that of the Democrats.

shoot the messenger *See* KILL/SHOOT THE MESSENGER.

shot heard round the world, the A brief, local act that achieves broad attention and influences major events elsewhere.

The expression appeared in Ralph Waldo Emerson's "Concord Hymn," sung at the dedication of a monument in Concord, Massachusetts, commemorating the battles of Lexington and Concord. The battles, on April 19, 1775, were the first military action against the British, the start of the armed insurrection that led to independence. The line notes the significance of the episode for the American Revolution, and the significance of the revolution for the world.

British troops had marched to Concord to seize weapons thought to be stored there. Thanks to the midnight ride of Paul Revere and his cohorts, the countryside was aroused and colonial militia met the British on the green at Lexington. A second confrontation took place at Concord Bridge, of which Emerson wrote:

By the rude bridge that arched the flood,
Their flag to April's breeze unfurled,
Here once the embattled farmers stood,
And fired the shot heard round the world.

In current use, the phrase is used to describe a brief but decisive or momentous action. A famous application was to Bobby Thomson's bottom-of-the-ninth home run on Oct. 3, 1951 that won the National League pennant for the New York Giants, considered to be one of the most exciting moments in baseball history.

And reported by columnist James J. Kilpatrick Jr., appearing in the *Richmond Times-Dispatch,* October 27, 1996:

Another splendid pun came from the *Cincinnati Enquirer* in June. Baseball owners had just forced Marge Schott, owner of the Reds, to give up day-to-day control of the team. Editor Peter Bronson was pleased. "It's a healthy change for the Reds and everyone in

Cincinnati who is bone weary of being embarrassed by the Schott heard round the world."

And a grimmer note, from Richard Price, in *USA Today,* May 18, 1994:

Four more shots heard round the world have left a German tourist dead, her husband critically wounded and the U.S. tourism industry again struggling to minimize the nation's growing image as an unsafe destination.

show trial A trial (as of political opponents) in which the verdict is rigged and a public confession is often extracted. Such trials are designed to discredit the defendant's views through a recantation or self-accusation.

The process is centuries old; the prosecution of witches and the procedures of the Inquisition were in this mold. But we owe the term itself to the 20th century, and specifically to the purges of Josef Stalin in the Soviet Union.

In the 1930s Stalin decimated the ranks of the Communist Party and the army. In a series of sensational trials, Old Bosheviks were accused of plotting to kill Stalin, restore bourgeois capitalism, and perpetrate numerous other offenses. To the amazement of the world, these men made full confessions, blaming themselves and recanting their views—and then they were executed. When Stalin had finished, there were no Old Bolsheviks left, no rivals to his rule.

The term in use, by Diane F. Orentlicher in the *Los Angeles Times,* May 19, 1996:

The trial of Dusan Tadic by an international war-crimes tribunal in The Hague will doubtless be a MORALITY PLAY, but it won't be a show trial. The tribunal's work, like the Nuremberg precedent it evokes, will be a lesson in universal conscience and individual responsibility.

And by Peter Schrag in the *New Republic,* October 2, 1995, on California Governor Pete Wilson:

Wilson and the Democrats who controlled the Legislature split the difference—half in program cuts, half in higher revenues, thus beginning the three-year spate of reductions in the state's once-generous welfare, health and higher-education programs that Wilson now touts as a model for national deficit reduction. But Republican presidential candidate Wilson, sounding like a defendant in a show trial, has now repudiated that act of moderation and compromise. . . .

And, in a use where getting at the truth is the issue, by Republican strategist William Kristol, on National Public Radio's *Weekend Edition,* January 21, 1995:

What I think Republicans on the Hill need to do is have lots of hearings, lots of what might be called "show trials" of different federal agencies and programs that have been around for decades and that have outlived their purposes or that are counter-productive, or the bulk of whose money goes to bureaucrats, rather than recipients and expose these facts, as they kill the programs.

shtick *or* **shtik** A show-business routine, gimmick, or gag; a bit.

The term is Yiddish and widely used in show business, where it means the "piece" employed by actors—grimaces, gestures—for calling attention to themselves.

The term in use, by Tom Teepen, columnist for the *Atlanta Journal and Constitution,* July 23, 1996, on the portrayal of Atlanta by out-of-town journalists:

> Far too many others don't report. They cavort. They don't do journalism. They do shtick. Take my wife—please. Take this city—please.

Another example from Ben Brantley, in the *New York Times,* May 3, 1997, reviewing a revival of Rodgers and Hart's *The Boys from Syracuse*:

> The show, and especially its shtick-driven, smirky book by George Abbott, may be firmly lodged in another era.

And in the *American Spectator,* July 1988, describing morning proceedings in the U.S. Senate:

> Senator William Proxmire, a notorious early-riser, wandered about, talking in a loud voice and casting an occasional glance to the gallery to see if he was being noticed. Proxmire's shtik as the crotchety-but-lovable eccentric, which at one time made him the object of an adoring press, has been wearing thin over the last several years; it is now mostly considered a petty annoyance.

And by Bill Ott in *Booklist,* December 12, 1992, describing dog photographer Kalman:

> No, Kalman's shtick isn't wearing thin. Far from it. The ongoing saga of Max the dog—in words, in pictures, in typography—has vaulted across genres, between audiences, and beyond expectations. It's the graphic novel of the nineties, and it's truly for all ages.

sick man of Europe Originally the decaying Ottoman Empire, which once extended from Hungary and the Balkan Peninsula to the Russian steppes and from Algeria to the Persian Gulf. Its decline sprawled over 200 years. The maneuvering of European governments to sustain a balance of power helped to maintain this huge, varied, and ancient entity, but its political and economic deterioration was inevitable despite efforts at reform led by "YOUNG TURKS."

Today the phrase is applied to a nation or institution suffering profound political, social, or economic difficulty.

The term in use, by Bob Ryan, in the *Boston Globe,* January 15, 1989:

> The Celtics are on the verge of becoming the NBA equivalent of the 1914 Ottoman Empire, a/k/a "The Sick Man of Europe." Clinging to the memory of past glories is no way to enter the '90s.

Another example, from George Will, in a column in the *Washington Post,* September 14, 1989:

> Italy, until recently the sick man of Western Europe, is so robust that social scientists should be dizzy.

And by Jeffrey Ulbrich, the Associated Press, November 28, 1997:

> Rare is the conversation with Turkish officialdom that doesn't include a reference to the "sick man of Europe"—once a description of the declining Ottoman Empire, but cited today as proof Turkey is really part of Europe.
>   And rare is the European Union official who doesn't think Turkey is still sick.

silent spring An ecological disaster; the death of nature from the unrestricted use of toxic chemicals.
    It refers to a spring without songbirds, caused by use of toxic chemicals that poison the FOOD CHAIN and destroy the balance of nature. It was the title of the 1962 book by Rachel Carson (1907–1964) that raised an early alarm about the environmental effects of herbicides and pesticides; the book helped launch the environmental movement.
    The term also applies, as illustrated in the second quotation, to groundbreaking books which have the same effect on public opinion as Carson's book.
    The term in use, by C.L. Sulzberger in the *New York Times,* June 12, 1970:

> The Caspian Sea is probably the most dramatic battleground of Soviet Russia's looming silent spring and to date this battle is being lost to oil, petroleum products, industrial and city sewage, ballast and waste from ships.

Also, by Frederic M. Biddle, in the *Boston Globe,* July 23, 1997, commenting on Gabriel Rotello's book *Sexual Ecology: AIDS and the Destiny of Gay Men* (1997):

> Rotello's ambitious book is the *Silent Spring* of the AIDS epidemic.

And in an editorial in the *Detroit News,* August 10, 1995:

> But for a really silent spring, consider the legacy of 70 years of communism in Russia.

And by Jane E. Brody in the *New York Times,* April 23, 1991:

While the threat of a silent spring may be abating, the danger of lifeless waterways looms ever larger, recent findings suggest.

Fish and other animals that live in North American waterways are disappearing much faster than land-based fauna, survey data indicate.

Simpson, Bart A character in *The Simpsons,* a long-running television cartoon series of the 1990s, created by Matt Gruening. Bart, the son of the family, is subversive and a menace to orderly society, with a bad attitude, bad manners, and a bad habit of describing things as they really are. Naturally, he has become something of a culture hero.

The term in use, by Valerie Takahama in the *Orange County Register,* December 17, 1995, on radio personality Howard Stern:

He's pure ID and inner child and a sophisticated parodist. He's Bart Simpson and Lenny Bruce.

In use again, by Evan Berland of the Associated Press, July 19, 1995, writing about efforts to censor Mark Twain's *The Adventures of Huckleberry Finn:*

It was first banned in 1885 in Concord, Mass., a year after its publication. Townspeople thought the pipe-smoking, insolent Huck was a bad role model—a 19th-century version of Bart Simpson.

And by Joseph Shapiro in *U.S. News & World Report,* February 22, 1993:

Twentysomethings are a generation in need of a press agent. Their elders think of them (when they think of them at all) as a generation of uppity, flesh-and-blood Bart Simpsons, so poorly educated that they can't find Vietnam on a map or come within 50 years of dating the Civil War.

sinister force Mocking term for an unlikely explanation for suspicious acts of obvious malefactors. An expression produced by the Watergate affair; it springs from the testimony of Alexander M. Haig, Richard Nixon's chief of staff, attempting to explain an 18½-minute gap—an erasure—in a key White House audio tape. The taping equipment, installed at Nixon's command in several places in the White House, was voice-activated and picked up conversations unbeknownst to virtually everyone.

Haig offered his theory—really a nontheory—in the Watergate trial presided over by Federal District Judge John J. Sirica. Sirica describes the moment in his 1979 memoir, *To Set the Record Straight:*

In court, Haig went on to offer what he called a "devil theory": ". . . perhaps some sinister force had come in and applied the other energy source and taken care of the information on that tape," he testified.

[H]is unhappy choice of words made headlines around the world. Quite by accident, Nixon's closest aide had supplied a description that many people all over the country thought probably fitted the president of the United States as well as anyone.

The term in use, by Lynn Darling, *Newsday,* November 10, 1989, on the abortion debate:

> Both sides talk of exploitation, and sinister forces fighting for the HEARTS AND MINDS of the American people. Both sides think the system is in thrall to the enemy.

And by Paul Hoffman in *Smithsonian,* February 1987:

> Those who suffer from morbid fear of the number 13 will want to go into hiding, because in any given year the maximum number of Fridays falling on the 13th that the sinister forces can serve up is three. There is at least one Friday the 13th in every year, but the faint of heart will be spared another triple dose of calendrical evil until 1998.

siren song An irresistible appeal; especially a deceptive and dangerous lure. A seductive woman may be called a siren. From a Greek word meaning "entangler." In classical mythology, sirens were sea nymphs: part woman, part bird. Their singing was so alluring that sailors forgot their duties and starved to death or were drawn to wreck themselves on rocky coasts. In the *Odyssey* [*q.v.*], Odysseus has his men wear earplugs to prevent them from wrecking the ship in response to the siren's song; he does not plug his own ears, but has himself lashed to the mast of his ship for safety.

The term in use, by Ann Louise Bardach in *Vanity Fair,* March 1995:

> Even Cuba's famed health-care system has been unable to resist the siren song of capitalism.

And by Mike Harris, AP Online, May 27, 1998:

> Jeremy Mayfield, a 28-year-old who stands second in the Winston Cup standings, heard the siren song of stock cars from his hometown of Owensboro, Ky.

And by Lawrence S. Ritter in the *New York Times Book Review,* September 8, 1991:

> Infatuated with the then-popular siren song of deregulation, Congress responded, as Mr. Lowry recounts, with a rescue operation that abolished many of the rules under which savings and loans had traditionally functioned.

Sisyphean Of, relating to, or suggesting the labors of Sisyphus, a king of Greek mythology condemned eternally to roll a heavy rock up a hill in Hades only to have it roll down again each time. A Sisyphean task is a burden or labor that never ends.

The term in use, in the *New Republic,* December 30, 1996:

The work of Nixon rehabilitators remains Sisyphean. Labori-
ously, they rebuild the Old Man's reputation until, inevitably,
their efforts come crashing down as each new Nixon tape is
released by the National Archives.

And by Lisa W. Foderaro in the *New York Times,* April 12, 1989, writing on state efforts to encourage New Yorkers to eat healthfully:

While undoing well-worn habits is something of a Sisyphean task,
the state is determined to try.

And by Norman Atkins in *Rolling Stone,* December 10-24, 1992, in a
profile of Marian Wright Edelman:

In the twenty-four years since then, Edelman has been engaged
in one of the heroic, Sisyphean struggles of our time, patiently
inching her rock up the mountain of poverty and showing
others that it isn't absurd to be spiritually optimistic. She accom-
plishes her work through the Children's Defense Fund, which
she founded nearly two decades ago.

skittles *See* BEER AND SKITTLES.

skunk works A usually small and often isolated department or facility
that functions with little supervision within a company.
    The name was applied to the Advance Development Project group estab-
lished within the Lockheed Corporation during World War II under
Clarence L. "Kelly" Johnson. Its mission was to build a jet airplane within 180 days in temporary quarters made from airplane engine packing
crates.
    Johnson, in his autobiography (*Kelly: More Than My Share of it All*),
offers this story: since everything the group did was secret, there was much
curiosity in the rest of the plant about its activities. An engineer responded to questions with "Oh, he's stirring up some kind of brew." Johnson
says, "This brought to mind Al Capp's popular comic strip of the day, 'Lil
Abner,' and the hairy Indian who regularly stirred up a big brew in his
Skonk Works, throwing in skunks, old shoes, and other likely material to
make his 'kickapoo joy juice.' Thus the Skunk Works was born and
named."
    The term in use, by John Holusha in the *New York Times,* July 16, 1989,
describing the use of innovative methods at Kodak:

Mr. Cole was authorized to set up a small design group outside
the company's normal structure, known in manufacturing as a
"skunk works."

And by Patt Morrison in the *Los Angeles Times,* November 6, 1994, in
a profile of the husband of gubernatorial candidate Kathleen Brown:

Van Gordon Sauter, by happy admission, is a "hostage" in California's governor's race, a "government-loathing, tax-abhorring,

bureaucrat-dreading Libertarian abducted by the wit, the charm, the intelligence and compassion of Kathleen Brown, my wife."

The skunk works at Fox Television, where Sauter, 59, is a consultant to the news division, could not have come up with a better plot device than this *Adam's Rib* casting.

slam dunk In basketball, a crowd-pleasing shot made by jumping high into the air and jamming the ball down through the basket. In a broader sense, the phrase refers to a spectacular success.

The term in use, by Dan Vierria in the *Sacramento Bee*, April 2, 1997, on the trendifying of tea:

> Tea's reputed health benefits may have been the slam dunk that finally caught the public's attention.

And by Christopher John Farley in *Time*, April 10, 1995:

> Stevie Wonder is a man whose accomplishments in music are as sparkling and intimidating as Michael Jordan's achievements on the basketball court. . . . When a guy like Wonder releases a new CD—his first in four years—we expect a slam dunk.

The verb ("to make a slam dunk") is *slam-dunk,* as in this example by Larry Dorman in the *New York Times*, December 18, 1994:

> He also birdied the eighth and ninth, making an 18-footer and a 15-footer. He hit a sand wedge to 8 feet at the 12th hole and made that. A sand wedge shot at the 16th stopped a yard from the hole and he made it and he then slam-dunked a 30-footer for eagle at the 17th.

slings and arrows Adversity, troubles, bad luck. Taken from Shakespeare's *Hamlet,* Act 3, Scene 1. The speech is Hamlet's famous soliloquy on death and suicide, which begins:

> To be, or not to be—that is the question;
> Whether 'tis nobler in the mind to suffer
> The slings and arrows of outrageous fortune,
> Or to take arms against a sea of troubles,
> And by opposing end them?

The term in use, by Bruce Fretts in *Entertainment Weekly,* December 5, 1997:

> [Dick Van Dyke] costar Mary Tyler Moore must've picked up a few ideas, because her self-titled office sitcom later ratcheted up the cranky quotient. Buffoonish anchor Ted (Ted Knight) was subjected to the slings and arrows of newswriter Murray. . . .

And by Carol Bishop Miller in *Horticulture,* June 1, 1997:

Horsetail is evergreen (though it may be laid low by the slings
and arrows of outrageous winter) and thrives in sun or shade in
either shallow water or, once established, most soils.

And by Michael Azerrad in *Rolling Stone,* February 23, 1995:

Kenny's witty, biting lyrics, delivered in a raspy purr or an
anguished squawk, paint everyday life as an onslaught of LIL-
LIPUTIAN slings and arrows: petty cruelties, crushes, jealousies,
greed.

slouching toward Bethlehem The slow but inexorable approach of something evil that will inevitably overwhelm what is good. This phrase from
William Butler Yeats' poem, "The Second Coming," describes a vision of
an ominous sphinxlike monster with "a gaze blank and pitiless as the sun":

And what rough beast, its hour come round at last,
slouches toward Bethlehem to be born?

The imagery suggests a frightening future imagined in a present in which
order is breaking down. Joan Didion chose the phrase as the title of an
essay describing the hippie scene in San Francisco's Haight-Ashbury district in the summer of 1967. She explained: "It was the first time I had
dealt directly and flatly with the evidence of atomization, the proof that
things fall apart. . . . "

The phrase in extended use, suggesting the inevitability of change for
the worse, by Ellis Henican, reviewing the McDonald's "Arch Deluxe"
sandwich in *Newsday,* May 10, 1996:

You can call this one MCFat. . . . Just what the cardiologist
ordered for all those aging boomers out there, slouching toward
middle age.

Another example, by Barrett Kalellis, in a commentary in the *Detroit
News,* June 18, 1996:

Whereas talk radio was once hailed as an alternative source for
news and information, it seems to be slouching toward [the]
philistinism that television, movies, literature and popular music
have long since exhibited. [*See also* PHILISTINE.]

And by the Associated Press, July 14, 1996, on economic revival in a
small Iowa town:

When this mite-size town seemed to be slouching toward oblivion, it found salvation in a most unlikely source: the local phone
book.

And by Peter Freundlich in *Harpers,* December 1987:

When the dream was done, there stood the yuppie: the smooth-
faced monster of consumerism, teeth like pearls, eyes like coals,
slouching toward Bloomingdale's to be born.

slough of despond \ˌslau̇ . . . di-ˈspänd, ˌslü-\ A state of extreme depression. The term comes from John Bunyan's 17th-century allegorical masterpiece *Pilgrim's Progress* [*q.v.*]. A slough is a bog, a place with deep mud into which the unwary may stray, become stuck, and sink. "Despond" is despondency, extreme discouragement, dejection, or depression. The Slough of Despond was one of the many hazards facing EVERYMAN on his way to the Celestial City. He wandered in and, weighed down by his sins, was unable to get out until rescued by Help.

The term in use, by Tom Junod in *Sports Illustrated,* April 10, 1995, on star professional athletes and their dogs:

> Jennifer Capriati, for instance, has credited her black Lab-boxer puppy with helping her emerge from her own slough of despond. . . .

And by Joseph Weber in *Business Week,* June 30, 1997, on Bristol-Myers Squibb CEO Charles A Heimbold:

> These days Heimbold is betting that the house—once-struggling Bristol—will win again. And he hasn't had to shout much to help it along. Bristol was in a "slough of despond" when he took the top job three years ago, says Heimbold, but now the company's bywords are such phrases as "competitive superiority" and "sense of urgency."

smoke–filled room A phrase originating in American politics, for the place where candidates are selected by cigar-puffing political bosses—the antithesis of the public and unpredictable process of political primaries. More generally, it is where the power brokers meet to make deals and settle things, safely away from the public eye.

The expression is attributed to Harry M. Daugherty, a political operative of Warren G. Harding. Daugherty predicted that the front-runners for the 1920 Republican presidential nomination would deadlock at the convention and that party leaders would "sit down about two o'clock in the morning, around a table in a smoke-filled room in some hotel and decide the nomination. When that time comes, Harding will be selected." Daugherty was exactly right; after nine ballots, the leaders met and agreed that Harding should be the nominee, and the senator from Ohio was selected on the tenth.

The convention surprised the bosses, however, when it nominated Calvin Coolidge for vice president. Daugherty became Harding's attorney general and was one of the "Ohio gang" of Harding cronies and associates implicated in various scandals. (*See* TEAPOT DOME.) He was tried twice for conspiracy to defraud the government but was saved by deadlocked juries.

The Democrats, true to form, had a much harder time, striving through 44 ballots to nominate James M. Cox. The vice presidential nominee was Franklin D. Roosevelt.

Electoral reforms moved the country away from the power-brokering

of party conventions to presidential primaries, thought to be more democratic, although the proliferation of primaries and escalating costs of campaigns have led to some nostalgia for the wild theater of the conventions
of the 1920s.

The term in use, by Curt Schleier in the *Detroit News,* August 16, 1996,
bemoaning the boredom of the year's conventions:

> There's a school of thought that suggests this system is prefer-
> able to a bunch of pols sitting in a smoke-filled room making the
> decision for us. But for me, those were the good old days.

And by Marshall Ingwerson in the *Christian Science Monitor,* March 12,
1992:

> The field of candidates is far more open and uncontrolled than
> half a century ago, when the legendary "smoke-filled rooms" of
> party politicos set the candidate field. But the nearest modern
> cousins to those power brokers now work in the news media.

And by H. Ross Perot, quoted by David Seideman in *Time,* October 5,
1992:

> Now that he is moving to return to the race, the Texas billion-
> aire is again posing as a selfless CINCINNATUS, standing ready to
> do the people's bidding. His decision to become a candidate again,
> he said last week, would come "from the bottom up." He added,
> "This is not three or four guys in a smoke-filled room deciding
> what we ought to be told to do."

smoking gun Incontrovertible evidence of guilt, often used in a political
context. The reference is to a device in detective fiction, in which a character is found standing over the corpse holding a smoking gun. This is
assumed to show guilt, although in fiction the detective hero often is able
to demonstrate that the obvious conclusion is wrong and that some other
malefactor committed the crime.

The expression is a legacy of the Watergate scandal. As evidence of
crimes accumulated, defenders of President Richard Nixon contended
that while there was ample evidence of impropriety, there was no direct
evidence that he had committed a crime.

That abruptly changed with the discovery of a taped conversation
between Nixon and chief of staff H.R. Haldeman on June 24, 1972, in
which there was agreement that the CIA should be used to block the FBI
investigation of the Watergate break-in, which had occurred the week
before. This evidence was proclaimed to be the "smoking gun" demonstrating Nixon's participation in efforts to obstruct the investigation.

The term in use, by Paul M. Barrett in the *Wall Street Journal,* June 26,
1990, on the savings and loan scandals of the time:

> The bottom line: There's no smoking gun or hidden-camera
> videotape in an S&L heist. The evidence is a complex paper trail,

a chain of evidence that's usually ice-cold by the time prosecutors lay their hands on it.

And from Tom Siegfried in the *Hartford Courant,* January 19, 1995:

> Long predicted by theory, BLACK HOLES are difficult to find because they are invisible. While indirect effects of their gravity had convinced many astronomers that black holes exist in the universe, only last May did astronomers find "smoking gun" evidence of a real black hole, in the galaxy M87.

And by Jane Sims Podesta in *People,* April 15, 1996:

> The result of Stewart's pit-bull perseverance is a bracing, 479-page plunge into a scandal so murky, it has become a COTTAGE INDUSTRY for lawyers. . . . Stewart immersed himself in the Whitewater land deal for two years, eventually interviewing some 300 people.
> No smoking gun emerged ("Life is never that simple"). . . .

snake oil Various mixtures sold as medicine usually without regard to their medical worth. A quack remedy. From the many medicine shows and traveling charlatans of the past who sold "miracle cures" to a credulous public. Now the term is applied to phony nostrums in all fields, and to poppycock in general. Anyone who purveys these dubious cures is a "snake-oil salesman," a con artist.

As Eugene O'Neill put it in *The Iceman Cometh* (1946): "I'll bet he's standing on a street corner in hell right now, making suckers of the damned, telling them there's nothing like snake oil for a bad burn."

The term in use, in a review by Madanmohan Rao, for the United Nations Inter Press Service bureau, of Clifford Stoll's 1995 book, *Silicon Snake Oil: Second Thoughts On The Information Superhighway:*

> The key ingredient of the silicon snake oil is the technocratic belief that computer networks will create a better society through access to information and better communications.

Another example, by Gwynne Dyer, in the Toledo, Ohio, *Blade,* February 21, 1997:

> Back then, the Communist empire was dying and Mr. Soros stood out as a beacon of intelligence and integrity among all the western CARPETBAGGERS and snake-oil salesmen who came to feast off the corpse.

And quoted in the *New York Times,* November 18, 1996, by David Barboza:

> "It's like selling snake oil," said Nye Lavalle, chairman of the Sports Marketing Group in Atlanta. "All it is is a newspaper clipping service transferred to television."

Snopes The name of a family of vicious characters in novels by William Faulkner. In Faulkner's tales of the American South, set in fictitious Yoknapatawpha County, the Snopeses are scoundrels, occasionally worse, and only seldom honest. More generally, a Snopes is an unscrupulous Southern businessman or politician.

The term in use, by Wesley Pruden, in the *Washington Times,* July 14, 1996:

> The White House is not really concerned about the reputations of either Clinton. It's too late for that.... At some point the wonderfully/woefully tolerant American public will decide that we've had enough of Flem Snopes' grandson and his unblushing parvenu bride.

And from Dave Rossie, Gannett News Service, November 16, 1994:

> What is happening to the GOP is roughly parallel to what happened to the South after the Civil War, when, with its best men either financially ruined or lying dead on fields from Pennsylvania to Georgia, it was taken over by Snopeses. Today's Snopeses are named Gingrich, Gramm, Helms and their AYATOLLAH Pat Robertson. And the ultimate Snopes is Sen. Richard Shelby, who, the day after the Republicans won the Senate, shed his Democratic skin and slithered over to the GOP.

snows of yesteryear The lost, transitory past. It is part of a line from the work of 15th century French poet François Villon. In French: "Mais ou sont les neiges d'antan?" ("But where are the snows of yesteryear?") The poet, just out of prison, invokes with both regret and appreciation the names of famous and beautiful women, both real and legendary, realizing that all must come to dust and memory, vanishing like the snow.

Villon was the great poet of his age, and one of the greatest of the French language. He was a hell-raiser and criminal, too. As a youth he was a brilliant student who also partook of the rowdier side of life in Paris, which was very rowdy indeed. He killed a priest in a street fight (he said the priest started it) and spent time in prison as well as on the run from the authorities. He disappeared in 1463; he had been sentenced to death for various transgressions, including robbery, but the sentence was commuted to 10 years of banishment.

Villon was something of a "gangsta." Robert Louis Stevenson called him "a sinister dog," while acknowledging his greatness as a poet. Stevenson, the author of *Treasure Island,* observed, "He was the first wicked *sans-culotte....* He is mighty pathetic and beseeching here in the street, but I would not go down a dark road with him for a large consideration." (*See* SANSCULOTTES.)

In the 19th century Villon was resurrected as a romantic rogue and outlaw hero. In the 20th century a musical was composed about him (*The Vagabond King*) by Rudolf Friml, which was made into a movie in 1956.

Two nonmusical movies were made about him, too: *The Beloved Rogue* (1928) and *If I Were King* (1938).

The term in use, by Murray Kempton, in *Newsday,* February 16, 1996, on presidential candidate Steve Forbes mushing through the contemporary snows of New Hampshire's presidential primary:

> Steve Forbes stood a few hundred yards away, pitiably misunderstanding his mishaps with a presence rendered more picturesque than usual by the snows of the day, and the suspicion was pressing ever more insistently that he must soon belong to the snows of yesteryear.

And from Neil Hickey in *TV Guide,* July 26-August 1, 1986:

> But—like the snows of yesteryear—the fish of Wyoming had disappeared. The guides were looking furtive. Hanging by a thread was the honor of their state and The Nashville Network's financial investment in this "piscicidal offensive" (in the coinage of the late sportswriter Red Smith). . . .

And by O.B. Hardison Jr., *Entering the Maze* (1981):

> A phrase like "radical . . . reordering of . . . priorities" activates a small PAVLOVIAN gong somewhere deep in the mind. It is familiar. It is the rhetoric of Stokely Carmichael, Rap Brown, Tom Hayden, Phil Berrigan, and all those other youths who have disappeared like the snows of yesteryear along with SNCC, SDS, and the whole alphabet soup of the radical sixties.

Sodom and Gomorrah \\'sä-dəm . . . gə-'mȯr-ə\\ Bywords for places notorious for vice or corruption.

In Genesis 19, these were the cities destroyed by God with FIRE AND BRIMSTONE because of their wickedness. As the story goes, Abraham persuaded the Lord to spare Sodom if ten righteous men could be found there. They couldn't. The lone righteous man, Lot, was warned to flee with his family to escape the city's destruction. God told them not to look back, but LOT'S WIFE disobeyed and she was turned into a pillar of salt.

The word *sodomy,* meaning "copulation with a member of the same sex or oral or anal copulation with a human or an animal," derives from Sodom and its reputation.

The term in use, quoted by Tovia Smith on National Public Radio's *Morning Edition,* September 24, 1997:

> Freshman Elisha Hack has been at Yale about three weeks now, but he has yet to set foot inside his dorm room. Hack says he went inside a residence hall just once, and he says he was shocked by the anything goes, promiscuous atmosphere that he compares to Sodom and Gomorrah.

And from *Newsweek,* March 13, 1989, on fallout from a partisan struggle in Congress:

Meanwhile the public is left with an image of the Senate as a cockpit of partisan squabbling, the White House as a center of questionable decision making, and the city of Washington as Sodom-and-Gormorrah-by-the-Potomac.

And by Mary McGrory in a *Washington Post* column, November 27, 1997, writing about why she opposed renaming Washington National Airport after Ronald Reagan:

Ronald Reagan, although an amiable man, had a considerable capacity for loathing few things more than the federal city. To him, it made Sodom and Gomorrah look like a bastion of family values.

solon \'sō-lən, -ˌlän\ A wise and skillful lawgiver. A member of a legislative body. Solon himself was an Athenian statesman and lawgiver of the 6th-century B.C.

He was granted absolute authority by the Athenian people to remedy an economic and political crisis, which he did by repealing most of the stern code of Draco (*see* DRACONIAN). He canceled debts on land, forbade debt-slavery (selling into slavery people who couldn't pay their debts), and opened political office to more citizens by creating citizenship rights based on modest wealth rather than aristocratic birth. His reforms are considered the basis of Athenian democracy.

The term in use, by Curt Suplee in the *Washington Post,* "Outlook," March 5, 1989, on changing public attitudes toward alcoholism:

The signs are ubiquitous, notably in the news media themselves. For generations, drinking was a taboo subject, and the press routinely overlooked the solons' most grotesque and conspicuous drunkenness. Now editors are closing the ethanol gap: the current *Newsweek,* for example, devotes a full page to famous Congressional sots.

And by Mike Cannon in the *Deseret News,* July 27, 1997, suggesting participation by state legislators in the 2002 Winter Olympics in Salt Lake City:

Need cushioning for ski jumpers who outjump the hill? There also are some pretty burly solons who—covered with a big net—could cushion any hard fall. Want more padding? Toss a few lobbyists onto the pile.

some are more equal than others A famous slogan from George Orwell's *Animal Farm* (1945). Orwell's satire on Stalinism tells the story of a farm animal revolution. One of their commandments is, "All animals are equal," a send-up of the American Declaration of Independence. (*See also* ORWELLIAN.)

The animals are betrayed by their leaders, the pigs, and end up in a worse situation than they were in before their revolution. All of their revolutionary commandments are rewritten and compressed into one: All Animals are Equal, But Some Animals are More Equal than Others. In other words, revolutionary slogans are fraudulent; all power and privilege is given to a small elite.

The term in use, by Andrew Neil in *Vanity Fair,* December 1996:

> When you work for Rupert Murdoch you do not work for a company chairman or chief executive: you work for a Sun King. All courtiers are created equal because all have access to the king, though from time to time some are more equal than others.

And by Carolyn Bates in *Gourmet,* November 1990:

> With dessert came the discovery that all tiramisu are not created equal. Three that are more equal than others are The Blue Fox's in San Francisco, Biba's in Sacramento, and Rex's. . . .

And by Alexander Wolff in *Sports Illustrated,* September 14, 1988:

> There persists in the world of East German sports a cold, matter-of-fact way of deciding which athletes are more equal than others.

something rotten A statement of suspicion or of the existence of corruption. Taken from Shakespeare's *Hamlet,* Act 1, Scene 4. Marcellus, an officer of the guard, having seen the ghost of the dead king on the guard platform of the castle, says, "Something is rotten in the state of Denmark." A ghost does not walk for frivolous reasons, after all; the widowed queen has remarried with unseemly haste, and to her husband's brother. The ghost tells Hamlet that his father was murdered by his brother. Rotten, indeed.

The term in use, by Jonathan Rauch, reviewing *Washington on $10 Million a Day: How Lobbyists Plunder the Nation* by Ken Silverstein in *Washington Monthly,* July 17, 1998:

> In 1998, to read a new book that is—SHOCKED, SHOCKED!—by corporate influence peddling is a slightly odd experience. . . . Silverstein is certainly right to smell something rotten in Washington's cynical lobbyist-for-hire culture.

And quoted by Rick Brand in *Newsday,* August 30, 1994, on political scandal on Long Island:

> "Even the Republicans are embarrassed and feel endangered by this deal and they want to save themselves," she said. "There's something rotten in Denmark, and they want to make sure the smell doesn't attach to them."

And by Randy Harvey in the *Los Angeles Times,* January 7, 1998:

> Something is rotten in college football's coaches poll. . . .
> An assistant coach for one of last week's bowl teams, assigned

to vote on behalf of his head coach, says he thinks so little of the responsibility he lets his ninth-grade son fill out the ballot.

sound and fury Great but meaningless noise and commotion. It is from Shakespeare's *Macbeth,* Act 5, Scene 5, spoken by Macbeth when he learns of the death of his wife:

> Life's but a walking shadow, a poor player,
> That struts and frets his hour upon the stage,
> And then is heard no more; it is a tale
> Told by an idiot, full of sound and fury,
> Signifying nothing.

William Faulkner chose it as the title of his 1929 account of the decline and fall of the Compson family, *The Sound and the Fury.* The first section of the novel, seen through the eyes of the idiot Benjy, is truly "a tale told by an idiot."

The term in use, by Richard Whittle and David Jackson in the *Dallas Morning News,* April 7, 1995:

> As promised, House Republicans raced through their Contract With America in less than 100 days of sound and fury.

And actor Robert Redford, quoted by Mark Woods, Gannett News Service, January 18, 1995:

> But it was Redford who before Super Bowl XIII—Dallas Cowboys vs. Pittsburgh Steelers in Miami—was asked if he planned to watch the game.
>
> "I'll be out skiing," he replied. "The Super Bowl is a lot of sound and fury signifying nothing."
>
> Exactly. What could be more American than a lot of sound and fury signifying nothing?

South Sea bubble A frenzy of financial speculation that inflates stock prices beyond their real value and ends in collapse when reality asserts itself.

In the early 18th century, Europeans and their governments were beginning to explore large-scale banking and credit in order to pay off huge war debts and raise money for new commercial ventures. In England, much of the government debt was to be paid off through government-chartered companies granted monopolies on particular activities.

The South Sea Company was one such enterprise; it was given a monopoly on British trade with South America. Rampant speculation developed in South Sea shares, fed by the apparent success of a similar scheme in France and by overblown promises of profits.

A rash of similar enterprises, called "bubbles" at the time, appeared. But in 1720 South Sea stockholders began to sell, and financial collapse and scandal ensued. Robert Walpole, a long-time critic of the South Sea scheme, became principal minister to the king. Parliament promptly passed "the Bubble Act" to limit such speculative activities, and Walpole's efforts preserved the credit of the British government.

In France the results were more dire. There the monarchy's inability to solve the country's financial problems helped bring on the French Revolution.

An Encyclopedia of World History calls the bubble "an introduction to modern speculative finance."

The term in use, by Martin Lipton, quoted in *Spy,* February 1989, on the leveraged buyout craze on Wall Street:

> "Our nation is blindly rushing to the precipice. As with tulip bulbs [and] South Sea bubbles . . . the denouement will be a crash." That's Marty Lipton talking—Marty Lipton, the best-known [leveraged buyout] lawyer in the world. . . .

And by columnist George Will, appearing in the *Kansas City Star,* September 25, 1995:

> Those people waiting in long lines for Colin Powell to inscribe his autobiography should first visit their bookstore's history section and then, while waiting in line, read about the South Sea Bubble. This autumn's Powell boomlet may be remembered as the South Sea Bubble of American politics.

sow dragon's teeth To incite strife; to plant the seeds of future conflict. From a Greek myth in which the teeth of a dragon, sown in the earth, yielded a crop of armed warriors.

The legendary hero responsible was Cadmus, who slew the dragon. The goddess Athena kept half the dragon's teeth and told him to plant the rest. Armed warriors then sprang up and fought each other until only five were left. These warriors then helped Cadmus build the city of Thebes.

Athena gave her share of the dragon's teeth to the king of Colchis, who in turn gave them to the hero Jason, who had sailed to Colchis with the Argonauts to capture the Golden Fleece. To retrieve the fleece Jason had to plow a field (with fire-breathing bulls), sow these dragon's teeth, and fight and kill the warriors who sprouted. He did get the fleece (and the king's daughter, Medea), although he must have been very, very tired.

The term in use, by Andrew J. Nathan, in the *New Republic,* August 22, 1994, reviewing *A Borrowed Place: The History of Hong Kong* by Frank Welsh:

> The Chinese suspected Britain of using democratic reform to sow dragon's teeth of chaos. . . .

Another example, from Emily Mitchell, in *Time International,* July 17, 1995, on a Brussels exhibit of World War II material, "I Was 20 in 1945":

> The dragon's teeth of the Second World War were sown in the First, and the show begins with artifacts and periodicals illustrating a single event that links past, present and future. The

place is Sarajevo; the date is June 28, 1914; the heir to the Austrian throne has been assassinated. . . . The murdered Archduke's uniform and the pistol that killed him restore a human dimension to a deed that has echoed across Europe ever since.

-speak A suffix used to form words denoting a particular kind of jargon. It is drawn from George Orwell's *Nineteen Eighty-four*. (*See* ORWELLIAN.) In the totalitarian society of Orwell's novel, there are two languages, Oldspeak and NEWSPEAK. Oldspeak is English as we know it; Newspeak is the new language of dictatorship, which erases the history and meaning of words and creates an ugly, clumsy language that serves the interests of the state.

The term in use, by Gerald F. Seib, the *Wall Street Journal*, June 21, 1989:

> Thus are the inquiring minds of foreign correspondents taxed these days as they try to interpret Bushspeak for their readers. . . . Mr. Bush . . . speaks in free-form Americanese, filled with pop-culture colloquialisms and Texas vernacularisms.

And from the *Economist*, July 29, 1989, on competing American and Canadian gold coins:

> Although the Eagle and the Maple Leaf contain the same amount of gold, the Eagle is padded with more alloys. . . . while the Maple Leaf is 99.99% pure gold or "four-nines" in goldspeak.

spear-carrier A member of an opera chorus or a bit actor in a play; a person whose actions matter little in an event or organization.

The term in use by Nixon aide John Ehrlichman, in his testimony before the Senate Watergate committee, quoted in the *Washington Post*, July 29, 1973:

> There were quite a few spear-carriers at the meeting from the White House staff and I was simply there to get information.

And by syndicated columnist Lars-Erik Nelson in *Newsday*, October 9, 1994:

> One reason for the mystery is that during all of his 33 years in Washington, Dole has been the loyal spear-carrier, submerging his own agenda—if he has one—to the needs of his party or his Republican presidents: Nixon, Ford, Reagan, and Bush.

And by Eleanor Clift in *Newsweek*, October 22, 1990:

> The moderate pragmatists who gravitate to Bush are by definition not passionately for anything. The GOP's spear carriers are on the right, and they have never fully trusted Bush.

Spillane, Mickey American writer (b. 1918) of pulp detective fiction whose popular work is characterized by violence and sexual licentiousness. His stories are called "hard-boiled fiction," with blunt, terse prose, sordid urban settings, and tough guys employing plenty of sex and violence.

Other more distinguished writers have written in this style, including Dashiell Hammett and Raymond Chandler, but it is Spillane's name which has come to describe this high-testosterone style. His best known creation is Mike Hammer; his novels include *I, the Jury* (1947), *Kiss Me Deadly* (1952), and *Tomorrow I Die* (1984).

The term in use, by Donna Jackson, for the Los Angeles Times Syndicate, in the *Arizona Republic,* June 13, 1995, describing her escapades masquerading as a man:

> I have to make an effort to keep up the Mickey Spillane glaze in my eyes. It seems to work only when I keep my mind on me, where I'm going, what I need and want.

And by John Bordsen in the *Charlotte Observer,* December 15, 1996, reviewing *Autobiography: My Dark Places,* by James Ellroy:

> In Mickey Spillane/*Dragnet* style, you meet the investigators and watch them swing into action.

star chamber A secret and often irresponsibly arbitrary and oppressive proceeding.

In England from the 10th-century until 1641, the Star Chamber was a notorious court that met in a room in London's Palace of Westminster where gilt stars decorated the ceiling.

The court was less bound by formal procedure than other courts: it required no juries for indictment or verdict and could act on individual complaints by simply hauling the accused in to testify under oath.

Opposition arose to such arbitrary use of power during the long struggle in the 17th century between King Charles I and Puritan forces in Parliament. For example, an attack by Puritan pamphleteer William Prynne on women actors as "notorious whores" was interpreted as aimed at the queen, who was theatrically inclined. (Prynne also objected to mixed dancing and face makeup and long hair on men.) The Court of Star Chamber sentenced Prynne to imprisonment for life, expulsion from the legal profession, an enormous fine, the pillory, and the "cropping" of his ears. For all that, Prynne continued agitating from his cell, and three years later the court had his face branded and the rest of his ears sliced off.

Such actions aroused Parliament, and the Star Chamber was abolished in 1641. Prynne and other political prisoners were freed.

The term in use, by George Stuteville in the *Indianapolis Star,* December 29, 1996, describing the rise of Rep. Dan Burton (R-Ind.) to the chairmanship of the House Government Reform and Oversight Committee:

> Burton almost certainly will continue using the power of this committee as a star chamber for assailing the presidency.

And quoted by Glenn Kessler in *Newsday,* December 1, 1994:

In a sometimes cerebral speech, Sen. Robert Byrd (D-W.Va) denounced the new World Trade Organization created by GATT to mediate trade disputes as a "new type of star chamber proceedings" and said Dole's deal with Clinton was "a fig leaf pasted onto a tyrannosaurus."

And by Mordecai Richler in *Atlantic,* June 1983:

What was singular about this episode was not the charge, or the ruling, but that the doctor in the case actually knew the name of his accuser. For it is in the nature of Bill 101 that, in true Star Chamber tradition, anyone can file a complaint anonymously. The accused has no right to confront his accuser.

stealth An aircraft-design characteristic that is intended to produce a very weak radar return. It is now applied as an adjective outside the military to persons or activities that are hidden or difficult to detect and are thus able to accomplish goals or purposes before opposition can mobilize.

The term in use, in *U.S. News & World Report,* October 23, 1995:

But a kind of stealth racism persists, unmistakable to every black but largely invisible to many whites who are appalled by a Mark Fuhrman or a cross burning.

Another example, from Edward Walsh, in the *Washington Post,* January 11, 1997:

But today, amid the storm of ethics charges that swirls around him, it was an almost furtive Gingrich, the stealth speaker, who slipped into Chicago for a few hours to pay tribute to a fallen comrade and do the least possible damage to himself.

stentorian Extremely loud. The word is usually applied to the human voice, but it may also be applied to extremely forceful expression by the printed word, such as a huge-lettered newspaper headline. It derives from the name of Stentor, who was a herald in the Greek army. Homer says in the *Iliad* that his voice was as loud as that of 50 men.

The term in use, by Joe Conason in the *Nation,* December 8, 1997:

Among the intrigued was the *Journal's* [John] Fund, whose paper had published a stentorian essay on October 10, with the stark headline "Impeach," by novelist and former Bob Dole speechwriter Mark Helprin.

And by Terry Baker in *Travel & Leisure,* March 1997:

We enter a small bar in Granada for tapas—calamari, langostinos—and dry Manzanilla sherry. We while away the time in the midday sun watching old men throwing shrimp shells on the floor and speaking in stentorian tones.

And by David Cole in *Newsday,* April 8, 1994:

The Supreme Court can be a very isolating place. Access is carefully controlled, decisions are made behind closed doors, and the justices speak to the outside world primarily through the stentorian tones of legal doctrine.

Stepford Unreal or false in a robotic, programmed, too-good-to-be-true way. It's derived from the 1972 novel *The Stepford Wives* by Ira Levin (and a 1975 movie). In suburban Stepford, Connecticut, all of the wives are the picture of domestic perfection: perfectly groomed Barbie dolls with spotless houses and no tattle-tale gray in their laundry. (*See* BARBIE AND KEN.)

All women's organizations in the town seem to have been disbanded; nonconforming newcomers go off for weekends with husbands and come back strangely changed, all ambition gone, and dedicated to waxing floors and ironing. Newcomer Joanna is puzzled, then frightened. Are the preternaturally perfect Stepford hausfraus the result of a male plot to substitute pliant robots for their flesh-and-blood wives? And now Joanna's husband wants to have a weekend getaway, too. . . .

The term in use, by humorist Dave Barry, describing the 1994 Winter Olympics in Lillehammer, Norway:

> Even the taxi drivers here are beautiful. Have you noticed there are no normal-looking people? I think they send the ugly ones away somewhere. It's a Stepford country.

Another example, from *USA Today,* July 30, 1996:

> At Saturn [auto dealerships], customers are greeted by Stepford-friendly salespeople.

And from from a theater review by Peter Marks, in the *New York Times,* March 3, 1997:

> In *Imagining Brad,* his 1990 surreal stage comedy, a Nashville Stepford wife, beaten black and blue by her husband, comes to believe the only trustworthy man is one without fists.

steroids, on Having unnaturally enlarged or strong muscles, or being unpleasantly large, loud, or aggressive; pushy or hostile; having physical qualities exaggerated. Taking anabolic steroids to enhance one's strength. Displaying the physical or mental effects of taking these manufactured forms of the hormone testosterone and other hormones.

Anabolic steroids were found to enhance athletic performance by promoting rapid growth of muscle mass. However, they also have extremely serious side effects, including aggressive, violent behavior and depression. Violent outbursts are known as " 'roid rage." Serious physical effects include masculinazation in women; growth of breasts in men; damage to bones and joints; and possible links to cancer.

The term in use, by Steve Rubenstein, in the *San Francisco Chronicle,* March 7, 1997, describing a human-vs.-machine contest between street-sweepers:

McGann conceded that the machine, which resembles a Shop Vac on steroids, can cover more ground on a level straightaway but noted that it lacks intelligence. A human, he observed, can tell when a cigarette butt is so firmly embedded in a sidewalk crack that it must be dug out and when it will yield to gentle pressure. The machine simply sucks.

And in the *Detroit News,* January 10, 1997, reporting on the highlights of the auto show:

The German convertible specialist said it could be a limousine, minivan or sport-utility vehicle. But it really looks like an armored Brinks truck on steroids.

And by Richard J. Cattani, editor of the *Christian Science Monitor,* March 10, 1993, on what he describes as "the fake combat of pundit gladiators":

Do the talk-show combatants, plied with ideological steroids, even listen to one another, let alone think to persuade?

Stockholm syndrome The process by which a hostage cooperates with or becomes sympathetic to or allied with his or her captor.

Psychologists say it is an automatic and unconscious defense mechanism for hostages to develop a sympathetic relationship with those who hold them captive, resulting from their total dependence on their captors and from extreme fear. The reverse sometimes occurs, too: hostage takers become emotionally attached to their prisoners.

The term takes its name from an incident in Stockholm, Sweden. On August 23, 1973, four employees of the Sveriges Kreditbank were taken hostage in the bank's vault by a gunman, Jan-Erik Olsson, a 32-year-old thief, burglar, and prison escapee who was later joined by his former cellmate. The hostages were held for 131 hours. After their release, it was found that the victims had come to fear the police more than their captors. The hostages had feelings of gratitude that their captors had "given their lives back," and after the incident visited the former captors in prison. One female hostage even married one of the hostage takers.

The term is used figuratively when someone changes sympathies as a result of contact with those who would normally be considered adversaries.

The term in use, by John Anderson in *Newsday,* November 27, 1994:

When bad movies happen to good actresses—never mind the multitude of barely tolerable ones—whose fault is it? Don't blame Hollywood, which has never pretended to be about anything but money. Blame the Stockholm syndrome: Female talent has been held hostage so long that the prisoners are beginning to sympathize with their jailers.

And by Frank Ahrens in the *Washington Post,* September 4, 1997:

Other new car dealers renovated their showrooms to eliminate what used to be known in the business as "closing booths": tiny cubicles where customers were trapped with salesmen who kept leaving to go "talk to their manager." This form of psychological terrorism often induced a Stockholm syndrome response— the customer actually began to believe the salesman was working on the buyer's behalf.

stonewall To be uncooperative, obstructive, or evasive; to refuse to comply or cooperate with. To be the stone wall into which an investigator or questioner must crash and go no further.

This term became the everlasting sobriquet of the Confederate General Thomas Jackson for the way in which his troops held their position at the First Battle of Bull Run when General Bernard E. Bee shouted to his wavering men, "Look, there is Jackson standing like a stone wall!"

The word came into widespread contemporary use from the testimony of former White House Counsel John Dean during the 1973 Senate Watergate hearings. Dean quoted President Nixon as ordering his men in to "stonewall" investigations, meaning to resist inquiries through vagueness or a lack of cooperation. Nixon's words, captured on his own tapes, were more to the point: "I don't give a shit what happens. I want you all to stonewall it, let them plead the Fifth Amendment, cover-up, or anything else."

An additional facet of "Stonewall" with a capital S: on June 28, 1969, in New York City, police raided the Stonewall Inn, a gay bar in New York City. Instead of submitting to what they considered harassment, the patrons fought back; the "Stonewall Rebellion" is now considered a watershed in the history of the gay rights movement.

The term in use, by Daniel Goleman in "How to Talk to Your Husband," *Good Housekeeping,* October 1, 1995:

> Stonewalling, in fact, is the male refuge of last resort: In his study Gottman found that 85 percent of stonewalling was done by husbands. Going blank and withdrawing sends a powerful, unnerving message of icy distance and distaste. . . .

And of course, the political context, in the *St. Louis Post-Dispatch,* January 4, 1997:

> Has Mr. Gingrich learned nothing from President Bill Clinton, whose administration has been characterized by successively stonewalling every allegation, even when telling the whole truth from the start would be less damaging?

And by John Gregory Dunne in the *New Yorker,* April 15, 1996:

> That cops sometimes lie on the witness stand is a fact that prosecutors will admit only after they leave the public sector; the name both they and cops have for it is "testilying," and it generally

involves either stonewalling or fudging evidence to make a good case better.

Strangelove A mad scientist who enthusiastically urges nuclear warfare; one who maniacally promotes wholescale destruction. Someone with these qualities is "Strangelovian."

Dr. Strangelove is one of the central characters in Stanley Kubrick's black-humored comedy of nuclear war, *Dr. Strangelove or: How I learned to Stop Worrying and Love the Bomb* (1964). Regularly listed as one of the greatest films of all time, *Strangelove* is the story of a nuclear attack launched against the Soviet Union by an insane American air base commander, and of efforts by the American command structure to recall the airplanes.

Dr. Strangelove (one of three roles in the movie played by Peter Sellers) is a sinister, deranged scientist who is called into the War Room as the president and his generals try to cope with the crisis. Dr. Strangelove, with his half smile and Teutonic accent, was chiefly inspired by figures like Dr. Edward Teller. Among the delectable details of Sellers' creation is Strangelove's black-gloved hand with a will of its own that alternately gives Nazi salutes or attempts to strangle him.

The term in use, by the *New Statesman & Society,* March 31, 1995, about a new book by Henry Kissinger, *Diplomacy:*

> Dr. Strangelove's magnum opus: damn lies and low cunning in world politics (no, it's not a memoir). More readable, and better balanced, than you'd expect.

And by William E. Burrows in *Popular Science,* August 1, 1994, on nuclear hazards in the former Soviet Union:

> While losing one or more nuclear devices to terrorists would be dangerous enough, it would pale in comparison with a Dr. Strangelovian doomsday system that was set up during the the height of the Cold War to ensure that the United States would not survive even if it launched a "decapitating" strike against the Soviet political leadership and the general staff. The computerized system, which is still in place, is called "dead hand" because it was designed to be switched on . . . to order all-out nuclear retaliation even if the whole hierarchy of Soviet leadership perished.

And by Hugh Sidey in *Time,* January 15, 1992, describing the equipment of the latest model of Air Force One:

> Refrigerator-freezers will hold provisions to feed the 23 crew and 70 passengers for about a week. The plane could function that long on the ground or be refueled in the air should the land be scorched or otherwise inhospitable—a Strangelovian concept the Air force will not abandon.

Sturm und Drang \ˌshtu̇rm-u̇nt-ˈdräŋ, ˌstu̇r-, -ənt-\ A late-18th-century German literary movement characterized by works of rousing action and high emotion that often deal with the individual's revolt against society. It is German for "storm and stress." Writers of the movement include Goethe and Schiller. Today, the term suggests turmoil or scenes heavy with emotion.

The term in use, by Edward Rothstein in the *New York Times,* October 26, 1997, on the ongoing battle over funding for the National Endowment for the Arts:

> It is too soon to say if the annual Sturm und Drang will achieve its threatened goal, but here is a working critic's confession: if this perpetual drama actually reaches its final wrenching cadences, it will be a relief.

And by Jerry Roberts in the *San Francisco Chronicle,* December 24, 1995:

> Despite all the Sturm und Drang, the GOP has yet to pass a single substantive piece of the Contract With America. . . .

And by Jeff Goodell in *Rolling Stone,* June 16, 1994, in a profile of Steve Jobs:

> Friends say the Sturm und Drang of the past few years has humbled Jobs ever so slightly; he is a devoted family man now, and on weekends, he can often be seen Rollerblading with his wife and two kids through the streets of Palo Alto.

Styx \\'stiks\\ The principal river of the underworld in Greek mythology. It is the river over which Charon the boatman ferries the spirits of the dead; the Greeks and Romans placed a coin in the mouth or the hand of the deceased to serve as fare. It is the river by which the gods would swear their most binding oaths; a god who broke faith would have to drink the dread waters of the river, and then would lie speechless for a year.

It was also the name of a rock group of the 1970s, which was revived in the 1990s.

The term in use, by Franz Lidz, *Sports Illustrated,* September 9, 1996:

> There may be no more potent a symbol of mythic malevolence than New York City's subway system. Many of us would rather cross the River Styx on a leaky inner tube than descend into underground Manhattan at, say, 2 a.m.

And from Stephen Hunter, film critic of the *Baltimore Sun,* describing Christopher Walken in *The Prophecy,* September 2, 1995:

> With henna-black hair and a chalky-white face and those haunted, depthless blue eyes, he seems less an angel than a hipster back from the jazz clubs on the other side of the River Styx.

sulk in one's tent To be moodily silent and refuse to take part in important activities because of a perceived slight or petty grievance.

This reference comes from the *Iliad,* Homer's epic poem of the Trojan

War. It wasn't his vulnerable heel that caused the Greek superhero Achilles to retreat to his tent, but a quarrel over honor and a girl. He and Agamemnon, king of Mycenae and one of the leaders of the Greek expedition against Troy, fought over personal honor manifested in a quarrel over a slave girl. Achilles, in a fit of pique, withdrew from the fighting. The Greeks suffered serious reverses as a result.

The term in use, by Barbara Tuchman in *The Proud Tower* (1966), describing the predominance of belligerent nationalism in imperial Germany at the beginning of the 20th century:

> The other Germany, the Germany of intellect and sentiment, the liberal Germany which lost in 1848 and never tried again, had withdrawn from the arena, content to despise militarism and materialism and sulk in a tent of superior spiritual values.

Another example, from David Falkner, writing in the *New York Times,* May 22, 1989, on difficulties experienced by Latin American baseball players in the United States:

> For more than a year after that, Valenzuela, an enormously proud man from Mexico, was reluctant to speak English. He declined all interviews with the English-speaking news media; he turned an impassive face to a public already swept up in "Fernandomania," and he cast a wary eye around the clubhouse.
>
> But what might have turned into an Achillean sulk turned out to be a relatively minor incident on an ascending slope of acculturation that some, but not all, Latin American ballplayers in the United States successfully negotiate.

Sunday, Billy William Ashley Sunday (1862–1935), a fire-eating evangelical preacher who achieved great fame in the United States from 1910 to 1920. His name is synonymous with a roaring style of fundamentalist preaching, and he is often compared to the fictional Elmer Gantry. He was a professional baseball player before he experienced a religious conversion and became an evangelist.

Sunday's forte was performance: he was *very* loud and tremendously active on stage. As he put it, he "slid into third base for the Lord," and jumped, walked, and ran from one end of the platform to another. What the church needed, he said, was fighting men, not "hog-jowled, weasel-eyed, sponge-columned, mushy-fisted, jelly-spined, pussy-footing, four-flushing, charlotte russe Christians."

He campaigned vociferously for Prohibition but was uninterested in or opposed to social reform of other kinds. Sunday prospered at the Lord's work; collection plates were the size of dishpans at his revivals.

Billy Sunday invoked, by Mike Lupica, *Esquire,* September 1, 1996, interviewing Dallas Cowboys owner Jerry Jones:

> "Lots of people can get A's in prosperity," Jones says. "I like to think I grade out higher in adversity...."

He is getting revved up, Billy Graham-style. Or maybe Billy Sunday.

Another example, reported by Mark Hermann of *Newsday,* in the *St. Louis Post-Dispatch,* March 16, 1997, on Branch Rickey's role in bringing Jackie Robinson to the major leagues:

> Rickey was known in a lot of ways: Ohio farmboy; conservative Republican; "a mixture of Phineas T. Barnum and Billy Sunday" (*Time* magazine, 1947). . . .

And finally, from C.W. Gusewelle, in the *Kansas City Star,* August 7, 1995, meditating on the connection between virtue and a good golf game:

> I have never thought of him as particularly righteous. But if, as I believe, character is everything, it is plain he is right up there in a class with Cotton MATHER, Billy Sunday and the Caliph of Khartoum.

Svengali \sven-'gä-lē, sfen-\ One who attempts, usually with evil intentions, to persuade or force another to do his bidding.

The term comes from a character in George DuMaurier's 1894 novel *Trilby.* Trilby is a beautiful woman who falls under the power of the musician Svengali, a sinister fellow who uses hypnosis to turn her into a great singer.

The term in use, by Jerry Roberts in the *San Francisco Chronicle,* December 24, 1995:

> Once reduced to whining that he was still "relevant" in Washington, Clinton began his latest comeback by leading the nation through the Oklahoma City tragedy, then added a few foreign policy successes and a well-pitched performance, designed by Svengali adviser Dick Morris, in seeking the elusive middle ground in the still unfolding budget drama.

Another example, from Alyn Brodsky's review of *If This Was Happiness: A Biography of Rita Hayworth,* by Barbara Leaming, in the *Miami Herald,* February 4, 1990:

> Rita's fourth marriage, and by far her most self-destructive relationship, was to crooner Dick Haymes—"Mr. Evil," as he was known. . . . This incredibly loathsome LOUNGE LIZARD almost destroyed her career, as well as her reputation, before she managed to break his Svengali-like hold.

And by *Washington Post* publisher Katharine Graham in her memoir *Personal History* (1997) on her relationship with her husband:

> I had learned so much from him that I felt like Trilby to his Svengali: I felt as though he had created me and that I was totally dependent on him.

sweetness *See* WASTE ITS SWEETNESS ON THE DESERT AIR.

sweetness and light A hallmark of culture, a harmonious combination of beauty and enlightenment; or a state of reasonableness and amiability, or a situation in which those qualities prevail.

The phrase was popularized by British poet and critic Matthew Arnold (1822–1888) in his collection of essays *Culture and Anarchy* published in 1869. He believed that culture should strive for a combination of upright behavior and intellectual truth-seeking through understanding the best that has been thought and said.

The expression was originated by Jonathan Swift in *The Battle of the Books,* (1704), comparing poets to bees whose honey and wax provide "the two noblest things, which are sweetness and light."

The term in use, by Tom Callahan in *Time,* September 19, 1988:

> She is the standard this time. The Olympics will be considered a success if the course of international sweetness and light runs and jumps and generally glides along as smoothly as Jackie Joyner-Kersee.

And by Olin Chism in the *Dallas Morning News,* March 11, 1997:

> Kathleen Battle is reputed to be a difficult artist—so much so that she and the Metropolitan Opera had a stormy parting of the ways. But that's only backstage. Onstage—as in the Morton H. Meyerson Symphony Center on Monday night—all is sweetness and light and, above all, sheer beauty of voice.

And harking back to the apian origin of the expression, by Irene Virag in *Newsday,* June 10, 1996:

> Life isn't all sweetness and light—even if you're a honeybee.
> Instead, life is a case of hives. An absolute monarchy ruled by a single queen. A caste system dedicated to procreation. A society in which free will isn't even a passing buzz.

sword *See* FALL ON ONE'S SWORD.

sword of Damocles \\'da-mə-ˌklēz\\ An impending potential disaster.

In a Greek legend, Damocles was a hanger-on of Dionysius, ruler of the city-state of Syracuse. According to the story, the ruler grew tired of Damocles' constant speeches about his good fortune and invited him to a banquet where he was seated under a sword suspended by a single thread or strand of hair. Damocles was too terrified to move as Dionysius demonstrated that the fortunes of those who hold power are as precarious as the predicament in which he had placed his guest.

The term in use, by President John F. Kennedy in a speech to the United Nations General Assembly, September 25, 1963:

> Today, every inhabitant of this planet must contemplate the day when this planet may no longer be habitable. Every man, woman

and child lives under a nuclear sword of Damocles, hanging by
the slenderest of threads, capable of being cut at any moment
by accident or miscalculation or by madness. The weapons of
war must be abolished before they abolish us.

And by economist Alan Sinai, quoted in the *Washington Post,* October
30, 1988:

But, Sinai said, "the legacies of deficits and debt hang like a sword
of Damocles over the financial markets and the economy."

And by David Einstein, in the *San Francisco Chronicle,* March 11, 1995:

The stock of Borland International jumped yesterday after a federal appeals court lifted a cloud that had hung over the struggling software company like a sword of Damocles.

swords into plowshares *See* BEAT SWORDS INTO PLOWSHARES.

 *. . . a raucous city-hall donnybrook that was part melodrama, part **theatre of the absurd**. . . .*
—Michael Satchell

Talmudic \tal-ˈmü-dik, -ˈmyü-, -ˈmə-; täl-ˈmü-\ Having to do with the Talmud, the authoritative body of Jewish law, tradition, and learned commentary. In current use, the word is also used to describe any analysis or commentary that is highly technical, overly scholarly, esoteric, or mysteriously arcane or cryptic.

The Talmud, whose name comes from the Hebrew word meaning "teaching" or "instruction," is a vast compilation of Jewish oral law and a compendium of debate and commentary (and commentary on commentary on commentary) by scholars who have exhaustively studied and interpreted the Torah (the first five books of the Bible).

The Talmud fills 63 books and goes back more than a thousand years. Leo Rosten says in *The Joys of Yiddish* (1968), "The Talmud embraces everything from theology to contracts, cosmology to cosmetics, jurisprudence to etiquette, criminal law to diet, delusions and drinking. . . . It illustrates the ways in which Biblical passages can be interpreted, argued over, and reinterpreted. For over the sprawling terrain of the Talmud disagreements rage, views clash, arguments are marshaled, advanced, withdrawn. (The effect on the young Jews who studied Talmud was to encourage questioning, arguing, refinements of distinction and analysis.)"

The term in use, by James K. Glassman in the *Washington Post,* September 30, 1997, writing about the tax code:

> Even expensive tax lawyers can't understand it. That leaves IRS agents free to make their own Talmudic interpretations—and then take away your house.

By John Liscio in *U.S. News & World Report,* April 20, 1992:

> Discussions about the money supply can quickly enter the realm of Talmudic debate.

By Warren I. Cohen in the *Nation,* May 8, 1995:

> I'm troubled by Steel's argument for aiding Rwandan and Cambodian victims of genocide, but not Bosnian. His contention that events in Bosnia are characterized first and foremost by a fight over territory and were not initially genocidal in intent strikes me as uncharacteristically talmudic.

And by George Steiner in the *New Yorker,* August 28, 1989:

But [Paul] Celan goes much farther. His best poems make haiku seem wasteful. Their conciseness is such that the only legitimate way of reading them is by Talmudic and Cabalistic methods.

Tammany \'ta-mə-nē\; **Tammany Hall** Of or relating to a political organization that seeks municipal control by methods often associated with corruption and bossism.

The Tammany society was founded in 1789, one of many groups established to champion democracy and oppose what was seen as a resurgence of aristocratic tendencies. Tammany was a 17th century chief of the Delaware Indians noted for his wisdom; "St. Tammany" was the name of anti-British groups before the revolution, ridiculing loyalist societies named for saints. Most of these groups died out, but "Tammany Society, No. 1" became a political machine under Aaron Burr and played an important role in the election of Jefferson as president in 1800.

Tammany Hall became identified with graft and corruption later in the 19th century, with the activities of the Tweed Ring and subsequent political crooks.

The term in use, by Steven Thomma, of Knight-Ridder Newspapers, in the *Seattle Times,* September 19, 1997:

> In a speech taped without his knowledge and released by Americans United for Separation of Church and State, [televangelist Pat] Robertson held up the corrupt Tammany Hall regime of New York as a model of political muscle, ridiculed Vice President Al Gore as "Ozone Al" and suggested members of the press shoot themselves.

And by Martin F. Nolan of the *Boston Globe,* October 30, 1994, describing a political rally at Faneuil Hall in Boston:

> Suddenly, the echoes of marching feet rattled the Greek granite pillars of the 168-year-old marketplace. The carpenters' union had arrived, 500 strong, shouting "Kennedy, Kennedy, Kennedy." The senator's gloomy entourage brightened, one of them saying, "This is like a Tammany Hall torchlight parade."

Tara \'tär-ə\ The fictional Georgia plantation, home of the O'Hara family of Margaret Mitchell's novel *Gone With the Wind* (1936). By extension, Tara sometimes refers to the opulent way of life of the antebellum plantation owners of the South.

Tara was built by Gerald O'Hara, the father of the novel's heroine, Scarlett. In times of crisis it is to Tara that Scarlett returns, and Tara which she fights to preserve. Tara survives the Civil War, thanks to the energy, adaptability and unscrupulousness of Scarlett.

The term in use, by Marshall Ingwerson, in the *Christian Science Monitor,* July 13, 1988:

If Scarlett O'Hara lived today, she might be a realtor in suburban Gwinnett County, selling tract Taras to Northerners, and never looking back.

And from Patricia Leigh Brown, for the New York Times News Service, in the *Deseret News,* January 5, 1997:

Jenrette's tastes run to Corinthian columns and killer staircases. A North Carolina native, he has restored seven houses of Tara-like grandeur. . . .

And from John Mariani, in *Wine Spectator,* June 30, 1996:

Couples out for the evening will find the opulent decor of gold curtains, marble pillars, pastoral murals and a grand staircase worthy of Tara . . . much to their romantic inclinations.

tar baby Something from which it is nearly impossible to extricate oneself.

In Joel Chandler Harris' famous *Uncle Remus* children's stories, the tar baby is a doll covered with tar. Brer Rabbit comes by and speaks to it, but the tar baby doesn't answer; Brer Rabbit gets angry and hits the tar baby, and sticks to it. The more Brer Rabbit struggles to get free, the tighter he sticks to the tar baby.

The term in use, by Richard T. Cooper in the *Los Angeles Times,* April 21, 1996:

Far from bestriding the Washington scene like a master or painting Clinton into corners, Dole last week looked a lot like the rabbit who wrestled with the tar baby.

And by Lance Morrow in *Time,* August 26, 1996:

Before Johnson fell for the tar baby of Vietnam, Americans believed their Presidents almost always told them the truth.

Teapot Dome A scandal involving government corruption. Also something of a measuring stick; newspaper writers like to say things like "the worst scandal since Teapot Dome." Watergate and more has come along since, but Teapot Dome still has some resonance.

Teapot Dome, Wyoming, and Elk Hill, California, are oil fields designated as reserves for the U.S. Navy. During the presidency of Warren G. Harding (1921–1923), Interior Secretary Albert B. Fall took jurisdiction over the reserves and then secretly issued leases allowing private oil companies to take oil out. The oil company executives showed their appreciation by paying Fall hundreds of thousands of dollars in gratuities.

The leases weren't secret for long; a Senate committee and special commission investigated. Fall, convicted of bribery, became the first Cabinet officer to be sent to prison.

The term in use, by Rep. James Leach (R-Iowa), discussing the savings and loan scandal of the 1980s, quoted in *Time,* June 12, 1989:

House Banking Committee member Jim Leach, an Iowa Republican who refuses to take PAC money, believes this may be the disgrace that brings down the current congressional establishment. "We're looking at an eleven-figure fraud story that's bigger than Teapot Dome," he says.

And by Ross K. Baker in the *Los Angeles Times,* January 31, 1997, on campaign financing scandals of 1996, under the headline "Perspectives on Campaign Finance: First, Teapot Dome; Now Coffee Pot Clinton:"

If the Teapot Dome was symbol of corruption in 1924, the kaffeeklatsch has become emblematic of the fund-raising excesses of 1996.

And by Marvin Kitman in *Newsday,* August 10, 1995:

What has been going on in Congress with this Telecommunications Act of 1995 is the biggest giveaway of public assets in history. It makes the Teapot Dome Scandal of 1921, the giveaway of oil reserves in Wyoming and California, seem like a tempest in a teapot dome.

tectonic plates The huge blocks that make up the crust of a planet, such as the earth, or moon. There are thought to be 12 or more immense plates that drift slowly on the molten rock far below the surface of the earth. The shifting apart or together of these plates results in the formation of continents, mountains, and volcanoes and such events as earthquakes. The expression has come to describe powerful and opposing social forces that produce profound changes and conflict.

The term in use, by political commentator Kevin Phillips in the *Los Angeles Times,* December 3, 1995:

That growing rumble from the tectonic plates of U.S. politics may keep building through next November's election.

And by Lance Morrow in *Time,* August 26, 1996, recalling the rioting at the 1968 Democratic convention in Chicago:

In front of the Hilton, on Michigan Avenue, two sides of America ground against each other like tectonic plates. Each side cartooned and ridiculed the other so brutally that by now the two seemed to belong almost to different species.

terpsichorean Of or relating to dance. The word is taken from the name of Terpsichore (meaning "dance-enjoying"), the inspiration and patroness of dancing and choral song, and the name is also applied to female dancers.

Terpsichore was one of the nine Muses of Greek mythology. The Muses were daughters of Zeus. Each Muse was identified with a branch of the arts and sciences. The chief of the muses was Calliope (meaning "beautiful-voiced"), who was the inspiration of heroic poetry and eloquence and after whom the tootling steam organ was named.

The term in use, by Jack Kroll in *Newsweek,* June 26, 1995:

> In an amazing dance sequence, Carrey envelops nightclub tootsie Cameron Diaz in a cyclonic fandango, his legs twisting into terpsichorean taffy as he whirls and hurls her in an ecstasy of motion.

And by Peter Steinhart in *Audubon,* July–August 1991:

> The birches are spotlessly white. The willows weep in terpsichorean chorus. The lawns are lush, emerald green and deep enough to swim in.

Also by Allan Ulrich in the *San Francisco Examiner,* August 10, 1987:

> Moscow's Bolshoi Ballet headed south to Los Angeles Sunday afternoon after infecting this town with six days of good, old-fashioned balletomania, the kind of terpsichorean frenzy the Bay Area hasn't experienced since Mikhail Baryshnikov's first visit with American Ballet Theatre more than a decade ago.

terrible beauty A phrase taken from "Easter 1916," a poem by William Butler Yeats.

The poem commemorates the Irish Nationalist insurrection against British rule at the Dublin post office, and other strategic points in the city, which resulted in several hundred deaths and the execution of the leaders. The event moved Yeats deeply, and he pays tribute to the ordinary men and women who were transformed by their action:

> All changed, changed utterly:
> A terrible beauty is born.

The expression is often used to refer to the unleashing of a destructive or transforming force, which nevertheless may be beautiful as it destroys—the mushroom cloud of an atomic bomb comes to mind.

The term in use, by Christopher Wintle in the *Times Literary Supplement,* October 5–11, 1990:

> Although it deploys a language reduced to a rubble of scatological shards, it never finds a terrible beauty within its vernacular, but remains rawly functional, and indeed, rather less witty than it might have been, given the resources of Cockney slang.

And by John Updike in *Hugging the Shore: Essays & Criticism* (1983):

> Vonnegut's come-as-you-are prose always dons a terrible beauty when he pictures vast destruction.

And in *Time,* March 9, 1998, in a description of the explosion of the space shuttle *Challenger:*

> A terrible beauty exploded like a primal event of physics—the birth of a universe; the death of a star; a fierce, enigmatic vio-

lence out of the blue. The mind recoiled in sheer surprise. Then it filled with horror.

Tet The Vietnamese New Year observed for three days beginning at the first new moon after January 20. The term *Tet offensive* describes a sudden, unexpected, and demoralizing assault that results in a material and a psychological defeat.

In the original, at 3 a.m. on January 31, 1968, Vietcong guerrillas and North Vietnamese attacked more than 100 military bases and civilian centers in South Vietnam, including the imperial capital of Hue. One assault team even managed to penetrate the U.S. embassy compound in Saigon.

Although the Tet offensive ended in a military defeat for the communists, the attack had a devastating psychological effect in the United States. Anti-war feelings had been growing, and the offensive seemed to belie government assurances of victory in the war.

An example of the term in use, by Reagan administration security advisor Robert McFarlane, as quoted in the *Washington Post,* May 14, 1984:

> Cuba has decided to roughly double the guerrilla force in El Salvador in hopes of mounting a "Tetlike" offensive there during the U.S. presidential race this fall, national security advisor Robert C. McFarlane charged yesterday.

And by Ed Siegel of the *Boston Globe,* October 4, 1993, reporting on a coup attempt against the Russian government of President Boris Yeltsin:

> Even as Yeltsin was responding to the crisis last night, there were indications that yesterday's events might be to Yeltsin what the Tet offensive in Vietnam was to Lyndon B. Johnson.

theater of the absurd Theater that seeks to represent the absurdity of human existence in a meaningless universe by bizarre or fantastic means.

This was the name of an avant-garde theatrical movement that developed after World War II. While playwrights dealt with timeless themes such as the human reaction to death, loneliness, and freedom, they presented them in shocking, outrageous, and nonsensical ways to reveal the absurdity of the human condition and the futility of trying to cope with it. Chief dramatists of the movement were Samuel Beckett (*Waiting for Godot*) [*q.v.*], Jean Genet (*The Maids, The Balcony, The Blacks*), Eugene Ionesco (*The Bald Soprano*), and Edward Albee (*The Zoo Story*).

The term in use, by Paul Johnson in his 1977 book, *Enemies of Society:*

> In a world where real distinctions are being deliberately eroded or inverted by pseudo-science, where reason is derided, knowledge assassinated and the most fundamental principles of civilization assaulted, we must not be surprised to find that the United Nations, the fount of international authority—such as it is—should have become the World Theatre of the Absurd, a global madhouse where lunatic falsehood reigns and the voices of

the sane can scarcely be heard above the revolutionary and racist din.

And by Michael Satchell in *U.S. News & World Report,* December 14, 1987:

> In the metropolis that traditionally sets the pace for bare-knuckled politics, backroom chicanery and unabashed power plays, Chicago's selection of a temporary successor to the late Mayor Harold Washington climaxed last week in a raucous city-hall donnybrook that was part melodrama, part theater of the absurd and—dare it be said—splendid public entertainment.

And in a variation, by Marianne Means of Hearst Newspapers, in the *Deseret News,* September 1, 1997:

> In the politics of the absurd, the clown is king. What else explains House Speaker Newt Gingrich's road test of what looks like a campaign for the GOP presidential nomination in 2000?

there's the rub *or* **here lies the rub** A phrase meaning, "there lies the difficulty." It usually refers to a stumbling block or the crux of a problem.

While this meaning was not coined by Shakespeare, the phrase was made famous in *Hamlet.* In Act 3, Scene 1, Hamlet speaks his famous "To be or not to be" soliloquy in which he muses on death as a sleep in which one may end life's heartaches and be at rest. But there's a catch:

> To sleep, perchance to dream. Ay, there's the rub;
> For in that sleep of death what dreams may come,
> When we have shuffled off this mortal coil,
> Must give us pause.

The term in use, by Jinx Morgan in *Bon Appetit,* August 1994:

> Of course, just because we don't feel like cooking doesn't mean we're ready to give up eating. And there's the rub. Yes, there are restaurants. And take-out emporiums can provide the wherewithal for a no-fuss feast on a sweltering evening. But in time, even those practical solutions begin to pall.

And by Sherry Roberts in *Compute,* November 1991:

> And there's the rub: How can a home office worker create a comfortable, efficient, and productive work environment next door to the laundry room with the rattling washer or adjacent to the nursery with the colicky baby?

And from Andrea Martin in *Utne Reader,* May–June 1996:

> Service-learning isn't really volunteering, though, when it is required for high school graduation—and there's the rub. Americans generally applaud community service, but make that service mandatory and sizzling controversy erupts.

Thermidor \\'thər-mə-ˌdȯr\ A moderately conservative reaction following the excesses of a revolution. The climactic events of the French Revolution that brought about the end of the REIGN OF TERROR are sometimes called a "Thermidorian reaction." Thermidor was the name of a month, running from July 19 to August 17, in the renamed revolutionary calendar. During that month in 1794 the Revolution finally snapped at its moment of greatest tension. Many of its leaders had already been sent to the guillotine and those left realized they would be next if ROBESPIERRE continued in power.

The deputies of the National Convention turned on him, and he was executed. The REIGN OF TERROR subsided, the Jacobin Club was disbanded, and the power of the Committee of Public Safety was reduced. Into the vacuum moved "men of Thermidor"—ex-revolutionaries and other opportunists—and a period of corruption and instability followed. The weak republic established in 1795 lasted until Napoleon's coup in 1799.

The term in use, by George Will, in the *Washington Post,* October 3, 1996:

> Conservative critics of the 104th Congress complain that it went directly from the ANCIEN RÉGIME to Thermidor, without any intervening revolution.

Another example, from Israel Spiegler, in the *Economist,* June 17, 1995:

> Two years ago Russia's government of radical reformers was replaced by the grey men who still surround Viktor Chernomyrdin, the prime minister. Will Russia's Thermidor turn out to be the prelude to rule by a soldier-turned-tsar?

And from Bruce Fein, in the *Washington Times,* July 11, 1995:

> The 1994–95 term of the U.S. Supreme Court has been lugubriously likened by many to a counterrevolution in constitutional law as dramatic as the 9th of Thermidor.

thermodynamics *See* SECOND LAW OF THERMODYNAMICS.

Thermopylae \(ˌ)thər-'mä-pə-(ˌ)lē\ The site in ancient Greece of one of history's great battles, the courageous stand of the Spartans, vastly outnumbered, against the invading Persians.

Thermopylae is a pass through the mountains on the east coast of central Greece.

In 480 B.C., a small army under King Leonidas of Sparta held the pass against the huge invading force of Xerxes, the Persian king. Guided to another path by a traitor, the Persians ultimately outflanked and overwhelmed the Spartans. Leonidas by then had sent most of his army to safety but remained to hold the pass as long as possible with his band of three hundred crack troops, joined by seven hundred Thespians. (Did Leonidas recruit unemployed actors to support his stand? Not quite. The Thespians were from the city of Thespiae.)

The defenders' valiant stand is still remembered and is commemorated in the epitaph composed by the poet Simonides:

Go tell the Spartans, thou who passest by
That here obedient to their laws we lie.

The term in use, by Francis X. Clines in the *New York Times,* October 2, 1997, writing about the fight led by Sen. Mitch McConnell, R-Ky., against campaign reform legislation:

"His opposition to campaign reform is not simply an innocent defense of the First Amendment," Ann McBride, president of Common Cause, insisted as Mr. McConnell unapologetically prepared for another Thermopylae stand next week against the passage of the bill.

And by Robert Reno in *Newsday,* Febuary 22, 1989, in a column on the federal budget deficit:

But you'd think Bush was defending the pass at Thermopylae. You'd think he was saving us from some hideous fate, from an invasion of carnivorous green slugs, from the toad that ate Nebraska. And all because he figured that a plea not to increase taxes to adequate levels was a pretty neat way to get elected.

And by John Borrell in *Time,* May 30, 1988, on fears about killer bees in Texas:

But the Texans' growing unease is understandable: unless the bees are headed off or at least slowed down, they may reach the Texas border as early as next year. Mexican and American scientists are doing their level best to keep that from occurring. Near the narrowest part of southern Mexico, where the rugged Sierra Madre sweeps close to the coast, they have prepared a stand against the marauders, a kind of apiarian Thermopylae.

thin red line A small but valiant line of defense; a small group standing between victory and defeat.

The term was probably coined by William Howard Russell of the *Times* of London, one of the first war correspondents, who applied it to the brave—and successful—stand of the 93rd Highlanders against the Russians at the battle of Balaclava in the Crimean War. (The war, 1853–56, pitted Russia against Turkey, England, France, and Sardinia over Russian influence in the Middle East. The allies won after a long siege of Sevastopol, the base of the Russian fleet. Balaclava was a key victory. The war is remembered for the disastrous CHARGE OF THE LIGHT BRIGADE, also at Balaclava, and for the nursing reforms of Florence Nightingale.)

Russell watched the battle from a distant hill and wrote: "The Russians charged in toward Balaclava. The ground flew beneath the horses' feet; gathering speed at every stride they dashed on towards that thin red streak

tipped with steel." (Russell later changed the wording to "line.") The Highlanders waited until the thundering ranks of horses were within range and
fired; the Russians retreated in confusion. After this incident, the regiment was called "the thin red line."

Rudyard Kipling immortalized the phrase in "Tommy," a tribute to the
unappreciated ordinary British soldier:

> Then it's Tommy this, an' Tommy that,
>   an' "Tommy, 'ow's yer soul?"
> But it's "Thin red line of 'eroes"
>   when the drums begin to roll. . . .

The title of a 1988 documentary-detective film, *The Thin Blue Line,*
makes a play on the phrase. A Dallas prosecuting attorney used the
amended version in the trial of a man accused of murdering a police officer: "the thin blue line of men and women who daily risk their lives by
walking into the jaws of death. . . ."

America's West Point has a related phrase, "the long gray line," referring to the generations of graduates of the United States Military Academy.

The term in use, by syndicated columnist Charles Krauthammer,
appearing in the *Charlotte Observer,* September 12, 1993:

> With the humanitarians in office, it is public opinion that is keep-
> ing us out of major trouble. Public opinion makes for a thin red
> line. But any red line is better than none.

And an example of *thin blue line* by Les Payne in *Essence,* November
1992:

> Integrating the force, however, won't completely eliminate police
> criminality or the so-called "thin blue line," the we-versus-them
> mentality that creates an insurmountable wall between cops and
> the citizens who pay their salaries.

third rail A metal rail through which electric current is led to the motors
of an electric vehicle such as a subway car. The electrical charge is lethal,
and in politics the term is applied to "killer issues," especially to any question of changing the Social Security system. Hence the characterization
of the program as the "third rail" of American politics: "Touch it and you
die."

The term in use, by Jason DeParle in the *New York Times Magazine,*
July 14, 1996, on the abortion issue:

> [Ralph] Reed's experience in touching the third rail eerily pre-
> saged Dole's.

And from Jerry Useem, in *Inc.,* December 1, 1996, on business success
among the Amish:

Lawyers, for example, constitute a sort of third rail in Amish business: get near one and you're toast, excommunicated by the church and shunned by all.

Also, from Jill Lawrence of the Associated Press, February 20, 1995:

But [Labor Secretary Robert] Reich's fellow Democrats in the Clinton Cabinet reacted as if "corporate welfare" were a political third rail, as untouchable as Social Security.

third-rate burglary, a An attempt at criminal activity so lacking in sense or intelligence as to be laughable—but devastating by its very existence. Specifically, the Nixon administration's characterization of the Watergate break-in that ultimately led to Nixon's resignation. The expression is since used with heavy irony to imply that any attempt to minimize a transgression (usually a political one) is asking for trouble and to remind the world that what seems like a low-grade burglary can bring down a president.

The Watergate burglars were caught in the offices of the Democratic National Committee in the early morning hours of June 17, 1972. On June 20 White House press secretary Ron Ziegler said, "I'm not going to comment on a third-rate burglary attempt." Further investigation revealed a web of lies and criminal behavior.

The term in use, by Dan Morain, in the *Los Angeles Times,* July 11, 1997:

In the annals of political intrigue, Assemblyman Carl Washington's statement earlier this week that he voted for one lawmaker's bill because that lawmaker supported one of Washington's bills wasn't even a third-rate burglary.

And by political commentator William Safire on corruption in the Clinton White House, in a *New York Times* column, June 26, 1996:

Only when threatened with jail for contempt of Congress did the former Gore aide hand over a document that led to revelations of political snooping into private lives, which the president tried to kiss off as a "bureaucratic snafu" (Clintonese for "third-rate burglary").

thirty pieces of silver The price of betrayal.

Thirty pieces of silver was the payment received by Judas Iscariot for betraying Jesus to the Roman soldiers with a kiss. He received his payment but repented and returned it to the priests and then hanged himself. Christian tradition and Western literature have made Judas an arch-villain; for example, he is at the center of the Earth in Dante's *Inferno,* chewed in Satan's mouth along with Brutus and Cassius, betrayers of Julius Caesar. The name Judas and a "Judas kiss" are terms attached to betrayers and traitors.

The term in use, by Pepsico chief Roger Enrico, quoted by Patricia

Sellers in *Fortune,* October 28, 1996, on the defection of an important Pepsi bottler to Coca-Cola:

> Roger Enrico is still trying to make sense of the caper in Caracas, a first-of-its kind raid. "This guy was a personal friend," Enrico says of Oswald Cisneros, 55, the Venezuelan who headed one of Pepsi's largest and oldest foreign bottling franchises. "Ozzie took his 30 pieces of silver and ran."

And again, from Larry Woody, Gannett News Service, September 9, 1994:

> After assuring Tennessee fans he wasn't leaving for the money, but rather to pursue his boyhood dream of playing in the NFL, [Tennessee quarterback Heath] Schuler promptly snubbed a $16 million offer and a starting job with the Washington Redskins in order to squeeze out an additional $3 million.
> He got his extra 30 pieces of silver, but sacrificed his dream starting job and a lot of fan admiration in the process.

thought police Intolerant enforcers of a narrow orthodoxy of ideas and action. Also the more diffuse but powerful social pressure or fear of reprisal that inhibit the free expression of nonconforming ideas.

Yet another term which originates with George Orwell's *Nineteen Eighty-four,* where the thought police rooted out nonconformist ideas ("thoughtcrime") in Oceania. They were able to spy on everyone everywhere through the ubiquitous telescreens. The telescreens could broadcast, but they could also watch and listen. Everyone was encouraged to inform the authorities of insidious thoughts or deeds. Children, who terrified adults with their zealotry in accusing others of mental crimes, were especially adept.

The term in use, by Karl Schoenbarger in *Fortune,* May 27, 1996:

> In the long run it's doubtful that Beijing's thought police have the manpower or the sophistication to muzzle the Internet. Insists maverick Hong Kong publisher Jimmy Lai: "They can pee on the Internet, but they can't control it."

And by columnist Lars-Erik Nelson in *Newsday,* February 7, 1995:

> BIG BROTHER Larry Pressler (R-S.D.) has been chairman of the Senate Commerce Committee for only five weeks, but he has already set himself up as head of the Thought Police. Pressler's target is public broadcasting, which he wants to bend to his own world view—on pain of death.

And by conservative journalist David Brock, on his conservative critics, quoted by Howard Kurtz in the *Washington Post,* July 22, 1997:

> Some conservatives, he says, didn't want to be bothered by the facts, and the "thought police" turned on him.

thousand cuts *See* DEATH BY A THOUSAND CUTS.

"thou shouldst be living at this hour" A line from William Wordsworth's "To Milton," "Milton! Thou shouldst be living. . . . " The name of another is frequently substituted for Milton, as in "You should see *this*!"

Wordsworth evoked Milton in his youthful enthusiasm for the French Revolution, which had just begun across the Channel. He considered Milton a kindred revolutionary spirit opposing the tyranny of kings.

The term in use, in the *National Review,* December 30, 1991, mocking the defense in the rape trial of William Kennedy Smith:

> [Sen. Edward] Kennedy showed up commendably clean and sober for the trial and recited a typical litany of tribal sufferings. . . . Prosecutor Moira Lasch showed considerable restraint in not guffawing at this performance. Most of us have lost family members, but it is not common for grief to set off an emotional chain reaction, months later, terminating in sex on the lawn. Rube GOLDBERG, thou shouldst be living at this hour.

Another example, from Stanley Kauffmann's praise for actress Emma Thompson's performance in the film *Much Ado About Nothing* in the *New Republic,* May 10, 1993:

> Thompson then speaks the two words with which Ellen Terry is said to have stabbed the audience with ice: "Kill Claudio." Ellen, thou shouldst be living at this hour—to hear Emma.

Three Musketeers A trio of fast friends bound by love and honor to stand by each other and the cause they served. Characters in the 1844 novel by that title written by Alexandre Dumas; the name was later adopted by a candy bar and the story adapted by Walt Disney.

The hero of Dumas' novel is D'ARTAGNAN, a dashing but impressionable young man from Gascony who goes to Paris to serve in the King's Musketeers. After being challenged to several duels, he makes friends with the three greatest fighters in the brigade: aristocratic, melancholy Athos; strongman Porthos; and handsome, dandyfied Aramis. Under the motto "All for one and one for all," they perform many brave deeds to save the queen and foil the evil machinations of Cardinal Richelieu, the king's minister.

The musketeers, begun in 1661, formed an elite corps in the service of the king of France. The name comes from the early muskets with which they were armed. They fought both as cavalry and infantry, and in times of peace served as the king's bodyguard. In the Dumas novel the musketeers were intense rivals of the Cardinal's Guards.

The term in use, by Richard Corliss, in *Time,* October 21, 1996, reviewing the film *Swingers:*

> Mike's pals, the most attentive male support group since the Three Musketeers, shed tears of joy when he's lucky and apologize when they do wrong.

And from Tom Teepen, in the *Deseret News,* April 27, 1997:

> Remember those one-each army squads in World War II movies? . . . It was all-for-one-and-one-for-all time, the Three Musketeers writ not just large but continentally. In the movies the social abrasions were slight, usually more amusing than scratchy, and easily resolved in a gush of fellow feeling.

And from Jennifer Files, in the *Dallas Morning News,* March 26, 1995, writing on a Mexican activist group:

> El Barzon works like the Three Musketeers, Ms. Flores said: "All for one, and one for all."

three yards and a cloud of dust Slow, slogging, but steady progress from which victory or sense gradually emerge. A football expression forever associated with coach Woody Hayes of Ohio State University. Hayes coached at Ohio State from 1951 through 1978, and the formula for his considerable success was a grinding ground game powered by a battering-ram running back. Forget aerial pyrotechnics; OSU powered its way to victory with inexorable progress on the ground, play after play after play.

As with so many football metaphors, the phrase has now moved into other realms to sum up ground gained by unglamorous, brute force.

The term in use, by the Christian Coalition's Ralph Reed, on National Public Radio's *All Things Considered,* November 9, 1994, describing their political organizing efforts:

> But I think—even more than those three-yards-and-a-cloud-of-dust, nonpartisan, get-out-the-vote efforts—the environment, the political environment was conducive to these voters wanting to send a message to Washington. . . .

A play on the expression, from Jim Toledano, Democratic Chairman of Orange County, California, quoted in the *Los Angeles Times,* July 31, 1996, characterizing a speech by the Republican candidate for president:

> "This was typical Bob Dole, no yards and a cloud of dust," Toledano scoffed. "He had nothing to say of substance."

And by Democratic strategist James Carville, ratcheting up the allusion, quoted by Joe Klein in *Newsweek,* September 21, 1992:

> "The way to the goal line is to keep running off-tackle," says James Carville, Clinton's intermittently colorful Cajun strategist, lapsing into Young Republican sports metaphor. "Four yards and a cloud of dust."

throw down the gauntlet *See* GAUNTLET, THROW DOWN/PICK UP THE.

tilting at windmills Waging an idealistic fight with little hope of victory, or a battle against an imaginary foe.

The expression comes from the 1605 novel *Don Quixote* by Miguel de Cervantes, in which a kindly man who reads stories of chivalric adventures decides he should go forth and right the world's wrongs. (*See* QUIXOTE, DON.) Among Don Quixote's misadventures is a jousting encounter with windmills, which he sees as threatening giants. Spurring his nag Rocinante, he charges them with his lance, which becomes caught on the sail of one of the mills. Horse and rider are lifted off the ground and fall painfully to earth. (To tilt is to engage in a medieval fight between armor-clad men mounted on horses and armed with lances.)

The term in use, by Tom Horton in the *Baltimore Sun*, June 17, 1995, describing former Congressman and EPA official Peter Kostmayer:

> Others, including EPA insiders not unsympathetic to Kostmayer, argue that his firing was no simple matter of good vs. evil. They say he was a cage rattler in an administration that wanted consensus builders. He had a bent for tilting at windmills. . . .

And by Jonathan Yardley, reviewing a Judith Krantz novel in the *Washington Post,* August 3, 1988:

> Krantz has achieved the status of brand name, and her books sell automatically; there is nothing that we reviewers, tilting at windmills with our silly little lances, can do either to help her along to greater riches or to arrest her progress in that direction.

Tinker to Evers to Chance A masterful three-way move or maneuver. It comes from the names of three players with the Chicago Cubs in the first two decades of the 20th century, shortstop Joe Tinker, second baseman Johnny Evers, and first baseman Frank Chance. They were famous for their short-to-second-to-first double plays.

The term in use, by Carol Richards in *Newsday,* August 24, 1995:

> The wonderful thing about sisters is that they grow up to be aunts. Between my husband and me, we have three, and this summer the aunts pulled off a Tinker-to-Evers-to-Chance routine with our kids. Handed from Aunt Ruthie to Aunt Alice to Aunt Sandra, our two daughters had one of those summers that you probably recall from your own childhood—one that seemed to go on forever.

And from Matt Lait and Eric Bailey, in the *Los Angeles Times,* March 24, 1995:

> Among the obstacles are environmental hurdles that could hinder the waste disposal plans, political difficulties in winning approval of the half-cent sales tax increase and the nagging reluctance of state lawmakers to embrace loan guarantees.
>
> If the proposal went smoothly, Craven said, it would be akin to "a triple play that's better than Tinker to Evers to Chance."

Titanic A huge "unsinkable" ocean liner that sank on its maiden voyage after colliding with an iceberg. Now synonymous with catastrophe, especially one brought about by arrogant confidence in the power of technology.

On her maiden voyage, with 2,200 people aboard, the British ship struck an iceberg and sank in the North Atlantic on the night of April 14–15, 1912. More than 1,500 lives were lost. The *Titanic* was the most opulent and elegant liner ever made; its watertight bulkheads and a double-bottomed hull led to its claim of unsinkability. Confidence was such that she carried only enough lifeboats for half the people on board. The disaster remains one of the most haunting and riveting stories of tragedy at sea. Indeed, only recently has the wrecked ship been found and an epic film been made telling her story.

The calamity also gave rise to the expression, "rearranging the deck chairs on the *Titanic*," that is, spending time on inconsequential details when disaster looms.

The term in use, by Walter Williams in the *Kansas City Star,* September 1, 1997, commenting negatively on the discarding of constitutional limitations on government:

> Our kind of congressman or president is the person who cares; and has the deepest contempt for constitutional limitations.
> None of this means that we're going down the tubes as a great nation right away. After all, when the Titanic struck that iceberg, everything was OK . . . for a while.

And from Janet Maslin in a *New York Times* review of *Titanic,* December 19, 1997:

> The irony is that Mr. Cameron's *Titanic* is such a Titanic in its own right, a presumptuous reach for greatness against all reasonable odds.

And by Denny Wolfe in *English Journal,* September 1995:

> But this is a low-level, band-aid approach to a profoundly complex, long-term problem. While it may be a necessary approach to coping with school violence, if it's the only approach, it's just moving deck chairs around on the Titanic.

Torquemada \tȯr-kə-'mä-də\ Tomás de Torquemada (1420–1498), first grand inquisitor of the Spanish Inquisition, appointed by Innocent VIII (1487). It was Torquemada who persuaded Ferdinand and Isabella to expel Jews from Spain (1492). His name has become synonymous with arbitrary, notorious severity of judgment and cruelty of punishment.

The Spanish Inquisition was instituted about 1480 in Spain, a little later in its European and Latin American domains, to detect and punish heretics and anyone suspected of offenses against Roman Catholic orthodoxy.

The Inquisition's procedures were secret and arbitrary: the accused was issued a sudden summons and could be imprisoned on the merest suspicion of wrongdoing, and the names of witnesses against the accused were withheld. Torture was allowed, including the torture of witnesses. Punishment ranged from fines to penances to imprisonment, with the most obstinate heretics handed over to the secular authorities for execution, usually by fire. (*See* AUTO-DA-FÉ.)

In Spain, the Inquisition was closely linked to the crown and was used by the government to centralize its authority during the reign of Ferdinand and Isabella. Through the Inquisition the state eliminated potential opposition and also seized the property of heretics, thus giving church and state a significant community of interest.

The term in use, by Alan Abelson, in *Barron's,* June 5, 1989:

> Perhaps we should have suspected long before that there was something different about the SEC [Securities and Exchange Commission]. Oh, sure, we were aware, of course, it had changed some since the days when Stanley Sporkin, a.k.a. Torquemada, was in charge of the rack and ate a broker for breakfast every morning.

And by columnist Nat Hentoff in the *Washington Post,* July 26, 1997, on efforts to impose content ratings on television programming:

> But Senator Joseph Lieberman (D-Conn.), the Torquemada of this censoring operation, could not restrain himself in a statement issued by his office: "We've tried to explain that you can put a label on garbage, but it's still garbage. . . ."

And by syndicated columnist Tony Snow in the *Detroit News,* January 6, 1997:

> Scandal has crept upon the U.S. Capitol ON LITTLE CAT FEET. . . . Democrats are turning Gingrich-bashing into an Olympic sport, and Republicans are preparing to conduct Torquemada-like inquisitions of Richard Gephardt, David Bonior, Bill Clinton, Hillary Rodham Clinton and anybody who has purchased so much as a frozen yogurt in the state of Arkansas.

totem An object such as an animal or plant, serving as the emblem of a family or clan, often as a reminder of its ancestry. Also a representation, usually carved or painted, of such an object. More generally, something that serves as a revered symbol. An Ojibwa word.

The tribes of what is now the Northwest of the United States and Canada carved these symbols into totem poles, which then filled such functions as commemorating the dead, identifying property, or mocking the mistakes of fellows or rivals.

In general use, the word is applied to the ways in which non-Native Americans display symbols—to make a point about themselves or to make points about others.

The term in use, from Jim Robbins in the *New York Times,* September 22, 1996:

Elk are a totem animal in Jackson [Wyoming]. The town square is decorated with four large arches made entirely from thousands of bleached white elk antlers.

And by David Broder in the *Washington Post,* March 9, 1992:

... every candidate in the Republican and Democratic primaries pledges his efforts on behalf of the children. Education is the totem to which they all bow.

Another example, by David Maraniss in the *Washington Post,* October 7, 1996, describing the scene at a presidential campaign debate in which each camp augmented the audience with people of symbolic importance to its issues:

As a totem of another sort, the Dole camp also found a seat for Frank Carafa, who as a young sergeant in the 10th Mountain Division pulled a wounded Dole to safety on Hill 913 in Italy back in April 1946.

to the manner born A phrase from Shakespeare's *Hamlet,* Act 1, Scene 4, meaning "accustomed to a practice from birth." Hamlet, hearing the off-stage revelry which celebrates each drink taken by his uncle, the usurping king, acknowledges that although such excess is customary, he does not approve:

But to my mind, though I am native here
And to the manner born, it is a custom
More honour'd in the breach than the observance.

Over time the phrase has been stretched to refer to an aristocratic style or bearing, or upper-class birth and education. Often the reference becomes "to the *manor* born," as in being born to a hereditary estate. The confusion is understandable because of Hamlet's princely birth, but remember that Shakespeare had Hamlet speak disapprovingly of custom, not of a life of privilege.

The term in use, in Shakespeare's sense, by the actor Sir John Gielgud (who should know, having memorably performed as Hamlet himself) in the obituary of the actress Gwen Efragcon-Davies, in the *Manchester Guardian Weekly,* February 2, 1992:

Her numerous successes in costume plays—Richard of Bordeaux, Queen of Scots, The Lady with the Lamp ... showed her rare instinct for wearing period clothes to the manner born.

In the sense of privileged background, by Edwards Park in *Smithsonian,* September 1984:

Dillon Ripley—he never uses his first name, Sidney—is nearly six-feet-four and has the presence of someone to the manner born. He is generally affable and relaxed, a man who can make people feel comfortable very quickly. But there is steel beneath the courteous tone and mild demeanor.

And finally, the family estate reference, from Ann Butler, in the *Pittsburgh Press,* July 16, 1990:

At 42, New Yorker Jim Erwin has the Gatsbyesque [*see* GATSBY] of a man to the manor born. Who knows what his background is? This man looks the part.

touchstone A type of smooth, fine-grained, black siliceous stone once used to test the purity of gold and silver by the streak left on the stone when rubbed by the metal. A touchstone is also a test, criterion, or standard for determining quality or genuineness.

The term in use, quoted by Ari L. Goldman, in the *New York Times,* February 9, 1997:

The Holocaust ties aside, that would be consistent with her experience as a Czech emigré; she has often said that her touchstone in thinking about foreign policy was the West's failure to step in and stop Hitler in time.

And in a story from *Newsday* in the *Seattle Times,* April 19, 1996:

The contributions that raise the most bristle from Oklahomans are the ones that went to families whose grief was played out in newspapers and on television. These families, who became touchstones for the country's grieving, as a result received thousands of dollars in personal contributions.

And by Michiko Kakutani, in the *New York Times Magazine,* May 11, 1997:

And bathroom humor, personal-hygiene insults and stupid sex jokes are no longer confined to *Beavis and Butt-head* and *Married . . . With Children* but have become touchstones for more and more movies and sitcoms.

trailing clouds of glory A line from a poem by William Wordsworth, "Intimations of Immortality from Recollections of Early Childhood." The poet reflects on the beauty of new consciousness, the touch of divinity present in the newborn that is lost or dimmed as we grow older:

Not in entire forgetfulness,
And not in utter nakedness,
But trailing clouds of glory do we come
From God, who is our home:
Heaven lies about us in our infancy!

The term in use, by Carol Dunlap in the *Los Angeles Times,* February 13, 1995:

545 trial by ordeal

Although he and his fellow philosophers believed that children are morally perfect, born into this world "trailing clouds of glory," Bronson Alcott seems to have made an exception of his daughters, and most particularly Louisa May, whose strong will he consistently sought to subdue.

Another, more playful example, from Joan Dames, in the *St. Louis Post-Dispatch,* September 24, 1995:

Also saw Mary Lou and Bob Hess, trailing clouds of glory from the success of the Tower Grove House party the night before, which netted $40,000.

trail of tears The original Trail of Tears was the journey of the Native American tribes forced to migrate (1829–43) to new homes in Oklahoma Territory. The Cherokees in particular had adopted many of white society's ways, including a written constitution, but emulation did not protect them when gold was discovered on their Georgia land.

Pressure was strong to move the Cherokees, and a small group of them was induced to sign a treaty ceding all their lands east of the Mississippi. Most resisted, and took their case all the way to the Supreme Court, which found on their behalf. The Court's decision was not enforced by President Andrew Jackson, and the Cherokees and others were evicted by federal troops, who forced them to march without opportunities to rest. About 4,000 died, one of every four, many from cold, disease, and exhaustion.

More generally, a trail of tears is a cruel, unjust ordeal endured by a group that consequently suffers great loss.

The term in use, quoted by Richard Reeves of the Universal Press Syndicate, October 12, 1992, on conditions in Bosnia:

The Womens' Commission report, "Balkan Trail of Tears: On the Edge of Catastrophe," was bleak. It estimated that more than 350,000 women and children could be expected to starve or freeze to death this winter in Bosnia if the world relief community cannot find the will and the way to deliver shelter, fuel and food.

And by Charlie Peek in the Columbia (S.C.) *State*, October 13, 1991:

For the fragile plants, it's becoming a trail of tears. They are dying under the crush of visitors along the side of Grandfather Mountain near the Linn Cove Viaduct.

trial by ordeal A test that presents great challenges to patience and courage or to physical and mental endurance. Originally, the practice in ancient Anglo-Saxon and German law to test the guilt or innocence of a defendant by subjecting him or her to various forms of torture. The theory was that God would protect the innocent.

In Anglo-Saxon days tests included plunging the accused's hand into boiling water; reddened skin indicated guilt. Alternatively, the accused was bound hand and foot and tossed into a pond; only the guilty floated. The innocent sank but by then the issue was often moot. Other tests involved carrying red-hot iron or walking across red-hot plowshares. If the accused was lucky the test consisted of swallowing the "Corsned" or consecrated bread; if he or she choked, guilt was proven.

Most of these tests were abolished in England in the 13th century with the establishment of trial by jury, although they continued to be used in witchcraft cases.

The term in use, by George Cantor in commentary in the *Detroit News,* September 9, 1995:

> We dropped off our daughter, the freshman, at her dorm in Ann Arbor last week.
>
> I say dropped off, but it really was sort of a 12-hour trial by ordeal. Lofts had to be installed, carpeting laid, last minute shopping at the mall, cars unloaded and the accumulation of 18 years carried into the dorm.

And by *Boston Globe* columnist Thomas Oliphant, June 5, 1996, on the Whitewater investigations:

> This isn't trial by evidence, it's trial by ordeal, and the fact is that each wave of speculative frenzy that has dissipated without result has been followed by a backlash.

And again, by Elizabeth Valk Long of *Time,* in "A Letter to Our Readers," August 28, 1995:

> The People v. O.J. Simpson has proved to be a trial by ordeal for almost everyone, including reporters.

troglodyte \'trä-glə-ˌdīt\ A member of a primitive people dwelling in caves. A person with reclusive habits or outmoded or reactionary attitudes.

The term in use, by columnist Murray Kempton in *Newsday,* October 31, 1993:

> The other day a visitor wondered aloud how in reason Giuliani could spurn the riches of this chance to stand before the cameras with Marlin calling him a closet liberal from his right hand and Dinkins calling him a Reaganite troglodyte from his left. The gods hold no richer boon for a politician than to set him in the center to shine under assault from both extremes.

And by Doug Ireland, in the *Village Voice,* January 23, 1990:

> Many in the gay community and among the HIV-infected, as well as their families and friends, gave their votes to Dinkins in the primary above all because they thought he was the only candidate who'd give New York City a compassionate health commissioner to replace that moral troglodyte, Stephen Joseph.

And by Marshall Loeb in *Fortune,* August 7, 1995, writing about the questions that executive job recruiters ask:

> . . . but they still want to know how computer-literate you are. Expect questions like "How do you write your letters and memos?" One troglodyte killed his chances forever by replying, "I call my gal in to dictate."

Trojan horse Someone or something intended to defeat or subvert from within. An innocent facade which conceals a conquering force and fools the enemy into allowing it through their defenses.

The original was the strategy devised by the Greeks to conquer the city of Troy, as recounted in Homer's *Odyssey* [*q.v.*] and Vergil's *Aeneid.*

After an unsuccessful 10-year struggle, the Greeks came up with the ploy. They constructed a huge wooden horse, filled it with Greek warriors and left it outside the city's gates. The rest of the Greeks pretended to sail away, leaving behind Sinon, who posed as a Greek traitor and convinced the Trojans that the horse was an offering to the goddess Athena. She would protect Troy if the Trojans would bring the horse into the city.

The Trojans were warned of trickery by CASSANDRA (ignored, as always) and the priest Laocoön ("I fear Greeks even bearing gifts"), who was inopportunely strangled by sea serpents. So the warnings did no good, the horse was brought in, and the Greeks hidden in it emerged and opened the gates to admit their army.

The term in use, by Sylvia Moreno in the *Washington Post,* October 5, 1997:

> NOW and other women's groups have characterized the Promise Keepers movement as a "Trojan horse" for ultra-conservative anti-feminists.

And quoted by Hugh Dellios, in the *Seattle Times,* March 23, 1997, on Laurent Kabila, the leader of a successful insurgency in the Congo:

> "Kabila is a manifestation of frustration, but he also is a Trojan horse, led and backed by Rwanda and Uganda," said Guillaume Ngefa, president of the Zairian Association for Human Rights. "Even in the past, he never had an agenda. He only was fighting Mobutu. He just wants power."

trouble in River City A suggestion that difficulties are brewing beneath a seemingly placid, utterly normal surface.

The term comes from the 1957 musical comedy *The Music Man* by Meredith Willson. Con man Professor Harold Hill persuades the people of River City, Iowa, that their children can be saved from "trouble" resulting in delinquency and worse only through the formation of a boys' band.

River City, a placid turn-of-the-century town, is the last place where youth is likely to go astray, but Hill warns: "Either you're closing your eyes to a situation you don't wish to acknowledge or you are not aware of the caliber of disaster indicated by the presence of a pool table in your community." He describes the horrors to follow, as foreshadowed by certain sure warning signs: "The moment your son leaves the house, does he rebuckle his knickerbockers *below the knee*? Is there a nicotine stain on his index finger? A dime novel hidden in the corn crib? That's trouble with a capital T, and that rhymes with P; and that stands for Pool!"

The term in use, in an editorial in the *Philadelphia Daily News*, March 3, 1994:

> Tradition is what the Mummers Parade is all about, so tampering with it isn't something to be done lightly. Nonetheless, there's been trouble in River City. Crowds have fallen off, even when the weather isn't rotten on New Year's Day (which isn't very often).

And by William J. Bennett in *Commentary,* November 1, 1995:

> But there is trouble in River City, MAIN STREET, and in the Hamptons, too. And while the problems there are somewhat different in nature (e.g., prolific divorce instead of illegitimacy), they pose no less a threat to the nation's long-term prospects.

And by Ross Anderson in commentary in the *Seattle Times,* April 16, 1997:

> For the gas tax, there's trouble in River City. It's being shouted to death by a few suburban Republicans who would rather sit in traffic and bluster than support anything that begins with a "t" and rhymes with "facts."

true minds *See* MARRIAGE OF TRUE MINDS.

tumbrel *or* **tumbril** \'təm-brəl\ A farm tipcart. A vehicle used especially during the French Revolution to carry those condemned to death to a place of execution. Ever since, the word has been used to evoke the image of those being borne to execution.

The term in use, by the *Economist,* May 6, 1989, in reporting international statistics on use of the death penalty by different nations:

> In the three years to mid-1988 the countries in which the tumbrels rolled most tirelessly were Iran (743 executions or more), South Africa (537+), China (500+), Nigeria (439+), Somalia (150+), Saudi Arabia (140), Pakistan (115+), the United States (66) and the Soviet Union (63+).

Another example, also from the *Economist,* July 8, 1989:

> Today's revolutionaries all want to overthrow the ANCIEN RÉGIME of communism bloodlessly. Hardly any want to set the tumbrels rolling—which is just one reason that communists and noncommunists alike should be glad if they succeed.

And by Henry Louis Gates Jr. in an essay appearing in *Lure and Loathing* (1993):

> And this, too, has been a consistent dynamic of race and representation in Afro-America. If someone has anointed a black intellectual, rest assured that others are busily constructing his tumbril.

Tweedledum and Tweedledee Two individuals or groups that are practically indistinguishable.

These two are particularly likely to show up at election time. Inevitably two opposing candidates with similar views are compared to Tweedledum and Tweedledee to underscore the assertion that scant difference exists between them.

The Tweedle boys appear as fat little identical twins in Lewis Carroll's *Through the Looking-Glass* (1872). Carroll used but did not coin the names himself; they come from a satiric verse by John Byrom (1692–1763) mocking a quarrel between two groups of musicians whose real differences were very small.

The term in use, by John Leo in *U.S. News & World Report,* July 20, 1992, on apathy among younger voters:

> Other generations feel that they should vote, and many often troop dutifully to the polls to pull the lever for Tweedledum over Tweedledee.

And in a *Philadelphia Daily News* editorial, June 19, 1997, urging the governor to veto a bill which in the paper's view would make it harder for third-party candidates to get on the ballot, thus protecting incumbent legislators in both parties:

> Tom Ridge must take his cue from the Federalist Papers: Veto this try at making Tweedledum, Tweedledumber and their heirs proconsuls of the commonwealth forever.

And by Joy Hakanson Colby, emphasizing visual rather than ideological similarity, in the *Detroit News,* October 2, 1997, describing two famous Detroit Prohibition agents:

> They made quite a team, that Izzy and Moe. Equally short and rotund, they must have resembled Tweedledum and Tweedledee when they chased Detroit's notorious Purple Gang during the Roaring '20s.

twist slowly in the wind The abandonment of a political subordinate to suffer prolonged and politically fatal public agonies alone.

This is a phrase that originated in the Nixon-Watergate era. It was coined by John Ehrlichman, assistant to President Richard Nixon, discussing the treatment of L. Patrick Gray, whose nomination to be director of the FBI was under bruising attack in the Senate during March 1973.

On July 26, 1973, Sen. Lowell Weicker (R-Conn.) referred to the phrase during Ehrlichman's appearance before the Watergate committee, reading from a transcript of a taped conversation with White House counsel John Dean. As published in the *Washington Post,* July 27, 1973, Erlichman said, referring to Gray: "Let him hang there. Hell, I think we ought to let him hang there. Let him twist slowly, slowly in the wind."

The term in use, by columnist Mary McGrory, appearing in *Newsday,* August 12, 1993:

> Washington is still gabbing: Was Bob Kerrey taking malicious pleasure in making Bill Clinton twist slowly, slowly, for two days, or was he that rarest of birds in Washington, a man with a conscience who had no price?

Another example, from Robert Dvorchak, of the Associated Press, June 27, 1990, reporting reaction of a radio talk show host to President George Bush's decision to renege on his campaign pledge of no new taxes:

> "It was the topic," O'Brien said. "There is a sense of disappointment among his supporters. Those on the other side had a sense of let him twist slowly in the wind."

And in a *San Francisco Chronicle* editorial summing up the favorite pratfalls of the year, December 31, 1995:

> Former Senator Robert (The Tongue) Packwood, the priapic Oregon legislator-diarist, who recorded in exquisite detail his awkward sexual exploits and political peccadilloes. He twisted slowly and deliciously in the wind for months before resigning in disgrace. . . .

Typhoid Mary One who is by force of circumstances a center from which something undesirable spreads.

Typhoid Mary was a real person; her name was Mary Mallon. She was an Irish immigrant to America in the early years of the 20th century at a time when great public fears about epidemics coincided with fears about immigration and crowded, dirty conditions in cities. Mary Mallon was the first documented healthy carrier of typhoid in the U.S., and the only one to be quarantined for life.

She was a cook, which meant that she spread the infection while earning her livelihood. In 1907, approached by a health inspector, she chased him out of the house with a carving fork. She was then forcibly put in quarantine. She was released after three years and told not to go back to cooking. In 1915, she was discovered cooking at a New York maternity hospital after an outbreak was traced to the hospital and was returned to quarantine, where she remained until her death in 1938.

The term in use, by Marilyn Goldstein in *Newsday,* April 9, 1995:

> We also got to catch a 24-hour virus as well. I was the Typhoid Mary, I fear.

And from Marilyn Chase in the *Wall Street Journal,* October 3, 1994:

"As far as we know, a case of pneumonic plague hasn't traveled by air," Dr. Dennis notes. Even if this happens, experts say the nightmare scenario of a plague carrier infecting many people isn't likely; plague patients fall too ill and need urgent care too quickly to pose a Typhoid Mary-type threat.

*If I had to advise Washington on its policy in Latin American, I'd say . . . please stop being the **ugly American**.*

—Oscar Arias

über alles \͵üe-ber-ʹä-les\ Supreme, completely dominant, or the best. Taken from the German national anthem, "Deutschland über Alles" or "Germany Over All." The expression is often used with some other word or concept substituted for "Deutschland."

"Deutschland über Alles" was the German national anthem from 1922–45 and is strongly associated with Nazis and goose-stepping tyranny. "Über alles" attached to an idea thus suggests that its user wishes to mock a bullying, overweening pushiness or a single-minded attachment to an idea or goal.

The term in use, by Gerri Hirshey in the *Washington Post Magazine,* February 14, 1988:

> Call them coupleniks, these fortunate folks, these devotees to Coupledom Über Alles. They tend to be between 30 and 45, married or cohabitating. They tend to "dialogue" for hours on all details of their coupleness, their twin corduroys bulging with tile samples and paint chips.

And by Rob Pegoraro, in the *Washington Post,* May 29, 1996, comparing competitors Netscape and Microsoft:

> The results—a 6–0 victory for Netscape, with one tie—will no doubt reassure those who fear *Microsoft über alles.*

Ugly American The boorish Yankee abroad.

The term comes from *The Ugly American,* a 1958 collection of stories by William J. Lederer and Eugene Burdick, and is used to describe any overbearing American being offensive to the people of a foreign country. In the book, however, the ugly American was so called because of his appearance. In fact, he was a compassionate man who went into rural areas and wooed Asian peasants away from communism. But the theme of the stories was the alienation caused by the ignorance, greed, and arrogance of Americans in foreign places. And not only Americans have earned the title. The ability to be an obnoxious visitor in a foreign land may be universal.

The term in use, by Costa Rican President Oscar Arias in an interview with Tad Szulc in *Parade* magazine, August 28, 1988:

> If I had to advise Washington on its policy in Latin America, I'd say, "Please be nice—please stop being the ugly American."

And by Roger E. Hernandez in the *Oregonian* of Portland, Oregon, January 22, 1996:

> The Ugly American of legend has always been a right-wing brute—the retired Green Beret colonel who trains death squads . . . or the rapacious manager of a multinational's banana plantation. . . . But the left produces Ugly Americans, too. They are the Jane Fondas who once posed behind Vietnamese anti-aircraft guns that were shooting down American fliers.

And in use by sportswriter Tony Kornheiser, in the *Washington Post,* October 1, 1988, describing Korean anger over the behavior of American fans and athletes at the 1988 Olympic games in Seoul:

> It hasn't deterred some Americans from practicing what is construed—particularly by the contentious European press—as Ugly Americanism. . . . This behavior is beyond patriotism. It's about rudeness and the automatic right of way that Americans consider their birthright as they travel the world in a clumsy exuberance that other cultures take for bullying.

Uncle Tom An epithet applied to blacks who are deemed over-eager to win the approval of whites.

Uncle Tom was a character in Harriet Beecher Stowe's *Uncle Tom's Cabin* (1852) which dramatized the sufferings of slaves in America. The book was an instant sensation and best-seller and aroused tremendous emotion; when President Abraham Lincoln met Mrs. Stowe during the Civil War, he said, "So this is the little lady who made this big war."

While the prose was ordinary, the characters of the novel were vivid, and Stowe presented the dilemmas and distributed the failings of North and South with remarkable evenhandedness. Of the white Northerners who give shelter to the fugitive slaves, only a Quaker family is really Christian in practice; it is Uncle Tom who is Christlike in his unselfish gentleness, courage, and ultimate martyrdom. Nevertheless it is as an insult that his name lives on.

The term in use, by Alice Steinbach in the *Baltimore Sun,* December 31, 1995, in a profile of critic Stanley Crouch:

> It has also earned him a reputation as—depending on where you stand on the complex issues of race and class in America—either an independent thinker who shuns ideology of any kind or a neo-conservative, retro-assimilationist Uncle Tom.

And from Karen Grigsby Bates, in commentary in the *Los Angeles Times,* November 9, 1994:

> When Supreme Court Justice Clarence Thomas attended a round-table discussion recently with a small, carefully chosen group of black men and women, he startled his select audience with this pronouncement: "I am not an Uncle Tom."

And by Earl G. Graves, publisher of *Black Enterprise* magazine, in *How to Succeed in Business Without Being White* (1997):

> Those I recognize as having stood up for fairness and inclusion have generally done very well in their careers. Selfishness doesn't last. Uncle Toms don't last. Fearful people don't last. It's rare for the individual who only cares about himself or herself to get very far in the modern business world where relationships are so important.

unkindest cut, the The cruelest, most personally devastating injury or insult; often one inflicted by a person who is thought to be a friend.

The phrase comes from William Shakespeare's *Julius Caesar*. In his famous oration over the dead Caesar (Act 3, Scene 2), Mark Antony fires up the mob against Caesar's assassins. He displays the cuts in Caesar's clothing made by the murderers' daggers, and points to one made by Brutus, Caesar's friend (*see* ET TU, BRUTE?):

> For Brutus, as you know, was Caesar's angel.
> Judge, O you gods, how dearly Caesar lov'd him!
> This was the most unkindest cut of all;
> For when the noble Caesar saw him stab,
> Ingratitude, more strong than traitors' arms,
> Quite vanquished him.

The term in use, by blue-chip divorce lawyer Raoul Felder, interviewed on National Public Radio's *Weekend Edition,* January 23, 1994, on the verdict in the infamous Bobbitt case, in which a woman had cut off her husband's penis:

> Lawyers mean it's a precedent that other cases are going to follow, and I don't think so, and I don't think many women are going to off and make that unkindest cut of all.

And in its extended sense from Anthony Scaduto, *Newsday,* December 18, 1996:

> Chanting "Don't go in!" and "Go to the Whitney"—the unkindest cut of all—scores of Museum of Modern Art employees from clerks to curators walked picket lines yesterday on what was planned as a one-day walkout.

And, extended, in the *Los Angeles Times,* May 29, 1996:

> Santa Monica College vegetarians are having a cow.
> A controversy has been simmering for months between student vegetarians and campus administrators, but the dissolution last week of the Vegetarian Club as a student activity was the unkindest cut of all, said Ryan Flegal, who takes his meals politically.

usual suspects *See* ROUND UP THE USUAL SUSPECTS.

utopia A place of ideal perfection especially in laws, government, and social conditions. It is Greek, meaning "nowhere." "Utopia" was the title of Sir Thomas More's (*see* MAN FOR ALL SEASONS) vision of an imaginary island in which society operates according to More's humanist principles, in social, legal, and political harmony. The word, usually not capitalized, has been extended to refer also to indefinitely remote or imaginary places.

More was by no means the first to consider these ideas, but his name for them stuck and is still applied to visions or plans for ideal communities. The United States has seen many such movements and communities, from the Shakers to the Harmony Society in New Harmony, Indiana, to Amana in Iowa, and many others, up to and including the communal living experiments of our own time.

Dystopia is the opposite of utopia: a place where things are as bad as they can be.

The term in use, by Stephen Clutter, in the *Seattle Times,* March 11, 1997:

> Actually, a jaunt into politics seems only natural for the former television salesman named Paul Erdman, whose powers of persuasion once drew as many as 400 followers, including people who turned over riches to fund his vision of a Christian Utopia.

And from Marianne Means, Hearst Newspapers, in the *Kansas City Star,* January 19, 1997:

> But the current fiddling is a piecemeal approach that can never satisfy those panting for a mythical low-tax utopia.

And from H. Ross Perot, quoted in the *Christian Science Monitor*, March 26, 1992:

> Still, Perot articulates the dimensions of voter anger: "Can we agree that going $4 trillion into debt [since 1980] did not create utopia?" he asks.

*But it can't stop the faithful fans . . . from won-dering whether there is hope beyond this **vale of tears** . . . for the joy of a world championship.*

—David Briggs

vale of tears Mortal life here on earth as opposed to the happier state of affairs in heaven. According to the *Oxford Book of Quotations* the phrase is from an 11th-century prayer to the Virgin Mary;

> To thee do we cry, poor banished children of Eve;
> To thee do we send up our sighs, mourning and weeping in this vale of tears.

The term in use, by Herbert Gold in the *New York Times Book Review,* April 15, 1984:

> Career crisis and the death of his mother have taught him much. This temporal world, this vale of tears and unexercised options, must be redeemed by individual virtue.

Another example, from David Briggs of the Associated Press, March 31, 1994, meditating on whether there is baseball in heaven:

> But it can't stop the faithful fans of teams like the Chicago Cubs and Boston Red Sox from wondering whether there is hope beyond this vale of tears on Earth for the joy of a world cham-pionship.

Valhalla \val-ˈha-lə *also* väl-ˈhä-\ The great hall in Norse mythology where the souls of heroes slain in battle are received. These heroes go out every day and fight each other just for fun, then return to Valhalla in the evenings, their wounds magically healed, to feast mightily on boar and quaff gallons of mead, a sweet wine made from fermented honey. The term is used today, often ironically, to describe the reward or place of honor for heroic (or very anti-heroic) combatants.

The term in use, by Rupert Christiansen in *Vanity Fair,* May 1989, describing the battle over the directorship of the Opera Bastille of Paris, playing full blast on the Nordic mythology themes of WAGNERIAN opera:

> Five months later the Wagnerian context for this meeting had come to seem all too appropriate. Valhalla, in the shape of a $350 million opera house, stood awaiting its finishing touches, but Daniel Barenboim was barred from crossing the rainbow bridge that led to its portals. From the wings, in apocalyptic unison, a chorus of front pages in Paris, London and New York rallied to his cause.

And by Ty Burr in *Entertainment Weekly,* August 22, 1997:

> We have our Valhalla in the late 20th century. . . . It's called the
> Web, and if it's more of an untidy democratic shopping mall than
> the Viking version, it's no less unreal. And it holds the digital
> ashes of our demigods just fine.
>   Take Jimmy Stewart. While the loving tributes that hit print
> last month will have long been recycled into fresh pulp come
> fall, the respectful Jimmy's Page (www.skynet.co.uk/~goddard/
> homepage.htm) . . . will be there as long as Britain's Merve God-
> dard keeps paying his server-host bill.

And by John le Carré in *Johns Hopkins Magazine,* August 1986, writing
about his fictional spy character George Smiley:

> Smiley has not been heard of since. If he has left the stage for
> good, then he has left it, for me, as an enigma, with the biggest
> question of his life and mine still unresolved—yet taking with
> him, as he lumbers away to his spies' Valhalla, the bulk of my
> work in his shabby briefcase.

Valley Girl A pampered, vacuous, suburban teenage girl with a passion
for shopping. She speaks a patois of high-school and surfer slang heavily
laced with sarcasm. The species was first observed in the San Fernando
Valley of Southern California and made famous by the satirical 1982 record
"Valley Girl" by Moon Unit Zappa. The movie *Clueless* (1995) recast Jane
Austen's heroine Emma as a Valley Girl.
   Tom Dalzell notes in *Flappers 2 Rappers* that "The Valley girl and her
speech were a fascinating case of life imitating art imitating life. The model
of the Valley Girl was firmly based in reality, then subjected to exagger-
ation and parody; teenage girls who were predisposed to the Valley Girl
ethic embraced and built upon the caricature."
   The term in use, in David Walton's review of Joan Didion's novel *The
Last Thing He Wanted* in the *Detroit News,* August 14, 1996:

> The description is vintage Didion, the aging Valley Girl about to
> slide in over her head.

And by Barry Garron, TV critic of the *Kansas City Star,* September 9,
1995:

> The script just isn't that funny. Other members of her brood are
> more like exaggerated TV types than real kids. Neal (Meghann
> Haldeman), her teenage daughter with an unexplained male
> name, is a Midwestern Valley girl.

And finally, from George Will, in the *Washington Post,* May 26, 1997:

> The Republican leadership's downhill slouch into ludicrousness
> accelerated with last Tuesday's spectacle of Trent Lott doing his

act as a Sensitive '90s Man and sounding like a Valley Girl doing
an impression of former Congresswoman Patricia Schroeder.

van Winkle, Rip Fictional colonial Dutch-American noted for having
slept for 20 years. One who is completely out of touch with contemporary developments.

Rip van Winkle is the creation of Washington Irving in his collection
of tales *The Sketch Book* (1819–1820).

In colonial New York, easygoing Rip van Winkle takes to the woods to
escape his nagging wife. He stops to help a gnomelike little man struggling to move a keg; the man invites him to join other little men who are
drinking and bowling at ninepins. The liquor is strong stuff, and Rip goes
to sleep for 20 years, right through the Revolutionary War. He finally
awakes and returns home, astounded by the changes around him.

To be a Rip van Winkle, then, is to awake suddenly to profound changes
in one's surroundings. This may be due to absence or to absence of mind.

The term in use, quoted in the *Christian Science Monitor* by Laura Van
Tuyl, January 3, 1992:

> American Public Radio (APR) has shifted into "rescue mode"
> and through an arduous campaign of pilot programs and exper-
> iments is hoping to help stave off, if not reverse, the decline in
> the number of listeners to classical music on the airwaves. . . .
>
> "I call it the Rip Van Winkle Syndrome, where we're just wak-
> ing up after a long sleep and realizing that our audiences are
> going away," says Ruth Dreier, project director of APR's Classi-
> cal Music Initiative.

And from Richard Reeves, in commentary in the *Baltimore Sun*, March
24, 1995:

> During a closed committee meeting considering Mrs. Clinton's
> health-care plans, a Democratic senator of tenure and stature
> blurted out a Rip Van Winkle theory: "Jesus Christ! What we're
> dealing with here are two VISTA volunteers who went to
> Arkansas 20 years ago and came back here thinking it's still the
> '60s."

vast wasteland A desolate, extensive, unproductive environment.

Newton Minow, chairman of the Federal Communications Commission in the Kennedy Administration, used the expression in a speech to
the National Association of Broadcasters in 1961 to describe what he considered the lowest-common-denominator offerings of television programming. The striking phrase is still used to describe television's
shortcomings as well as failures elsewhere.

The term in use, by Lester Bernstein in the *New York Times Magazine,*
February 26, 1989, writing on the business empire of Time, Inc.:

> Whether or not it can intimidate an acquirer, the attempt to
> clothe Time Inc.'s huge television franchises in public-service

virtue recalls the noble blather with which the networks once defended the vast wasteland of TV.

And by Frank Deford in commentary on National Public Radio's *Morning Edition,* February 17, 1993, on television sports programming:

> Sports was clean, sports was prestige, sports was the shining light in that vast wasteland, and television big shots convinced themselves that you can sucker sports fans into watching other programs on your network if you merely promoted them during a TV game.

And by David Leon Moore in *USA Today,* March 28, 1997, on the University of Arizona's basketball team:

> From out of the West, from the vast wasteland of college basketball, from the giant junkyard of off-target bricks and silly turnovers, from the region of playground castoffs and no-talent wanna-bes, comes . . . The national champs?

vaudeville A light, often comic theatrical piece frequently combining pantomime, dialogue, song, and dance. Also, stage entertainment consisting of such pieces. Popular in the United States in the 19th and early 20th centuries, vaudeville featured many types of light individual acts. Many famous performers began their careers in vaudeville—the Marx Brothers, Sophie Tucker, the Three Stooges, and George Burns and Gracie Allen among them.

The term comes from the French "vau-de-vire," applied to popular satirical songs composed in the valley (vau) of Vire in Normandy, France.

The term in use, by Mark Sandalow in the *San Francisco Chronicle,* June 18, 1997, describing Washington events observing the 25th anniversary of the Watergate break-in:

> On the silver anniversary of the break-in, Washington marked the event with equal parts vaudeville and reflection. . . .
> The Howard Johnson's hosted a display of "authentic Nixon-era collectibles" and a party that was to include Bob Woodward and Carl Bernstein, the *Washington Post* sleuths who broke the story. Convicted Watergate felon G. Gordon Liddy, now a shock jock of the conservative airwaves, broadcast his daily show in the lobby.

And by Tim Keown, also in the *Chronicle,* July 9, 1997, reporting on the baseball All-Star Game:

> So, for the most part, not much was going on in Cleveland, unless you count the wacky antics of Johnson and Walker. Former teammates in the Expos' minor-league organization, they put on a little vaudeville routine in the second inning.

verdict afterwards *See* SENTENCE FIRST, VERDICT AFTERWARDS.

voice crying in the wilderness, a A lone protester, a solitary prophet whose predictions and warnings are ignored until it is too late.

The phrase comes from the Old Testament prophet Isaiah, 40:3, and from Matthew, 3:3, in the New Testament:

> The voice of him that crieth in the wilderness, Prepare ye the way of the Lord, make straight in the desert a highway for our God.

According to Matthew, Isaiah was referring to John the Baptist.

The term in use, by the *Detroit News,* March 13, 1997, quoting Thomas Reese, author of *Inside the Vatican,* on efforts to stop the sale of cigarettes in Vatican stores:

> "The American Cardinal Edmund Szoka has argued that the sale of cigarettes by the Vatican is wrong, but he is still a voice crying in the wilderness since the Vatican is in the middle of Italy, where heavy smoking is still common," said Reese, a senior fellow at Georgetown University.

And by W. Bradley Stock, in an essay in the *Christian Science Monitor,* April 19, 1995:

> What sort of new world order is this? The West may have won the cold war, but it forgot to plan the peace. . . . The few people who planned a post-cold-war peace (including a few members of the Bush administration) were voices crying in a wilderness of utopians and cynics. This helps explain the initial lack of an exit strategy for the cold war. [*See also* UTOPIA.]

vox populi, vox Dei Popular opinion of ordinary people reveals God's will and should be obeyed. Used most often in political contexts, it's a Latin phrase meaning "the voice of the people is the voice of God." The phrase is often used negatively, in the sense that the popular voice may not be wise or good and may in fact be the lowest common denominator but is nonetheless an irresistible force. The phrase is often simply shortened to vox populi or even to vox pop. Its first appearance was in a letter to the Frankish emperor Charlemagne from his adviser Alcuin.

Civil War General William Tecumseh Sherman, that master of the tersely turned phrase, wrote in a letter to his wife, "Vox populi, vox humbug."

The term in use, by Judith Dunford in *Newsday,* January 29, 1995, reviewing Robert James Waller's *Border Music:*

> Written by anyone but the author of a phenomenon, *Border Music* would be a pleasant enough read at the dentist's. Since Waller is the author, who knows what can happen. Vox populi, vox Dei. But not always.

And in its shortened form from TRB, editorialist in the *New Republic,* reprinted in the *Baltimore Sun,* February 3, 1995:

> For a man who considers himself the vox populi, Mr. Gingrich was slow to fathom public sentiment toward PBS. He started out assuming that a routine incitement of class resentment would carry the day.

... the anchorman looked for an instant like Wile E. Coyote when, gimlet-eyed, he understands he is about to plummet into the abyss.
—Lance Morrow

Wagnerian \väg-'nir-ē-ən, -'ner-\ Of, relating to, or suggestive of the music or theory of German composer Richard Wagner (1813–1883). The word, sometimes used in a jocular fashion, suggests grandiose Teutonic themes and a stout soprano with spear and horned helmet singing fortissimo. Wagner was notable for his megalomania and extreme German nationalism; his operas (or music dramas, as he called them) were generally based on Norse and Teutonic mythology and include *The Flying Dutchman, Tannhaüser, Lohengrin, Tristan und Isolde,* and the four-part *Der Ring des Nibelungen.*

He introduced innovations to opera, including the LEITMOTIV; he also wrote operas consisting of continuous music rather than alternating aria and recitation.

The term in use, by Alan Jay Lerner, in his lyrics for *My Fair Lady* (1956), in which Professor Henry Higgins sings of the dangers of letting a woman in your life: "She'll have a large Wagnerian mother, with a voice that shatters glass!"

Another example, from Stephen Holden in the *New York Times,* July 16, 1989, on the soundtrack for the 1989 film *Batman:*

> Jack Nicholson's fiendish Joker and Michael Keaton's Caped Crusader aren't the only forces that collide in the smash-hit movie *Batman.* The film's noisy soundtrack presents a pitched battle between the two strains of music that have accompanied movies since the dawn of the sound era: one derived from high culture, the other from pop. The majority of the film's score is loud, post-Wagnerian action music composed by Danny Elfman. Sly, subterranean funk songs by Prince make up the rest.

And by Pope Brock, profiling Warner's cartoon director Chuck Jones in *People,* November 13, 1989:

> Yet in his 30-year career at the studio, this master artist created WILE E. COYOTE, the Roadrunner and Pepe Le Pew, and strongly influenced the development of Bugs Bunny, Daffy, Porky and other American ICONS. Boundlessly versatile, he also created an Oscar-winning abstract short and mini-epics such as *What's Opera, Doc?,* which featured a Wagnerian Elmer Fudd on a mountain peak invoking the elements. ("Typhoons! Huwwicanes!")

And by Rob Norton in *Fortune,* February 22, 1993:

> For Germany's politicians, accomplishing that with elections
> looming in 1994 could prove a task of Wagnerian proportions.

Wailing Wall In Jerusalem, a surviving section of the ancient enclosure
of Herod's temple, destroyed in A.D. 70, near the Holy of Holies where
Jews gather for prayer and lament. By extension the term, not capitalized, means a source of comfort and consolation in misfortune.

The term in use, by Universal Press Syndicate, in the *Deseret News,* January 12, 1996, profiling advice columnist Dear Abby:

> She explained that although she had taken journalism in college,
> she had never written professionally, but she knew she could
> write an advice column because all her life she had been an ama-
> teur "wailing wall without portfolio."

Another example, from author Paul Theroux, whose book *My Other
Life* is quoted by Sven Birkerts in a review in the *Detroit News,* September 27, 1996:

> Theroux (well known for his travel books) travels, tries to out-
> run his pain; he even moves back to Massachusetts, his home
> place. But despair stalks him at every turn. "A bank of phones,"
> he observes, "now looks to me like a wailing wall."

And from Lewis W. Diuguid, in the *Kansas City Star,* June 1, 1996:

> Today people nationwide will take such problems to the Stand
> for Children rally in Washington—the city that has become the
> Wailing Wall for all of America's woes.

waiting for Godot To wait endlessly, and in futility, for something to happen. *Waiting for Godot* (1952, translated in English, 1954) is a play by
French playwright Samuel Beckett in which, famously, "nothing happens," according to outraged critics.

Two tramps meet in a bare, unidentifiable place. They are waiting for
Godot, who sends word that he is coming, but does not. The only passersby are a rich man and his servant, whom he treats cruelly. The tramps
pass the time in meaningless conversation; they agree to leave and meet
the next day, but stand still. There is no sense of progress, nor any understanding of who Godot is, or why anyone should wait for him.

The term in use, by Don McLeese in the *New York Times Book Review,*
December 28, 1986:

> These days, waiting for someone to reignite that rock-and-roll
> explosion—as Elvis did in 1954, as the Beatles did in 1963—has
> become something like waiting for Godot.

And by Allan Fotheringham in *Macleans,* August 8, 1994:

"In any world menu, Canada must be considered the vichyssoise of nations—it's cold, half-French and difficult to stir."

The analysis by the late and witty *Vancouver Sun* publisher [Stuart Keate] still applies. We are in the August of our years. As we swore as a nation never to do again, we are once more Waiting for Godot, paralyzed while we sit in resignation for the result of the Quebec election.

And by Robin Finn in the *New York Times,* August 6, 1990:

The Millers are also waiting for Karin, 4 feet 9 inches, to sprout another 6 inches; although waiting for her to grow may turn out to be as futile as waiting for Godot, the Millers aren't to be dissuaded from their dream.

wall *See* HIT THE WALL.

Walpurgis Night \väl-'púr-gəs\ The Eve of May Day on which witches are held to ride to an appointed rendezvous. Also, something having a nightmarish quality.

It is an ancient German pagan festival, a night for witches and fiends to carouse in the Harz Mountains of Germany.

The night is named for St. Walpurgis, considered a defense against witchery, whose feast is celebrated on May 1. She was an Englishwoman of the 8th century who went to Germany as a missionary when she was called from her abbey at Wimborne to go with her brothers Willibald and Wunibald to the monastery at Heidenheim.

The term in use, by Herbert London in an opinion piece in the *Washington Times,* November 24, 1996:

Most people do not realize that they dwell inside an epistemological inferno, a veritable Walpurgis Night of hollow ideas and relativistic beliefs.

And by Glenn Lovell, reviewing *Batman Returns* for the *San Jose Mercury News,* June 19, 1992:

And when Catwoman and Penguin find some quality time alone—look out! This "Batman" adventure plumbs perverse new depths only dreamed of by its predecessor.

Will fantasy buffs hail this as Peng-ultimate entertainment, or will they emerge from Burton's cartoonish Walpurgis Night feeling Bat-tered and Cat-atonic?

The alternative form of this word, *Walpurgisnacht,* preserves the German word, and it too often appears, as in this example by John Aldridge in the *New York Times Book Review,* October 26, 1986, describing a particularly nightmarish chapter in Joseph Heller's novel *Catch-22* (1961):

Through a complicated process, involving countless repetitions of references and details and a looping and straightening inch-

worm progression, the moment is finally reached in the Walpurgisnacht "Eternal City" chapter when the humor is stripped away
and the terrified obsession with death, from which the humor
has been a hysterical distraction, is revealed in full nakedness.

Walter Mitty *See* MITTY, WALTER.

war of all against all A situation in which all order has broken down and
random violence prevails in which each person fights only for his or her
own advantage against everyone else. In such circumstances, all vestiges
of civilization and morality disappear.
     The line is adapted from Thomas Hobbes in *Leviathan* (1651), Part I,
chapter 4 (*see also* HOBBESIAN; NASTY, BRUTISH, AND SHORT):

> During the time men live without a common power to keep them
> all in awe, they are in that condition which is called war; and
> such a war, as is of every man, against every man.
>   To this war of every man against every man, this also is con-
> sequent; that nothing can be unjust. The notions of right and
> wrong, justice and injustice have there no place.
>   Where there is no common power, there is no law, where no
> law, no injustice. Force, and fraud, are in war the cardinal virtues.

The term in use, quoted by Glenn Garvin in the *Miami Herald,* August
4, 1997:

> In fact, El Salvador's horrifying annual murder rate of 140 per
> 100,000 inhabitants ties it with South Africa as the globe's most
> homicidal country. El Salvador's rate is almost seven times the
> average for Latin America and the Caribbean—a region that a
> World Bank study calls "among the most violent in the world,"
> where society's rules are collapsing into "the war of all against
> all."

And by E.J. Dionne Jr., in the *Washington Post,* April 24, 1994:

> Clinton is right to think his nastier enemies ought to be ashamed
> of themselves. The best way to shame them is to acknowledge
> that all sides have some responsibility for stoking this political
> war of all against all and that all sides have a duty to end it.

waste its sweetness on the desert air To allow an undiscovered talent to
lie dormant; to labor in obscurity or allow someone' genius to go unno-
ticed, as a beautiful flower may bloom in a wilderness where there is no
one to appreciate its lovely scent.
     This is a phrase from Thomas Gray's *Elegy in a Country Churchyard,*
source of several familiar phrases. (*See also* FAR FROM THE MADDING
CROWD; MUTE INGLORIOUS MILTON; PATHS OF GLORY). As he speculates
on lives lived out in the obscurity of a rural village, Gray muses:

Full many a gem of purest ray serene
The dark, unfathomed caves of ocean bear,
Full many a flower is born to blush unseen,
And waste its sweetness on the desert air.

The term in use, by Enid Saunders Candlin, in the *Christian Science Monitor,* August 26, 1991:

It appears, however, that most botanical artists must be content to "blush unseen" (and this includes [Isaac] Sprague, who is quite unknown to the general public and is hard even to find in libraries). This is perhaps not inappropriate; we know that their subjects must often also "waste their sweetness on the desert air."

And quoted by Renee Kaplan in *Newsday,* March 1, 1996, although the phrase is mistakenly attributed to Timothy Dwight, president of Yale:

"To Blush Unseen, 19th-Century Long Island Women" at the Hofstra Museum focuses on the life of female Long Islanders a century ago by examining samplers, books, journals, wedding gifts, pottery and paintings of the era. The exhibit takes its title from a passage written by Yale college president Timothy Dwight in 1823, when he visited a Smithtown family and remarked about the charm and beauty of the daughter: "I was ready to believe as all my companions were when we left the spot, that some flowers were born to blush unseen, and waste their sweetness in the desert air."

And by poet and critic Donald Hall in the *New York Times Book Review,* June 5, 1988, writing about Ernest Lawrence Thayer's poem *Casey at the Bat* [*q.v.*]. (*See also* NO JOY IN MUDVILLE):

The poem's biography is richer than the poet's. At first "Casey" blushed unseen, wasting its sweetness on the desert air, until an accident blossomed it into eminence.

waterloo A decisive or final defeat or setback.

Waterloo, nine miles from Brussels, Belgium, was the scene of Napoleon's final defeat. He had slipped out of exile on the island of Elba in March 1815 and marched in triumph to Paris, where he reestablished his rule. The European allies who had defeated and exiled him in 1814 dropped their own quarrels and rushed into position; the Duke of Wellington concentrated his British, Prussian, Dutch, and Belgian forces at Brussels.

Seeking to defeat his enemies before they could join forces, Napoleon crossed swiftly into Belgium on June 14. He forced the Prussian troops to fall back and on June 17 reached Wellington's lines at Waterloo. The following day, Napoleon made a critical error when he waited for the ground to dry out before launching his attack. The delay enabled the Prussians to reinforce Wellington and tip the balance in favor of the allies.

The French defeat was total. Napoleon was exiled again, this time to a more stern and isolated venue, the island of St. Helena, where he died in 1821.

The term in use, by Melinda Bargreen in the *Seattle Times,* September 21, 1997, describing the Seattle Opera's return to financial health:

> Jenkins is unquestionably the idea man and the company's Napoleon—to use an image from the opera's ultra-successful *War and Peace.* But he's a Napoleon who listens closely to his marshals and his generals, who are all collectively keeping him and themselves well away from any waterloos.

Another example, from Megan Rosenfeld, in the *Washington Post,* June 18, 1989, in an article about spas:

> What I had was a bad case of the My Second Child is 14 Months Old and I Still Can't Fit Into My Old Clothes Blues. . . .
> That, plus the desire for a short break from the adorable children who had brought me to this plump waterloo—not to mention the husband who, when losing weight is mentioned, says "What's the big deal? Just stop eating"—led me to think of going to a spa.

wave the bloody shirt Use inflammatory rhetoric that exploits public prejudice and resentment. The phrase was applied in the 19th century to Republicans who fanned post-Civil War bitterness by blaming the Democrats for the struggle, a tactic that caused such moderate Republicans as Horace Greeley to break with the GOP.

The term in use, by Dave Rossie, Gannett News Service, June 12, 1996:

> Democrats might want to remember that had they nominated Bob Kerrey in 1992, they would not today be awash in Whitewater. Bob Dole would not be waving the bloody shirt at every whistle stop—not with a disabled Medal of Honor winner for an opponent—and Republicans would be enjoined from tossing around such terms as "pot-smoker," "draft dodger" and "womanizer" for fear of embarrassing the Speaker of the House of Representatives.

And by Stanley Crouch, in a comment in the *Los Angeles Times,* October 27, 1996:

> But when we fumble down into the idea that every activity within the black community is the result of forces from the outside, it is easy to wave the bloody shirt of all-encompassing blame at the government, the system, the majority, big business, etc.

And a whimsical application from Sam Howe Verhoek, in the *New York Times,* May 19, 1988:

> Nobody is waving a bloody shirt in this year's campaign for the board of directors at Co-op City, but mysterious stains in the laundry are a key rallying point.

we few, we happy few An elect band of true heroes who prevail despite enormous odds. A line from Shakespeare's *Henry V,* Act 4, Scene 3. Before the battle of Agincourt (1415) young King Harry addresses his men, sick and exhausted and facing a French army that overwhelmingly outnumbers them. Henry tells them:

> We few, we happy few, we band of brothers;
> For he today that sheds his blood with me
> Shall be my brother. . . .
> And gentlemen in England now a-bed
> Shall think themselves accurs'd they were not here,
> And hold their manhoods cheap whiles any speaks
> That fought with us upon Saint Crispin's day.

Henry won a stupendous victory that day. The French lost thousands, close-packed in ranks that forced them into sharpened stakes planted by the English. Heavily armored knights and horses staggered in deep mud and were mowed down by the famous "arrow cloud" of Agincourt, launched by English longbows.

The term in use, by David Thomson in the *New Republic,* April 25, 1994, reviewing *The Lion Roars: Ken Russell on Film:*

> At least that frightens off Hollywood money—so then the few, the happy few, can soldier on in brave penury, singing a lonely song. Who knows, a day may come when grim and overpriced American professionalism has been surpassed by technology, while British eccentrics keep filming in their garden with antique cameras, watching the flowers explode.

By Sandra Gilbert in *The State of the Language* (1990):

> In humanities departments on university campuses . . . arcane and esoteric vocabularies—those that sound like the language of astrophysics or brain surgery—will always trump clear and simple speech because they will always function to foster self-certification for the marginalized few, who necessarily must define themselves (ourselves) as the fortunate few, the happy few.

And by Arthur M. Schlesinger Jr. in *The Cycles of American History* (1986):

> Over the long run, this historian finds it hard to believe that the instinct for political and civil freedom is confined to the happy few in the North Atlantic littoral.

we're not in Kansas anymore A humorous statement implying that circumstances have changed dramatically, usually from the ordinary and familiar to the exotic or weird.

The line comes from the 1939 movie *The Wizard of Oz.* As Dorothy emerges from the ordinary house the tornado has carried from dull sepia-toned Kansas into the Technicolor brilliance and lush flowers of the Land of Oz, she gazes about in wonder and says to her little dog, "Toto, I have a feeling we're not in Kansas anymore." The movie is based on the L. Frank Baum novel, but these words are from the screenplay.

The term in use, by Richard Lacayo in *Time*, February 26, 1996, on the Republican presidential primary contest:

> In a speech to the New Hampshire legislature, Dole, as steadfast an example of Republican orthodoxy as the party has ever produced, was suddenly Woody Guthrie. "Corporate profits are setting records and so are corporate layoffs," he said. "The real average hourly wage is 5% lower than it was a decade ago."
>
> Toto, I don't think we're in Kansas anymore. When Republicans talk this way, it means they have a problem on their hands.

And by Gary Van Sickle in *Sports Illustrated*, May 26, 1997, on golf phenomenon Tiger Woods:

> If you get the feeling we're not in Kansas anymore, Toto, you are so right. Woods has taken the PGA Tour to a new address, a strange and wonderful place where golfers hang out with Kev and Mike (as in Costner and Jordan) and chat with Oprah and Barbara Walters and tell the President, not now man, I'm going to Mexico for a couple of days.

And an extended use by Mike Littwin, describing his luxury flight aboard MGM Grand Air, in the *Baltimore Sun*, January 1, 1995: "I don't think we're flying Continental anymore, Toto."

whammy; double whammy A supernatural power bringing very bad luck; an irreversible curse or spell; a completely paralyzing or lethal blow. The expression was popularized in the 1950s by cartoonist Al Capp in his strip "Li'l Abner."

Capp's character Evil-Eye Fleegle could disable his victims with the power of his eyes: the single whammy was a look from one eye; the dreaded double whammy "which I hopes I never hafta use" brought both eyes to bear. "Double whammy" now describes a two-part blow, a one-two punch.

The term in use, by Julie Hinds in the *Detroit News*, December 17, 1996, on the shopping frenzy for "Tickle Me Elmo" dolls:

> What bothers discerning adults about the toy is the double whammy of media hype and consumer frenzy surrounding it.

And quoted by Frank Donnelly in *Newsday*, October 19, 1995:

> Riders in two-fare zones, mainly in Queens, will be among the hardest hit by the proposed 25-cent fare hike the Metropolitan Transit Authority is expected to approve today.
>
> "Obviously, it's a double whammy for anyone in a two-fare zone," said Gene Russianoff, staff counsel for the Straphangers Campaign, an advocacy group.

And by James Gannon, Gannett News Service, May 22, 1994:

> Instead of another drop of chinese water torture, the Fed on Tuesday unleashed a double whammy. It raised two key rates—the discount rate and the federal funds rate—and not by a mere quarter-point as before, but by a half-point each.

whiff of grapeshot A show of force, especially one intended to intimidate the opposition. A phrase from Thomas Carlyle's account of the French Revolution, describing how easily young General Bonaparte was able to disperse insurrectionists in 1795: "Six years ago this whiff of grapeshot was promised." He was describing the behavior of Bonaparte's opponents.

Grapeshot, by the way, consists of small cast-iron balls packed in an arrangement of iron plates. When fired from a cannon they produce a wide spray of shot, and thus wreak carnage on attacking troops.

The term in use, by Ian Aitken, in the *New Statesman & Society,* June 23, 1995:

> Against this background, the surprising thing is not that [British Prime Minister] John Major is beginning to look rattled, but that so far he doesn't seem absolutely petrified. . . . After all, Lady T [former Prime Minister Margaret Thatcher] turned and ran at the first whiff of grapeshot.

And in the *Los Angeles Times,* November 2, 1994, quoting historian Rosalind Miles on how Queen Elizabeth I would have handled quarreling royals Charles and Diana:

> "She would've sent Charles off to conquer new worlds—heroic action is always good. Give him a whiff of grapeshot and he would've had plenty to do. Today, he's just a man without a function."

And from Martin Walker in the *Manchester Guardian Weekly,* August 23, 1992:

> Politicians in trouble are understandably tempted by the whiff of grapeshot, particularly when it seemed to work so well before. But Desert Storm was a temporary triumph.

whimper *See* NOT WITH A BANG BUT A WHIMPER.

whip the offending Adam To punish someone and leave him or her virtuous; to administer a drubbing that produces a KINDER, GENTLER attitude.

Adam, the first man, was also the first sinner—"the offending Adam." Shakespeare used the phrase in *Henry V,* Act 1, Scene 1, to describe the transformation of rascally Prince Hal into virtuous monarch:

> The breath no sooner left his father's body
> But that his wildness, mortified in him,
> Seemed to die too; yea, at that very moment,

Consideration like an angel came
and whipped the offending Adam out of him,
Leaving his body as a paradise
T' envelop and contain celestial spirits.

The term in use, by Leonore Fleischer in her "Talk of the Trade" column in *Publishers Weekly,* June 9, 1989:

Birch Lane Press will be publishing Stephen Hanks's *The Game That Changed Pro Football* in September. The game of the title is the 1969 Superbowl III, in which, sparked by star quarterback Joe Namath, the New York Jets of the upstart American Football League whipped the offending Adam (16–7) out of the Baltimore Colts, leaders of the super-heavy National Football League.

whited sepulcher Someone or something that is inwardly corrupt or wicked but outwardly virtuous.

The expression comes from the Bible. A sepulcher is a tomb constructed of stone or set in a cave. In biblical times, Jewish tombs were whitewashed so that people would know they were there and not approach too closely. Jesus says in Matthew 23:27:

Woe unto you, scribes and PHARISEES, hypocrites! for ye are like unto whited sepulchres, which indeed appear beautiful outward, but are within full of dead men's bones, and of all uncleanness.

The term in use, by Barry Hillenbrand in *Time International,* August 21, 1995, on the state of the Catholic Church in Ireland:

The faithful continued to attend Mass in encouraging numbers, and Rome could always count on the Irish bishops for unswerving support of the Vatican line. Not anymore. In the past few years, the Pope's Emerald Isle has more resembled a whited sepulcher. A series of sex scandals has sapped the church's moral authority, and now even the Irish bishops, who always spoke with a single voice, are in a major public fracas with one another—and with Rome.

And by Karal Ann Marling in the *New York Times,* June 22, 1997:

. . . a recent book of lurid revelations about Elvis's addictions and predilections written by three members of his entourage, had the effect of turning the dead King into a freak, the whited sepulcher of pop culture. Like Elvis himself, Graceland seemed just fine on the outside, all columns and spurious dignity, but on the inside horror lurked.

Whitehall The British government. (*See also* FOGGY BOTTOM.) For the French government, especially the foreign office, *Quai D'Orsay,* the name of the site along the River Seine in Paris of government offices, is used in a similar sense.

Whitehall is a thoroughfare in London, near the Houses of Parliament. The street was named for a royal palace that stood there from the time of Henry VIII to William III. The palace burned except for the Banqueting Hall in 1698.

The term in use, by columnist Mary McGrory, appearing in the Portland *Oregonian,* February 17, 1996, on attempts to negotiate peace in Northern Ireland:

> The Irish nationalists thought it was another dodge to put off the evil day when Whitehall would treat the terrorists as equal.

And by Tony Collins in the *New Statesman,* June 27, 1997, on the British government's mistakes in acquiring computer technology:

> Since Britain began spending in earnest on computers in the 1970s, there has been relentless pressure on Whitehall to pursue the efficiencies promised by information technology.

white man's burden The alleged duty of the white peoples to manage the affairs of the less developed nonwhite peoples. Used by Rudyard Kipling in an 1899 poem by that title. Today the phrase, unless used ironically, suggests the condescending, racist elitism of the imperial era and the persistence of such attitudes.

Kipling addressed his poem to the American people as the United States acquired the Philippines in the Spanish-American War:

> Take up the white man's burden—
> Send forth the best ye breed—
> Go bind your sons to exile
> To serve your captive's need;
> To wait in heavy harness
> On fluttered folk and wild—
> Your new-caught sullen peoples,
> Half devil and half child.

The term in use, by Stanley Cloud, profiling former President Jimmy Carter in *Time,* September 11, 1989:

> He's productive again, and seems finally at peace with the conflicts between his well-known born-again Christianity and his life as a public man. Says he ... "My Christian faith is just like breathing to me or like being a Southerner or an American. It's all part of the same thing—the sharing, the compassion, the understanding, the dealing with the poor and the destitute and the outcasts." If there is a bit of the white man's burden in that and if Carter sometimes falls victim to Christianity's age-old CATCH-22, the sin of pride, well, it doesn't seem very important in the scale of things.

A play on the term, by Paul Johnson, in his 1988 book *Intellectuals,* referring to British writer Cyril Connolly:

Connolly's accounts of these visits [to the Spanish Civil War], mainly in the *New Statesman,* are acute and a refreshing contrast to the field-grey committed prose most other intellectuals were producing at the time. But they indicate the strain he found in carrying the Left Man's Burden.

white noise A mixture of sound waves extending over a wide range of frequencies. It has the effect of masking other sounds. By extension, it has come to refer to a steady stream of meaningless messages that one learns to ignore.

The term in use, by Greg Kot, Knight-Ridder News Service, in the *Wichita Eagle,* November 13, 1994, in a description of Elvis Presley:

From the start the crowd would be in his face, a white-noise blur of screaming and crying, and he would break into a half-smile crossed with a sneer. It is a look of calm and bemusement in a maelstrom, the look of an entertainer and a tease, a provocateur and a crowd-pleaser, a pleasure merchant and a menace.

And by Robin Abcarian, in the *Los Angeles Times,* June 5, 1996, on the Stand for Children march in Washington, D.C.:

I give Edelman credit for recognizing this unpleasant truth: When a drumbeat is steady enough, it disappears from consciousness, becomes white noise, something to go to sleep by. What better way to cut through the white noise than to commandeer the nation's capital, to summon thousands on behalf of children?

And quoted by Anna Quindlen in the *New York Times,* December 11, 1991:

"I work in midtown," says Mr. Brown, who is a vice president in futures and options at Dean Witter, "and I saw these poor souls on the subway grates. We're just trying to do what Christ asked us to do." That is to do good. Boy, does that seem distant from the white noise of modern life.

white smoke The outward sign of a critical decision having been reached in a closed meeting or organization.

The expression comes from the election of the popes of the Roman Catholic Church. When a new pope is to be elected, the cardinals meet in the Vatican in secret as the world watches. After each round of voting, the ballots are burned. The smoke is black until a final decision is made, when a substance is added to make the burned ballots produce puffs of white smoke, the signal that a new pope has been named.

The term in use, by Ian Williams in the *New Statesman,* September 6, 1996, on the selection of a new secretary-general of the United Nations:

Some time before midnight on New Year's Eve, in the diplomatic equivalent of white smoke from the Vatican chimney, the president of the Security Council should announce the unanimous choice to be presented to the UN General Assembly.

And Kansas legislator Tom Sawyer quoted by John Petterson in the *Kansas City Star,* March 23, 1997, on negotiations for tax cuts: "After about 1-1/2 hours, white smoke came up."

And again, by Peter C. Newman, *Maclean's* magazine, March 4, 1996:

Canada's bank chairmen customarily succeed one another in a seamless web reminiscent of the papacy—except that there isn't even the telltale sign of a puff of white smoke to mark the transition.

wilderness, in the In exile. The phrase occurs over and over in the Bible; the most familiar is the 40 years of wandering after the Jews fled Egypt. The phrase also often describes years of adversity or unpopularity, such as the time spent by defeated politicians out of office. Generally, it refers to isolation from the centers of power in politics or society.

The term in use, by Hugh Dellios of the *Chicago Tribune,* March 23, 1997:

The rebel leader whose troops have captured Zaire's third-largest city is seen as the savior who finally rallied Zairians against Mobutu after so many others failed. But he also is an opportunist who wandered for 30 years in Zaire's wilderness before Mobutu's troubles dawned.

And by House Majority Leader Dick Armey (R-Texas), quoted in the *Christian Science Monitor,* June 10, 1997:

Looking back on that landmark shift in power and the rocky partisan battles that ensued, Armey observes during a Monitor interview that "there were two big emotional problems with the [104th] Congress. . . . One was the Democrats' inability to manage their disappointment, and the other was our inability to manage our enthusiasm," he says.

He blames the GOP demeanor on the "40 years we wandered in the wilderness."

Wile E. Coyote A character doomed to endless, fruitless pursuit of the unattainable. Wile E. Coyote is the creation of Chuck Jones of Warner Brothers cartoons, first introduced in 1949. In the Roadrunner and Coyote cartoons, the Roadrunner is never caught; Coyote's attempts to capture the speedy bird (often aided by elaborate technology ordered from the ACME company) end only with injury to himself. Coyote's pratfalls often involve plunges off towering cliffs or singed fur from backfiring explosive devices. One of the richnesses of the series is Coyote's look of sudden realization of his fate in the split second before disaster strikes.

The term in use, by Stephan Wilkinson in *Air & Space,* April–May 1991:

Why on earth test wingless airplanes that maneuvered as handily as a Mack truck on ice? That had the glide-angle of Wile E. Coyote going off a cliff? Simply to prove that it was possible to take an airplane that flew about as well as a cartoon villain and land it neatly.

And by Lance Morrow in *Time,* February 8, 1988:

When Bush slugged Rather with the line about Rather's once walking off the set of the CBS Evening News, the anchorman looked for an instant like Wile E. Coyote when, gimlet-eyed, he understands he is about to plummet into the abyss.

And by Doug Gamble in the *Los Angeles Times,* March 29, 1998:

We in the VRWC [Vast Right-Wing Conspiracy] have been left looking like a pathetic collection of cartoon characters. Every time the president escapes a new trap, the more we resemble the hapless Wile E. Coyote failing once again to snare the elusive Roadrunner. No matter how many Acme presidential traps we assemble and deploy, none of them is going to stop Bill Clinton.

windmills *See* TILTING AT WINDMILLS.

win one for the Gipper An emotional appeal to go all out this one last time, for the sake of an inspiring but absent teammate.

The Gipper was George Gipp (1895–1920), a legendary football player at Notre Dame under legendary coach Knute Rockne.

As he was dying of pneumonia at age 25, December 14, 1920, he—according to oft-repeated accounts—made this entreaty to Rockne: "I've got to go, Rock. It's all right. I'm not afraid. Some time, Rock, when the team is up against it, when things are wrong and the breaks are beating the boys—tell them to go in there with all they've got and win just one for the Gipper. I don't know where I'll be then, Rock. But I'll know about it, and I'll be happy."

Opportunity knocked eight years later. On November 10, 1928, after losing two of its first six games, the injury-plagued Irish traveled to Yankee Stadium to face unbeaten Army. The day before Rockne told sportswriter Grantland Rice, "He's been gone a long time but I may have to use him again tomorrow."

Rockne told his team of Gipp's deathbed wish and added, "This is the day and you are the team." It worked. Notre Dame won 12–6 on a pair of second-half touchdowns. Jack Chevigny scored the first of them on a one-yard run, and on reaching the end zone said, "That's one for the Gipper." Rice wrote up the story and pulled out the stops in his usual style. (*See* FOUR HORSEMEN OF THE APOCALYPSE.).

"Even now," says Notre Dame on its Internet Web site, "every aspiring football player, or anyone facing insurmountable odds, hears the tale of the Gipper."

The tale and the nickname are inextricably merged with the persona of

Ronald Reagan, because of his portrayal of Gipp in 1940 in *Knute Rockne—
All-American,* one of his most successful roles in a 20-year, 50-plus-movies
acting career.

Reagan carried the line to good effect into his political career: he used
it to close out his own campaigns, and when he was kept by the Constitution from seeking a third term, he used it to appeal at the 1988 Republican National Convention for votes for his successor, George Bush. "Win
one," he pleaded, eyes glistening, "for the Gipper."

Some facts clumsily get in the way of the Gipp legend. While he was a
brilliant athlete and still holds a handful of Notre Dame records, and was
named by Walter Camp the outstanding college player in America in 1920,
he also smoked and drank, cut class and skipped exams and practices,
secretly played professional football, and gambled on Notre Dame games
(as did Rockne). Moreover, he never called himself "the Gipper."

The term in use, by Mark Coomes, Gannett News Service, January 7,
1994:

> If ever coach Rick Pitino was to give a "Win one for the Gipper"
> speech, Thursday night was his big chance. Everything was in
> place for the sappiest of soliloquies.

And quoted by Sandra Sobievaj of the Associated Press, an account of
presidential candidate Bob Dole's visit to the Reagans, July 4, 1996:

> Leaving the meeting, [Republican strategist Ken] Khachigian said
> he assured Reagan, "We're gonna win one for the Gipper one
> more time."
> "He lit up and said, 'All right,' " Khachigian said.

winter of our discontent Period of dark resentment, dissatisfaction, or
restless unhappiness. The phrase is from the opening line of Shakespeare's
Richard III. Richard, Duke of Gloucester, appears in a London street and
comments acidly on the triumph of his family (the Yorkists) over its rival,
the House of Lancaster—"Now is the winter of our discontent/Made glo-
rious summer by this sun of York. . . . "

Richard goes on to speak of his physical deformity but reveals his more
deformed soul with his cold, malevolent plots to take the throne now held
by his brother. Richard does become king, briefly, and is one of the most
monstrously evil figures of literature. Shakespeare wrote the play during
the reign of Elizabeth I, whose grandfather Henry Tudor overthrew
Richard and founded the Tudor line; a balanced portrayal of a defeated
foe was not the bard's intent.

The term in use, by Robert Shogan in the *Los Angeles Times,* February
26, 1996:

> GOP legislative leaders, once heralded for their boldness and
> cunning, have been outmaneuvered and upstaged on Capitol Hill.
> The party's presidential campaign has turned into a winter of dis-
> content and disarray—a disarray that only deepened Saturday

as Steve Forbes revived his campaign by winning the primary in Delaware.

And from Humphrey Taylor of Gannett News Service, writing in the same winter season, January 23, 1996:

> The overall picture is clearly bleak for all political leaders in Washington. Americans' long winter of discontent deepens as the budget debate continues. The poll sends a message that comes close to "a plague on all your houses." [*See* PLAGUE ON BOTH YOUR HOUSES.]

And by William F. Reed, in *Sports Illustrated,* February 6, 1995, recounting the woes of the Boston Celtics (datelined "Boston, Mess"):

> Even if the Celtics were still their normal winning selves, this would have been a winter of discontent in New England.

witch-hunt The searching out for persecution of persons accused of witchcraft. Also, the searching out and deliberate harassment of those, such as political opponents, with unpopular views. The term often characterizes what is considered an unjust, malicious, or hysterical persecution, as with the Salem witch trials, which took place in Salem, Massachusetts in 1692.

The term comes from the rampant pursuit of witches in Christian Europe in the 15th century and continuing for the next three hundred years. The witches were pursued in the belief that they had made a pact with Satan.

The hysteria finally ran its course; as modern commerce and government emerged, the disruption and fear the persecutions caused were undesirable. The last executions for witchcraft were in the late 17th and early 18th centuries.

The term in use, by Gregg Easterbrook in an opinion column in the *Los Angeles Times,* June 15, 1997:

> Maj. Gen. John F. Longhouser, commander of the Army's Aberdeen Proving Ground, was just compelled to retire at reduced rank because of the disclosure that he had an affair with a civilian woman while separated from his wife. . . . And how did this private matter become known? The Army has set up a nationwide hotline for sexual allegations. Someone who doesn't like Longhouser called to lodge an anonymous accusation against him. In the manner of witch-hunts, that an accusation was made was all that mattered.

And from Congressman Albert Wynn (D-Md.) characterizing hearings on the Whitewater scandal, quoted in the *Baltimore Sun,* August 8, 1995:

> This is basically a partisan witch-hunt. It's fueled by conspiracy theories and conspiracy fantasies.

And by Brent Staples in the *New York Times Book Review,* March 23, 1997:

> Slavery and the Declaration of Independence can in no way be reconciled. Even so, the debate on slavery over the last decade or so has taken on the character of a witch hunt into the past—with Jefferson as its sole object, as if burning him at the stake would purge us of racial poison.

witching hour A time, usually night, appropriate for witchcraft; a time for significant, weird happenings. As Shakespeare puts it in *Hamlet,* Act 3, Scene 2: " 'Tis now the verie witching time of night,/When Churchyards yawn, and Hell itself breathes out/Contagion to this world."

In the financial world, the term refers to the moment at which stock option contracts and other stock-index futures expire. At the witching hour, as traders change their positions, dramatic price swings are apt to occur with great speed. It is a moment of uncertainty, when things may run out of control.

The term in use, by Daryn Eller, for the New York Times Syndicate, appearing in the *Arizona Republic,* February 19, 1995, on the pitfalls of obsessive low-fat dieting:

> "I can't go out to dinner with her anymore," a woman complains about a friend. "She's trying to lose weight, so she won't eat anything after six o'clock." How 6 p.m. became the witching hour is unknown, but many people seem to think that eating after the nightly news is a sure route to getting fat.

And by George Vecsey in the *New York Times,* August 31, 1997, describing events at the U.S. Open tennis tournament:

> The main stadium has been generally bland, even Friday night, normally a major witching hour at the Open. The unseeded Venus Williams—"I'm tall. I'm black. Everything's different about me. Just face the facts."—came out and pulverized the pouty eighth-seeded German, Anke Huber, but the new stadium never quivered.

Wonderland *See* ALICE IN WONDERLAND.

woodshed A place, means, or session for administering discipline. Sometimes used as a verb, as "to woodshed" someone. In American mythology, the woodshed was where father meted out punishment (usually with his belt) to an erring son.

The phrase entered the contemporary political lexicon in 1981 when Reagan budget director David Stockman spoke frankly and indiscreetly with journalist William Greider. Stockman confessed to his doubts about Reaganomics—the economic theories President Ronald Reagan was pursuing—and added that when it came to assessing the budget deficit, "none of us really understands what's going on with all these numbers."

An uproar followed, and the White House engaged in some spin control to get off the hook. Stockman met with the president, then told the White House press corps that he had been "taken to the woodshed."

Writes Christopher Matthews, recounting the episode in his book *Hardball* (1988):

> In one small but elegant bit of stagecraft, the West Wing PR folks, running with Stockman's naughty-boy metaphor, shifted the entire media focus from an earth-shaking revelation of unsound public finance to a small soap opera: the betrayal by one bright young man of his trusting mentor.

The term in use, by Jonathan Yardley in the *Washington Post,* June 1, 1997, commenting on the 1,600 book reviews of his career:

> Lay them all end to end and they would stretch from here to Tedium. Think of . . . all the memoirists whose ventures into publicly self-administered psychology have been mocked; all the writers of this and that and the other who have been taken to the woodshed and made to suffer their just desserts.

And used as a verb, by Tony Kornheiser in the *Washington Post,* June 10, 1997, describing an episode in which pro golfer Greg Norman chastised a tournament announcer:

> After smacking his drive into the rough, Norman continued to seethe, and motioned McGuire into a small tent to woodshed him, like some errant child.

Wooster, Bertie \\'wús-tər\\ A fictional character, an inane English gentleman in several comic novels by British writer P.G. Wodehouse (1881–1975). Bertie is invoked to suggest genial incompetence and good-hearted simple-mindedness.

Wodehouse wrote numerous whimsical novels and stories featuring Bertie and his ilk; among the best known are *Jeeves* (1925), *Leave It To Psmith* (1923), and *The Code of the Woosters* (1938).

Bertie, evoked by David Nyhan in the *Boston Globe,* February 28, 1989:

> The ever-affable Bush, our Bertie Wooster in the White House, trusts that John Sununu and Bob Dole will pull this one out.

And from *People,* January 22, 1996, describing Queen Elizabeth's private secretary, Sir Robert Fellowes:

> Indeed, with his impeccable dress and manners, the tall, thin, bespectacled Fellowes—who is often compared in the press to P.G. Wodehouse's mildly twittish Bertie Wooster—seems increasingly pained by the entire messy scene.

worship the golden calf To sin against God, an action by rebellious Hebrew wanderers who cast the golden calf from their own jewelry and worshipped it. Thus, to bow down to a new god, the false idol of wealth; to sell out one's principles for money.

This expression comes from one of the most famous episodes from Exodus (32:1–6) in the Bible. Moses, having led the Hebrews out of slavery in Egypt, leaves his followers to ascend Mt. Sinai. There he receives the stone tablets of the Ten Commandments, but when he returns to camp, he finds his people worshipping a new idol, a golden calf, the pagan Baal, in thanks for their deliverance. Moses smashes the tablets, then leads his people in repentance, after which he is issued a new set of tablets.

The term in use, frequently by Patrick Buchanan in his 1996 presidential campaign, here quoted from his "On the Issues":

> Rather than making "global free trade" a golden calf which we all bow down to, and worship, all trade deals should be judged by whether: a) they maintain U.S. sovereignty, b) they protect vital economic interests and c) they ensure a rising standard of living for all our workers.

And again, by the *Onion,* a Web humor publication, quoted by Gannett News Service, February 19, 1997:

> "Golden Calf to Unite Nation," said another, picturing Clinton in the streets of Washington calling for national unity under the golden calf. "World Death Rate Holding Steady at 100 Percent," headlined another, complete with a chart going back to 1992.

wunderkind \\'vùn-dər-ˌkint\\ A child prodigy. One who succeeds in a difficult or competitive field at an early age. The word means "wonder child" in German.

The term was often applied to David Stockman, appointed director of the Office of Management and Budget in the Reagan Administration at the age of 34. (Of course, Stockman was also characterized as an enfant terrible and, after his candid statements about economic policies (*see* WOODSHED) and his 1986 book, *The Triumph of Politics: How the Reagan Revolution Failed,* probably as a QUISLING, too.) Others frequently receiving the accolade include computer mogul Bill Gates and Olympic gold medalist figure skater Tara Lipinsky.

The term in use, by critic Andrew Sarris in *American Film,* November 1988:

> If Orson Welles (1915–1985) was famous even before he made *Citizen Kane,* the onetime (and allegedly one-shot) wunderkind was notorious ever after. (Welles produced, directed, partly wrote, and starred in *Citizen Kane,* all at the age of 25.)

Another example, described by movie critic Rita Kempley in the *Washington Post,* August 11, 1989:

Sex, lies, and videotape is inspired chitchat, a barefaced Louisiana gabfest written and directed by Steven Soderbergh, a 26-year-old wunderkind preoccupied with *l'amour.*

And by Bill Vilona, Gannett News Service, December 6, 1996:

Six years ago, Chris Weinke was Florida State's first wunderkind quarterback prospect, before being lured away by a professional baseball contract.

*In his lonely **Xanadu** on Pennsylvania Avenue, the
Citizen Nixon . . . is left to contemplate what history has
in store.*

—Janet Maslin

Xanadu \\'za-nə-ˌdü, -ˌdyü\\ An idyllic, exotic, or luxurious place. It is a
poetic idealized version of the city of Xandu, or Shangtu, in Mongolia,
which is celebrated in Samuel Taylor Coleridge's 1797 poem, *Kubla Khan.*
The city was founded by Kublai Khan (1215–1294), a Mongol general and
statesman who became emperor of China. Stories of the wealth and power
of Kublai Khan were brought to the West in the (now suspect) writings
of Marco Polo.

Here are the opening lines, themselves often alluded to or imitated:

> In Xanadu did Kubla Khan
> A stately pleasure-dome decree:
> Where Alph, the sacred river, ran
> Through caverns measureless to man
> Down to a sunless sea.

Coleridge—poet, essayist, critic, free spirit, and drug addict—claimed
to have dreamed the poem in an opium-induced sleep. He began to write
it down when he awoke, but was interrupted; when he returned to the
work he could no longer remember it. The unfinished poem is nevertheless considered one of his best. Coleridge is also remembered for *The Rime
of the Ancient Mariner.* (*See* ANCIENT MARINER.)

The term in use, by Janet Maslin in the *New York Times,* December 20,
1995, reviewing the film *Nixon:*

> In his lonely Xanadu on Pennsylvania Avenue, the Citizen Nixon
> of Oliver Stone's sprawling new biography is left to contemplate
> what history has in store.

And by Hilary DeVries in the *Christian Science Monitor,* November 14,
1983, describing a luxury Florida hotel:

> This is the Boca Raton Hotel and Club, one of the oldest grand
> hotels in America. And it is indeed a Xanadu among the trailer
> parks—a pink stucco pleasure palace left over from the jazz
> age. . . .

Also by Susan Ram, a British writer, in a *New York Times* travel article
on Nepal, October 15, 1995:

Mass tourism has also left its stamp. A quarter of a century ago, it was the drug-seeking counterculturalist who came here in search of Xanadu.

Xanthippe \zan-'thi-pē, -'ti-\ An ill-tempered woman. Xanthippe was the wife of the Greek philosopher Socrates, and a shrewish nag furious at his indifference to her and to earning a living.

The term in use, in the *Los Angeles Times,* December 17, 1994:

Electric woodworking tools turn at furious speeds and are less forgiving than Socrates' wife, the ultimate shrew Xanthippe.

And by Francine Du Plessix Gray in the *New Yorker,* August 8, 1994:

For many decades, there was a tendency to see the marriage exclusively through Leo's eyes and to denigrate Sonya as a shrewish Xanthippe, who was the source of most of Tolstoy's torments.

*. . . stocks that could have sent you on the **Yellow Brick Road** to Riches. . . .*

—Steve Sakson

yahoo A boorish, crass, or stupid person. The word comes from Jonathan Swift's *Gulliver's Travels;* Gulliver visits the country of the Houyhnhnms, rational, intelligent, civilized horses who had tamed the bestial men they called Yahoos. Today the word, uncapitalized, means someone who is a PHILISTINE.

The capitalized term in use, by transplanted English writer Jonathan Raban, in *Harpers,* August 1, 1993, writing about his new home in Seattle:

> My own car, a low-slung, thirsty, black Dodge Daytona with a working ashtray, marked me out as a Yahoo among the Houyhnhnms—too old, dirty, and wasteful to pass as a member of Seattle's uniquely refined middle class.

And by Sid Stapleton in *Motor Boating & Sailing,* October 1, 1995:

> Recreational skippers don't enjoy the best of reputations among commercial captains, many of whom consider us ignorant yahoos.

Another example, quoted by Kurt Shillinger, in the *Christian Science Monitor,* January 11, 1991:

> "Artificial walls have produced a generation of very skilled climbers who can not climb safely," says Paul Casaudoumecq, who learned to climb in Yosemite Valley in California.
> "You get some yahoo who jumps on a real wall who doesn't know what he's doing, there are a potential number of problems," says [a second climber] Yardley.

Yalta Decisions about the fate of the many made by the few under circumstances that suggest duplicity. Yalta, an old Russian resort on the Black Sea, gained fame as the site of the meeting of Joseph Stalin, Winston Churchill, and Franklin Roosevelt in February, 1945.

The World War II Allied leaders met to determine the shape of the postwar world. Many analysts contend that an ailing Roosevelt—who died two months later—gave too much to Stalin, allowing Soviet influence to prevail in postwar eastern and central Europe. Roosevelt biographer Nathan Miller, on the other hand, notes that Soviet armies were already in the region and that Churchill and FDR could have done little to change that overwhelming fact.

Stalin also agreed to enter the war against Japan in exchange for the Kurile Islands and concessions in Manchuria lost in the Russo-Japanese War (1904–1905). As it turned out, Russian entry into the Pacific war was of little consequence; it came two days after the atomic bomb was dropped.

As MUNICH stands for appeasement of rapacious dictators, so Yalta connotes naïve trust in treacherous opponents.

The term in use, by the prime minister of Poland, quoted by Barry Schweid of the Associated Press, February 23, 1990:

> It is unthinkable in today's democratic world to have this form of Yalta, where one group of countries could decide about another.

And by Peter Gammons in the *Boston Globe,* August 8, 1993, on a meeting of major league baseball team owners:

> While last week the auction of the Orioles jacked the price $18.5 million in 10 minutes and in Pennsylvania Vince Piazza has begun another challenge to the anti-trust exemption, Sheboygan is baseball's Yalta.

yawp *See* BARBARIC YAWP.

yellow brick road A path that leads to the end of troubles, an end that may not be as expected at the outset.

The term is from *The Wonderful Wizard of Oz,* L. Frank Baum's story published in 1900 and made into a movie musical in 1939. In the story, Dorothy, a little girl from Kansas, is transported to the magical land of Oz by a tornado. She sets out to find the Wizard of Oz, who she hopes will help her return home. To get there she is told to follow the "road paved with yellow brick." In the movie, she and her friends sing "follow the yellow brick road" as they set out.

The term in use, by Laurent Belsie and Scott Armstrong, in the *Christian Science Monitor,* January 13, 1994:

> America's Information Superhighway is a lot like the Yellow Brick Road.
> Everyone sees the bricks already in place. They know the direction the road-builders are taking. But Oz is still distant, and nobody has seen the Wizard.

Another example, from Bob Herzog, *Newsday,* June 2, 1996, recalling the 1972 Olympics in Munich:

> Soviet Olga Korbut, nicknamed the "Munich Munchkin," followed the yellow brick road to gold in three events, added a silver and was one of the most popular athletes of the Games. [*See also* MUNCHKIN.]

And from Steve Sakson of the Associated Press, January 1, 1995:

What follows is a by-no-means definitive list of the stocks that could have sent you on the Yellow Brick Road to Riches or the Garden Path to the Poorhouse in 1994.

yellow journalism Sensationalism and irresponsible, inventive reporting in the press.

The term was born in the newspaper circulation wars of the 1890s. To bolster street sales, big city papers, especially William Randolph Hearst's *New York Journal* and Joseph Pulitzer's *New York World,* engaged in flashy, exaggerated reporting, lavish illustrations, and screaming headlines.

The term comes from the color and comics added to further pique interest. In 1896, Pulitzer's *New York World* experimented with printing the color yellow for the first time. According to *A History of the Comic Strip* (1968) by Pierre Couperie, et al., (translated from the French by Eilleen [sic] B. Hennessy), a rascally character in the strip "Down Hogan's Alley," drawn by Richard Outcault, always wore a long white shirt. On February 16, the printers colored the shirt yellow. The gambit was a great success; the character immediately became the "Yellow Kid." Colored comic sections soon developed in the competing papers.

Various intriguing theories are advanced for the term's origins. As Coulton Waugh describes it in *The Comics* (1991), the success of the Yellow Kid began a series of raids, counter-raids, and lawsuits between Pulitzer and Hearst. Hearst hired Outcault; Pulitzer bought him back, and Hearst bought him back again. Pulitzer then hired another artist to draw a competing Yellow Kid, and the resulting competition between the two strips excited so much attention that the rivalry between the two newspapers was referred to as yellow journalism.

Bill Blackbeard rebuts the Outcault theory in his introduction to *R.F. Outcault's The Yellow Kid: A Centennial Celebration of the Kid Who Started the Comics* (1995). Several weeks before the Outcault raid, Hearst's California and New York newspapers sponsored a coast-to-coast bicycle marathon: the "Journal-Examiner Yellow Fellow Transcontinental Bicycle Relay." A relay of cyclists dressed head-to-toe in yellow carried a yellow dispatch pouch from the *Examiner* office in San Francisco to the *Herald* office in New York. It was promotion, of course, but Hearst's papers covered it as big news. More respectable newspapers fumed, and Ervin Wardman of the *New York Press* used the expression in an editorial on September 2, 1896.

The term in use, by Bob Sussman, Deputy Director of the Environmental Protection Agency in a letter to the editor of *Mother Jones,* March 1, 1994, objecting to an article in the magazine:

> The *Mother Jones* article on the East Liverpool incinerator adds heat, not light, to an already heated situation. Your study in black-and-white is, in the end, merely yellow journalism.

And by John Huey in *Fortune,* December 13, 1993, reviewing Porter Bibb's biography *It Ain't As Easy As It Looks: Ted Turner's Amazing Story:*

Like [Citizen] Kane, Turner manages along the way to build one of the world's great media empires, combining his incredible stomach for risk with a gut instinct for what the public really wants: in Kane's case, yellow journalism; in Turner's case, old movies, wrestling, and lots of baseball.

yin and yang In Chinese philosophy, two cosmic forces that combine to produce all that comes to be. Yin is the passive, feminine principle—dark, cold, wet; yang is the active, masculine principle—light, warm, dry. These forces are not opposites as we understand them in the West but more like a continuous cycle of balance and harmony. The symbol of the two forces is a circle divided into light and dark fields by an S-shaped curve, as seen on the South Korean flag.

The terms in use, by Richard Harrington, in the *Washington Post,* September 25, 1989, on Rolling Stones Mick Jagger and Keith Richards:

> They have inspired much definition—Siamese twins with two strong heads pulling in opposite directions, a ship with two mastheads plowing into the sea, the rock-and-roller and the superstar, the warrior and the dilettante, one taking the high road, one the low—but in the mid-Eighties, Yin/Yang became Yin vs. Yang, the Glimmer Twins slid to Grimmer, RIFFS turned to rifts.

And by Orlando Ramirez, in the Portland *Oregonian,* April 16, 1996, on Thai cookery:

> The recipes are similar in their use of coconut cream and salt. The latter addition seems odd in terms of Western desserts, but Thai cooking seeks a balance of flavors—a yin and yang, as it were—and the salt helps balance the sweetness of the sugar and the cream.

Also, from Michael Brus' review of *A Prayer for the City* by Buzz Bissinger in the *Washington Monthly,* December 1997, in a description of Philadelphia Mayor Ed Rendell and his chief of staff David Cohen:

> The impulsive pol and precise, punctual chief of staff are the yin and yang of the mayor's office, one handling the rhetoric, the other the details.

Young Turk An insurgent in a political party; a radical. One who advocates changes within an established group.

The original Young Turks were young Turks who, at the beginning of the 20th century, sought to reform and modernize the decaying Ottoman Empire (*see* SICK MAN OF EUROPE). The movement was largely supported by students, and in 1908 they deposed the sultan, replaced him with his brother, and introduced a number of reforms, hoping to prevent the breakup of the empire. That hope proved futile; territories were lost in the Balkan wars and World War I. Massive changes came with the proclamation of the Turkish Republic in 1923 under the leadership of Mustafa Kemal (who took the name Atatürk, or "father of the Turks").

The term in use, in its most familiar and hackneyed form, from Jeffrey Birnbaum in the *Wall Street Journal,* March 21, 1989, describing the fight among Republicans in the House of Representatives over the position of minority whip—between old-line Republican Edward Madigan and up-and-coming Newt Gingrich:

> The 45-year-old Mr. Gingrich, though gray-haired and a 10-year veteran of the House, considers himself the GURU of the insurgent "Young Turks."

And by Alice LaPlante in *Computerworld,* June 1, 1996, describing the new generation of computer experts:

> Indeed, Cuccia is only echoing what seems to be the universal MANTRA of these so-called Young Turks: Don't bore me.

And by John Heilemann of the *Economist,* in a column appearing in *Newsday,* March 21, 1995, on the conflicts between senior congressional Republicans and their recently elected colleagues:

> The GOP's Old Bulls need their Young Turks to help pull off the revolution. But tensions between the generations are growing fast and getting ugly.

*Finding C-SPAN fully restored in your neighborhood
is a little like finding Zuzu's petals. . . . A magical moment
of disbelief, relief, renewal and ecstasy. . . .*
—Michelle Malkin

Zelig \\'ze-lig\\ A seemingly ordinary person who nevertheless constantly turns up near famous people or in fabulous contexts. A chameleon. Zelig is a fictional character created by Woody Allen in his 1983 movie *Zelig*. Special effects in the film show Zelig batting for the New York Yankees, as a Chicago gangster, and with Calvin Coolidge, Pope Pius XI, and Adolf Hitler.

The term in use, in the *Deseret News*, October 18, 1996:

> After Kemp's uncharacteristically brief remarks, Gore tickled the dinner crowd of about 1,200 with a slide presentation that attempted to show how he has "tried to break the vice presidential mold."
>
> It featured images of Gore popping up like Zelig in photographs: carrying injured Olympic gymnast Kerri Strug; as a New York Yankee baseball player, celebrating a victory; in the football field with Kemp; and in the now-famous photograph of a young Clinton shaking hands with President Kennedy.

And in *Newsday,* Richard Eder reviews Calvin Tomkins' biography of artist Marcel Duchamp, November 24, 1996:

> Since 1942 he was a permanent resident here—his friends, his many affairs, two or three real loves and a late, flowering marriage, he is a kind of Zelig. His face is in every gathering, but who is he?

Zen A sect of Buddhism that aims at enlightenment by direct intuition through meditation.

Zen Buddhism developed in China in the 6th century and spread to Japan in the 12th and 13th. Zen strives for truth or enlightenment through a stroke of insight called *satori,* rather than through ritual or good works. The breakthrough often comes through meditation, including concentration on problems, called *koan,* usually paradoxes such as, "What is the sound of one hand clapping?" Thinking about such problems is a way for the mind to break free of the constraints of conventional logic.

Recent western interest in eastern cultures and religions has brought the word into the English language as a conceptual breakthrough, a spiritual elevation, or a state of euphoria.

The term in use by Steven S. King in the *Washington Post,* September 2, 1988:

> When conditions approach ideal, though, biking can transcend the realm of mere physical endeavor and affect mental or even spiritual planes. For lack of formal terminology, I call this experience the Zen bike ride.

And by Jim Molnar in the *Seattle Times,* November 19, 1997:

> The name itself seems to be a Zen-like enigma: Point-No-Point. A place that simply is, and a place where people can shed all their concerns about the past and the future and simply be.

In use again, by Benjamin J. Stein in the *American Spectator,* December 1988, writing on the success of the Disney company:

> If the Disney managers are in Zen synch with their audiences and attendees, they are in even greater synch with their stockholders, who have gotten rich, despite a stock market crash, off Michael [Eisner] and Mickey [Mouse]'s efforts. The Zen bond between stockholder wishes and management wishes is truly profound.

zero–sum game A situation in which a gain for one side entails a corresponding loss for the other side. A term from game theory, a branch of mathematics that analyzes competitive situations by looking at the decision making of each player. The theory assumes that the players will act rationally but also considers such factors as conflicting interests, incomplete information, and chance, and is now applied in many fields, from economics, business, and law to strategic planning for national security.

In a zero-sum game, the winner wins at the expense of the loser(s). In the politics of the nuclear age, policy makers try to avoid this situation; it is much safer to introduce face-saving factors so both sides can back away from confrontation and claim gains.

The term in use, by President Bill Clinton, quoted in the *Los Angeles Times,* May 28, 1997:

> "This new NATO will work with Russia, not against it," the president continued, adding that the goal is to "create a future in which European security is not a zero-sum game where NATO's gain is Russia's loss and Russia's strength is our alliance's weakness."

And by Russ Dondero in the Portland *Oregonian,* February 19, 1996, on the political landscape in Congress:

> In this environment, congressional politics may become more of a zero-sum game of winner take all, not a search for the political center. Coalition building gives way to the demands of partisanship and ideology.

And quoted by Keith Ervin in the *Seattle Times,* October 14, 1997, on the highways vs. mass transit arguments in the region:

> For many transportation advocates, there is a middle ground. Transit and roads needn't be an either/or choice, says Mike Vaska, an attorney who spent several years working through the Greater Seattle Chamber of Commerce to craft a more cost-effective transit plan. "There has been an assumption that it's a zero-sum game where you improve transit at the expense of roads or vice versa," Vaska observes. "That's wrong."

And by Wendy Kaminer in the *Atlantic,* October 1993:

> Feminism and the careerism it entails are commonly regarded as a zero-sum game not just for women and men but for women and children as well, Ellen Levine believes: wage-earning mothers still tend to feel guilty about not being with their children and to worry that "the more women get ahead professionally, the more children will fall back."

Zurich *See* GNOMES OF ZURICH.

Zuzu's petals \\'zü-(ˌ)züz-\\ Restored contact with reality; a symbol of the real, normal world. This phrase comes from *It's a Wonderful Life,* the 1946 film by Frank Capra. (*See* CAPRAESQUE.)

In the film, hero George Bailey (Jimmy Stewart) is overwhelmed by the difficulties of his life and on Christmas Eve wishes he had never been born. At this, his guardian angel whisks him into a world as it would have been without him.

George's daughter Zuzu had brought a flower home from school under her coat. The flower had dropped some petals, and Zuzu had asked her father to put them back. He had pretended to do so while stuffing the petals into his pocket. After his encounter with the angel, he discovers that the petals are no longer there and realizes that he has truly been removed from his own life.

Shocked by the grim vision of the world without him, George begs to return; he sees that he really did have a wonderful life. He knows he is back when he find's Zuzu's petals in his pocket. Overflowing with joy and relief, he rushes home through the snow, delighted with every familiar face and landmark, and at home he finds that friends from far and wide have rallied to help him.

The term in use, in an editorial by Michelle Malkin, in the *Seattle Times,* February 11, 1997:

> Finding C-SPAN fully restored in your neighborhood is a little like finding Zuzu's petals. It happened here in Seattle last Thursday evening. A magical moment of disbelief, relief, renewal and ecstasy: Brian Lamb! Booknotes! Moscow Nightly News! You're back? Are you real?

And by Phil Kloer, previewing Christmas television fare—"A Beavis and Butt-head Christmas"—in the *Atlanta Journal and Constitution,* December 19, 1995:

> In "It's a Miserable Life," Butt-head's guardian angel shows him how the town of Highland would have fared without him—far better than it did with him, in fact.
>
> You've got to hand it to B&B that they haven't gone all Capra-corny just because it's Christmas. Their SHTICK is so limited, however, it's gotten tiresome—and as familiar as Zuzu's petals.

Bibliography

In our research, we relied constantly on the updated editions of these classic reference works: *Brewer's Dictionary of Phrase and Fable,* the *Oxford English Dictionary, Second Edition,* and *Encyclopædia Britannica,* as well as *Merriam-Webster's Collegiate Dictionary, Tenth Edition, Webster's Third New International Dictionary,* and *Merriam-Webster's Encyclopedia of Literature.*

Other invaluable sources included *The Facts on File Dictionary of Classical, Biblical and Literary Allusions,* by Lass, Kiremidjian and Goldstein; *An Incomplete Education,* by Jones and Wilson; William Safire's *Political Dictionary; The Dictionary of Cultural Literacy,* by Hirsch, Kett and Trefil; *Le Mot Juste: A Dictionary of Classical & Foreign Words & Phrases,* Buchanan-Brown, et. al.; *The Joys of Yiddish,* by Leo Rosten; *The Morris Dictionary of Word and Phrase Origins,* by William and Mary Morris; *The Barnhart Dictionary Companion* and *The Barnhard Dictionary of New English Since 1963; Black's Law Dictionary;* I. Moyer Hunsberger, *The Quintessential Dictionary; Bartlett's Familiar Quotations;* George Seldes, *The Great Thoughts; Benét's Reader's Encyclopedia.*

About the authors

Elizabeth Webber is a native of Ottumwa, Iowa, transplanted to Washington, D.C. A lawyer by training but not inclination, she worked several years in Congress, but managed to make a clean getaway.

She is now a freelance writer and editor and devotes her time to the basics: reading, writing, and rowing on the Potomac River.

Mike Feinsilber, a Pennsylvanian, has been putting words in print ever since the 5th grade when he established *The Daily Stink,* which partially lived up to its name although it did not come out every day.

Feinsilber, assistant chief of bureau for news with The Associate Press in Washington, has been a newsman for more than 30 years, first in Pittsburgh, Columbus, Harrisburg, Newark, New York, Saigon, and Washington for United Press International and since 1980 in Washington for The AP.

He is married, bicycles, gardens and bakes bread.